Human Trafficking

Sara Miller McCune founded SAGE Publishing in 1965 to support the dissemination of usable knowledge and educate a global community. SAGE publishes more than 1000 journals and over 800 new books each year, spanning a wide range of subject areas. Our growing selection of library products includes archives, data, case studies and video. SAGE remains majority owned by our founder and after her lifetime will become owned by a charitable trust that secures the company's continued independence.

Los Angeles | London | New Delhi | Singapore | Washington DC | Melbourne

Human Trafficking

A Comprehensive
Exploration of Modern-Day Slavery

Wendy Stickle
University of Maryland

Shelby Hickman
University of Maryland

Christine White
University of Maryland

Los Angeles | London | New Delhi
Singapore | Washington DC | Melbourne

FOR INFORMATION:

SAGE Publications, Inc.
2455 Teller Road
Thousand Oaks, California 91320
E-mail: order@sagepub.com

SAGE Publications Ltd.
1 Oliver's Yard
55 City Road
London, EC1Y 1SP
United Kingdom

SAGE Publications India Pvt. Ltd.
B 1/I 1 Mohan Cooperative Industrial Area
Mathura Road, New Delhi 110 044
India

SAGE Publications Asia-Pacific Pte. Ltd.
18 Cross Street #10–10/11/12
China Square Central
Singapore 048423

Acquisitions Editor: Jessica Miller
Editorial Assistant: Sarah Manheim
Marketing Manager: Jillian Ragusa
Production Editor: Veronica Stapleton Hooper
Copy Editor: Rachel Keith
Typesetter: Hurix Digital
Proofreader: Lawrence W. Baker
Indexer: Sheila Bodell
Cover Designer: Scott Van Atta

Printed in the United States of America.

Library of Congress Cataloging-in-Publication Data

Names: Stickle, Wendy, author. | Hickman, Shelby, author. | White, Christine (Christine Andrea), author.

Title: Human trafficking : a comprehensive exploration of modern day slavery / Wendy Stickle, Shelby Hickman, Christine White.

Description: Los Angeles : Sage, [2020]

Identifiers: LCCN 2019020138 | ISBN 9781506375038 (paperback)

Subjects: LCSH: Human trafficking.

Classification: LCC HQ281 .S844 2020 | DDC 364.15/51—dc23

LC record available at https://lccn.loc.gov/2019020138

This book is printed on acid-free paper.

19 20 21 22 23 10 9 8 7 6 5 4 3 2 1

Brief Contents

Detailed Contents

Preface

Designing and teaching a class on human trafficking is challenging. The goal of this book is to make it less so.

When we first embarked on designing a course on human trafficking, it was complicated. To begin with, we had to develop our own understanding of the topic. Human trafficking is not well studied or attended to in academia. No textbook existed at the time, and full-semester courses on the topic were also in short supply. Nevertheless, piecing together mainstream books, technical reports, and guest speakers, a class on human trafficking was born. Students' feedback was encouraging, but they were shocked. Like us when we first focused on the topic, they knew what sex trafficking was. They knew this terrible crime happened on continents they might never visit. But learning that this crime was much more complex than originally thought, that the same explanations we use for other forms of crime might apply to human trafficking, and that the crime was happening in their own backyards was almost too much to take in. While other crime-related topics, such as juvenile delinquency, the role of punishment, and race relations, were rehashed in some capacity in nearly all their classes, the study of human trafficking was completely novel to these students. And it continues to be for the students who register for our classes every semester.

After a couple of years of teaching the course, it became more than a class to us. We became involved in our local communities, in task forces, research, and awareness campaigns. As our knowledge grew, our passion for exposing students to the drivers and consequences of human trafficking also grew. While victim testimonies and documentaries were powerful resources for our courses, they fell short in really exposing students to the complicated nature of this crime and the importance of context. Thus, we designed study-abroad programs to take students to different parts of the world to study human trafficking. One conclusion we hope comes out in this book is that the causes and reactions to trafficking look very different depending on where you are in the world. What behavior is acceptable or not looks different. What types of services are in demand varies. Understanding human trafficking and how to prevent it requires understanding the context in which it takes place. For this reason, study-abroad opportunities provided a powerful complement to our courses.

The impact of the courses and study-abroad programs could be replicated. Thus, from an academic standpoint, we felt there was more to do. Empowering students with knowledge is one of the greatest gifts we can give them. Not only is it critical to understand human trafficking for the immoral violent crime that it is, but providing citizens of the world with this information can only help to put a stop to this criminal enterprise. Increasing the number of full-semester courses dedicated to the topic of human trafficking will not only expose a new generation of service-oriented students to this crime but exponentially raise the larger community's awareness. As we tell our students on the first day of class, their most important homework every week is to go home and share something that surprised them with three different people.

We hope the publication of this book will provide its audience with an accurate understanding of all forms of human trafficking and current responses to this crime. We hope having a book such as this will promote the creation of more classes, lectures, brown bags, and other events that spur conversation on this topic.

We hope the readers of this book will further the world's knowledge of this topic. To help accomplish this, we have included several features throughout the text:

FOCUS ON boxes offer the reader an opportunity to delve into a specific issue related to the chapter topic. These boxes are found throughout each chapter, highlighting debatable topics, controversial issues, and unique challenges.

CASE STUDIES provide a human context to the issue of human trafficking. Also found throughout each chapter, this feature aims to remind readers that human trafficking is not simply an academic or political issue. Human lives are at stake.

Finally, **CHALLENGE YOURSELF** boxes offer readers a chance to think critically about what they are reading. Readers are asked to formulate opinions and assess critical issues. The goal of this feature is to remind readers to remain critical. Ask questions. Pave the way for progress in understanding and fighting this crime.

So often while writing this text, we were dumbstruck by the lack of information available. While anecdotal information is plentiful, the academic community's empirical knowledge of this topic is notably limited. There may be times when you are reading this book and think that something is missing and wonder why we didn't include a discussion of that. Why didn't the authors speak to this topic or that one? Asking questions is exactly what we hope you will do. For the most part, we provided information as it was available. For some of these topics, the information simply isn't available yet. Maybe you, the reader, will be the one to answer those unanswered questions?

To date, we have yet to see a comprehensive introductory overview of human trafficking from a nonpractitioner perspective. For students, policy makers, criminologists, and those simply attempting to better understand this topic, we think you will find this book useful. While many books focus primarily on sex trafficking and labor trafficking, we will also present what is currently known about organ trafficking, child marriage, and child soldiers. The text also explores the topic within the borders of the United States as well as across the world. The reality is that this problem is not limited to one country or even one continent. Technology and globalization have made this an international crisis that requires a collaborative and cooperative international response.

The themes described above are reflected throughout the book:

Chapter 1, "Human Trafficking in Context," introduces readers to the definition of human trafficking. It tracks slavery through time and clarifies what human trafficking is and is not.

Chapter 2, "Challenges, Resources, and Recommendations," covers challenges faced when estimating the magnitude and complexities of human trafficking domestically and globally. Additionally, it provides descriptions of existing resources, their purposes and data collection strategies, criticisms they face, and their general contributions to the understanding of human trafficking.

Chapter 3, "Do Traditional Theories Help Us Understand Human Trafficking?" describes the ways theory can be applied to appreciate the why and how of the trafficker's role and the trafficked person's role, as well as the higher-level ecological complexities that permit this illegal and unethical enterprise to successfully operate. Such an application of theory will elevate our understanding of human trafficking beyond the relationship between offender and victim to an improved understanding of the intricacies that create an environment ripe for exploitation.

Chapter 4, "The Victims of Human Trafficking," explores the broad factors that make victims more vulnerable to traffickers.

Chapter 5, "The Traffickers," describes the traffickers: their motivations, their roles or job functions, and what we know about their demographic characteristics, criminal histories, occupations, and educational backgrounds.

Chapter 6, "The Colliding Worlds of Prostitution and Human Trafficking," defines and describes prostitution. Who becomes a sex worker? What motivates a person to enter prostitution? It also discusses how prostitution is handled legislatively, domestically, and internationally.

Chapter 7, "Moving Past the Prostitution Debate: An Examination of Sex Trafficking," explores the prevalence of sex trafficking and leads the reader through the stages of sex trafficking. Finally, it reviews special populations, including children, males, and LGBTQ individuals.

Chapter 8, "Sex Trafficking: Demand and Prevention," focuses on some of the unique factors that drive the demand for sex trafficking. The chapter will conclude with attention on the varying approaches to reducing sex trafficking.

Chapter 9, "More Than Unfair Labor Practices," reviews definitions of labor trafficking and its components, the extent of labor trafficking in the United States and abroad, laws and legislation affecting our ability to identify and prosecute labor traffickers, and characteristics of labor traffickers and their victims.

Chapter 10, "Responses to Labor Trafficking," reviews the ways that individuals, nongovernmental agencies (NGOs), law enforcement, and government agencies work to prevent labor trafficking, stop it where it continues to exist, and serve and protect victims.

Chapter 11, "Child Soldiers," explores child soldiers. What regions of the world are they most often found? What are the risk factors for and consequences of such violent experiences during a vulnerable period of child development? Finally, what is currently being done to control and eliminate this terrible practice, and what challenges do we face?

Chapter 12, "Organ Trafficking," reviews the history of organ transplantation, definitions of distinct types of organ trafficking, legal frameworks and considerations related to organ trafficking, and the prevalence of trafficking globally and in the U.S. It also discusses factors that facilitate vulnerability to trafficking, characteristics of traffickers, and responses to organ trafficking.

Chapter 13, "Forced and Child Marriage," reviews forced marriages and child marriages. It highlights the issue in the United States as well as the rest of the world. It challenges the reader to assess the ethics and morality of condemning child marriage.

Chapter 14, "Conclusion," provides a summary of lessons learned throughout the text.

Acknowledgments

The path to this book has been long and admittedly more challenging than first anticipated. It definitely would never have come to fruition without the help of many. We are most grateful for and proud of the undergraduate students who assisted with this book. Not only was their help invaluable, but we believe the research experience was equally invaluable to them. These students include Karen Carrillo, Maria Chesnos, Duc Duong, Petra Farkas, Brenda Garcia, Katie Heil, Carlos Orellana, Camila Thorpe, Tyissha Walters, and Sara Yassin. Jessica Miller has been a wonderful support, offering a perfect balance of encouragement while also reminding us that there are deadlines to meet! Also, we want to thank the reviewers of this text for their helpful comments:

Valerie Anderson, University of Cincinnati

Jane H. Bayes, California State University, Northridge

Jan Bourne-Day, Manchester Metropolitan University, Cheshire

Mary Breaux, Sam Houston State University

Natasha Chubbock, Nottingham Trent University

Jeff Dailey, Sam Houston State University

Dawn Eccleston, University of Central Lancashire

David F. Ericson, Cleveland State University

Amy Farrell, Northeastern University

Theresa C. Hayden, University of Louisville

Lin Huff-Corzine, University of Central Florida

Iryna Malendevych, University of Central Florida

Tatyana Nestorova, Ohio State University

Jillian Noel, Germanna Community College

Elizabeth Perkins, Morehead State University

Lynne Reynolds, University of Bedfordshire, UK

Tazreena Sajjad, American University

Nadia Shapkina, Kansas State University

Roberta Villalón, St. John's University

Kali Wright-Smith, Westminster College

Manuel F. Zamora, Angelo State University

And of course, we would be remiss not to acknowledge our personal circles of support—family, friends, and colleagues who regularly reminded us of the importance of our work.

Lastly, this book was a labor of love for all three authors. We hope readers find the book informative, thought-provoking, and action-inducing.

About the Authors

Wendy Stickle is a senior lecturer for the Department of Criminology and Criminal Justice at the University of Maryland. She received her bachelor's degree in psychology from St. Mary's College of Maryland and her PhD in criminology and criminal justice from the University of Maryland. She has interest and expertise in the areas of domestic and international human trafficking. She coleads student trips abroad to understand human trafficking in context and teaches a semester-long course on the topic for UMD. Her recent research explores the role of the hospitality industry in perpetuating and preventing human trafficking in the United States.

Shelby Hickman is a doctoral student in the Department of Criminology and Criminal Justice at the University of Maryland and a research scientist at Child Trends, an independent research organization. She received her bachelor's and master's degrees in public health from the George Washington University. Her research interests focus on improving the lives and well-being of vulnerable youth, including those affected by human trafficking.

Christine White is a lecturer for the Department of Criminology and Criminal Justice at the University of Maryland. She received her bachelor's degree in sociology from the University of Pennsylvania and her JD from American University's Washington College of Law. She has interest and expertise in the areas of domestic and international human trafficking. She coleads student trips abroad to understand human trafficking in context and teaches a semester-long course on the topic for UMD. Her recent research explores the impact of human trafficking in local communities.

Fundamentals

Human trafficking is one of the fastest-growing criminal enterprises in the world. Every country in every region of the world is impacted by this crime. At an individual level, neither gender nor race nor socioeconomic status nor citizenship status can eliminate one's risk of victimization. Part I of this text will introduce you to our current understanding of human trafficking, including the different forms of trafficking. An in-depth analysis of existing resources and data as well as the challenges we face in understanding and combating this crime is presented in Chapter 2. Chapter 3 encourages readers to examine the crime of human trafficking from theoretical perspectives. Readers will be exposed to criminological theories, economic theories, and psychological theories. As with other forms of crime, theoretical explanations may improve our understanding of the crime while also driving future research on the crime. Finally, Chapters 4 and 5 delve more deeply into risk factors for victimization as well as the factors that drive humans to traffic other humans. As you read these chapters, consider your current understanding of human trafficking changes. Where can the global community go from here to reduce human trafficking around the world?

Human Trafficking in Context

Slavery is what slavery's always been: About one person controlling another person using violence and then exploiting them economically, paying them nothing. That's what slavery's about.

—Kevin Bales

Every nation in the world has laws abolishing slavery, yet the International Labour Organization (ILO) estimates that 21 million men, women, and children are exploited for profit (ILO, 2013c). This means that three out of every 1,000 people experience human trafficking, and this estimate is conservative (ILO, 2013c); the Global Slavery Index (2018) suggests that the prevalence of individuals in human trafficking is closer to 45 million. Human trafficking is pervasive; while two-thirds of victims are determined to have come from the Asia-Pacific region, slavery has been identified in every single country. Human trafficking generates substantial profits for traffickers: upwards of $150 billion per year (ILO, 2014b). Annual profits range from $3,900 to $34,800 per victim.

No-So-Modern Slavery

People sometimes refer to **human trafficking** as "modern slavery," but there is some debate about whether this distinction is appropriate. In many ways, human trafficking is a continuation of historical slavery. **Slavery** as an institution has existed in various forms throughout history, as shown in Figure 1.1. The concept of forcing some people to complete certain tasks in order to benefit another group of people has been implemented by nations across the globe. The transatlantic slave trade traces back to the 1400s. During that time, more than 12.5 million people, over a quarter of whom were children, were purchased in countries like Ghana, Sierra Leone, and the Ivory Coast (Gates, 2014). In fact, Africans living in countries all along the western coast were bought by the British, the French, the Portuguese, and the Spaniards.

Over the course of hundreds of years, Europeans used the people they purchased to accomplish goals of cultural imperialism by transporting these individuals to countries in the Western hemisphere. This process was embraced by European countries including France, England, Portugal, and Spain. These countries bought and sold individuals in order to profit financially and politically. This process of buying and selling people continued even as the United States of America achieved and declared itself an independent nation.

In fact, instances of slavery continued to prevail throughout the 1900s. As a result, both the United Nations and the United States proclaimed protection of victims and prosecution of perpetrators in 2000 with the United Nations Protocol to Prevent, Suppress and Punish Trafficking in Persons Especially Women and

Children (United Nations General Assembly, 2000c), and the Trafficking Victims Protection Act of 2000 (TVPA). Since passage of these laws in 2000, the TVPA has been authorized several times. With each reauthorization—in 2003, 2005, 2008, and 2013—the goals of the Department of State's annual Trafficking in Persons (TIP) Report have been heightened.

Often when we think about slavery, we think about a dichotomy between when slavery was legal and when it was abolished, as linearized in the timeline presented in Figure 1.1. The dates in the timeline do not paint a full picture of the reality of slavery. The economic, psychological, cultural, and legal effects of slavery persist through generations. The idea that there exists a binary between "slavery" and "freedom" is overly simplistic.

For example, slavery was officially abolished in the United States in 1863 with the Emancipation Proclamation, and the United States moved into Reconstruction after the Civil War finally ended two years later in 1865. Even with these milestones toward equality, slavery persisted. In fact, courts evaluated whether individuals had been subjected to slavery various times since the passage of the Thirteenth Amendment. In *United States v. Ingalls* (1947), the court defined a slave as "a person in a state of enforced or extorted servitude to another," and it also included psychological coercion within the definition of slavery. However, over forty years later, the Supreme Court decided in *United States v. Kozminski* (1988) that

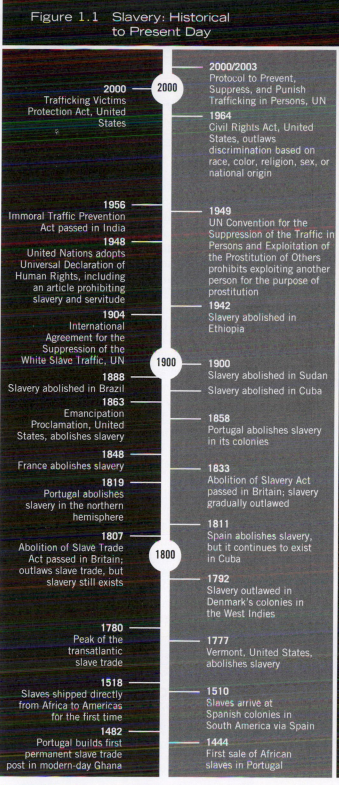

Figure 1.1 Slavery: Historical to Present Day

2000/2003
Protocol to Prevent, Suppress, and Punish Trafficking in Persons, UN

2000
Trafficking Victims Protection Act, United States

1964
Civil Rights Act, United States, outlaws discrimination based on race, color, religion, sex, or national origin

1956
Immoral Traffic Prevention Act passed in India

1948
United Nations adopts Universal Declaration of Human Rights, including an article prohibiting slavery and servitude

1949
UN Convention for the Suppression of the Traffic in Persons and Exploitation of the Prostitution of Others prohibits exploiting another person for the purpose of prostitution

1942
Slavery abolished in Ethiopia

1904
International Agreement for the Suppression of the White Slave Traffic, UN

1900
Slavery abolished in Sudan
Slavery abolished in Cuba

1888
Slavery abolished in Brazil

1863
Emancipation Proclamation, United States, abolishes slavery

1858
Portugal abolishes slavery in its colonies

1848
France abolishes slavery

1833
Abolition of Slavery Act passed in Britain; slavery gradually outlawed

1819
Portugal abolishes slavery in the northern hemisphere

1811
Spain abolishes slavery, but it continues to exist in Cuba

1807
Abolition of Slave Trade Act passed in Britain; outlaws slave trade, but slavery still exists

1792
Slavery outlawed in Denmark's colonies in the West Indies

1780
Peak of the transatlantic slave trade

1777
Vermont, United States, abolishes slavery

1518
Slaves shipped directly from Africa to Americas for the first time

1510
Slaves arrive at Spanish colonies in South America via Spain

1482
Portugal builds first permanent slave trade post in modern-day Ghana

1444
First sale of African slaves in Portugal

Sources: "Chronology—Who banned slavery when?," 2007; United Nations Treaty Collection, n.d.

How was imperialism used to justify slavery?

Most anti-trafficking efforts today are located in modern, Western societies. How can that affect anti-trafficking movements? In what ways might modern anti-trafficking efforts suffer from the influence of imperialism?

involuntary servitude exists only when the master subjects an individual to (1) threatened or actual physical force, (2) threatened or actual state-imposed legal coercion, or (3) fraud or deceit where the servant is a minor or an immigrant or is mentally incompetent. This ruling therefore limited the Thirteenth Amendment's prohibitions to physical or legal coercion. These interpretations controlled definitions of modern-day slavery until the year 2000 brought passage of the TVPA, which includes psychological coercion.

True "anti-slavery" efforts cannot end when legislation is passed. They must continue to question policies, ideologies, and motives to examine in what ways societies promote systemic discrimination and exploitation. When we look at modern-day human trafficking, we must push ourselves to consider whether it is distinct from historical slavery or just a continuation of it.

The world has watched as wars have been fought, as leaders have been overthrown, and as human rights violators have been prosecuted. With such a vivid memory of our involvement and movements toward destroying a one-sided and oppressive system, many questions abound as we contemplate the global crime of human trafficking.

Human trafficking as a crime emerged during the twenty-first century during a time when we thought we were finished with having to figure out why some people in the world were exploiting other people in the world. We might have believed that, after the Civil War in the United States ended, and especially after the apartheid regime in South Africa was dismantled, we no longer needed to discuss this atrocity.

Human trafficking has been at the center of conversations, concern, and public awareness campaigns for the past two decades. There has been a push for further discussion and movement to combat this complex and dynamic global human rights issue. Presidents have made pledges and speeches promising to eradicate such an atrocity. Human rights activists have organized public awareness campaigns. Lawyers have represented victims and perpetrators of this varied crime. Celebrities have made public service announcements.

Root Causes of Human Trafficking: Supply, Demand, and Globalization

Root causes of human trafficking vary by trafficking type. Accordingly, we will discuss these in more detail throughout the book. Central to all types of human trafficking, however, are principles of supply and demand and the globalization of the international economy.

Globalization refers to the increasingly integrated nature of global economies (sometimes called "shrinking of the global economy"), cultures, and people (Kolb, 2018). It is characterized by free trade, utilization of cheaper foreign labor markets, and the movement of individuals across country lines to fill the demand for low-cost labor (Brewer, 2009; A. Jordan, 2004). Globalization brings positive and negative changes to the world economy and individual quality of life. Because it increases the transmission of ideas and technologies across cultures and across country lines, globalization facilitates innovation, business scale-up, and new job opportunities. Globalization is the reason it is easy to travel the world, have products shipped to our doorsteps from anywhere in the world, and buy more things for lower prices.

However, globalization also displaces low-skilled workers and depletes environmental resources, and many experts argue that it is has widened the income gap between the richest and poorest members of society. Some argue that "the lesser developed countries of the world have become the factories and workshops for the developed countries" (Brewer, 2009). When job markets are displaced to other countries, domestic workers are left with few options for survival. This results in huge rates of out-migration as people search for job opportunities. In 2015, 244 million people—3.3% of the world's population—lived outside their country of origin; this represents a 40% increase since 2000. Most migrants cross borders in search of better economic and social opportunities, while others are forced to leave their countries because of conflict and war (United Nations, 2016). As conflict plagues the Middle East, for example, millions of people have been displaced, providing traffickers a prime opportunity for exploitation.

When people discuss modern-day globalization, they are typically referring to the massive changes that occurred following the end of the Cold War in 1990. However, there was a similar period of globalization brought about by the transatlantic slave trade. Today modern globalization facilitates trafficking in the same way that globalization in the 15th through 19th centuries facilitated the slave trade. Then and now, slavery is ultimately propagated by laws of supply and demand. Trafficking, then, is not just a negative consequence of globalization but a main factor facilitating globalization.

Human trafficking is a multibillion-dollar industry, driven by demand for cheap goods and services and for paid sex with men, women, and children. Traffickers leverage this demand and maximize profits by exploiting humans for little or no pay. Globalization increases the supply of vulnerable workers who are unable to compete in the rapidly changing workforce. Marginalized people are left looking for any job to support themselves and their families. Traffickers take advantage of this desperation, promising job opportunities and hope for economic advancement. Traffickers take advantage of the increased flow of people, goods, and services across countries. This is exacerbated by low prosecution rates around the world for human trafficking, which allow traffickers to engage in this business with little risk of identification or punishment.

Globalization has also improved anti-trafficking efforts, however. Anti-trafficking efforts limited to one country are often insufficient when traffickers move between borders. The development of international institutions like the United Nations' International Labour Organization allow for more coordinated efforts to combat trafficking. Below, we describe key policies that promote a coordinated, global response to trafficking.

International Definition of Human Trafficking

As shown in Figure 1.1, anti-trafficking legislation is relatively modern. There was not international consensus around the definition of human trafficking until 2000, when the United Nations included a definition in its Protocol to Prevent, Suppress and Punish Trafficking in Persons Especially Women and Children, hereafter referred to as the trafficking in persons protocol (one of three supplements to the UN Convention Against Transnational Organized Crime known as the **Palermo protocols;** United Nations General Assembly, 2000c). The United Nations sought to highlight the need to prevent and protect against human trafficking in its various forms. The trafficking in persons protocol identifies the multiple types of exploitation that qualify as human trafficking. In addition, this policy seeks to explain the processes by which these crimes can take place.

The trafficking in persons protocol (United Nations General Assembly, 2000c) defines human trafficking as follows:

(a) "Trafficking in persons" shall mean the recruitment, transportation, transfer, harbouring or receipt of persons, by means of the threat or use of force or other forms of coercion, of abduction, of fraud, of deception, of the abuse of power or of a position of vulnerability or of the giving or receiving of payments or benefits to achieve the consent of a person having control over another person, for the purpose of exploitation. Exploitation shall include, at a minimum, the exploitation of the prostitution of others or other forms of sexual exploitation, forced labour or services, slavery or practices similar to slavery, servitude or the removal of organs.

(b) The consent of a victim of trafficking in persons to the intended exploitation set forth in subparagraph (a) of this article shall be irrelevant where any of the means set forth in subparagraph (a) have been used; . . . The three key elements that must be present for a situation of trafficking in persons (adults) to exist are therefore: (i) action (recruitment, . . .); (ii) means (threat, . . .); and (iii) purpose (exploitation).

The **Trafficking Victims Protection Act** also defines human trafficking by focusing on actions, means, and objectives:

(A) sex trafficking in which a commercial sex act is induced by force, fraud, or coercion, or in which the person induced to perform such act has not attained 18 years of age; or

(B) the recruitment, harboring, transportation, provision, or obtaining of a person for labor or services, through the use of force, fraud, or coercion for the purpose of subjection to involuntary servitude, peonage, debt bondage, or slavery.

The creation and passage of these definitions were not the beginning, nor are they the end, in regard to revealing who can be a victim and how one can be trafficked. In fact, the United States passed the Mann Act, also known as the White Slave Traffic Act, in 1910. This law illegalized the transportation of women across state lines "for the purpose of prostitution or debauchery, or for any other immoral purpose." In 1978 and again in 1986, the act was amended to criminalize the movement of minors and adults through coercion across state or national lines for the purposes of engaging in commercial sex. The United States passed the Tariff Act in 1930 prohibiting the importation of goods produced with force or indentured labor. In 2016, the United Nations passed a human trafficking resolution, which recognized that people fleeing armed conflict are among the most vulnerable to trafficking (United Nations Office on Drugs and Crime, 2016). We will discuss these and other laws relevant to specific forms of trafficking throughout this book.

Key Elements of Human Trafficking

The **trafficking in persons protocol** recognizes that modern-day slavery takes many forms. However, many myths about what constitutes human trafficking pervade public opinion and efforts to combat trafficking. Below we review important elements of the protocol's definition of human trafficking.

Trafficking Involves a Broad Range of Exploitive Practices and Is Not Limited to Sexual Exploitation

Human trafficking used to be understood as sexual exploitation of women and girls. As we discussed above, many of the precursors to modern-day anti-trafficking legislation focused on preventing forced prostitution of women and girls. Further, discussions of human trafficking tend to revolve around commercial sexual exploitation, although victims of sexual exploitation account for just 22% of all trafficking victims (ILO, 2013b).

As shown in Figure 1.2, however, human trafficking encompasses a broad range of exploitive practices. Notably, individuals can be exploited in different ways simultaneously.

Figure 1.3 provides definitions for the forms of human trafficking that we will explore in future chapters.

Case Study

"Cristopher"

Cristopher was thrilled to be fulfilling his lifelong dream to work in the United States. After his labor recruiter in the Philippines showed him a signed job offer at a resort in the Appalachian mountains, he paid them nearly $5,000 for the opportunity.

But when he arrived in the U.S., he was told the job didn't exist. He was told to get on a bus to a Gulf state and traveled for 3 days with no money for food or water. When he arrived, he had to clean hotel rooms for 15–18 hours per day at a significantly lower wage, was constantly monitored, and was threatened with deportation.

Cristopher was worried for his family and unsure how he would repay his debt to his recruiter.

Cristopher is a client of Polaris and wanted to share his story.

Source: Polaris, 2014b.

Figure 1.2 Forms of Human Trafficking

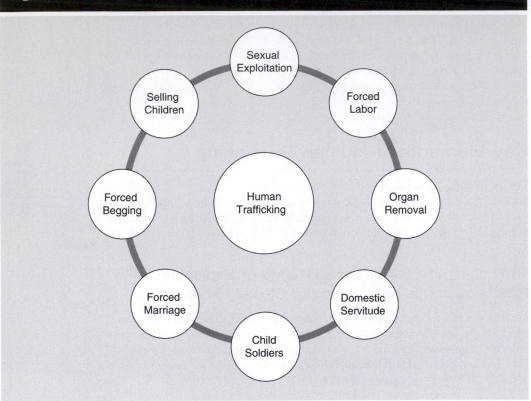

Trafficking Does Not Require Movement

To define trafficking in persons on the basis of movement is to create an artificial and unfounded distinction between victims who are exploited without being moved and those who are moved prior to and during their exploitation.

—TIP Report (Office to Monitor and Combat Trafficking in Persons, 2007)

Although the word *trafficking* connotes images of movement across state and/ or country lines, it is not a required element of human trafficking. If we look at the definition provided by the trafficking in persons protocol, transportation is only one of many means by which exploitation can occur. For example, in the book *The Slave Across the Street,* Theresa Flores provides details of how she was trafficked for sex throughout her time in high school in a suburb of Detroit, Michigan. Theresa describes how she was initially manipulated by another high school student, and because she was afraid of her parents' response and for the lives of her entire family, she went to school every day and went home every day but was sold in exchange for money she was not allowed to keep.

Traffickers may use transportation to facilitate crime. Moving victims across borders can help decrease detection by law enforcement and isolate victims serving

Figure 1.3   Definitions for Different Forms of Human Trafficking

Forced Child Labor

Although children may legally engage in certain forms of work, children can also be found in slavery or slaverylike situations. Some indicators of forced labor of a child include situations in which the child appears to be in the custody of a nonfamily member who requires the child to perform work that financially benefits someone outside the child's family and does not offer the child the option of leaving.

Forced Labor

Labor trafficking occurs in numerous industries in the U.S. and globally. In the United States, common types of labor trafficking include people forced to work in homes as domestic servants, farmworkers coerced through violence as they harvest crops, and factory workers held in inhumane conditions. Labor trafficking has also been reported in door-to-door sales crews, restaurants, construction work, carnivals, and even health and beauty services.

Domestic Servitude

As defined by the Tip report, involuntary domestic servitude is a form of human trafficking found in unique circumstances—work in a private residence—that create distinct vulnerabilities for victims. It is a crime in which domestic workers are not free to leave their employment and are abused and underpaid, if paid at all.

Organ Trafficking

The challenge inherent in combating organ trafficking is rooted in confusion over the scope of the problem itself. News reports on the subject frequently focus on the kidnapping that results in stolen organs, drawing more attention to human trafficking for the purpose of organ removal than the larger problem of trafficking in organs, tissues, and cells (OTC). Human trafficking for the purpose of organ removal involves the coercive transport of an individual and subsequent organ removal. By contrast, in OTC trafficking organs are obtained by coercion and then sold for transplant.

Child Soldiers

A child soldier is "trafficked" when there is forced recruitment or no genuine voluntary recruitment; when the recruitment is done without the informed consent of the person's parent or legal guardians; and when such persons were not fully informed of the duties involved in the military service. Child soldiering is a form of child trafficking because the acts required of a child soldier are dangerous enough to interfere with a child's fundamental human right to education, health, and development.

Data sources: Office of the High Commissioner for Human Rights, 2014; U.S. Department of State, 2018.

as a barrier to escape. When victims are transported outside their communities, they face exacerbated mental, physical, and social consequences.

Trafficking Does Not Require Physical Bondage

As mentioned earlier, slavery is no longer purely about shackles and physical abuse. Like transportation, physical bondage tactics can facilitate trafficking but are just one of many ways traffickers can exert control over victims.

Challenge Yourself 1.2

What types of things would make it easier or more difficult for someone to exert control over another person without using physical force?

Figure 1.4 Means of Control Used by Traffickers

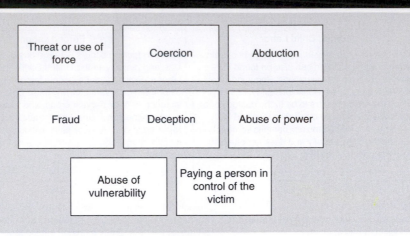

Traffickers can creatively identify a host of strategies to use against an unsuspected individual, as shown in Figure 1.4.

Trafficking Is Distinct From Migrant Smuggling

Human trafficking is not another term for *human smuggling*. **Human smuggling** refers specifically to violating a nation's laws regarding entry and may be performed with the consent of the individual being smuggled (U.S. Department of State, 2017a).

The United Nations Protocol Against the Smuggling of Migrants by Land, Sea and Air (United Nations, 2000) defines smuggling as follows:

(a) "Smuggling of migrants" shall mean the procurement, in order to obtain, directly or indirectly, a financial or other material benefit, of the illegal entry of a person into a State Party of which the person is not a national or a permanent resident;

(b) "Illegal entry" shall mean crossing borders without complying with the necessary requirements for legal entry into the receiving State.

Figure 1.5 identifies some of the key similarities and differences between human trafficking and human smuggling. While human trafficking and smuggling both involve a financial or commercial component, smuggled individuals typically give permission to the smugglers to be moved across borders in violation of the entering nation's laws. In fact, people agreeing to be smuggled generally pay smugglers large amounts of cash to enter another country illicitly. In human trafficking, victims have no say or cannot provide consent to be victimized. Therefore, it is important to understand that in smuggling, everyone involved is a party to a crime, but in human trafficking we have violators and victims.

While trafficking and smuggling are distinct violations, the two can be interrelated. What begins with voluntary involvement in a smuggling scheme can at times turn into transportation to achieve the objective of exploitation. Additionally, a critical distinction between smuggling and trafficking of humans is the relationships between the smuggler and the trafficker. The smuggler and the client/immigrant typically go their separate ways once entry into the new nation has

Figure 1.5   Human Trafficking Versus Human Smuggling

	Human Trafficking	Human Smuggling
Action	✓ Does not necessarily include transport at all	✓ Includes transport across country lines
Means	✓ Contains an element of force, fraud, or coercion ✓ Victim does not consent	✓ Smuggled person free to leave ✓ Smuggled person usually cooperates
Purpose	✓ Forced labor, services, or commercial sex acts ✓ Traffickers financially profit	✓ Illegal entry into a country ✓ Involves financial profit

occurred. In contrast, a trafficker maintains physical and psychological control over the victim, and the trafficker continues to earn profits from the victim's work (U.S. Department of State, 2017a).

There Is No Such Thing as Consenting to Human Trafficking

Once it is established that deception, coercion, force or other prohibited means were used, consent is irrelevant and cannot be used as a defence.

—Protocol to Prevent, Suppress and Punish Trafficking in Persons Especially Women and Children (United Nations General Assembly, 2000c)

A defining feature of human trafficking is that traffickers employ some form of control over their victims. As we have already discussed, not all forms of control are overt. While many instances of human trafficking are hidden from public view, many victims of trafficking engage with the public and may appear to lead normal lives, working in beauty salons, restaurants, hotels, or nearly any other industry. Just because the ways traffickers control victims are hidden from the public eye does not mean that victims are complicit with or consenting to their situation.

Additionally, many victims of trafficking often do not immediately seek help or self-identify as victims of crime for myriad reasons, including but not limited to feeling ashamed, feeling guilty, lacking familiarity with laws in the area where they are trafficked, or being socially or linguistically isolated. Further, because of the complicated dynamics between traffickers and victims, some victims develop a bond similar to that of Stockholm syndrome, known as trauma bonding. Trauma bonding is the combination of psychological control and physical control, which creates a strong sense of fear and loyalty that traps victims and makes them too scared to leave (Office for Victims of Crime, Training and Technical Assistance Center, n.d.a).

Thailand has a thriving commercial fishing industry. In fact, in recent years seafood exports that end up on our tables have totaled $7.3 billion and the industry as a whole has employed over 650,000 people. With high profits and a high supply of workers, Thailand emerged as a ripe environment for poor working conditions, forced labor, and ultimately human trafficking. The elevated demand for Thailand's fish and shrimp from people near and far has also contributed to the creation of a perfect storm of vulnerability.

Working in the fishing industry means extremely long hours (up to 24-hour shifts) of physical labor along with unpredictable pay. Because of these undesirable working conditions, Thailand began to see a labor shortage in 2011. While Thailand typically enjoys a low unemployment rate, one of its neighboring countries, Myanmar, experiences just the opposite. Due to political unrest and persecution, residents flee their home country and travel to Thailand seeking financial opportunities. However, what they

have run into is great promises for employment that are largely unmet. The workers are sent out on long-haul fishing boats into international waters for months at a time for uncertain wages and thus with no financial stability.

Migrant workers who consciously leave their homes and their families may appear to choose to enter legitimate employment in the fishing industry, but what we discover is that they may make arrangements for a job with a labor broker in exchange for a portion of their future pay. This exchange is known as debt bondage, which involves a complex system of contractors and subcontractors who all take a cut from the wages of the indebted workers, who thus may work years before receiving an income (Office of the High Commissioner for Human Rights, 2016).

These practices and others are implemented as strategies to pull unsuspecting workers in only to intentionally not fulfill the promises made to them. They end up stuck, afraid, and broke.

Anyone Can Be a Trafficker or a Victim of Human Trafficking

As we discussed earlier in this chapter, it is important to challenge our preconceived notions about who is versus who is not at risk for trafficking. It is harmful to anti-trafficking efforts to fall into the routine of conceptualizing either traffickers or victims as a group of people distanced from society—particularly imperialistic notions of what constitutes mainstream society—because of factors like socioeconomic status, education, race, gender identity, or sexuality. Trafficking affects people in every country, of all racial and ethnic backgrounds, and from all socioeconomic backgrounds. Trafficking is perpetrated by men, women, parents, doctors, lawyers, business owners, managers, truck drivers, accountants, and people of all ages, in every country of the world. Victims are similarly diverse.

In this book we will highlight risk factors for each of the various forms of human trafficking. **Risk factors** refer to characteristics that increase someone's likelihood of experiencing a risk—in this case, human trafficking victimization or perpetration. The presence of a risk factor does not mean a person will engage in trafficking or be victimized by trafficking. The absence of any of the common risk factors also does not ensure that someone could not be a trafficker or could not be exploited by a trafficker. The purpose of studying risk factors is to better understand the motives and ways that traffickers succeed in human exploitation. It is not to contribute to the marginalization of all people to whom the risk factor may apply.

Poverty can motivate people to take risks when seeking employment opportunities, which is one way that poverty increases the risk for trafficking victimization and perpetration.

What are some other ways that poverty may increase someone's risk of becoming a trafficker or being a victim of human trafficking? What social, cultural, and political factors might interact with poverty to increase someone's risk of being involved in trafficking?

For example, poverty (having relatively low income or financial resources) is a strong risk factor for trafficking victimization, but certainly not everyone in poverty is a victim of human trafficking and not all victims of human trafficking come from low socioeconomic backgrounds.

In Chapter 4 we will discuss factors that make potential victims vulnerable to human trafficking, and in Chapter 5 we will discuss risk factors for traffickers.

Approaches to Combating Human Trafficking

Violations of human rights are both a cause and a consequence of trafficking in persons. Accordingly, it is essential to place the protection of all human rights at the centre of any measures taken to prevent and end trafficking. Antitrafficking measures should not adversely affect the human rights and dignity of persons and, in particular, the rights of those who have been trafficked, migrants, internally displaced persons, refugees and asylum seekers.

—Office of the High Commissioner for Human Rights, 2014

Human trafficking is inextricably linked to **human rights**. The actions associated with human trafficking are explicitly prohibited by international human rights laws. While it may seem unnecessary to even distinguish human rights violations from human trafficking violations, doing so can help to identify the role of governments in protecting victims (Office of the High Commissioner for Human Rights, 2014).

Most governments and anti-trafficking organizations use the 4-P framework, shown in Figure 1.6, to guide anti-trafficking efforts (United Nations Office on Drugs and Crime, 2009b; U.S. Department of State, n.d.a). We will discuss the 4P framework more throughout this book as we delve into the different forms of trafficking. It is important to review these principles now, because the U.S. State Department, the UN, and other international organizations use this framework to determine how countries and other localities rank in terms of addressing human trafficking.

Prevention. Prevention is fundamental to anti-trafficking efforts. Prevention efforts include providing general interventions to communities and strategic interventions to high-risk groups to prevent victimization and revictimization.

Figure 1.6 Select Trafficking in Persons Protocol Requirements Related to the Four *P's*

Prevention	Protection	Prosecution	Partnership
• International standards to prevent trafficking in persons • Media campaigns and social and economic initiatives to prevent trafficking in persons • Policies and programs that prevent trafficking and protect victims from revictimization	Protection, assistance, and reintegration for victims, including: • Housing • Medical, psychological, and material assistance • Employment, education, and training opportunities • Facilitation and acceptance of the return of victims • Participation of victims in proceedings • Protection of the privacy of victims and witnesses • No detention of trafficked persons	• Definition and criminalization of human trafficking at national and local levels • Criminalization and measures against corruption • Special investigative techniques	• National coordination/ cooperation among all stakeholders • International cooperation . . . to increase capacity to prevent, investigate, prosecute, adjudicate, and punish traffickers • Support of extradition mechanisms

Source: Adapted from United Nations Office on Drugs and Crime 2009.

Prevention efforts may include increasing awareness of the prevalence and nature of trafficking as well as knowledge about the tactics used by traffickers.

Protection. Many victims go undetected, and thus unprotected. Protection efforts focus on identifying victims and referring victims to legal, social, and health services that will help them rebuild their lives.

Prosecution. Many traffickers are never prosecuted or punished. While nearly every country has some legislation outlawing human trafficking, few have provisions that comprehensively cover all aspects of the trafficking in persons protocol. Prosecution efforts focus on developing and strengthening legal frameworks to comply with the protocol, building the capacity of actors at every stage in the criminal justice system to address human trafficking, and establishing specialized institutions to identify, prosecute, and punish traffickers.

Partnership. Lack of coordinated efforts, collaboration, and communication among different groups serves as a primary barrier to combating human trafficking. Partnership refers to the coordination of multiple actors to execute prevention, protection, and prosecution efforts. Partnerships can include collaboration among many groups, including governments, victim service providers, law enforcement, health care personnel, financial institutions, researchers, and the general public.

Conclusion

Human trafficking is a profitable criminal enterprise and a grave threat to individuals' fundamental human rights. Human trafficking refers to a broad range of exploitive practices, including debt bondage, forced labor, child marriage, organ removal, sexual exploitation, and child soldiering. International consensus on the definition of human trafficking is relatively recent; it was established in the trafficking in persons protocol of 2000. Our understanding of human trafficking and the populations most vulnerable to it is continually evolving.

KEY WORDS

globalization 5
human rights 13
human smuggling 10

Palermo protocols 6
risk factors 12
slavery 2

human trafficking 2
trafficking in persons protocol 7
Trafficking Victims Protection Act (TVPA) 6

DISCUSSION QUESTIONS

1. Navigate to www.slaveryfootprint.org. What is your slavery footprint? What are three things the average person can do to reduce their slavery footprint?

2. How might someone's gender increase their risk for human trafficking?

3. What is the punishment for human trafficking in your home community? Did you know this offhand or did you have to look it up? How might the ways we publicize or fail to publicize punishments associated with human trafficking affect traffickers' behaviors and decision making?

RESOURCES

Environmental Footprint

-   This site allows you to enter numerous resources you use (shelter, food, transportation) to get an estimate of how many Planet Earths it would take to provide you with enough resources to sustain your lifestyle: http://www.earthday.org/take-action/footprint-calculator/? gclid=Cj0KEQjwpNm-BRCJ3rDN mOuKi9IBEiQAlzDJH9w6pClsswfHtqMGpszz 8QvZCLRz_B5_HZHHtjcC1mYaAikn8P8HAQ

Human Rights

-   Human rights and human trafficking footprint: https://www.ohchr.org/Documents/Publications/FS36_en.pdf

Historical Slavery

-   Transatlantic slave trade: http://www.unesco.org/new/en/social-and-human-sciences/themes/slave-route/transatlantic-slave-trade/

-   Slave trade database: http://www.slavevoyages.org/

Understanding Globalization

-   *What Is Globalization?*: https://piie.com/microsites/globalization/what-is-globalization.html

-   World Economic and Social Survey 2017: https://www.un.org/development/desa/dpad/wp-content/uploads/sites/45/publication/WESS_2017-FullReport.pdf?_ga=2.217782431.883992601.1545514570–1258121075.1545514570

Challenges, Resources, and Recommendations

The tools to crush modern slavery exist, but the political will is lacking.

—**Sheryl WuDunn**

The term *human trafficking* is becoming increasingly familiar among the general public in the United States and perhaps even globally. However, a precise understanding of the magnitude of human trafficking is more difficult to grasp. Definitional disagreements, limited data, and unreliable measurement all result in a grave misunderstanding of the scope of human trafficking and its causes. Such misconceptions result in a lower prioritization of trafficking in policy and a misallocation of resources for trafficking victims. There are some data and reports, however, that are considered reliable and informative, including the U.S. Department of State's annual Trafficking in Persons Report, the United Nations Office on Drugs and Crime's (UNODC's) Global Report on Trafficking in Persons, reports from the International Labour Organization, and reports from well-known nonprofit organizations such as Walk Free. While these resources are not without their own criticisms, they are the best resources we have to date.

This chapter will review the general challenges faced when estimating the magnitude and complexities of human trafficking domestically and globally. Additionally, it will provide descriptions of the existing resources, their purposes, data collection strategies, criticisms they face, and their general contributions to the understanding of human trafficking. The chapter will conclude with a discussion of future directions for data collection and analyses.

Challenges to Understanding Human Trafficking

The general population in the United States, and perhaps even the world, does not understand what human trafficking is, its complexities, and its massive reach. Several challenges exist when it comes to understanding human trafficking. Perhaps one of the biggest challenges relates to inconsistent definitions of trafficking. While increased legislation has improved uniformity in definitions across countries and regions, definitional inconsistencies remain. Additional challenges come from an inherent misunderstanding of trafficking. Smuggling and trafficking are often confused; discriminating between the two is inherently difficult. Further, the acceptance of males and boys as victims requires a paradigm shift that is challenged by cultural norms and tools that may not be as effective at identifying male victims. Finally, data and methods, hindered by definitional issues, pose an enormous barrier to understanding and eliminating human trafficking. More on these issues follows.

Definitions of Human Trafficking

Consider your own definition of the term *human trafficking*. You could refer to a dictionary to understand what *human* means if you are confused. But what about the term *trafficking*? What does this word mean to you?

Words like *trafficking*, *slavery*, and *discrimination* are contextualized. Your definition may come from personal and observed experiences, random pieces of information, culture, religious beliefs, and so forth. As you might imagine, when we incorporate our own values into definitions, this can lead to variations in the definition. This is exactly what has happened with human trafficking. Internationally, values vary widely. What types of behavior are okay in one country or region may be quite different in another. Take, for example, child marriage. While in some countries this is acceptable (see Focus on Child Marriage on page 18), it is not okay in others (Neumann, 2015). Similarly, child labor is acceptable and routine in Brazil and Guyana, and debt bondage is a formal part of the Nepali economy (Schartz, 2017). However, in the United States we would never condone either of those behaviors. Such disagreement results in serious challenges to formulating an agreed-upon international definition of human trafficking.

Challenge Yourself 2.1

What do these terms mean to you: *trafficking, slavery, racism, discrimination*? Do you have the same definitions as your peers? Your instructors? Your parents? How might definition disagreements impact measurement? How might it impact policy?

U.S. State Department

Photo 2.1 Yemeni schoolchildren held up this poster outside the parliament in Sana'a, Yemen, to denounce child marriage.

Focus On

Child Marriage: An Example of Cultural Differences

Girls Not Brides is "a global partnership of more than 700 civil society organizations from over 90 countries committed to ending child marriage and enabling girls to fulfill their potential." Organizations associated with Girls Not Brides come from all continents and work to change laws and policies as well as create programs to reduce child marriage. Child marriage occurs in many countries and across various cultures and religions. According to Girls Not Brides, several factors contribute to marriage for individuals under age 18, including gender inequality, culture and tradition, poverty, and insecurity.

The organization has some startling facts to share:

- At the current rate there will be 1.2 billion women married as a child by 2050.

- 1 in 3 girls in the developing world is married before age 18.

- Over 700 million women alive today were married as children.

Girls Not Brides ranks countries in two ways—those with the highest rates of child marriage and those with the highest absolute numbers of child marriage. Child marriage occurs most often in African nations. Nearly all of the 20 countries with the highest rates of child marriage are in Africa. Niger is at the top, with 76% of women having been married before the age of 18. India and Nicaragua, the only two non-African countries on the list, have the tenth- and fourteenth-highest rates of child marriage in the world, respectively. Forty-seven percent of Indian women and 41% of Nicaraguan women were married before the age of 18.

When considering the highest absolute numbers, India ranks the highest of the top-20 countries, with a total of 26,610,000 girls in child marriage, as compared to Bangladesh, ranked in second place, with 3,931,000 girls.

These numbers indicate extreme differences of opinion regarding the acceptability of child marriage. While desperation seems to provide some explanation for child marriage, it does not explain it all. Whether it be due to gender discrimination or tradition, the practice is accepted in some cultures. We see child marriage occurring even in the United States. Girls Not Brides estimates that over 248,000 girls were married, mostly to adult men, between 2000 and 2010.

Culture and tradition play a role in defining acceptable behavior. Definitions of child marriage, like those of human trafficking, are also susceptible to culture and tradition, making its elimination all that much more challenging.

Source: Girl Not Brides website: http://www.girlsnotbrides.org/.

Lack of an agreed-upon definition is by far one of the greatest challenges we face in combating human trafficking (Aroma, 2007; Kessler, 2015; Laczko & Gramegna, 2003). Without compatible definitions, it becomes nearly impossible to measure trafficking across countries. As nearly all countries have become a source, transit, and destination for trafficking, multi-country analyses are critical to fully understand the problem (Aroma, 2007). Further, cross-country investigative cooperation is also hindered by definition disagreement. Fortunately, definitional challenges have been minimized, albeit not at all eradicated, by the formation and ratification of international laws and, domestically, the Trafficking Victims Protection Act.

International Laws on Human Trafficking

The United Nations Convention Against Transnational Organized Crime provides the main international guidance on how to define, prevent, and prosecute human trafficking, adopted in 2000 and entered into force in 2003 (King, 2008; United Nations General Assembly, 2000c, 2001): This guidance comes specifically from two relevant protocols, the United Nations Protocol to Prevent, Suppress and Punish Trafficking in Persons Especially Women and Children, entered into force in 2003 (United Nations General Assembly, 2000c), and the United Nations Protocol Against the Smuggling of Migrants by Land, Sea and Air, adopted in 2004 (United Nations, 2000). You may see either of these termed the Palermo protocol, as they comprise two of the three protocols supplementing the Palermo convention, that is, the **UN Convention Against Transnational Organized Crime** (see Figure 2.1). The main convention, at its adoption, signified the seriousness of the issue of international organized crime and provided the groundwork to encourage international collaboration and cooperation. States that ratified the convention committed to defining trafficking as a domestic criminal offense, designing frameworks for extradition, cooperating with law enforcement, and promoting training and technical assistance to increase domestic capacity for fighting organized crime (United Nations General Assembly, 2001).

The **UN Protocol to Prevent, Suppress and Punish Trafficking in Persons Especially Women and Children** offered the first globally agreed-upon definition of human trafficking and carried the intention of creating comparable definitions within domestic frameworks. This definition implies the absence of human agency in trafficking instances. One cannot choose to be trafficked. Such a specification is important, as it provides a distinction between trafficking and smuggling (King, 2008). Another central theme of the definition is to specify that trafficking does not require direct force or threat. Simply having no other alternative to compliance is means for labeling a situation human trafficking. Further, the protocol provides guidance on how to protect and assist victims of human trafficking within a human rights framework (United Nations General Assembly, 2001).

As described by the United Nations, the **UN Protocol Against the Smuggling of Migrants by Land, Sea and Air,** adopted in 2004, recognized the growing

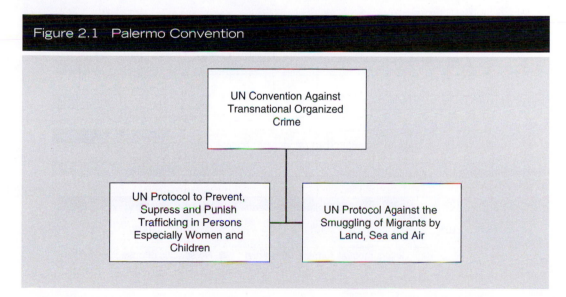

Figure 2.1   Palermo Convention

issue of smuggling and the high risk for exploitations experienced by those being smuggled (United Nations General Assembly, 2001). The protocol provides a concrete definition of smuggling and encourages states to collaborate to end smuggling and the extreme forms of exploitation often present during the smuggling process. More discussion on the definitions of smuggling and human trafficking are discussed below.

While the existence of international laws is a first step, adherence is perhaps even more challenging. As of July 2018, 189 UN member states were party to the UN Convention Against Transnational Organized Crime (United Nations General Assembly, 2001). Upon adopting the convention, a country's adherence is monitored by the UN and the country is expected to submit reports regularly describing its compliance with the convention (King, 2008). There has been a distinct upward trend in countries signing on. In 2008, only 143 countries were party to the convention, compared to 189 today (King, 2008). In 2018, countries not signing on to the convention, or signing on but not ratifying it, included Bhutan, Republic of the Congo, Iran, Palau, Papua New Guinea, the Solomon Islands, Somalia, South Sudan, and Tuvalu (United Nations General Assembly, 2001).

There has been a surge in support specifically for the Protocol to Prevent, Suppress and Punish Trafficking in Persons. As of 2018, 173 countries had adopted the protocol. Country-specific analyses are available and assess countries' inclusion of specific laws against human trafficking and how well those laws coincide with the UN's definition. The UN is looking to ensure that laws encompass crimes against men, women, boys, and girls and acknowledge domestic and transnational victims. Further laws should acknowledge all elements of trafficking, including the act, means, and purpose, as specifically described in Article 3 of the protocol (United Nations Office on Drugs and Crime, 2016a). As apparent in Figure 2.2,

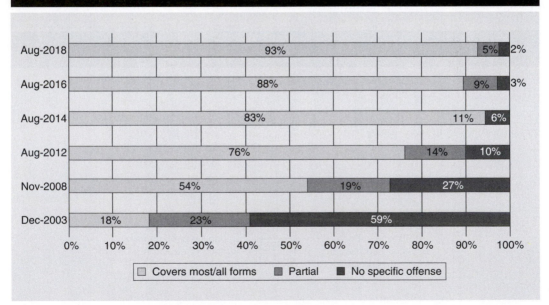

Figure 2.2 Criminalization of Trafficking in Persons With a Specific Offense Covering All or Some Forms as Defined in the UN Protocol, Shares of Countries, 2003–2018

Source: UNODC, 2018; UNODC elaboration of national data.

by 2018, 168 out of 181 countries included a definition of human trafficking consistent with the protocol. Only four of the 181 countries for which data were available do not criminalize trafficking in persons today.

The emergence of international law is a major contributor to reducing definitional issues. By providing a clearer distinction between smuggling and trafficking and acknowledging the trafficking of males as well as forms of trafficking other than sex, these laws have addressed many issues relating to variations in the definition of trafficking (Laczko & Gramegna, 2003). That being said, not all countries use a definition consistent with the protocol, although more and more do. And even when using a consistent definition, challenges can still exist in the minutiae. For example, as will be discussed in Chapter 4, at what point does a smuggled person become a victim of human trafficking? While the definition of human trafficking and human smuggling may be agreed upon, the gray area between may be disputed. Related, the concept of human agency, also discussed in Chapter 4, may be interpreted differently in different cultures. What is considered force? When is it reasonable to assume a person had no alternative options? Legislative specifications can only go so far in defining every possible act, means, and purpose.

United States Trafficking and Violence Prevention Act

As stated in Chapter 1, the Trafficking Victims Protection Act (2000) and its subsequent reauthorizations provide a definition of human trafficking in the United States. The law states that trafficking includes:

(A) sex trafficking in which a commercial sex act is induced by force, fraud, or coercion, or in which the person induced to perform such act has not attained 18 years of age; or

(B) the recruitment, harboring, transportation, provision, or obtaining of a person for labor or services, through the use of force, fraud, or coercion for the purpose of subjection to involuntary servitude, peonage, debt bondage, or slavery.

The law seeks to define the necessary requirements to conclude human trafficking has occurred. These requirements have been labeled the AMP model, requiring evidence of the action, means, and purpose of the trafficker (as shown in Figure 2.3). The AMP model is also used in the UN trafficking in persons protocol (United Nations General Assembly, 2000c). The Trafficking Victims Protection Act of 2000 (TVPA) specifies what elements must be present to prove someone has broken the law—proof of force, fraud, and coercion are necessary elements to convict someone of human trafficking (the "means" in the AMP model). The TVPA specifically states the forms of trafficking that are considered illegal—sex trafficking (of adults and minors) and labor trafficking (the "purpose" in the AMP model). The TVPA also specifies that evidentiary requirements are less stringent for the sex trafficking of children.

Although the AMP model, focusing on evidentiary requirements, takes on a punitive emphasis, the TVPA specifies more than just punishment. Punishment, in fact, is only one of the three Ps focused on in the TVPA. The others include *prevention* of trafficking internationally and *provision* of services to victims (Sheldon-Sherman, 2012).

Preventatively, the TVPA orders the monitoring of human trafficking around the world through the State Department's Office to Monitor and Combat Trafficking in

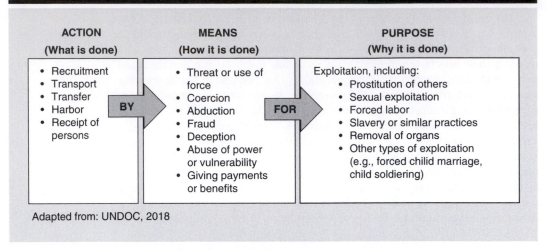

Figure 2.3 The AMP Model

ACTION (What is done)		MEANS (How it is done)		PURPOSE (Why it is done)
• Recruitment • Transport • Transfer • Harbor • Receipt of persons	**BY**	• Threat or use of force • Coercion • Abduction • Fraud • Deception • Abuse of power or vulnerability • Giving payments or benefits	**FOR**	Exploitation, including: • Prostitution of others • Sexual exploitation • Forced labor • Slavery or similar practices • Removal of organs • Other types of exploitation (e.g., forced chiild marriage, child soldiering)

Adapted from: UNDOC, 2018

Source: Adapted from UNODC, 2018.

Persons and the President's Interagency Task Force to Monitor and Combat Trafficking in Persons (Reiger, 2007; U.S. Department of State, n.d.c). Finally, in regard to provision, the law provides legal and social benefits to victims, including visas and support services.

The law is not without controversy. There are two different schools of thought when it comes to combating trafficking—those who are prosecutorial-minded and those who approach trafficking from the victim's perspective (Sheldon-Sherman, 2012). Prosecutors believe the law should go further in criminalizing trafficking and specifying more provisions for public safety trainings. Alternatively, victim advocates want to see more attention and focus in the law on victim services, for both domestic and foreign-born victims. They would like to see the foundation of the law be victim centered rather than focused on criminal justice.

Dang (2014) suggests that a victim-centered modification would improve the country's understanding of the complexity of the crime. She offers the following definition:

> Slavery is a social phenomenon existing on the far end of a continuum of oppression, where human beings completely dominate and exploit other human beings and this domination results in physical, psychological, and interpersonal trauma; financial and social instability and inequities; and dilution of the fundamental principles of democracy.

Challenge Yourself 2.2

Write your own definition of human trafficking. Read your definition. Is it consistent with the UN's definition? Is it punitive? Does it accurately portray the complexities of the crime (social and economic impact)? Is your definition more similar to the TVPA's or to Dang's (2014)? Why did you choose to write the definition in the way you did?

The controversies surrounding the TVPA go beyond its focus. The effectiveness of the law has often been called into question, specifically due to the lack of federal prosecutions since the law's implementation, the lack of follow-through on the part of individual states in engaging in anti-trafficking efforts, and insufficient victim services (Reiger, 2007; Sheldon-Sherman, 2012). There is specific concern regarding the prosecution of labor trafficking cases. At the federal level, there has actually been a decline in the number of federal prosecutions for labor trafficking. In 2010, labor trafficking represented 60% of all human trafficking cases. That number dropped to 27% in 2014. The Human Trafficking Prosecution Unit, within the Department of Justice, cited a lack of funding as the explanation for the drop in prosecutions. Labor cases are especially resource-intensive. Their unique complexities require more time, staff, and interagency collaboration than sex trafficking cases (Febry, 2013). Febry (2013), an associate for the Human Rights First's Bankrupt Slavery campaign, advocates for future TVPA reauthorizations to focus on labor trafficking. Statistics show that labor trafficking is most certainly not on the decline. A decline in enforcement is not reflective of a decline in trafficking. Improved regulations should designate special prosecutors and trainings that focus on labor trafficking issues, especially in regions most vulnerable to this form of trafficking.

Despite criticism, progress has undoubtedly been made since the adoption of the TVPA, specifically regarding state engagement (see Focus on State-Level Attention to Human Trafficking on page 25). An increase in state legislation has prompted an increase in state-level enforcement and prosecutions. Nevertheless, prosecutions at a federal level as well as victim services continue to struggle to keep up. In regard to prosecutions, federal law enforcement officials express challenges to combating human trafficking at a federal level. The most pressing challenges include lack of victim cooperation, limited availability of victim services, and difficulty in identifying human trafficking (U.S. Government Accountability Office [GAO], 2016). The best chance of alleviating these challenges is believed to be through increased grant-based programming. The GAO (2016) identified 42 grant programs, awarded to 123 organizations in 2014 and 2015, used to combat human trafficking and assist victims. The primary purposes of these grant programs were to provide technical assistance to service providers and law enforcement, support task forces, and provide direct service (GAO, 2016).

Although not as recently, Polaris also produced a report grading the states on their human trafficking legislation, including all forms of trafficking. Their ranking system assigned states and the District of Columbia to four different tiers, with Tier 1 states having the most promising legal frameworks for combating trafficking (Polaris, 2014a). Polaris evaluated and ranked states on the following categories: laws criminalizing (1) sex trafficking; and (2) labor trafficking; laws focused on (3a) asset forfeiture for trafficking offenses; (3b) investigative tools such as including human trafficking in the state racketeering statute or authorization of interception of communications during investigations into trafficking; (4a) training for law enforcement; (4b) development of a task force; (5) lower burden of proof for the prosecution of child sex trafficking offenses; (6) posting information about a human trafficking hotline; (7) providing safe harbor to minor victims of trafficking; (8) victim assistance plans or services; (9) a civil remedy for human trafficking victims; and (10) vacating convictions.

Shared Hope International (SHI) has made a commitment to ending domestic minor sex trafficking (DMST). One way it has invested in the cause is to assess the work being done on a state level to reduce DMST. Assessment of state-level legislation is central to its work, as states that do not have the appropriate trafficking laws in place have fewer resources at their disposal to address the problem. SHI's Protected Innocence Challenge identifies laws that are necessary in establishing an aggressive response to DMST (SHI, 2016b). All 50 states and the District of Colombia are scored on whether they have laws in the following categories:

1. Criminalization of domestic minor sex trafficking

2. Criminal provisions addressing demand

3. Criminal provisions for traffickers

4. Criminal provisions for facilitators

5. Protective provisions for the child victim

6. Criminal justice tools for investigation and prosecution

States are graded within each of these categories. Category grades are tallied to assign a total grade to each state (SHI, 2016b). The good news is that as of 2016, every state and the District of Columbia had criminalized DMST. Five states had even gone so far as to eliminate criminal liability of minors under state prostitution laws (SHI, 2016b). As illustrated in Figure 2.4, great improvements have been made in state-level legislation regarding DMST. Organizations like SHI provide a valuable resource in engaging state leaders to improve their legislation and engagement in combating human trafficking. However, more work needs to be done.

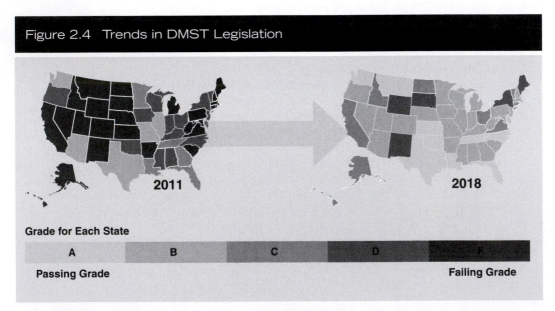

Figure 2.4   Trends in DMST Legislation

2011

2018

Grade for Each State

| A | B | C | D | F |

Passing Grade

Failing Grade

Source: Reprinted by permission of Shared Hope International. (2018).

Figure 2.5 Number of States Fulfilling Polaris Legislative Categories

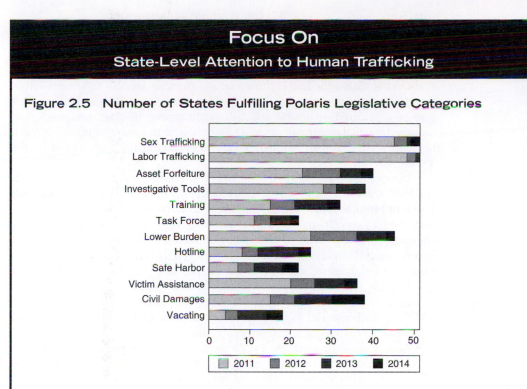

Source: Polaris, 2014a.

As evident in Figure 2.5, all states have some form of legislation regarding sex trafficking. Trends show improvement across all 10 categories. The maps shown in Figure 2.6 support the findings of SHI as well. Generally, states are improving in their legislative efforts to reduce human trafficking.

Figure 2.6 Trends in State Rankings

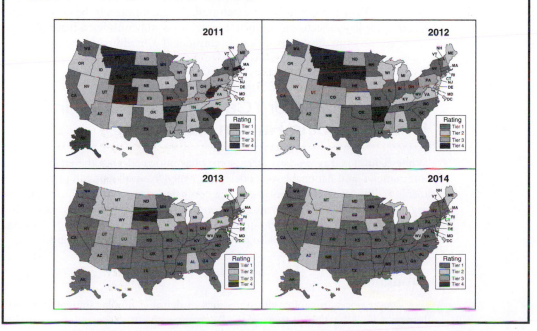

It appears evident, based on the GAO (2016) as well as other sources, that while the TVPA does use a prosecutorial framework, there are specifications for victim services. Sheldon-Sherman (2012) suggests that, given this point, discussion needs to move away from changing the foundation of the law to focus more on working within the law. Is there a way to improve services to victims within the prosecutorial focus of the TVPA? Sheldon-Sherman (2012) suggests another P to be considered—*partnership*. Collaboration among agencies, nonprofits, and nongovernmental organizations (NGOs) would lead to a more cohesive approach to victim services and an increased likelihood of meeting the goals set forth in the TVPA.

Increasingly, it appears as if this strategy is receiving some buy-in. At the federal level, the TVPA mandated the emergence of the **President's Interagency Task Force to Monitor and Combat Trafficking in Persons**. In 2013, this task force published a five-year strategic plan to promote collaboration for the purposes of aligning efforts, improving understanding of human trafficking, expanding access to services, and improving outcomes. The GAO (2016) report indicates a commitment to a collaborative approach at the federal, state, and local levels as well as across levels. Their data show collaboration among federal agencies including the Departments of Health and Human Services, Homeland Security, Justice, Labor, and State. Such agencies work together for federal cases and work with state and local agencies to investigate and prosecute cases.

Also, at the state level, there is an increased focus on multidisciplinary task forces. It seems logical that the emergence of task forces increases and encourages collaboration among the different players around the table. Polaris (2014a) includes legislatively mandated human trafficking task forces as one of the categories for its state rankings. As of fall 2015, 20 states had legislation requiring or encouraging the creation of a statewide task force (Polaris, 2015c). It is believed that many more states than that have nonmandated task forces. While such task forces are more vulnerable to dissolution, they provide an important step toward coordination and collaboration.

In summary, the TVPA faces challenges, especially related to the framework of the law. How the law defines human trafficking continues to be debated. The fact that the law's effectiveness, albeit improving, is still considered inadequate by some gives victim advocates reason to consider if a modified framework might alleviate some of those challenges.

Additional Factors Causing Confusion in Understanding Human Trafficking

While definitional issues have been somewhat mitigated with the emergence of international and national laws modeled after the UN's trafficking in persons protocol, additional issues contribute to the confusion surrounding human trafficking. Distinguishing between smuggling and trafficking as well as issues in how we define victims all contribute to the misunderstanding of human trafficking. Measurement and data issues also play a significant role in the confusion.

Smuggling

One major source of confusion comes in defining human smuggling versus human trafficking. One purpose of the Palermo protocols, discussed earlier in this chapter, is to distinguish between smuggling and trafficking. The protocols define trafficking as:

> . . . the recruitment, transportation, transfer, harbouring or receipt of persons, by means of the threat or use of force or other forms of coercion, of abduction, of fraud, of deception, of the abuse of power or of a position of vulnerability or of the giving or receiving of payments or benefits to achieve the consent of a person having control over another person, for the purpose of exploitation. Exploitation shall include, at a minimum, the exploitation of the prostitution of others or other forms of sexual exploitation, forced labour or services, slavery or practices similar to slavery, servitude or the removal of organs. . . . The consent of a victim of trafficking in persons to the intended exploitation . . . shall be irrelevant where any of the means set forth (above) have been used. The recruitment, transportation, transfers . . . of a child for the purpose of exploitation shall be considered "trafficking in persons" even if this does not involve any of the means set forth (above). (Bhabha, 2005)

In contrast, the term *smuggling* refers to consensual transactions between individuals who want to cross borders and individuals willing to provide means to cross borders without adhering to proper immigration protocols. The smuggling protocol (United Nations, 2000) defines "smuggling of migrants" as "the procurement, in order to obtain, directly or indirectly, a financial or other material benefit, of the illegal entry of a person into a State Party of which the person is not a national or a permanent resident" (Napier-Moore, 2011, p. 5). Figure 2.7 compares the two definitions.

As Chapter 4 will point out, those who are smuggled are extremely vulnerable to traffickers. But smuggling on its own is not trafficking. That being said, it can be

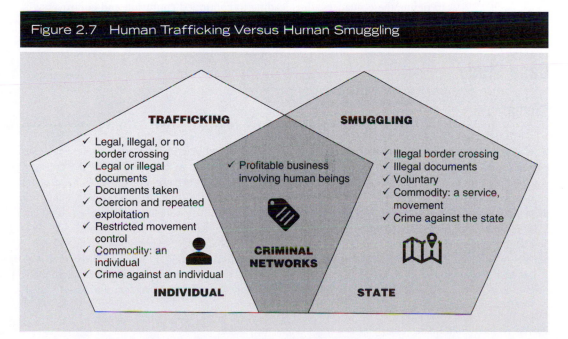

Figure 2.7   Human Trafficking Versus Human Smuggling

Source: Adapted from BlueBlindFold.Gov (http://www.blueblindfold.gov.ie/en/bbf/pages/trafficking_or_smuggling).

difficult to tell the difference, especially without in-depth investigation. Further, a case may start out as smuggling and end as trafficking. Laws may not be specific in defining when the appropriate time is to label an act—when the smuggled person departs or at the point of arrival. While the state may prefer assessing the situation from the point of departure, most victim advocates prefer defining the crime from the point of arrival. Their perspective is that intentions and reality are often different. While the smuggled person may have consented to illegally crossing the border, upon arrival, the conditions of the smuggling agreement may have changed. For example, the smuggler may demand more money for release or force the smuggled person into an employment situation he or she did not consent to. The smuggled person may go from criminal to victim status. Further, even at the point of departure, the consensual agreement may be based on fraudulent promises of work, schooling, or other opportunities (Bhabha, 2005).

The possibility of consensual agreements being based on fraudulent promises brings up the issue of human agency. When attempting to define an act as smuggling or trafficking, the decision maker (policy maker?) must assess the line between consent and coercion. Some forms of **coercion** are clear—kidnapping, blatant lying, and falsehoods. But some forms of coercion are blurrier—for example, if a family has absolutely no money, no means to make money, and no hope for survival in their current situation. If a smuggler comes offering an opportunity for work, schooling, and a generally better life, the family may have no other option than to take the risk of trusting the smuggler. In a situation such as this, does a policy maker define this as trafficking or smuggling? While the smuggled person consented to crossing the border, what option did they have?

The trafficking in persons protocol (United Nations General Assembly, 2000c) includes the following in its definition of coercion—"the abuse of power or of a position of vulnerability." Thus, if a smuggler takes advantage of his or her position and offers fraudulent opportunities to vulnerable individuals and families living in extreme poverty, is this trafficking or smuggling? There are no laws in place to define these nuances, thus leading to continued confusion and controversy in discriminating between trafficking and smuggling.

Case Study

"Sonia"

Would you define this as human smuggling or human trafficking?

Sonia was invited to come to the United States by family friends and told that she could work for them as a housekeeper and they would pay her $100 a week. Sonia was provided with fraudulent documents and departed for the United States with her new employer. She knew this was illegal, but she needed the money and was willing to take the risk.

Was Sonia smuggled or trafficked?

Upon arriving in the United States, Sonia was kept in isolation, given a place to sleep in the basement, and told not to speak to anyone or she would be turned over to Immigration Services. Sonia was never paid for her work and felt that she had no one to turn to for help.

Was Sonia smuggled or trafficked?

At this point, Sonia was restricted from leaving the house, threatened with deportation if she attempted to talk to anyone, and forced into involuntary servitude.

Source: Adapted from Human Smuggling and Trafficking Center, 2006.

Focus On

The Human Smuggling and Trafficking Center

The United States is aware of the confusion law enforcement may experience when investigating potential smuggling and trafficking cases. To provide more clarification and understanding, the **Intelligence Reform and Terrorism Prevention Act** of 2004 established the **Human Smuggling and Trafficking Center.**

The center serves as a clearinghouse for all information related to human smuggling and trafficking. Subject-matter experts with expertise in intelligence analysis, law enforcement collaboration, and support and diplomacy staff the Center.

The center performs five main functions:

- **Facilitates broad dissemination of all source information:**

  o The center integrates and disseminates raw and finished tactical, operational, and strategic intelligence to member U.S. agencies' operational components, U.S. policy makers, and appropriate foreign partners. This intelligence provides actionable leads for U.S. law enforcement agencies.

- **Prepares strategic assessments:**

  o The center prepares strategic assessments related to important aspects of human smuggling and trafficking in persons and clandestine terrorist travel. Assessment topics include global smuggling and trafficking organizations and networks; the extent of progress in dismantling organizations; smuggling and trafficking schemes, patterns, and trends; and proven law enforcement and other approaches for countering smuggling and trafficking.

  o The center may issue intelligence bulletins, reports and notes, longer analysis products, and target packages about human smuggling organizations and networks, which are provided to appropriate U.S. agencies for action. These strategic assessments provide policy makers with accurate, objective analysis about threats, vulnerabilities, and opportunities for action.

- **Identifies issues for interagency coordination or attention:**

  o The center identifies issues related to migrant smuggling or trafficking in persons for referral to relevant agencies or interagency organizations for consideration and action, as appropriate.

- **Coordinates select initiatives and provides support:**

  o Where appropriate, and upon the request of relevant members of the community, the center may coordinate anti-smuggling or anti-trafficking initiatives.

- **Works with and exchanges information with allied foreign governments and organizations:**

  o The center serves as a centralized U.S. point of contact for similar allied foreign centers, multinational organizations, and national law enforcement and intelligence authorities that combat international illicit travel. The center actively exchanges information with allies and partners—including Interpol, Europol, and Frontex—regarding human smuggling, human trafficking, and terrorist mobility.

Source: Adapted from U.S. Immigration and Customs Enforcement, n.d.c.

Men and Boys

As mentioned, the UN's trafficking in persons protocol is formally named the Protocol to Prevent, Suppress, and Punish Trafficking in Persons Especially Women and Children. Such a title nearly eliminates the possibility of male victims. The TVPA has been criticized for its focus on women and children when describing the trafficking issues faced in the United States (Greve, 2014). Section 102 of the law specifically highlights women and children as the primary populations of concern when it comes to trafficking. It states, "At least 700,000 persons annually, primarily women and children, are trafficking within or across international borders. Approximately 50,000 women and children are trafficked in the United States each year" (Trafficking Victims Protection Act, 2000). Moreover, while, it is true that women and children are more likely to be trafficked than men, it is inaccurate to assume that males are only perpetrators of trafficking and cannot be victims. Similarly, it would be false to assume that women are only victims and never traffickers. Chapter 4 provides statistics and trends concerning the number of women, men, girls, and boys believed to be victims of trafficking. The point to be made here is that the intense focus on women and children has made the identification of male victims more challenging. First responders and service providers may not be properly trained or have the most accurate tools for identifying and serving male victims. The growing realization that male victims exist may change the way we identify trafficking. Our understanding of the male victim population is still being realized but with that will come a recalibration of assessment tools and services, which is absolutely needed to meet the unique needs of this population.

Data and Measurement

Issues with data and measurement also play a role in our misunderstanding of human trafficking. As not all countries use the United Nations' definition of trafficking, there is no universal definition. What may be considered trafficking in the United States may not be so in other countries. A lack of agreed-upon definitions makes collecting data across countries very challenging, and given that human trafficking often results in the crossing of borders, this limitation results in a serious barrier to our understanding of trafficking in general (Aroma, 2007; Laczko & Gramegna, 2003). Many believe that our ability to accurately measure trafficking is quite possibly our best chance at eliminating it (Weiner & Hala, 2008). More attention must be given to creating regional and country-level definitions that may help us see the trafficking situation more clearly (Aroma, 2007).

In addition to measurement weaknesses, existing data is limited (Gozdziak & Bump, 2008; Schartz, 2017). Even in the process of writing this book, we were shocked at the limited number of high-quality peer-reviewed articles available on the topic. The Institute for Study of International Migration at Georgetown University completed a comprehensive study of all the available literature on human trafficking. Their findings indicated that most of our knowledge on human trafficking comes from intragovernmental reports, NGOs, and the United Nations. Further, the methodological quality of this research is weak. They concluded that our misunderstanding of human trafficking is multilayered and complex. Their findings showed that a lack of high-quality and reliable data results in

> . . . limited understanding of the characteristics of victims (including the ability to differentiate between the special needs of adult and child victims, girls and boys, women and men), their life experiences, and

their trafficking trajectories; poor understanding of the modus operandi of traffickers and their networks; and lack of evaluation research on the effectiveness of governmental anti-trafficking policies and the efficacy of rescue and restore programs, among other gaps in the current state of knowledge about human trafficking. (Gozdziak & Bump, 2008, p. 4)

The conclusions of Gozdiak and Bump's (2008) research are overwhelming but consistent with the findings of others (Kangaspunta, 2010; Laczko & Gramegna, 2003; Weiner & Hala, 2008). It is challenging to understand something when we may not know what we don't know. Our understanding can only be based on human trafficking cases we have identified. Moreover, we know that underreporting is especially problematic when it comes to human trafficking. Victim identification is particularly difficult, hampered by many factors, including fear of coming forward (due to distrust of government, fear of retribution by the trafficker, and fear of deportation) (Weiner & Hala, 2008).

Further, some victims may not even identify as victims (Neumann, 2015). Take, for example, sex trafficking in the United States. A common recruitment strategy is for a male trafficker to act as his potential victim's boyfriend. He gains her trust and makes her fall in love with him. He asks her to have sex for money as a favor to him. The girl may not even realize that what is happening is very wrong. Other reasons victims may not identify as victims include financial needs and family pressure. Ask yourself the questions in Challenge Yourself 2.3. Understanding a victim's decision to come forward or not, and understanding how he or she may not identify as a victim, even if it is clear to everyone else, is impossible without understanding the context in which the victim is experiencing his or her trafficking.

The challenges to understanding human trafficking are great. While laws have improved, they are by no means complete. Labor trafficking is not well specified domestically or internationally. Males are underacknowledged in laws and service provisions. And the murky distinctions between smuggling and trafficking exist on every continent. But perhaps the most devastating challenge to our understanding of trafficking is a lack of data and valid measurement. Without data to compare trafficking within and across countries, we cannot have an effective counterstrategy (Aroma, 2007; Schartz, 2017). Efforts must be made to quantify vulnerabilities. The Heritage Foundation has been able to compare the rankings from the United States Trafficking in Persons (TIP) Reports to indices of economic freedom. The results are unsurprising, with those countries that are the most repressed having the lowest TIP rankings. Understanding economic freedom as well as poverty can hugely aid in driving interventions to reduce trafficking (Schartz, 2017).

The reality is that until we have consistent international definitions and laws, agreed-upon data collection methods, sophisticated data, and comparable statistics

Challenge Yourself 2.3

If your family said something was okay, would you think it was wrong? If you had no money and were being paid a small amount—perhaps not what you should have been paid, and the work conditions seemed very restrictive—would you think this was wrong? Would these situations, within context, make you define yourself as a victim?

on victims, trafficking reports, prosecutions, and convictions, human trafficking will continue to exist, if not flourish. Victims need to feel comfortable coming forward. This means that laws must specify service and visa provisions as well as resources to increase awareness, especially among vulnerable populations. These recommendations will improve our understanding of the magnitude of trafficking as well as the vulnerabilities driving human trafficking domestically and internationally.

Existing Resources to Improve Our Understanding of Human Trafficking

Despite the many challenges we face in defining human trafficking, assessing the magnitude of the problem, and targeting specific risk factors for prevention, resources exist that provide some clue as to the state of human trafficking, both domestically and internationally.

The Trafficking in Persons Report

The TVPA specified the creation of the Trafficking in Persons (TIP) office within the United States Department of State as well as the formation of an annual TIP Report. The Department of State indicates that the TIP Report provides "the world's most comprehensive resource on governmental anti-human trafficking efforts" (U.S. Department of State, n.d.b). There appears to be some agreement that this is the case—the TIP Report is considered one of the most reliable resources available today. Its efforts and contributions to the world's understanding of human trafficking are undeniable (Enos, 2015; Schartz, 2017; Szep & Spetalnick, 2015; Wooditch, 2011).

"Trafficking in Persons Report" (2018)

TRAFFICKING IN PERSONS REPORT

Photo 2.2
Cover of the
U.S. Department
of State's
Trafficking in
Persons Report
2018.

The first TIP Report was published in 2001, and annual reports have been released ever since. Although the exact methodologies and data sources are not explicitly stated in the annual reports (see more on this issue below), the methodology section of the 2018 report indicates that the report was prepared based on "information from U.S. embassies, government officials, nongovernmental and international organizations, published reports, news articles, academic studies, research trips to every region of the world, and information submitted to tipreport@state.gov" (U.S. Department of State, 2018b, p. 38).

The primarily goal of the report is to rank countries based on "the extent of government action to combat trafficking" (U.S. Department of State, 2016, p. 36). Less focus is given to the size of the countries' problems. Countries' efforts are compared to the minimum standards set forth in the TVPA, which are also consistent with the standards of the Palermo protocols (U.S. Department of State, 2018b). Countries are ranked into four tiers—Tier 1, Tier 2, the Tier 2 Watch List, and Tier 3. The Focus on the U.S. Department of State Trafficking in Persons Report Tier Rankings (see page 33) provides an explanation of each tier. Tier 1 indicates the closest adherence to the TVPA standards.

Tier 1

The governments of countries that fully meet the TVPA's minimum standards for the elimination of trafficking.

Tier 2

The governments of countries that do not fully meet the TVPA's minimum standards but are making significant efforts to meet those standards.

Tier 2 Watch List

The governments of countries that do not fully meet the TVPA's minimum standards but are making significant efforts to meet those standards, and for which:

i.   the absolute number of victims of severe forms of trafficking is very significant or is significantly increasing;

ii. there is a failure to provide evidence of increasing efforts to combat severe forms of trafficking in persons from the previous year, including increased investigations, prosecutions, and convictions of trafficking crimes; increased assistance to victims; and decreasing evidence of complicity in severe forms of trafficking by government officials; or

iii. the determination that a country is making significant efforts to meet the minimum standards was based on commitments by the country to take additional steps over the next year

Tier 3

The governments of countries that do not fully meet the TVPA's minimum standards and are not making significant efforts to do so.

The TIP Report: Is It Effective?

As a student, you are learning how to be critical. You are learning how to question research, question facts. So, what about the TIP Report? Does it seem odd to you that the United States has an entire office in the State Department fully committed to policing the rest of the world on their level of human trafficking? Why do they do it? Is it worth the resources it requires? If you are asking these questions, you are not alone.

There is no doubt that the TIP Report has positively impacted the battle to end human trafficking around the world. It is believed to have forced Switzerland to improve its laws to protect child prostitutes. It caused the Dominican Republic to improve its prosecutorial efforts and conviction rates of child traffickers (Szep & Spetalnick, 2015). In 2016, the number of rescued slaves nearly doubled although the rate of trafficking increased (Schartz, 2017). If the TIP Report's goal is to publicly embarrass countries into improving their efforts to curb human trafficking, it is successful. Public rankings create awareness, and the threat of sanctions (albeit typically waived) motivates many countries into action. And improvements have been made to the report since its first release in 2001 (Gallagher, 2010). Data sources are slightly more transparent, and the United States subsequently began including itself in the rankings.

Nevertheless, human trafficking seems to be on the rise. The TIP Report hasn't made the kind of impact it set out to make. Critics have some ideas on why this is. Although there are many reasons why the TIP Report may not be as effective as it could be, such as poor policy directives or the lack of inclusion of all countries, there are three primary criticisms of the report this text will focus on—the politicization of the TIP Report, the authority of the United States to publish such a report, and the methodology of the report.

Politicization of the TIP Report

Vague methodologies and a lack of transparent data (discussed below) result in critics questioning the independence of the TIP Office and its annual report. In particular, some have wondered if certain country rankings are in any way influenced by political ties between the U.S. and those countries (Gallagher, 2010; Schartz, 2017; Wooditch, 2011). An explosive report by Reuters gave credence to these beliefs in 2015 (Szep & Spetalnick, 2015). The Focus on the Reuters Investigative Report Into the 2015 TIP Report box provides details on the countries involved in the controversy, but essentially it came to light that in 2015 several countries received TIP rankings higher than what was recommended by the TIP Office. Reuter attributed this to pressure from high-up officials and diplomats within the U.S. Department of State (Enos, 2015; Szep & Spetalnick, 2015). Accusations indicated that the TIP Office was unable to produce independent assessments of diplomatically important countries. This controversy drew the attention of the U.S. Congress. Representative Chris Smith (NJ-R) concluded that the TIP Office was being influenced by the president's agenda. He publicly called the report politicized (Szep & Spetalnick, 2015).

Focus On
The Reuters Investigative Report Into the 2015 TIP Report

In preparing the 2015 TIP Report, Reuters reported disagreements between the TIP Office and various U.S. diplomatic bureaus regarding 17 different countries, resulting in multiple countries receiving higher rankings than the TIP Office had recommended, as noted in the figure below. Countries that the TIP Office (labeled "J/TIP" in the table) believed should be downgraded remained the same, such as India and Mexico. Some countries were even promoted to higher rankings despite recommendations from the TIP Office, including Cuba, Malaysia, and Uzbekistan.

Table 2.1 Disputed Rankings

	2014 Ranking	J/Tip Recommended Ranking for 2015	Final 2015 Ranking
China	TIER 2 WATCH LIST	TIER 3	TIER 2 WATCH LIST
Cuba	TIER 3	TIER 3	TIER 2 WATCH LIST
India	TIER 2	TIER 2 WATCH LIST	TIER 2
Malaysia	TIER 3	TIER 3	TIER 2 WATCH LIST
Mexico	TIER 2	TIER 2 WATCH LIST	TIER 2
Thailand	TIER 3	TIER 3	TIER 3
Uzbekistan	TIER 3	TIER 3	TIER 2 WATCH LIST

Note: J/TIP refers to the U.S. Department of State's Office to Monitor and Combat Trafficking in Persons
Source: Trafficking in Persons Report, Reuters Graphics.

This information was especially troubling, as it brought to light the involvement of diplomats and embassies in the rankings. Given the serious consequences of a Tier 3 ranking, including sanctions such as limited access to aid from the U.S., the International Monetary Fund, or the World Bank, the participation of diplomats influencing the report certainly reduced the legitimacy of the report's rankings (Schartz, 2017).

According to the Reuters investigative reporting, senior officials within the State Department disagreed with the TIP Office and pressured it to elevate the rankings of countries such as Malaysia, possibly due to a proposed new free-trade deal the U.S. was trying to negotiate with Malaysia and 11 other countries.

State Department official John Kirby insisted the rankings were not politicized, responding to Reuters that "as is always the case, final decisions are reached only after rigorous analysis and discussion between the TIP office, relevant regional bureaus and senior State Department leaders" (Szep & Spetalnick, 2015).

Of course, there are two sides to every debate. In the face of this criticism, and in addition to blatant denial of politicization, diplomats shared their perspective. They argued that poor TIP rankings hurt their ability to form strong relationships in unstable and corrupt countries. They advocated that their on-the-ground experience and expertise should be considered in the ranking assessments. Further, they stressed the importance of looking at the big picture. The TIP Report is just one piece of information. Goals to reduce authoritarian governments and bring about trade deals that may reduce poverty could be just as effective as, if not more effective than, a poor ranking in reducing trafficking (Szep & Spetalnick, 2015).

U.S. Authority

Although the TIP Report has continued to be published annually since its first publication in 2001, there has been a mixed reaction from "activists and governments alike, who object to the USA appointing itself supervisor and arbiter of a complex international issue that remains both contested and controversial" (Gallagher, 2010, p. 382). Some of the frustration was alleviated in 2010 when the U.S. began assessing their own anti-trafficking efforts; however, questions remain as to why they waited so long to do so (Gallagher, 2010; Schartz, 2017). Finally, some have criticized the U.S. for placing its own cultural standards on other countries. As discussed earlier in this chapter, countries vary in their approval of, or at least their complicity in, certain behaviors such as child marriage, child labor, and so forth. Is it the place of the U.S. to judge countries on traditions and practices that have been in place for many, many years (Schartz, 2017)?

Data and Methodological Challenges

The TIP Report is not exempt from the data and methodological challenges that plague nearly all existing reports on human trafficking. Poor data and methodology are unequivocally one of the biggest challenges to trafficking reduction efforts. Given the U.S. Department of State's confidence (perhaps insistence?) that the TIP Report offers the most comprehensive and accurate depiction of human trafficking available, its lack of transparent methodology and rich data is that much more disappointing and troublesome.

Critics highlight the inconsistent and murky methodology as being especially troublesome to the report's legitimacy (Enos, 2015; Gallagher, 2010; Weiner & Hala, 2008). Early on in the methodology section of the report is a vague list of resources, which are said to be the basis for each country's ranking. Few specifics in regard to sources of information are provided by country. Little is known about exact resources or analyses used in calculating the rankings of each country.

Data is another serious issue. The TIP Report does not include raw data files. There is little to no transparency regarding the specific evidence being used to determine rankings. The lack of both quantitative and qualitative data limits the TIP Report's ability to truly make an impact on human trafficking (Gallagher, 2010; Schartz, 2017).

Global Resources to Monitor Human Trafficking

As Gozdziak and Bump (2008) pointed out in their review of the existing literature on human trafficking, 90% of publications on the topic come from intergovernmental agencies, NGOs, and the United Nations. There is very little empirical data available to improve our understanding of the foundational causes of human trafficking (Schartz, 2017). While this in itself is a weakness, it is important to review the sources that provide the most reliable information. There is a lot of misinformation available. The TIP Report offers one reliable, if not biased, resource on human trafficking. But others also exist.

The United Nations

The United Nations (UN) has committed itself to being a compass when it comes to directing nations on how to react to and combat human trafficking. The UN's Office on Drugs and Crime (UNODC) provides a global database

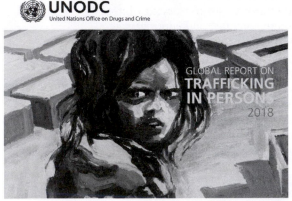

of international case law and legislation that offers immediate public access to information on specific instances of human trafficking (Kangaspunta, 2010; UNODC, 2016a). The information gathered in the database includes details on the nationalities of the perpetrators and victims as well as the stories of the victims. The UNODC hopes that the database can offer precedent for policy makers, judges, and prosecutors as they set forth to improve laws and prosecutorial efforts (UNODC, 2011b).

Moreover, the UNODC publishes a Global Report on Trafficking in Persons, complete with profiles of 142 countries. The original report was published in 2009 and garnered international attention. It was said to provide an "unprecedented view of the available information on the state of the world's response to trafficking, including near-comprehensive data on national legislative and enforcement activity" (Gallagher, 2010, p. 390). In its fourth edition, in 2018, the report was touted as proving "an overview of patterns and flows of trafficking in persons at global, regional and national levels"

Photo 2.3 Cover of the UNODC's Global Report on Trafficking in Persons 2018.

© Yasser Rezahi/UNODC/UN.org

in 142 countries, based primarily on trafficking cases detected between 2014 and 2016 (UNODC, n.d.e). Unlike the TIP Report, the Global Report on Trafficking in Persons includes quantitative and qualitative data gathered from a questionnaire distributed to governments, and the collection of official information available in the public domain, such as police reports and Ministry of Justice reports (UNODC, 2016a). Country profiles provide specific data based on detected cases of human trafficking. Despite its more data-driven reporting, as compared to the TIP Report, the Global Report on Trafficking in Persons suffers from similar criticisms, including methodical and analytical weaknesses (Gallagher, 2010).

The UNODC acknowledged certain weaknesses it its data-collecting efforts. Specifically, the lack of consistent definitions of human trafficking, as identified in country legislation, eliminated some countries from being included in analyses. For example, data from countries that criminalized only sex trafficking, transnational trafficking, or child trafficking could not be combined with data from countries that criminalized all forms of trafficking, as defined by the UN's trafficking in persons protocol. Thus, those countries with narrower definitions of human trafficking were eliminated from regional and global analyses (UNODC, 2016a).

The report provides a lengthy description of methodology and weaknesses. While too lengthy and complicated to cover in this text, the limitations are unsurprising given what we know about the challenges to high-quality data collection on human trafficking.

Another branch of the UN, the International Labour Organization (ILO), also commits a good amount of attention to bringing awareness to and assessing forced labor, including forced sexual exploitation. In 2014, the ILO adopted the forced labor protocol (ILO, 2014c). It encourages countries to adopt this protocol, standardize the measurement of forced labor, and design comprehensive legislation to prevent forced labor, punish perpetrators, and identify and serve victims (ILO, 2016b, 2016c). The ILO's data efforts have resulted in many publications, specifically in an attempt to measure the number of victims forced into labor as well as the profits resulting from forced labor (Kangaspunta, 2010). Further, the ILO has produced a broad awareness campaign, complete with videos and information available in multiple languages (ILO, n.d.a, n.d.b).

The collaborative report between the ILO and Walk Free Foundation, the *2017 Global Estimate of Modern Slavery and Child Labour*, also offers a valuable estimate of human trafficking worldwide (International Labour Organization, n.d.d). This collaboration between an NGO and the UN is encouraging and offers a valuable contribution to our understanding of trafficking using improved methodology and partnership.

The Global Slavery Index

NGOs provide a wealth of information on human trafficking. While much of it is focused on awareness efforts, a worthy cause most certainly, there are a few nonprofit organizations that provide quantitative assessments of human trafficking domestically and globally. One such assessment comes from the Global Slavery Index (GSI). The index includes assessments of human trafficking in 167 countries based on surveys conducted in 25 countries with over 42,000 respondents. The GSI has a database with over 17,000 data points covering 161 government

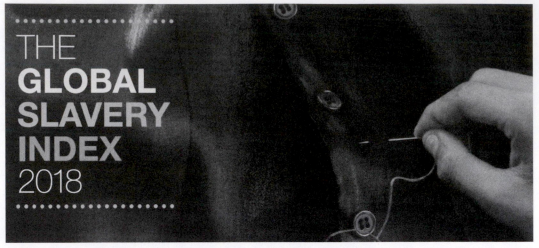

| Photo 2.4 The Global Slavery Index 2018 provided country rankings of human trafficking.

responses (GSI, n.d.). The GSI is produced by the Walk Free Foundation. It aims to provide information on how many slaves are in each country as well as the strengths and weaknesses of individual countries. However, critics offer serious concerns regarding the methodology used to collect and assess data (Guth, Anderson, Kinnard, & Tran, 2014; Kessler, 2015). Simplistically, these concerns regard the use of primary and secondary data and the possibility that data sources may have used different definitions of human trafficking (Kessler, 2015). The U.S. State Department admits that a concrete number of slaves is elusive and warns that elevated numbers such as those provided by the GSI may not be accurate. The State Department has indicated frustration in the media's attention to the GSI, posing the possibility that its estimates are more frequently advertised because of their larger magnitude (Kessler, 2015). Kevin Bales, the lead author on the GSI and a leading human trafficking expert, believes in the accuracy of the GSI.

Conclusion

The GSI makes big claims. Although its validity is contested, so is the validity of all sources of data, and rightfully so. Estimating the magnitude of the problem is challenging. There is general agreement that without improved data and methodologies, we will make limited progress in ending human trafficking (Enos, 2015; Schartz, 2017). So where do we go from here? If methodologies and data were so easy, this problem wouldn't exist.

First, let's focus on the TIP Report. Albeit controversial, it does offer one of the best, and only, annual assessments of human trafficking. Enos (2015) specifies that the TIP Report must design an empirical framework from which to develop a methodological plan. Improved transparency in regard to methodology will prevent pressure from above and promote discretion in ranking countries. Empirical data that track numbers of victims and the effectiveness of existing anti-trafficking programs will most certainly add legitimacy to this report.

Other suggestions regarding TIP Report methodology include looking to other data models, validating the data by comparing them to other indices, and looking at the methodologies used in successful studies on human trafficking (e.g., Gausman, Chernoff, Duger, Bhabha, & Chu, 2016). Validation of the TIP Report could come from comparison to the Global Report on Trafficking in Persons, the GSI, or smaller, more localized assessments of human trafficking.

Additionally, universal definitions of human trafficking will greatly improve the quality of available data. Challenges in combining data from different countries to assess regional and global patterns was indicated in all three major reporting efforts on human trafficking—the TIP Report, the Global Report on Trafficking in Persons, and the GSI. Kangaspunta (2010) suggests the need for a human trafficking severity index. Similarly, Aroma (2007) concluded that a "structured monitoring system" would allow for comparable data to be collected across the trafficking in persons protocol. It stressed the importance of using standardized procedures and consistent methodologies in order to permit valid and reliable cross-country comparisons. Such a system would permit a greatly improved understanding of victims and traffickers as well as reveal domestic and international solutions to trafficking.

KEY WORDS

coercion 28
Human Smuggling and
   Trafficking Center 29
Intelligence Reform
   and Terrorism
   Prevention Act 29

President's Interagency
   Task Force to Monitor
   and Combat Trafficking in
   Persons 26
smuggling 16
UN Convention Against
   Transnational Organized
   Crime 19

UN Protocol Against the
   Smuggling of Migrants by Land,
   Sea and Air (the smuggling
   protocol) 19
UN Protocol to Prevent, Suppress
   and Punish Trafficking in
   Persons Especially Women and
   Children (the trafficking in
   persons protocol) 19

DISCUSSION QUESTIONS

1. What is the key distinction between trafficking and smuggling.?

2. In what ways are the definition you created for human trafficking (see Challenge Yourself 2.2 on p. 22) and the definitions provided in different international laws different? In what ways are they similar?

3. How do measurement and data present misunderstandings of human trafficking?

4. According to Sheldon-Sherman (2012), what are the two schools of thought for combating trafficking, and how do they differ?

5. How does the Trafficking in Persons Report improve our understanding of human trafficking, and what are some criticisms regarding the transparency of its data?

6. Pick two international reports on human trafficking. What are some of the strengths and weaknesses of each of these resources?

RESOURCES

The National Institute of Justice (NIJ) has taken a keen interest in improving detection and prosecutorial efforts as related to human trafficking. Through funding research, NIJ has focused specifically on:

- The nature and extent of human trafficking
- Detecting and investigating traffickers
- Prosecuting traffickers
- Services for trafficking victims

On its website, NIJ stresses the need for improved data efforts focused on the characteristics of victims and perpetrators, the mechanism of operations, and assessment of trends. Even more importantly, NIJ points out the need for changes in the cultural, legal, and organizational barriers that limit its ability to investigate and prosecute trafficking cases.

Source: National Institute of Justice, n.d.

Public websites such as these, as well as nonprofit organizations such as Polaris and Shared Hope, remind us of the importance of high-quality data. This is a complex problem that requires rigorous methods and valid data if we have any hope of eradication. Such research can assist law enforcement in allocating resources, emergency rooms and first responders in identifying victims, and service providers in providing services specific to the victims they are working with. While global estimates are most definitely important, as is understanding transnational trafficking patterns, learning more about intracountry characteristics and barriers to detection should not be set aside. NIJ's efforts to focus on the United States and to understand how the problem presents itself here specifically are valuable and should be modeled globally.

The following websites are either mentioned in this chapter or relevant to topics discussed in the chapter. These sites offer valuable resources in understanding human trafficking as well as recognition of the limitations in our understanding.

- 2018 Global Slavery Index: https://www.globalslaveryindex.org/

- Blue Blindfold: http://www.blueblindfold.gov.ie/en/BBF/Pages/Trafficking_or_Smuggling

- Girls Not Brides: https://www.girlsnotbrides.org/

- Shared Hope International, "Policy Research and Resources": http://sharedhope.org/resources/policy-research-resources/

- Thomson Reuters Foundation's fight against modern slavery: http://www.trust.org/thought-leadership/modern-slavery/

- United Nations Convention Against Transnational Organized Crime, including the United Nations Protocol to Prevent, Suppress and Punish Trafficking in Persons Especially Women and Children and the United Nations Protocol Against the Smuggling of Migrants by Land, Sea and Air: https://www.unodc.org/documents/middleeastandnorthafrica/organised-crime/UNITED_NATIONS_CONVENTION_AGAINST_TRANSNATIONAL_ORGANIZED_CRIME_AND_THE_PROTOCOLS_THERETO.pdf

- United Nations Global Initiative to Fight Human Trafficking: http://www.ungift.org/

- UNODC Human Trafficking Knowledge Portal: https://www.unodc.org/cld/en/v3/htms/index.html

- UNODC on human trafficking and migrant smuggling: https://www.unodc.org/unodc/en/human-trafficking/index.html

- U.S. Department of State's annual Trafficking in Persons Report: https://www.state.gov/j/tip/rls/tiprpt/

Do Traditional Theories Help Us Understand Human Trafficking?

> *. . . let's recommit to addressing the underlying forces that push so many into bondage in the first place. With development and economic growth that creates legitimate jobs, there's less likelihood of indentured servitude around the globe. A sense of justice that says no child should ever be exploited, that has to be burned into the cultures of every country. A commitment to equality . . . so societies empower our sisters and our daughters just as much as our brothers and sons.*

> **—President Barack Obama to the Clinton Global Initiative, September 25, 2012**

The plethora of literature, websites, documentaries, and other forms of information available on human trafficking is encouraging. As discussed in the previous chapter, human trafficking is an issue garnering growing global awareness. People across the world are beginning to, literally, "see" trafficking. Often in our academic course on human trafficking, we witness students' adverse reactions when the magnitude and seriousness of this issue clicks in their heads.

It may be accurate to say that more and more people are aware of the existence of human trafficking. But what exactly does that mean? Perhaps they follow the CNN Freedom Project (https://www.cnn.com/interactive/2018/specials/freedom-project/) or "learn" about trafficking through the compelling stories that appear on their social media outlets. Perhaps they have read some of the better-known books on the topic, such as *Half the Sky*, *The Slave Next Door*, or *Disposable People* (Kristof & WuDunn, 2010; Bales & Soudalter, 2010; and Bales, 2012, respectively). It may be safe to say that for the majority of the population, their understanding of trafficking comes from passing images and stories they encounter, quickly react to, and then forget or let lodge in the backs of their minds. As mentioned, our intention with this book is to provide more than just a passing encounter with human trafficking. We aim to provide a thorough and accurate depiction of the problem, without minimizing or overstating the issue. One way to do this is to develop a theoretical framework from which to understand human trafficking.

The framework provided in this chapter uses criminological and psychological theories as a foundation for understanding how human trafficking is sustained and proliferates. Theory can be applied to appreciate the why and how of the trafficker's role, the trafficked person's role, and the higher-level ecological complexities that permit this illegal and unethical enterprise to successfully operate. Such an application of theory will elevate our understanding of human trafficking beyond the relationship between offender and victim to an improved understanding of the intricacies that create an environment ripe for exploitation (Parmentier, 2010).

Throughout the chapter, you will be provided with a snapshot of what human trafficking looks like around the world. Consider the characteristics that drive human trafficking in each region. This should be helpful in assessing different theories and their applicability to human trafficking. If we are to apply theory to solve the problem of trafficking, we need to know what the problem is to begin with. When considering each theory, do you think the theory explains trafficking equally well in different regions? If not, what does this mean for the effectiveness of theories to explain and drive trafficking policies?

This chapter will begin with an overview of criminological theories at the individual level, which strive to understand the motives of the trafficker and the reasons many trafficked persons fall into their situations. Staying at the individual level, the chapter will continue with an examination of the psychological theory of trauma bonding. Moving on to a more macro-level perspective, the chapter will explore potential theoretical causes of trafficking at national and international levels. The chapter will conclude with a proposal of theoretical integration in order to create a concise "ecology" of human trafficking (as advocated by Parmentier [2010]). This chapter will assume some level of understanding of criminological and psychological theory.

Assessing the Cost/Benefit Ratio: The Motivations of the Trafficker, Victim, and Buyer

Although research linking criminological theory to human trafficking is infrequent, when it does appear, neoclassical theories are typically the theories applied (Aronowitz, Theuermann, & Tyurykanova, 2010; Gianni & Di Fillipo, 2015; Hodge, 2008; Wheaton, Schauer, & Galli, 2010). These theories focus on the rationality of the actor, in this case the trafficker. Internal assessments of the risks and benefits of certain acts, combined with identification of appropriate opportunities, are assumed in these theories. Especially relevant to understanding the behavior of traffickers are the rational choice and routine activities theories.

Rational Choice Theory

Rational choice theory (RCT) is often applied to understanding the motivations of a human trafficker. The theory's premise is that all behavior is intentional and rational. Consistent with RCT, the trafficker is assumed to be attempting to gain maximum benefit while reducing the potential risks associated with his or her behavior (Gianni & Di Fillipo, 2015). As the authors of this revitalized classical theory, Derek B. Cornish and Ronald V. Clarke (1986), explain, "Crimes are broadly the result of rational choices based on analyses of anticipated costs and benefits" (p. vi). The basic assumptions of this approach include that offenders are motivated and crimes are committed for the sole purpose of benefiting the offender. Free will and assessment of opportunities are also assumptions of the rational choice theory (Cornish & Clarke, 1986, 2003; Green, 2002; Lutya & Lanier, 2012). Critical to the theory is the belief that decisions are based in

Exhibit 3.1

A Snapshot of Human Trafficking by Region: North America, New Zealand, Australia, and Western Europe

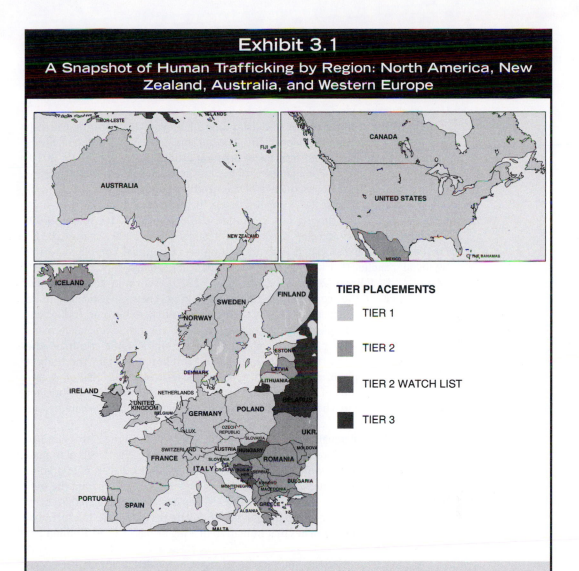

TIER PLACEMENTS

- TIER 1
- TIER 2
- TIER 2 WATCH LIST
- TIER 3

With some exceptions in Europe, all of these countries are ranked in Tier 1 in the 2018 TIP Report.

- These regions are characterized by higher prosecution rates, human trafficking awareness campaigns, trained law enforcement, victim identification, victim protection services, and adoption of national plans to combat human trafficking.

- In 2015, the United Kingdom passed the Modern Slavery Act. It requires large corporations to report steps they are taking to eliminate trafficking from their supply chains.

Sources: U.S. Department of State, 2016.

- In 2000, the United States passed the Trafficking Victims Protection Act. It was signed by President Clinton and reauthorized by both Presidents Bush and Obama.

Prostitution: Criminalization of the purchase (not the selling) of sex in Sweden in 1999 (followed by Norway, Iceland, Canada, and Northern Ireland) has decreased human trafficking in these countries. In 2002, Germany legalized prostitution, and this country has seen increases in human trafficking. The Netherlands, where prostitution is legal, has also seen an increase in the number of trafficking victims.

limited and bounded rationality (e.g., E. Rosen & Venkatesh, 2008). Decisions are made only within the confines of what the individual knows to be true. This knowledge may be accurate or not. Understanding the context in which the individual is behaving is critical to understanding the decision making of both the trafficker and those who choose risky employment that easily leads to trafficking (e.g., sex workers).

Especially relevant to the understanding of human trafficking is Cornish and Clarke's focus on crime specificity. The authors believe that different needs and desires lead to the commitment of different crimes (Aronowitz et al., 2010; Lutya & Lanier, 2012). For example, robbery is the result of the need for money, while rape may be the consequence of the need for control, power, and/or sexual gratification (Clarke & Cornish, 2001). In the case of human trafficking, financial gain is the driving factor (Hodge, 2008; Kortla, 2010; Rand, 2009; Samarasinghe, 2009; Steele, 2010; Williamson & Prior, 2009; Zhang, 2011). Further, the costs associated with trafficking seem minimal compared to the financial benefits (Cockbain & Wortley, 2015; Finckenauer & Chin, 2010; Gianni & Di Filippo, 2015; Wheaton et al., 2010). Wheaton and colleagues (2010) explored the economics of human trafficking. Their assessment applied a rational choice framework to explaining why traffickers become traffickers. After considering all possible costs associated with the trafficking of humans (including monetary/operational, physical, psychological, and criminal—the risk of being caught), the benefits prevail. In an effort to obtain the highest possible level of profit, the trafficker experiences relatively little risk or consequence. Prosecutions of traffickers are rare. The consequences simply are not felt. Traffickers go to where people are the most vulnerable: places where people want to get out.

Generally, individuals escaping their own country want to travel to a country with more economic development, stability, and safety and higher levels of human rights. Generally, these countries have stricter immigration laws. As immigration laws get stricter, those attempting to escape become more desperate, and the trafficker makes more profit. According to the U.S. Department of Homeland Security (n.d.), human trafficking brings in billions of dollars per year. The International Labour Office (2014) estimates that human trafficking brings in $150.2 billion per year in profits.

As a reader of this text, you may be trying to rationalize the trafficker's decision. While the gain is huge, the risks are still grave. However, be reminded that RCT acknowledges the bounded rationality of the individual (Cornish & Clark, 1986; Green, 2002). The trafficker is making decisions based on her or his own and others' experiences. Without evidence of consequences related to the force, fraud, or coercion of others, the trafficker has little reason to consider these risks when participating in an opportunity to traffic.

Assuming rational decision making plays a central role in understanding the actions of a trafficker, simply changing the cost/benefit balance should deter subsequent trafficking (Aronowitz et al., 2010; Gianni & Di Fillipo, 2015; Yuko, 2009). Of course, it may not be that simple, as noted by Arsovska and Zabyelina (2014). In their analysis of trafficking of small arms in the Balkans and North Caucasus, Arsovska and Zabyelina (2014) explored the effectiveness of the rational choice theory in understanding the motivations of traffickers. Their application of RCT to weapons trafficking seems useful for human trafficking as well. Should the risks associated with the trafficking of humans become too high, the tracker will likely desist from the activity. At that point, the financial gain is not worth the consequences (including, perhaps, apprehension and punishment). Thus, in order to

Exhibit 3.2

A Snapshot of Human Trafficking by Region: Latin America and North America

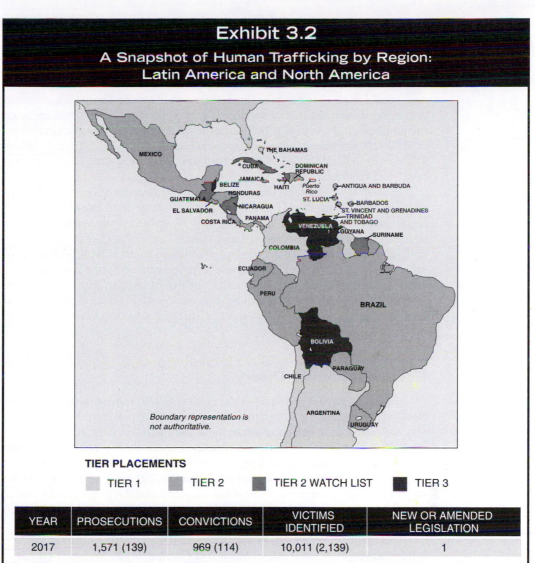

Boundary representation is not authoritative.

TIER PLACEMENTS

TIER 1   TIER 2   TIER 2 WATCH LIST   TIER 3

YEAR	PROSECUTIONS	CONVICTIONS	VICTIMS IDENTIFIED	NEW OR AMENDED LEGISLATION
2017	1,571 (139)	969 (114)	10,011 (2,139)	1

The above statistics are estimates derived from data provided by foreign governments and other sources and reviewed by the Department of State. Aggregate data fluctuates from one year to the next due to the hidden nature of trafficking crimes, dynamic global events, shifts in government efforts, and a lack of uniformity in national reporting structures. The numbers in parentheses are those of labor trafficking prosecutions, convictions, and victims identified.

Data source: Seelke, 2016.

- Poverty, high birth rates, machismo culture, history of slavery, little opportunity, government corruption, and organized crime explain the high rates of trafficking in this region.

- Children are often forced by their families to contribute to the household income, making them vulnerable to traffickers.

- Child pornography production and sex tourism are common in this region.

- Many victims are smuggled or trafficked across northern borders in their search of greater opportunity.

- Many children are forced into gangs in Central America.

- Most countries in this region are taking steps to combat human trafficking but lack the resources, political will, or stability to move forward.

reduce trafficking, the risks and consequences must be elevated. As Arsovska and Zabyelina (2014) hypothesized, "a combination of an improvement in the security environment, a reduction in ethnic conflict, severe and swift punishment, better legislation, and an increase in law enforcement capacity will lead to a decrease in arms trafficking as well as demand for illicit firearms" (p. 402). It seems likely that, should those changes come about, there would also be a reduction in human trafficking. Fewer individuals would feel they needed to escape, thus reducing the profitability of trafficking. Trafficking thrives on vulnerable people (Aronowitz et al., 2010; Cockbain & Wortley, 2015; Wheaton et al., 2010; United Nations Office on Drugs and Crime, 2008a). With fewer vulnerable people, there are fewer benefits to traffickers.

Interestingly, Arsovska and Zabyelina (2014) found evidence that rational thinking did not necessarily reduce the demand and trafficking of arms in the highly unstable regions under their review. In spite of arms reduction tactics designed to increase consequences and reduce opportunity, seemingly "irrational" behavior ensued. The authors suggested than in areas with high levels of other sociocultural factors, cost/benefit analyses cannot be the only consideration in understanding behavior. Such conclusions support our belief that an integrated theory of human trafficking is necessary to understand the multilevel complexities of the issue. A discussion on theory integration follows at the end of this chapter.

Routine Activities Theory

Consistent with RCT, L. Cohen and Felson's (1979) **routine activities theory** (RAT) acknowledges the importance of location and opportunity. Situational factors are critical and well incorporated into the offender's decision-making process. While a rational and motivated offender is necessary, it is not sufficient. RAT extends our understanding of why, even with a motivated offender, crime does not always occur. Specifically, Cohen and Felson (1979) explain that crime occurs when three factors are present: motivated offenders, suitable targets, and a lack of capable guardians. In contrast to RCT and other theories, Cohen and Felson (1979) highlight the role of the victim and location in understanding predatory crime.

RAT has been applied to various forms of trafficking (Cockbain & Wortley, 2015; Kenyon & Schanz, 2014; Warchol & Harrington, 2016) but is especially relevant when trying to understand human trafficking. We have established that the trafficker is a rational, motivated offender through our application of RCT. However, in this section we delve more into the role of the victim in understanding trafficking. Walsh and Ellis (2007; as cited in Warchol & Harrington, 2016) suggest that the more disorganized an environment is, the more likely it is that routine activities will lead to criminal behavior. This certainly can explain why the levels of human trafficking are so high in countries with unstable governments and high levels of conflict, poverty, and statelessness (Gianni & Di Fillipo, 2015). Given vulnerable individuals (those in need of shelter, money, food, etc.) in the absence of capable guardians (e.g., governmental oversight), it is no wonder that traffickers are highly successful in these environments.

Can RAT still hold muster when applied to more developed and stable countries, such as the United States or Great Britain? Albeit with relatively low sample sizes, two different studies suggest that RAT can explain human trafficking in developed regions (Cockbain & Wortley, 2015; Kenyon & Schanz, 2014). Cockbain and Wortley (2015) examined the role of RAT in explaining internal domestic sex trafficking of British children. Their study involved in-depth reviews of six high-profile police investigations from 2008 to 2012. They found that traffickers

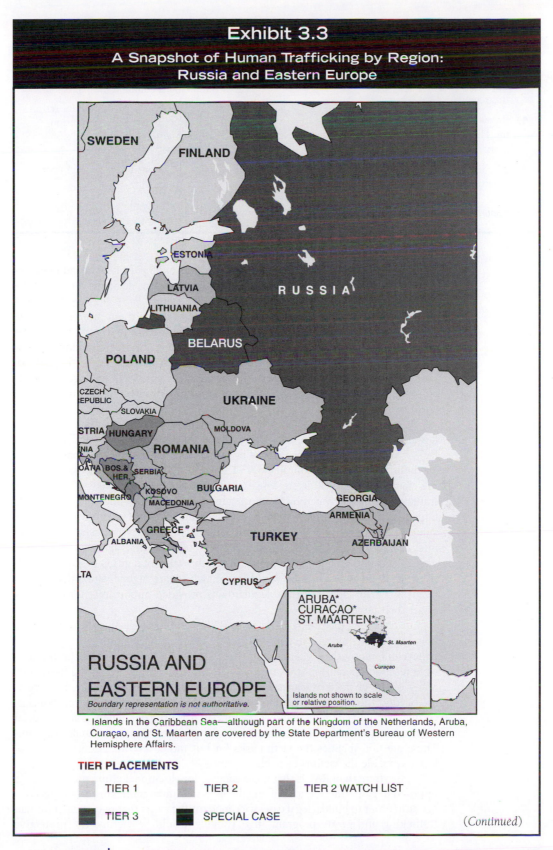

Exhibit 3.3
A Snapshot of Human Trafficking by Region: Russia and Eastern Europe

RUSSIA AND EASTERN EUROPE
Boundary representation is not authoritative.

ARUBA*
CURAÇAO*
ST. MAARTEN*

Aruba   *St. Maarten*

Curaçao

Islands not shown to scale
or relative position.

* Islands in the Caribbean Sea—although part of the Kingdom of the Netherlands, Aruba, Curaçao, and St. Maarten are covered by the State Department's Bureau of Western Hemisphere Affairs.

TIER PLACEMENTS

TIER 1	TIER 2	TIER 2 WATCH LIST
TIER 3	SPECIAL CASE

(Continued)

exploited children who lacked guardians, and this exploitation occurred in everyday activities. Even in seemingly organized communities, a lack of oversight at the community level can allow trafficking to occur.

Several characteristics of the victim may have made them more susceptible to the auspices of a motivated trafficker, including friends' involvement with the trafficker, lack of economic power, poor relationships at home, boredom, loneliness, and perceived attachment to the offender (Cockbain & Wortley, 2015). Traffickers were especially opportunistic, targeting primarily teenagers. This is consistent with RAT, as this age group has newfound independence and thus less adult oversight.

Kenyon and Schanz (2014) found consistent results based on interviews with law enforcement in the United States. A desire for money, drug dependence, and a lack of awareness on the existence of prostitution and sex trafficking made victims all the more vulnerable to traffickers. The authors offered evidence to show that the elements of trafficking are consistent with RAT. Their interviews showed that traffickers were motivated by financial gain as well as power and control. Suitable targets came in the form of victims. L. Cohen and Felson (1979) focused on the value of the target as influencing their suitability. The law enforcement officers interviewed by Kenyon and Schanz (2014) noted that the value of a target may vary by location. While in the United States the value of a girl is based on attractiveness, in other parts of the world, age may be more highly valued than attractiveness. Finally, a lack of capable guardians provided opportunity for traffickers to get their targets.

In reviewing the findings related to RAT, it is easy to disregard this theory as blaming the victim. One might interpret this section as suggesting that if victims behave differently, they will not be as susceptible to traffickers. While this is a possible reaction (Cockbain & Wortley, 2015), we would argue that it is a hasty one. Many of the characteristics that make victims vulnerable (i.e., a suitable target) are beyond their control, such as factors occurring at the country level (policies, conflict, etc.). Even individual-level factors such as drug dependency, lack of social attachments, and loneliness are not exactly qualities that individuals seek out. These are not qualities the victim asks for but rather are often consequences of factors outside the victim's control.

One strength of RAT is that it is a catalyst for situational crime prevention. As opposed to gathering and identifying the facts of human trafficking cases *after* they occur in order to build a legal case, we can identify factors that may predict human trafficking and create programs that provide would-be victims the protective

Exhibit 3.4

A Snapshot of Human Trafficking by Region: South and Central Asia

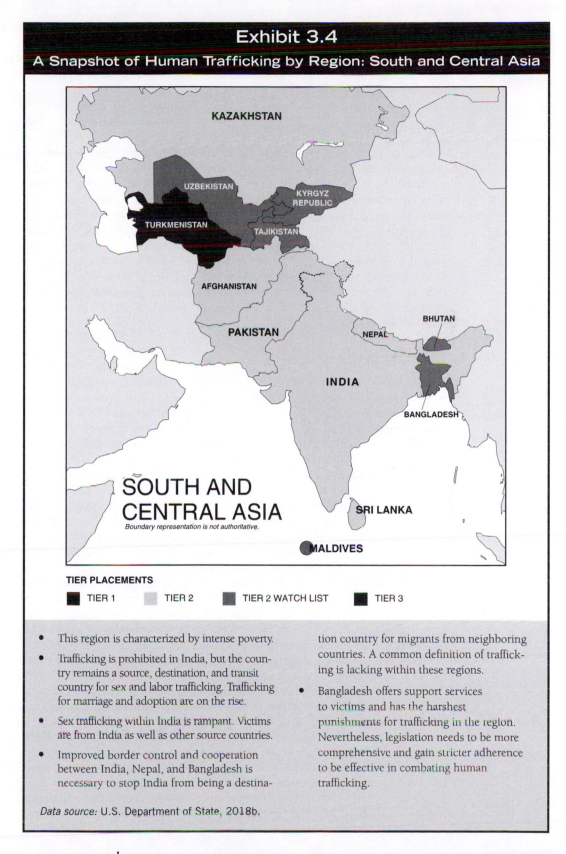

SOUTH AND CENTRAL ASIA
Boundary representation is not authoritative.

TIER PLACEMENTS

TIER 1   TIER 2   TIER 2 WATCH LIST   TIER 3

- This region is characterized by intense poverty.

- Trafficking is prohibited in India, but the country remains a source, destination, and transit country for sex and labor trafficking. Trafficking for marriage and adoption are on the rise.

- Sex trafficking within India is rampant. Victims are from India as well as other source countries.

- Improved border control and cooperation between India, Nepal, and Bangladesh is necessary to stop India from being a destination country for migrants from neighboring countries. A common definition of trafficking is lacking within these regions.

- Bangladesh offers support services to victims and has the harshest punishments for trafficking in the region. Nevertheless, legislation needs to be more comprehensive and gain stricter adherence to be effective in combating human trafficking.

Data source: U.S. Department of State, 2018b.

factors they need to avoid victimization (Gianni & Di Fillipo, 2015). L. Cohen and Felson (1979) specify that if any of the three factors—motivated offenders, suitable targets, or a lack of capable guardians—is absent, then the crime is not likely to occur. Thus, the use of situation crime prevention could be a viable approach to reducing human trafficking.

Situational Crime Prevention

Situational crime prevention (SCP) attempts to reduce the opportunity to commit crime that occurs due to common routines (Clarke, 1995). Common methods of SCP include increasing risk to the offenders, reducing rewards, reducing provocations, and removing excuses (see Table 3.1). In essence, these tactics should increase the risks and difficulties associated with crime and reduce the rewards (Clarke, 1995). Although not often applied to trafficking in the academic literature, there are a couple of applications available to highlight the potential effectiveness of this method in reducing human trafficking, specifically on the demand side. Research has shown that applying SCP tactics to both the traffickers, buyers of sex, and the victims themselves can potentially be effective in reducing trafficking (Cockbain, Brayley, & Laycock, 2011; Finckenauer & Chin, 2010).

Traffickers

Cockbain and colleagues (2011) explored the effectiveness of social network analysis in investigating child sex trafficking in Great Britain using case reviews from two major child sex trafficking investigations. They explored relationships between both traffickers and victims. They mapped the social relationships in both groups, classifying relationships into the following categories: relative, colleague/classmate, neighbor, friend, associate, and acquaintance. Their application of social network analysis found support for the use of SCP techniques. Cockbain and colleagues (2011) concluded that the use of social network analysis during the investigative stage (rather than after the fact) could reduce the opportunity for further crime. The development of a social network database would further help to increase the risk to traffickers and improve our ability to identify traffickers. Inherently this would reduce the benefits of participating in trafficking behavior.

Cockbain and colleagues' (2011) major findings indicated that trafficker organizations were not as organized as one might expect. The relationships between traffickers did not necessarily appear centralized. However, within the social network, trafficking behavior was socially acceptable. Traffickers did not always have a direct link to their victims but rather used snowballing techniques to identify them. Cockbain and colleagues (2011) made several suggestions to increase risk to traffickers and reduce opportunity. In addition to increasing the awareness of victims (as discussed below), the authors suggested two additional tactics: (1) target hardening at the locations where the sex transactions were occurring, and (2) intercepting the gatekeepers of the social networks to reduce access to victims.

Target hardening would involve identifying where the trafficking was taking place and making it less easy to conduct "business" in that location. For example, the investigations reviewed for Cockbain and colleagues' (2011) research indicated that sexual transactions were taking place in the park. Thus, with knowledge of specifically when and where the crimes were occurring, sprinklers could be put in those locations to deter subsequent crime.

Table 3.1 Cornish and Clarke's (2003) Detailed List of 25 Different SCP Techniques

TWENTY FIVE TECHNIQUES OF SITUATIONAL PREVENTION

Increase the Effort	Increase the Risks	Reduce the Rewards	Reduce Provocations	Remove Excuses
1. Target harden • Steering column locks and immobilisers • Anti-robbery screens • Tamper-proof packaging	6. Extend guardianship • Take routine precautions: go out in group at night, leave signs of occupancy, carry phone • "Cocoon" neighborhood watch	11. Conceal targets • Off-street parking • Gender-neutral phone directories • Unmarked bullion trucks	16. Reduce frustrations and stress • Efficient queues and polite service • Expanded seating • Soothing music/muted lights	21. Set rules • Rental agreements • Harassment codes • Hotel registration
2. Control access to facilities • Entry phones • Electronic card access • Baggage screening	7. Assist natural surveillance • Improved street lighting • Defensible space design • Support whistleblowers	12. Remove targets • Removable car radio • Women's refuges • Pre-paid cards for pay phones	17. Avoid disputes • Separate enclosures for rival soccer fans • Reduce crowding in pubs • Fixed cab fares	22. Post instructions • "No Parking" • "Private Property" • "Extinguish camp fires"
3. Screen exits • Ticket needed for exit • Export documents • Electronic merchandise tags	8. Reduce anonymity • Taxi driver IDs • "How's my driving?" decals • School uniforms	13. Identify property • Property marking • Vehicle licensing and parts marking • Cattle branding	18. Reduce emotional arousal • Controls on violent pornography • Enforce good behavior on soccer field • Prohibit racial slurs	23. Alert conscience • Roadside speed display boards • Signatures for customs declarations • "Shoplifting is stealing"
4. Deflect offenders • Street closures • Separate bathrooms for women • Disperse pubs	9. Utilize place managers • CCTV for double-deck buses • Two clerks for convenience stores • Reward vigilance	14. Disrupt markets • Monitor pawn shops • Controls on classified ads • License street vendors	19. Neutralize peer pressure • "Idiots drink and drive" • "It's OK to say No" • Disperse troublemakers at school	24. Assist compliance • Easy library checkout • Public lavatories • Litter bins
5. Control tools/weapons • "Smart" guns • Disabling stolen cell phones • Restrict spray paint sales to juveniles	10. Strengthen formal surveillance • Red light cameras • Burglar alarms • Security guards	15. Deny benefits • Ink merchandise tags • Graffiti cleaning • Speed humps	20. Discourage imitation • Rapid repair of vandalism • V-chips in TVs • Censor details of modus operandi	25. Control drugs and alcohol • Breathalyzers in pubs • Server intervention • Alcohol-free events

Source: Theory for Practice in Situational Crime Prevention, edited by Martha J. Smith and Derek B. Cornish. Copyright © 2003 by Lynne Rienner Publishers, Inc. Used with permission of the publisher.

Cockbain and colleagues (2011) observed that the traffickers' "girlfriends," also known as the gatekeepers into trafficking, were highly involved in the recruitment of additional girls. These girlfriends were made to think they were important and/or special to the trafficker, when all the while they were being manipulated to recruit more victims. If police could target these girlfriends and get them to understand what they were doing, this would, in essence, increase risk to the trafficker once again by breaking up the social network of victims and reducing the traffickers' access to those victims. Awareness campaigns targeting these "girlfriends" would also increase risk to traffickers and lessen access to victims.

Focus On

Proposed Application of SCP in Turkey to Reduce the Sex Trafficking of Females

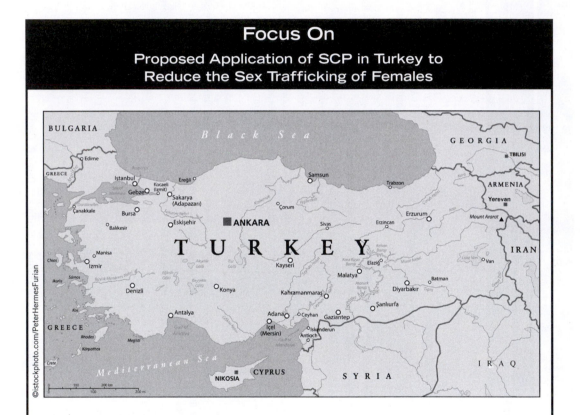

©istockphoto.com/PeterHermesFurian

Akbas (2009) presents an analysis of how situational crime prevention tactics can be applied to the prevention of female trafficking in Turkey. Turkey is considered to be a Tier 2 country in the most recent publication of the U.S. Department of State's (2018b) Trafficking in Persons Report. It is considered primarily a destination and transit country for men, women, and children for sex and labor trafficking. Turkey has experienced an uptick in trafficking victims from Syria, Afghanistan, Iraq, and Iran due to the instability and crises occurring in those countries. Although the Turkish government does not currently meet the minimum standards set forth to eliminate trafficking, it is making concerted efforts to do so. Increased law enforcement efforts, identification of victims, and improved legislation indicate Turkey's commitment to reducing trafficking within its border. However, its efforts to protect vulnerable refugees are deficient.

Consistent with Cornish and Clarke (2003), Akbas (2009) specifies SCP techniques that can be used to increase the efforts required of the trafficker (see Figure 3.1). Such techniques include making it more difficult to attract female victims, strengthening border control, and using awareness campaigns. Awareness campaigns impact both traffickers and victims. Traffickers may feel less "invisible," and victims will be more informed of the risks they may face should they become involved in a trafficking situation, such as sexually transmitted diseases and violence.

SCP tactics can also be used to increase risk to venues that support trafficking. Closed-caption televisions can assist venues in ensuring that trafficking is not occurring on their property. Law enforcement can shut down those venues that choose to turn a blind eye to trafficking. A requirement that hotels register every guest in a room is another suggested policy to increase risks to the trafficker. Finally, if all countries were to use citizen identification numbers on passports, this could be an easy way to track movement and identify whether, for example, women who have previously been deported for prostitution are returning to Turkey, a problem cited by Akbas

(2009). These actions would also reduce rewards, as would informing women that they will not make money by being trafficked.

Increased regulation of venues, employment, and advertising will reduce trafficker and consumer excuses as well as provocations of all involved.

While Akbas's (2009) focus was on Turkey, these methods are globally applicable. To date, no comprehensive evaluation of SCP tactics is available to assess their effectiveness in combating trafficking. While the recommendations by Akbas (2009) seem promising, applied research is imperative.

Akbas (2009) describes the application of SCP techniques at multiple stages in the trafficking process, including recruitment, transportation, and exploitation. As shown in Figures 3.1 through 3.3, she believes these efforts can be applied to victims, traffickers, and consumers. Of course, in the case of consumers, SCP tactics are applicable only at the exploitation stage.

Figure 3.1   SCP Tactics to Influence Traffickers

	Recruitment	Transportation	Exploitation
Effort	• Get rid of illegal recruitment agencies • Monitor legal recruitment agencies • Regulate and monitor entertainment businesses • Launch public awareness campaigns	• Prevent people from entering (or reentering) under false pretenses using: • Fingerprints • Interviews (for visas and at the border) • Citizen identification numbers	
Risk	• Help lines + awareness campaigns related to the help lines		• Monitor individuals involved in trafficking • Monitor repeat offenders and potential recruiters • Place cameras in high-risk venues like hotels and nightclubs
Reward	• Cancel licenses and/or fine businesses and agencies that violate regulations		• Fine businesses where trafficking takes place

(Continued)

Figure 3.1   (Continued)

Excuses	• Increase awareness of trafficking among managers of recruitment agencies		• Create and enforce guidelines for managers and employees in businesses likely to be involved in trafficking
Provocation	▪ Remove false employment advertisements		

Figure 3.2   Tactics to influence consumers

	Exploitation
Risk	• Place cameras in high-risk venues like hotels and nightclubs • Launch public awareness campaigns • Require hotels to register all guests
Reward	• Educate potential consumers on: • Consequences of trafficking • Negative effects on family values • Potential to spread disease or illness to their families
Excuses	• Hold people legally responsible for engaging in sex with victims of trafficking (and sex workers where it is illegal)
Provocation	• Remove advertisements for prostitution

Figure 3.3   Tactics to influence victims

	Recruitment	Transportation	Exploitation
Effort	• Get rid of illegal recruitment agencies • Monitor legal recruitment agencies • Regulate and monitor entertainment businesses • Launch public awareness campaigns		• Support victims trying to escape from traffickers using: • Multilanguage help lines • Awareness campaigns • Targeted interviews at airports

Risk ⚠	▪ Help lines + awareness campaigns related to the help lines	▪ Prevent people from entering (or reentering) under false pretenses using: ▪ Fingerprints ▪ Interviews (for visas and at the border) ▪ Citizen identification numbers	
Provocation ⚙	▪ Remove false employment and advertisements		▪ Remove advertisements for prostitution

Source: Adapted from Akbas, H. (2009).

A broader prevention effort has to do with documentation. Finckenauer and Chin (2010) pointed out how easy it currently is to get counterfeit documentation, making passage across country borders reasonably unchallenging. Countries that make their documents more secure and border crossings that can better detect counterfeits will reduce the ability of traffickers to seemingly travel legally for illegal purposes. In essence, this increase in guardians hinders the ability of the trafficker and his or her victims to cross borders.

Victims

SCP techniques can also be applicable to victims (see Table 3.4). Finckenauer and Chin (2010) point out that push and pull factors exist that put girls at especially high risk of being trafficked. Unemployment, economic challenges, marital problems, and so forth push the victim into situations where trafficking is likely. Further, the trafficker makes the life of a sex trafficking victim appear glamorous. Victims are promised an improvement in lifestyle, escape from a bad living situation, and material goods that the victim may not otherwise be able to afford. Dispelling these lies and exposing girls to the risk factors for trafficking are critical. Helping the potential victim better understand the costs and benefits to them is a viable way to reduce the targets of trafficking (Akbas, 2009; Finckenauer & Chin, 2010).

The current literature notes that messaging is important. Public messaging to raise awareness is not likely to be as effective with this population as messaging through trusted individuals within the potential victims' networks (Cockbain et al., 2011; Finckenauer & Chin, 2010). These trusted individuals are better able to caution girls that traffickers are not honest and cannot be believed. Further, the girls can be warned that certain behaviors, such as getting in cars willingly, taking alcohol or drugs, or being paid money, will increase their risk of being trapped in trafficking situations (Cockbain et al., 2011). As mentioned above, by increasing the awareness

Exhibit 3.5
A Snapshot of Human Trafficking by Region: Southeast Asia

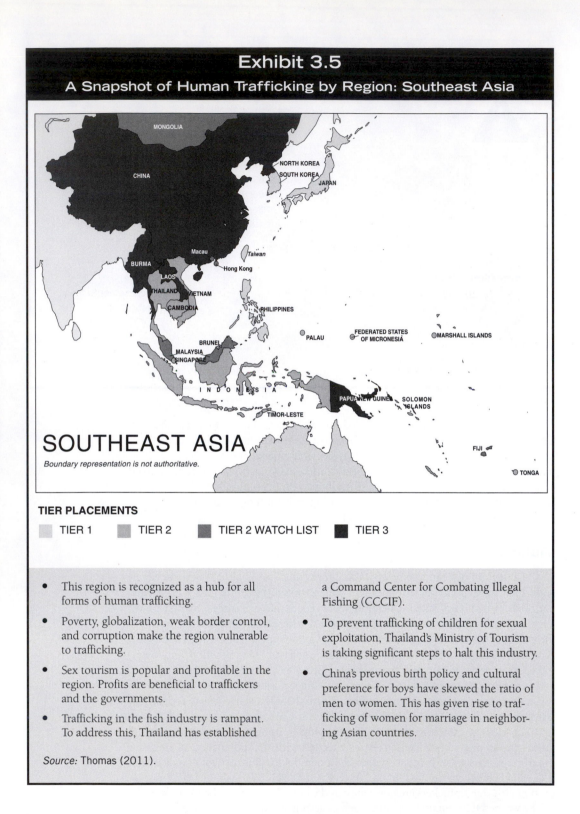

SOUTHEAST ASIA

Boundary representation is not authoritative.

TIER PLACEMENTS

	TIER 1		TIER 2		TIER 2 WATCH LIST		TIER 3

- This region is recognized as a hub for all forms of human trafficking.

- Poverty, globalization, weak border control, and corruption make the region vulnerable to trafficking.

- Sex tourism is popular and profitable in the region. Profits are beneficial to traffickers and the governments.

- Trafficking in the fish industry is rampant. To address this, Thailand has established a Command Center for Combating Illegal Fishing (CCCIF).

- To prevent trafficking of children for sexual exploitation, Thailand's Ministry of Tourism is taking significant steps to halt this industry.

- China's previous birth policy and cultural preference for boys have skewed the ratio of men to women. This has given rise to trafficking of women for marriage in neighboring Asian countries.

Source: Thomas (2011).

of potential victims, there is an opportunity to increase the risks to the trafficker. When potential victims are encouraged to partake in risky behavior, they may be more likely to grow suspicious of and report the potential trafficker's behavior.

Sex Buyers

In addition to focusing on traffickers, much attention has been given to the demand side of purchasing sex. The demand for sex workers promotes, or at least tolerates, a culture where sex trafficking is acceptable. Consistent with this belief, to reduce sex trafficking, there must be a focus on demand reduction. Although Part II of this text will explore in depth the relationships between demand, prostitution, and sex trafficking, our focus here will be on tactics to more generally reduce the demand for purchasing sex. As mentioned in earlier sections of this chapter, to develop policies to stop the buyer from purchasing sex, we need to understand the context and motivations of the buyer (Cornish & Clarke, 1986). Through its research, Shared Hope International (Allen, 2007) offers three different categories of sex buyers (also known as *johns*). The cost/benefit ratio varies for each category of buyers, thus necessitating different strategies to reduce sex-buying behavior (Allen, 2007; Finckenauer & Chin, 2010). The **"situational" buyer** simply purchases sex because it is available and the practice is accepted. **Opportunistic buyers** are those who purchase sex indiscriminately. These individuals are raised in a culture that normalizes and even values commercial sex. These buyers don't care about the willingness of the girl and do not discriminate between adult and minor victims. Finally, the **preferential buyer** is looking for a specific type of victim. According to Shared Hope International (Allen, 2007), these buyers shop in specialized markets to identify victims that meet their specific needs and desires.

While the motivations of the buyer are important when implementing specific SCP strategies to reduce demand, it is a good reminder that when applying SCP, dismantling of any of the three components of RAT (motivated offenders, suitable targets, and a lack of capable guardians) will reduce crime (L. Cohen & Felson, 1979). For example, Finckenauer and Chin (2010) note that any interventions that reduce individuals' likelihood of becoming victims are going to effectively impact demand, regardless of the motivations of the buyer. Thus, consistent with the classical criminology theories discussed in this chapter and the practical interventions that stem from these theories, the potential exists to reduce trafficking by interrupting any one of the contributing factors that allow trafficking to occur. Further, by incorporating an understanding of the individual-level factors that contribute to the behavior of the traffickers, the victims, and the potential buyers of humans (for sex or labor), we can target all of these factors to create a more comprehensive reaction to trafficking.

Moving Beyond Rational Thinking: Additional Considerations in Explaining the Behavior of Traffickers and Victims at the Individual Level

Most of the academic literature, albeit limited, linking criminological theory to human trafficking focuses on the classical perspective, as described above. However, other individual-level causes can aid in the explanation of trafficker and victim behaviors. These causes stem from both criminological and psychological disciplines.

Neutralizing the Decision to Traffic

Sykes and Matza (1957) developed their theory of the **techniques of neutralization** to explain how individuals can "drift" in and out of crime. These techniques, including (1) denial of responsibility, (2) denial of injury, (3) denial of victims, (4) condemnation of the condemners, and (5) appeal to higher loyalties, allow individuals to justify their criminal behavior so as not to allow the behavior to define the individual.

While there are only a few publications that test the applicability of this theory to human trafficking, these findings indicate that the theory may be relevant in explaining trafficking behavior (Antonopoulos & Winterdyk, 2005; Aronowitz et al., 2010; Parmentier, 2010). According to Aronowitz and colleagues (2010), traffickers can *deny their responsibility* in contributing to the victimization of another by blaming forces bigger than themselves for putting the victim in the position to be trafficked. The findings of Antonopoulos and Winterdyk's (2005) qualitative study support this perspective. Antonopoulos and Winterdyk (2005) engaged in a case study with a single male trafficker who trafficked women from the former Eastern Bloc to Greece. The trafficker stated that it was the dismal life circumstances of the victims that forced them into prostitution and exploitation and that it was not the fault of the trafficker himself.

Sykes and Matza's (1957) *denial of injury* neutralization technique is also fitting for explaining the behavior of traffickers, specifically those who are doing the recruiting. These recruiters have convinced themselves that they are helping the victims improve their lives. They are taking the girls out of terrible living conditions and giving them jobs and money (Aronowitz et al., 2010). This attitude was confirmed through the interviews with the Greek trafficker (Antonopoulos & Winterdyk, 2005). He reported that the girls were being taken care of. Typically, these girls had been sex workers in their countries of origin, so they were doing the same job but were now better off in Greece. Of course, the girls hadn't known the level of exploitation that would be occurring once they were working in Greece or any destination country (Antonopoulos & Winterdyk, 2005; Aronowitz et al., 2010). This reasoning is also consistent with the neutralization technique of *denial of a victim*. The trafficker does not identify as a victimizer but rather believes he is providing the victim with an opportunity to better her or his situation.

Another technique used by the trafficker is *condemnation of the condemner*. Corrupt governments and police drive the trafficking industry, thus making those entities equally at fault for the trafficking situation, as confirmed by the Greek trafficker (Antonopoulos & Winterdyk, 2005; Aronowitz et al., 2010). Note that this line of reasoning is not as applicable when the trafficking is occurring in countries where government corruption is less present.

The only neutralization technique that does not seem consistent with our understanding of the trafficker is the belief that traffickers can excuse their behavior by *appealing to higher loyalties*. While such a technique may work in highly centralized trafficking rings, we know that oftentimes human trafficking is not centralized (Cockbain et al., 2011). The interviewed Greek trafficker described most trafficking as opportunistic and carried out for the purposes of quick money. He noted, however, that in Albania the trafficking rings are family run, and thus there is some obligation to the family to cooperate (Antonopoulos & Winterdyk, 2005).

Although the findings of Antonopoulos and Winterdyk (2005) and Aronowitz and colleagues (2010) are compelling, they certainly don't indicate that the techniques of neutralization offer the exact explanation needed to understand the behavior of a trafficker. That said, this preliminary evidence is intriguing and warrants more attention.

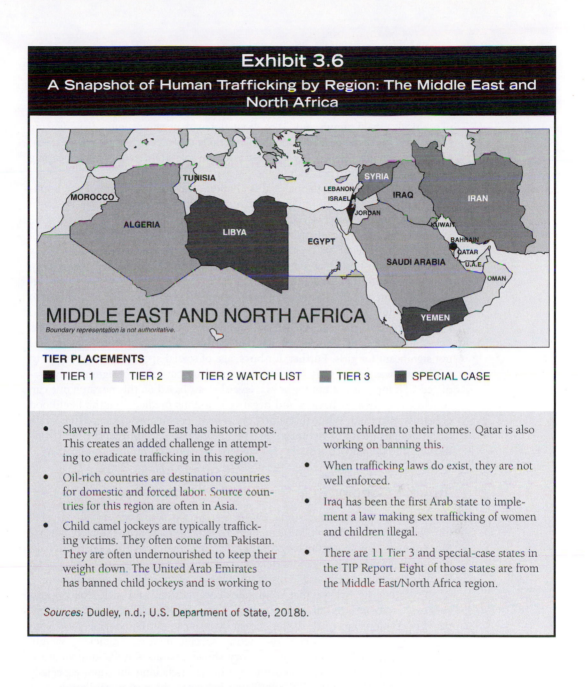

Exhibit 3.6

A Snapshot of Human Trafficking by Region: The Middle East and North Africa

TIER PLACEMENTS

■ TIER 1   TIER 2   TIER 2 WATCH LIST   TIER 3   SPECIAL CASE

- Slavery in the Middle East has historic roots. This creates an added challenge in attempting to eradicate trafficking in this region.

- Oil-rich countries are destination countries for domestic and forced labor. Source countries for this region are often in Asia.

- Child camel jockeys are typically trafficking victims. They often come from Pakistan. They are often undernourished to keep their weight down. The United Arab Emirates has banned child jockeys and is working to

- return children to their homes. Qatar is also working on banning this.

- When trafficking laws do exist, they are not well enforced.

- Iraq has been the first Arab state to implement a law making sex trafficking of women and children illegal.

- There are 11 Tier 3 and special-case states in the TIP Report. Eight of those states are from the Middle East/North Africa region.

Sources: Dudley, n.d.; U.S. Department of State, 2018b.

The Role of Strain in the Life of a Trafficking Victim

Vulnerability is a key factor in identifying victims of human trafficking. However, not everyone who is vulnerable to being trafficked becomes victim to it. Merton and later Agnew developed the strain and general strain theories, respectively (Agnew, Brezina, Wright, & Cullen, 2002; Agnew, Cullen, Burton, Evans, & Dunaway, 1996; Merton, 1938). Merton's (1938) original theory hypothesized that individuals without legitimate means to achieve socially defined goals experience strain. Individuals experiencing strain are forced to come up with alternative, often illegal, means of achieving socially defined goals.

Agnew's **general strain theory** (GST) further developed Merton's theory to define the varying sources of strain (Agnew et al., 1996, 2002). Merton was criticized for his theory's inability to explain criminals who did not have financial struggles. The revived theory explained noneconomic strain as well. Agnew and colleagues identified three sources of strain: (1) failure to achieve positively valued goals, (2) removal of positively valued stimuli, and (3) confrontation with negative stimuli. Experiencing strain combined with negative emotional reactions to strain were the cause of delinquent and criminal behavior. Agnew posed that chronic strain leads to limited coping skills and thus criminal behavior (Agnew et al., 1996, 2002).

Consistent with the theme of this chapter, our understanding of the applicability of GST to human trafficking is limited. However, there is some evidence to suggest that increased levels of strain due to life circumstances can increase vulnerability and, subsequently, trafficking (de Pérez, 2015; Reid, 2011; Reid & Piquero, 2016). Reid (2011) examined the relationship between maltreatment as a juvenile and prostitution as a minor. She found support for GST. More specifically, maltreated youth (i.e., those experiencing child neglect, juvenile sexual victimization, and more general measures of maltreatment) were more likely to enter into risky behavior (i.e., running away) and experience negative emotions. Reid and Piquero (2016) further parceled these findings by gender. Negative emotion was linked to commercial sexual exploitation (CSE) for boys, but the relationship was not significant for girls. Further, for boys, age of sexual appearance was linked to CSE, but it was not for girls. Early exposure to drugs and alcohol significantly predicted CSE for girls but not for boys. Nevertheless, based on this research one can conclude that risky behaviors and negative emotions predict a youth's likelihood of being prostituted. While this is not, on its own, convincing evidence that strain is the primary cause of victimization, the findings do suggest that further investigation into the impact of strain and vulnerability on victimization is necessary.

Trauma Bonding

The vulnerabilities discussed above may suggest how victims of trafficking fall into the traps of traffickers, but can such a theory explain why the victims stay? More often than not, a victim is not physically restrained. So, what keeps a trafficking victim linked to his or her trafficker? According to psychologists, trauma bond theory can explain the invisible restraints tying a victim to his or her trafficker.

Psychologists believe that a unique, complicated, and sick bond forms between a trafficker and his or her victim. This complex relationship, often compared to relationships made dysfunctional by intimate-partner violence, develops while the trafficker is "wooing" the victim, specifically a sex trafficking victim. Evidence supporting **trauma bond theory** shows that a sex trafficking victim is not typically kidnapped or forced into her or his trafficking situation, especially in the United States. Instead, the trafficker befriends the victim, spoiling him or her both emotionally and materialistically (see Case Study: "Tiffany" on page 61; American Psychological Association, 2014; Reid, 2010, 2016). The victim, often deprived of strong, healthy relationships, craves the attention she or he is being given. After gaining the victim's trust, the trafficker incorporates sporadic violence and abuse into the relationship (Mehlman-Orozco, 2017; Reid, 2010, 2016). Reid (2010) describes this relationship as "a mixture of reward . . . and punishment, freedom and bondage, acceptance and degradation, all used to produce loyalty and trauma bonding to the trafficker" (p. 158). The trafficker's gifted ability to manipulate and gain complete control (emotionally and economically) over the victim supports the trauma bonding hypothesis (Reid, 2010).

Case Study: "Tiffany"

An Illustration of the Development of Trauma-Coerced Bonds

Having run away from her group home, Tiffany, a 12-year-old African American girl, went to New York City. At the NYC terminal, a neatly dressed, polite young man approached her and asked if she was all right; Tiffany, grateful for the attention, smiled. The young man asked if she would like to get something to eat. Tiffany accepted, and over the meal she began to tell him about running away, her troubled family life (father in jail, mother's drug addiction, multiple foster/group homes), and her dilemma of not having anywhere to go. He invited her to live with him and to be his girlfriend, promising he would take care of her and they could be like "family." Tiffany readily accepted, thinking she had found what she had always been hoping for, "a home." The first few weeks were wonderful; her "boyfriend" took her shopping and bought her clothes, even a pair of high heels and a sexy dress. Tiffany felt like a grown-up wife, cooking and cleaning and having sex nightly. Her boyfriend asked her to dance for him in just her underwear and high heels. Initially she felt awkward, but in time, with his encouragement and praise, she felt proud to do it for him. After a few weeks, her boyfriend told her that they were going out to a club. He instructed her to dress sexy and gave her two drinks before they left. Tiffany woke the next morning with a hazy memory of the night before, barely recalling dancing and stripping. While miserable and feeling like she never wanted to do anything like this again, her boyfriend was excitedly counting money and verbally praising Tiffany for her actions. Unable to let him down, Tiffany began her life of sexual exploitation.

Source: Adapted from American Psychological Association, 2014. Originally published in *From Girls Like Us*, by R. Lloyd, 2011, New York, NY: HarperCollins.

Trauma bonding is defined as a strong emotional attachment where the relationship is characterized by both positive treatment and abuse (Dutton & Painter, 1981, 1993). Victims caught in these relationships are especially vulnerable to the whims of the trafficker due to poor family relationships and prior exposure to violence and sexual abuse (Miller-Perrin & Wurtele, 2017; Reid & Jones, 2011). These victim characteristics are not coincidental, as the abuser identifies possible victims based on their vulnerabilities. Once the relationship is formed, the abuser (in this case, the trafficker) further isolates his or her victims and takes complete control over all aspects of their lives. One may question why the victims don't recognize and react to the abusive part of the relationship. Often, the victims feel dependent on the trafficker and don't necessarily have alternative positive relationships to retreat to. Further, perceived positive aspects of the relationship, combined with isolation, threats, and negative responses from the outside community and family, make the victim that much more vulnerable to the trafficker (Hossain, Zimmerman, Abas, Light, & Watts, 2010; Lutya & Lanier, 2012). Although the trafficker is the primary cause of discomfort, fear, and danger, she or he may be the sole source of comfort to the victim as well.

The trauma bond can also transform the self-identity of victims, causing them to see themselves as culpable and deserving of the trafficker's mistreatment (Dutton & Painter, 1981, 1993). This change in identity can make it that much more difficult for victims to recognize the dangerous situation they find themselves in. Further, financial dependency on the trafficker makes leaving difficult, similar to the economic factors that drive victims of intimate-partner violence to stay with their abusers (Dutton & Painter, 1981, 1993).

Exhibit 3.7
A Snapshot of Human Trafficking by Region: Africa

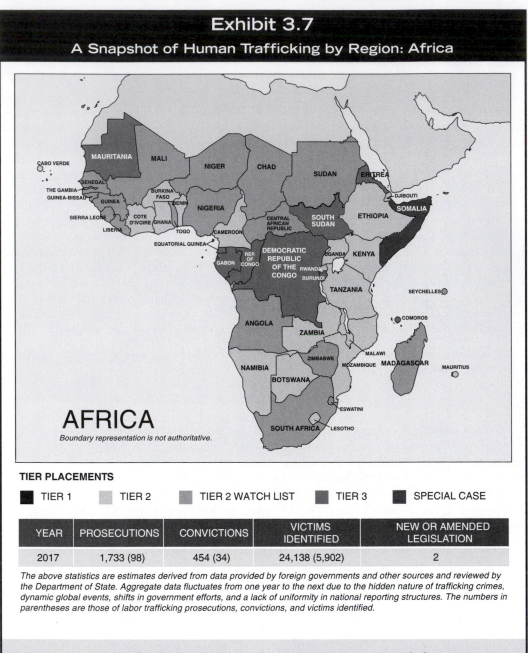

TIER PLACEMENTS

- ■ TIER 1
- ■ TIER 2
- ■ TIER 2 WATCH LIST
- ■ TIER 3
- ■ SPECIAL CASE

YEAR	PROSECUTIONS	CONVICTIONS	VICTIMS IDENTIFIED	NEW OR AMENDED LEGISLATION
2017	1,733 (98)	454 (34)	24,138 (5,902)	2

The above statistics are estimates derived from data provided by foreign governments and other sources and reviewed by the Department of State. Aggregate data fluctuates from one year to the next due to the hidden nature of trafficking crimes, dynamic global events, shifts in government efforts, and a lack of uniformity in national reporting structures. The numbers in parentheses are those of labor trafficking prosecutions, convictions, and victims identified.

- Poverty, regional conflict, limited education (especially for girls), high numbers of refugees, open borders, corruption, organized crime, and the HIV/AIDS crisis all are factors in human trafficking in this region.

- War and conflict create child soldier trafficking, labor trafficking for military service, and sex trafficking to service the soldiers. War and conflict also displace people and families.

- Governments in turmoil often cannot address the human trafficking. Two of the three special cases in the 2017 TIP Report came from this region.

- Rituals play a role in Africa, and human trafficking for body parts exists.

- Trafficked children working in the mineral-enriched mines of Africa face a number of health problems and seldom get treatment.

- Victim support is limited, as law enforcement is found to harass victims rather than help them.
- Paying families to take a bride increases the risk of trafficking, as traffickers may pose as potential husbands.

Sources: IOM (2008). Human trafficking in eastern africa. (2008). Geneva, Switzerland. International Organization for Migration. Retrieved from http://publications.iom.int/system/files/pdf/kenyahumantrafficking-baselineassessment.pdf.

Research specifically focused on sex trafficking supports the application of this hypothesis to trafficking victims, especially child victims (Mehlman-Orozco, 2017; Miller-Perrin & Wurtele, 2017; Reid, 2010, 2016; Reid & Jones, 2011). In fact, child victims are particularly susceptible to the manipulations of traffickers due to their immaturity and less-developed psychosocial development (Reid & Jones, 2011).

While the convincing research applying trauma bond theory to intimate-partner violence makes it a reasonable explanation of the trafficker–victim relationship (e.g., Dutton & Painter, 1981, 1993), evidence directly relating trauma bond theory and human trafficking is insufficient. Further research applying trauma bond theory to trafficking is required to create a precise, evidence-based theoretical framework for human trafficking around the trauma bonding concept (Stein, 2012). Once this framework is developed, we can better develop interventions to give potential victims of sex trafficking the emotional armor they need to protect themselves from the fraudulent offerings of a trafficker.

Moving Beyond the Trafficker and Victim: Exploring the Impact of Ecological Factors

To fully understand the drivers of human trafficking, we must look beyond the individual push and pull factors leading traffickers and victims into the trafficking web. As Parmentier (2010) suggests, an ecological explanation of human trafficking will allow us to view the issue outside the current framework of victim and offender. We must understand the intricate causes and consequences of human trafficking, its cyclical nature, and the country-level factors that play into its proliferation. To understand human trafficking at an individual level, as an issue involving only a victim and the victimizer, prevents us from creating policy at a broader level.

For human trafficking to occur at the rate at which it does, there must be environmental factors at play. The culture, government, and general population condone, at least implicitly, this behavior. Two specific criminological theories appear to be especially relevant to our understanding of the ecological factors that promote the occurrence of human trafficking. These theories include Sampson and Groves's (1989) theory of **collective efficacy** and Chambliss's (1996) **political economy theory**.

Community and State Disorganization: Creating an Environment Fertile for Trafficking

Shaw and McKay (1942), the original founders of **social disorganization theory**, believed, simplistically, that three ecological factors—heterogeneity, socioeconomic status, and mobility of the population—could explain crime within the community. Sampson and colleagues extended Shaw and McKay's work to further define the impact of ecological factors on crime, using the concept of collective efficacy (Sampson & Groves, 1989; Sampson, Raudenbush, & Earls, 1997). Essentially, those communities that have high levels of collective efficacy have high levels of trust, cooperation, and connection among the individuals living in the community. Collective efficacy can act as a protective factor against the negative impacts of social disorganization.

Consistent with this theory, countries with low levels of social control (i.e., collective efficacy) are going to be more susceptible to human trafficking (Bush, 2010; Jiang & LaFree, 2016). Ecological factors, such as high levels of mobility, poverty, transiency, and unemployment, coupled with low income levels, create a highly disorganized environment in which individuals feel unstable, groups compete for power, and state officials (such as law enforcement) are unable to protect community members. Jiang and LaFree (2016) identified an additional measure of social control by noting the curvilinear relationship between international trade openness and social control. Those countries with very high and very low levels of trade displayed high levels of social control, while those countries that fell in the middle of the trade continuum displayed low levels of social control. Low levels of social control were correlated with deviance and crime, including human trafficking.

As such, countries with high levels of instability (and thus low levels of collective efficacy) are at risk for becoming both a destination and a source country for human trafficking victims. Such countries have less border control, less control over falsification of identifying documents, and more vulnerable individuals willing to take some risk in order to be offered better opportunities.

Parmentier (2010) advocates that while these same ecological factors may not fully explain the causes of human trafficking, they should be acknowledged when trying to understand this crime. Although social disorganization theories were originally intended to explain violence-ridden communities, those same factors may be relevant, albeit on a larger scale (e.g., countries rather than neighborhoods), in our attempt to understand human trafficking.

Social disorganization and other ecological factors appear to offer a reasonable explanation of the varying levels of human trafficking across countries and regions of the world. In every country there are motivated offenders. In every country there are potential victims desperate to make connections, looking for additional income, and looking for "too good to be true" opportunities. But where the country climate does not provide such opportunities, where traffickers offer victims opportunities they have never been offered before, and where the government protects those who wish to profit at any cost (or at least fails to protect those most in need of protection), it is understandable that human trafficking flourishes.

This next section expounds on Chambliss's economy of crime theory to better understand how the impact of ecological factors proliferates as globalization makes our world smaller.

Globalization: Increasing the Options for Maximizing Profit While Reducing Protections to the Vulnerable

Chambliss (1996) theorizes that the government in power defines who is criminal and who is not. Those in power create the laws. Such laws often result in inequality between the upper and lower classes of society. While the upper class may also be criminal, they are advantaged and are given more leniency in their behavior. Further, should they be accused of a criminal act, they are more likely to have the means to pay off the government representative and avoid the consequences of their behavior. The population not in power does not have such luxuries.

How can this conflict perspective shed light on human trafficking, especially while acknowledging that trafficking knows no race, socioeconomic status, gender, and so forth? It is applicable in understanding how globalization offers new ways for those in power to profit while simultaneously stripping the vulnerable of protections, essentially making them invisible players in this new business arena.

Wonders (2016) extends Chambliss's perspective to explain transnational crime in the increasingly globalized world we live in. Wonders (2016) postulates that globalization has essentially allowed those in power to design a space where laws can be completely disregarded. Powerful nations, such as the U.S., have strict and specific policies regarding labor, unions, taxes, and so forth. Profitable businesses from these countries have learned that if they operate in transnational spaces, they are relieved of the requirement to meet the same labor and union expectations as in their home countries. Nations often support this move to international soils in an effort to promote "global capitalism." Such actions on the part of businesses reduce the transparency of labor choices and limit legislative oversight (Wonders, 2016).

In this context, the benefits to companies as well as the dangers to workers become apparent. Businesses want to reduce costs and maximize profits. By going to countries where poverty is extensive, people are desperate for work, and labor laws are nonexistent, businesses increase profits and avoid their home countries' more stringent laws. Victims are in vulnerable positions and are eager for employment. Wonders (2016) notes that transnational spaces limit protections to the rights of individuals and groups, which exacerbates the problem. Further, transparency is reduced, as labor practices and agreements are often brokered in a virtual world. Once businesses move production to foreign countries, standards, practices, and intentions become nearly untraceable. Wonders (2016) poses the problem most effectively by suggesting "that the greatest danger at this moment may be what we do not know, what is hidden from public accountability, what is beyond the public gaze" (p. 214). His conclusions appropriately highlight that we are in a unique moment where we are realizing the potential pitfalls of a globalized economy and have the momentum and power to rectify the situation. "We have, perhaps, a brief moment to reveal and interrupt the move toward spaces without law and to reveal the 'unseen offenses' that are too often occurring in these spaces" (Wonders, 2016, p. 214). Coinciding with these comments, we see more and more public movements begun and reports written with the intent to bring awareness to unethical business practices abroad. FRDM (https://frdm.co/) is one such movement and will be highlighted in the labor trafficking section of this book (Part III). All of this being said, we find ourselves in this current precarious position because we live in a culture that promotes profit at all costs. It is not just the traffickers that allow trafficking to occur. It also requires the accountants and tax lawyers who do the books for corporations and traffickers, the law enforcement and government officials who turn a blind eye, and the consumers who demand low prices at the expense of fair wages for all commodities (Parmentier, 2010). We, as a society, must acknowledge how we contribute to the problem of human trafficking. We must reconcile our want for low-cost goods, and businesses' (and countries') want for maximum profits, with the reality that these wants are resulting in unethical labor practices and human-rights violations on an international scale.

Conclusion

According to Polaris (n.d.a), 20.9 million people are trafficked globally per year. It is reasonable to assume that individual, familial, and ecological factors all play a role in predicting the occurrence of human trafficking. Understanding variations in these factors, especially the ecological ones, helps us to explain variations in the severity of trafficking around the world.

Parmentier (2010) argues that, as a society, we have come to the point of needing a concise "ecology" of human trafficking. We struggle today with the varying definitions of human trafficking in different regions of the world (as reviewed in Chapters 1 and 2 of this text). These different definitions prevent us from making a broad and real impact on this crime. Just as the Chicago school gave credence to the ecological causes of urban violence (Shaw & McKay, 1942), criminologists today need to design an ecology of human trafficking.

Extending beyond an ecological model, Lutya and Lanier (2012) promote an integrated model of theoretical understanding of the multidimensional nature of human trafficking. Such an integrated model can borrow ideas from multiple schools of thought, including deterrence, economic, conflict, control, social disorganization, strain, and schools outside the reach of criminology, such as psychological and human rights theories (Lutya & Lanier, 2012; Yuko, 2009). Further, to really prevent human trafficking, theory developers must be able to explain not only the role of the traffickers but also the roles of the victims and the community/country. An integrated theory must be able to discriminate between *and* integrate the individual-level and ecological factors playing into this crime, as shown in Figure 3.4.

Figure 3.4 Multi-Level Factors That Predict Trafficking Victimization

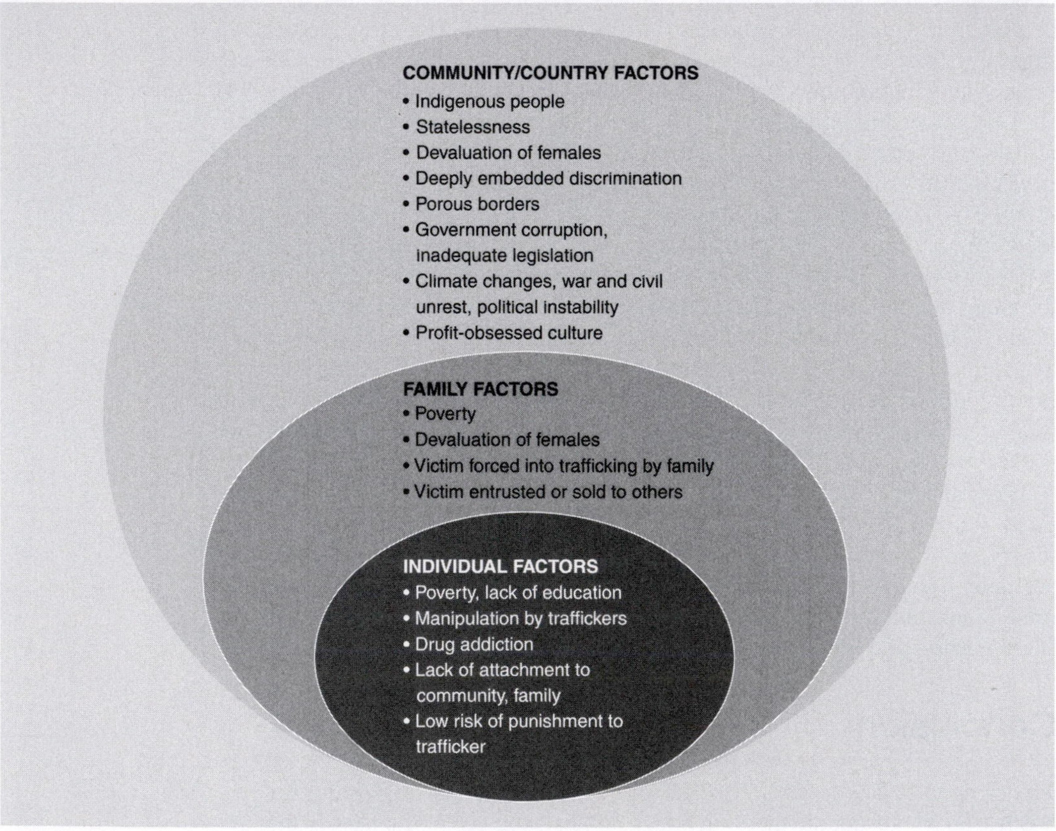

COMMUNITY/COUNTRY FACTORS
- Indigenous people
- Statelessness
- Devaluation of females
- Deeply embedded discrimination
- Porous borders
- Government corruption, inadequate legislation
- Climate changes, war and civil unrest, political instability
- Profit-obsessed culture

FAMILY FACTORS
- Poverty
- Devaluation of females
- Victim forced into trafficking by family
- Victim entrusted or sold to others

INDIVIDUAL FACTORS
- Poverty, lack of education
- Manipulation by traffickers
- Drug addiction
- Lack of attachment to community, family
- Low risk of punishment to trafficker

Sources: Bales, 2016; Department of Homeland Security, 2016; International Labour Office, 2014; Kristo and WuDunn, 2010.

Challenge Yourself 3.2

You have read about the various theories applicable to explaining human trafficking. Defend the theory you think best explains human trafficking.

Do you think integration is important? Do you think different theories are needed to explain different forms of trafficking?

KEY WORDS

collective efficacy 63

general strain theory 60

opportunistic buyer 57

political economy theory 63

preferential buyer 57

rational choice theory 42

routine activities theory 46

situational buyer 57

situational crime
    prevention (SCP) 50

social disorganization theory 63

target hardening 50

techniques of neutralization 58

trauma bond theory 60

DISCUSSION QUESTIONS

1. How does rational choice theory help criminologists understand the motivations of human traffickers? What factors hinder the application of rational choice theory to understand motivations of the trafficker?

2. List some of the ways in which situational crime theory reduces opportunities to commit crime that occur during common routines.

3. How does routine activities theory act as a catalyst for supporting a situational crime prevention approach?

4. Compare and contrast the three different categories of sex buyers. Regardless of which category a sex buyer belongs to, why is it ultimately important to incorporate an understanding of the individual-level factors contributing to behaviors of the trafficker?

5. In your own words, explain Sykes and Matza's (1957) theory of techniques of neutralization on how individuals can drift in and out of crime.

6. How do the elements contained in trauma bond theory transform the self-identity of victims?

7. Describe the ecological factors of human trafficking and explain how environments can become susceptible to high volumes of human trafficking.

RESOURCES

- Arizona State University, Center for Problem-Oriented Policing: "Situational Crime Prevention": https://popcenter.asu.edu/content/situational-crime-prevention-0

- Blue Campaign: https://www.dhs.gov/blue-campaign

- FRDM: https://frdm.co/

- Shared Hope International: https://sharedhope.org/

- Urban Institute's human trafficking research: https:w//www.urban.org/research-area/human-trafficking

The Victims of Human Trafficking

A key part of prevention is learning from survivors what would have helped them avoid victimization.

—Susan Coppedge, U.S. Ambassador-at-Large to Monitor and Combat Trafficking in Persons

Case Study

"Jana"

Jana, 18, is from a country in Eastern Europe known to be a major source for trafficked women. She has just completed secondary school and works in a confectionery factory. Her older sister, Lydia, was trafficked two years ago. After being arrested in a brothel raid, Lydia agreed to testify against her traffickers and was given temporary residence for the duration of the trial. Although her testimony contributed to the prosecution's obtaining a conviction and a sentence, Lydia was told she needed to go home. Rather than face the shame and stigma of returning as a criminal and a prostitute, she hanged herself.

Now her four-year-old daughter lives at home with Lydia's mother, who also works in a confectionery factory, and Jana. The father is a migrant laborer and is often away from home for long periods of time. Extensive conversations with the family revealed feelings of deep shame about what had happened to Lydia. Her pictures had been removed from the house and her name was not mentioned.

Jana admitted that, while being afraid of what could happen to her, she still wanted to work overseas because there was nothing for her at home, other than to stay in the confectionery factory and "marry a worthless alcoholic like my sister did." A small foundation offered to pay for Jana's university education over four years, including a subsidy to make up for lost wages as well as all books and fees. Although definitely bright enough, Jana declined the offer, saying that she did not know anyone who had gone to the university and she didn't think it was her place. She asked, instead, to be sent to a vocational program to study hairdressing, following the example of many of her friends.

Jana is a potential victim of trafficking. She is vulnerable because she faces limited employment opportunities in a country with a volatile economy and a limited job market. She is also vulnerable because she feels no support to pursue a university education, because of the expectations of her community that overseas jobs are the only option and because she can see little opportunity for either personal or professional fulfilment at home.

Source: Trafficking in Persons, 2016 Trafficking in Persons Report. United Nations Office on Drugs and Crime, 2008a, p. 70.

The Case Study opening this chapter highlights the realities of human trafficking. A lack of opportunities, combined with cultural and other contextual factors, puts individuals at risk of becoming victims.

While today there is intense focus on prosecutorial and reactionary responses to trafficking, it is critical to understand the vulnerabilities that create a victim.

Improved understanding of the risk factors for victimization will result in more focused and more intentional prevention efforts. The Department of State, in its annual Trafficking in Persons (TIP) Reports, reinforces the importance of implementing prevention tactics and suggests that to implement prevention strategies, we must understand the problem sufficiently (U.S. Department of State, 2016). The 3P paradigm—prosecution, protection, and prevention—originally presented in the 2000 Protocol to Prevent, Suppress and Punish Trafficking in Persons Especially Women and Children, one of the Palermo protocols—offers guidance on how to implement prevention strategies (United Nations General Assembly, 2000c).

Building on the Palermo protocols, the United Nations Office on Drugs and Crime (UNODC) and the United Nations Global Initiative to Fight Human Trafficking (UN.GIFT) also stress the importance of acknowledging the vulnerability of individuals in their defining background paper (UNODC, 2008a). They state that understanding the vulnerabilities some individuals face will provide the "missing link" to effective prevention strategies. With an improved understanding of the vulnerabilities faced by individuals, countries can better inform vulnerable populations of their options. In other words, prevention activities should result in alternatives to being trafficked (UNODC, 2008a).

Strengthening individuals and communities to resist the advances of traffickers will reduce the available supply of victims. While specific vulnerabilities are fluid and will vary by country (and this is something researchers, policy makers, and practitioners should focus on identifying and fortifying), this chapter will explore the broad factors that make victims more vulnerable to traffickers. The specific factors exist at the individual, country, and regional levels. These factors are complex and interrelated. Some factors are better understood than others. For some, such as gender discrimination, an entire book could be written on the topic. Nevertheless, this text will provide a comprehensive overview of the factors listed in Figure 4.1. Prior to delving into these vulnerability factors, however, the chapter starts with an overview of what trafficking victimization looks like.

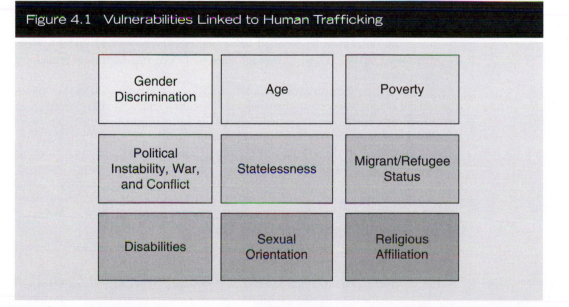

Figure 4.1 Vulnerabilities Linked to Human Trafficking

Who Is a Victim?

This section will explore the demographics of identified victims, both within the United States and globally.

The United States

The National Human Trafficking Resource Center (NHTRC; 2016) offers statistics on survivors[1] identified through the **National Human Trafficking Hotline**. These number are based on calls coming in to the National Human Trafficking Hotline, texts from Polaris's **BeFree Textline,** and communications regarding overseas cases. In 2015, 21,947 calls, 1,275 emails, and 1,535 online tip reports were received, resulting in 5,961 potential human trafficking cases (Polaris, n.d.d). In 2016, there was a 35% increase in numbers of reported cases. In total, 8,042 unique cases of trafficking were reported to the hotline in 2016 (NHTRC, 2016). Seven thousand, five hundred seventy cases came from within the United States on the National Human Trafficking Hotline, 301 cases were reported from overseas, and 169 came through the BeFree Textline. In 2016, 2,042 survivors directly reached out, representing a 24% increase from 2015 (NHTRC, 2016). Table 4.1 describes both the breakdown in forms of trafficking and the demographics of identified trafficking survivors.

In 2016, sex trafficking cases characterized the dominant form of trafficking reported in the United States (73%). Labor trafficking accounted for 14% of all reported cases. Despite the smaller proportion of labor trafficking cases reported as compared to sex trafficking, from 2015 to 2016 there was a 45% increase in the number of reported labor trafficking cases (717 and 1,057, respectively). Cases in which victims were forced into both labor and sex trafficking accounted for 4% of all cases. Nine percent of reported cases were not specified.

As listed in Table 4.1, over a quarter of identified survivors were minors. The 2016 report provides more refined information on age when sex or labor trafficking began. In 2016, nearly half of all sex trafficking survivors (49%, based on 1,164 survivors for whom exact age was disclosed) were between the ages of 12 and 17 when their victimization began; however, the average age when victimization began was 18 years old. For labor trafficking, 36% of survivors (based on 238 survivors) reported being between the ages of 12 and 17 when their trafficking began. The average age when trafficking began for labor trafficking survivors was 23.

The majority of survivors were female (83.4%). Although citizenship status was not often disclosed, survivors who did disclose this information identified as U.S. citizens as well as foreign nationals. Of the 3,664 survivors for whom nationality information was available, nearly half were from Mexico (n = 359), as shown in Figure 4.2. Nearly a quarter were from China (n = 159), and the remaining were from the Philippines (n = 119) and Guatemala (n = 114). Some survivors had multiple nationalities. In regard to ethnicity, Latinos represented the highest number of survivors at 42% (n = 1,040 out of 3,116 survivors for whom ethnicity was available), followed by Asian (n = 715), white (n = 577), African American (n = 553), and multiracial survivors (n = 139).

---

[1] For the purposes of this section, we will refer to victims as survivors, consistent with the National Human Trafficking Resource Center reporting. All of the statistics presented in this section refer to those who survived their trafficking experience.

Table 4.1 Human Trafficking Hotline Statistics for 2016

Form of trafficking[1]	# of cases	% of cases
Sex trafficking	5,551	73%
Labor trafficking	1,057	14%
Labor and sex trafficking	268	4%
Unspecified	696	9%
Survivor demographics[2]		
Adult	5,297	62.0%
Minor	2,297	26.9%
Female	7,128	83.4%
Male	1,115	13.1%
Gender minority	51	0.6%
U.S. citizen/legal resident	2,190	25.6%
Foreign national	1,726	20.2%

[1]Based on 7,572 cases where the form of trafficking was identified.

[2]Based on 8,542 survivors who were identified or described to hotline staff. Age is based on time of first contact with Polaris.

Source: Statistics reported in the National Human Trafficking Resource Center 2016 Report (NHTRC, 2016).

Figure 4.2 Nationality and Ethnicity of Survivors of Human Trafficking

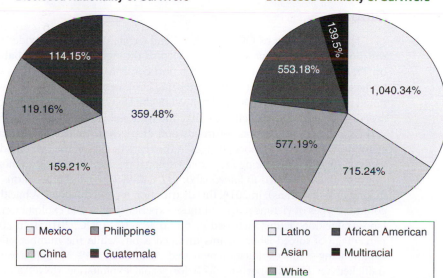

Disclosed Nationality of Survivors

- Mexico: 359.48%
- China: 159.21%
- Philippines: 119.16%
- Guatemala: 114.15%

Disclosed Ethnicity of Survivors

- Latino: 1,040.34%
- Asian: 715.24%
- White: 577.19%
- African American: 553.18%
- Multiracial: 139.5%

Source: Adapted from National Human Trafficking Resource Center (2016).

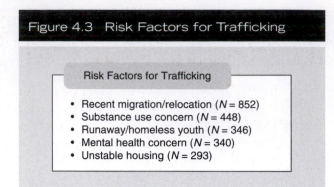

Figure 4.3 Risk Factors for Trafficking

Risk Factors for Trafficking

- Recent migration/relocation ($N = 852$)
- Substance use concern ($N = 448$)
- Runaway/homeless youth ($N = 346$)
- Mental health concern ($N = 340$)
- Unstable housing ($N = 293$)

Data source: Adapted from National Human Trafficking Resource Center, 2016.

While the bulk of this chapter goes into depth on the vulnerabilities that result in individuals becoming victims of human trafficking, the National Human Trafficking Resource Center (2016) reported on the most frequent reasons survivors gave for falling into trafficking situations, as described in Figure 4.3. The factors, while based on U.S. data, are consistent with our understanding of the vulnerabilities for trafficking globally. Perhaps unsurprisingly (once you read the rest of this chapter), migration and relocation are a driving factor. Substance abuse is common among human trafficking victims and a frequently stated reason for returning to a trafficking situation. In *Half the Sky*, Kristof and WuDunn (2010) offer an effective account of the power of drug addiction to keep a trafficking victim linked to his or her trafficker. Running away from home and homelessness are also driving factors for youth, especially in the United States, as are mental health and housing issues. Like drug addiction, mental health challenges and lack of adequate housing can force victims to return to traffickers.

As discussed in Chapter 2, reliable large-scale statistics can be difficult to capture. While the statistics cited above come from concrete reports of trafficking, the actual rate of trafficking is most certainly underestimated, as these reports exclude unidentified cases of trafficking in the United States. That said, the National Human Trafficking Hotline offers a central source of data on trafficking in the United States. The same cannot be said for the rest of the world. Although Polaris and other organizations are working to develop regional hotlines and improved networking across nongovernmental organizations, in other countries there is no centralized way to gather statistics on human trafficking (Polaris, n.d.b).

Global

The United Nations Office on Drugs and Crime (UNODC) provides perhaps the most reliable account of trafficking victims through its annual **Global Report on Trafficking in Persons.** The 2018 report confirms that no country is without trafficking victims and that victims are being exploited in many different ways, as noted in Figure 4.4 (UNODC, 2018a). While the UNODC report does not confirm specific incidences of trafficking, unlike the National Human Trafficking Hotline, it does provide observations of trends and changes in trafficking patterns. For example, the report describes changes in the types of exploitation among detected victims. In 2007, trafficking for sexual exploitation was the most common (59% of victims) as compared to forced labor (32% of victims) and other forms of trafficking (9% of victims). In 2014, this distribution looked different. While the most common types of victims remained those experiencing sexual exploitation (54%), labor trafficking victims increased by 6% to 38% (UNODC, 2016a). In 2018, the percentage of forced-labor victims dropped a bit, while the number of victims experiencing sexual exploitation increased. As of 2016, 34% of victims were being trafficked for forced labor and 59% for sexual exploitation (UNODC, 2018a). However, as noted in Figure 4.4, this trend is not consistent across regions. The balance between forced labor and sexual exploitation varies depending on the

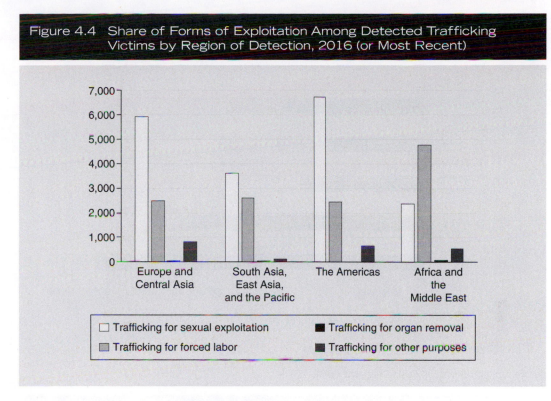

Figure 4.4 Share of Forms of Exploitation Among Detected Trafficking Victims by Region of Detection, 2016 (or Most Recent)

Legend:

☐ Trafficking for sexual exploitation
■ Trafficking for forced labor
■ Trafficking for organ removal
■ Trafficking for other purposes

Source: United Nations Office on Drugs and Crime, 2018.

region, with forced labor being the more common form in Africa and the Middle East in 2016.

The report also highlighted an upward trend in the identification of male victims. While in 2004 only 13% of victims were identified as male, in 2014 that number increased to 29% (including men and boys). In 2016 the number remained relatively consistent, with 28% of victims being identified as male (UNODC, 2016a, 2018a). Later in the chapter, we will explore the concept of men as victims as well as the continued disparities between men and women that make women especially vulnerable to traffickers.

In regard to the age of victims, the UNODC (2018a) reports consistent increases in the trafficking of children for the past seven years. While the report states that more than a quarter of trafficking victims are in fact children, the trafficking of children actually surpasses that of adults in two different regions—West Africa, and Central America and the Caribbean (see Figure 4.5).

Finally, when exploring trends in the movement of trafficking victims, the 2016 Global Report on Trafficking in Persons (UNODC, 2016a) reported that 42% of detected victims had been trafficked within the borders of their home country. This number increased to 58% in 2016 (UNODC, 2018a). Cross-border trafficking patterns are, unsurprisingly, consistent with the flow of migration (discussed further below). Trafficking victims are often of the same nationality as their trafficker. The UNODC (2016) suggests this is intentional, as in such cases traffickers can more effectively develop trust with their victims. Improved border control and greater awareness of domestic trafficking are also possible explanations of the increase in identification of domestic trafficking victims.

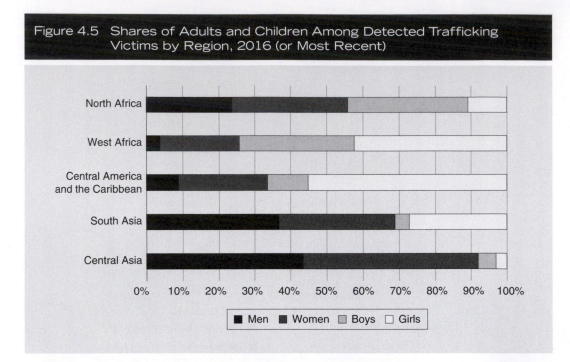

Source: United Nations Office on Drugs and Crime, 2018a.

Figure 4.6   Distribution of International Forced Labor (Including
              Sexual Slavery)

Source: International Labour Organization, 2013c.

These statistics are generally helpful in providing a raw understanding of trafficking on an international level. The UN's International Labour Organization (ILO; 2013c) also offers a global perspective with its global estimate of forced labor in 2012 (see Figure 4.6). Using a combination of secondary sources and four national surveys, it estimated that 21 million people were living enslaved, with over half come from the Asia-Pacific region (56%), 18% from Africa, 9% from Latin America, 7% from developed nations and the European Union, 7% from Central and Southeast Europe, and 3% from the Middle East. It estimates individuals are experiencing forced labor at a much higher rate than sexual slavery (77% and 22% of slaves, respectively). Twenty-six percent of slaves are under the age of 18. A large minority of slaves are boys and men 45% (ILO, 2013a).

So what can we take away from this discussion? Human trafficking happens everywhere. Men, women, boys, and girls are all at risk. Individuals from every society and culture can be impacted. Given that this terrible fate can happen to anyone, let's delve deeper into why some individuals fall prey to traffickers and others do not. As you will observe, many of these factors exist at the individual level and country/regional level. As the number of individuals experiencing any of these vulnerabilities increases, the country/regional level destabilizes.

Turning Vulnerabilities Into Victimization

As Chapter 5 will point out, the trafficker is a cunning master of manipulation. Any sign of weakness in a potential victim will be taken advantage of. In the United States, this weakness could take the form of a runaway with no access to housing. In the hills of Thailand, it might be a family desperate for income. Without education, documentation, or employment prospects, the family's only option to survive may be to send a child into the city with the promise of a job. A key component to ending trafficking involves identifying and preventing characteristics that make victims vulnerable to traffickers.

In Part I of UNODC's background paper on human trafficking (2008a), Clark specifies a definition of **vulnerability** in regard to trafficking: "a condition resulting from how individuals negatively experience the complex interaction of social, cultural, economic, political, and environmental factors that create the context for their communities" (p. 69). Consistent with this notion, it is important to explore not only the individual-level vulnerabilities but also how these vulnerabilities are perpetuated in higher-level contexts, such as the country and region.

The 2016 TIP Report acknowledges the role that vulnerabilities play in creating trafficking victims (U.S. State Department, 2016). It mentions several characteristics that make an individual more vulnerable to a trafficker, including specific sexual orientations and gender identities, certain religious affiliations, migrant status, disability status, and statelessness. UNODC and UN.GIFT provide an even more comprehensive list of factors that give a trafficker the advantage, including gender, age, poverty, social and cultural exclusion, limited education, political instability, war and conflict, social/cultural and legal frameworks, movement under duress, and demand (UNODC, 2008a). The remainder of this chapter will provide an overview of how the most damaging vulnerabilities play a role in turning individuals into trafficking victims. While these lists are by no means comprehensive, nor does having any of these traits guarantee that an individual will be trafficked, understanding general risk factors can help in providing a foundation and direction for the implementation of prevention programming. As you will see, there is more information available for some of these risk factors than for others.

Figure 4.7 Trafficking Victims by Gender and Age

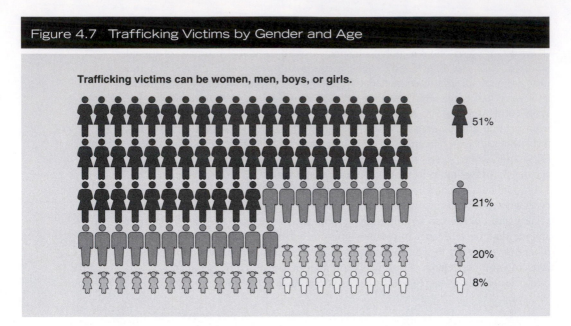

Trafficking victims can be women, men, boys, or girls.

51%

21%

20%

8%

Source: United Nations Office on Drugs and Crime, 2016a.

This fact, in its own right, indicates the need for an improved understanding of who is most vulnerable to trafficking.

The remainder of this chapter will review selected vulnerabilities that result in trafficking. These factors require more attention both in policy and advocacy.

Gender

The ILO (2013c) predicts that approximately 55% of all human trafficking victims are women and girls. The UNODC (2018a), using more recent data, estimates this number to be even higher at approximately 72%. No form of trafficking excludes women. While mostly found in commercial sex services, women are forced into marriage, domestic servitude, and other forms of labor as well (Voronova & Radjenovic, 2016). And while the UNODC (2016a) reports an increase in the number of males being trafficked,[2] the number of females far surpasses that of males, likely due to the continued disparities that exist between men and women in every country (International Organization for Migration [IOM], 2015; UNODC, 2016; see Figure 4.7). A collaborative report published by the Clinton Foundation and Bill and Melinda Gates Foundation (2015) points out that while the status of women has improved on all continents, women, especially impoverished women, still lag behind men in regard to status, pay, and access to health care and education. While this does not necessarily speak directly to the status of women in regard to human trafficking, it provides a foundation for understanding the unique challenges women face as compared to men when avoiding human trafficking.

---

[2] The number of identified male victims of trafficking appears to remain steady in comparing the data presented by the UNODC in 2016 and 2018.

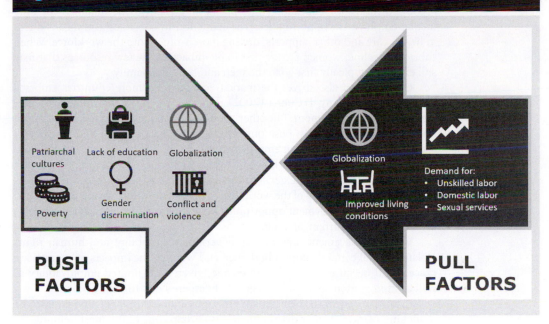

Figure 4.8 Push and Pull Factors Driving the Trafficking of Women and Girls

PUSH FACTORS

Patriarchal cultures

Lack of education

Globalization

Poverty

Gender discrimination

Conflict and violence

PULL FACTORS

Globalization

Improved living conditions

Demand for:
- Unskilled labor
- Domestic labor
- Sexual services

Further, the widespread acceptance of violence against women makes them all the more vulnerable to traffickers. According to the Half the Sky Movement, gender-based violence is as pressing a public health crisis as cancer and heart disease. In fact, the Half the Sky Movement suggests that women age 15 to 45 are more likely to die or be severely injured due to gender-based violence than from cancer, malaria, traffic accidents, and war combined (Half the Sky Movement, n.d.b). Similarly, lack of employment opportunities, drug addiction, and pressure from families, pimps, and traffickers can all lead women into forced prostitution, a form of trafficking (Half the Sky Movement, n.d.a).

Vulnerabilities faced by women and girls can be broken down into **push** and **pull factors** (D'Cunha, 2002; United Nations General Assembly, 2000c; Voronova & Radjenovic, 2016). These complex factors indicate that while sometimes simply being a woman is an inherent vulnerability, the combination of being a woman and having other risk factors, such as being impoverished or uneducated, results in women being especially vulnerable to traffickers (Clinton Foundation & Bill and Melinda Gates Foundation, 2015; D'Cunha, 2002; Voronova & Radjenovic, 2016). The reason is that when there are disparities between the status of men and women, women's voices are limited, if not completely silenced. Women are less able to advocate for themselves and thus become less empowered and more oppressed.

Push Factors

As mentioned above, there are both push and pull factors that result in increased numbers of women being trafficked. D'Cunha (2002) refers to these factors as supply and demand factors. She cites globalization, displacement, and gender discrimination as the driving factors resulting in a bountiful supply of women available to be trafficked. Cost-cutting measures in the wake of globalization have resulted in many low-paying, low-security, and intensive-labor jobs, aimed at women. Coupled with the reduction in state subsidies, this means women have less opportunity for education, thus positioning them to be qualified for only menial employment opportunities. The reduction in subsidies also means a loss in health care and other supports, driving more women into the workforce. When subsidies decline, women are the first to be impacted; the few resources that may still exist will typically first go to the men and boys in a family.

Globalization also drives the market economy. As more countries embrace this form of economy, D'Cunha (2002) describes the need for women to enter **"facilitated job placement."** In other words, women gain assistance (often from traffickers) to be placed in positions. This reliance on others to find them work lessens their control over their employment situation. Further, as a result of globalization, women are exposed to how others live. They may become dissatisfied with their living situations—the extensive domestic work and family care don't seem as attractive as what the rest of the world has to offer. Unfortunately, women's limited experience and employment opportunities give them few choices when attempting to leave their current situations.

While displacement (due to war, government instability, and human rights violations) will certainly impact both men and women, the impacts on women are exacerbated because their ability to escape, given their limited employability as well as immigration restrictions, is greatly hampered due to their gender.

Finally, in regard to characteristics that put a large supply of women into the trafficking market, gender discrimination is perhaps one of the most defining. As noted by the Clinton Foundation and Bill and Melinda Gates Foundation (2015), the status of women is far less equal to men in certain parts of the world, especially in South Asia and Sub-Saharan Africa. The World Bank (n.d.) estimates that 62 million girls between the ages of 6 and 15 are not enrolled in school globally. Further, even when girls are enrolled in school, their completion rates lag behind those of boys, especially their completion rates for secondary school. The impact of gender disparities in education is cyclical and is occurring in some form in every county (United Nations Educational, Scientific and Cultural Organization [UNESCO], 2012).

Poverty is a likely cause of the ineducation of girls, coupled with cultural norms dictating that limited resources go to boys and men. Consequences (and possibly causes) of being uneducated include poorer health, lower income, marriage at an earlier age, more children, and worse health care and education for offspring (Clinton Foundation & Bill and Melinda Gates Foundation, 2015; Lerch, 2015; World Bank, n.d.; UNESCO, 2012). In some societies it is customary for young girls to be married off at a young age. In such situations, the families often feel it a waste to invest in education for the girl (UNESCO, 2012). Further, the girl knows her fate and takes no initiative to perform well in school when given the opportunity.

As displayed in Figure 4.9, gender disparities and discrimination extend beyond education. Child marriage and early maternal age independently put girls at risk for human trafficking. Families often feel the financial and cultural burden of girls due to the expectation of purity and the obligation of dowries for marriage (D'Cunha, 2002). Any opportunity parents have to marry off a girl without the demand for a dowry will often be accepted. Getting married at a young age often results in a poor-quality marriage and/or abandonment. Consequently, this produces a young woman with no means to support herself, creating an attractive possibility for a trafficker.

Figure 4.9 Gender Inequality Index 2013

The European year for development: Women and girls

Gender Inequality Index 2013

The index measures equality between men and women.

It is composed of indicators on reproductive health (maternal mortality and adolescent fertility rate),
empowerment (women's secondary school attendance and parliamentary seats) and labour market (women's share in labour force).
A value of 0 means maximum equality and 1 means maximum inequality.

■ More than 0.60   ■ Between 0.45 and 0.30   Less than 0.15
■ Between 0.60 and 0.45   ■ Between 0.30 and 0.15   No data

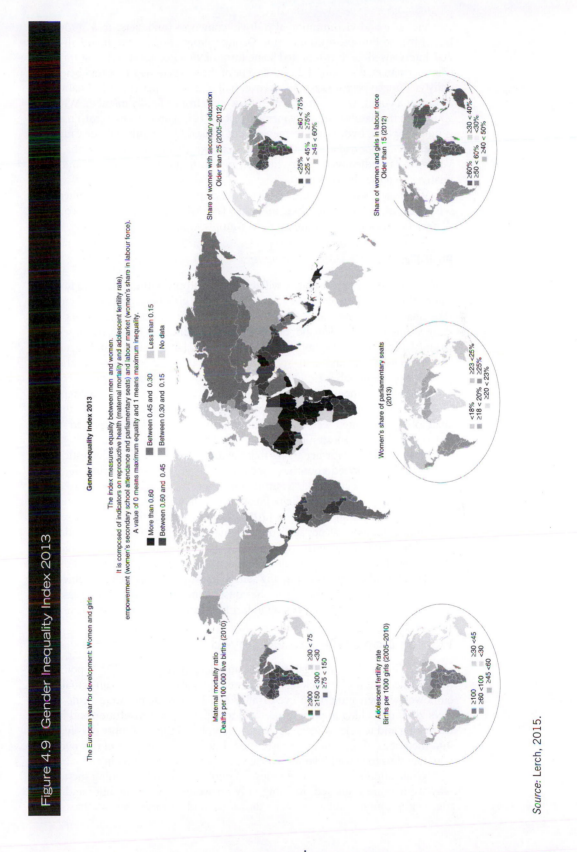

Share of women with secondary education
Older than 25 (2005–2012)
<25%   ≥45 < 60%   ≥60 < 75%
≥25 < 45%   ≥45 < 60%   ≥75%

Share of women and girls in labour force
Older than 15 (2012)
≥60%   ≥30 < 40%
≥50 < 60%   <30%
≥40 < 50%

Women's share of parliamentary seats
(2013)
<18%   ≥23 <25%
≥18 < 20%   ≥25%
≥20 < 23%

Maternal mortality ratio
Deaths per 100 000 live births (2010)
≥300   ≥30 < 75
≥150 < 300   <30
≥75 < 150

Adolescent fertility rate
Births per 1000 girls (2005–2010)
≥100   ≥30 <45
≥60 <100   <30
≥45 <60

Source: Lerch, 2015.

Violence and victimization also drive women to traffickers. In a study published by the European Commission Daphne Programme, more than half of the 207 interviewed victims reported some form of violence prior to being trafficked (Zimmerman et al., 2006). Fifteen percent of the interviewees reported being sexually victimized prior to age 15. And over half of those experiencing sexual victimization at a young age reported abuse or coercion from a family member. When the abuse is at the hands of a family member, escape is imperative and returning home is not an option. Even when women are not abused by a family member, rape and domestic violence can leave them with low self-worth and shame (D'Cunha, 2002; Voronova & Radjenovic, 2016). Further, rape can embarrass a family and cause relatives to reject the victim.

When women experience gender discrimination, resulting in limited skill sets, and violence, often resulting in limited familial support, it is easy to conclude that traffickers enjoy a seemingly endless supply of victims.

Pull Factors

As a basic economics course will teach you, supply without demand holds no value. The growing demand for women and young girls is apparent in all cultures. D'Cunha (2002) states that "the development of certain economic sectors with a more women-specific demand, circumscribed by gendered occupational segmentation[;] gendered perceptions of attributes, skill, [and] value[;] and [gendered] perceptions of body and sexuality," promotes the demand for women in the form of both sexual and labor exploitation (p. 17; Voronova & Radjenovic, 2016). The assumption of women's submissiveness makes them ideal for the menial repetitive jobs emerging due to the increase in the export production market. Unfortunately, such jobs offer limited security for their employees due to low wages and no collective bargaining opportunities.

D'Cunha (2002) further argues that the increased demand for domestic workers, even in developed countries, stems from more women entering the workforce. As women begin working outside the home, they have less time for keeping house, thus requiring outside help. Finally, the demand for sex inherently requires women. As Kristof and WuDunn (2010) have observed, the spread of sexually transmitted diseases has not slowed this demand but simply changed the demand to younger and younger girls. Traffickers are well aware that they can charge more for a virgin due to her lower likelihood of carrying a sexually transmitted disease.

The state of women is improving across the world. Nevertheless, women continue to be mistreated globally, and the consequences are dire. However, assumptions about women by activists may in fact be contributing to the problem.

Women Don't Need to Be Saved

The Global Alliance Against Traffic in Women (GAATW; 2010) points out that our definition of trafficking and assumptions about women can actually disempower women more than even traffickers. Improvements were made to the UN's 2000 trafficking in persons protocol to separate out prostitution and human trafficking and to acknowledge consent. Chapter 6 of this text more deeply delves into the issues of consent and prostitution, but for the purposes of this overview, you may start to consider your own views on consent and coercion.

While attention to vulnerabilities is important to understanding the reasons why women are trafficked, focusing only on women's vulnerabilities and ignoring their autonomy, ability to make decisions, and so forth narrows the voice of women as much as the structural causes limiting women's opportunities. There is no reason to dispute that the status of women is variable in different countries and cultures. That being said, to design and implement effective solutions, it is imperative to acknowledge and expect that women can, in fact, be active participants in their escape. In other words, women need not to be saved but rather to be provided with tools that they themselves can use to escape.

Further, as noted in the GAATW (2010) report, examining the role of women only as victims does not adequately portray the many roles women can play in the human trafficking process. Women have been known to traffic, recruit, and otherwise benefit from the exploitation of others. In fact, the recent report by the UNODC (2018a) indicates that in some regions, specifically Eastern Europe and Central Asia, and Central America and the Caribbean, the number of convicted female traffickers supersedes that of males (nearly 60% in both regions). In East Asia and the Pacific, the numbers of male and female traffickers are equal at 50% each.

Could it also be possible that the narrow focus on women has not allowed for the acknowledgment of males in trafficking?

Males Are Trafficked Too

While there is no denying that women have unique vulnerabilities that make them especially susceptible to traffickers, there is a notable uptick in the number of male victims. The UNODC (2016a) reports that 16% of victims in 2004 were men or boys. By 2014, the number had increased to 29%. The number of males steadied by 2016, when 28% of victims were identified as male (UNODC, 2018a). Between 2012 and 2014, one in five victims was male. Regional statistics better parse out this increase. The number of male victims exceeded 50% in North Africa and approached 50% in Central Asia. The number of male victims was larger than the global average in West Africa and South Asia, likely due to the frequency of forced labor in these regions (UNODC, 2018a). In 2014, men were predominantly trafficked for forced labor (82%); however, 10% were trafficked for sexual exploitation and another 7% for other forms of trafficking. One percent of male victims were trafficked for organ removal. Half of boy victims were trafficked for forced labor, with the other half being trafficked for sexual exploitation (27%) and other purposes (23%; UNDOC, 2018a).

While females are stereotyped as the weaker gender, does stereotyping prevent us from seeing that males can also be trafficked? Do gender norms prevent males from coming forward to report victimization? O. Edwards (2015) of the End Slavery Now organization believes this is the exact reason why males have been overlooked as human trafficking victims. The unfortunate consequence of this is a lack of assessment tools and services available for male victims. The techniques and assessments we use to identify female victims may not work to identify male victims.

Challenge Yourself 4.1

If I mentioned to you a recent case of trafficking and said a male was involved, would you automatically assume the male was the trafficker? Why or why not?

Youth

The National Human Trafficking Resource Center (2016) statistics, referenced earlier in this chapter, highlight the unique challenges faced by youth trying to avoid victimization at the hands of a trafficker. It goes without saying that minors' status inherently makes them vulnerable to many forms of exploitation. Children are considered unable to make decisions for themselves when it comes to sex, marriage, work, and so forth. Further, children are developmentally and physically different from adults (UN.GIFT, n.d.). They are less able to protect themselves, may be less aware of laws, and, perhaps most notably, are at a disadvantage when being asked to do something by an authoritative figure (UNODC, 2008a). Finally, the massive demand for younger victims, both for sexual exploitation and forced labor, make this group all the more vulnerable (UN.GIFT, n.d.).

In spite of a goal to eliminate the worst forms of child labor by 2016, child labor continues, albeit reduced (Connell, 2013; ILO, 2013d). The ILO cites Asia and the Pacific as having the largest number of child laborers—approximately 9.3% of the child population in those locations. Even in other locations, including Latin America, the Caribbean, the Middle East, and North Africa, millions of children are involved in labor, and often in hazardous forms of work, including sexual exploitation (ILO, 2013d). The involvement of minors in specific forms of trafficking will be addressed throughout this text.

While youth are inherently more vulnerable to traffickers, a few characteristics and policies that exacerbate these vulnerabilities are explored in in the remainder of this section.

Children Traveling Alone

Perhaps the youths most at risk for trafficking are unaccompanied minors (UACs) (IOM, 2015). The United Nations Refugee Agency (2016a) estimated that 98,400 UACs, from 78 different counties, applied for asylum in 2015. These youths are often limited in their abilities to communicate and are not safeguarded by the presence of parents or relatives. As tens of thousands of UACs enter Europe and the United States, the immense risk these youths take are becoming more apparent.

The general risk factors for migration are discussed later in this chapter; however, youth traveling alone are uniquely vulnerable to trafficking. As cited in a *Huffington Post* article, research conducted by the UN Refugee Agency showed that 50% of UACs interviewed indicated that they had been threatened in their home country by criminal groups, including gangs and cartels. Nearly a quarter of girls interviewed reported having experienced or having been threatened with sexual violence (Roenigk, 2014).

A study on the factors driving UACs out of Afghanistan provides a further nuanced understanding of why UACs take such risky journeys alone (Echavez, Bagaporo, Pilongo, & Azadmanesh, 2014). The findings indicated that most UACs (from Afghanistan) were males between the ages of 13 and 17 years old and made the solitary journey as a result of poverty, insecurity, inadequate opportunities for education and employment, and family and peer expectations. Youths from provinces that were frequent producers of UACs often had the support of family. Families financed the youths' journey by borrowing money and mortgaging properties. Youths coming from provinces that did not often produce UACs more frequently had to convince family members to support their journeys. Most indicated a goal of relocating to Europe, possibly with stops in Iran. Smuggling rings were often involved in the transport of UACs.

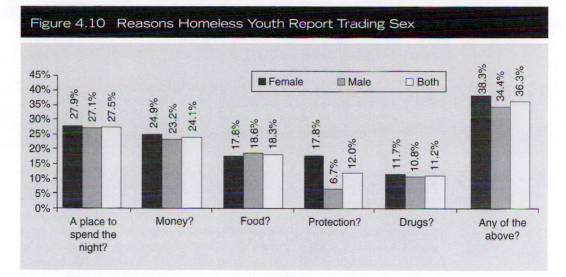

Figure 4.10   Reasons Homeless Youth Report Trading Sex

Legend: ■ Female   ▨ Male   □ Both

- A place to spend the night?: Female 27.9%, Male 27.1%, Both 27.5%
- Money?: Female 24.9%, Male 23.2%, Both 24.1%
- Food?: Female 17.8%, Male 18.6%, Both 18.3%
- Protection?: Female 17.8%, Male 6.7%, Both 12.0%
- Drugs?: Female 11.7%, Male 10.8%, Both 11.2%
- Any of the above?: Female 38.3%, Male 34.4%, Both 36.3%

Source: Family and Youth Services Bureau's Street Outreach Program, 2016.

The Intersection of Child Welfare and Trafficking

Youth involved in the U.S. child welfare system are especially at risk for being trafficked, specifically those who have experienced abuse or neglect (Child Welfare Information Gateway, 2015). Wilson and Butler (2014) offer a review of existing research that uniformly show involvement with child welfare services to be a precursor to forced prostitution of minors and adults.

Homelessness also poses a huge risk factor for youth. In fact, the NHTRC's (2016) findings indicated that being a runaway or homeless was one of the top five risk factors for human trafficking in the U.S. The Family and Youth Services Bureau's Street Outreach Program (2016) found, in their study of homeless youth, that 36% reported having traded sex for something they needed. This is consistent with the statistics displayed in Figure 4.10, which shows the types of resources that drove homeless youth into the trafficking business.

Weak Child Protection Laws and Policies

While attention needs to be paid to the specific vulnerabilities youth face, especially UCAs and those involved in child welfare, more attention must also be paid to protecting children once they have been victimized. In the U.S., we have laws in place to specifically protect children. For example, the threshold for defining sex trafficking in the U.S. is much lower for children than for adults. Anytime a person under the age of 18 is sold for sex in the U.S., it is considered trafficking (Trafficking Victims Protection Act, 2000). Further, the U.S. has strict labor laws that prevent the exploitation of youth in the U.S. labor market (U.S. Department of Labor, n.d.). That said, these laws don't effectively eliminate the trafficking of minors in the U.S., nor do they extend to the rest of the world. And while most countries have adopted some sort of legislation prohibiting or restricting child labor, these policies have not succeeded in eliminating child labor, even in hazardous conditions (ILO, n.d.c). Thus, more needs to be done not only in prevention of but also in reacting to child trafficking.

The UNODC (2008a) articulates the struggle trafficked children face in identifying and communicating their victimization. Improved protocols designed specifically for children should be developed in order to better identify and serve victimized children (Hartinger-Saunders, Trouteaud, & Matos Johnson, 2016; Wilson & Butler, 2014). To improve protocols, awareness of the issue must be increased. Hartinger-Saunders and colleagues (2016) recently found that mandatory reporters in the U.S. have little training to recognize the signs of domestic minor sex trafficking. Without proper identification and services, the risk of revictimization is high, especially given a youth's vulnerable status.

Poverty

It goes without saying that extreme poverty, both at the country level and at the individual level, creates a vulnerable situation for potential victims. The melodious promises of escape and employment spewing from the trafficker are compelling to those lacking basic needs such as food, clothing, and shelter. **The Borgen Project,** a nonprofit fighting for the world's poorest citizens, plainly states the devastating impact extreme poverty has on communities. Extreme poverty is a predictor of migration patterns—wherever you find extreme poverty, you will find citizens attempting to escape (Wright, 2015). Such individuals are prime candidates for trafficking, desperate to escape but with no means to do so. Traffickers make grand promises to these desperate individuals, all the while knowing they have no intention of keeping said promises.

A trafficker's persuasion can make families do risky things. Parents struggling to meet basic needs for themselves and their children may arrange for children to leave with a trafficker in hopes that employment of and income from the child will provide relief for the family (Dottridge, 2006). Female-headed households may all go with a trafficker simply to survive. Perhaps more disturbing, poverty sometimes forces families to sell their children, knowing what fate awaits them, as described in the Focus on the CNN Freedom Project box highlighting families in Cambodia.

Focus On
The CNN Freedom Project

The CNN Freedom Project profiles a family living in Svay Pak, Cambodia, who were forced to sell their daughter's virginity to pay back a threatening loan shark. The loan, originally $200 borrowed to maintain the nets of the family's fishpond after the patriarch of the family was diagnosed with tuberculosis, swelled into a $9,000 loan with the attached extortion rates. To pay back the burgeoning debt, the family felt their only choice was to sell their 12-year-old daughter's virginity and subsequently sell her into local brothels. This story is not unique, especially in Svay Pak, Cambodia. The CNN profile describes the impoverished town, indicating that half the population lives on less than $2 per day. Many are undocumented migrants from Vietnam. The mothers interviewed for the CNN piece were certainly remorseful and regretful but could offer no alternatives to their decisions. Cambodia has become a hotbed of pedophiles posing as tourists due to the desperation of impoverished families.

Source: Adapted from Hume, Cohen, & Sorvino, 2013.

While poverty alone can provide a constant supply to traffickers, poverty combined with any of the other vulnerabilities introduced in this chapter makes individuals that much more susceptible to the recruitment tactics of a trafficker. An effort by more well-off countries to provide support for those in extreme poverty would greatly reduce the supply of potential trafficking victims.

Statelessness

Imagine you do not have a driver's license or a valid ID. Imagine you don't have a passport, social security card, or birth certificate. You know you exist, but do you have any documentation to prove it? When you die, will anyone know you were alive? And how about your kids? If you don't have citizenship, how will they?

While to you, presumably a college student, these questions may seem hypothetical, to the nearly 10 million individuals who were stateless at the end of 2015, these questions couldn't be more real (United Nations Refugee Agency, 2016a).

To be stateless means to not be a citizen of any country (United Nations Refugee Agency, 2016a). When one is stateless, one is often denied basic needs such as housing, employment, and health care. One cannot legally marry or obtain citizenship for a child (United Nations Refugee Agency, n.d.).

How does this happen? Several factors can explain why **statelessness** continues to persist. Although many states (i.e., countries) are parties to international conventions aimed at reducing statelessness, states still ultimately control whom they deem citizens. Thus, complex laws can be designed to eliminate people from meeting the requirements for citizenship. As states are broken up (e.g., the Soviet Union and the Yugoslav federation in the 1990s) and borders are redefined, as new laws regarding citizenship are created, individuals may not fit into any citizenship category. Tens of thousands are still stateless today in Eastern Europe and Central Asia due to major boundary changes that occurred nearly 30 years ago. Similarly, with frequently changing state boundaries in Africa, statelessness is a regular occurrence. And, even when laws do permit citizenship, obstacles may stand in the way of obtaining that citizenship. For example, when a baby is born, if the parents are unable or choose not to obtain a birth certificate, that child has no documentation proving where he or she was born, who his or her parents are, or the citizenship of his or her parents (United Nations Refugee Agency, n.d.).

Discrimination is perhaps one of the most commonly cited reasons for the continued existence of statelessness. While in many developed countries citizenship is linked to where one is born—the jus soli method of determining citizenship—this is not common globally. The **jus sanguinis method** of determining citizenship dictates that citizenship is based on that of the parents. And in some countries, only the male can pass on citizenship, not the woman. In fact, 27 countries have nationality laws that do not allow women to pass their nationality to their children (United Nations Refugee Agency, 2015a). In these countries, in the event that the father does not obtain proper documentation of a child's citizenship, dies, is stateless, or abandons the family, the child is left stateless, regardless of the mother's citizenship status. Thus, the **jus soli method** of determining citizenship can be an effective way to eliminate gender discrimination in citizenship and the passing of statelessness from generation to generation (Rijken, van Waas, Gramatikov, & Brennan, 2015; United Nations Refugee Agency, 2015a).

Discrimination is also aimed at racial and ethnic minorities. When the state government has the power to dictate citizenship, it can also strip citizenship from minority groups as it sees fit. Saddam Hussein stripped the Faili Kurds of

The hill tribes of Northern Thailand warrant attention due to the size of their population (over half a million); their rural, remote location; and the diversity among the tribes, both in dialect and cultural traits (Rijken et al., 2015). The tribes are indigenous to the land, yet most are not recognized as Thai citizens. This group constitutes one of the largest groups of stateless individuals in the world. Statelessness continues from generation to generation. Interviews with members of the hill tribes indicate their most significant challenges to be travel restrictions, discrimination, and access to employment (Rijken et al., 2015). Discrimination in education is especially apparent, as undocumented youth have limited access to primary school and higher education and see little value in it, as discrimination prevents employment regardless of level of

education (Quinnell & Perri, n.d.; Rijken et al., 2015). Further, stateless girls are very vulnerable to criminal gangs and sex traffickers (C. Becker, 2008). Table 4.2, created by Rijken and colleagues (2015) based on their interviews with members of the Thai

Photo 4.1
A small hill tribe in Northern Thailand, 2016.

Table 4.2 Consequences and Root Causes of Statelessness and Trafficking in Persons

Consequences of Being Stateless	Root Causes of TIP
Fear of being arrested	Lack of awareness
Travel restrictions	Pursuit of adventure
Lack of land rights	Becoming independent / risk tolerance
Drug abuse	To enhance life chances / materialism
Not going to the police	Family responsibility
Being trafficked	Crisis / situation of conflict
Poverty	
Lack of employment opportunities	
Lack of (access to) education	
(Gender) discrimination	
Corruption	
Lack of access to health care / acute need of medical treatment	

Source: Rijken et al., 2015. Reprinted with permission from Wolf Legal Publishers.

hill tribes, highlights the dangers of statelessness. As you can see, several factors including poverty, lack of employment and access to education, discrimination, corruption, and lack of access to health care are both consequences of statelessness and causes of trafficking. It is these characteristics that are especially important in explaining why statelessness is a risk factor for trafficking.

To fully understand how this can happen in Thailand, one can compare citizenship requirements for Thailand and the United States. Though citizenship in the U.S. is based on jus soli, that is not the case in Thailand. Further, Thailand makes getting documentation to prove citizenship difficult. For example, registration of a newborn child must be completed within 15 days of the birth (Becker, 2008). For hill tribe members, this may be nearly impossible, given their remote location and lack of transportation. Further, a birth certificate can be obtained only from a registered hospital, doctor, or midwife and must be delivered to the local registrar's office for validation. Hill tribe babies are born at home. Rarely are doctors or midwives present. These roadblock policies make it nearly impossible to end the cycle of statelessness among the hill tribes of Thailand.

citizenship in 1980 (United Nations Refugee Agency, n.d.). Myanmar, despite giving citizenship to 135 different ethnic groups, took citizenship status from Rohingya, a Muslim ethnic minority group that has since mostly fled the persecution they experienced in Myanmar ("Statelessness," 2014).

Statelessness and Human Trafficking

The relationship between statelessness and human trafficking is clearly articulated in the Focus on Statelessness in Thailand box (see pages 86–87). While Thailand is used as an example given that it has one of the highest populations of stateless individuals in the world, the characteristics that make stateless individuals vulnerable to traffickers apply globally.

Consider what proof of citizenship gets you. Employment? A free public education? Access to higher education? Housing? Without documentation proving citizenship, smugglers and traffickers may provide the only options for housing, employment, and so forth. Of course, the consequences of statelessness go beyond the individual. At a macro level, high levels of statelessness create conflict and forced migration, which consequently impact both the country experiencing high levels of statelessness and the international community.

Now consider another question. Up to this point, human trafficking has been described as the consequence of statelessness, but consider that it could also be a cause. This is especially common if the trafficker takes the citizenship documentation from the victim. Without this documentation, it can be challenging to prove citizenship in the country of origin.

This next section will focus on forced migration and smuggling. Stateless individuals are prime targets for smugglers.

Migrants and Refugees

Measured against the world's population of 7.4 billion people, one in every 113 people [or 65.3 million people] globally is now either an asylum-seeker, internally displaced or a refugee—putting them at a level of risk for which the UNHCR [United Nations Refugee Agency] knows no precedent.

—U.S. Department of State, 2016, p. 20

Picture a young Syrian woman and her child getting on an overcrowded boat—a boat ill qualified to travel across the Mediterranean Sea. Imagine finding the child washed up on the beach of Turkey, the boat having capsized ("Migration to Europe," 2015). This is happening all too regularly due to the surge in illegal migration coming from the Middle East and Africa. The refugee crisis in Europe is a fluid and unsustainable situation. The situation isn't much better on the hot desert southern border of the United States, where one can find passages littered with the lifeless bodies of migrants hoping for successful entry into the U.S. What do these images conjure up to you? A quick Internet search can provide a visual depiction of the refugee crisis, but who are these people? And why are we using precious space in this book on human trafficking to talk about the voluntary, yet illegal, crossing of borders?

What Is Smuggling? Where Is It Happening?

You may have heard the term *smuggling* in the news. We know that many different commodities can be smuggled, including weapons, drugs, wildlife, and, most relevant to this discussion, humans. U.S. Immigration and Customs Enforcement (ICE) is the lead U.S. law enforcement agency responsible for fighting human smuggling and human trafficking. ICE defines smuggling as "the importation of people into a country via the deliberate evasion of immigration laws. This includes

Figure 4.11 Migrant Routes in the Mediterranean

Source: IOM's Missing Migrants Project (2016), licensed under CC BY 4.00, https://creativecommons.org/licenses/by/4.0/.

Figure 4.12   Migrant Routes in the Americas

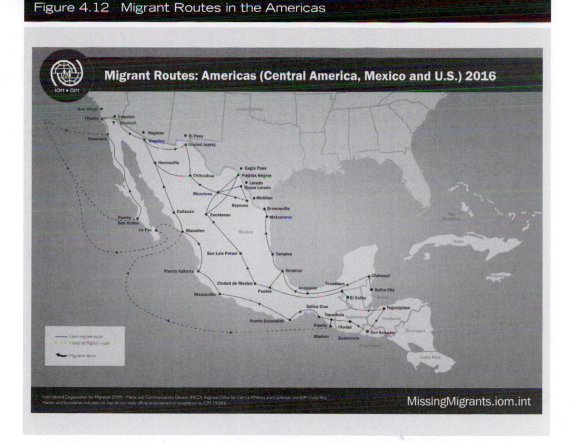

Source: IOM's Missing Migrants Project (2016), licensed under CC BY 4.00, https://creativecommons.org/licenses/by/4.0/.

bringing illegal aliens into a country, as well as the unlawful transportation and harboring of aliens already in a country illegally. Some smuggling situations may involve murder, rape and assault" (ICE, n.d.b, para. 1).

Although the concept of smuggling and illegal movement across borders is nothing new, international instabilities are pushing more and more individuals to consider the option of migration. According to the Migration Policy Institute, prospects of a better life abroad, poverty, economic marginalization, political and social unrest, and conflict are all incentives to move (Bhabha, 2005). Further, in the past, the idea of moving may have seemed unrealistic. However, in an increasingly interconnected world, the prospect of movement comes within reach. Unfortunately, those wishing to migrate more and more frequently are abruptly stopped by inflexible immigration policies that industrialized countries have put in place. Thus, we have the current situation. A lack of legal migration channels, coupled with growing instability in the Middle East, Africa, and parts of South America, drive some of the best-paved international smuggling routes (Fargues, 2016). Figure 4.11 shows the most common pathways between the Middle East, Africa, and Europe as well as between South and North America. The United Nations Refugee Agency (2016a) estimates that approximately 24 persons were displaced from their homes every minute of every day in 2015.

As the maps in Figures 4.11 and 4.12 indicate, a lot of movement is occurring. However, maps don't illustrate the extreme conditions that push people into agreements with smugglers nor the harsh conditions experienced en route to destination countries. Let's consider the current refugee crisis playing out in Europe to clarify what a refugee experiences and how this may relate to human trafficking.

Since the surge in the refugee crisis in 2011, the State Department reports, nearly 11 million refugees have had to leave their homes due to any number of dangerous home country conditions, with an estimated 9 million of them hailing from Syria (as cited in Ross, 2015). The Migration Policy Center in Florence reports even more robust numbers, with 11 million fleeing Syria alone since the start of the war in 2011 (as cited in Achilli, 2016).

Since 2011, Syria has been in the depths of a violent and brutal civil war, resulting in nearly half the population of Syria becoming displaced and desperate to escape the ensuing human rights emergency. The government is fighting against strong insurgents, with international support on both sides. The terrorist group ISIS operates within the country. The complex and layered war includes the claimed purpose of fighting terrorists. However, there is also a splintering of opinions on whether the current political party in power should remain. The consequences of the war could be massive, including the spread of terrorism and major changes to Middle Eastern borders (Gilsinan, 2015).

Perhaps even more consequential than changes in borders is the massive loss of life resulting from the conflict. According to Andrew Tabler (2015), a policy expert from the Washington Institute, "the Syrian Civil War is arguably the worst humanitarian crisis since the Second World War, with over a quarter million killed, roughly the same number wounded or missing, and half of Syria's 22 million population displaced from their homes" (as quoted in Gilsinan, 2015).

Let's move past the basic need for survival that pushes people into the arms of smugglers. What happens to someone once she or he decides to be smuggled across the border? Refugees coming from the Middle East and Africa pay large sums of money to smugglers to transport them across the Mediterranean. An examination of the top three countries producing refugees in 2015—Syria, Afghanistan, and Somalia—found that many traveled to Europe via the Mediterranean Sea (Refugee Project, n.d.). Countless articles chronicle the plights of these migrants, in unfit and overcrowded boats. According to the United Nations Refugee Agency (2015b), 137,000 refugees successfully crossed the Mediterranean (compared to 75,000 in 2014). Many more did not survive the trip. In April 2015, a boat capsized, drowning the 800 on board. During the first four months of 2015, 479 sea passengers were documented as drowned or missing, compared to 15 during the same period the previous year. Over 1,000 refugees drowned or went missing during April 2015, a shockingly high number (United Nations Refugee Agency, 2015b). This unprecedented loss of life garnered national attention and demanded an international reaction.

When the Smuggled Become the Trafficked

For those individuals who survive the trip and arrive in Europe, the challenges continue. The smuggler is both professional and merciless. The goal of the smuggler is to make money, not to help desperate individuals escape horrific situations. The UNODC (2010) provides some insight into smugglers, as highlighted in Figure 4.13. Smugglers have many tactics to stay invisible and retain control over the individuals they are smuggling. Their ability to change routes

Figure 4.13 Smuggling Trends

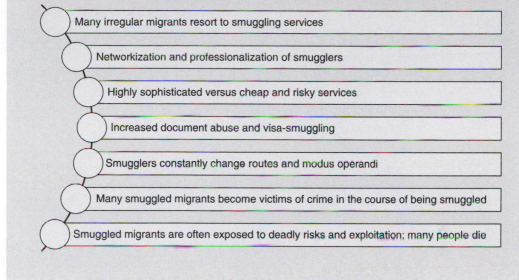

What Do We Know: Smuggling Trends

- Many irregular migrants resort to smuggling services
- Networkization and professionalization of smugglers
- Highly sophisticated versus cheap and risky services
- Increased document abuse and visa-smuggling
- Smugglers constantly change routes and modus operandi
- Many smuggled migrants become victims of crime in the course of being smuggled
- Smuggled migrants are often exposed to deadly risks and exploitation; many people die

Source: United Nations Office on Drugs and Crime, 2010.

and modes of transport, retain control of the smuggled person's documents, and use violence as necessary allow them to be successful. Perhaps smugglers' financial control is their strongest tool—the refugees arrive without money and often in debt due to the large sums they originally paid their smugglers.[3] With nowhere to go and no money, many of those who do reach their destinations find themselves locked in cycles of violence, exploitation, and abuse. The smuggler sells the individual to a trafficker or traffics the individual him or herself. The smuggler instills immense fear into his or her victim, making the victim convinced that he or she will be deported if he or she contacts any authorities. This fear, coupled with not knowing the language of the destination country and certain other threats by the smuggler, result in many human rights violations going unreported. Often the victims fear arrest and deportation on one hand, and retribution by smuggling gangs on the other.

Is This Human Trafficking?

This section has provided a definition for smuggling, the patterns of smuggling, and the justification for smuggling. It is evident that being smuggled is an unpleasant experience and that only the most desperate would take on such a

---

[3] To give some perspective on this, the International Organization on Migration (2016) reported migrants needing to pay $13,000 to a smuggler for travel from Bangladesh to France and between €500 and €2,500 to travel from Turkey to Greece. The costs only increase as migrants leave Greece or Italy to travel north.

dangerous and potentially deadly endeavor. But what does this have to do with human trafficking, you may ask? You may be thinking that while the refugee crisis is terrible, these are individuals who wish to escape their current situations. They do so by choice. Can smuggling be defined as human trafficking, given the requirement of the use of force, fraud, and coercion for such a definition?

The Palermo protocols were instated by the UN Convention Against Transnational Organized Crime at the end of 2003 and beginning of 2004, in part to deal with the blurred lines between smuggling and trafficking (Bhabha, 2005). The protocols provide explanation around the dichotomy of coerced and consensual migrants who illegally cross borders. The protocols define trafficking, providing more explicit definitions for the terms *force*, *fraud*, or *coercion*. It is in these definitions that the vulnerabilities of smuggled persons become more transparent. As Bhabha (2005) writes,

> coercion is not simply brute force, or even mental domination, but it includes the "abuse of a position of vulnerability[,]" . . . [which] can encompass a very broad range of situations, since poverty, hunger, illness, lack of education, and displacement could all constitute a position of vulnerability.

The mere assigning of a smuggling event into either the consensual or the coercive category can be complex. The smugglers' goals, paired with the vulnerabilities of their clientele, make for precarious situations. Smuggling exists in the shadows. Often the circumstances of an arrangement appear **consensual** at the start of the relationship but quickly change as the destination nears (see Case Study box). Many activists and lawmakers struggle to define consent. Should consent occur at the beginning of the relationship and hold regardless of whether circumstances change? This distinction in the definition of consent becomes critical, as different services are available to victims of trafficking versus illegal migrants (Bhabha, 2005).

Case Study

The Life of Migrants Crossing the U.S. Southern Border

© U.S. Customs and Border Protection, CBP

Photo 4.2
U.S. Border Patrol identified undocumented migrants living in a stash house in Laredo, Texas.

In 2011, the Associated Press published a report on the increasing number of stash houses lining the American border cities (Spagat, 2011). The *New York Times* did an exposé in 2012 on what goes on in a stash house. Stash houses are one of the major obstacles faced by smuggled migrants upon arrival in the U.S. but not something commonly reported on (Fernandez, 2012). According to the *New York Times*, once smuggled, migrants were placed in a "drop house" for a few days until arrangements were made for their final destination or final payments were made. The smuggled were packed tightly into these houses, enduring prisonlike conditions, often accompanied by beatings, rape, and starvation. The

New York Times described one of the "drop" or "stash" houses in its story as an 800- to 1,000-square-foot cinder-block house complete with chains on the doors and bars on the windows. Escape was not an option to those inhabiting the house. There were at least 50 people trapped in this house with no electricity or air conditioning. (Recall that South Texas in May averages temperature in the high 80s to low/mid–90s.) When freed by Border Patrol, the migrants reported poor conditions and having not eaten in several days. Caught smugglers admitted to holding migrants under these conditions to extort more money from families or to ensure no one escaped before payment was fulfilled.

In addition to **consent,** Bhabha (2005) considers the importance of **human agency.** Often individuals appear to be consenting when in actuality they are victims of fraud or coercion. After all, coercion is defined as "the abuse of power or a position of vulnerability." Thus, when the conditions people find themselves in are literally unlivable, do they have any choice but to consent to the smuggler's conditions? Further, the smuggler often promises more opportunities for work and income in the destination country. The reality is that many of the "jobs" given to illegal migrants do not meet international labor standards (Bhabha, 2005). When the new employee is given no opportunity to leave a job or advocate for the employer to meet labor standards, the originally consensual relationship quickly transforms into coercion. In other words, even if the relationship started out as consensual, if the smuggled person has no option but to stay with the smuggler or whomever the smuggler passed the individual on to, the relationship has morphed into a coercive one.

To summarize, the distinction between smuggling and trafficking can be blurred at times due to the vulnerability of the migrant population. Although not all migrants become trafficking victims, their situations put them at grave risk of exploitation and victimization. A recent report shows that with the surge of migrants entering Europe, criminal gangs are on the prowl, looking for their next vulnerable victim (Rankin, 2016).

The current situation in Europe demands international attention. International policy makers and activists struggle with how to react to this population. How can destination countries protect refugees and prevent them from becoming victim to traffickers? Is it even the responsibility of destination countries?

Disabilities

While there is little concrete data informing our understanding of the relationship between trafficking and disability, the National Disability Rights Network (2017) recently published a press release bringing awareness to this growing issue. The timing of the press release signals a growing realization that disabled individuals are one of the most at-risk populations for traffickers.

Challenge Yourself 4.2

The Palermo protocols require different provisions for trafficking victims versus migrants who illegally cross borders. Should migrants and trafficking victims be treated the same or differently in regard to the services provided upon rescue or arrival at their destination?

This notion is reinforced by the 2016 TIP Report (U.S. Department of State, 2016), which lists disability as a quality that puts someone at additional risk of becoming trafficked. Any form of disability, including physical, sensory, mental, cognitive, or behavioral, makes an individual more vulnerable to entering a trafficking situation and makes it more challenging to escape from that situation. A disability may limit a person's independence and may also hamper an individual's ability to detect when trafficking and/or exploitation is occurring (Office for Victims of Crime, Training and Technical Assistance Center, n.d.d; U.S. Department of State, 2016). Should the caregiver choose to exploit a disabled individual, there may be little the disabled person can do. Further, disabled individuals are more at risk of experiencing isolation (United Nations Children's Fund, 2007b; Yea, 2009). Promises of relationships may persuade the disabled individual to perform sexual acts, even for payment. Also complicating matters, individuals living with a physical disability may be desensitized to touch, as caregivers frequently physically assist them. This desensitization may make the identification of inappropriate touch more confusing. The person may not know whether inappropriate touch should warrant a complaint.

The Ohio Department of Developmental Disabilities (2014) published a fact sheet listing the specific risk factors individuals with intellectual disabilities face, including social powerlessness, communication skill deficits, diminished ability to protect themselves due to lack of instruction and/or resources, and inability to detect who is safe to be around.

Once involved in a trafficking situation, it may be more difficult for the disabled person to escape that situation. Challenges in communication may make it difficult for the individual to report what is happening to him or her (Office for Victims of Crime, Training and Technical Assistance Center, n.d.d). Further stigmas associated with disability may make it more difficult for the disabled person to be believed in the event that she or he does report the victimization.

Trafficking of the disabled is especially common in countries where social support services are limited for disabled people. The 2016 Trafficking in Persons Report (U.S. Department of State, 2016) indicates that disabled children are especially at risk of being trafficked. It is common for parents to unknowingly, or out of shame, give their disabled child to a trafficker who has promised education and work for the child (Yea, 2009). Traffickers take advantage of the fact that disabled children will pull the heartstrings of most people who see them. Thus, placing a disabled child in the street as a beggar will be more profitable than using a healthy child or adult. The United Nations Children's Fund (UNICEF) reports that internationally organized beggar rings target deaf children and women specifically due to the fact that they are less able to report their victimization (Yea, 2009). The Human Trafficking Pro Bono Legal Center (2016) believes that in many instances, relatives and strangers have trafficked individuals with disabilities in order to take advantage of their disability benefits.

In the U.S. the courts are well aware of the challenges disabled individuals face when protecting themselves from traffickers. In fact, the case that prompted creation of the Trafficking Victims Protection Act of 2000 (TVPA) involved two farmworkers with mental disabilities (*United States v. Kozminski*, 1988). The two farmworkers were being held against their will and were required to work seven days per week for 17 hours a day for no pay. The trafficker threatened physical abuse and return to a mental institution if the workers did not meet the trafficker's demands. The men also reported the use of psychological coercion. Although the defendant was originally found guilty of conspiring to prevent the men from exercising their Thirteenth Amendment right to be free from involuntary servitude and knowingly holding the men in involuntary servitude, the convictions were overturned on appeal based on the conclusion that the definition of involuntary servitude was too broad due to the inclusion of psychological coercion.

Subsequently, prosecutions of traffickers involving disabled victims have been successful, including the 2014 case from Ohio where a man was sentenced to 30 years in prison for holding a cognitively disabled woman and her child against their will and forcing the woman to perform manual labor (U.S. Attorney's Office, 2014).

Religious Vulnerabilities

Religious affiliation is also a risk factor that increases the chances of being trafficked, particularly for women from religious minorities (U.S. Department of State, 2016).

Religious Belief Systems

In Nigeria and other countries in Africa, **voodoo**, a form of witchcraft, induces fear in victims and is used as a coercive tactic to keep victims under the control of their traffickers and ensure obedience, often for the purposes of forced prostitution (Baarda, 2016; Garcia, 2013; Ikeora, 2016). Ninety percent of African women trafficked into Europe participate in an oath ceremony, where victims are sometimes raped and are made to take an oath to be obedient and keep the victimization secret (Garcia, 2013; Ikeora, 2016). Baarda (2016) notes that this use of fear equates to psychological coercion and manipulation by taking advantage of the victims' beliefs in supernatural forces. Traffickers imply to victims that disobedience will result in angering the gods and that very bad things will happen to them, such as illness and death (Garcia, 2013). This manipulation allows the trafficker to maintain control of victims at all times, even when the trafficker is not physically present. Unlike other trafficking victims, African women are often left physically unharmed by their trafficker.

Similar to victims who experience language barriers and unfamiliarity with their surroundings, coercion based on religious affiliation can result in victims' mistrust of authorities or others wishing to assist them in leaving their situations. When voodoo is used as a coercive tactic, investigations are compromised by the victim's refusal to testify in court against the trafficker because he or she legitimately fears what might happen if the oath is broken, even after being told that voodoo is not real (Ikeora, 2016). In other instances, law enforcement who first come in contact with victims are strangers to the victim's belief system and may discount their stories or may be unsure how to handle them (Ikeora, 2016).

Religious Minorities

The TIP Report also states that in some cases, members from religious minorities are forced into marriages that ultimately lead them to trafficking situations of domestic or sexual servitude (U.S. Department of State, 2016). As is the case with minority groups, affiliation with a minority religious group can place an individual in a vulnerable position of powerlessness, marginalization, persecution, inequality under the law, and discrimination (Lederer, 2011). It has been reported that in Burma, for example, the Karen people and other Christian minorities are targeted and sold by traffickers to other nearby countries for the purposes of sex or domestic trafficking as well as forced labor and involuntary servitude (Lederer, 2011).

Further, as mentioned previously, a country's prerogative in declaring citizenship rights may be based on ethnicity and religious beliefs. In the case of the Rohingya, a Muslim sect from Burma, they are excluded from citizenship in Burma and frequently trafficked into the fishing industry in Southern Thailand from the Burmese/Thai border.

Other countries in which religious minorities are impacted include Egypt, Pakistan, and Sudan. Lederer (2011) discusses how Christian and Hindus in these countries have been abducted and subjected to abuse, forced to convert to Islam, and forced into marriages. Finally, in countries in which religious affiliation leaves a particular group marginalized from the rest of society, women's vulnerabilities to trafficking and other physical abuses such as genital mutilation are heightened (Lederer, 2011).

The United States is not exempt from the vulnerabilities caused by religious affiliation. In *Headley v. Scientology International*, a couple in California filed a lawsuit against the Church claiming that the Church had violated the TVPA. They stated that they had joined the Church as teenagers and had been forced to work more than 100 hours per week, received payment of only $50 per week, were prevented from having children, and were subjected to physical and verbal abuse. The Headleys alleged that they were psychologically coerced by the Church to stay. This case is an example of how the doctrine of ministerial exception, which protects religious institutions in their hiring practices, could be harmful to trafficked individuals in forced-labor situations. The court ultimately dismissed the plaintiff's claim without addressing their argument of psychological coercion and "may have established unduly restrictive precedent for future applications of the TVPA" ("First Amendment," 2013, p. 2129).

Sexual Orientation and Gender Identity

While the research is scant on the intersection of sexual orientation, gender identity, and human trafficking, the 2016 TIP Report highlights sexual orientation and gender identity as a concerning vulnerability to human trafficking (U.S. Department of State, 2016). In many parts of the world, including the United States, lesbian, gay, bisexual, transgender, and intersex (LGBTI) individuals are persecuted for their gender identity. These individuals face grave human rights violations that motivate them to flee their homes and home countries. Forced migration among this population puts these individuals at increased risk for human trafficking (United Nations Refugee Agency, 2016b).

The 2016 TIP Report (U.S. Department of State, 2016) specifically mentions the United States in their treatment of LGBTI youth. This population is overrepresented in the number of homeless and runaway youth (more on homeless and runaway youth can be found earlier in this chapter). In fact, while LBGTI youth constitute only 10% of the general youth population, they represent 20% of the youth homeless population. Further, this population has a higher rate of victimization, with 58.7% reporting sexual exploitation while homeless as compared to 33.4% of heterosexual homeless youth (National Coalition for the Homeless, 2009).

Available support services are especially limited for this population (Polaris, 2015a). When these young people have no shelter and no resources for survival, they are pressured into working conditions with a high potential for exploitation. Polaris (2015a) reports that they are also less likely to identify as victims, further limiting their access to appropriate resources. Due to the stigma, and in certain countries, the illegality of same-sex prostitution, this form of trafficking is less likely to be reported than heterosexual forced prostitution (O. Martinez & Kelle, 2013).

Male victims are an especially challenged population, as victimization is often a taboo topic. Shame and embarrassment further limit male victims from reporting their victimization.

Political Instability, War, and Conflict

The International Organization for Migration (2015) conducted field and desk research between November 2014 and June 2015 on Syria, Iraq, the Philippines, Haiti, Eastern Africa, and countries impacted by the 2004 tsunami. The purpose of the research was to assess the unique vulnerabilities that make individuals living in unstable environments (those exposed to highly unstable governments, armed conflict, and natural disasters) more susceptible to traffickers. Their main finding was that in these crisis situations, "the erosion of rule of law, development of criminal activities, corruption, and involvement of official impunity, and the enhanced reliance on negative coping mechanisms and risky survival strategies, are . . . important risk factors for trafficking in persons" (International Organization for Migration [IOM], 2015, p. 7).

Traffickers have the ability to be largely in control in areas of instability. Such areas often lack economic opportunities and are characterized by a weak government incapable of protecting its citizens from the disingenuous promises of traffickers. The IOM's (2015) research found that traffickers would take advantage of the increase in humanitarian efforts in areas in crisis. They would pose as individuals trying to offer employment or other opportunities, when in reality their offers were fraudulent or exploitative in nature.

The IOM's (2015) research indicated that the individuals most vulnerable were unaccompanied minors, women and children, and ethnic, racial, religious, and social minorities as well as other vulnerable populations residing in refugee and displacement camps, transit locations, and informal places of employment.

D'Cunha (2002) describes how women are especially impacted in areas of instability due to their limited ability to migrate. As countries often limit women's abilities to migrate alone (in an effort to protect them from traffickers), desperation to escape a war-torn country may force these women directly into the arms of traffickers. The unique situation caused by war and conflict results not only in a large supply of potential victims but also the emergence of trafficking gangs, looking to prey on this new and limitless supply. Often in these situations, children are picked up by traffickers and used as combatants in the conflict (UNODC, 2018a). Chapter 11 will go into more depth on child soldiers.

Conclusion

This chapter has provided an overview of the general characteristics of trafficking victims. By no means is this a complete picture. As mentioned previously, an entire book could be written explaining some of these complex relationships, such as the interaction between gender and trafficking. Many of these traits will be revisited as you move through the different types of trafficking. For now, continue on to the next chapter to explore the manipulation and deceit of the masterful trafficker.

KEY WORDS

DISCUSSION QUESTIONS

1. What are some factors that may make an individual vulnerable to human trafficking?

2. What populations, if any, do you think may be undercounted in estimates of labor trafficking? Why?

3. Do you think a person of Christian faith in Spain and a person of Christian faith in Egypt have the same or different levels of risk for human trafficking victimization? Why?

RESOURCES

Interesting websites and relevant reports for further investigation:

- The CNN Freedom Project: http://www.cnn.com/specials/world/freedom-project

- Free the Slaves: https://www.freetheslaves.net/

- Global Action Plan to End Statelessness: https://www.unhcr.org/ibelong/global-action-plan-2014–2024/

- International Organization for Migration: http://www.iom.int/

- Missing Migrants Project: https://missingmigrants.iom.int/

- No Ceilings: The Full Participation Project: http://www.noceilings.org/

- Refugee Project: http://www.therefugeeproject.org/

- Syrian Refugees Timeline: http://syrianrefugees.eu/timeline/

- UN Refugee Agency: http://www.unhcr.org/

The Traffickers

I had girls from the whole country. I had a guy in a nearby village, and he was looking for the girls for me. He was asking for 500 euros [about $750 at the time] per girl. . . . In the worst night, a woman would make you 300 euros. There were some nights when a woman made 1,500 to 2,000 euros.

—**Matthew, convicted sex trafficker**
(U.S. Department of State, 2016)

Many anti-trafficking efforts focus on identifying victims and reintegrating them into the community. These efforts are critical to stopping trafficking once it has begun. To prevent trafficking from occurring in the first place, however, we must also focus our efforts on the traffickers themselves.

It is nearly inevitable, when studying human trafficking, to wonder, "What kind of person would exploit another human being?" A natural response is to assume that only a truly evil person could get caught up in the industry of human trafficking. This reaction is reassuring; it distances what we think of as "normal" or typical human behavior from the devastating act of human exploitation.

The reality, however, is that **traffickers** are ordinary people: parents, siblings, teachers, government officials, doctors, teachers, and neighbors. We cannot mentally distance ourselves from traffickers because there is no one-size-fits-all description for human traffickers. Consider institutionalized slavery. When slavery was legal, people in power controlled, often through physical assault, every move another human being made day in and day out. These were the behaviors of everyday people, not some statistical aberration of evildoers.

Another, perhaps unsatisfying, reality is that most human traffickers get involved in trafficking because it is profitable. They are largely driven by a simple desire to earn money. Traffickers are not a mutant strain of human on a warpath to cause misery. They did not die out after slavery was outlawed, and they will not go away as society ages and younger, more progressive generations rise to power. It is important, then, for us to understand the motivations and characteristics of traffickers so that we can better design policies and programs that seek to stop traffickers, or that make trafficking an unviable or undesirable way to earn money.

Challenge Yourself 5.1

Draw or describe in words what you think a trafficker looks like.

In this chapter, we will describe the traffickers: their motivations, their roles or job functions, and what we know about their demographic characteristics, criminal histories, occupations, and educational backgrounds.

Motivation

Traffickers are motivated by two factors: high profits and low risk. Human trafficking is tied with arms trafficking as the second-most profitable criminal industry in the world (behind drug dealing). Human trafficking generates $150 billion dollars annually (International Labour Office, 2014). The global demand for cheap labor and marginalization of individuals or groups of people contribute to the profitability of human trafficking. Factors that contribute to the low risk of trafficking include lack of legal sanctions against traffickers, weak enforcement of trafficking legislation, and inadequate funding allocated toward identifying and prosecuting traffickers.

Offenders' Self-Reported Justifications and Risk Mitigation Strategies

There is extremely limited information on traffickers, in part because many traffickers are never caught. One study of convicted traffickers in the U.S. (primarily sex traffickers) asked traffickers to report their reasons for trafficking. All but two denied engaging in human trafficking but admitted to criminal offenses, such as pimping (Shively, Smith, Jalbert, & Drucker, 2017). Their justifications included:

- It was a means of earning money

- They felt pressure from family or friends

- The victims were voluntarily involved (in the case of sex trafficking with adult victims)

- They did not know the victims were minors (in the case of sex trafficking with child victims)

- It was a means of survival

Among traffickers prosecuted in the U.S. who worked as part of an **organized crime** group, motivations included power, control, and esteem. Many of these traffickers reported childhood abuse or neglect, low levels of education, criminal histories, and substance abuse (Bouché, 2017).

Traffickers also reported that they were afraid of being caught by police (Shively et al., 2017). While about one-third did nothing to prevent being caught by police, others employed a variety of strategies, including:

- Coaching victims to avoid or evade police

- Keeping a minimal number of collaborators, and maintaining direct contact with them

- Avoiding exploitation of minors

- Frequently changing location

- Committing offenses only internationally

Roles

An individual who knowingly participates in trafficking of another person is considered a human trafficker. There are several critical roles in trafficking operations, including recruitment, transportation, exploitation, supervision, and management. In many cases there is also a primary beneficiary who fronts money for the operation and receives most of the profits. The beneficiary may take on any of these roles or be removed entirely from the trafficking operation. Trafficking operations can be part of larger criminal networks where each role is delegated to a different person or group of people or conducted by an individual or small group of individuals who take on multiple roles. A study of traffickers convicted in the U.S. found that more than half operated alone, with no known support; most offenders in this study were convicted for sex trafficking, however, so this may not be as representative of other types of trafficking (Shively et al., 2017; United Nations Office on Drugs and Crime, 2016a).

Recruiters

Recruiters are responsible for identifying victims. Recruiters generally promise a better life, often through employment, education, transit to a new location, or marriage. In some cases, traffickers use forcible recruitment and abduct victims against their will (U.S. Department of State, 2018b). Victims often have a personal relationship with their recruiter. A study of trafficking in the United Kingdom, for example, found that someone known to the victims was the recruiter in about half of cases; in 6% of cases it was a close relative and in 3% a close friend (United Nations Global Initiative to Fight Human Trafficking, 2008). The Counter Trafficking Data Collaborative (2017) has found that roughly 10% of adult victims and 37% of child victims have a relationship with their recruiter.

Abusive Recruitment Practices

Recruitment agencies are critical to ensuring appropriate and adequate staffing across industries. They are particularly important for companies that require staffing in different countries or time zones, that have a seasonal demand for labor, and where employers and staff don't share a common language. In addition to identifying and screening potential candidates, recruiters help employers obtain work visas, housing, transportation, and contract negotiation. Recruiters can be individuals or companies of various sizes. Many countries have a high degree of regulation governing recruitment agencies, including licensing requirements. In some countries, however, there is little to no oversight of recruiters. This lack of oversight makes it easier for recruitment agencies to engage in unethical practices (International Labour Organization, 2016).

Unfortunately, despite widespread regulation of recruitment agencies, it is difficult to distinguish ethical from unethical recruiters. Many recruitment agencies, across sectors, company size, and geographic locations, engage in practices coercive of workers (International Labour Organization, 2016; United Nations Office on Drugs and Crime [UNODC], 2015b; U.S. Department of State, 2017b). **Unfair recruitment practices** include:

- Debt bondage

- Isolation

- Surveillance

- Withholding wages

- Threats of violence and/or violence

- Contract substitution

- Exploitation of workers' visa status

- Withholding travel documents

- Recruitment fees

Migrant workers are typically more reliant on recruitment agencies because of a lack of connection to the destination country or limited familiarity with the process of obtaining a visa and work permit. Unethical recruiters exploit these vulnerabilities through coercive practices, such as exploitation of visa status or withholding travel documents. If migrant workers attempt to leave an exploitive work environment without their documents, they become undocumented and have no access to legal protections, which may increase their risk for subsequent abuses. Further, once migrant workers are in the destination country, they have limited social support and may be unfamiliar with the culture and language. The trafficker, or "employer," can then exploit migrant workers' legal status to keep them from leaving the workplace (UNODC, 2015b; U.S. Department of State, 2017b).

Recruitment agencies or recruiters involved in human trafficking commonly charge workers **recruitment fees**. Recruiters may tell workers that fees are for costs associated with travel, passport and visa processing, or unspecified services. Workers agree to these fees because recruiters promise the opportunity to more than recover the fee once they begin work. Recruiters typically charge above and beyond the actual costs of providing these services, which lends substantial profits to the recruitment agencies. Many times, workers cannot afford to pay recruitment fees, so recruiters offer loans with exorbitant interest rates— as high as 80% per year (UNODC, 2015b). Workers may also leverage their families' assets, such as a home, to pay recruitment fees. Coercing workers to take on huge debts makes it easier for traffickers to exploit them. Once workers establish this debt, other actors in the trafficking chain convince them to take on additional work, lower pay, unsafe living conditions, excessive working hours, or other abuses to pay down their debts (UNODC, 2015b; U.S. Department of State, 2017b).

In May 2009, "Allain," a 31-year-old from Central Asia, and 11 codefendants were indicted by a federal grand jury in the U.S. for their participation in a racketeering conspiracy spanning almost a decade and involving numerous crimes, including, most notably, trafficking for forced labor exploitation.

Allain was the leader of a criminal enterprise that recruited hundreds of foreign workers from Latin America, Southeast Asia, Eastern Europe, Central Asia, and elsewhere, through false promises of good employment, free housing, transportation, food, and so forth.

When the workers arrived, Allain and his codefendants compelled them into service in various jobs in the United States. The defendants forced the workers to live in greatly overcrowded apartments with exorbitant rents and coerced their labor through threats of deportation and by withholding their wages. Recruitment fees of up to $5,000 were charged, as well as visa renewal fees of $3,000, and families were threatened with additional fees. This case was the first instance of trafficking in persons for forced-labor exploitation charged as part of a Racketeer Influenced and Corrupt Organizations Act, or RICO, conspiracy.

On October 20, 2010, Allain pleaded guilty to racketeering conspiracy, fraud in foreign labor contracting, evasion of corporate employment tax, and identity theft, and on May 9, 2011, he was sentenced to 12 years in prison and 3 years of supervised release. He and the codefendants were also sentenced for their respective roles in this criminal enterprise.

Source: Adapted from United Nations Office on Drugs and Crime, 2015b.

Policies and Legislation Against Unfair Recruitment Practices

Because of the dangers associated with charging workers recruitment fees, this practice is banned by international and country-specific regulations. Such measures are supported by various advocacy organizations (International Labour Organization, 2016). Some of these policies are outline in Table 5.1.

The International Organization for Migration developed the International Recruitment Integrity System (IRIS) to help job seekers and employers identify recruiters who are committed to the ethical recruitment practices laid out in the policies in Table 5.1. For recruiters to be accredited in this system, they must agree not to charge fees to job seekers, misrepresent job descriptions or wages, confiscate passports or other documents, or engage in other unethical practices (International Organization for Migration, n.d.).

Table 5.1 Policies Regulating Recruitment Fees	
Private Employment Agencies Convention, Article 181 (International Labour Organization, 1997)	*Private employment agencies shall not charge directly or indirectly, in whole or in part, any fees or costs to workers.*
General Principles & Operational Guidelines for Fair Recruitment (International Labour Organization, 2016)	*No recruitment fees or related costs should be charged to, or otherwise borne by, workers or jobseekers.*

(Continued)

Table 5.1 (Continued)

Dhaka Principles (Institute for Human Rights and Business, 2011)	*No fees are charged to migrant workers.*
U.S. Federal Acquisition Regulation; Ending Trafficking in Persons (2015)	*E.O. 13627 [prohibits] contractors and subcontractors from engaging in prohibited practices such as destroying, concealing, confiscating, or otherwise denying access by an employee to his or her identity or immigration documents; using misleading or fraudulent recruitment practices; charging employees recruitment fees; and providing or arranging housing that fails to meet the host country housing and safety standards.*
Leadership Group for Responsible Recruitment, Employer Pays Principle (Institute for Human Rights and Business, 2016)	*No worker should pay for a job—the costs of recruitment should be borne not by the worker but by the employer.*
Business Actions Against Forced Labour (Consumer Goods Forum, 2017)	*No worker should pay for a job.*

Source: International Labour Organization. (2016).

Transporters

Transporters are responsible for moving victims to their destination, whether within or across country lines. Transporters may stay with the victims, physically bringing them to the new location, or provide tickets or documentation for transit. Oftentimes, however, traffickers continue to need to transport victims from where they are lodged to the work site. In these cases, transporters may be part of the trafficking operation or unknowing participants. Some traffickers also employ drivers, typically someone known to the trafficker through a friend or family network. In some cases drivers go on to start their own operation (Bouché, 2017).

> *I had a cab driver that was on payroll. He came and got me and the other girls . . . around 9:30 [pm] so that I got to the track by 10 every night and coming back he would meet me at the store around 2 am. Every night.*
>
> **—Polaris (2018)**

It is also common for the transporter to be unaware of their involvement in a trafficking operation. A survey of survivors of human trafficking in the U.S. found that traffickers used a variety of transportation methods, including private or rental vehicles, mass transit, ride sharing, and even cruise ships (Polaris, 2018).

Recruiters also take advantage of transportation stations (such as bus or train stations) because of the high proportion of vulnerable youth and adults that congregate there (U.S. Department of State, 2018). A survey of trafficking victims in the U.S. found that 63% of victims used mass transit, and 16% of these victims said they used mass transit very frequently. There is also some evidence that sexual exploitation takes place at truck stops (Polaris, 2018).

Case Study

Recruiter Working in a Transit Station

As part of the United Nations Office on Drugs and Crime project "Criminal Justice Responses to Trafficking in Human Beings in Poland," United Nations Interregional Crime and Justice Research Institute–coordinated researchers completed detailed interviews with 15 female Polish trafficking victims. In most cases, the means of transport to the destination was by private car; otherwise it was by bus. The shortest journey took four hours, whereas the longest journey to the destination country lasted four months (with a few weeks' break during the transportation). Some women traveled with a person who helped to organize the journey and were also accompanied by other possible victims. Most of the victims had either tourist visas or their own passports. Only one person crossed the border illegally using a fake passport. In the majority of cases, the traffickers immediately seized the victim's documents once the border had been crossed. Some women acknowledged the use of starvation, violence, and forced administration of psychotropic drugs as means to intimidate them. Several respondents were confined by force during the journey, while only 3 out of the 15 women had permission to leave their escorts or the places they were kept en route. The others could not move about alone. None of the trafficked victims had been aware of the dangers they would experience during transportation.

Source: Adapted from United Nations Office on Drugs and Crime, 2006.

Buses and Trains

Long-distance buses and trains provide more discretion in the ticket-buying process and have substantially less security and law enforcement presence than do airports. Buses and trains are also commonly used by victims attempting to escape from their trafficker. These transit options are low-cost, accept cash as payment, commonly do not require proof of identification, and depart at regular intervals.

Airplanes

Airlines are a necessary means of travel for many traffickers transporting victims into a new country. Traffickers may travel with victims by airplane. According to the U.S. Department of Transportation (n.d.), some of the warning signs that someone is a trafficker include:

- Holding victims' travel and identification documents

- Paying for tickets in cash

- Answering questions for the victim

- Providing evasive answers to questions

- Constantly monitoring the victim

Traffickers may also arrange travel for individuals to the destination country, promising a job opportunity. In this scenario, these individuals have not yet been trafficked. One study found that 71% of labor trafficking victims arrived in the U.S. by airplane. Trainings targeting airline personnel may not capture these victims, who are not exploited until they arrive (Polaris, 2018).

Case Study

Transportation Used by Trafficker to Exploit Victim, and Used by Victim for Escape

When Pamela accepted an offer from a neighbor's friend to help her go to Italy, she thought she was accepting a chance for a brighter future. She was 21, and the promise of a job in Europe was an attractive option compared to the limited prospects in her native Nigeria. She was introduced to a man who told her she must take part in a traditional Nigerian juju ritual that would ensure her protection—as long she did everything he said. The man then handed Pamela over to a Nigerian bus driver and gave her a bus ticket and a telephone number for his contact in Italy.

Pamela traveled across Nigeria and Niger in a bus packed with other women and men, arriving one month later in Libya. There they were brought to a house run by a group of Nigerian and Middle Eastern men, who told the group they were forbidden to leave while awaiting the boat journey to Italy. After one month of confinement in the house, where she witnessed beatings, rape, and other abuses, Pamela and the other migrants were taken to the shore, where they boarded a boat for Italy

Upon arriving in Sicily, she and the other women on the boat were met by a man who brought them to Naples and to the apartment of a Nigerian woman. She gave the women some clothes and condoms and explained they would have to work as prostitutes on the street and earn on average €100 per day in order to repay their debt of €35,000 for their journey to Europe. They were to bring their clients to a nearby "connection house" and give their earnings to the woman supervising the house.

Within days of her arrival in Italy, Pamela was forced to work day and night selling sex on the streets, and between work shifts was kept locked in the apartment. A typical workday began at 10 in the morning and lasted until 9 at night, and after a few hours of rest, they were back on the street for the late-night shift, from after midnight until 6 in the morning.

One week later, after hiding away some money for herself, Pamela left for work one morning and headed instead to the train station and boarded a train to Rome. She asked for assistance from an Italian woman, who contacted the police, who then referred Pamela to a local nongovernmental organization called BeFree Social Cooperative, which runs a number of shelters for trafficked women.

"Pamela was extremely traumatized. Like most victims of trafficking, she was in terrible shape. They have seen hell, and they have survived," said Loretta Bondi, director of International Projects at BeFree, an organization supported by the UN Voluntary Fund on Contemporary Forms of Slavery.

According to the organization, about 75% of trafficking victims in Europe are women, mostly from Nigeria and other parts of western Africa; many are subjected to sexual violence and other human rights abuses throughout their travels; and as many as two-thirds of them are forced into prostitution and are enslaved by their traffickers upon arrival.

Source: United Nations Office of the High Commissioner, n.d.

Response

Importantly, the transporter is often not complicit with the trafficking operation. In fact, various actors in the transportation and travel industries have taken proactive steps to identify trafficking when it occurs.

In 2018, for example, the International Civil Aviation Organization partnered with the UN's Office of the High Commissioner for Human Rights to release "Guidelines for Training Cabin Crew on Identifying and Responding to Trafficking in Persons." This document provides indicators for airline crews to help them identify traffickers and victims and information on how to respond if they suspect trafficking (International Civil Aviation Organization, 2018).

Case Study

Flight Attendant Identifies Trafficker and Trafficking Victim

"Something in the back of my mind told me that something was not right," Shelia Fedrick, a flight attendant working for Alaska Airlines, told reporters. "The girl looked like she had been through hell." Fedrick was working on a flight from Seattle to San Francisco, United States, when she noticed on board a well-dressed older man travelling with a teenage girl that she said looked "dishevelled and out of sorts."

Fedrick tried to speak to the pair but the girl remained silent and the man became defensive.

It was at that moment that the flight attendant decided to leave a note for the girl in the restroom and instructed her discreetly to go to the restroom.

"She wrote on the note that she needed help," said Fedrick who immediately informed the pilot. Police officers were waiting at the plane's terminal in San Francisco on arrival and were able to confirm that the young girl was a victim of human trafficking.

Source: Office of the High Commissioner for Human Rights, 2018.

The U.S. Department of Transportation's (DOT's; 2016) Transportation Leaders Against Human Trafficking Initiative provides training and education for stakeholders in the transportation industry on identifying and preventing trafficking. In 2012, the DOT implemented mandatory training for all 55,000 of its employees every three years. This initiative includes raising public awareness through media campaigns. It also launched the Blue Lightning Initiative, which requires airlines to provide annual trainings for flight attendants on recognizing and responding to human trafficking. Over 100,000 airline personnel have been trained since its inception (U.S. Department of Transportation, n.d.). Similar trainings are available for large bus companies.

The International Air Transport Association's #Eyesopen media campaign targets the public and airline staff. This campaign includes videos, infographics, and free online trainings (International Air Transport Association, n.d., 2018).

Other Roles in Trafficking Operations

Traffickers may also take on other roles that are less compartmentalized, such as exploitation, supervision, and management. The lines are less clear in the distinction of these various roles. In many cases, supervisors and managers are simply considered exploiters. It is less important to be able to classify specific behaviors and more important to understand the different actions traffickers use to control and exploit victims.

Exploiter: Exploiters include a range of actors, including those who, through force, fraud, or coercion, make the victim engage in sexual exploitation, forced labor, removal of organs or parts of the body, forced marriage, illegal adoption, or any other act or service. An exploiter can also be the "end user"—the person benefiting from the service the trafficked person provided.

Supervisor: The supervisor is the person who maintains control of the victim in some form of living accommodations. This person is responsible for keeping the victim from escaping.

Manager: The manager oversees business aspects of the trafficking operation, such as collecting money, allocating funding for transportation, paying other members of the operation, and laundering money.

Case Study

Manager in a Trafficking Operation

The following information, concerning the most common patterns of exploitation among women being trafficked from Romania into Germany, was compiled by an interdisciplinary research team in Germany:

- Appointments were arranged by pimps. For example, in certain cases, the women victims concerned were regularly brought to a nearby petrol station, and then they would either walk alone to the apartment they were kept in after an agreed-on time or would be picked up by the pimp.

- Romanian women lived and engaged in prostitution in the traffickers' flats, and clients were found through the Internet.

- Upon arrival in Germany, the victim would be taken to a bar or club and forced into prostitution using psychological or physical violence. She would be subjected to verbal assault and forced to pay off a debt.

- In most cases, the money earned would be taken by the trafficker. In a few cases, the victims were allowed to keep half the amount.

- The rotation of victims between cities, such as between Cologne and Dortmund, was quite common. The transfer of women between countries also occurred in order to avoid the risk of deportation if the victim was identified in a police raid.

- In brothels, women underwent constant surveillance through video cameras.

- In some cases, women tried to escape. They were then physically assaulted and threatened by traffickers with harm to their families so as to deter the other women.

- Women were forced to prostitute themselves with numerous clients a day, in some cases the whole week long.

- Seizure of documents, threats, and psychological and physical violence were used to control the victims. The level of psychological control held by the traffickers over the victims was generally so high that the victims were often not able to act on any opportunity to escape.

Source: Adapted from United Nations Office on Drugs and Crime, 2006.

Primary beneficiary/funder: The beneficiary fronts the money for transportation, purchasing victims, and other pieces of the operation. This person receives most of the profits from the trafficking operation.

There is some debate about who should be considered an exploiter. As mentioned above, traffickers are individuals who knowingly engage in the exploitation of human beings. Thus, consumers who purchase goods made with forced labor are not considered traffickers. What about "johns," or individuals who purchase sex from trafficking victims in a country where prostitution is illegal? International legislation provides some clarity. Article 19 of the European Convention on Action Against Trafficking in Human Beings on "criminalization of the use of services of a victim" specifically criminalizes "the use of services which are the object of exploitation, where the user has knowledge that the person is a victim of trafficking" (quoted in Sembacher, 2005). This makes it hard to prosecute exploiters who may falsely claim that they thought the victim was voluntarily involved in the trafficking operation.

Organizational Structure of Trafficking Operations

As previously mentioned, many traffickers operate individually or in small collaborations of a few people. Sometimes trafficking is spontaneous, with no preplanning at all. There is not enough information about traffickers to determine what proportion of trafficking operations are part of an organized criminal network and what proportion are individuals operating alone. A report of traffickers prosecuted in the United States found that just over half (58%) of defendants were part of an organized crime group (Bouché, 2017). In cases where trafficking is part of an organized criminal network, there are several organizational structures that can be used. Research finds that different hierarchical structures lend themselves better to certain types of crimes and methods of exploitation (United Nations Global Initiative to Fight Human Trafficking, 2008).

A UN study of organized crime groups in 16 countries classified five structural models, which are summarized in Table 5.2. This report identified six criminal groups engaged in human trafficking as well as other crimes; five were classified as rigid hierarchies. The two groups for which human trafficking was the primary activity were both classified as core criminal groups. Core criminal groups decide which activities they will pursue based on opportunities for profit. In both of the core criminal groups, a separate gang member was assigned to each specific role in human trafficking (recruitment, transport, supervision, exploitation). Members of both of these groups did not share a social or ethnic identity, and members had nationalities that matched the countries where they worked (United Nations Office on Drugs and Crime, 2002).

Focus On
Human Trafficking by MS-13

The Mara Salvatrucha, or MS-13, is perhaps the most notorious street gang in the Western Hemisphere. While it has its origins in the poor, refugee-laden neighborhoods of 1980s Los Angeles, the gang's reach now extends from Central American nations like El Salvador through Mexico, the United States, and Canada.

The MS-13 groom the girls with two different tactics. The first is the boyfriend technique, where the trafficker will pretend to be in a relationship with the victim and shower her with gifts and attention. Lonely, homesick, and far from home, the young girls from Central America feel comfortable around the MS-13 because they speak Spanish and oftentimes even know their family members back home. Gang members approach the girls in a variety of strategic places, such as malls, schools, subway stations, and house parties.

They analyze a girl's insecurities, look for vulnerabilities to exploit, and overwhelm the girl with attention, affection, and gifts. Soon the girl believes she is in a loving relationship, and that's when the gang member asks her to have sex with another gang member to make money. The girls often live at home and attend school, engaging in prostitution only part-time as a way to prove their love for their gang-member boyfriend. Eventually the gang member uses "violence and other coercive tactics to intimidate the girl into continuing her sexual activity for the gang and public." Oftentimes girls trapped in this type of human trafficking do not see themselves as victims and instead insist their participation is a voluntary choice. The MS-13 typically traffic Latino and Spanish-speaking girls, specifically targeting newly arrived unaccompanied minors from the Northern Triangle.

Source: Adapted from Lillie, 2017.

Table 5.2 Types of Structural Models in Criminal Organizations

Structure Type	Key Characteristics
Rigid Hierarchies	✓ Single leader ✓ Clear hierarchy ✓ Strong internal discipline systems ✓ Known by a specific name ✓ Strong social or ethnic identity (usually) ✓ Violence essential to activities ✓ Clear control over a specific area
Regional Hierarchy	✓ Single leadership structure ✓ Line of command from center ✓ Regions have independence ✓ Geographic distribution ✓ Strong social or ethnic identity (usually) ✓ Violence essential to activities
Clustered Hierarchy	✓ Consists of multiple criminal groups ✓ There is a governing body for the groups ✓ Cluster has a stronger identity than member groups ✓ Member groups have independence ✓ Formation linked to social/historical context ✓ Relatively rare
Core Criminal Group	✓ Core group surrounded by loose network ✓ Limited number of individuals ✓ Organized flat structure ✓ Small size lends itself to internal discipline ✓ Rarely has a social or ethnic identity ✓ Not typically known by a specific name
Organized Network	✓ Defined by activities of key individuals ✓ Personal loyalties more important than social or ethnic identities ✓ Rarely known by any name ✓ Network will re-form if a key individual leaves

Source: Adapted from United Nations Office on Drugs and Crime, 2002.

Case Study

Human Trafficking in a Regional Hierarchy—the Fuk Ching

The Fuk Ching has a sophisticated hierarchical structure and is primarily involved in smuggling illegal migrants, human trafficking, and kidnapping. The group is based on strong ethnic ties and, apart from the core areas mentioned above, engages in a wide range of activities. Violence (or the threat thereof) is an essential component of the group's operations, both to ensure internal discipline and in relation to activities such as extortion. The group is reputed to have some political influence in China, has made relatively significant investments in the economy of the United States, and cooperates with a number of other criminal groups. In the United States the group is predominantly involved in extortion. Victims are largely business owners in New York's Chinatown.

The group also smuggles Chinese migrants from Fujian Province to the United States and engages in drug trafficking and kidnapping for ransom. In addition, the Fuk Ching is involved in armed robberies, money laundering, organized prostitution, and environmental crimes. The Fuk Ching in New York comprises 35 members, all of whom are male. Another 20 members are currently in prison. Most of the members are of Chinese origin. In the mid-1980s, young men from Fujian province in China, many of whom had criminal records, founded Fuk Ching in New York. New members are still recruited among Fujianese teenagers. Similar to other Chinese criminal groups, street **gangs** such as the Fuk Ching are affiliated with an organization or tong (in this case the Fukien American Association), which provides a venue to operate from, criminal opportunities (for example, by protecting gambling operations) and, where necessary, money and guns. Behavior within the group is governed by strict rules, such as respect for seniors, not using drugs, following orders without question, and not betraying the gang.

Violators of these rules are punished, sometimes severely, by physical assault or even death. Violence within the group and against other criminal groups is common, although the available evidence suggests that such incidents are more likely to be random street-level violence than targeted attacks. Disputes over territory and market access with other criminal groups are typically resolved using *kong so*, a process of peaceful negotiation. If this fails, resolution is sought through violence.

Although gang members are involved in legitimate business activities in New York's Chinatown, they have no significant role in the broader economy. At a local level, some gang members own or operate restaurants, retail stores, or car services, while more senior-level members own wholesale supply firms, factories, and banks. The gang is closely connected to criminal groups in China and Hong Kong. Although the Fuk Ching is regarded as having political connections in China's Fujian Province, there is little evidence that such activities are a significant feature of the gang's activities in the United States.

Source: Adapted from United Nations Office on Drugs and Crime, 2002.

Characteristics of Traffickers

Traffickers typically have characteristics similar to those of their victims, whether in terms of gender, citizenship, country of origin, religious affiliation, hometown, or other cultural identifier. These shared characteristics sometimes serve practical purposes. For example, shared languages facilitate exploitation in a practical way. Shared backgrounds and experiences can also facilitate exploitation by increasing trust or rapport between victims and traffickers.

Racial, Ethnic, and Cultural Background

Most traffickers operate in their home countries. As shown in Figure 5.1, 70% of traffickers are citizens of the country where they are convicted, and an additional 21% are from countries in the same region where they are convicted. This pattern holds in nearly every region of the world, with a few exceptions. Foreigners account for the majority of traffickers in Western and Southern Europe and nearly all traffickers in the Middle East. In nearly all (known) cases, traffickers share a common language with their victims.

Even when traffickers do not share a common citizenship, they often share a nationality. For example, traffickers may be second- or third-generation immigrants to a country but share a common heritage. In some cases, these individuals may be assisted by family members who still live in their country of origin.

Figure 5.1 Proportion of National and Foreign Citizens Convicted of Trafficking Relative to the Country of Conviction, 2016

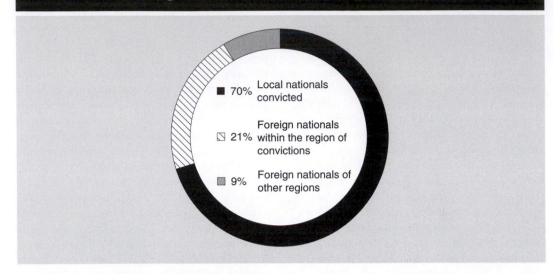

Figure 5.1 Proportion of National and Foreign Citizens Convicted of Trafficking Relative to the Country of Conviction, 2016

- 70% Local nationals convicted
- 21% Foreign nationals within the region of convictions
- 9% Foreign nationals of other regions

Source: United Nations Office on Drugs and Crime, 2018a.

Figure 5.2 Proportion of Prosecuted Traffickers by Sex (Data From 70 Countries)

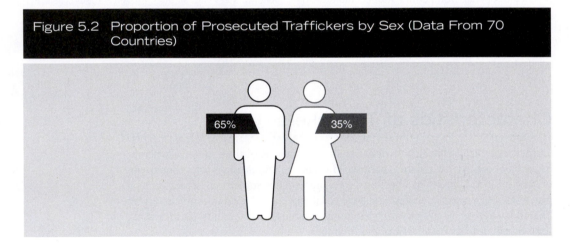

65%   35%

Source: United Nations Office on Drugs and Crime, 2018a.

Gender

In line with trends for nearly all crime types, most traffickers are male (see Figure 5.2). In contrast with other crime types, however, women account for a notable portion of traffickers.

Women make up the largest proportion of traffickers in 30% of countries for which data are available (United Nations Office on Drugs and Crime, 2016a). Women account for the majority of individuals investigated for human trafficking in Eastern Europe and Central Asia as well as about half of those investigated in Sub-Saharan Africa. As depicted in Figure 5.3, women account for the

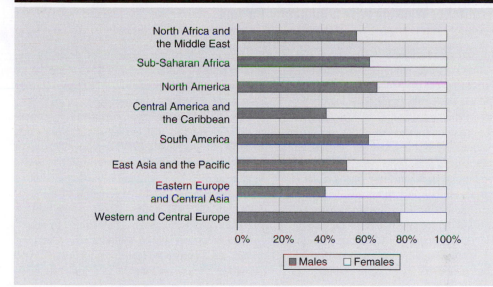

Figure 5.3 Individuals Prosecuted for Human Trafficking by Region and Sex

Source: United Nations Office on Drugs and Crime, 2018a.

majority of prosecuted traffickers in Eastern Europe and Central Asia as well as Central America and the Caribbean (United Nations Office on Drugs and Crime, 2018a). They account for nearly half of prosecuted traffickers in East Asia and the Pacific. Country-specific investigations find that women may be less likely to be prosecuted because of paternalism in the criminal justice system, where judges have more sympathy for female perpetrators. In Israel, for example, research finds that women are especially likely to be treated with leniency if they are mothers, are arrested in conjunction with a male partner who is abusive or coercive, or were victims of trafficking themselves (Levenkron, 2007; United Nations Global Initiative to Fight Human Trafficking, 2008). A report on sex traffickers of minors in the United States found that 24% of traffickers were women, over half of whom had been victims of sex trafficking themselves (Roe-Sepowitz, Gallagher, Hogan, Ward, & Denecour, 2017). Among traffickers convicted in the U.S. who worked as part of an organized crime group, over two-thirds were male, and women were more likely to be involved in labor trafficking than sex trafficking (Bouché, 2017).

Women can play various roles in trafficking operations. When traffickers are the same gender as their victims, it can enhance trust. Traffickers take advantage of this and often use women to recruit other women and girls. When women and men are involved in trafficking operations, their victims include men, women, and children. In male-led criminal organizations, women are often delegated lower-level tasks, such as recruitment, transportation, or supervision. Women, then, are more likely to be identified and convicted because victims are able to identify them, while men remain unseen (United Nations Office on Drugs and Crime, 2016a).

When men and women work together in trafficking operations that are not part of a larger criminal organization, they are often domestic partners or family members. In a study of 155 cases of human trafficking, women were involved in traffickers in 54% of cases. In 33% of the cases in which women were involved, they worked together with male traffickers and in the remaining 21% they worked alone or with other women.

Case Study

Female Trafficker Working With a Romantic Partner

Yulia Shomrenko Weicherman arrived in Israel illegally, and, after [arriving], entered into a fictitious marriage with [a Jewish person] and [acquired citizenship]. Shortly thereafter, she became the domestic partner of another individual, Genady Bosolowitz, the head of a crime syndicate who, among his other criminal pursuits, also trafficked in women. In August 2004, when Bosolowitz was abroad, she stood in for him at work, and transferred sums of money to his associates based on his instructions.

The court notes that Yulia "had been exposed" to Bosolowitz's activities and was intimately familiar with the details of the business, and, among other things, would explain to the women the conditions under which they would be employed in prostitution, and accompany them to various government offices.

She expressed her opinion of some of the women held by Bosolowitz as follows: "They're all like that. You take them out of the garbage, and they forget that they only got hit here."

Despite her active involvement in sex trafficking, the court ruled that her activity did not reach the level of trafficking in persons or membership in a criminal organization. In the end, of all the counts pending against her, including managing a criminal organization, only the charges relating to her fictitious marriage held weight—those being using a forged document and obtaining something by deceit.

The court was satisfied with time served, and further imposed a suspended sentence and a fine of 20,000 NIS (about $5,400), despite the fact that in astoundingly similar and less serious cases, the court had convicted defendants of trafficking, or at least of abetting.

Source: Levenkron, 2007.

When trafficking operations are run exclusively by women, the victims are typically also exclusively women and girls, and they are typically trafficked for sexual exploitation (United Nations Office on Drugs and Crime, 2016a).

Victims Who Become Traffickers

It is common for trafficking victims, particularly female victims, to be used to recruit and traffic new victims. A report on sex traffickers of minors in the U.S. found that of the women traffickers, over half were identified as the most trusted victim of the sex trafficker who was given the role of recruiting new victims and establishing and enforcing rules (Roe-Sepowitz et al., 2017).

Victims are often used to recruit new victims. Victims-turned-traffickers are motivated by their desire to transfer their debts to traffickers to new victims, fear or intimidation from their trafficker, or the chance to free themselves from exploitation. In some cases victims develop a dependent or sympathetic relationship with their trafficker, commonly known as Stockholm syndrome, in which case becoming a trafficker can be viewed by the victim as a promotion.

Traffickers benefit substantially from using victims in their operations. For example, victims involved in trafficking are less likely to seek assistance for themselves or assist law enforcement.

When traffickers are recognized as victims, they should not be prosecuted. This policy comes from Article 26 of the Council of Europe's Convention on Action Against Trafficking, which states, "Each Party, shall, in accordance with the basic principles of its legal system, provide for the possibility of not imposing penalties on victims for their involvement in unlawful activities, to the extent that they have been compelled to do so."

Age

Traffickers can be any age, including children and older adults. Traffickers tend to be older than their victims, except in the case of children. Trafficking operations typically use children to recruit other children. This is often the case in child soldiering, for example, which is covered in more detail in Chapter 11. In a case study of sex trafficking in Las Vegas, Nevada, the average age of traffickers was 29 years, and sex traffickers of minors were younger and closer to the age of the victims than traffickers of adults (Spencer, Peck, & Dirks, 2014). A study of traffickers prosecuted in the U.S. who were working as part of an organized crime group found that the average age of traffickers was 33 years, though defendants engaged in minor sex trafficking and defendants who were members of a gang were significantly younger (Bouché, 2017).

Family/Marital Status

Traffickers can be married, in relationships, or single. Traffickers can have children. In some cases, a trafficker's family is unaware that their relative is involved in trafficking; in other cases, family members are complicit or do nothing to stop their relative's involvement in trafficking; and in other cases family members engage in trafficking activities together.

Traffickers may exploit their own family members; this is more common with child trafficking. Global estimates suggest that 40% of child trafficking cases begin with family members, compared to just 9% of adult trafficking cases; an additional 14% begin with an intimate partner, and 11% begin with friends (Counter-Trafficking Data Collaborative, 2017). Family members are slightly more likely to be involved in the trafficking of boys than girls. Child trafficking cases that begin with a family member are less likely to include sexual exploitation than those that do not begin with a family member.

Case Study

Family Involvement in Trafficking

Carlos was 16 when some members of his family invited him to move to the U.S. from Guatemala under the pretense of getting a better education.

When he made the journey, he soon discovered that instead of going to school, he was going to be forced to work. Carlos's mother told him she had spent $10,000 to get him into the U.S. and that he would need to repay this debt.

Carlos worked in construction 12 hours a day, 6 days a week. He never knew the name of the company he worked for because his employment was arranged entirely by his stepfather, who took Carlos's money and told him this was in return for rent, food, and the debt associated with Carlos's journey to the U.S.

One day, after several months, Carlos confronted his mother and stepfather and refused to return to work. At this point, they left him behind, and Carlos began working odd jobs but could not pay the rent. Soon he had nowhere to live.

Carlos found a phone number for a government agency that helps undocumented minors in the U.S. He reached out and received a caseworker. Thanks to the U.S. National Human Trafficking Hotline, operated by Polaris, Carlos is now receiving government services, and his case has been referred to law enforcement for investigation.

Source: International Organization for Migration, 2017.

Occupation

We do not know a lot about traffickers' legitimate work activities. In some cases, traffickers are unemployed and facing extreme financial hardship. Traffickers are also known to have regular professions, including work as lawyers, medical professionals, law enforcement, government officials, mechanics, chefs, or drivers. Some types of trafficking may necessitate specific occupations more than others. For example, organ trafficking requires the expertise of medical personnel, child soldiering often involves corrupt government officials, and as noted above, sex trafficking often requires a driver to move victims throughout a city. The involvement of law enforcement and other government officials in trafficking operations has received more exploration than the involvement of other professionals.

Government Corruption

Substantial research has been dedicated to understanding the role of government **corruption** in trafficking operations. According to the Organisation for Economic Co–operation and Development (OECD; 2016), organized human trafficking cannot take place without systematic corruption. This statement is supported by international trends. For example, a

> woman trafficked from Southeast Asia to Western Europe mentioned . . . that she was instructed by the trafficker to stand in a particular queue at her home country's main airport. When she moved to a shorter one, she was moved back to the original queue[,] and it was pointed out to her that the particular immigration official serving this queue was "one of them" and [would] not ask any questions about her documents. (UNODC, 2011a, p. 36)

As shown in Figure 5.4, countries that make the least effort to combat human trafficking also have the highest levels of corruption (OECD, 2016; D. Siegel & Nelen, 2008; UNODC, 2011a).

There are several ways that traffickers benefit from government corruption. Figure 5.5 shows how corruption facilitates the cycle of human trafficking.

Perceived Corruption

Traffickers use perceived levels of corruption to control victims. When victims perceive corruption to be high, they are less likely to question traffickers when they claim a middleman is needed to arrange visas, travel, and work permits. Traffickers may also tell victims that attempted escape is fruitless because they have law enforcement on their side. When victims come from countries with high levels of corruption, they are also more likely to believe these claims.

Corruption is highly correlated with the rule of law within countries; in countries where the rule of law is not a guarantee, there is higher perceived corruption and also higher levels of trafficking. When the rule of law is not strong, victims may also be less likely to report, either for fear of a negative reaction from authorities or because they assume it will not be taken seriously (UNODC, 2011a).

Involvement of Corrupt Government Officials

Traffickers may bribe government officials to assist in all roles of a trafficking operation, including recruitment, transfer, transport, and preventing victims from escaping. Government officials may facilitate trafficking by admitting victims

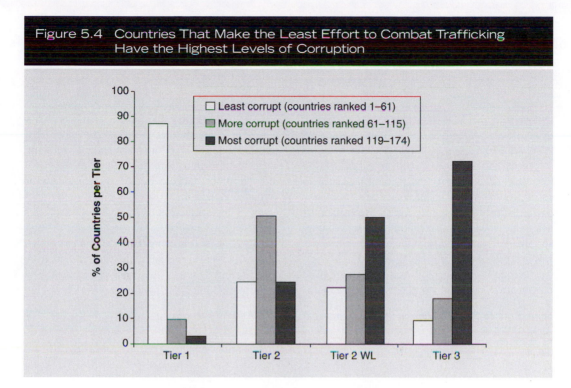

Figure 5.4   Countries That Make the Least Effort to Combat Trafficking Have the Highest Levels of Corruption

Source: Organisation for Economic Co-operation and Development, 2016.

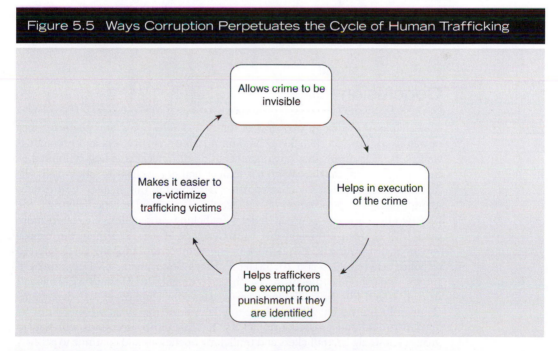

Figure 5.5   Ways Corruption Perpetuates the Cycle of Human Trafficking

Source: Adapted from Organisation for Economic Co-operation and Development, 2016.

Case Study

Corruption at Multiple Levels of Government

M. was a minor female from Moldova who was trafficked to the Balkans, where she was sexually exploited and held in a brothel until she was rescued by a human trafficking task force operating with the assistance of the international community.

M.'s trafficking had been allegedly facilitated by corruption in three different ways. First, actual blank passports had been allegedly corruptly obtained by her traffickers from a neighboring Balkan country and used to transfer her into the location where she was sexually exploited.

Second, even though the passports were filled out incorrectly and obviously improper, with the wrong official stamps and other glaring mistakes, and even though M. did not speak any of the local languages of where she was exploited, she was passed through several border crossings without question, allegedly through corrupt facilitation.

Third, the brothel where M. was exploited was across the street from the local police station. No action to investigate was taken; some police officers were allegedly obtaining sexual services from M. and other victims of trafficking. M. was freed based on a national-level investigation undertaken with international support without the participation of the local authorities.

Source: United Nations Office on Drugs and Crime, 2011a.

through immigration without visa checks; facilitating access to illegitimate passport or visa documents; or turning a blind eye to trafficking when they witness it. There are also accounts of government officials benefiting from the services of trafficking victims, particularly in the case of sex trafficking. Government officials can also prevent victims from escaping by apprehending and returning victims to traffickers, or by forcing victims or their families to pay a bribe for their release (OECD, 2016; UNODC, 2011a).

Conclusion

This chapter provided an overview of the motivations, roles, and characteristics of traffickers. Data on traffickers come from trafficking survivors and prosecuted traffickers. This means that our understanding of traffickers is largely limited to traffickers who are caught. We do not know whether the characteristics of all traffickers are aligned with the characteristics described in this chapter. Fortunately, identification and prosecution of traffickers has increased substantially over the past two decades. For example, federal trafficking prosecutions increased more than 40% between 2011 and 2015 (Motivans & Snyder, 2018). In the United Kingdom there was a 159% increase in the number of trafficking cases referred to police between 2015 and 2016 (Her Majesty's Government, UK Department of Justice, Scottish Government, & Welsh Government, 2017). In 2017, Thailand held its largest human trafficking trial to date, convicting 62 of 102 defendants (Human Rights Watch, 2017). These trends indicate that what we know can be applied to find and prosecute traffickers. Increases in prosecutions will lead to greater knowledge of traffickers and trafficking operations and continue to accelerate anti-trafficking efforts.

KEY WORDS

DISCUSSION QUESTIONS

1. What are three benefits of studying traffickers?

2. What are three things that make it difficult to research traffickers?

3. What are two primary motives for trafficking?

4. What are two factors that make human trafficking easier?

5. What are two policies or programs that make human trafficking more difficult?

6. How can media campaigns like #Eyesopen prevent trafficking?

RESOURCES

Trends in identifying traffickers:

- 2017 UK Annual Report on Modern Slavery: https://assets.publishing.service.gov.uk/government/uploads/system/uploads/attachment_data/file/652366/2017_uk_annual_report_on_modern_slavery.pdf

- "Federal Prosecution of Human-Trafficking Cases, 2015": https://www.bjs.gov/content/pub/pdf/fphtc15.pdf

- "Thailand: Trafficking Convictions Important Step Forward": https://www.hrw.org/news/2017/07/24/thailand-trafficking-convictions-important-step-forward

Organized crime and human trafficking:

- *An Empirical Analysis of the Intersection of Organized Crime and Human Trafficking In the United States*: https://www.ncjrs.gov/pdffiles1/nij/grants/250955.pdf

- "The Connection Between the Mara Salvatrucha (MS-13) and Human Trafficking": http://humantraffickingsearch.org/wp-content/uploads/2017/09/MS-13-Publication.pdf

Sex Trafficking

Part II and the remaining sections of the text will focus on specific forms of trafficking. Many readers may find this section, focused on sex trafficking, rather provocative. While sex trafficking is more talked about, and possibly more understood, than any other forms of trafficking, the complexities surrounding this crime are still perplexing and controversial to many. The prostitution debate, the focus of Chapter 6, pushes the reader to conclude that although human trafficking and prostitution are different, in reality the distinctions can be difficult to identify. Readers will parse out the different approaches to prostitution across the world and how these approaches impact sex trafficking. From there, the remaining chapters will focus specifically on sex trafficking—the laws, special populations, and current responses to these crimes.

Readers may begin these chapters thinking they know about sex trafficking, thanks to the media's attention to the issue. However, after covering these chapters, readers of this text should have a better understanding of the relationship between prostitution and sex trafficking. Readers will also be able to explain the unique challenges special populations, such as children, males, and transsexuals, face in avoiding and/or recovering from their trafficking experiences.

The Colliding Worlds of Prostitution and Human Trafficking

We, the survivors of prostitution and trafficking . . . declare that prostitution is violence against women. Women in prostitution do not wake up one day and "choose" to be prostitutes. It is chosen for us by poverty, past sexual abuse, the pimps who take advantage of our vulnerabilities, and the men who buy us for the sex of prostitution.

—**Manifesto, Joint CATW-EWL Press Conference (2005; as cited in O'Connor & Healy, 2006)**

The beach is behind me, waves crashing onto the sand, clear water streaming back into the massive body that is the Pacific Ocean. I sit in an open-air restaurant with my family and friends, and notice out of the corner of my eye a young woman. She is across the street, just standing around, alone. She is dressed provocatively, following the cars with her eyes as they pass by. I have no idea what her purpose is, although I have suspicions. Beach town, provocative clothes, interest in who is driving by. The girl looks barely 18.

As I sit down to write this chapter, I am relaxing in the apartment of close family friends. The apartment is in a posh part of Mexico City. I am far from my cozy home on the East Coast of the United States. I am relishing in my good fortune in having been able to take my young children on a vacation they could never have dreamed of, filled with beaches, mountains, and the sights and sounds of one of the most historic cities in the world. Overtired, over-sugared, and overindulged, they've gotten a summer experience we all want to be able to give our kids.

For my daughter, about to enter second grade, I gently but regularly remind her of how lucky she is. I point out to her young children begging and selling trinkets on the street. Young girls her age, working the street to support their families, being "managed" by an unseen employer. My daughter will, with any luck, never experience the extreme poverty felt in Mexico, many other countries in Central and South America, and around the world. In Chapter 4, we spoke about the extreme vulnerabilities associated with living in poverty. This link to poverty is also closely related to becoming a prostitute or sex worker.

This chapter will define and describe prostitution. Who becomes a sex worker? What motivates a person to enter into prostitution? It will also discuss how prostitution is handled legislatively, domestically and internationally. It will conclude with an exploration into the relationship between prostitution and sex trafficking. With first-world countries falling on both sides of the legalization debate, case studies focusing on how different countries handle the intersection of prostitution and human trafficking will be presented. A debate on whether legalized prostitution reduces or escalates human trafficking will challenge you, the reader, to draw your own conclusions on the best ways to react to prostitution and sex trafficking.

You may wonder what the authors' personal opinions are on the relationship between prostitution and human trafficking. Does legalized prostitution hinder or exacerbate opportunities for human trafficking? Are those being prostituted better protected from exploitation if prostitution is criminalized or legalized? I suspect our opinions will become transparent, but it is important to stress that, as the reader, you should not underestimate the complexities of this debate. As the author of this chapter, I often ponder this issue and reassess right and wrong for myself. And every time I think I have landed on a viewpoint, something causes me to question my beliefs. Issues of feminism, agency, and basic moral values will all come into play in this chapter.

What Is Prostitution?

Prostitution is known as the "world's oldest profession" and occurs "when an individual engages with another person in a sexual activity for a fee" (Capaul, 2013, p. 16). While considered morally reprehensible (not to mention illegal) in many circles, the opportunity to engage in prostitution is readily available, albeit typically underground. Prostitution is often called a victimless crime, as those selling themselves for sex choose the lifestyle they live. In some cases, this is true. In others, it is not. Often sex trafficking goes unidentified due to the assumption that sex workers are willing participants in their prostitution. Nevertheless, from 2008 to 2010, a U.S. federal anti-trafficking task force examined 2,515 possible human trafficking cases. Of those cases, 82% involved sex trafficking, and nearly half of them included victims under the age of 18 years old (Banks & Kyckelhahn, 2011).

Both domestically and internationally, laws have been put in place to criminalize prostitution (the consensual sale of sex) and related acts (Batsyukova, 2007; Deady, 2011; Hennigan, 2004). Much is debated on the best way to go about dealing with prostitution. Should the prostitute be punished or helped? Should the "john"—the person purchasing sex—be punished? Should the establishments knowingly allowing prostitution to take place on their properties be punished?

Some question even the language used to discuss sex for pay. *Prostitution* and *sex work* are terms used interchangeably when speaking about the sale of sex. Some prefer to label the act *sex work*, as it has a less negative connotation. The term *prostitute* is sometimes viewed as a victimizing term. However, there are instances when sex workers make purposeful choices to enter into sex work, albeit often based on bounded rationality (E. Rosen & Venkatesh, 2008). For the purposes of this chapter, we will refer to those who sell their bodies as sex workers. We understand that some sex workers are actually victims of human trafficking—discussed later in this chapter. However, to respect those who make the difficult choice to enter into prostitution, we will use the term considered more respectful of those individuals—sex workers.

Prevalence

Prostitution assumes consensual sex. For an act of prostitution to be considered sex trafficking, there must be evidence that the sex act was not consensual. This can sometimes be difficult to determine. Sex workers, especially in countries where prostitution is illegal, such as the U.S., do not identify publicly as prostitutes. And if arrested, they rarely report their victimization, even if they are victims, and accept the prostitution charges (Bayhi-Gennaro, 2008). A lack of proper legal assistance, a lack of awareness that what is happening to them is not okay, and fear often play into their decisions to plead to criminal charges rather than report victimization.

Patience and awareness on the part of the first responders and those dealing with sex workers are required to accurately label situations as prostitution or sex trafficking. The blurry line between prostitution and sex trafficking makes it especially challenging to estimate the number of sex workers involved in prostitution in the U.S. and internationally. The data on both prostitution and sex trafficking are limited and of questionable accuracy (Dank et al., 2014).

In this section, descriptive information is provided regarding the numbers of prostitutes internationally as well as the revenue made by prostitution. However, I encourage you to be cautious. These numbers are estimates at best. It is very likely that these numbers reflect individuals selling sexual services for a fee. This is inclusive of both consensual sex workers and victims of sex trafficking.

Havocscope (2015), a popular website that reports on underground crime, estimates the number of sex workers in the world to be 13,828,700 persons. This number was based on public data provided by criminal justice agencies, public health programs, global criminal justice programs, and security services estimates. As shown in Table 6.1, China is estimated to have the highest number of sex workers—approximately 5 million. India and the United States round out the top three with 3 million and 1 million estimated sex workers, respectively (Havocscope, 2015).

Table 6.1   Estimated Number of Prostitutes and Revenue by Country

Country	Number of Prostitutes	Prostitution Revenue
China	5 Million	$ 73 Billion
India	3 Million	$ 8.4 Billion
United States	1 Million	$14.6 Billion
Philippines	800,000	$ 6 Billion
Mexico	500,000	—
Germany*	400,000	$ 18 Billion
Brazil	250,000 (Children)	—
Thailand	250,000	$ 6.4 Billion
South Korea	147,000	$ 12 Billion
Turkey	118,000	$ 4 Billion
Taiwan	100,000	$ 1.84 Billion
Cambodia	70,000	$ 511 Million
Ukraine	67,5000	$ 1.5 Billion

United Kingdom	58,000	$ 1 Billion
Kenya	50,000 (Children)	—
Vietnam	33,000	—
South Africa	30,000 (Children)	—
United Arab Emirates	30,000	—
France	20,000	—
Switzerland*	20,000	$ 3.5 Billion
Poland	19,000	—
Mongolia	19,000	—
Israel	17,500	$ 500 Million
Costa Rica	15,000	—
Netherlands	7,000	$ 800 Million
New Zealand	3,500	—
Denmark	3,200	—
Ireland	1,000	$ 326 Million
Indonesia	—	$ 2.25 Billion
Bulgaria	—	$ 1.3 Billion
Italy	—	$ 600 Million
Czech Republic	—	$ 200 Million
Jamaica	—	$ 58 Million
Australia	—	$ 27 Million

*Prostitution is legal in these countries.

Source: Havocscope, 2015.

China also leads in amount of prostitution revenue. Germany, where prostitution is legal, comes in a far second for revenue with $18 billion. With $14.6 billion in revenue, the United States has the third-highest amount of revenue produced from prostitution (Havocscope, 2015).

A 2014 landmark study, published by the Urban Institute, provides the most reliable data to date exploring the size and impact of prostitution in the United States (Dank et al., 2014). The study explored the revenue made by the underground sex industry in eight U.S. cities: Atlanta, Dallas, Denver, Kansas City, Miami, San Diego, Seattle, and Washington, DC. It also compared the revenue made in the underground sex industry to revenue collected from the illegal sale of drugs and guns. Their findings indicated that, in 2007, revenue in the eight cities ranged from $39.9 million to $290 million, with Atlanta having the highest revenue. The revenue made in the underground sex industry in Atlanta was 2.5 times larger than the payroll of the Atlanta Falcons in 2013 (Dank & Johnson, 2014)!

The sex industry in Atlanta also produced higher revenues than the gun and drug industries in 2007 ($290 million, $146 million, and $117 million, respectively).

Atlanta was one of two cities, Seattle being the other, that experienced a rise in prostitution revenue from 2003 to 2007 (Dank et al., 2014). Washington, DC, experienced the greatest drop in revenue, going from $155 million in 2003 to $103 million in 2007. This was a 34% decline in revenue.

Commercial sex venues, including massage parlors, **brothels**, escort services, and street- and Internet-based prostitution were found in all cities included in the study. Pimps and traffickers interviewed for the study reported a weekly income ranging from $5,000 to $32,833.

There are a few studies available that examine country-specific prostitution data (e.g., J. M. Edwards, Iritani, & Hallfors, 2006; Vanwesenbeeck, 2013). In the Netherlands, the percentage of the adult population that reported exchanging money for sex was between 1% and 3%. Three percent was considered high but reasonable, given policies in the Netherlands that provide regulations and protection for sex workers, discussed further in this chapter (Vanwesenbeeck, 2013). Generally, the estimate has been around 1% of the adult population in other countries. Using a nationally representative sample of youth in the United States, J. M. Edwards and colleagues (2006) found that 3.5% of youth reported exchanging sex for money and drugs.

The next few subsections examine the limited information available on the demographics of sex workers as well as the push factors that result in individuals becoming sex workers.

Demographics

What are the demographic characteristics of a sex worker? This is a tough question to answer. Once again, there are few reliable data that examine the demographics of people who enter the world of prostitution.

Gender

There is a general view, supported by data, that men make up a smaller proportion of sex workers in the world (e.g., International Labour Organization, 2013d; International Organization for Migration, 2015; National Human Trafficking Resource Center, 2016; United Nations Office on Drugs and Crime [UNODC], 2018a). Nevertheless, the number of males in the sex industry grew at a pace quicker than that of females through 2014 and appeared to become steadier by 2018 (UNODC, 2016a, 2018a). A recent study found that the percentage of adult men and women reporting receiving payment for sex was approximately the same (Vanwesenbeeck, 2013). Interestingly, Vanwesenbeeck (2013) cited multiple studies showing that in interviews with juveniles, boys actually are the dominant gender reporting involvement in the commercial sex industry. In Norway, 2.1% of boys and 0.6% of girls reported involvement in the sex industry. In a sample of youth in the U.S., two-thirds of those that reported exchanging sex for money or drugs (grades 7 through 12) identified as boys (J. M. Edwards et al., 2006). More discussion on males in the sex industry can be found in Chapter 7.

While male sex workers are certainly a population that has been overlooked and deserves acknowledgment, this should not minimize the historical global view of women as responsible for providing sex and pleasure to the male population. Reactions to prostitution, as well as the debates and controversies surrounding prostitution, are primarily focused on female sex workers. Patriarchal versus feminist views on prostitution often clash as woman gain equal standing domestically and in many countries internationally. This will become more apparent as reactions to prostitution are discussed later in the chapter.

Age

Many organizations and nongovernmental organizations (NGOs) believe that most prostitutes began their careers in the sex trade around 12 to 15 years old (e.g., McCartin, 2016; L. Smith, Vardaman, & Snow, 2009). **Shared Hope International**, a large and respected nonprofit whose goal is to end domestic minor sex trafficking, provided data from an unpublished survey of youth in Clark County, Nevada, who were arrested for prostitution. In this sample, the average age of entry into prostitution was 12 to 14 years old (L. Smith et al., 2009; see Figure 6.1 for the age distribution of the arrested youth).

First-responder data also support the belief that the age of entry into prostitution is quite young. Findings from surveys of first responders indicated the average age of contact with the police to be 15 years old (L. Smith et al., 2009). In fact, a report on domestic minor sex trafficking in New Orleans found victims as young as eight years old (Bayhi-Gennaro, 2008). This is also consistent with a Department of Justice (DOJ) report from 2015 that gave age 15 as the average age of entry (McCartin, 2016).

Polaris (2015e), based on data from the National Human Trafficking Resource Center hotline and Polaris's BeFree Textline, found the average age of entry in the U.S. to be slightly older at 19 years old. However, 44% of survivors who reached out to the hotline reported being 17 years old or younger at age of entry. This is by no

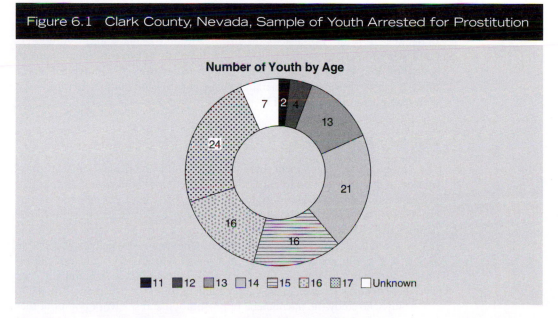

Figure 6.1 Clark County, Nevada, Sample of Youth Arrested for Prostitution

Source: Adapted from Smith, Vardaman, and Snow, 2009.

means an insignificant number. Kennedy, Klein, Bristowe, Cooper, and Yuille (2007) conducted an interview-based study with 44 women involved in the sex trade. The age range of the women was 19 to 45, with the average age being 34.5. The women reported entering into sex work between the ages of 10 and 45 years old, with the average age being 21.3 years old. Note that Polaris (2015e) and Kennedy and colleagues (2007) sampled only adults, so they might not have captured youth who hadn't yet self-identified as victims of trafficking. Nevertheless, sample selection is critical when examining this issue. If the sample is limited to youth, it will produce a younger average age of entry than adult samples. Similarly, if the sample includes only adults, the age of entry will skew older. One can assume that the average is somewhere between 14 and 19, given the available data. However, a more robust sample is required to truly understand the age of entry into prostitution/trafficking.

Ultimately, prostitution is an ugly job. Whether you are a child or an adult, male or female, it is dangerous and demoralizing. While one might like to believe sex workers are kidnapped and forced into the life, more often than not this is *not* the case. Oftentimes, sex work is voluntarily chosen, typically because no alternative exists. For most, prostitution is a last resort (Burnette, Lucas, & Ilgen, 2008; Kennedy et al., 2007; E. Rosen & Venkatesh, 2008).

The next subsection will explore the push factors that drive individuals into prostitution. You will find these to be similar to the push factors that result in people becoming victims of trafficking. Understanding these push factors will help you, the reader, to understand why people choose prostitution and how easily prostitution turns into human trafficking.

Push Factors for Prostitution
....

What puts people into such a desperate position? In Chapter 4 you heard the terms *push* and *pull factors*. These were the factors that explained how people enter trafficking, or for the purposes of this discussion, prostitution. You will see several of the push factors discussed in Chapter 4 mentioned again in this chapter. However, in this chapter the factors will be related specifically to prostitution and sex work. Demand is the primary pull factor driving prostitution. Demand for prostitution is particularly important in understanding the longevity of prostitution on a global scale. For now, let's focus on the push factors that explain why individuals enter into sex work. These factors generally consist of social and cultural factors, along with manipulation (Capaul, 2013).

Poverty and Gender

There is general agreement that financial strain is the driving cause of prostitution. If *any* other option to make money existed, individuals would avoid this profession (O'Connor & Healy, 2006). However, note that this can be a complicated decision. A person who chooses to become a sex worker, in spite of the dangers and risks associated with that line of work, may have other job options (e.g., fast food). However, those job options are not nearly as flexible or profitable as sex work (E. Rosen & Venkatesh, 2008). As E. Rosen and Venkatesh (2008) observed in their qualitative study of sex workers in an urban environment, "sex work has become a solution to the employment needs of the urban poor" (p. 417).

Many who study the phenomena of prostitution and sex work point out that females involved in sex work are especially vulnerable to the consequences of poverty. Generally, females have fewer alternative options to sex work than males. The feminism of poverty is a reality and an important factor when considering ways to reduce the number of individuals entering into sex work (Franklin, 2008; Vanwesenbeeck, 2013). Vanwesenbeeck (2013) describes the sex work business as "firmly rooted in (unequal) gender relations in sex and finance" (p. 12). While males who live in poverty are certainly at risk for turning to sex work, the reality is that gender discrimination and cultural norms more specifically limit the financial opportunities offered to women. In many cases, cultural norms place expectations on women that sex work is their designated role (Kennedy et al., 2007; O'Connor & Healy, 2006; Vanwesenbeeck, 2013). Similarly, while limited opportunities for education and work make all individuals vulnerable to entering into sex work, women are uniquely impacted by limited opportunities for education and conventional employment (Kennedy et al., 2007; O'Connor & Healy, 2006).

Abuse and Addiction

In addition to structural challenges such as poverty and gender discrimination, individual-level characteristics can also be predictive of one's likelihood of entering into sex work. A history of sexual abuse is a major risk factor for entering into sex work (Kennedy et al., 2007; E. Rosen & Venkatest, 2008; J. A. Siegel & Williams, 2003; Simons & Whitbeck, 1991; L. Smith et al., 2009; Vanwesenbeeck, 2013). In fact, in a study of the impact of sexual abuse, those individuals who reported a history of sexual abuse were 27.7 times more likely to be arrested for prostitution compared to non–sexually abused individuals (as described in E. Rosen & Venkatesh, 2008). Simons and Whitbeck (1991) found that prior sexual abuse increased the probability of entry into sex work even for those individuals who had also experienced drug abuse and runaway status. In other words, prior sexual abuse had an independent impact on entry into sex work, even when other risk factors were present. An interviewee from a study conducted in a Vancouver safe house stated, "A friend of mine . . . she got out and got money and I had been approached while I was waiting. And I figured I'm getting molested at home so why not get paid for it and get my rent covered" (Kennedy et al., 2007, p. 14).

Drug addiction is another common characteristic observed among sex workers. Drug addiction not only limits the opportunity for jobs in the formal economy, but oftentimes sex work offers a means to sustain one's addiction—through financing or trading drugs for sex (J. M. Edwards et al., 2006; Kennedy et al., 2007; L. S. Murphy, 2010; E. Rosen & Venkatesh, 2008; Silbert, Pines, & Lynch, 1982). As reviewed previously in this chapter, J. M. Edwards and colleagues (2006) found that 3.5% of a representative sample of students exchanged sex for money or drugs. In addition to drugs, this study found running away from home, depression, and risky sexual behaviors to be predictors of trading sex for money or drugs.

The challenges associated with drug addiction result in similar consequences for consensual sex workers and sex trafficking victims. The National Human Trafficking Resource Center (2016) cited drug involvement as one of the top five characteristics of those identifying as trafficking victims. Addiction can be the result of the sex work (consensual or not) or the cause. At times pimps and traffickers supply their prostitutes with drugs to make them more pliable and more easily manipulated. In many cases traffickers and pimps use drugs to maintain control. It is one of the factors that makes escaping trafficking and prostitution so difficult. Drug addictions are all-consuming and often force sex workers back into a life of sex work even when they try to get out (Kristof & WuDunn, 2010; Silbert et al., 1982).

Socialization

Sex workers are looking for something. Whether it be personal connections, parental figures, love, financial support, drugs . . . the list goes on. Nevertheless, sex workers are missing something in their lives. Sometimes they are so desperate to find whatever they are looking for, they don't see situations clearly. Take, for example, a young woman who observes her friend engaged in prostitution. She sees that her friend has this boyfriend who takes care of her. He says he loves her. He buys her gifts, provides her housing, keeps her hair and nails maintained. This young woman thinks to herself, "I want this. I want someone to take care of me, to buy me things." What this young woman fails to see is the obsessive level of control this "boyfriend" has over her friend. This young woman doesn't see the deep betrayal of this boyfriend, who sells his "girlfriend" to others so that he can make money. Her friend never sees the money, never controls her own situation.

Prostitution becomes normalized, if not glamorized. Vulnerable people who are exposed to this life fail to see the negative aspects (Capaul, 2013; Dank et al., 2014; E. Rosen & Venkatesh, 2008). Networks and connections produce opportunities for sex work, almost like networking in any other career field. Music and media have also normalized the idea of pimps, prostitutes, and the exploitation of women, resulting in a desensitization of the issue even in mainstream culture.

While prostitution and human trafficking are not the same thing, the gray area between them is substantial. Research shows that factors that push individuals, especially women and girls, into sex trafficking also predict their participation in the sex industry (i.e., as consensual sex workers). Such factors include poverty, sex abuse, drug addiction, and homelessness (O'Connor & Healy, 2006). Prior victimization is an especially common characteristic of sex workers. A San Francisco study of sex workers revealed that over half reported being sexually abused during childhood, while 49% reported being physically assaulted (Farley & Barkan, 1998).

Challenge Yourself 6.1

How do you see the mainstream media playing into the glamorization of prostitution? What are the consequences of how prostitutes and pimps are characterized in movies, music, television, and social media? What is the responsibility of those producing this media in terms of providing a more accurate depiction of prostitution?

Focus On
Why and How Pimps Do What They Do

The Urban Institute published a lengthy report exposing the realities of the underground commercial sex economy (UCSE) in eight U.S. cities (Dank et al., 2014). In addition to gathering information on the experiences of the sex workers, the organization of this underground economy, and the staggering amount of money flowing through these networks, the authors drew some conclusions regarding the ringleaders of these organizations—the pimps and traffickers.

The authors interviewed 73 individuals charged and convicted with crimes related to **pimping** and trafficking. Following are the exact findings reported in the study report (Dank et al., 2014, p. 131).

- **Identity**: The majority of respondents reported that the media inaccurately portrays all pimps as violent. While fifteen percent of respondents to this study reported using violence to control their employees, respondents felt that popular interpretations of pimp-managed sex work exaggerate the use of force perpetrated by pimps against employees.

- **External influences on entry into pimping**: Extant literature has offered some insight on how pimps first engage in the facilitation of sex work. Studies have suggested that individuals that grew up in neighborhoods where prostitution was prevalent or have family members engaged in sex work sometimes enter the field. Other research has found that individuals working in other illegal underground economies, such as drug dealing, sometimes move into the facilitation of underground sex markets. Our findings corroborate earlier studies and shed light on new ways that individuals start pimping. Pimps cited multiple influences on their own choices, and thus different factors are not mutually exclusive.

- **Internal motivations for entry into pimping**: Pimps cited self-perception of business-related strengths as a factor in the decision to become a pimp. Beyond the impact of external influences, pimps believed that their capacity to convince or manipulate other people to engage in activities, their focus on making money, and their leadership skills were reasons to become involved in pimping.

- **Perceptions of business-related risks**: As prior research on pimping and sex trafficking has focused on the perspectives of law enforcement and victims, little information is documented about how perpetrators perceive and interpret the risks associated with the facilitation of sex work. Respondents cited multiple risks they recognized due to their involvement in pimping. Arrest was the primary consequence feared by pimps, followed by personal safety, and employee safety.

- **Risk mitigation**: Pimps employed multiple tactics to mitigate business-related risks. To control against law enforcement detection, pimps avoided hiring minors and worked proactively to identify law enforcement stings prior to making transactions. To ensure personal safety, some pimps reported carrying weapons. To protect employee safety, pimps armed employees, enforced safety-related rules, and remained close to employees when they met customers.

Additional findings regarding the networks, relationships, and management of pimping included the following (Dank et al., 2014, p. 151):

- **Business structure**: Findings support research suggesting that pimps manage pre-transaction preparation including finding clients, establishing locations and times, and determining the price of the transaction (Levitt and Venkatesh 2007). However, this study also indicates that the duties of a pimp vary drastically across facilitators; while some pimps take full control of business management, others provide only limited oversight and leave much of the business operations in the hands of their employees.

- **Employee recruitment**: No previous study explores the process of employee recruitment from the perspective of pimps or sex traffickers. Finds from this report detail the locations where pimps recruit, the individuals who are targeted, and the methods employed to recruit individuals into sex work.

- **Demographics of recruited individuals**: Pimps recruited individuals of all ages, genders, and races. However, multiple pimps noted that white women are more profitable in the sex market and easier to manage. Pimps also reported that law enforcement has placed a heightened emphasis on arresting and prosecuting individuals who pimp underage women. As a result, many offenders avoided minors, in part due to fears of arrest and prosecution.

- **Location**: Pimps recruited sex workers in different spaces. Findings from this study corroborate earlier studies that suggest pimps and traffickers recruit women in a variety of locations—advertisements, businesses, online, malls and shopping venues, social events, bus stations, and night clubs.

- **Methods of recruitment**: Prior research has suggested that pimps appeal to individuals' emotional dependencies and economic needs through "finesse pimping." This

(Continued)

study supports this literature by finding that different forms of coercion and fraud, sometimes independent or even free of physical violence, are used by pimps to recruit and control employees. These forms of coercion and fraud included feigning romantic interest, emphasizing mutual dependency between pimp and employee, discouraging women from "having sex for free," promising material comforts, and establishing a reputation as a "good" pimp.

- **Women in recruitment**: Pimp-managed employees played a critical role in recruiting individuals to engage in sex work. Employees approached individuals, encouraged friends to engage in sex work under the pimp, bolstered the pimp's reputation, and explained the business to recruited individuals.

- **Rules and regulations**: Sixty percent of respondents reported imposing rules on employees. Findings from this study offer insight into the rules imposed by pimps on employees, including: the role of drugs and alcohol in the control of sex workers; limitations on clientele; restricted communications with other pimps; and earning quotas.

- **Punishment**: Pimps responded to rule violations in multiple ways, including physical violence, isolation, and confiscating possessions. Even in the absence of clearly articulated rules, pimps used discipline to exert control over employees and encourage dependency. Fifteen percent of respondents to this study reported using violence to control their employees, though study findings rely on self-reported information and it is possible that the use of violence was under-reported. Those that discussed using violence indicated that physical violence was always used in conjunction with other forms of coercion. Coercion through psychological and emotional abuse was cited by respondents as the most common form of punishment.

- **Competition between employees**: Pimps relied on competition between employees to maintain control and drive earnings. Competition also provided an "incentive program" among employees, which included more personal time with the pimp and spending money.

- **Relationships between pimps**: Some respondents claimed that pimping was an independent and competitive business, and that other pimps could not be trusted; whereas, other respondents stated that they looked to other pimps for support and partnership. These respondents looked to their pimp partners as family and felt that they could go to them when in trouble.

- **Travel**: Travel was an essential business practice for some respondents. Seventy percent of respondents reported working in more than one city. Reasons for travel included recruitment, police crackdowns, special events, tragedy, and employee appeal. Pimps relied on networks in other cities to provide advice on where to find clients and how to navigate the UCSE in that city.

- **Relationships with legal businesses**: Some pimps enjoyed lucrative relationships with legal businesses. Hotel employees and managers often turned a blind eye to prostitution occurring within their establishment. In some cases, legal business employees would actively support a pimp in order to earn additional income.

Are Prostitution and Sex Trafficking the Same Thing?

The quote at the beginning of this chapter brings into question the agency (free will) of a sex worker. Does any man, woman, or child ever *choose* to be a sex worker? Human trafficking is defined internationally and domestically as the use of force, fraud, or coercion for the purpose of profiting off the backs of human beings. Many would argue that those who choose to prostitute themselves have no alternative options or are pressured due to social and/or culture constraints, and thus they are coerced into their actions (Capaul, 2013; Kennedy et al., 2007). This perspective holds that all

Case Study

The Challenges Faced by a Prostitute by Choice

Despite all the interviews and, perhaps, our desire to believe that prostitution is not a choice and is a miserable life, there are some who refute this belief. Barb Brents, a well-known sociologist who studies prostitution, posed, "It's curious to me that the most stigmatized employment for women is also the highest paid employment for women" (Lopez, 2016). Brents continues, "Prostitution can be empowering for certain women—not just financially, but gives them confidence. I've had a lot of women tell me that it's not the work that is bad; it's the stigma that it carries."

The blog entry below highlights some of these issues, specifically the benefits of sex work; the many consequences of this type of work, driven by stigma; and the irony of what options are left for an individual trying to get out of sex work. This blog entry was originally published on the pro–sex work blog *Tits and Sass* on August 24, 2017, by Kelly Michaels.

Warning: The text is graphic and potentially disturbing.

In the last four months, I have been in the most unusual employment circumstances of my life. I am kept in a small box with no access to even basic human needs like hot meals and showers. I am forced to stay there until my employers are ready to use me again. I am only permitted to shower when my employers are not using me. Up to a week in between showers has passed. I am not paid for all of the work that I have performed. I am forced to share my small box with strange men when my employers demand it. These men have become aggressive and verbally abusive toward me. I am not allowed to know if the men have been violent to others before I work with them. I have been harassed sexually by my employer and I'm viewed as a sexual object by an overwhelming number of the men that surround me.

I am paid less than minimum wage for the hours that I work. I am kept apart from my family and do not see my home for months at a time. In fact, since taking this job I have not seen my home once, though I was promised I'd be brought home every three to four weeks.

I do not have access to healthcare despite having been the victim of a violent physical assault by one of the people they had living with me in my box. I've asked repeatedly to go home to see a doctor, but my employers keep me in my box. They keep moving my box around the nation so that I am too far away to escape and return home. I suspect they keep my pay minimal so that I cannot afford to escape.

I first saw the signs from Truckers Against Trafficking at truck stops around the nation. They were your basic public awareness flyers with signs about how to recognize human trafficking. Then at the port of entry in Wyoming, I saw a different poster from Polaris asking, "Do you want out of the life?" I thought for a moment and realized that I do feel as if I am being trafficked and I do want out of "the life."

For the first time in my life, I feel like I should call Polaris for help, but I can't. Because I am no longer a sex worker.

This all began after I left sex work.

For most of my life I have earned an honest living as a sex worker. From the age of 15, I have been involved in one form of sex work or another. I began working the street as a homeless teenager, waiting to turn 18 so an escort service would hire me. At 18 I upgraded to being an escort, then quickly began advertising on my own as an independent. I married for 13 years, but when the housing market crashed I returned to sex work to save my family from certain homelessness.

Until recently, my work life was satisfactory. I made good money, was treated well, and had the freedom to do as I pleased when I pleased. Until this latest round of human trafficking hysteria began, I was happy at work.

(Continued)

Then things changed. I began to feel hunted. I began to fear publicly broadcast police stings, and FBI investigations that changed the charges I would face from the previous charge of prostitution to frightening things like felony promotion of prostitution because I used a computer to commit my crime. The prospect of being charged for violating the Mann Act for crimes involving "crossing state lines for immoral purposes" and earning myself a ten year sentence haunted me.

I lost my children to a violent man with a long history of domestic violence because I was a sex worker. The court did not view him as a wife beater, they viewed him as a whore beater, and that wasn't nearly as bad. The courts refused to view important evidence and left the children in his care despite overwhelming evidence that they were being abused and neglected in his home.

The losses that I suffered due to the criminalization of my work are inconceivable: three children whose lives I will never again be a part of. Then I lost my main source of income when Backpage executives were forced to shut down the Adult Services section of their website.

Sure, I could have moved my business to the casual dating section, or gone to another website. But for me, the closure of Backpage meant yet another loss—the loss of my successful business model. It was too much for me to bear. I finally threw in the towel.

What would come next was unimaginable.

First, I tried to go to college for the first time in my life. I applied to the University of Florida, having been awarded FAFSA funding. But the university declined my application to their online curriculum, citing my criminal background.

My criminal background has prevented me from achieving many of my goals in my life. I stayed in that abusive marriage far too long because of the lack of economic opportunity that I have always faced. I went to domestic violence shelters for help on two occasions based on

their promises to help me find work and become independent, but their promises failed because of my background.

Having been denied employment, a college education, and custody, I had little chance to survive. I was suicidal when I decided there was one thing I had not yet tried: CDL (Commercial Driver's License) school. I had not tried to get a job in the trucking industry. They often hire felons, so I put suicide on hold, and made one last effort to make my life sustainable. I spent three months on a black top training pad, with instructors screaming at, swearing at, name calling, and body shaming me.

I never imagined how much whore-bashing I would face entering the workforce, either. It began with my first female lead driver, the person charged with the on-the-job-training I was to complete following CDL school graduation. I listened for hours as she told me how vile and disgusting prostitutes are. She occupied the drive time telling me that her husband gave her MRSA after getting it from a prostitute. When I asked her how she knew he got it from a prostitute, she said, well, if you think about it, they have sex with 50 to 100 men per day.

"Really? You think that is even possible?" I replied. It was shocking to hear what she imagined being a prostitute involved. I knew at that moment that I had to conceal who I really was to make life on a truck with a stranger possible.

I did try tried to conceal my ties to sex work when I was at CDL school, but ultimately I found it unbearable to keep it up. For me personally, the hardest part was the truck driver talk about "lot lizards"—the derogatory trucker term for the sex workers who work truck stops. Every day, several times a day, I listened to these veteran-truckers-turned-instructors telling stories and making jokes about "lot lizards" and "dirty whores." Every day I came to school to huge "Truckers Against Trafficking" logos on the parked trailers.

I was so down about it that a friend tried to cheer me up by sending me a pro–sex work t-shirt that said, "Hookers of the world, Unite and Take Over!" I loved it and wore it to school under my jacket. I planned only to take a photo discreetly and not let anyone see my shirt. I was waiting for lunchtime to come so I could enlist a friend to snap a quick pic of me wearing the shirt while standing by the Truckers Against Trafficking logo when an instructor asked a group of us if he'd ever told us about the time he poured hot coffee on a hooker's head. I was the only woman in the group of people he addressed.

He told us that a lot lizard knocked on his door and he told her that he was married and tired and not to knock on the door again. He said she knocked again an hour later and he opened his window and poured hot coffee on her head. Everyone laughed. I said, "I guess she let you sleep after that."

He said, "No, about an hour later, there was another knock. This time it was the police. Can you believe that dirty whore called the cops on me?"

I asked if he got arrested, and he said, "No, the cops asked me if I poured hot coffee on her head, and I said, 'Yes I did, and if you take me to jail for it, maybe I can get some sleep there because I can't hear when that hooker keeps banging on my door.' So the cops turned around, put her in handcuffs, and drove her to jail."

I was infuriated by his boastful account of abuse and the fact that his behavior was perfectly acceptable to all those listening— except me. Empowered by my t-shirt, I slipped out of my jacket and saw his eyes dart back and forth from the words on my shirt to my eyes several times when I said, "Cool story. Tell it again."

If for no other reason but to do something to stand against his pride at what he had done to that woman, I stood up to him. I began feeling a need to be true to who I really am, a sex worker, even during these difficult times when I am displaced from my industry.

I eventually graduated with a CDL, and the transphobic, whore-hating rhetoric on the job was not quite as bad as it was in training, but it was still present. If I wasn't listening to negativity about sex workers, it was negativity toward the LGBTQ community, of which I am also a member. Most of the time, I learned to hide being a whore, and hide being a lesbian.

I was hired by the company that put me through school. It seemed like a good offer when I accepted it. They would pay for my school, and deduct the costs from my paychecks at a rate of no more than $40 at a time. I would be home one day for every week out, and never out more than four weeks at a time. I would be paid $0.25 per mile for the first six months. That is significantly below average, but I attributed it to being debt bonded to the company. My income was projected at $52,000 my first year.

That didn't happen.

Debt bondage. I know this phrase from my early days working for a pimp. He paid for my legal costs after an arrest and then put me into an apartment he paid for and kept almost all of my earnings until I "repaid" my debt. To be exact, I was able to keep $20 per $200 call. He kept track of my payments, and it was a very long time before I realized that he kept conflating new debt with old debt to keep me in a constant state of confusion about the repayment. This allowed him to exploit me for far longer than the debt alone would have called for.

The same thing is happening to me today with the company I work for. They keep changing things and coding repayments in a very confusing way to keep me working without being paid for the work that I am actually doing. Mileage is not accurate, log books are faked to misrepresent the amount of time I actually work, and so far, I am making only an average of $150–$200 per week for being held captive in this little box without being allowed to go home.

This is not what I agreed to, but I am debt bonded to the company. If I leave before completing ten months of this indentured servitude, my CDL will be useless due to the agreement major carriers have with each other not to hire debt-bonded individuals.

(Continued)

(Continued)

I am left now in a worse situation than I ever felt I was in as a sex worker. I feel terribly exploited, and there is no "Truckers Against Trafficking Truckers" to help me safely return to the freedom and independence of sex work.

Prohibitionists do not understand that for women who are consenting adult sex workers, transitioning into life outside the sex industry is a painful process. I am facing abuse, shame, ridicule, and far worse working conditions than I ever experienced when I traveled the country as a tantra provider.

Exploitation in the workforce is real and rampant. But to admit this or give it any attention would require that prohibitionists admit that it isn't exploitation that they are concerned with, or they would fight all exploitation. It seems what they are interested in is controlling who is permitted to do the exploiting.

I am now being exploited by a multibillion dollar company. Does that make it acceptable, or just invisible?

Trucking in my experience has been extremely exploitative. However, for many in the trucking industry the experience is far different. To focus only on my experience in trucking would not be a fair representation of the industry as a whole. To demonize and criminalize trucking based on my experience would force many out of a career that is lucrative and loved. It depends on individual circumstance—much like sex work.

Prohibitionists focus solely on individuals in the sex industry who were coerced or abused. This is not a fair representation of the majority of consenting adults that find their livelihood in the sex industry. In the effort to "rescue" trafficked individuals they are driving many more sex workers out of a career that is lucrative and loved, or is even just the best of many bad options. And as many trafficking survivors can attest, prohibitionists don't help them by "rescuing" them via arrest, either.

Prohibitionists offer no apology or assistance when rescue goes wrong. I know because I asked. In an email to a leading activist in the prohibition movement, I wrote,

> . . . What do you tell women like me? What do I do when I am ostracized from society due to a felony and cannot find suitable employment?
>
> Where are all of the sex workers that leave and find jobs? Why isn't there anyone lobbying to give incentives to hire women attempting to leave prostitution rather than laws that make it harder than ever for a prostitute to start a new life? I noticed prostitution is the only misdemeanor on the list of crimes that prohibit someone from having their record sealed, why?

In her reply she stated simply, "I wish I had fast answers but I don't, I'm sorry."

It seems prudent to think of these answers prior to leading a campaign to force change in an industry you don't understand and then proceeding to abandon the individuals you proclaim to save when they are lost in the transition.

I have lost a great deal to the stigma associated with my work. So much that I threw in the towel and tried it their way. I went to school. I got a job. I was "saved" from sex work and now I am a prisoner. Unless I can pay $6,000 while earning $200 a week to buy my freedom, I will be a prisoner of this company until March of 2018.

For me, sex work was my best option. I had done it my whole life. In my heart and my soul I am deeply connected to the industry and I proudly self-identify as a whore. I just want to have my freedom back and do what I love. I don't want to be saved.

I miss the admiration and gratitude of my clients, and hope that one day I can return to my true calling—sharing love and teaching the sex positive lessons of the Tantras—if I can only figure out a way to escape from the debt bondage that I've been trafficked into since accepting this "real job."

sex work is forced in some way. However, others argue that it is a woman's right to become a sex worker, and that to take that right away is misogynistic (Deady, 2011).

Kelly's story (see Case Study: The Challenges Faced by a Prostitute by Choice on page 133) highlights the intricacies in defining an act as prostitution (choosing to be a sex worker) versus human trafficking (being forced into sexual slavery).

While it is most definitely reasonable to suggest that sex work is an undesirable field, only selected in the direst of conditions, ultimately, if an individual can make the choice to leave sex work, legally this is not human trafficking. In other words, if the sex worker can quit, this is not human trafficking (Batsyukova, 2007). Nevertheless, the differences between the sex worker who can't leave his or her situation and the sex worker who can may be barely visible. For this reason, many wonder whether prostitution and sex trafficking can ever be considered completely independent (Lee & Persson, 2015).

Batsyukova (2007) provides a useful table comparing and contrasting prostitution and human trafficking, arguing that the roles are completely separate. Prostitution does not cause human trafficking; rather, it is the exploitation of sex workers that drives prostitution. Choice seems to be the distinction between prostitution and sex trafficking. However, consider the description of the sex worker in relation to choice (second row, third column of Table 6.2). Batsyukova (2007) suggests that while prostitution is considered voluntary, the worker may not be able to choose the client or the form of sexual activity. One may ask, how, then, is this voluntary? If the sex worker does not feel comfortable with the client, is he or she allowed to refuse to provide service?

Consider other services, albeit less exploitative ones, such as housecleaning. Like prostitution, this isn't an enviable occupation. Nevertheless, a housecleaner chooses what houses to clean, perhaps based on how much they will pay, how long it will take to clean the house, and so forth. The housecleaner can refuse to

Table 6.2 Batsyukova's Comparison of Sex Work to Prostitution

Criteria	Human Trafficking for Sexual Exploitation	Prostitution
Nature	Exploitative	Exploitative
Choice	Individuals are forced to provide sex services; they are forced to work even if sick—involuntary involvement.	Voluntary involvement. But women man not have control over which clients they serve or the nature of sexual activity.
Compensation	Victims are not paid or their compensation is very limited.	Workers are paid for the services they provide.
Concept of consumers	Both are highly dependent on the male demand for sex services.	
Vision of service providers	Women are likely to be seen as commodified bodies.	
Legal status	Always illegal	It may be legal, illegal, or regulated.

Source: Batsyukova's (2006, p.48).

take a job if he or she feels it is not advantageous. Can the sex worker do the same? If so, is this human trafficking? Is this prostitution? These are the tough questions that U.S. states as well as other countries must consider as they design their prostitution and human trafficking laws.

Regulating Prostitution

The United States

The "world's oldest profession" has been present in the United States for hundreds of years. In the 19th century, prostitution was frowned upon but considered a necessary evil by many, resulting in red-light districts where women prostituted themselves in an underground world (Hennigan, 2004). During this time period, prostitution was generally controlled primarily through common laws such as those involving lewdness and disorderly conduct (Deady, 2011). The public had conflicting views of sex workers. While generally public opinion was sympathetic, believing that these women had no option other than to prostitute themselves, the public concurrently judged sex workers for choosing such a lowly and humiliating line of work (Capaul, 2013; Hennigan, 2004).

However, throughout the 20th century, there was a concerted effort to more formally deal with prostitution. Prostitutes gradually were understood to be victims. The term *white slave trade* became accepted, and no longer was prostitution viewed as a choice (Hennigan, 2014). As early as 1910, the United States made illegal the transport of women and youth across states lines for the purposes of commercial sex, otherwise known as the **Mann Act** or the White Slave Traffic Act. This law was upheld in *Hoke v. United States* (1913), a Supreme Court case that also gave states the right to regulate prostitution at state and local levels. By 1971, prostitution was made illegal across all states in the U.S. except for 13 counties in Nevada (Drexler, 1996; Law, 2000).

During the early part of the 20th century, there was a focus on regulating red-light districts. Both the new concern over the welfare of prostitutes and concerns regarding the protection of military men (who were understood to rely on prostitution) resulted in the regulation of brothels and red-light districts at state and local levels (Deady, 2011; Hennigan, 2004).

The Mann Act was refined in 1986 to narrow its language. In its original form, the law made illegal the transport of women across state lines for the "purposes of prostitution, or debauchery, or any other immoral purpose" (Mann Act, 1910). This broad language allowed for a wide application of the law. Not only were traffickers punished based on this law, but more commonly, adulterers were also punished for bringing girlfriends across state lines. The latter was not the intent of the law. Nevertheless, the law was not amended to exclude "any other immoral purpose" until 1986 (Deady, 2011)!

Today, several federal laws outlaw the selling of sex as well as related behaviors including soliciting sex, arranging for prostitution, and houses of prostitution

Challenge Yourself 6.2

What are the laws on prostitution in your state? Who are the laws aimed at? In other words, who is being punished? How do you feel about that? In your opinion, are these laws effective in reducing crime?

Given states' autonomy in creating laws, some states have more refined prostitution laws than others. Capaul (2013) asserts that prostitution can operationally be defined as incorporating three characteristics: level of engagement, sexual activity, and a fee. States vary on how well they specify these three characteristics in their laws. In regard to level of engagement, some states require the act to occur. In other words, a sexual act must be performed and a fee exchanged. In other states, the threshold for a crime is lower. Only an agreement to purchase a sexual act or an offer to provide a sexual act for a fee is necessary to be charged with prostitution.

Sexual activity is also defined differently in different states. Some states specifically list, in their statute, the forms of sexual contact that are included in the definition of prostitution. States may employ different terminology to describe sexual services, such as "sexual intercourse," "sexual conduct," "sexual contact," "deviant sexual activity," or "sexual intrusion" (Capaul, 2013).

Finally, regarding the fee, a small number of states require a monetary exchange for an act to be considered prostitution. Most are broader in their definition of a fee, allowing for payment in forms other than money (Capaul, 2013).

As apparent in this discussion, the components that are required to define the crime of prostitution vary by state. Nevertheless, in all states, prostitution is a crime. In all states, sellers and buyers of sex can be charged with crimes relating to prostitution. Not until 2000, with the passage of the Trafficking Victims Protection Act, did the U.S. acknowledge that the sex worker might not be acting on her own accord.

(e.g., brothels). Laws also exist to prohibit prostitution on or near U.S. military bases or travel outside the United States for the purposes of prostitution (U.S. Government Publishing Office, 2009a, 2009b, 2009c). Federal laws are transparent and certain in their treatment of prostitution. Prostitution is illegal. Those participating in the act as the seller, purchaser, or organizer will be punished. The U.S. federal government is intent that prostitution is demeaning, dehumanizing, and detrimental to the health of those involved, as noted in the 2007 Trafficking in Persons Report (U.S. Department of State, 2007).

While federal laws are important in defining the United States' position on prostitution, state-level laws are critical to ensure that prostitution is illegal. Aside from laws related to interstate commerce, such as the Mann Act (1910), states are given the responsibility of regulating commercial sex, thanks to *Hoke v. United States* (1913). While federal laws apply across the country, state laws specify what is considered criminal behavior within state lines. Each state has its own system of laws and infrastructure for handling criminal matters. Every state in the United States has laws criminalizing prostitution and the selling of sex except Nevada (see Focus on How What Happens in Vegas Stays in Vegas on page 140 for more on Nevada; Law, 2000).

Acknowledging the Nonconsenting Sex Worker in the U.S.

If you are reading this book and were raised in the United States, it may seem obvious that prostitution is a criminal offense in all states (except a few counties in Nevada). Prostitution is a crime, after all. But should prostitution be a criminal offense? And if you answer yes, should all parties be punished?

In 2000, the Trafficking Victims Protection Act (TVPA) acknowledged that prostitution is not always a choice. The emergence of this act validated the idea

You likely didn't blink at the title of this excerpt. Perhaps you even found it humorous. This popular tag line insinuates, if not encourages, bad behavior in Las Vegas. Las Vegas is known for excess—excess in alcohol, excess in food, excess in women. In actuality, prostitution is illegal in the city of Las Vegas. Nevertheless, it is an impossible problem to eliminate. Alan Feldman, spokesperson for MGM's Mirage, says that in spite of perceptions, hotels work hard to keep prostitution and sex work off their properties. Even with the help of security and surveillance, fully eliminating prostitution from hotels is a relentless task (LasVegasNow.com, 2007).

However, not far from Las Vegas, prostitution is legal. In counties with fewer than 700,000 residents, prostitution offered in brothels (and only brothels) is considered legal. As of 2016, 19 brothels were operating in Nevada (M. Martinez, 2016). To legally work in a brothel, prostitutes are required to receive sexually transmitted disease testing, including monthly HIV and syphilis testing. Patrons of the brothels are required to wear condoms. Brothel owners are required to disclose financial records and pass a background investigation. Prostitutes are able to negotiate their own fees, sometimes pricing out the client if they don't want to serve a specific client (Brents & Hausbeck, 2006). Brothel rooms have panic buttons and the doors don't lock from the inside, for the protection of the sex worker (Lopez, 2016).

Christine Parreira, a PhD student at the University of Nevada, Las Vegas, chose to start working at a legal brothel in Nevada while doing her research. She reported that the women in the brothel were content and in control of the clients they worked with and what they did with those clients. Parreira reported that of 50 sex workers she interviewed, only five reported having experienced violence as a sex worker (Lopez, 2016). Parreira also noted the benefits of legalized brothels, including revenue to the county they are located in.

Of her time as a sex worker, Parreira said,

This work helped me pay for school and helped me pay for really everything. It's afforded me a better lifestyle without a doubt. People need to know that this is a job just like any other. Yes, some of us had drug problems, and others have been molested, but there are also doctors, lawyers and secretaries that have been molested and do drugs. These stereotypes don't just exist in sex work. (Lopez, 2016)

Brents and Hausbeck (2005), in their continued research on the topic of legalized prostitution in Nevada, found support for the claim that legalized prostitution protects sex workers through regulation and policy. Based on interviews with prostitutes, managers, and policy makers in Nevada, they found that the current regulations of brothels in Nevada reduce the risk of three forms of violence: interpersonal violence against prostitutes, violence against community order, and sexually transmitted diseases as violence.

Legalized prostitution in Nevada is not without its critics. The *Los Angeles Times* wrote a scathing article in 2015 condemning legal brothels. The article described the legalization of sex work in Nevada as antiquated, unpopular, and likely to be abolished soon (Glionna & Panzar, 2015). Interviewees for the articles indicated that the brothels are not profitable and have been relegated to the "cow counties." A woman interviewed by the *New York Times Magazine* agreed with some of these criticisms, stating that the Nevada brothels were too regulated and the sex workers had few freedoms compared to prostitutes in Australia (Bazelon, 2016).

Sex workers corroborate the excessive regulations controlling the Nevada brothels. In fact, there are more sex workers working illegally in Las Vegas than in the legal brothels. The reality is that most of these sex workers are desperate for money and don't have a better way of earning it.

The allure of not sharing money with the "house" and the elimination of health check requirements entice some to take on the risks of prostituting in illegal markets. Further, regulations in Nevada, while perhaps enhancing the health and safety of sex workers, also result in financial benefits to the counties. This leaves some questioning whether the focus of regulation is on protecting sex workers or bringing in revenues (Law, 2000).

While there may be opponents to Nevada's policies on prostitution, others see it as progressive and consistent with European countries that embrace legalized prostitution. Brents and Hausbeck (2001), well-informed sociologists on the topic of legalized prostitution, acknowledge both sides of this debate. Nevada's prostitution laws are seemingly contradictory. Brothels are legal but not treated the same as other service-based businesses. Sex workers are within their rights to practice their professions but still experience challenges because of their chosen profession. Brents and Hausbeck (2001) argue that Nevada is caught between "old boy" policies and modern thinking when it comes to legalized prostitution. At some point the state will need to determine if it intends to maintain its legalized prostitution in a framework consistent with forward-thinking ideas (consistent with countries such as Australia) or cast the policies off as relics from a time gone by and amend policies to be more consistent with the rest of the U.S.

that prostitution is not so simple. There are times (more than we are comfortable admitting) when someone labeled a consenting sex worker is not, but rather a victim. There are times when an entrepreneurial pimp is actually a trafficker. The TVPA provides a way to distinguish between these roles criminally. However, distinguishing that fine line between a consenting sex worker and a victim can be nearly impossible at times. Some believe it is because the line doesn't exist. Others disagree.

The United States has come a long way in its regulation of prostitution. From acceptance to use of common law to specific federal and state laws, the U.S. has taken a hard stance on prostitution statutorily. However, many question whether the focus of these laws is misguided. What we have historically defined as prostitution is rampant in the U.S. Perhaps our focus on punishing the prostitute is ineffective? Perhaps punishment is not sufficient, or even appropriate, for reducing prostitution, especially given our understanding now that oftentimes prostitution is really trafficking. High demand, minimal consequences for pimps and traffickers, and the push and pull factors that result in an endless supply of humans willing to enter the ugly life of prostitution are all factors that must be tackled if we are to eliminate exploitation of persons for the purposes of commercial sex. The TVPA is a start. But often it is difficult to know whether prostitution laws or the TVPA should be applied to a crime. Is the sex worker a criminal or a victim? This challenge makes it especially critical to consider the impact of prostitution laws in the United States on the rate of human trafficking (Cho, Dreher, & Neumayer, 2013).

After reviewing international laws on prostitution, this chapter will explore the most popular approaches to controlling prostitution.

Global Perspectives

International law is somewhat confusing on its prostitution messaging. While the UN Convention for the Suppression of the Traffic in Persons (United Nations General Assembly, 1949) explicitly calls for the suppression of prostitution, the more recent international Protocol to Prevent, Suppress and Punish Trafficking in Persons Especially Women and Children, Supplementing the United Nations Convention Against Transnational Organized Crime (United Nations General Assembly, 2000c) does not directly comment on the role of prostitution in the prevalence of trafficking.

Figure 6.2 Analysis of Legalized Prostitution in 100 Countries

Illegal		Limited Legality	Legal	
39 Countries Combined Population: 2.05 billion		12 Countries Combined Population: 1.91 billion	49 Countries Combined Population: 1.41 billion	
Afghanistan	Lithuania	Australia	Argentina	Guatemala
Albania	Malta	Bangladesh	Armenia	Honduras
Angola	North Korea	Bulgaria	Austria	Hungary
Antigua and	Philippines	Canada	Belgium	Indonesia
Barbuda	Romania	Iceland	Belize	Ireland
Bahamas	Rwanda	India	Bolivia	Israel
Barbados	Saint Kitts and Nevis	Japan	Brazil	Italy
Cambodia	Saint Lucia	Malaysia	Chile	Kyrgyzstan
China	Saint Vincent and	Norway	Colombia	Latvia
Croatia	Grenadines	Spain	Costa Rica	Luxembourg
Cuba	Saudi Arabia	Sweden	Cyprus	Mexico
Dominica	Slovenia	United States	Czech Republic	Netherlands
Egypt	South Africa		Denmark	New Zealand
Grenada	South Korea		Dominican Republic	Nicaragua
Guyana	Suriname		Ecuador	Panama
Haiti	Thailand		El Salvador	Paraguay
Iran	Trinidad and Tobago		Estonia	Peru
Iraq	Uganda		Ethiopia	Poland
Jamaica	United Arab Emirates		Finland	Portugal
Jordan			France	Senegal
Kenya			Germany	Singapore
Liberia			Greece	Slovakia
				Switzerland
				Turkey
				United Kingdom
				Uruguay
				Venezuela

Source: Adapted from ("100 Countries," 2016).

A study of 100 counties, selected based on their diversity in regard to religion, geographic location, and prostitution policies, examined policies related to prostitution, brothel ownership, and pimping (ProCon.org, n.d.). As apparent in Figure 6.2, over a quarter of the population in these 100 countries lived where prostitution was acceptable. Countries were identified as having legal, illegal, or limited legality prostitution. Legal prostitution was defined as legalized prostitution, brothel ownership, and pimping. Those countries identified as having limited liability defined one of the included measures of prostitution as illegal or had varying prostitution policies across jurisdictions. For example, in Australia, states range from having decriminalized prostitution to legal prostitution to illegal prostitution. Australian states also vary in their legality of brothels. In India, while brothel ownership and pimping are illegal, prostitution has limited legality. **Solicitation** is illegal, as is prostitution in public spaces. But prostitution is not inherently illegal.

International Trends in Regulating Prostitution

All Asian countries criminalize prostitution, specifically the selling of prostitution (Godwin, 2012). In Europe, various models are applied to prostitution, best described by Czech mathematician Jakub Marian (H. Miller, 2017). Those countries using the German model, described in more depth below, regulate prostitution in a similar manner as they do any other "service" profession. Brothels are legal, but regulated, in most of these countries. The laissez-fair model operates in several European countries where prostitution operates outside the legal realm (H. Miller, 2017). Prostitutes work, but the profession is unregulated. Operating brothels and pimping are criminal offenses, but brothels are typically in operation under the guise of hourly motels and spas. The Swedish model, also known as the Nordic model, focuses more on payment for sex rather than selling. While prostitution is not legal, in the event that sexual services are traded for money, the client, not the sex worker, is punished. The prohibitionist model is the most severe, with prostitution being illegal and the sex worker punished. Figure 6.3 shows the countries that fall into each of these categories.

Prostitution in Central and South America is less defined, with prostitutes operating in the gray areas between legal and illegal. Except in Uruguay, where prostitution is regulated and prostitutes are eligible to receive protections by the government, prostitution is a very dangerous and unprotected profession in this region of the world (T. Rogers, 2014). RedTraSex (n.d.), the Network of Women Sex Workers for Latin America and the Caribbean, advocates the recognition and protection of sex workers in Central and South America.

At this point one could argue, as an academic debate, that it is a complicated task to determine whether prostitution is truly a choice. The debate becomes even more complicated as we move past a hypothetical discussion into the "real" world. Beyond the discussion of whether the label of prostitution requires agency (free choice) is the discussion of how we react to prostitution. If we assume that sex workers have no choice, or that their options for income are so limited that prostitution is their only option, then prostitution is in fact synonymous with human trafficking. However, if we believe individuals have the free will to choose to enter into sex work, then one should ask, how do we regulate this type of work? Should it be legal to engage in sex work? Should it be legal to purchase sex? As noted earlier in the chapter, prostitution is illegal in nearly all jurisdictions in the U.S. and is frowned upon internationally. However, it is quite prevalent. The debate on whether or not prostitution should be legal is ongoing.

Figure 6.3   Reactions to Prostitution in European Countries

German Model	Laissez-faire Model	Swedish Model	Prohibitionist Model
• Austria	• Belgium	• France	• Andorra
• Germany	• Bulgaria	• Iceland	• Albania
• Greece	• Cyprus	• Ireland	• Belarus
• Hungary	• Czech Republic	• Northern Ireland	• Bosnia and
• Latvia	• Denmark	• Norway	Herzegovina
• Netherlands	• Estonia	• Sweden	• Croatia
• Switzerland	• Finland		• Kosovo
• Turkey	• Italy		• Liechtenstein
	• Luxembourg		• Lithuania
	• Poland		• Macedonia
	• Protugal		• Moldova
	• Slovakia		• Montenegro
	• Slovenia		• Russia
	• Spain		• Serbia
	• United Kingdom		• Ukraine

Data source: Marian, 2017.

Advantages and Disadvantages of Regulation

This section discusses the advantages and disadvantages of varying levels of prostitution regulation. Figure 6.4 highlights the overlap between prostitution and sex trafficking. Figure 6.5 maps country-level prostitution regulations to the U.S. State Department's rankings for countries. Interestingly, there appears to be little relationship between U.S. Department of State rankings and prostitution regulations. More countries than not legalize prostitution. Countries with legalized prostitution fall into Tier 1, Tier 2, Tier 2 Watch List, and Tier 3 categories. What some may find interesting is that only five countries that make prostitution illegal fall into the Tier 1 category (assigned to those countries identified as effective

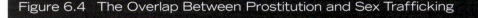

Figure 6.4 The Overlap Between Prostitution and Sex Trafficking

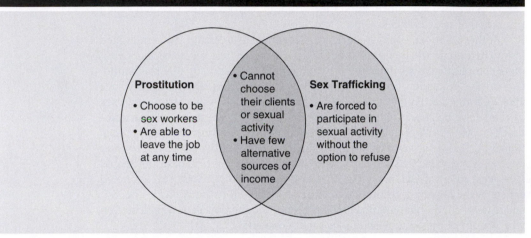

Figure 6.5 Legal Status of Prostitution by U.S. State Department Rankings

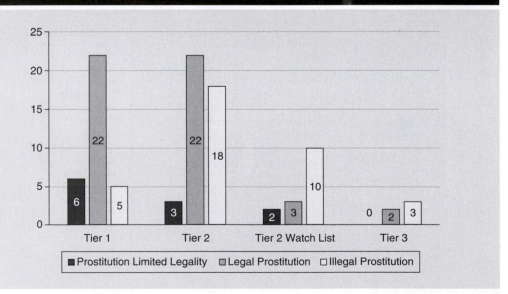

at combating trafficking). Findings such as this help to explain why advocates on both sides of the debate argue that their position will slow the slippery slide from consensual prostitution into trafficking from sex work. Any factors that limit an individual's agency in choosing sex work make that person vulnerable to sex trafficking. Inarguably, a relationship exists between prostitution and human trafficking, as noted in Figure 6.4. Following will be a discussion on the different viewpoints regarding the regulation of prostitution and the impact of regulation on sex trafficking.

Efforts to Control Prostitution and Their Impacts on Sex Trafficking

Although the legalization of prostitution has been widely debated, it appears that conclusions are based on "anecdotal evidence, but little in terms of systematic and rigorous research" (Cho et al., 2013). Even without strong data, it is apparent that the demand for prostitution seems insatiable. Regulations that prohibit prostitution both domestically and internationally don't appear to be effective. Prostitution is a booming business, often at the expense of the sex worker. With no way out and serious mental and physical health consequences, the situation, globally, is dire (Burnette, Lucas, & Ilgen, 2008; V. J. Greenbaum, 2014). There are many different ways to put the prostitution puzzle together (reviewed below), with some models fitting all the pieces better than others.

While the trigger response may be to argue for keeping prostitution illegal, it may not be so simple. As observed in Table 6.2, the legal status of prostitution does not seem to predict the TIP Report ranking. Both countries that legalize and criminalize prostitution are ranked as Tier 1 countries. One may argue that this table isn't useful, as the TIP Report focuses less on the amount of human trafficking than on the response to trafficking. The table can't allow conclusions regarding the prevalence of prostitution and trafficking in a country. Rather, it shows that however a country reacts to prostitution is not predictive of how it reacts to human trafficking. Both countries that criminalize and countries that legalize prostitution are making serious efforts to reduce human trafficking. This is an important point to make. This table suggests that human trafficking reduction efforts can be successful even when prostitution is legal. Thus, the trigger response to say that prostitution is bad, and that the only way to reduce it—and human trafficking—is to make it illegal, may not be accurate.

Given the reality that the legal status of prostitution does not necessarily predict human trafficking, it is appropriate to consider the various ways prostitution is handled throughout the world. The debate on the legalization of prostitution can be divided into four viewpoints—criminalization, abolition, decriminalization, and legalization (Brents & Hausbeck, 2001, 2005; Capaul, 2013; Deady, 2011; Weitzer, 2000). This next section considers each of these viewpoints and provides case studies on how the policies are implemented.

Criminalization

Those who embrace the **criminalization model** believe that prostitution should be considered illegal and criminally prosecuted. Most in this camp, including the U.S. government and most countries in Asia and the Pacific, believe that prostitution exacerbates the human trafficking problem (Bureau of

Public Affairs, 2004; Deady, 2011; Farley, 2009; Godwin, 2012; Hughes, 2000; U.S. State Department, 2007). They believe that legalization will not decrease sex trafficking because prostitution is "almost always forced and rarely voluntary" (Cho et al., 2013). Sex workers are exposed to violence, sexually transmitted diseases, and psychological manipulations (Law, 2000; O'Connor & Healy, 2006). Further, research shows that when prostitution is legalized, the largest profits still go straight to traffickers and there is an increased demand for sex slaves and foreign women (Hughes, 2002; Swedish Ministry of Industry, Employment, and Communications, 2004). In short, the context in which individuals enter into prostitution, combined with a lack of evidence showing that alternative policies such as regulation are effective, results in the conclusion that the act of prostitution should be criminalized.

The criticisms of criminalization are plentiful and legitimate. Moral opponents to criminalization argue that selling sex is not immoral but rather a purely economic transaction, like the sale of other commercial goods. A sex worker should have the right to support himself or herself with the sale of sex. To disallow that delegitimizes a sex worker's autonomy.

Further, the current U.S. policy, which criminalizes prostitution, does not seem to be effective (e.g., Deady, 2011; Law, 2000). Millions and millions of dollars are spent annually prosecuting sex workers as they cycle through the criminal justice system over and over again. Additionally, sex trafficking continues to occur in the U.S. in spite of the criminalization of prostitution.

Opponents also note that criminalizing prostitution does little to protect sex workers. It fails to prevent the sex worker from returning to prostitution and in fact may make it more difficult to leave the life of sex work. It fails to offer the sex worker protection from victimization or a means of escape in the event that the sex work is not consensual. Further, prostitution has a stigmatizing label. While street prostitution is less common (as most solicitation has moved online), communities that still have street prostitution are largely stigmatized and broken down (Weitzer, 2000). Ultimately, the benefits of criminalization are unclear. What seems more likely is that the criminalization of prostitution has done little to reduce prostitution or mitigate the health consequences associated with prostitution domestically or internationally (Godwin, 2012; Law, 2000). Perhaps it is time to look to other policies.

Challenge Yourself 6.3

Bazelon (2016), in a compelling article on whether or not prostitution should be a crime, details the policies of President George W. Bush. Nongovernmental organizations that wanted funding to combat international trafficking or to conduct AIDS research had to show they did not support the legalization or practice of prostitution. These policies are still in practice today; however, the Supreme Court concluded that the policy could not apply to U.S. organizations, as it limited their right to free speech. Nevertheless, foreign entities that receive federal funding to combat AIDS and trafficking must still sign anti-prostitution pledges. Bazelon (2016) questions whether Bush's relationship with Evangelicals and other religious groups influenced this policy. What do you think of this policy? Do you think politics plays into the U.S.'s policies on prostitution? If so, is this a problem? Why or why not?

Abolition

In the continuum from criminalization to legalization of prostitution falls the viewpoint of abolition. Otherwise known as the Swedish or Nordic model (Aleem, 2015; Cho et al., 2013), this viewpoint retains the concept of criminalizing prostitution but changes the focus of punishment. In the case of criminalization, everyone involved in the prostitution is at risk of being punished, including the prostitute. Given the many consequences that befall a sex worker with a criminal record, abolitionists believe that those who purchase sex should be punished but the sex worker should not (Brents & Hausbeck, 2001, 2005).

Those who hold this perspective generally believe that sex workers will be safer should the abolitionist model be implemented (Brents & Hausbeck, 2005). Where prostitution is criminalized, sex workers are less likely to come forward if they are victimized out of fear of arrest. Those who are victimizing sex workers know this sad truth. If sex workers did not fear the consequences of their behavior, they would be more likely to come forward and report victimization. Further, the sex worker is provided support and services to allow her to exit prostitution.

Supporters of this perspective believe it is also more effective than legalizing prostitution, as legalization would require regulations, and regulations would further stigmatize women and possibly label them (as we have seen in Brents & Hausbeck's [2001] research). Hobson (1990, as cited in Brents & Hausbeck, 2001) suggests that any regulation of prostitution designed within a patriarchal society will unavoidably stigmatize women in some way.

Of course, there are those who do not believe this model offers the best approach to prostitution. While Sweden reported a reduction in street prostitution ten years after the law was implemented, evidence showed that the reduction could simply be the result of solicitation moving online. The abolitionist model generally assumes that the sex worker is the victim (Aleem, 2015; Batsyukova, 2007). However, feminists and other advocates take issue with such a viewpoint. To label prostitutes as victims takes away their agency and ability to make choices about their own bodies (Aleem, 2015; Cho et al., 2013). For those who truly choose to prostitute themselves, the criminalization of paying customers prevents them from being able to support themselves (Anwar, 2007; Bazelon, 2016).

Further, Bazelon (2016) interviewed Swedish sex workers, who highlighted some of the unanticipated consequences associated with the abolitionists' movement. Their findings indicated that criminalizing the demand side forced the industry to go more underground, as sex purchasers wanted to avoid getting caught. Additional challenges associated with being a sex worker in an abolitionist country included getting deported, losing custody of children, and being evicted. The evictions stemmed from landlords' fear of being punished for knowing a sex worker was selling sex. Sweden's response to these issues was to consider this a form of deterrence. Ultimately, the goal of the abolitionist movement is to reduce prostitution. These challenges faced by sex workers may force them to look for other forms of employment and means to support themselves. It seems, according to some opponents of the abolitionist model, that the focus still needs adjusting. Rather than punishing buyers, more attention needs to be paid to supporting sex workers (Bazelon, 2016).

Nevertheless, this type of model is likely not viable in the U.S. Sweden and other countries provide a much more stable safety net for those looking to exit the sex industry. The U.S. simply does not offer the same resources, such as family services, state-funded universities, and so forth, as those offered in countries like Sweden (Bazelon, 2016).

Prior to 1999, prostitution was legal in Sweden, although brothels were illegal (Cho, Dreher, & Neumayer, 2014). In 1999, the Swedish government passed a law banning prostitution and making the purchase of sex illegal and punishable with prison, fines, or both. This model is known as the Nordic model, the Swedish model, or the abolitionist model (Aleem, 2015; Cho et al., 2013). The model focuses on shifting criminal liability away from sex workers, who in many cases come from vulnerable backgrounds, and instead punishes the johns and the pimps (Cho et al., 2013).

In addition to a change in punishment strategy, this approach focuses on protecting the prostitute, including providing a strong welfare state, as well as offering services and strategies for those who do not want to remain in the sex-selling industry. Extensive training of police officers and a general education campaign are also important to the abolitionist movement. Sweden invested in raising awareness that prostitutes were victims rather than criminals (Aleem, 2015).

Almost a decade after the law went into effect in Sweden, data showed a significant decline in the number of sex trafficking victims and prostitutes in the country, especially in comparison to neighboring countries in Europe (Aleem, 2015). More specifically, data showed a reduction in prostitution between 1999 and 2002 (Cho et al., 2014). Consequently, Sweden concluded that their new laws reduced the demand for prostitution, and thus the demand for trafficking (Batsyukova, 2007). The perceived success of the law prompted other countries, including Norway, Iceland, Canada, and Northern Ireland, to adopt similar laws (Aleem, 2015; Bazelon, 2016).

According to the 2016 TIP Report, Sweden continues to be ranked as a Tier 1 for the country's government's efforts to combat human trafficking (U.S. Department of State, 2016). However, the number of prosecutions and convictions continues to remain very low, there having been only two sex trafficking prosecutions and convictions in 2016. One of the reasons prosecutions have proved difficult has to do with the fact that johns have to be caught receiving or about to receive services, and that can be challenging. Another reason is the apparent lack of understanding about human trafficking by judges, which according to the 2016 TIP Report could lead to "fewer convictions and less stringent sentences" (p. 355).

Decriminalization

Decriminalization offers another approach to prostitution, moving down the continuum of policies toward legalization. In this scenario, prostitution is neither legal nor illegal but is regulated through traditional employment and health policies (Brents & Hausbeck, 2001; Deady, 2011). All laws associated with prostitution are eliminated. Many prefer this approach to legalization, which could be viewed as simply allowing the State to act as the pimp rather than individuals (Law, 2000).

During the 1970s there was an impressive push to decriminalize prostitution, aligned with the movement to improve the rights of women more generally. Prostitutes began to organize and vocalize their desire to be able to operate in the same way as other independent businesses. Decriminalization gained traction, and major organizations have come out in favor of this approach to prostitution, including the United Nations, the American Civil Liberties Union, Human Rights Watch, Amnesty International, and the National Organization for Women (NOW; Amnesty International, 2016; Bazelon, 2016; Brents &

Hausbeck, 2001). Advocates today believe that decriminalization will assist in reducing the health risks associated with prostitution, including AIDS and other sexually transmitted diseases, as well as allow the criminal justice system to focus their resources on traffickers rather than consenting adults (Bazelon, 2016; Lee & Persson, 2015). In spite of strong support for the **decriminalization model**, there is no evidence to suggest that it reduces human trafficking (Lee & Persson, 2015).

In fact, there are some who believe decriminalization has had little impact on improving the lives of sex workers. A woman interviewed for the *New York Times Magazine* reported that even in New Zealand, when prostitution is decriminalized, prostitutes are still hesitant to come forward due to the stigma related to being a sex worker (Bazelon, 2016). She opined that the legal status of prostitution will never fully protect sex workers and that the culture will need to change in order for prostitutes to truly feel no retribution for their chosen line of work. At the same time, she conceded that the police do assist if called upon and help to keep the sex workers safe.

Focus On
New Zealand

An example of decriminalization can be found in New Zealand. New Zealand neither condones nor condemns the prostitution of adults. The Prostitution Reform Act (PRA) of 2003 provides safeguards for sex workers, prevents individuals under the age of 18 from prostituting themselves, and states that prostitution against the will of the sex worker is prohibited. It further provides requirements, including background checks, for those who wish to own a brothel or employ sex workers. Sex workers are considered to be "at work" when engaging in sex work and fall under New Zealand's health and labor laws (Deady, 2011). Sex workers are permitted to take advantage of legal remedies in the event of being mistreated by an employer (e.g., forced to perform sexual acts), and the sex worker will experience no legal repercussions when coming forward to report victimization or other forms of harm.

The PRA further engaged the sex worker community by requesting aid from the New Zealand Prostitutes Collective (NZPC), which provides sex education to sex workers and acts as a union. The NZPC was able to advise and make recommendations in employment disputes for sex workers.

Perhaps most relevant to the current discussion, the PRA mandated an oversight committee whose responsibility, in part, was to assess whether decriminalization resulted in more vulnerable persons entering into prostitution. It also monitored changes in the number of sex establishments, and whether the new policy created a safe haven for traffickers. Five years after decriminalization was implemented, there was no evidence of an increase in sex establishments or that the motivation for entering sex work was anything other than financial. In other words, there was no increase in the number of individuals entering into prostitution. The committee also noted that there was no evidence of an increase in the number of trafficking victims. They attributed this to the country's stringent legal system and the prohibition on non-residents working as prostitutes. Nevertheless, the U.S. criticized New Zealand in 2009 for not adequately acknowledging the possibility that sex workers were not engaging in prostitution willingly and for failing to implement an adequate human trafficking awareness campaign. New Zealand argued that sex workers retained employment protections that would encourage them to report any trafficking situation to the NZPC; the industry essentially polices itself (Deady, 2011).

Case Study

India's Sex Work Collectives

In India, street prostitution and brothels are illegal. However, indoor prostitution is legal. Sex workers have created collectives in India that have garnered some political power, thanks to the support of the Gates Foundation (Bazelon, 2016). In addition to offering political security, the collectives have changed the landscape of sex work in parts of India. In Karnataka, over 60,000 sex workers organized to engage policy makers and police officers on an education campaign about sex work. This campaign resulted in fewer arrests, less violence, and fewer reports of HIV.

Bharati Dey is the head of the Durbar Mahila Samanwaya Committee, a collective organizing 75,000 sex workers from the West Bengal region. She told her story to Amnesty International in 2016.

I was a sex worker at one time, but I am retired now. I went into sex work because my husband left and I had to feed myself and my two sons. Sex work offered me a good amount of money and flexible working hours. I worked in a rural area, in a brothel. At that time we had so many problems; from police raids to violence from these *goondas* (hooligans) who would come to the brothels and beat the sex workers.

That is why Durbar was formed—because these problems, violence and discrimination, were being faced by all sex workers in all red light districts. Now we stand together fighting these things. With the formation of the collective, violence has gone down and almost stopped. Relations with the police [are] much better now too—they will listen if sex workers have something to say.

Organizing and being in a collective is very important when you are a sex worker because otherwise you can be vulnerable.

Durbar has really made a big difference for sex workers in this area, and for their children too. When I was working in a brothel, I had my two boys with me because there was no [other] option. Usually in a brothel, a sex worker only has one room so when we are with a client, the children have nowhere to go. The environments in the red light districts are not good for children and especially not if they are trying to study. We also used to find that the children of sex workers were bullied at school, leading to high drop-out rates.

One of Durbar's missions is to support the children of sex workers—to open opportunities for them and to end discrimination. So very early on we opened a residential home. At the moment there are 86 children at the home and they attend the government school nearby. At the hostel there are provisions for vocational training and computer skills training. There are also provisions for sports—football training, yoga training, dance training, basketball, volleyball and all these things and a few indoor games.

The facilities are so good that boys and girls from the local area come to the hostel to take part in our various sporting activities that are going on. So the children are able to mix with mainstream society and the stigma is reducing. Now children can say "I am the child of a sex worker."

For over 10 years Durbar has been fighting against the amendment of the Immoral Traffic Prevention Act [to make buying sexual services illegal in India] because these laws create tension and problems for sex workers. We know that the proposals before Parliament since 2006 to criminalize buying sex will make things harder for us and give us more problems with the police. When the police used to raid us, it was very frightening for the children; and if a client behaves badly you cannot report it. More laws against us may bring these problems back. When it was first proposed we mobilized 9,000 sex workers to march on the Parliament [in the capital New Delhi] to protest. The amendment was not passed but still today we are doing advocacy in the Parliament to ensure that no further legal sanctions are placed on us. Sex workers are workers and we need our rights. This should be recognized as a profession rather than as a crime.

One of the things I am most proud of is the self-regulatory boards that we have set up in some of the red light districts. These are committees of sex workers who, among other things, conduct peer to peer education on issues like safe sex and identifying anyone who is below 18 years of age or who might be working as a sex worker against their will.

We do not want minors working as sex workers, or anyone who is not doing it as their own choice.

Sometimes we find girls who are too young, or slightly older women who have not been able to pay off their dowry and so the husband has sent them out to earn money in the brothels. We talk with all the newcomers and try to find out how they have come into sex work. We can offer them counselling or, if they are too young, a place at the residential home where they can learn vocational skills or computing. Only if they are over 18 and willing can they join the profession.

We have come a very long way in 20 years as Durbar. Whenever we go anywhere now, we introduce ourselves as sex workers. If we aren't able to tell people we are sex workers, how will we ever be able to fight for our rights? First we need to introduce ourselves as sex workers and then we can get people to listen. Previously we did not even have the courage to speak with someone at a senior level like the policymakers. But when we go under the banner of Durbar we are given the time, we are given the due respect, and we are able to speak to these people on better terms.

Source: Excerpt taken from Amnesty International blog in 2016, written by Bharati Dey (https://www.amnesty.org/en/latest/news/2016/05/rita-roy-and-bharati-dey-sex-worker-testimony-india/).

Legalization

Like the other approaches to prostitution, there are those in favor and those against the legalization of prostitution. Legalization of prostitution essentially makes the act permissible under state-enforced regulations.

Supporters of legalized prostitution cite the benefits, as described earlier in the discussion of Nevada sex workers. Those benefits include increased safety to the sex worker in terms of health[1] and reduced violence, tax revenues to the state, and control over brothel owners (Batsyukova, 2007; Brents & Hausbeck, 2005). Those in favor of legalization cite research showing that women and men do sometimes choose this lifestyle (Kennedy et al., 2007; Vanwesenbeeck, 2013). Legalization has sometimes been seen as a symbol of women's sexual liberation (Batsyukova, 2007; Cho, 2016). It is further argued that by legalizing prostitution, there will be more willing sex workers, thus reducing the number of forced workers (Cho et al., 2014). Ultimately, liberal feminists believe that the focus should be on reducing forced prostitution rather than eliminating prostitution more generally. This sentiment is in direct conflict with the criminalization and abolitionist movements, which both focus on reducing prostitution (Outshoorn, 2005). Interestingly, both sides of this debate believe their solution will protect sex workers from violence, health risks, and forced prostitution.

---

[1] However, these benefits are effective only when they are mandated, as they are in Nevada. When health benefits such as health checks and condom usage are not mandated, such as in Germany and the Netherlands, concerns exist (Seals, 2015).

Opponents to legalization object to the desensitization that comes with legalization. They argue that legalization legitimizes sex work and the sex industry more generally. Language such as "clients," "sex entrepreneurs," "state sex economy," "suppliers" and "supply" becomes acceptable (O'Connor & Healy, 2006). Is this good, bad, or doesn't it matter? That is an opinion that you, the reader, will need to formulate for yourself. Nevertheless, many believe that legitimizing this language also legitimizes pimps, traffickers, the profit of the state from the sex industry, and the stance that prostitution is acceptable work. For some, prostitution is a legitimate choice, but for many, prostitution is a last resort. Do we want to say that if no other option exists, prostitution should be on the table as a reasonable option? Is it really the same as other independent businesses such as owning a shop, running a restaurant, or consulting?

In regard to human trafficking, opponents of legalized prostitution adamantly believe that legalization increases human trafficking, and they have evidence to back up these claims. While it is difficult to truly understand the impact of prostitution on human trafficking, due to the clandestine nature of both, there is some evidence to show that rates of human trafficking increase in those countries that have legalized prostitution (Cho, 2016; Cho et al., 2013; Jakobsson & Kotsadam, 2013). Further, recent research shows that policies put in place to protect sex workers under a legalized approach may not actually provide protection, and in some cases may make the sex workers' situations worse (Cho, 2016). It is suggested that the legalized approach to prostitution makes the assumption that by legalizing prostitution, forced prostitution will be eliminated. This assumption informs protection policy and results in protection efforts that are not attentive to the unique abuses and challenges faced in situations of forced prostitution.

Further, there continues to be evidence of forced prostitution, even in countries with legalized prostitution (e.g., Germany and the Netherlands). Cho and colleagues (2013) found that legalization was no more effective than the abolitionist movement in reducing trafficking, based on a comparison of Germany, Denmark, and Sweden. In fact, in countries where prostitution is legalized, the underground market competes with the regulated sex workers and legal venues. This **black market** offers lower prices and unprotected sex, as seen in countries such as the Netherlands, where prostitution is legal (Batsyukova, 2007). Oftentimes, this black market is filled with women who have migrated (often illegally) from other countries.

Another factor, yet to be discussed in this chapter, is the movement, specifically of women (and some men), across borders for the purposes of sex work. Often, even when prostitution is legal, it is legal only for citizens. However, those are not the only individuals acting as sex workers in any country, including countries with legalized prostitution. Due to the many vulnerabilities discussed in this book, women are coerced or fraudulently taken across borders and end up in forced prostitution. These women are rarely protected by the policies in place for legal sex workers. In fact, these women are often criminalized for illegal migration. Instead of being offered protections, they are often punished for their efforts to support themselves through sex work (Cho, 2016; Outshoorn, 2005). The situation of foreign sex workers offers further ammunition to those who oppose legalization of prostitution.

A New Model?

Lee and Persson (2015) propose a new model that may allow for prostitution to occur but eliminate the forced supply that often comes with it. Essentially, the debate over prostitution stems from a desire to protect women. As noted in the discussion above, each position believes that its approach will best protect women. However, none of these positions has been able to eliminate the supply of sex workers forced into prostitution. Lee and Persson's (2015) analysis confirmed the inability of the criminalization and **abolition models** to minimize trafficking. Criminalization increases the costs associated with prostitution, more so for voluntary sex workers than for traffickers. Thus, while the aim of criminalization is to eliminate prostitution, it is effective only at reducing voluntary sex work and less effective at reducing trafficking. In fact, Lee and Persson (2015) find a modest increase in trafficking when prostitution is criminalized in certain contexts. Further, the criminalization of prostitution is damaging to both the voluntary sex worker and the victims of trafficking.

One might think, then, that reducing the penalties experienced by the sex worker and refocusing those penalties on the purchaser would sufficiently reduce demand, thus eliminating trafficking. While evidence shows that punishing the prostitute has no impact at best and increases trafficking at worst, strong enforcement on the demand side can be effective at reducing trafficking. However, increased penalties on the demand side often result in the movement of prostitution to the underground market, thus failing to eliminate trafficking. Further, the model reduces the opportunity for voluntary sex work.

Lee and Persson (2015) describe another model where sex workers become licensed. This comes closest to what we have described as legalized prostitution. In this case, trafficking is reduced, as more sex workers wish to become licensed and those interested in purchasing sex from a licensed sex worker are not penalized. Resources are then more available to tackle unlicensed sex workers—typically victims of trafficking.

Lee and Persson (2015) conclude that the abolitionist model may be the most effective at eliminating trafficking, but it is at the expense of voluntary sex workers. The legalized model, while still reducing trafficking, may be less effective, but it permits the existence of voluntary prostitution. Thus, Lee and Persson (2015) propose a new model, combining the abolitionist and legalization approaches to prostitution. In the **legalization model**, licensed sex workers and their clients would experience no penalties; however, those purchasing sex from unlicensed sex workers would be susceptible to criminal penalties. They suggest that a model such as this would reduce trafficking while increasing voluntary prostitution.

While Lee and Persson's (2015) findings are based on a hypothetical model of voluntary and involuntary prostitution, they are consistent with what the few actual studies have found regarding human trafficking and the various reactions to prostitution. Their proposed approach to prostitution is a provocative one, as it acknowledges the position that prostitution is a valid choice should it be voluntarily selected while still creating policies that directly impact human trafficking. Nevertheless, without any country actually implementing this model, we are left with the reality that the existing reactions, on their own, appear at best to have had minimal positive impacts on human trafficking.

Conclusion

Prostitution is a booming business in the United States and around the world. The costs associated with prostitution are high for the sex worker in terms of health, safety, criminal, and financial consequences. Does legalizing sex work hurt the status of women? Does legalizing sex work make women safer and empower them to make their own decisions? The contradictions are deep-rooted and divisive. All sides promote their viewpoint as helping to reduce involuntary prostitution—human trafficking.

While there are distinct viewpoints for and against the legalization of prostitution, the reality is that it can be difficult to assess the relevance of legalized prostitution to human trafficking, with research often finding conflicting results (e.g., Akee, Bedi, Basu, & Chau, 2010; Cho et al., 2013; Jakobsson & Kotsadam, 2013). As pointed out by Cho and colleagues (2013), legalized prostitution does not mean weaker human trafficking laws or enforcement. Similarly, outlawing prostitution does not mean that human trafficking laws are stricter. Reactions to prostitution and human trafficking are independent of one another and should be viewed in that manner. Tangling the two policies may result in a distortion of the cause-and-effect order. Countries with legalized prostitution and those where prostitution is criminalized both sit in the top tier of the U.S. State Department's annual Trafficking in Persons Report. Ultimately, prostitution and human trafficking are distinct concepts. If a person chooses to engage in sex work, there are valid moral, ethical, and legal debates as to the appropriateness of this job choice. However, there is much less debate, if any, on whether it is okay to force a person into prostitution. It is how countries criminalize human trafficking that will impact the prevalence of human trafficking in that country. Legalizing prostitution, criminalizing prostitution, or anything in between does not substitute for strong, enforceable human trafficking laws.

KEY WORDS

DISCUSSION QUESTIONS

1. What is your view on prostitution?

2. How do you feel about the quote at the start of the chapter?

3. Is prostitution equivalent to human trafficking?

4. If the sex worker has no control over which clients he or she services or the type of sexual activity engaged in, is this still voluntary? Explain your response.

5. If a sex worker truly chooses to work in this field, should it be stigmatized? Explain your response.

6. In the Focus on Why and How Pimps Do What They Do box on page 130, you read about pimps. How similar or different is this portrait of pimps from how pimps are displayed in the media?

RESOURCES

- European prostitution map: https://jakubmarian.com/prostitution-laws-in-europe/

- Fondation Scelles—Anti-Prostitution Foundation: http://www.fondationscelles.org/en/

- ProCon.org's description of legalized prostitution internationally: https://prostitution.procon.org/view.resource.php? resourceID=000772

Moving Past the Prostitution Debate

An Examination of Sex Trafficking

There are situations where you have to force girls by using rape, abuse or torture. When she begins to fear for her life, she stops resisting and starts working.

—South African brothel owner and human trafficker
(U.S. Department of State, 2017c)

Case Study

"Tonya"

Tonya spent night after night in different hotel rooms, with different men, all at the command of someone she once trusted. She was held against her will, beaten and made to feel like she had no other option at the time, all by the man she thought she loved.

She felt she deserved it. Tonya felt she couldn't escape. Afraid and confused, she thought the emotional and physical abuse she endured was her own doing.

Tonya (a pseudonym) was a victim of human trafficking. "He made me feel like I was doing it because I loved him, and in the end, we'd have a really good [financial] reward," Tonya said.

When Tonya was 13, she met Eddie (a pseudonym) at the apartment she was living in with her mother in the Dallas, Texas, area. His estranged wife was the property manager. Tonya was classmates with Eddie's stepdaughter, so the two would often see each other at the apartment and in the local grocery store. It was there that the two first exchanged numbers.

"It was a casual relationship at first. You could see there was a mutual connection. I thought he was cute," Tonya recalled. "I could tell he was really flirtatious with me. We would talk and flirt a

lot, but it was not much more than that until we met again when I was 15."

Things began to change one night when Tonya ran into Eddie at a bar. The two reconnected, the flirting picked up where it left off, and Tonya went home with Eddie that night. Tonya was a runaway at the time, so she eventually moved in with Eddie and the two began a relationship.

It was a "normal" arrangement at first. Tonya would cook, clean and look after Eddie's kids from time to time. However, it was when the two were at a party filled with alcohol and drugs that the relationship took a turn.

"He approached me and told me in so many words, 'I want you to have sex with this guy for money,'" Tonya said. "I was very uncomfortable and I kept saying no, I didn't want to do it. He kept telling me, 'If you love me, you'll do this. It's just one thing. Just try it.'"

After nearly 30 more minutes of constant pressure, Tonya agreed to have sex with the man. What she thought would be a one-time thing became an everyday routine for the next few weeks. Night after night and bar after bar, Tonya would go

(Continued)

(Continued)

out with Eddie while he advertised her to potential "suitors." Tonya thought she loved him. She felt she could deal with the physical toll the trafficking took on her body. It turned out that the hardest part to deal with was the emotional and psychological effects.

"Being able to sleep with that many people and live with myself and get up every day and keep doing it and just lying there being helpless was so hard," Tonya said.

Help eventually came for Tonya in the form of U.S. Immigration and Customs Enforcement's (ICE) Homeland Security Investigations (HSI) Special Agent Keith Owens. The Grand Prairie, Texas, police department had received a tip about Eddie's crimes and passed the case on to HSI Dallas. Owens and his team took over, moved in, and arrested Eddie.

Eddie pleaded guilty and was sentenced to 12 years in prison on May 29, 2015. During the sentencing hearing, Tonya had to testify. Having to hear and see the man who trafficked her was difficult, especially not knowing what the outcome would be and whether he would be convicted.

"Telling people publicly about what I'd been through made me feel more ashamed because I'd never told anyone or was open about it," Tonya said. "Keith and [HSI Dallas special agent] Allison [Schaefer] were the only two people I've really told everything to."

Tonya feels her life is a little better now. She doesn't think or talk about what she's been through and doesn't want people to know that was once a part of her life. Her focus is on moving forward.

"I want to finish getting my GED and go to community college, take on journalism, go to college and study political science and pre-law," she said. "I just want to live a normal life, accept my past, and not run from it."

Eventually, Tonya knows that she will have to talk about her experience again. If she has kids one day, she wants to be able to tell them what their mother went through. She wants them to know what to look out for and how to avoid going through something as awful as she did.

Until then, she passes along her words of encouragement to anyone who may be experiencing what she did. She wants any victims out there to know they are not alone.

"You're worth something. You're very important to someone," Tonya said. "No matter what he says, it's not true. You're worth something."

Tonya's story was shared by U.S. Immigrations and Customs Enforcement to raise awareness of human trafficking during National Human Trafficking and Slavery Prevention Month.

Source: Retrieved from https://www.ice.gov/features/human-trafficking-victim-shares-story

An Introduction to Sex Trafficking

Sex trafficking occurs when an individual involuntarily performs commercial sex acts. These acts are performed under force, fraud, or coercion. If the individual performing the acts is under 18 years old, force, fraud, or coercion is not required to define the act as sex trafficking. Individuals forced into sex trafficking live ugly and traumatic lives. This chapter opens with Tonya's story. Tonya was only a child when she entered into what she through was a loving, exclusive relationship. Her age and homeless status contributed to her vulnerability to her trafficker. Tonya's story reflects many of the vulnerabilities known to be linked to human trafficking, including poverty, homelessness, and age. More description of these vulnerabilities can be found in Chapter 4.

Stories like Tanya's are not uncommon. Accounts of sex trafficking, found in the mainstream media, on the websites of nongovernmental organizations (NGOs), and in empirical research, all indicate that the experience of being trafficked for sex is nothing if not traumatic. Before delving too far into the topic of sex trafficking, the text explores its prevalence globally. Following this, the reader will be led through the stages of sex trafficking. Finally, special populations, including children, males, and LGBTQ individuals, will be reviewed.

Explaining the Prevalence of Sex Trafficking

While the media has greatly improved the accuracy and frequency of its reporting on human trafficking during the past 15 years, it still is biased toward reporting on sex trafficking (Austin & Farrell, 2017; U.S. Department of State, 2017c). This has greatly raised the general public's awareness of this form of trafficking. As a result, sex trafficking globally may be more transparent than other forms of trafficking. As depicted in Figure 4.4 in Chapter 4, sex trafficking is the dominant form of trafficking internationally, with the exception of a few regions (United Nations Office on Drugs and Crime [UNODC], 2018a).

The estimated number of trafficking victims varies widely. While the Trafficking in Persons Report (TIP Report) estimates the world slave population to be somewhere between 600,000 and 800,000, nonprofits such as Free the Slaves estimate numbers well into the millions. As Kristof and WuDunn acknowledge as part of the Half the Sky Movement (n.d.c), all the estimates, though they vary, reflect an enormous population of victims. Kristof and WuDunn (2010) estimate that there are approximately 3 million women and girls being trafficking for sex around the world.

Data from the National Human Trafficking Resource Center (NHTRC, 2016) and the United Nations Office on Drugs and Crime (UNODC; 2018a) offer more nuanced descriptions of the rates of sex trafficking domestically and internationally. As explained in Chapter 4, sex trafficking appears to be the dominant form of trafficking in the United States, representing nearly three-fourths of cases reported to the Human Trafficking Hotline. However, this could be a consequence of a lack of tools to effectively identify instances of labor trafficking. From 2015 to 2016, labor trafficking increased at a rate of 45% (NHTRC, 2016). Improving our understanding of other forms of trafficking may change these patterns of detection domestically and globally.

Kristof and WuDunn (2010) estimate that sex trafficking generates approximately $27.8 billion every year globally, and that number is on the rise. The authors propose several factors that drive the uptick in sex trafficking. Those factors include the fall of the Soviet Union, globalization, and AIDS awareness. The fall of communism has resulted in extreme poverty across Eastern Europe, making girls and

Challenge Yourself 7.1

As with other crimes, awareness, changes in definition, and so forth impact our ability to identify the prevalence of human trafficking. In the case of sex trafficking, a greater awareness of the crime may be influencing the detection of it. How does this impact the reliability of estimates of sex trafficking (vs. labor trafficking) worldwide?

women from this region especially vulnerable to sex traffickers. Globalization is making travel and communication easier and cheaper, resulting in the trafficker's ability to provide supply (trafficking victims) to the demand (purchasers of sex) also becoming easier and cheaper. Finally, as individuals become more aware, and thus fearful, of AIDS, there is a growing demand for younger girls. Young virgins, it is assumed, are less likely to have contracted the virus than a woman who has had many sexual partners and (assumedly) frequent unprotected sex.

Stages in Sex Trafficking

When we think of **sex trafficking,** we often assume (or want to assume?) that the victims have been viciously kidnapped from their tranquil lives and thrown into nightmares. However, research tells us this is not the case (Burnette, Lucas, & Ilgen, 2008; Kennedy, Klein, Bristowe, Cooper, & Yuille, 2007; Lyneham & Richards, 2014; E. Rosen & Venkatesh, 2008; Vindhya & Dev, 2011; Zimmerman, Kiss, Hossain, & Watts, 2009). Rather, victims' introductions into the world of sex trafficking occur in a far less dramatic, but equally traumatic, manner. Research indicates that victims' experiences in sex trafficking typically occur in stages, starting with recruitment.

Recruitment

Generally, sex trafficking victims are recruited in a manipulative and intentional manner (Carpenter & Gates, 2016; Hom & Woods, 2013; Kennedy et al., 2007; Meshkovska, Siegel, Stutterhein, & Bos, 2015). Identifying vulnerable individuals, especially women and children, is the first step in the recruitment process. From there, the recruitment stage typically plays out in one of two ways. As discussed in the previous chapter, a common method of recruitment is through a pimp (aka, trafficker).[1] The trafficker acts as a boyfriend to a woman or girl wanting love and affection. After trust is gained, the trafficker asks the woman or girl to enter into commercial sex. Oftentimes violence and rape are used to condition a new recruit and prep her for her new role (Hom & Woods, 2013; Zimmerman et al., 2009). In these situations, the trafficker is capitalizing on the woman's or girl's want for love and affection. This emotional attachment can cause a good deal of trauma once the victim is "turned out" or prostituted. The victim often still feels love toward the trafficker while at the same time experiencing fear, confusion, and betrayal (Kennedy et al., 2007). Hom and Woods (2013) label this process **"pimp enculturation."**

A vice officer interviewed by Kennedy and colleagues (2007) indicated that a trafficker typically takes three to six months to recruit a new girl. However, the officer noted that he had seen a trafficker manipulate a girl into her trafficking situation in as little as 24 hours. The same vice officer observed that trafficking victims recruited through a trafficker were typically not coming from abusive childhoods but stable middle- and middle-upper-class homes. However, Hom and Woods's (2013) qualitative research, in which they interviewed providers who directly served sex trafficking victims, found evidence that prior trauma, including child abuse, rape, and violence, was a common precursor to trafficking experiences.

---

[1] Although the term *pimp* was used in Chapter 6 in the context of a discussion of prostitution, pimps will be referred to as traffickers in this chapter and Chapter 8. Victims of trafficking do not work for pimps. Traffickers force them into their trafficking situations. Although the traffickers may identify as pimps, their behavior is more consistent with that of a trafficker.

These competing findings just go to show that while prior abuse may be part of the profile of the trafficking victim, it is not the only predictor.

Dysfunctional and insufficient relationships in the background of victims typically trigger the use of emotional attachment by traffickers. However, Kennedy and colleagues' (2007) qualitative research also indicated that traffickers attempted to capitalize on women's debt, drug addictions, and lack of authority figures.

A second common recruitment strategy is to offer the potential victim employment (Jani & Anstadt, 2013; Jones, Engstrom, Hilliard, & Sungakawan, 2011; Meshkovska et al., 2015; Vindhya & Dev, 2011; Zimmerman et al., 2009). The vulnerability being attacked with this strategy is economic hardship, as depicted in Figure 7.1 (Meshkovska et al., 2015; Vindhya & Dev, 2011). In these scenarios, the potential victim and the trafficker do not always know each other. Traffickers utilize newspapers, the Internet, and radio ads to attract victims. Sometimes traffickers are honest that the employment opportunity involves sex work. Other times traffickers are deceitful, implying that the employment involves babysitting, hospitality, or some other innocuous service when in actuality the work is sex work (Jones et al., 2011).

Trafficking Experience

The trafficking experience can be described in terms of time, working conditions, and the detrimental effects of the experience. In regard to time, interview and survey research with different samples of sex trafficking victims provides some understanding of how long trafficking experiences tend to last. As might be expected, there is a range. Identified sex trafficking victims report being in their trafficking situations anywhere from a day to more than a year (Meshkovska et al., 2015; Zimmerman et al., 2008).

The working conditions of sex trafficking victims are dismal. The driving force behind these conditions is the traffickers' desire to retain complete control over the victim. Essentially, the trafficking experience can be characterized by control. Generally, this control extends to all parts of the victims' lives, from general things such as when

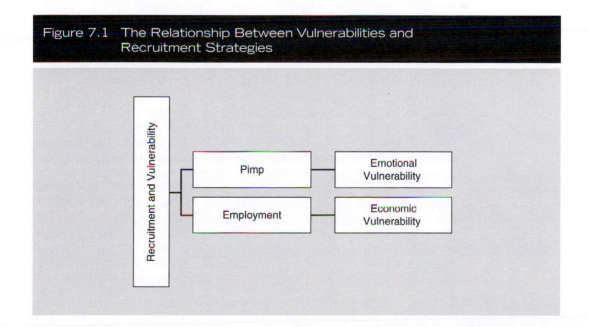

Figure 7.1   The Relationship Between Vulnerabilities and Recruitment Strategies

Case Study: Through the Eyes of the Victim

The Experiences of Four Thai Girls Trafficked to Japan

Through the next couple of sections, you will follow the lives of four Thai girls—Noi, Gogk, Pom, and Kwan (not necessarily their real names)—as described in the qualitative work of Jones and colleagues (2011). The women ranged in age from 31 to 38 at the time of the interview. They appeared to be in their late teenage years when trafficked to Japan. All lived in poverty, were poorly educated, had parents with health issues or drug addiction, or had a deceased parent. Given that the recruitment efforts took place in Chiang Rai, one can assume the girls came from Northern Thailand. Prior to being recruited for trafficking to Japan, three of the girls has engaged in sex work. The recruiters assured the girls they would not need to pay for anything to get to Japan and they would be provided with travel documents. Kwan, the fourth girl, was told

she would be working as a maid and believed the trafficker. None of these girls had opportunities at home, and all felt pressure to help support their families. Promises of free travel and good money were enticing to the girls.

Travel to Japan took one week to one month. The girls traveled with other trafficked women and were met by smugglers when arriving in Japan. The smugglers were to take them to their work locations. Upon arrival in Japan, the girls' travel documents were taken from them. They were also informed of their large debt (700,000 to 800,000 baht, or $17,500 to $20,000), including all of their travel expenses and travel documents. Daily living expenses would be added to their financial obligation. Debt, coupled with no travel documents, eliminated the option of escape.

Source: Jones, et al., 2011, p. 207.

the victim eats, what she wears, and her general appearance, to more serious matters such as working hours, medical care, selection of clients, sexual services, and the decision to use a condom (Hom & Woods, 2013; Meshkovska et al., 2015).

The trafficker maintains control over victims in a variety of ways. Financial debt is a central method of control used by traffickers, as illustrated in the four Thai girls' stories highlighted in this section (Jones et al., 2011; Lyneham & Richards, 2014). Debt bondage, a means of control we see in both sex and labor trafficking, often requires the trafficking victim to work off the debt accrued from travels, provision of false travel documents, daily living expenses, medical care expenses, and so forth. In the case of sex trafficking, compliance with the trafficker's demands increases the chances of repaying the debt and being released (Jones et al., 2011).

Isolation is another tactic applied to maintain control. In the case of the four Thai girls trafficked to Japan, the girls were taken to another country where they did not speak the language. The only people they could communicate with, aside from each other, were their traffickers and the traffickers' employees (Jones et al., 2011). Language barriers, restricted movement, and fear all play into the isolation trafficking victims feel (Hom & Woods, 2013; Lyneham & Richards, 2014; Zimmerman et al., 2009).

Violence is a central means of garnering control of the traffickers' victims (Carpenter & Gates, 2016; Comacho, 2013; Hom & Woods, 2013; Kennedy et al. 2007; Lyneham & Richards, 2014; Meshkovska et al., 2015; Miller-Perrin & Wurtele, 2017; Raphael, Reichert, & Powers, 2010; Vindhya & Dev, 2011). The sex workers interviewed by Kennedy and colleagues (2007) reported regular violent interactions with their traffickers, typically for no specific reason. Violence was used to maintain control and to scare the sex workers. This is especially true early on in the trafficking

Case Study

Violence in Brothels

Below are excerpts from women who experienced violence at the hands of their brothels and/or clients. These excerpts were originally published as part of a study of 78 sex trafficking victims in India.

(a) For one whole year, I was kept imprisoned by the sethani (brothel madam). I was not allowed to even step across the threshold. Every day I had to put on makeup, and she forced me to go to at least 30 men per day . . . If I did not listen to what the sethani said, she would beat me up. If I did not listen to what the customers asked me to do, they used to slice me with knife cuts all over my body.

(b) I was once sent to an "English man." He wounded my body by biting me because I did not listen to him. He forced himself on me even when I had bleeding injuries. I had to entertain 100 clients per day. By the end of the day I had to give 100 tokens to the sethani. The money that was given by clients was collected by the sethani only. Twenty-five women who were staying in the brothel were forced to serve clients in the same room. Drunken customers abuse in different ways. Customers used to force oral sex. I had to tolerate this kind of torture; otherwise they used to scratch me with a blade all over my body. If I did not do as these violent customers asked me to, the sethani would beat me. The sethani wrote out a five-year agreement instead of a one-year agreement as she had told us initially. She forced me to consume all types of drugs. She forced me to serve customers even during my menstrual periods.

(c) I was forced to be in my undergarments only. When I refused, the gharwali (brothel madam) kept me locked up in the bathroom for 10 days. . . . She said that every day 10 customers would come and that I would have to be nice to them; otherwise she would parcel my body home.

(d) I was forced to wear a small skirt and short blouse and beaten severely when I refused to wear such clothes. I was not provided food due to my unwillingness to serve clients. She beat me severely if a client complained about noncooperation. She made the police also beat me up. I was forced to serve customers even during menstrual periods. Once I could not serve clients due to fever and she beat me for that. When my family members called me up, I was forced not to complain about my situation.

(e) _____ forced me to drink alcohol and sent me to a room to serve clients.

(f) The brothel madam forced me to put on makeup and confined me to a room and forced me to earn ₹40,000 in a month. When she found that I was falling short by ₹10,000, her husband beat me and broke my leg.

(g) I was forced to put on makeup and sit on the road along with other women and asked to call men "oye." When I refused, she beat me up severely. I was forced to serve many clients for long hours and to take tablets for abortion.

(h) As I'm a beautiful girl, many customers used to choose me. Sometimes I used to hide in the bathroom to escape from them. The brothel madam then used to beat me with a stick through the window and made me serve clients. I was forced to serve 50 to 100 clients per day. I used to earn ₹5000 to ₹10,000 per day. The brothel madam did not provide food and water if the money was less than that.

Source: Excerpts adapted from Vindhya & Dev, 2011, pp. 155–156.

The Experiences of Four Thai Girls Trafficked to Japan

Their traffickers did not allow them any control of their situations. They had no say in the number of "johns" they saw or the type of sex work they engaged in. All four girls reported their families being threatened as well as their own lives. All of the girls reported experiencing violence at the hands of their traffickers, and one of the girls reported experiencing violence from the johns.

Noi became pregnant, hoping it would end her trafficking situation. Instead the cost of medical care was added to her debt. Gogk reported,

I realized something was wrong when they took away the passport. They said I was indebted and I was not allowed to go away until I cleared the debts. They threatened that if we did not comply with the rules, we would be killed or sold to other people, or dumped in the sea. I was so frightened and tried to behave myself the best I could. . . . (Jones et al., 2011, p. 207)

experience. Intimidation, in the form of rape and violence, is used to ensure the victim knows her place and to scare her into compliance (Hom & Woods, 2013; Zimmerman et al., 2009).

Identification

Reports of how women escape their trafficking situations vary. When identification does occur, it may not always look the same. Victims who reach out for help do so in different ways. Some may reach out to friends, neighbors, relatives, or colleagues—essentially self-identify to those they have personal relationships with. Others will take a more formal approach to self-identification, reaching out to the police or official authorities (K. Richards & Lyneham, 2014). Most are identified in the country in which they are being trafficked. And most escape their situations after realizing the danger they are in (Brunovskis & Surtees, 2012b; Vindhya & Dev, 2011). Interviews with 78 sex trafficking victims in India indicated that most escaped on their own or with the help of other women in the brothels (Vindhya & Dev, 2011). In the story of the four Thai women highlighted in this chapter, the assistance of other victims played a role in the escape of one of the girls (Jones et al., 2011). Other women from the India study indicated that they were rescued through police raids or with the assistance of NGOs.

In those cases where the victim does not self-identify as a victim or chooses not to report victimization, identification becomes challenging (Richards & Lyneham, 2014). Several factors may prohibit victims from reaching out for assistance, including fear of deportation, fear of criminal justice consequences for what may be identified as prostitution, and mistrust of the criminal justice system (Richards & Lyneham, 2014).

Identification is further hampered by misidentification. In their research of sex trafficking in Australia, Richards and Lyneham (2014) found that sex trafficking victims were often misidentified as domestic violence (DV) victims. While even as domestic violence victims they are separated from the offender, the DV identification does not acknowledge the exploitation a sex trafficking victim has endured. The failure to accurately identify a sex trafficking victim hampers the assessment of treatment options and needs, may preclude her or him from certain visa options, and limits the criminal charges available to the assailant.

Case Study

Escaping From Brothels

....

Below is a continuation of excerpts from women's experiences in brothels.

(a) Brothel madam's daughter understood my feelings and one day informed me that her mother had gone to the temple and allowed me to escape from there. One girl among us gave me ₹40. I met an old man and explained my situation [to him] and he dropped me at the railway station. There I met a police constable and revealed my plight. He asked me to sit in a room and when the train to Andhra arrived he informed me and I boarded the train. [After] looking at my dress some passengers offered me money. . . . I collected ₹500 on the train. With that money I reached my native village.

(b) In that house there were 10 girls and we thought "at least one girl should escape from here." One day when the gate-keeper was asleep, I jumped over the wall and ran away. One of the girls gave me ₹50. With that money I went to the police station and lodged a complaint against the brothel madam. The police took me back to the brothel madam's house, saying, "How come you complain against your owner who provides food to you?" After that the harassment increased. It was only in a rescue operation by the police and REDS [an NGO] that I finally came out.

(c) One day she [the brothel madam] forgot to lock the door. So I escaped and reached the railway station. I boarded one train and I found some people from Andhra inside and they told me that the train goes to Dharmavaram. I pleaded with the ticket collector and he allowed me to travel. I reached Dharmavaram.

(d) When all of them were asleep I came out of that place and stayed under a tree till morning. I went to the bus-stand—I sold my gold earrings and bought a dress, and went to the Delhi railway station and boarded a train to Anantapur.

Source: Vindhya, U., & Dev, V. S. (2011).

Recovery and Reintegration

Once the victim has escaped and is identified, the physical and mental trauma caused by the trafficked experience typically come to the surface (Burnette et al., 2008; Hom & Woods, 2013; Meshkovska et al., 2015; Vindhya & Dev, 2011; Zimmerman et al., 2008). Zimmerman and colleagues (2008) found that out of 192 women receiving post-trafficking assistance, more than three-fourths experienced headaches and fatigue. More than half reported dizzy spells, back pain, and gynecological symptoms such as pelvic pain and infection. Over half of the women were also diagnosed with post-traumatic stress disorder and exhibited symptoms of depression, anxiety, and hostility. The study found that many of these issues had to be dealt with immediately and before any discussion of reintegration and cooperation with authorities could be considered.

Women who escape their trafficking situations do not often escape with money or the security they would need to inoculate them from subsequent trafficking experiences. Those same vulnerabilities continue to exist when the women return home, in the event that they do return home. Such vulnerabilities, of course, include poverty, family dysfunction, abusive relationships, and the like. After the trafficking experience, stigmatization is also common (Brunovskis & Surtees, 2012a; Jones et al., 2011). Families may be judgmental of the girls' loss of

Case Study Continued: Through the Eyes of the Victim

The Experiences of Four Thai Girls Trafficked to Japan

Kwan eventually worked off her debt and was released from her trafficking situation. When she attempted to return to Thailand, she was refused entry because she had no proof that she was a Thai citizen. The Thai embassy provided her with a Thai passport only after a district officer from her hometown vouched for her identity.

Gogk [also] gave birth to a baby. The other Thai workers sympathized with her and pooled their money to pay her debt. She returned to Thailand to find her father had cancer. She again accumulated debt being trafficked to karaoke bars and massage parlors.

Noi's debt was paid off by a john, who then sold her to another brothel. After escaping the second brothel, Noi worked as an independent sex worker in Tokyo until she was arrested and deported back to Thailand. She became depressed in Thailand. As an independent sex worker in Tokyo, Noi made 400,000 baht ($10,000). She left Thailand eventually to work as a bonded laborer in Taiwan.

Pom worked off her debt and engaged in independent sex work in Japan until she had enough money to return to Thailand. After the money ran out in Thailand, she arranged to return to Japan to work in a bar. However, upon her arrival, her trafficker sold her to a brothel. In a botched attempt to escape her brothel, the brothel owner was accidently killed. Pom and three other Thai women were convicted of murder. Feminist organizations brought attention to Pom's story, and the Japanese government was pressured into releasing her and allowing her to return to Thailand.

Focus On

The Challenge of Housing in the U.S.—Where to Place Sex Trafficking Victims Immediately After Identification

A major challenge in aiding the recovery process of sex trafficking victims is immediate housing (Meshkovska et al., 2015; Office for Victims of Crime, Training and Technical Assistance Center, n.d.b). With nowhere to turn, these individuals are often placed in shelters, specifically domestic violence shelters. The are several problems with this solution. First, unless the shelter is specifically designed for victims of trafficking, it likely will not offer the necessary services, nor be equipped with the most qualified service providers to meet the unique needs of trafficking victims. Secondly, placing sex trafficking victims in domestic violence shelters creates safety concerns for those in the shelter. Additionally, shelters are very controlled. They typically offer little privacy and limit the comings and goings of their residents. Unfortunately, there is an extreme shortage of safe and appropriate housing options for victims of sex trafficking. This not only puts these victims in danger but also limits the likelihood of their fully exiting their trafficking situations and successfully recovering from their victimization.

Fair Girls, an education, prevention, and policy advocacy nonprofit in Washington, DC, works to prevent the trafficking of girls and others. Its mission statement is "Ending human trafficking one life at a time through trauma and survivor informed services, prevention, and advocacy" (Fair Girls, n.d.a).

Fair Girls offers the only safe home that exclusively serves female survivors of trafficking in the Washington, DC, area. Vida Home (Fair Girls, n.d.b) is open to female victims between the ages of 18 and 26. The girls are mostly U.S. citizens, but the home can service non–U.S. citizens as well. The home can serve up to six women at a time. Residents receive round-the-clock care, including access to warm beds and meals, counseling and survivor support groups,

emergency clothing, fully furnished town-home accommodations, transportation, and field trips based on resident interest. Residents also have access to the Fair Girls crisis line, intensive case management, and the organization's confidential drop-in center. Residents can stay for up to 90 days. Specific attention is given to ensuring that residents of the Vida Home remain integrated with their community so as to assist in successful transitions back into the community. Anecdotally, residents have reported that entering the Vida Home provided their first opportunity to exit their trafficking situation safely. More information on the Vida Home can be found on the Fair Girls website at http://www.fairgirls.org/vida-home/.

While the Vida Home offers a valuable resource to the DC area, it is insufficient to serve the entire population of victims in Washington, DC, and its surrounding area.

Photo 7.1 Fair Girls is an anti-trafficking nonprofit organization.

© FairGirls.org

virginity or apparent prostitution. The returning women are often met with shame, making the reintegration process that much more challenging and retrafficking that much more likely. Addressing the family situation is critical to ensuring a successful recovery and reintegration process (Brunovskis & Surtees, 2012a).

One woman, interviewed as part of a study of sex trafficking in India, stated, "My life is ruined because I listened to others' words. No one should go through what I experienced. I spoiled my life by listening to others" (Vindhya & Dev, 2011, p. 150).

For successful recovery and reintegration to occur, several steps must be taken on the part of service providers. Hom and Woods (2013) interviewed service providers on their experiences in working with victims of sex trafficking. During the aftermath of trafficking, the trauma may present itself in various forms, both physical and psychological. Those interviewed by Hom and Woods (2013) stressed the importance of street outreach during the early stages of recovery. Not only does this outreach allow for the identification of victims, but it cultivates a positive relationship that will begin the foundation for recovery. An outreach worker has the ability to establish a trusting relationship with the victim, drawing the victim out of isolation and allowing her to see that there are people to support her aside from her trafficker.

Once a victim is identified and ready to receive assistance, the recovery process must engage the victim where she is at. The treatment must be individualized and specific to the victim's experiences. The victim, used to being controlled and told what to do, must be empowered to control her own path to recovery.

Another important component to recovery and eventual reintegration is the acknowledgment of trauma. Trauma-informed treatment is especially important with victims of sex trafficking (Hom & Woods, 2013). Not only do victims experience the trauma associated with their trafficking situation, but this trauma may be coupled with trauma from childhood and other violent experiences.

A service provider must be able to break down this trauma, acknowledge and treat traumatic events separately, and treat the cumulative effects of the trauma.

Finally, successful reintegration requires a holistic approach to recovery (Hom & Woods, 2013). Trauma-informed care is critical, but it must be combined with medical attention, vocational training, housing, and any other supports the victim requires to live independently and without exploitation.

Data tell us that most identified victims of sex trafficking are adult females; however, this may vary by region internationally (NHTRC, 2016; UNODC, 2016a). Thus far this text has laid out a general description of women's involvement in trafficking and the challenges we face in identifying these trafficking victims. However, we know that others are also entrapped in the sex trafficking world. Neither age nor gender protects an individual from being trafficked. The final two sections of this chapter will explore our current understanding of the involvement of children in sex trafficking as well as that of less recognized populations, including male and transgender individuals.

Child Sex Trafficking

The trafficking of minors for sex is likely not an unfamiliar concept. It is an act that disgusts most, combining the inhumane exertion of power of one human over another with the innocence and immaturity inherent to youth. This section will explore how trafficking laws change when children are involved, as well as the unique risk factors that make some youth more vulnerable. Forms of sex trafficking of minors include prostitution, pornography, stripping, and other sexual acts (Miller-Perrin & Wurtele, 2017; Reid & Jones, 2011; Shared Hope International, n.d.a).

Special Legislative Attention to Child Sex Trafficking

United States

The federal statue on trafficking, the Trafficking Victims Protection Act of 2000 (TVPA), defines sex trafficking as "the recruitment, harboring, transportation, provision, or obtaining of a person for the purpose of a commercial sex act where such an act is induced by force, fraud, or coercion, or *in which the person induced to perform such act has not attained 18 years of age*" (emphasis added). For victims identified as under age 18, the use of force, fraud, and coercion is not required to charge an offender with human trafficking.

Human trafficking laws are on the books in all 50 states (Child Welfare Information Gateway, 2016; National Center for Prosecution of Child Abuse, 2012). These laws require a lower threshold to identify human trafficking if the victim is under age 18, similar to the TVPA (Shared Hope International, 2017). However, simply acknowledging that youth are incapable of giving consent and are therefore victims of trafficking isn't effectively protecting children from prostitution charges and convictions. Further legislation is required to fully protect youth. Shared Hope International (2017) assesses states on an annual basis to evaluate their responses to domestic minor sex trafficking. Their Protected Innocence Challenge focuses on laws categorized into six areas: (1) criminalization of domestic minor sex trafficking; (2) criminal provisions addressing demand; (3) criminal provisions for traffickers; (4) criminal provisions for facilitators; (5) protective provisions for the child victim; and (6) criminal justice tools for investigation and prosecution. Chapter 8 will provide a discussion of further legislation that is required to fully protect youthful victims.

International Law

Obviously, there is no clear singular law to define human trafficking outside the United States. Instead, countries, including the U.S., look to the United Nations to provide guidance on how to handle human trafficking and other crimes within their own borders. The **United Nations Convention Against Transnational Organized Crime** and one of its related protocols, the **United Nations Protocol to Prevent, Suppress and Punish Trafficking in Persons Especially Women and Children**, set expectations for the world regarding how to define, prevent, and prosecute human trafficking (King, 2008). The convention states, "The recruitment, transportation, transfer, harboring or receipt of a child for the purpose of exploitation shall be considered trafficking in persons even if this does not involve any of the means set forth in subparagraph" (United Nations General Assembly, 2000c).

Those that are party to the convention and related protocol agree to adhere to the guidelines. Examining child sex trafficking legislation by country is too cumbersome a project for this text, but the Department of State's annual Trafficking in Person Reports would be a good starting place to assess sex trafficking of minors by country. The Focus on the **Council of Europe Convention on Action Against Trafficking in Human Beings** box describes the European Union's attention to the trafficking of children.

Focus On
The Council of Europe Convention on Action Against Trafficking in Human Beings ("the Convention")

Each Party shall take specific measures to reduce children's vulnerability to trafficking, notably by creating a protective environment for them.

—**Council of Europe (2005)**

The convention was adopted by the Committee of Ministers of the Council of Europe on May 3, 2005, and was entered into force on February 1, 2008. The convention applies to men, women, and children; national and transnational victims; and all forms of human trafficking (Council of Europe Portal, n.d.). As of 2016, 46 European countries had signed onto the convention.

Council of Europe members as well as non-members and the European Union are eligible to become party to the convention. The European Union formed a **Group of Experts on Action Against Trafficking in Human Beings (GRETA)**. This group is mandated through the convention to engage in activities related to monitoring and implementing the convention. After previous GRETA evaluations found gaps in identification and assistance of child victims of trafficking, the most recent GRETA evaluation has chosen to investigate these gaps (Council of Europe, 2017).

Magnitude

The sex trafficking of minors receives special attention both within and outside the United States. But what does the problem look like? How many children are being trafficked for commercial sex? What are the age ranges of these children? What is the gender breakdown? Generally, the most reliable statistics to understand magnitude come from the National Human Trafficking Resource Center (2016), the UNODC (2018a), and the **International Labour Organization** (2012; International Labour Office & Walk Free Foundation, 2017). The NHTRC indicated that 27.2% of reported sex trafficking cases in 2016 involved child victims.

According to the United Nations Office on Drugs and Crime (2018a), sex trafficking is the most frequently detected form of trafficking in nearly all regions of the world, with the exception of Africa and the Middle East (where forced labor is more frequently detected; UNODC, 2018a). In 2016, approximately 23% of trafficking victims globally were girls and 7% were boys. When looking at just victims of trafficking for sexual exploitation, girls represented 26% of victims. Three percent of victims were boys (see Figure 7.2).

The number of child victims can also be identified by region, as shown in Figure 4.5 in Chapter 4. Children represent more than a quarter of trafficking victims in all regions of the world, with the exception of Central Asia, where children represent less than 10% of victims. Understanding that sex trafficking is the most detected form of trafficking in most regions, combined with our understanding of the rate of children being trafficking for sexual exploitation globally, allows for assumptions to be made regarding the number of children being trafficked for sexual purposes by region.

Take Central America and the Caribbean as an example. Over 50% of detected victims in this region are girls. Approximately 87% of detected trafficking in the region is sex trafficking. Given girls' disproportionate status as victims in this region, one can assume that many are victims of sex trafficking (UNODC, 2018a).

Figure 7.2   Detected Victims of Trafficking for Sexual Exploitation Internationally, 2016

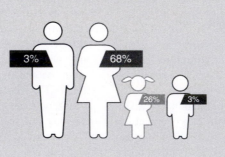

Source: United Nations Office on Drugs and Crime, 2018a.

The ILO provides more specific demographic indicators of sex trafficking victims. In 2012, 21% of victims of sexual exploitation were children (ILO, 2012). More recently, the International Labour Office collaborated with the Walk Free Foundation (2017) to publish new global estimates. They reported that 21.3% of victims of forced sexual exploitation were children.

Vulnerabilities

The vulnerabilities linked to the sex trafficking of minors are plentiful. Child welfare involvement, homelessness, childhood maltreatment, race, young age, poor mental health, addiction, and financial pressures have all been indicated as predictors of sex trafficking during childhood (e.g., Barnett et al., 2017; Comacho, 2013; Countryman-Roswurm & Bolin, 2014; Fedina, Williamson, & Perdue, 2016; National Center for Missing and Exploited Children, 2017; Reid & Piquero, 2014).

The ecological model, presented in Figure 7.3, highlights the broad categories of risk factors that make youth vulnerable to traffickers (Institute of Medicine & National Research Council, 2013). These factors are organized by level—individual, relationship, community, and societal. This categorization highlights the complexity of factors that result in trafficking. Note that independently, factors may not explain sex trafficking victimization. However, interactions between these factors make children more vulnerable to traffickers. This section will review a selection of vulnerabilities. Prevention efforts targeted at these vulnerabilities would help to protect the most vulnerable from being trafficked and retrafficked.

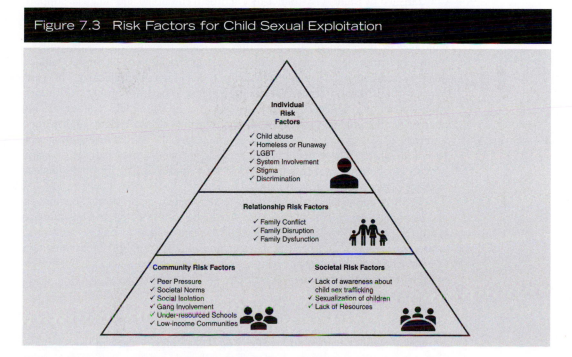

Figure 7.3 Risk Factors for Child Sexual Exploitation

Individual Risk Factors
- ✓ Child abuse
- ✓ Homeless or Runaway
- ✓ LGBT
- ✓ System Involvement
- ✓ Stigma
- ✓ Discrimination

Relationship Risk Factors
- ✓ Family Conflict
- ✓ Family Disruption
- ✓ Family Dysfunction

Community Risk Factors
- ✓ Peer Pressure
- ✓ Societal Norms
- ✓ Social Isolation
- ✓ Gang Involvement
- ✓ Under-resourced Schools
- ✓ Low-income Communities

Societal Risk Factors
- ✓ Lack of awareness about child sex trafficking
- ✓ Sexualization of children
- ✓ Lack of Resources

Source: Institute of Medicine & National Research Council, 2013.

Child Welfare Involvement

For the purposes of this text, the child welfare population includes runaways, children in foster care and adoptive families, and children experiencing neglect and abuse (physical, mental, and sexual). Although child welfare status is a global risk factor for sex trafficking (see Figure 7.3), most research on the relationship between child welfare status and sex trafficking status comes out of the United States. The National Center for Missing and Exploited Children (2017) states that one in seven reported runaways in 2017 were victims of sex trafficking. Of those, 88% were in the care of social services when they went missing. Running away and social services involvement are serious risk factors for sex trafficking in the United States (Countryman-Roswurm & Bolin, 2014; Fedina et al., 2016; Miller-Perrin & Wurtele, 2017; Moore, Hirway, Barron, & Goldberg, 2017; L. Smith, Vardaman, & Snow, 2009). In fact, Fedina and colleagues (2016) found that survivors of child sex trafficking were five times more likely than their nontrafficked counterparts to have ever run away as a child.

There is mixed evidence on the impact of child sexual abuse and trauma on subsequent child sex trafficking (Fedina et al., 2016). Fedina and colleagues (2016) found that these risk factors were not significantly related to child sex trafficking. However, others have found strong support for the link, as well as for the relationship between sex trafficking and other characteristics of child-welfare-involved kids (e.g., Child Welfare Information Gateway, 2017; Children's Bureau, n.d.; Countryman-Roswurm & Bolin, 2014; L. Smith et al., 2009). In fact, some studies identify 50% to 90% of child sex trafficking victims as individuals involved in the child welfare system (Administration for Children and Families, 2013). Children experiencing abuse and dysfunction in their home lives may be specifically targeted by traffickers. Traffickers offer them emotional and financial support they may not be receiving at home.

While not always consistent, there is compelling evidence to suggest that child welfare involvement, at a minimum, increases the vulnerability of youth to becoming trafficking victims. Once this population has become victims of traffickers, they require special care and protection to avoid being retrafficked. This care may come in the form of medical health, behavioral health, housing, education, employment, or legal services. It is imperative that no matter what the service, no matter who the provider, all care is trauma-informed (Child Welfare Information Gateway, 2017). Victims of human trafficking, especially sex trafficking, may not be willing victims. They may not ask for help, or worse, they may be resistant to receiving help. Only with a trauma-informed approach will a provider have a fighting chance at being able to help these victims.

Further, specifically related to the child welfare population, an analysis and assessment of child welfare services must be implemented and appropriate resources provided to strengthen the child welfare system to reduce runaways, abuse, and neglect among biological, foster, and adoptive families. Eliminating this as a vulnerability, albeit a challenging task, will likely contribute to a reduction in sex trafficking of youth in the United States.

Age

Age presents a particularly challenging vulnerability. A lack of development and immaturity make this population especially vulnerable to traffickers all over the world (Reid & Jones, 2011). More than half of the children in the media images cataloged in the International Child Sexual Exploitation (ICSE) database were of prepubescent and younger children, as noted in Figure 7.4 (ECPAT International & Interpol, 2018). The global demand for younger and younger girls, specifically, is linked back to the fear surrounding AIDS. As consumers of sex become aware of the danger of AIDS (it is still a death sentence in many regions of the world), there is a greater demand for virgin girls (Kristof & WuDunn, 2010). Virgins are less likely to be infected by a previous sexual partner.

Shared Hope indicates that the common age for entering into sex trafficking in the United States is 14 to 16 years old (Shared Hope International, n.d.b; L. Smith et al., 2009). This nonprofit organization, focused on reducing the commercial sexual exploitation of youth, specifically believes preteen and adolescent girls are most at risk of the manipulation of sex traffickers; however, all children carry some risk.

In a sample of 115 U.S. sex trafficking survivors (average age of 36 at the times of data collection), over a quarter indicated participating in their first commercial sex act at age 12 or 13. Another 28% of the sample indicated engaging in their first commercial sex act at age 14 or 15 and the remaining 34% at age 16 or 17 (Fedina et al., 2016).

Reid and Piquero (2014) found, in a sample of serious delinquent offenders in the U.S., that the age of onset into commercial sexual exploitation ranged from 11 to 25 years old, with the mean age being 17.09. Fifty-one percent of the sample reported age of onset to be between 11 and 16 years old, while the remaining 49% reported age of onset to be between 17 and 25 years old. Some predictors of earlier entry into sexual exploitation included family dysfunction, psychological disorders, and drug addiction during early childhood.

Figure 7.4   International Child Exploitation Database Description of Unidentified Victims

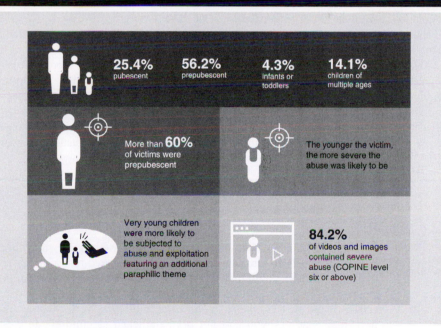

Source: EPCAT and Interpol, 2018.

HIV infection is of particular concern for human trafficking victims, specifically in sex trafficking. There is a higher prevalence of HIV in sex trafficking victims, caused by many contributing factors, including a lack of control in the selection of sexual partners, use of condoms, or choice of sexual activities (Gupta, Raj, Decker, Reed, & Silverman, 2009). The physical nature of commercial sexual activity can also increase the risk of infection with AIDS. Sex trafficking victims are subject to physical and sexual violence, creating a higher likelihood of vaginal or anal tearing and increased vulnerability to contracting HIV. Limited opportunities to receive medical care often result in undiagnosed cases of HIV or the advancement of HIV into AIDS (Gupta et al., 2009).

Asia has a particularly high occurrence of HIV/AIDS infections among sex trafficking victims. Sex tourism in Sri Lanka and Thailand has a high demand for young male sex workers from their western customers (United Nations Development Programme [UNDP], 2007). Male-with-male unprotected sex carries the highest risk of contracting HIV/AIDs (Centers for Disease Control and Prevention, n.d.). One NGO in Karnataka, India, reports 45.8% of the rescued female sex trafficking victims testing positive for HIV (Gupta et al., 2009). India has a high HIV rate in the general population, with 2.5 million people infected. This results in commercial sex workers having a higher chance of meeting a john or customer that is infected and contagious (UNDP, 2007).

There are many misconceptions about HIV/AIDs, resulting in a higher demand for virgins. With HIV/AIDs affecting people around the world, the demand for sex trafficking of younger girls and boys has been widespread globally. There is a perception that the younger the girl is, the less likely she is to be infected. This perception is especially prominent in southern Africa due to the large-scale AIDs epidemic that has been ongoing in the region (Adepoju, 2005).

There are also myths and inaccurate beliefs that sex with a virgin or sexual cleanses can cure AIDS (AIDS InfoNet, 2014; Ayikukwei et al., 2008; Oluga, Kiragu, Mohamed, & Walli, 2010). This baseless belief has resulted in younger and virgin girls becoming a selling point for sex traffickers. This, in turn, is infecting many young sex trafficking victims with HIV, which makes life even harder should these victims manage to escape. They will have trouble finding a partner, with the double stigma of prostitution and AIDS hanging over them, and illness may prevent them from certain kinds of work. If they have no access to proper medicine, they will most likely develop AIDS, and an opportunistic infection could easily kill them.

The AIDS epidemic creates a demand for sex trafficking while at the same time making the victims of sex trafficking even more vulnerable and stigmatized. Additionally, there is evidence that sex trafficking is integral to the continued spread of AIDS in certain regions, including Africa and parts of Asia. Ending sex trafficking would undoubtedly result in a reduction in the spread of HIV/AIDS (Kloer, 2010).

Race

In the United States, child sex trafficking victims are more likely to be nonwhite. The 2016 Uniform Crime Reports indicated that a higher percentage of Africa American youth than white youth were arrested for prostitution (57.5% versus 39.7%; Federal Bureau of Investigation, n.d.). Fedina and colleagues (2016) found that survivors of child sex trafficking were twice as likely to be nonwhite as adults who had not been trafficked as children. Interestingly, in examining the ICSE database, over two-thirds of the more than 1 million images in the database showed white victims. It is important to note, however, that this database could be biased toward certain regions, as less than half the world's population lives in countries included in the ICSE database (ECPAT International & Interpol, 2018).

There also appears to be an interaction between LGBTQ and racial minority youth who identify as homeless, further increasing the vulnerability of that population (Cray, Miller, & Durso, 2013). Data show a higher rate of racial minorities (specifically Black and Hispanic) who identify as LGBTQ among the New York City homeless population than other racial subpopulations among NYC's homeless youth (Cray et al., 2013).

Drug Addiction

The drug addiction of either children or parents makes children more vulnerable to traffickers (Countryman-Roswurm & Bolin, 2014; Miller-Perrin & Wurtele, 2017; Moore et al., 2017; Smith et al., 2009). Drug-addicted parents have been known to sell their child for sex in exchange for drugs. These parents also expose their children to drug use and are unable to adequately supervise their children while under the influence of drugs (L. Smith et al., 2009; Sprang & Cole, 2018).

In the case of the youth, there is little evidence available to prove causal order (Institute of Medicine & National Research Council, 2013). Does the drug addiction result in trafficking, or does the trafficking increase the likelihood of drug addiction? Drug addiction may drive someone into the commercial sex industry as a source of money to purchase drugs. Traffickers also supply their victims with drugs as a way to keep them compliant. Drug addictions that develop during exploitation also entice victims to stay in their trafficking situation, as that may be the only way for them to obtain drugs.

Homelessness

As noted in a *New York Times* article, there is an army of people combating human trafficking and a separate army combating homelessness. However, the link between the two demands that these armies combine forces (Mzezewa, 2017). Our best evidence showing the link between homelessness and human trafficking comes from a study by the Covenant House (n.d.) using a U.S. sample. According to data collected at 30 Covenant House shelters between 2014 and 2016, one in five of the 911 interviewed homeless youth identified as victims of human trafficking. Twenty-one percent of women, 10% of men, and 26.9% of LGBTQ homeless youth reported being trafficked for commercial sex. Thirty-two percent reported engaging in the sex trade at some point in their lives.

LGBTQ Youth

LGBTQ youth represent 40% of the homeless youth population and only 7% of the general youth population in the United States (Schmitt, 2016). Typically, LGBTQ identification is an especially strong predictor of the involvement of boys in the commercial sex industry (Figlewski & Brannon, 2013; Miller-Perrin & Wurtele, 2017). These kids are at extreme risk of being trafficked due to their lack of safe shelter and social supports. Even those LGBTQ youth who are not homeless experience more vulnerability to traffickers due to their experiences with higher rates of discrimination, bullying, and violence as well as less familial support and opportunities for employment than their non LGBTQ peers (Cray, 2013; Hunt & Moody-Mills, 2012; Institute of Medicine & National Research

Focus On
Gang Involvement and Sex Trafficking

The relationship between gang involvement and sex trafficking has been given little attention in empirical research. While there is speculation that gang involvement is tied to sexual exploitation (e.g., Courture, 2017; Shared Hope International Staff, 2014), there are few methodologically rigorous studies available to prove this link. A recent National Institute of Justice (NIJ) study, however, shows some support for the relationship (Carpenter & Gates, 2016). Using quantitative and qualitative methods, the researchers were able to establish the existence of a booming sex trafficking business as well as an active gang culture in San Diego County. Multiple data sources indicated that 110 gangs were profiting, in some fashion, from the commercial sex industry. Of those offenders interviewed (all of whom were in jail at the time of interview), 33% identified as sex trafficking facilitators. Of those facilitators, 80% were affiliated with a gang. All of those gang-member facilitators were interviewed. Findings from the interviews indicated that the level of the gang's involvement in the facilitation of sex trafficking varied. At one end of the spectrum, gang members facilitated sex trafficking for their own personal gain, while at the other end, the gang directly profited from commercial sexual activity.

This NIJ study, journalistic accounts, and case studies, combined with what we know about gangs, makes it reasonable to assume that sex trafficking offers a source of financial support to gangs (Shared Hope International Staff, 2014). The crime is relatively low risk and carries the probability of high levels of profit.

Journalistic investigations have shown that the MS-13 gang relies on sex trafficking as a major source of revenue, specifically exploiting girls and young women (Arthur, 2018; Wilber, 2011). Girls often have little power in a gang, especially in the United States. For that reason, it is safe to assume that females identifying as gang members or hanging around with a gang are being sexually exploited or are being used to transport other trafficked goods such as drugs and/or weapons (Shared Hope International Staff, 2014).

Source: Human Trafficking Search Staff, 2017.

Human Trafficking Search described how MS-13 recruits and exploits its members:

> In the United States, victims of MS-13 tend to be Latino immigrant girls or girls from the Northern Triangle countries who came into the country as unaccompanied minors. Once the unaccompanied minors are smuggled into the United States, they become prime targets for human trafficking. HHS places minors either in foster care, with family or a sponsor. The majority of unaccompanied minors end up in California, New York, Texas, and the Washington DC area that includes Maryland and Virginia—states that have large Central American populations and thus large MS-13 populations. . . . MS-13 preys on the vulnerability of the unaccompanied minors; some have previously suffered sexual abuse either in their home country or during the trip north; others lack a community and do not speak English. Members of MS-13 seek out the vulnerable young girls, using violence and other coercive tactics to intimidate the girls into having sex for money to help financially support the gang. Runaways are also appealing to the MS-13. Family problems, transitions from foster care, and economic problems are some of the reasons that unaccompanied minors run away from their homes. Many of the unaccompanied minors may have experienced sexual abuse, exploitation, or physical abuse in their home countries or during their migration to the United States, and even more suffer from poverty and lack of a stable social network. These are all factors that make young girls more susceptible to human trafficking. (Lillie, 2017, para. 2)

Council, 2013). LGBTQ victims experience stigma due to both their LGBTQ status and their exploitation, resulting in a reduced likelihood that they will report their exploitation (Nichols, 2010).

The LGBTQ youth population experiences discrimination not only among their peers but also within the juvenile justice system. LGBTQ youth represent 13% to 15% of those involved in the juvenile justice system (Hunt & Moody-Mills, 2012). They commit the status offense of running away at a higher rate than other youth due to familial rejections and the child welfare system's inability to be sensitive to this population's unique challenges (Cray et al., 2013). LGBTQ youth are also more likely to be labeled as sex offenders, often for age-appropriate consensual sexual activity, limiting their ability to gain employment and adding to their social stigma (Cray et al., 2013; Hunt & Moody-Mills, 2012).

It is especially important that LGBTQ youth service providers are aware of the indicators of sex trafficking (Dank et al., 2015; Schmitt, 2016). Not only can they raise awareness among this vulnerable population but they can recognize and stop exploitation when they identify it. Their role within the LGBTQ community brings with it trust and social support, making providers prime candidates to assist and protect this population. Safe-harbor laws can also be helpful in protecting LGBTQ youth and reducing their vulnerability to exploitation, as discussed in Chapter 8.

Women and Children Are Not the Only Victims

Males

Men and boys are increasingly being recognized as victims of sex trafficking (ECPAT International & Interpol, 2018; Figlewski & Brannon, 2013; O'Brien, Li, Givens, & Leibowitz, 2017; T. Richards & Reid, 2015). Referring back to Figure 7.2, earlier in this chapter, men and boys account for approximately 6% of sex trafficking victims. In data from the International Child Sexual Exploitation (ICSE) database, which includes more than 1 million media files of child sexual exploitation, 31% of unidentified media images represented male children, as indicated in the gender infograph in Figure 7.5.

The limited information available on male sex trafficking victims indicates that males typically operate without a pimp/trafficker. They may be introduced into the commercial sex industry by peers, as a solution to financial and/or housing challenges (Curtis, Terry, Dank, Dombrowski, & Khan, 2008; Figlewski & Brannon, 2013; M. D. Smith, Grov, Seal, & McCall, 2013). **"Survival sex"** is common among this population, characterized by older men providing younger men shelter in exchange for sexual activities (Figlewski & Brannon, 2013). This model of trafficking is inconsistent with how women and girls enter into and remain in their trafficking situations. For this reason, it can be more challenging to recognize male victims of commercial sexual exploitation. First responders and service providers must be able recognize trafficking, even when a trafficker isn't part of the equation.

While the trafficking situation may look different for male victims, the risk factors are similar. Broken homes, homelessness, involvement in the child welfare system, child sexual abuse, personal drug abuse and/or drug abuse of parents, and peers involved in prostitution are all factors that make males vulnerable to traffickers (Figlewski & Brannon, 2013). As noted in the Child Sex Trafficking section, LGBTQ status is a unique risk factor for males. The most compelling risk

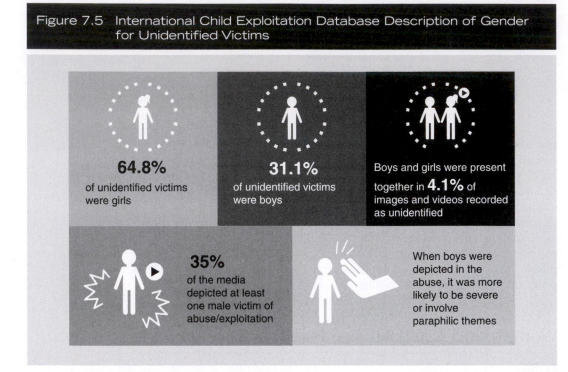

64.8% of unidentified victims were girls

31.1% of unidentified victims were boys

Boys and girls were present together in **4.1%** of images and videos recorded as unidentified

35% of the media depicted at least one male victim of abuse/exploitation

When boys were depicted in the abuse, it was more likely to be severe or involve paraphilic themes

Source: EPCAT and Interpol, 2018.

Challenge Yourself 7.2

Consider a scenario where a young, impoverished male is encouraged by his peers to enter into the commercial sex industry. He has no apparent trafficker but finds an older man to provide him shelter in exchange for sex.

Do you believe there is evidence of force, fraud, or coercion? Is this human trafficking?

factor predicting male victimization is poverty. Both living in poverty and limited opportunities to escape poverty explain much of male involvement in the commercial sex industry.

As the previous few paragraphs have indicated, recognizing male victims of trafficking can be particularly challenging. The tools used to identify victims typically focus on female victims. Further, male victims who do not identify as LGBTQ may be hesitant to admit victimization if their exploiter was male. Assessment tools must be amended or unique tools designed to be more sensitive to male victimization. Further, because male victims, specifically children, are not tied to an adult trafficker, they are often seen as complicit in their trafficking and may be identified as a criminal rather than a victim (Figlewski & Brannon, 2013). All of these issues result in male victims not being recognized. Consequently, serving these victims is also challenging. Oftentimes, programs geared towards sex trafficking victims prohibit male participants (Figlewski & Brannon, 2013).

Case Study

Urban Light

Photo 7.2
Urban Light is a nonprofit organization located in Chiang Mai, Thailand, focused on male victims and potential victims of sex trafficking.

Urban Light is a nonprofit based in Chiang Mai, Thailand, committed to serving young men who are victims of trafficking and exploitation. The organization's founder, Alezandra Russell, describes her introduction to the gap in services being offered to vulnerable young men working in the red-light district during her first trip to Thailand in 2009:

> Finding refuge at a table, I immediately befriended one working boy. Through broken English, a love of soccer and the ability for me to lose gracefully at Connect Four, a friendship was quickly formed. I had unexpectedly befriended a young, kind and protective hilltribe boy—his name, "Oi." The friendship and trust between myself and Oi—two complete strangers from two completely different worlds— would only grow over the next 5 days. On my fifth and last day in Chiang Mai, the desperation of knowing that there would

be no one to play Connect Four with Oi, and no one to talk soccer stats with him other than the male customers in the boy bars, left me frantic. (Urban Light, n.d.)

Three months after that first encounter with Oi, Alezandra went on to open Urban Light. From a small organization dedicated to helping male sex workers and victims of human trafficking, to a holistic movement to fight for the rights of boys, men, and communities in Chiang Mai, through prevention, protection, partnership, Urban Light embraces a policy that it's never "too late" and that every individual matters, regardless of their past.

Located in the center of Chiang Mai, the organization focuses on filling a gap in services by providing health, employment, housing, education, harm reduction services (e.g., clean needles and drug treatment education and awareness), prevention, outreach, and legal support. UL by way of the UL Drop-In Center allows for vulnerable young men to access daily meals, a washroom with complimentary hygiene products, and a safe place to rest and recharge. UL's core purpose is to provide male clients with a consistent space, a safe outlet for healing, and a support system of trained professionals. The organization, one of the few in the world that focuses on young men, is attempting to change a culture both in Thailand and abroad that consistently overlooks the needs and vulnerabilities of boys and men.

Source: Urban Light (n.d.).

LGBTQ Individuals

The LGBTQ community, children and adults, is not immune from victimization relating to human trafficking (Boukli & Renz, 2018). In fact, this population is one of the most vulnerable to traffickers. As discussed in previous sections related to child sex trafficking and the sex trafficking of males, this population may experience unique hardships such as homelessness, disconnection with family, and stigmatization that may force them into sex work (Cray, 2013; Figlewski & Brannon, 2013; Hunt & Moody-Mills, 2012; Institute of Medicine & National Research Council, 2013; Miller-Perrin & Wurtele, 2017).

Evidence suggests that this is especially true in more conservative cultures where homosexuality and gender fluidity are very stigmatized and in some cases criminalized (e.g., Darlington, 2017; Nichols, 2010). In these situations, sex workers engaging in homosexual commercial sex may be criminalized on multiple levels. They may experience punishment and abuse by law enforcement more than even female sex workers (Nichols, 2010). There is evidence of more extreme treatment of homosexual and transgender sex workers in many countries, including Sri Lanka, Israel, Palestine, Peru, Brazil, Lebanon, Spain, and Italy (Nichols, 2010; Office to Monitor and Combat Trafficking in Persons, 2017b).

As with many other human trafficking–related topics, research and data on this population and their specific sex trafficking experiences are limited to policy papers and research using small sample sizes (e.g., Boukli & Renz, 2018; Nichols, 2010). There is also little research conducted in more conservative countries, such as those in Asia and South America.

This population is vulnerable in many ways due to the stigmatization that comes from their sexual identification. The population requires special attention, not only to protect them from traffickers but also in regard to how they are recovered from their trafficking situations and the kind of care and treatment they receive post-trafficking. This population, like males, may present signs of trauma differently than female victims. More attention must be given to understanding this population, their vulnerabilities to traffickers, and the unique challenges associated with recovery and reintegration.

Conclusion

Sex trafficking leaves an indelible print on those who survive the seemingly unbreakable chains of this form of slavery. Whether the victim is female, male, adult, child, or transgender, the experience of sex trafficking is dangerous, terrifying, and seemingly insurmountable. The precise recruitment tactics of traffickers and their control over victims, as reviewed in this chapter, share similar qualities in every region of the world. While variations in culture, laws, and corruption influence who are most vulnerable to becoming victims of sex trafficking, those who survive are left with the same complicated emotions and basic needs. They require intense and personalized support to recover from their traumatic experiences. Chapter 8 will examine the role of demand in the proliferation of sex trafficking as well as the various ways the United States and global community currently react to sex trafficking and its victims.

KEY WORDS

Council of Europe
  Convention on Action
  Against Trafficking in
  Human Beings 167
Group of Experts on
  Action Against
  Trafficking in
  Human Beings
  (GRETA) 167

International Labour
  Organization 168
pimp enculturation 158
sex trafficking 158
survival sex 175
United Nations
  Convention Against
  Transnational Organized
  Crime 167

United Nations Protocol
  to Prevent, Suppress and
  Punish Trafficking in Persons
  Especially Women and
  Children 167

DISCUSSION QUESTIONS

1. What factors do the authors attribute to the increase in sex trafficking, and which factor(s) do you believe have greater influence?

2. What two methods do pimps use to capitalize on women sex trafficking victims? Which method is used more and why?

3. Consider the trafficking experience described in this chapter. Compare sex trafficking victim experiences to those of domestic violence victims. Consider the power and control wheel (http://www.ncdsv.org/images/PowerControlwheelNOSHADING.pdf) that is often used in discussions of domestic violence. What similarities do you see between domestic abusers and sex traffickers?

4. How do trafficking laws change when children are involved, and what are the risk factors that make children more vulnerable to sex trafficking?

5. How does the victim experience for men and women differ? What are the differences with respect to their reasons for entering and staying in their trafficking situations?

6. What are some of the challenges in recognizing male victims of sex trafficking? Identify an organization not reviewed in the text that deals specifically with male victims. What is the organization? How does it attempt to overcome the unique challenges faced by male victims?

RESOURCES

- Equality Now: https://www.equalitynow.org

- Fair Girls: http://www.fairgirls.org/

- Half the Sky Movement: http://www.halftheskymovement.org/

- Safe Harbor: https://dps.mn.gov/divisions/ojp/forms-documents/Documents/!2012%20Safe%20Harbor%20Report%20%28FINAL%29.pdf

- SOLWODI: https://www.solwodi.de/

Sex Trafficking
Demand and Prevention

By engaging and training law enforcement, religious leaders, teachers, tribal elders, business executives, and communities, we become more vigilant . . . [and] strengthen our ability to protect our most vulnerable and weaken a criminal's ability to infiltrate, recruit, and exploit.

—Secretary of State Michael Pompeo
(U.S. Department of State, 2018)

Throughout this text, the role of supply and demand is discussed in explaining the proliferation of human trafficking around the world. Chapter 4 discusses the factors that drive the supply of victims as well as the more general factors that drive demand. This chapter will focus on some of the unique factors that drive the demand for sex trafficking. It will conclude by giving attention to the varying approaches to reducing sex trafficking. These reduction initiatives will be organized using the 3P framework, the international paradigm outlining a three-pronged approach to reducing human trafficking—*prevention, protection,* and *prosecution* (Office to Monitor and Combat Trafficking in Persons, 2017a).

Demand

Many would argue that reducing **demand** would be one of the most effective ways to reduce trafficking (Franzblau, 2013). Demand comes in many forms. Chapter 6 explored the general demand for sex. Men's need/want for sex, and cultures that accept this as a right of being a man, explain the acceptance, if not the proliferation, of the commercial sex industry. The spread of HIV/AIDS, discussed in Chapter 7, offers another significant example of how demand influences the portrait of human trafficking. In those regions where HIV/AIDS is still widespread, the demand for younger and younger girls continues to grow. Throughout the entire text, the role of globalization has been discussed, although primarily to explain the supply side of trafficking.

Globalization has increased not only the supply of trafficking victims but also the demand for commercial sex. Use of the Internet to find opportunities to participate in commercial sex and to communicate with potential sex workers or those they are working for, and the ability to travel to remote and exotic places to participate in commercial sex without detection, have all resulted in a growing demand for commercial sex worldwide.

Sex Tourism

Demand comes in many forms. **Sex tourism** is one of the more glamorized ways in which we have come to accept the commercial sexual exploitation of others. Generally, sex tourism is more prevalent in underdeveloped countries, which may advertise themselves as "exotic" and culturally different from Western nations. Individuals from more developed countries travel to those less fortuitous countries to engage in the exploitation of others (Gezinski, Karandikar, Levitt, & Ghaffarian, 2016; T. Richards & Reid, 2015; Wonders & Michalowski, 2001). Countries with legalized prostitution are also popular sex tourism destinations (Yates, 2016). Interestingly, there is some posturing on whether the more recent influx of Easterners traveling to the West may create a pattern of sex tourism going in the opposite direction (Bandyopadhyay, 2013). While individuals traveling for the purpose of sexual entertainment are typically looking for prostitutes, not sex trafficking victims, there is little way for customers to distinguish between the two. Consequently, the sex tourism demand drives the sex trafficking business in those areas where sex tourism is popular.

Child sex tourism is exceptionally concerning. Certain countries attract tourists based on the perceived availability of underage child sex workers. In these cases, the sex purchaser likely knows he or she is participating in illegal and nonconsensual activity. There is no mistaking these situations for consensual prostitution when the sex work is selected due to the worker's underage status. This is of particular issue in parts of Asia as well as in the Caribbean (e.g., Chemin & Mbiekop, 2015; T. Richards & Reid, 2015). In the Caribbean, there is evidence of foreign females purchasing sex with underage boys, consistent with the unique demand for male sex workers discussed in Chapter 7 (T. Richards & Reid, 2015).

Travel and tourism does not make sex offenders. The tourism industry, however, is in a position to identify sex offenders and it is important that the industry itself addresses these issues—rather than being a vehicle for abuse.

—Dorothy Rozga, executive director at ECPAT International (ECPAT, 2018)

End Child Prostitution and Trafficking (ECPAT) is a leading organization fighting the expanding business of sex tourism, specifically that involving children.

Challenge Yourself 8.1

Individuals from Western nations often see themselves as separate from those from Eastern nations. However, much of the world's population stems from Asia, and tourism and migration have brought many from Asia to western parts of Europe and North America (Castles & Miller, 2009). While the East and West are undeniably distinct in terms of culture, they share many commonalities when it comes to the demand for sex trafficking. Can you explain these similarities in light of cultural distinctions between the East and West? Does globalization blur the distinctions between East and West?

In 2018, at an ECPAT-cosponsored summit, more than 400 participants from 25 countries agreed to engage in several actions over the next few years to raise awareness of and reduce sex tourism. Those attending the summit, including representatives from the UN, nongovernmental organizations, and travel businesses, agreed to the following:

- Launching a joint global campaign against the sexual exploitation of children by travelling child sex offenders, which includes targeting media so they use appropriate terms and report the issue with sensitivity;

- Creating a central repository of existing resources to make them accessible—especially to the private sector—to provide practical guidance;

- Training—especially for hotel, hospitality, and other tourist-facing workers so they can identify sexual exploitation and help implement standards on child protection across the sector;

- Strengthening or developing reporting systems such as helplines, hotlines and online reporting platforms, establishing standards to report cases of the sexual exploitation in travel and tourism, and engaging the public to actively use reporting mechanisms; and

- Ensuring that law enforcement is well resourced and trained to identify, investigate, and use child-friendly methods when dealing with child victims and witnesses. (ECPAT, 2018, para. 4)

Sex tourism creates a particular demand for male sex workers (T. Richards & Reid, 2015). While stereotypes may drive readers to assume the buyer of sex is male and the seller of sex is female, evidence shows this is not always the case (T. Richards & Reid, 2015). Specifically, in the Caribbean, men and women are changing roles. Women are becoming the sex tourists, while men are the exploited population. T. Richards and Reid (2015) reviewed several studies to provide a profile of the Caribbean male sex worker. These males range in age from 15 to 35. As one might expect, they typically have limited education and few legitimate employment opportunities. Sex work may not be a full-time job but rather is used to supplement other meager income sources. These males often experience stigmatization for their selected line of work. Other research shows that male sex workers are in demand in the Caribbean for the purpose of homosexual sex tourism (Padilla & MPH, 2007). Consistent with our understanding of male sex workers, those in the Caribbean are typically not being forced into commercial sexual exploitation by a trafficker. Rather, their financial situation and lack of employment opportunities leave them little choice but to enter the commercial sex industry (T. Richards & Reid, 2015).

The Use of the Internet to Drive Demand

The "streetwalker" prostitute no longer really exists. Instead, those looking to sell sex rely on the Internet to market their product. Those looking to purchase sex, whether it be locally or abroad, also rely on the Internet to search for a sex worker or a locale to travel to in order to engage in commercial sex (Dank et al., 2014; Gezinski et al., 2016; Newman, Holt, Rabun, Phillips, & Scott, 2011). The sharing of child pornography has also increased with the regular use of the Internet (Dank et al., 2014; Newman et al., 2011; Niveau, 2010).

Booking your next vacation . . . have you considered a sex tourism package?

Even before you picked up this book, I suspect, you had heard the term *sex tourism*. However, did you know this isn't just an underground business? You can find services and resorts to plan sex tour vacations with a simple Google search. A recent study found 21 websites that were offering sex tourism services on popular search engines such as Google, Yahoo, and Bing (Gezinski et al., 2016). These websites contained information regarding the cost and duration of the tour; types of services available; target client population; pictures of sex workers, often categorized by physical descriptors; FAQs and testimonials; and legal information. Most services were offered in the Caribbean, specifically the Dominican Republic, and Southeast Asia. However, websites also offered services in Europe, South America, Central America, and North America.

Are you surprised at the openness and availability of sex tourism? Do you feel the same about local online prostitution advertisements?

The 2017 Trafficking in Persons (TIP) Report (U.S. Department of State, 2017c) included as one of its topics of special interest information on the online sexual exploitation of children. This exploitation often includes live-streaming of child sexual abuse using cell phones or web cameras. The mainstream nature of smartphones makes the exploitation of children easy and inexpensive, even for the novice exploiter. As websites such as Craigslist and Backpage are being targeted and shunned for their advertising of commercial sex, various social media apps (e.g., Facebook, Instagram, Snapchat, Twitter, Vine) provide new and innovative options for the distribution of child pornography and advertising of exploitation. Social media is also a primary resource for the targeting and recruitment of potential exploits. Evidence indicates that children of any gender, socioeconomic status, or ethnic background could be victims to **online exploitation** (U.S. Department of State, 2017).

> *That could be anybody's daughter. . . . That could be your neighbor.*
> *That could be your daughter's or your son's friend at school.*
>
> **—FBI agent Bob Parker, on a victim lured into child sex trafficking via Facebook (U.S. Department of State, 2017c, p. 32)**

So what does this online exploitation look like? Generally, the trafficker grooms his or her victims for sexual exploitation. Using a cell phone or web cam, the trafficker can connect with an interested client anywhere in the world. The client pays anonymously, often through wiretap. The 2017 Trafficking in Persons Report indicates that a growing number of highly protected online communities exist and are dedicated to the sexual abuse of children (U.S. Department of State, 2017).

The 2017 TIP Report (U.S. Department of State, 2017) draws special attention to the Philippines, where a large proportion of the population experiences extreme poverty and limited access to the Internet. Those who exploit family members often justify the behavior by noting that the acts are not harmful to the children, especially when there is no physical contact, such as cases where a child is recorded exposing themselves. Both in the Philippines and elsewhere, online exploitation proliferates due to a lack of understanding of the consequences, complicity or direct involvement of family members, and profitability of the behavior.

The 2017 TIP Report (U.S. Department of State, 2017) notes another trend related to online sexual exploitation. The report labels the behavior *sextortion*. **Sextortion** occurs when an offender obtains incriminating photos or information about a child and then uses those photos or information to coerce a child into performing sexual acts on web cams.

The number of cases of online sexual exploitation and sextortion are likely to rise due to the lost cost of the enterprise and the lower risk of begin caught. Those factors, coupled with the high profitability, make this an ideal option for traffickers. Governments will need to develop legislation and design trainings for both police officers and prosecutors on recognizing and collecting evidence related to these online crimes.

Focus On
FOSTA: The Takedown of Backpage

In 2016, 16-year-old Desiree Robinson ran away from home. Charmed by Joseph Hazley, she moved in with him in November. By Christmas Eve of that same year, she was found dead, beaten and stabbed (Jackman & O'Connell, 2017). During the time Desiree was living with Hazley, he began posting pictures of her on Backpage.com, a classifieds website known for publishing ads for the purchase of sex. Desiree's mother, Yvonne Ambrose, filed a wrongful-death suit against Backpage. Past attempts to prove Backpage's culpability for the death of trafficking victims had been previously unsuccessful. But new facts showing that Backpage had done more than just allow individuals to post ads on its site brought new attention to the Ambrose case and the culpability of Backpage, the go-to website for posting and finding sex advertisements.

A U.S. Senate report in January 2017 provided evidence that Backpage edited ads to ensure advertisements did not imply the advertiser as underage. Additional evidence became public showing that Backpage was soliciting sex-related ads and redirecting customers from competing sites to Backpage. Although Backpage had always insisted it had no control over content posted on its page, convincing evidence was coming out to the contrary (Jackman & O'Connell, 2017).

In the spring of 2017, some anti-trafficking advocates got a big win with the signing of new legislation by President Trump. The FOSTA bill (the Allow States and Victims to Fight Online Sex Trafficking Act) allows prosecutors and victims to file charges and lawsuits against any website that hosts sex trafficking ads. The bill, which went into effect immediately after being signed, resulted in the immediate shutdown of Backpage and similar websites (Jackman, 2018).

Of course, the passage of this bill is not without controversy. Civil liberties advocates take issue with increasing the liability of websites (Jackman, 2018). There was also pushback from anti-trafficking advocates. "Shutting down every service provider and website will not end sex trafficking" argued Jean Bruggman, executive director of Freedom Network USA (Jackman, 2018). By shutting down Backpage and like websites, sex workers lost a safe place to screen clients and investigators lost the ability to use Backpage as a valuable source of evidence on pimps and missing girls, among other pieces of information. Backpage had historically been cooperative to subpoena requests (Jackman, 2018; McCombs, 2018), and the evidence collected from Backpage had secured many convictions of traffickers and aided in identifying victims.

Nevertheless, Backpage had been complicit, and more likely actively engaged, in the sex trafficking of adults and minors, showing a $100 million plus annual profit in recent years.

Reactions to Sex Trafficking

As noted in the quote at the beginning of the chapter, reactions to sex trafficking must be multifaceted and include many different groups of people. The 3P paradigm (*prevention*, *protection*, and *prosecution*) is used worldwide as a guide to human trafficking reduction efforts (Office to Monitor and Combat Trafficking in Persons, 2017a). Human trafficking reduction efforts must target all three areas to effectively combat the problem. During her term as secretary of state, Hillary Clinton added a fourth paradigm to the list—*partnership* (Miller-Perrin & Wurtele, 2017). In this concluding section on sex trafficking, the existing efforts to reduce sex trafficking will be explored, organized using the 3P paradigm with the addition of *partnership*. Moving forward, this will be referred to as the 4P paradigm.

Prior to delving into the four *p*'s, a discussion on legislation is particularly important. Although a brief review of legislation relating specifically to children is presented earlier in the chapter, a broader focus on legislation is critical, given its relevance to the 4P paradigm. Legislation is one of the most critical ways we can prevent sex trafficking, provide a basis for prosecution, ensure the protection of all victims and potential victims, and incorporate partnerships more structurally into responses to trafficking. Miller-Perrin and Wurtele recommended several common themes that should exist in all human trafficking–related laws:

- All underage persons should be protected against commercial sexual exploitation regardless of gender or nationality.

- Adults who are responsible for the exploitation should be punished by law, with sentences appropriate to the severity of the damage caused.

- It is the State's responsibility to ensure that victims are protected.

- The "consent" of persons under the age of 18 to participate in commercial sexual activities cannot lift the illegality of the exploitation; children are victims and any so-called consent does not waive their right to protection.

- Victims of human trafficking and commercial exploitation need, and are deserving of, efforts to help their recovery and reintegration into society.

- Addressing and preventing the problem of human trafficking and commercial exploitation will require collaboration and cooperation among various governmental and nongovernmental constituents. (2017, p. 138)

Legislatively, there is continuous oversight, through nonprofits such as Polaris and Shared Hope, as well as the regular reports published by organizations such as the UN, the U.S. Department of State, and the International Labour Organization (ILO). However, specific measures must be taken to improve our ability to protect victims, as discussed below. The specific strategies addressed below are aimed at targeting sex traffickers and victims of sex trafficking.

Prevention

Prevention requires an understanding of the factors that make individuals vulnerable to traffickers. Human trafficking is an issue of supply and demand. Many factors drive the seemingly endless supply of trafficking victims. Preventative strategies must target those vulnerabilities.

In addition to focusing on the supply of victims, some approaches can be considered preventative (Karlsson, 2013). Demand reduction, specifically the use of johns' schools and "naming and shaming" tactics (publishing the names of those who get caught purchasing sex), are popular methods of reducing demand in the U.S., with minimally consistent research findings on their effectiveness. Criminalization of sex buyers and increased prosecutions of traffickers are also reactive demand-reduction strategies, but still preventive ones. These strategies lessen the power and profit of traffickers.

Additionally, the global culture needs to change to reduce the demand for commercial sex. Sexual exploitation needs to be viewed as unacceptable. Presently, sexual exploitation is viewed by the general public as something negative but nevertheless an unavoidable consequence of prostitution and the commercial sex industry. Even in countries where prostitution is illegal, the public outcry against prostitution is weak, if it exists at all. Cultural norms must be adjusted to reject sexual exploitation in all forms (Karlsson, 2013).

Relating to both supply and demand, one of the strongest prevention strategies is raising awareness (Karlsson, 2013). Awareness strategies will look different depending on the audience. Efforts need to be made to raise the awareness of vulnerable people—to let them know the risks associated with employment promises, smuggling, and so forth. Sex purchasers need to be made more aware as well. While it may not be their intention to exploit sex trafficking victims, that may very well be what they are doing. These buyers need to be more aware of the likelihood that the people providing the sex may not be doing so by choice. Whether or not a person supports the legalization of sex work, few support the idea of individuals being forced or pressured to perform commercial sexual services.

Finally, the general public needs to be more aware. In wealthier countries, such as the U.S., there is widespread disbelief around the concept that sex trafficking, or any form of trafficking, for that matter, occurs. Once the public is more accepting of this unfortunate news, they may be more impassioned to stop it. The general public has the power to lobby for better laws, call the human trafficking hotline when they see suspicious activity, and reject friends and family who purchase sex. Raising awareness is a powerful tool in reducing sex trafficking on a global scale.

Under the umbrella of prevention, this text reviews three additional areas that require more attention in order to become effective prevention strategies. These include the use of trauma-informed care, the improvement of research methodologies, and the use of technology to investigate trafficking cases.

Trauma-Informed Care

It is becoming more apparent that preventive efforts must extend beyond the initial victimization. Escaping one's trafficking situation and staying out of that lifestyle can be incredibly challenging. The physical and mental consequences of sex trafficking victimization are especially traumatizing (e.g., injuries from violence, STDs, pregnancy, addiction, post-traumatic stress disorder, anxiety, and suicidality; Barnert et al., 2017). Traumatic bonding, or Stockholm syndrome, can make victims of sex trafficking especially difficult to treat (Leidholdt, 2013). Additional emotions, including fear, shame, isolation, and adaptation (to their exploitation), must also be acknowledged by those working with these victims, including service providers, attorneys, and the court systems. **Trauma-informed care** and individualized reintegration strategies are critical in preventing individuals from being retrafficked (Barnert et al., 2017; Leidholdt, 2013).

Trauma-informed care requires "working to maximize the patient's sense of safety, empowerment, and trust, while maintaining transparency and encouraging collaboration among service providers" (Barnert et al., 2017, p. 827). Providing this care can be especially challenging. Awareness within the medical field is limited. In one study, 63% of urban, suburban, and rural health facilities reported no specific training on sex trafficking victims (Barnert et al., 2017).

While research exploring the effectiveness of specific trauma-informed models of treatment is limited, there appears to be an increased focus on the topic. A Google search on "trauma-informed care for human trafficking" returned multiple webinars, governmental agency guides, and training opportunities (e.g., Administration for Children and Families, n.d.a; American Hospital Association, 2018; National Human Trafficking Resource Center, 2015; Office for Victims of Crime, Training and Technical Assistance Center, n.d.c). This is an encouraging step forward in improving our care of sex trafficking victims and reducing their likelihood of revictimization.

Research

Another source for prevention is research. Improving our understanding of sex trafficking, the risk factors and vulnerabilities associated with sex trafficking, and the micro and macro factors driving this highly consequential victimization will enhance our ability to prevent it. High-quality research is lacking, as are valid and reliable data. While a Google search or academic database search of sex trafficking will provide a researcher with a bounty of information, most of it is policy related or research based on small sample sizes, case studies, and ethnographies (Barnert et al., 2017). These data are informative; however, it is critical that future research use representative samples and be able to speak to various subpopulations of victims (adults vs. children, victims from different nationalities, etc.).

Research on the prevalence of sex trafficking is improving. More recent data sources are providing promising exploration into sex trafficking, including the International Child Sexual Exploitation (ICSE) database; the Global Estimates of Modern Slavery, developed by the ILO and Walk Free; and the Human Trafficking Knowledge Portal, a global database of human trafficking prosecutions (ECPAT International & Interpol, 2018; International Labour Office & Walk Free Foundation, 2017; United Nations Office on Drugs and Crime, n.d.c). These major data sources will aid researchers in better understanding, descriptively, what human trafficking looks like. However, as informative as these data sources are, they are not sufficient. Evaluative research, using stronger sampling strategies and more rigorous methodologies, is also critical for better understanding and improving our responses to sex trafficking and human trafficking more broadly.

Using Technology for Good

DARPA

While sex traffickers have taken full advantage of the Internet and other forms of technology, technology can be used to prevent sex trafficking as well. This section presents some of the recent technological advances attempting to disrupt trafficking efforts.

The Defense Advanced Research Projects Agency (DARPA) is developing new search technologies that will aid in identifying individuals using the Internet for the purposes of human trafficking (Pellerin, 2017). Using a tool—Memex—law enforcement will be able to conduct more-advanced online investigations to identify traffickers, even those using the dark web. This will most likely target sex traffickers, as commercial sexual activity is most often sold online. Memex will be able to identify sex-related advertisements on both the dark and open webs. The technology will identify "online behavioral signals in the ads . . . that help us detect whether or not a person is being trafficked" (Pellerin, 2017, para. 7). Examples of indicators that may represent human trafficking are descriptors such as "new in town" or "fresh" (which often means underage). The technology also recognizes phone numbers that are repeatedly listed in different ads and branding tattoos in media images.

The DARPA heat map, shown in Photo 8.1, was created using the Memex technology. It represents human trafficking activity across the world. This technology could become a powerful tool for investigators, as it eliminates the need to visually review each prostitution ad. The possibility that a big-data resource could computationally identify patterns could save resources as well as offer a more powerful tool for identifying traffickers and trafficking rings.

Since the Memex program began in 2014, it has grown in capability and application. The program has been adopted by over 33 agencies worldwide and resulted in hundreds of arrests and convictions (Pellerin, 2017). DARPA offers this technology free to federal, state, and local law enforcement agencies in the U.S. and works with agencies outside the U.S. to make sure they can use the technology or design their own versions of the technology.

© DARPA graphic

| Photo 8.1 Human Trafficking Heat Map

Thorn

Thorn is a nonprofit organization that has taken a collaborative approach to understanding the commercial sexual exploitation of children, working with individuals from the tech field, law enforcement, nongovernmental organizations (NGOs), and government to eliminate the spread of materials associated with child sexual abuse and to identify child traffickers. Readers of this text may be familiar with two of the cofounders of Thorn—Hollywood actors Ashton Kutcher and Demi Moore. The primary goals of Thorn are to accelerate victim identification, deter abusers, and disrupt platforms (Thorn, n.d.a).

One of the most effective tools designed by Thorn is its online tool, Spotlight. More than 5,000 law enforcement officers across the U.S. and Canada use this tool, designed based on data from a survey of survivors. In 2016 and 2017, Spotlight was used in over 21,000 cases and assisted in identifying 12,328 adults, 5,791 children, and 6,553 traffickers (Thorn, n.d.b). Spotlight allows law enforcement to collaborate beyond jurisdictional, state, and national borders. It allows law enforcement to see patterns of movement as well as identify victims advertised on the dark web.

Project Vic

Thorn partners with several entities to support **Project Vic**. This organization has "created an ecosystem of shared and standardized technologies specifically chosen to combat crime involving massive amounts of images and videos" (Project Vic, n.d.). It essentially aggregates the individual collections of media jurisdictions. VICS (Video Image Classification Standard) is a private open-source data model managed by technical experts from the Project Vic community. Project Vic has several other technologies that help law enforcement read images and videos that are hidden in obscure formats. They use PhotoDNA, a Microsoft technology that gives images a unique "signature" so they can be tracked as they are copied or shared, even when the images have been altered.

This brief overview of technology suggests that the future of fighting human trafficking, sex trafficking specifically, requires technology. While reacting to trafficking after it has occurred is necessary, it is by no means sufficient. Providing law enforcement with big-data resources will provide more efficient and smarter ways to prevent trafficking through identification of victims and traffickers. Those who are engaged in developing these technologies acknowledge that trafficking is a moving target. Communication and collaboration on a global level, through the use of technology, is necessary to reduce and prevent trafficking.

Protection

Protection comes in many forms. Protection could mean protecting survivors from their traffickers or protecting the most vulnerable from being trafficked. There are many interpretations of protection. This section will introduce some specific legislation that is slowly being implemented in the United States to protect victims of sex trafficking, namely safe-harbor laws and **vacatur**. It will also focus on different temporary visa options victims are eligible for in the United States, Canada, and the United Kingdom.

Safe Harbor

Children engaged in commercial sex acts are automatically considered victims of human trafficking under the Trafficking Victims Protection Act of 2000 (TVPA). In spite of this, some states allow for minors to be charged with prostitution, in turn prosecuting victims of sex trafficking (Polaris, 2015b; Shared Hope International, 2016a). There are a variety of negative outcomes that can come from children being arrested and charged with prostitution. Stigmatization and the process of criminalization (physical restraint, interrogation, etc.) often lead to revictimization and "traumatizing consequences" (Shared Hope International, 2016a). Due to the negative consequences associated with criminalizing child sex trafficking victims, the American Bar Association Commission on Youth at Risk passed a resolution urging states not to charge children under the age of 18 with prostitution or related crimes. Instead, states should develop and provide services to support these youth (Wasch, Wolfe, Levitan, & Fink, 2016). **Safe-harbor** laws do just that.

Safe-harbor laws are laws put in place to prevent children who have been forced into prostitution from being prosecuted. These laws serve two main goals— to provide youth with legal protections and to provide youth with services to prevent their reentry into the commercial sex industry (Polaris, 2015b).

> *I was arrested for prostitution, and put in jail. The John was released.*
> *I was sentenced and sent upstate for a year. He was sent to a special*
> *school [for a couple of evenings] and his case was dismissed. There was no*
> *school for me.*
>
> **—A youth arrested on prostitution charges in New York City,**
> **circa 2003 (Mullen & Lloyd, 2013, p. 129)**

Shared Hope International, a well-known NGO, provides an annual report card on how effective U.S. states are in their efforts to combat the commercial sexual exploitation of youth. The Protected Innocence Challenge assesses all 50 states and the District of Columbia on a variety of aspects in each state's legislation and policy. These include:

- Section 1. Criminalization of Domestic Minor Sex Trafficking

- Section 2. Criminal Provisions Addressing Demand

- Section 3. Criminal Provisions for Traffickers

- Section 4. Criminal Provisions for Facilitators

- Section 5. Protective Provisions for the Child Victim

- Section 6. Criminal Justice Tools for Investigation and Prosecution (Shared Hope International, 2017)

Safe-harbor laws are evaluated under Section 5— "Protective Provisions for the Child Victim." The specific components States are evaluated on, related to Section 5, are:

- Victims include all types of child commercial sex exploitation including prostitution, pornography, or sexual performance.

- A defendant cannot claim the willingness of the minor as a defense for sexually exploiting the minor.

- Prohibiting the criminalization of minors for prostitution.

- Special services available with non-punitive entry routes. (Diversion programs cannot include charges or lasting arrest records.)

- Child sex trafficking is identified as a type of abuse and neglect within child protection statutes.

- The definition of "caregiver" or another related term in the child welfare statutes is not a barrier to a sex trafficked child accessing the protection of child welfare.

- There is compensation available for victims of child sex exploitation.

- Courts provide victim-friendly procedures and protections for minors.

- Victims of child sex trafficking must be able to get rid of criminal charges related to prostitution and trafficking victims (i.e., vacate delinquent status, expunge criminal records) without a waiting period.

- Victim restitution and civil remedies available to victims of child sexual exploitation.

- Statute of limitations eliminated or lengthened against perpetrators so victims can pursue charges and civil actions. (Shared Hope International, 2017, p. 16)

In 2017, Florida was the only state to receive full points in Section 5. South Dakota had the lowest ranking for Section 5.

Research conducted by the National Conference of State Legislatures (NCSL) assessed safe-harbor laws in the U.S., resulting in findings consistent with those of Shared Hope International (2017). The NCSL identified six themes typically found in safe-harbor laws and which states had employed these themes as of 2016 (Williams, 2017). States did not consistently implement safe-harbor laws incorporating all six themes.

- Theme 1: Collaboration and coordination of state entities and resources.

- Theme 2: Decriminalization and/or diversion for actions of trafficked youth.

- Theme 3: Funds for anti-trafficking efforts and survivor services.

- Theme 4: Provision of services for youth survivors. State laws may also specify the services available to young victims of trafficking. As discussed below, and measured by Shared Hope, provisions are critical for the success of safe-harbor laws.

- Theme 5: Increased penalties for traffickers of children. As of 2016, 44 states had increased penalties for trafficking children.

- Theme 6: Training to recognize and respond to trafficking crimes and its victims.

State legislation is fluid and constantly changing (hopefully improving). For the purposes of this text, it is necessary to note that, to date, states are in varying stages of implementation of safe harbor.

While it seems logical to simply support the passage of safe-harbor laws and other protections for child victims of commercial sexual exploitation, it is futile to pass such laws without the proper support systems in place (Barnert et al., 2016; Wasch et al., 2016; Williams, 2017). Diversion and prevention programs must be implemented and sustainable for protective measures to work. In other words, a sound plan to avoid the criminalization of youth must be in place and cannot be developed concurrently with the passage of the laws. Such planning and implementation should be completed prior to the passage of safe-harbor laws. This implementation would include training of those working directly with victims as well as first responders and employees of the child welfare and juvenile justice systems. A greater awareness of trauma and trauma-informed care would be necessary for all those coming into contact with the child victim.

A 2016 study on the effectiveness of safe-harbor laws, one of the first of its kind, found that the existing laws were all similarly focused (Barnert et al., 2016). They all aimed to treat youth as victims rather than criminals. However, the nine states included in the qualitative analysis varied greatly in the legal and support provisions. The authors made the following recommendations based on their analysis:

1. Implementation: Safe-harbor laws should be implemented over time to allow for adequate training and program funding.

2. Types of Protection: Of the different approaches observed in the study, decriminalization-plus-diversion appeared to be the most closely related to the goals of safe-harbor laws (as opposed to decriminalization-only or diversion-only approaches).

3. Penalties: Clear procedures must be in place to ensure that fines and other monies collected from traffickers, pimps, and johns are actually applied to victim funds and used by those serving victims.

4. Training: Adequate training on commercial sexual exploitation is imperative for all first responders and prosecutors for safe-harbor laws to be effective.

5. Coordination: There must be coordination between all who work with victims, including health professionals, lawyers, law enforcement agents, and child welfare providers. They must also work in coordination with lawmakers.

More recommendations, based on states currently implementing safe-harbor laws, can be found in Table 8.1.

Barnert and colleagues (2016) acknowledged that there can be unintended consequences to safe-harbor laws, specifically when the laws are not properly implemented. When the diversion options are insufficient, victims may continue to be detained. While this is done in an effort to separate the victim from the trafficker, it can still retraumatize the victim. For this reason, a best-practices model must be implemented (Barnert et al., 2016; Williams, 2017).

Safe-harbor laws are designed to protect youth when prostitution is criminalized. One would assume that in countries where prostitution is decriminalized or legal, services would be in place for youth who are being sexually exploited. While there would not be risk of criminalization in these countries, services and support

Table 8.1 Provisions for Model Safe-Harbor Legislation

Implementation Timeline	Incorporate stages of implementation, especially in states currently lacking services and placements.
Prevention	Support the development of evidence-based prevention programs.
Penalties	Strengthen legal penalties for traffickers and buyers, including the collection of fees and fines to fund victim services.
Training	Mandate repeated training on commercial sexual exploitation of children for law enforcement and child welfare providers.
Age	Apply protection to all commercially sexually exploited youth under 18 years old.
Type of Protection	Create diversion pathways. If decriminalization is pursued, diversion programs need to be in place.
Guidance for Diversion	Establish clear diversion criteria.
Placement	Establish short- and long-term placement options, including shelters, safe houses, inpatient mental health facilities, substance abuse treatment centers, and foster care placements.
Services	Establish diversion services. Priorities are mental health care, case management, medical care, mentoring programs, and educational and vocational training.
Funding	Establish sustainable funding streams to support training, placements, services, data collection, and an overseeing agency.
Data Collection	Incorporate a plan for data collection on child sex trafficking and program outcomes to allow for evaluation of safe-harbor laws.
Coordination/Task Force	Establish a plan for coordinated, interagency response led by the state child welfare agency or state task force to ensure a locally informed, effective, multidisciplinary response.
Accountability/Oversight	Establish statewide oversight and accountability of the safe-harbor programs with a central agency (e.g., task force or state child welfare agency plus legislature and /or governor). Plan for ongoing evaluation of safe-harbor protections and programs.

Source: Adapted from Barnert et al., 2016, p. 259.

Challenge Yourself 8.4

Does your state or country have safe-harbor laws or something similar? If so, do the laws meet the elements listed in Table 8.1? If not, how would you improve upon the law?

are still necessary to ensure that youth can transition out of the sex industry. The European Union provides guidelines for member states, instructing them to protect youth victims from penalties, especially in those member states that criminalize prostitution, similar to the safe-harbor laws being implemented in the United States (European Parliament & Council of the European Union, 2011). Similar language has been incorporated into Canadian federal law as well (Barrett, 2013).

Post-Conviction Relief

The Honorable Fernando Comacho (2013) reported vacating

> numerous criminal convictions of girls who were eleven, twelve, and thirteen years old when they took adult pleas. They lied about their ages on the instructions of traffickers who found it difficult to secure their release from the juvenile justice system. The ugly truth is that many of those charged with prostitution are in fact kids, not mature adults, and their decisions are far from knowing and intelligent. (p. 142)

Human trafficking victims who are misidentified as consenting sex workers collect criminal convictions for their involvement in prostitution (Barnard, 2014; Emerson, Kroman, Mogulescu, & Sartori, 2014; Shdaimah, 2017). As discussed in Chapter 6, criminal convictions relating to prostitution can be particularly stigmatizing and limit the sex worker's ability to find employment outside the commercial sex industry. Perhaps even more frustrating than limiting the ability of a consenting sex worker to exit his or her current profession, these criminal convictions essentially punish victims of sex trafficking. Those who are being forced into participating in the commercial sex industry are convicted of prostitution-related crimes, crimes they had no choice but to commit.

New York was the first state in the U.S. to implement legislation to vacate prostitution-related charges (Emerson et al., 2014). The legislation, effective August 13, 2010, allows a judgment to be vacated where

- the judgment is a conviction where the arresting charge was under section 240.37 (loitering for the purpose of engaging in a prostitution offense . . .) or 230.00 (prostitution) of the penal law; and

- the defendant's participation in the offense was a result of having been a victim of sex trafficking under section 230.34 of the penal law or trafficking in persons under the Trafficking Victims Protection Act.

Additionally, the legislation:

- Does not require the survivor to prove that she or he has left the sex industry or "rehabilitated";

- Does not explicitly offer confidentiality provisions to protect the client's identity but is able to do so under civil rights law provisions;

- Provides for vacatur, the most complete remedy possible under the law;

- States that the Court must vacate the convictions and dismiss the accusatory instrument if an individual meets the elements;

- Allows the Court to take additional appropriate action beyond the mandate of the statute such as vacatur of additional charges;

- Is retroactive and inclusive of those with older convictions as long as the motion is made with "due diligence." (Emerson et al., 2014)

Prostitution-related charges are not limited to the sale of sex in New York, or in any other jurisdiction, for that matter. Sex workers are often tasked with participating in other illegal activities by their pimps and traffickers. Loitering, vagrancy, disorderly conduct, drug possession, trespassing, and possession of a weapon are just some of the charges sex workers are also convicted of. These convictions can have detrimental effects similar to those of prostitution charges and should be acknowledged in all vacatur legislation (Barnard, 2014; Emerson et al., 2014). A list of effective components to effective vacatur laws is described in Table 8.2.

Vacatur laws are not without criticism (e.g., Barnard, 2014; Shdaimah, 2017). In some states (e.g., Maryland), vacatur laws are limited to prostitution charges. In all states, vacatur is only considered should the victim's attorney bring motions to vacate convictions. The victim isn't always aware of this option and/or encounters challenges in filing the motion, thus limiting the effectiveness of this legislation (Barnard, 2014). Further, vacatur legislation does not provide a defense to imminent charges. Vacatur is reactionary. Human trafficking courts may offer an opportunity to reduce the number of prostitution-related convictions; however, this option is not without challenges, as described below.

Table 8.2 Components of Effective Vacatur Laws

Include prostitution and other offenses	Laws should apply to individuals arrested for these crimes as well as to those convicted.
Do not require official documentation of trafficking	Such documents may include a T visa or letter from the Department of Health and Human Services "certifying" someone is a trafficking victim. If documentation is presented, the law should presume that the individual's conviction(s) resulted from his or her having been trafficked.
Do not require rehabilitation	Requiring survivors to prove they have left the sex industry shifts the blame from the trafficker to the victim.
Ensure confidentiality	This reduces potential stigma and the risk of identifcation by the trafficker.
Offer the strongest remedy possible	Vacatur is a stronger remedy than expungement because it fully erases the criminal convictions.
Require that if all conditions are met, the court must vacate convictions	The judge has no discretion.
Allow the court to take additional actions	For example, allow the court to vacate offenses not explicitly covered in the law.
Ensure retroactive application	Laws should apply to convictions that occured before their passage.
Attach funding provisions	Legal services must be funded to bring these motions.

Source: Adapted from Emerson, Kroman, Mogulescu, & Sartori, 2014.

Human Trafficking Courts

In the United States, there is a trend to implement human trafficking intervention courts (Barnard, 2014; New York State Unified Court System, Office of Policy and Planning, n.d.). While the idea is consistent with the popularity of other specialty courts (e.g., drug courts, mental health courts, domestic violence courts, etc.), the primary difference is, in all of those other courts, the defendant did indeed break the law. In the case of human trafficking courts, the sex worker has to be arrested and charged in order to benefit from the court. This is counter to the widespread belief that these victims should not be arrested in the first place (Barnard, 2014). Further, as with other specialty courts, some of these courts require the defendant to plead guilty, and thus to have some kind of criminal record (Barnard, 2014; Shdaimah, 2017). Again, this is counter to the argument that these victims should not be criminalized.

Human trafficking courts could be revamped to offer a victim defense, rather than forcing defendants to plead guilty to be eligible for the courts (Barnard, 2014). Should this become the procedure, these courts may offer an improved way to deal with prostitution-related charges.

Temporary Visas

Temporary **visas** are offered in several different countries to protect victims of trafficking.

United States

Non-U.S.-citizen victims of human trafficking are eligible to receive a temporary visa to remain in the United States, known as a T Visa. The visa allows victims, and possibly their families, to remain in the U.S. for up to four years should they meet the following conditions (Barbagiannis, 2017; Trafficking Victims Protection Act, 2000):

1. Applicant must be a victim of a "severe form" of human trafficking, as defined by the TVPA.

2. Applicant must be "physically present" in the United States as a direct result of human trafficking.

3. Applicants must cooperate with any "reasonable requests" for assistance in the investigation of human trafficking from law enforcement.

4. Victim must show that she or he will experience "extreme hardship" if removed from the state.

While in the U.S., applicants are eligible for federal services and benefits (Barbagiannis, 2017). Applicants may eventually be eligible for Green Card status, allowing them to stay in the U.S. permanently (Kamhi & Prandini, 2017; U.S. Citizenship and Immigration Services, n.d.b). There is a cap of 5,000 T visas per year, but that cap has yet to ever be reached.

There are some exceptions to the requirement to cooperate with law enforcement for T visa recipients. If the victim is under 18, cooperation is not required. If the request for cooperation is unreasonable, or if the victim experienced extreme physical or psychological trauma, the expectation of cooperation may be waived. Further, if cooperation is not requested, obviously it is not required (Kamhi & Prandini, 2017).

The motivation behind the creation of the T visa was twofold. In addition to improving human trafficking investigations and prosecutions, the visa protects individuals by allowing them to avoid returning to potentially dangerous and violent situations in their home countries. There is little chance for successful rehabilitation in returning victims to dangerous, unstable, and violent home countries. What is more likely is that they will be retrafficked (Barbagiannis, 2017). Remember, many end up in their trafficking situations while attempting to escape and/or improve a dismal situation at home.

While the T visa is a valid source of protection to noncitizens of the U.S., it is not without its issues. It is continuously underutilized, often due to a lack of awareness and the difficult application process. The cooperation clause can also be problematic, as traffickers brainwash their victims to not trust law enforcement. Victims are also fearful of the threats of their traffickers (Barbagiannis, 2017).

Canada

Canada allows victims of human trafficking to remain in the country for 180 days using a temporary resident permit (TRP). It is possible to reissue the permit once it has expired. The permit allows the victim to receive health care and trauma counseling (Government of Canada, 2016). Victims are not required to testify against their traffickers, and the permit is free of cost, as is a work permit. Victims using a TRP are able to work legally in Canada while residing there (Government of Canada, 2016).

The Canadian response to trafficking victims has been criticized nevertheless. NGOs claim that Canadian governmental agencies often disagree on whether someone is a victim, and the TRP is not provided in those situations. Further, because there is no pathway to permanent residence with the TPR, nor the option to bring family members over, this permit is deemed less effective than the T visa (Barbagiannis, 2017).

United Kingdom

The UK uses the National Referral Mechanism (NRM) to identify victims of trafficking and collect data about these victims (National Crime Agency, n.d.). The UK uses the Council of Europe's definition of human trafficking to determine a victim's status. The NRM allows victims of human trafficking to remain in the UK for a 45-day period. Situations such as police cooperation or personal circumstances may result in the victim being able to remain in the UK for longer periods of time. The NRM also may offer financial assistance to return home, should that be the preference of the victim (National Crime Agency, n.d.).

Research by Barbagiannis (2017) indicates that the NRM option is fairly ineffective in terms of protecting victims. The 45-day period is insufficient for protecting victims or aiding prosecutions. The NRM provides no pathway to citizenship. Further, there have been accusations of nationality biases and inconsistent conclusions in determining who are victims and eligible for the NRM options (Barbagiannis, 2017).

While all three of the models have their benefits, the T visa is perhaps the most effective at providing protection, thanks to the length of the visa and its pathway to citizenship. That being said, it could borrow from the other models described to become even more effective. Adding financial assistance to return home for those who want to go home would be a huge benefit to some victims. Further, not requiring cooperation, or making the exceptions to cooperation broader and more explicit, may make the visa more accessible. Identifying "reasonable compliance" with law enforcement is vague and confusing. Furthermore, the trauma exception is also unclear and narrowly defined (Barbagiannis, 2017).

Nevertheless, providing some sort of temporary status to trafficking victims is an important part of protection.

Challenge Yourself 8.5

How should countries respond to noncitizen victims of human trafficking? Is it their responsibility to provide permanent residence to these individuals? Their families? Does it matter whether the victim entered the country legally?

Prosecution

Jennifer's story (see Case Study on page 199) highlights the challenges faced when attempting to prosecute human trafficking cases. Among many obstacles, the traumatization of victims, due to their experiences, often prevents them from being able to adequately support prosecutors' cases (Hersh, 2013). As in domestic violence cases, prosecutors must rely on concrete evidence, often taken from traffickers' computers, victims' phones, photographs, wiretaps, and so forth. Cooperation and collaboration with first responders and service providers can also aid prosecutors in their trafficking cases.

Prosecutorial practices as related to human trafficking are a central indicator of the effectiveness of a country in fighting human trafficking. One of the factors used by the U.S. Department of State (2018b) to assign tier rankings for the annual Trafficking in Persons Report is an assessment of the "implementation of human trafficking laws through vigorous **prosecution** of the prevalent forms of trafficking in the country and sentencing of offenders" (p. 39). Foreign governments are required to provide the U.S. Department of State with data on trafficking investigations, prosecutions, convictions, and sentences.

As shown in Table 8.3, the number of prosecutions globally has steadily grown between 2009 and 2016. While these are not all sex trafficking cases, it is encouraging to see this pattern.

The Human Trafficking Knowledge Portal (United Nations Office on Drugs and Crime, n.d.c) offers an even more nuanced examination of prosecutions and additional information on documented cases of human trafficking, by country. This resource, supported by the United Nations, includes several databases, as described in Figure 8.1.

The Case Law Database is especially helpful, as one can parse out the different types of trafficking occurring in different regions of the world as well as the nationalities of victims and traffickers, case findings, and laws that stem from the cases. This is a valuable resource to practitioners and researchers alike.

Case Study

Jennifer

Jennifer, fifteen years old, was having a difficult time adjusting to her family's move to Georgia. She was lonely and fought with her mother constantly. Jennifer took refuge online. That is where she met Roslyn, a 25-year-old living in New York City. The two developed a fast friendship. Jennifer explained her circumstances, telling Roslyn she wanted to leave Georgia. After seeing Jennifer's photos, Roslyn told Jennifer that she could make her a successful model. Roslyn, sensing Jennifer's urgency, encouraged her to come to New York City. Roslyn arranged for Jennifer's bus ticket and picked her up from Port Authority one Thursday afternoon.

The two spent the next week dining out, shopping, and partying. In addition to introducing Jennifer to new people, Roslyn introduced Jennifer to marijuana, ecstasy, and cocaine.

Jennifer lived in Roslyn's apartment for several weeks. Jennifer was happy, enjoying her new life in New York City. One afternoon Roslyn told Jennifer she was having trouble paying the rent. She asked her to help out. Roslyn suggested that Jennifer start dancing at a club that Roslyn knew about; it would be good money and a good way for Jennifer to meet people. Eager to help and fearful of losing her place to stay, Jennifer agreed.

A few more weeks passed. Roslyn's demeanor changed. She grew hostile. Roslyn began restricting Jennifer's movement and monitoring her telephone conversations. With increasing urgency, she insisted that Jennifer pay off the debt she was accumulating. Then she proposed a solution. She would set Jennifer up with a friend who would pay Jennifer to have sex with him. When Jennifer protested, Roslyn threatened to call Jennifer's mother and tell her about Jennifer's drug use. Jennifer reluctantly agreed.

That was the beginning of the cycle. In several weeks, Jennifer was having sex with approximately three men a week. About a month later, Jennifer could no longer take it. She fled Roslyn's apartment and called her mother. Her mother contacted the Kings County District Attorney's Office, where I work, and we contacted the New York Police Department. Fortunately, we were able to rescue Jennifer and over time we learned her story, but Jennifer refused to testify before the Grand Jury. Consequently, the Kings County District Attorney's Office has been unable to prosecute the case.

Source: This account was taken from Hersch (2013, p. 255–256). Reprinted with the permission from the New York State Judicial Committee on Women in the Courts. All rights reserved.

Table 8.3	Global Law Enforcement Data			
Year	Prosecutions	Convictions	Victims Identified	New or Amended Legislation
2011	7,909 (456)	3,969 (278)	42,291 (15,205)	15
2012	7,705 (1,153)	4,746 (518)	46,570 (17,368)	21
2013	9,460 (1,199)	5,776 (470)	44,758 (10,603)	58
2014	10,051 (418)	4,443 (216)	44,462 (11,438)	20
2015	19,127 (857)	6,615 (456)	77,823 (14,262)	30
2016	14,939 (1,038)	9,072 (717)	68,453 (17,465)	25
2017	17,880 (869)	7,045 (332)	100,409 (23,906)	5

Source: U.S. Department of State, 2018b, p. 43.

Figure 8.1   The Human Trafficking Knowledge Portal Databases

Source: UNODC Human Trafficking Knowledge Portal, https://sherloc.unodc.org/cld/en/v3/htms/index.html.

Focus On
The Human Trafficking Knowledge Portal Case Law Database

Case of Bondar, Günter and B.

Belarus

UNODC No.: BLR001

Fact Summary

In March 2012, the undertaken investigative measures blocked the channel of trafficking of Belarusian girls to Germany. A. E. Bondar made a criminal conspiracy with German citizens Alexander Günter and P. B., who were permanently residing in Hamburg. At their request, he recruited two women for sexual exploitation in an illegal brothel in Germany. He was promised a reward of EUR 1000 for each of them. After that, the German citizens arrived in Belarus by car to transport the victims to the site of exploitation. The three traffickers were arrested red handed while trying to transport the victims abroad.

Sentence Date:
2012-09-18
Author:
Office for Drug Control and Combating Trafficking in Human Beings, Criminal Police, Ministry of Internal Affairs of Republic of Belarus

Victims / Plaintiffs in the first instance

Victim: 2 Individuals
Gender: Female

In this criminal case, 2 victims were identified (adult women), whom the criminals had recruited and tried to transport to Germany for sexual exploitation. Factually, they have not been sexually exploited.

Defendants / Respondents in the first instance

Defendant: P. B.
Gender: Male
Nationality: German
Born: 1984
Legal Reasoning:
P. B. was found guilty of committing an offense under Art. 14 Part 1 and Art. 171 Part 2 of the Criminal Code of Republic of Belarus (attempt to exploit the prostitution of others committed by a group, combined with transportation of a person outside of the country for prostitution).

Defendant: Alexander Günter
Gender: Male
Nationality: German
Born: 1992
Legal Reasoning:
Alexander Günter was found guilty of committing an offense under Art. 14 Part 1 and Art. 171 Part 2 of the Criminal Code of Republic of Belarus (attempt to exploit the prostitution of others committed by a group, combined with transportation of a person outside of the country for prostitution).

Defendant: Artem Eduardovich Bondar
Gender: Male
Nationality: Belarusian
Born: 1991
Legal Reasoning:
A. E. Bondar was found guilty of committing an offense under Art. 14 Part 1 and Art. 171 Part 2 of the Criminal Code of Republic of Belarus (attempt to exploit the prostitution of others committed by a group, combined with transportation of a person outside of the country for prostitution).

Charges / Claims / Decisions

Defendant: P. B.
Verdict: Guilty
Charge / Claim:
Exploitation of the Prostitution of Others

Legislation / Statute / Code:
Criminal Code of Republic of Belarus, Art. 171

Term of Imprisonment:
7 years

Compensation / Payment to Victim:
No
Fine / Payment to State:
No
Appellate Decision:
Upheld
The Minsk Court upheld the decision of the court of 1st instance and dismissed the appeal.

(Continued)

(Continued)

Defendant: Alexander Günter

Verdict: Guilty

Charge / Claim:
Exploitation of the Prostitution of Others

Legislation / Statute / Code:
Criminal Code of Republic of Belarus, Art. 171

Term of Imprisonment:
7 years

Compensation / Payment to Victim:
No

Fine / Payment to State:
No

Appellate Decision:
Upheld
The Minsk Court upheld the decision of the court of 1st instance and dismissed the appeal.

Defendant: Artem Eduardovich Bondar

Verdict: Guilty

Charge / Claim:
Exploitation of the Prostitution of Others

Legislation / Statute / Code:
Criminal Code of Republic of Belarus, Art. 171

Term of Imprisonment:
7 years

Compensation / Payment to Victim:
No

Fine / Payment to State:
No

Appellate Decision:
Upheld
The Minsk Court upheld the decision of the court of 1st instance and dismissed the appeal.

Photo 8.2 Images taken directly from the Case Law Database, detailing a sex trafficking case in Belarus.

Source: UNODC Human Trafficking Knowledge Portal, https://sherloc.unodc.org/cld/en/v3/htms/index.html.

Trends in the U.S. also show a marked improvement in successful prosecutions. As indicated in Figure 8.2, between 2004 and 2013, the number of commercial sexual exploitation cases referred to the U.S. Attorney's Office increased, as did the number of cases filed in federal court and the number of convictions related to these cases (Adams & Flynn, 2017).

Nevertheless, there are many challenges to prosecuting human trafficking cases. While most countries have laws against human trafficking, using those laws to prosecute traffickers proves difficult all over the world. The UN, as part of its online Toolkit to Combat Trafficking in Persons, provides guidelines on investigating instances of human trafficking and prosecuting traffickers (United Nations Office on Drugs and Crime, 2008b). Guidelines such as these are absolutely

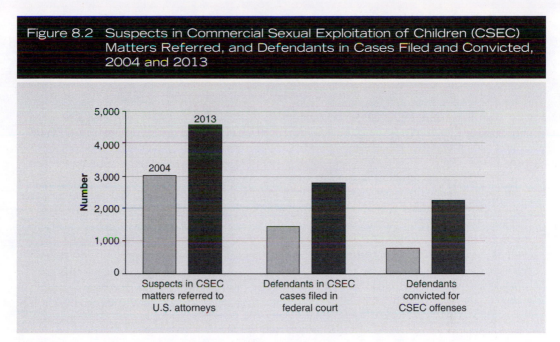

Figure 8.2 Suspects in Commercial Sexual Exploitation of Children (CSEC) Matters Referred, and Defendants in Cases Filed and Convicted, 2004 and 2013

Source: William Adams and Abigail Flynn (October 2017).

imperative to aid countries in improving their investigating methods and prioritizing prosecutions and sentencing of traffickers. Without proper investigations, prosecutions are nearly impossible (United Nations Office on Drugs and Crime, n.d.d). The UNODC works with countries to ensure they effectively investigate trafficking cases. This includes developing strategies to protect victims and witnesses, as both are critical to prosecuting trafficking cases.

A quantitative study of human trafficking prosecutions in the United Sates described challenges in identifying victims, investigating cases, and prosecuting cases (National Institute of Justice [NIJ], 2016). The covertness of human trafficking, combined with limitations in training first responders, explains the challenges in identifying victims. A lack of resources, lack of training, and lack of preparation in dealing with traumatized victims were cited as reasons that investigating cases was so difficult. Finally, the backgrounds of victims, combined with a lack of application of human trafficking laws, cause prosecutors to avoid human trafficking prosecutions or drive them to opt to charge offenders with crimes they are more familiar with (NIJ, 2016).

The data on prosecutions of trafficking cases are telling. While the number of prosecutions are on the rise, there is still more work to do. There must be more investment on a global level in prosecuting traffickers and those who engage in the commercial sex industry, especially when it is obviously a trafficking situation (i.e., underage victim). Even when human trafficking is happening in a different country, countries have the ability to control the behavior of their own citizens, using case law.

Sex tourism is discussed in this chapter as impacting women, men, and children. Sex tourism drives the demand for sex workers in many countries. Countries have the ability to make laws that make it illegal for their citizens to travel to other countries to engage in commercial sex, particularly with children (Chemin & Mbiekop, 2015; Newman et al., 2011). Once a law is in place, prosecutors are able to go after individuals who have traveled abroad for the purposes of sex tourism. The United States passed the PROTECT Act in 2003 to establish jurisdiction in

Case Study

the event that a U.S. citizen engages in sexual relations with a child abroad. While many countries, such as Costa Rica and the UK, are cooperative in providing sex registries and limiting the travel privileges of sexual offenders, strict laws must be in place in every country to extend the country's jurisdiction over its citizens to include prohibitions on engaging in sex with children while abroad (Newman et al., 2011).

Partnership

Partnership is an important component of any jurisdiction, state, or country's human trafficking reduction strategy. Partnerships should occur among many players, including NGOs, advocates, district and state attorneys' offices, and local and state task forces.

Task Forces

As of 2015, at least 20 states had human trafficking **task forces** (Polaris, 2015c). These task forces serve a variety of roles, including identifying best practices, coordinating efforts to prevent and combat trafficking, advocating legislation and policy changes, and providing an opportunity for collaboration, coordination, and awareness among agencies, nonprofits, and the local community.

Other Forms of Partnership

Interpol provides an example of a collaborative effort to combat sex trafficking by working with ECPAT and other NGOs. Its goal is to identify sex tourists within destination countries through collaboration, national alerts, and assisting local law enforcement. These NGOs also work with Internet service providers to identify sex tourists and sometimes recover victims as well (Miller-Perrin &

Focus On

Strategies to Reduce Sex Trafficking Between Nepal and India

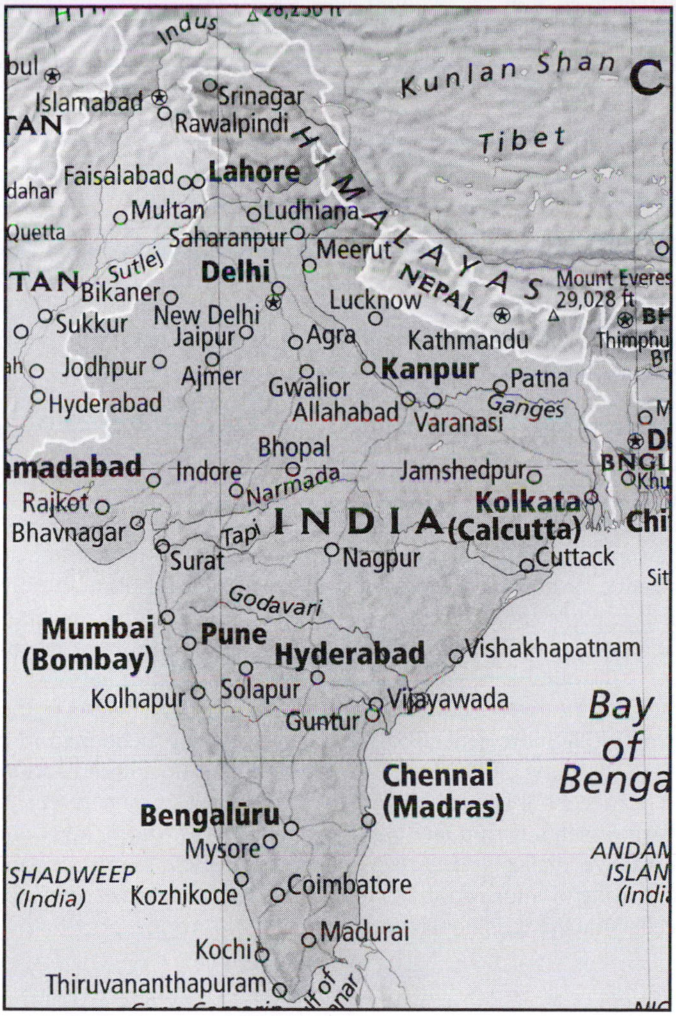

©istockphoto.com/AlpamayoPhoto

Photo 8.3 Map of India and Nepal.

Violence, gender discrimination, and poverty all result in Nepali women being trafficked to India for the purposes of performing commercial sex. While this happened for many years, it did not receive public attention until 1996. At that time, 200 underage Nepali girls were identified in Bombay brothels (Kaufman & Crawford, 2011). The Nepali government was unwilling to help the girls (e.g., no repatriation or reintegration), who sat in shelters in India until NGOs were able to get the girls and rehabilitate them. The incident brought a lot of attention to Nepal's policies on human trafficking.

The reaction of the public, combined with cooperation by government and a commitment to change by NGOs, highlights the importance of collaboration and partnership in combatting trafficking. Since that time, efforts have been put in place to improve the Nepali response to all forms of human trafficking. NGOs are relied on to provide prevention as well as trainings and awareness campaigns. Awareness comes in the form of community surveillance and more attention to suspicions of trafficking at the border (Kaufman & Crawford, 2011).

Victims of trafficking also receive increased attention. Far from the complete abandonment by the Nepali government of 200 of their underage citizens, more recent efforts by NGOs and the government provide opportunities for victim rehabilitation, including seed money to help make them self-sufficient (Kaufman & Crawford, 2011). NGOs also offer housing and medical care when necessary. Many girls are unable to return

(Continued)

(Continued)

home due to the stigmatization of prostitution, making their rehabilitation that much more challenging.

The Nepali police and government are now more responsive to demands for stronger anti-trafficking policies. Efforts are made to improve Nepali anti-trafficking laws, although these laws

still fail to meet that standards set forth by the UN, resulting in a Tier 2 ranking (U.S. Department of State, 2017c). Political instability and a lack of resources limit the country's ability to take full advantage of the collaborative opportunities that will result in a reduction of trafficking of Nepali citizens (Kaufman & Crawford, 2011).

Wurtele, 2017; Newman et al., 2011). Similarly, the U.S. works with foreign governments to identify and prosecute U.S. citizens engaging in commercial sex with underage youth outside the U.S.

Albeit limited, there is research available to show that partnerships will not only improve awareness and investigative opportunities but can also reduce the occurrence of sex trafficking. When examining the high rates of child sex tourism in India, researchers sought to explore the reactions to sex tourism in India, examining efforts to curb both supply and demand. Findings of the research indicated that isolating supply or demand efforts was ineffective in reducing child sex tourism in India (Chemin & Mbiekop, 2015; Newman et al., 2011). Rather, coordinated efforts to reduce the supply (through programs aimed at getting children off the streets) while also targeting the demand seemed most effective. Demand efforts required the coordination of multiple countries. The interaction of programming targeting street youth combined with effective child sex trafficking laws in other countries resulted in a reduction of the number of sex offenses against children in India.

Partnership is a relatively new term when it comes to reducing sex trafficking, and human trafficking more generally. That being said, it is mentioned in nearly every chapter of this book. The importance of communication, coordination, and collaboration may seem obvious, but privacy laws, lack of case management systems, and disagreements within and between jurisdictions, states, and countries make this a massive challenge. Legislation must be in place in every country to allow for the sharing of information as well as the creation of task forces or other avenues to collaboration and cooperation.

Conclusion

There is more information available on sex trafficking involving women and girls than perhaps on any other form of trafficking or victim. This information comes primarily from the media and a bounty of governmental and NGO reports. This information may make an uninformed reader believe that human trafficking is primarily a problem of sexual exploitation of women and girls. Hopefully, this books shows you the inaccuracy of this assumption. Labor trafficking is real, albeit less recognizable, as is the sex trafficking of males and transgender individuals. Undeniably, less is known about the sex trafficking of men and boys, but that is changing. Increased attention on these populations is resulting in improved screening tools and trainings. What also needs to expand, however, is the focus on empirical research on sex trafficking and prevention efforts (Jani & Anstadt, 2013; J. Jordan, Patel, & Rapp, 2013). While the limitations on research were previously mentioned, the magnitude of the issue warrants further discussion here.

As an example of the lack of research in this area, a recent systematic review found only 119 articles focusing on domestic minor sex trafficking since 2000 (Twis & Shelton, 2018). This seems like a relatively small number, given the outcry and attention focused on this specific population of victims. Of those 119 students, fewer than half of them (47.9%) were considered empirical (meaning the article has "prescribed, replicable methods and answered one or more specific research questions" (Twis & Shelton, 2018, p. 442). Of the empirical articles, only 49% were quantitative. The rest were qualitative or ethnography. There was one case study. Of the nonempirical articles, 48% were literature reviews, with the remaining being legal/policy related or conceptual papers. All of this to make the point that there is simply not enough research or data to apply evidence-based strategies to our understanding of and efforts to combat sex trafficking.

Improvements can be made to the global datasets we currently use as well. Earlier in this chapter, research was discussed as a way to improve our ability to prevent human trafficking. For this to be effective, we need to strengthen our current global data collection efforts. For example, the ICSE database, produced by ECPAT International and Interpol (2018), currently collects data from only 53 countries, Europol, and Interpol. Broader data collection efforts, combined with standardized definitions and categorizations, can greatly enhance our understanding of sex trafficking and responses to sex trafficking.

Our understanding of sex trafficking and responses to sex trafficking is at a crossroad. As awareness of this issue increases, funding and other resources are becoming available. Research is imperative to ensure that resources are targeting the right populations, prevention and rehabilitative programs, and investigation strategies. This, combined with investment in developing relationships across borders as well as common definitions and laws, will undoubtedly result in a reduction in sex trafficking of women, men, and children (J. Jordan et al., 2013).

KEY WORDS

Defense Advanced Research Projects Agency (DARPA) 188
demand 180
End Child Prostitution and Trafficking (ECPAT) 181
online exploitation 183
partnership 204

prevention 186
Project Vic 189
prosecution 198
protection 189
safe harbor 190
sex tourism 181
sextortion 184

task forces 204
Thorn 189
trauma-informed care 187
vacatur 189
visas 196

DISCUSSION QUESTIONS

1. Sex trafficking can be understood in terms of supply and demand. Explain. Make sure to respond to this prompt using a global context.

2. Explain how sex tourism impacts special populations such as males and children.

3. The Internet has changed the way sex is sold. Explain this progression and current legislative initiatives in the U.S. that aim to stop the advertising of sex online.

4. Safe harbor seems like an obvious strategy to protect young people from the consequences of sex trafficking and prostitution. However, safe harbor is not always legislatively supported or implemented. Why is this? What is the status of safe harbor where you live?

5. Visit the Human Trafficking Knowledge Portal online (https://sherloc.unodc.org/cld/en/v3/htms/index.html). Select a couple of countries. How do they compare in terms of prosecutions? Explain. Do the prosecutorial practices evident in this database coincide with the Department of State's TIP Report descriptions of prosecutions in those countries?

RESOURCES

- 3P Paradigm: https://www.state.gov/j/tip/3p/

- ECPAT International: http://www.ecpat.org/

- Human Trafficking Knowledge Portal: https://sherloc.unodc.org/cld/en/v3/htms/index.html

- Shared Hope International: https://sharedhope.org/

- Thorn: https://www.thorn.org/

Labor Trafficking

Labor trafficking takes on many forms. Like all types of human trafficking, labor trafficking is underreported and often goes undetected. In this section we will review why experts believe labor trafficking is even more likely to go unreported than sex trafficking. One reason is that labor trafficking pervades the spectrum of possible work environments. In the U.S., for example, many individuals are trafficked through immigrant work programs in agricultural and hospitality settings; in the Middle East, many individuals are trafficked through domestic servitude; and in southeast Asia, labor trafficking is prevalent in fishing boats. To help understand the differences in prevalence of distinct forms of labor trafficking, we will review political and legal infrastructures, or lack thereof, as they pertain to global labor trafficking. We will then discuss the prevalence of labor trafficking worldwide. We will also review risk factors for labor trafficking victimization and perpetration. Finally, we will discuss global responses to labor trafficking. As you read these chapters, think about the similarities and differences between labor trafficking and other forms of trafficking that you have learned about. Think about why the response to labor trafficking must be distinct from the response to other forms of trafficking and what additional research, legislation, or interventions could be used to combat labor trafficking.

More Than Unfair Labor Practices

Right now, there is a man on a boat, casting the net with his bleeding hands, knowing he deserves a better life, a life of dignity, but doesn't know if anybody is paying attention. Right now, there's a woman, hunched over a sewing machine, glancing beyond the bars on the window, knowing if just given the chance, she might someday sell her own wares, but she doesn't think anybody is paying attention. Right now, there's a young boy, in a brick factory, covered in dust, hauling his heavy load under a blazing sun, thinking if he could just go to school, he might know a different future, but he doesn't think anybody is paying attention. . . . And so our message today, to them, is—to the millions around the world—we see you. We hear you. We insist on your dignity. And we share your belief that if just given the chance, you will forge a life equal to your talents and worthy of your dreams.

—President Barack Obama to the Clinton Global Initiative, September 25, 2012, Sheraton New York Hotel and Towers, New York, New York

I got my first job at a fast-food restaurant when I was 13 years old. I had to sign several contracts acknowledging that I understood my rights as a worker and as a minor. I signed documents confirming that I would not work more than 18 hours per week, or 8 hours per day during the school year. I agreed not to work after 7 p.m. I also couldn't prepare food or perform several other tasks that were deemed too dangerous for my age. Every four hours when I clocked out for a mandatory break, I sat in a room next to a laminated poster describing compulsory compensation for injuries incurred on the job. At the time, I resented all of these restrictions. I wanted to earn more money. I didn't realize how lucky I was to have these protections as a minor and to work for an employer that abided by them. In the absence of workplace protections, millions of people work at arduous, often dangerous tasks for endless hours. For many children, work may come at the expense of their education. Entire families are forced to work, earning hardly enough money to stay alive. As a teenager, however, my privileges afforded me the luxury to know nothing of forced labor.

What, if anything, comes to mind when you imagine labor trafficking? For many people, my younger self included, labor trafficking never comes to mind at all. One reason for this is that forced labor takes place in isolated or private locations and disproportionately impacts the most vulnerable and disconnected populations. Many victims of labor trafficking are kept out of the view of direct service providers, law enforcement, and the general public in agricultural settings, mines, in private homes as domestic servants, and in factories. Other victims work right in the public eye in restaurants, sales crews, and in the entertainment and beauty industries. Labor traffickers are also difficult to detect, in part because law enforcement providers are not familiar with the characteristics or legal definitions of labor trafficking and are often unaware that their country, state, or locality has laws specific to labor trafficking (United Nations Office on Drugs and Crime [UNODC], 2016a).

In this chapter, we will review definitions of labor trafficking and its components, the extent of labor trafficking in the United States and abroad, laws and legislation affecting our ability to identify and prosecute labor traffickers, and characteristics of labor traffickers and their victims. At the end we will highlight populations that are particularly vulnerable to labor trafficking, including populations that are likely underreported.

What Is Labor Trafficking?

Labor trafficking is the "use of force, fraud, or coercion to make someone perform labor or a service," and is a pervasive form of human trafficking worldwide (International Labour Office & Walk Free Foundation, 2017). Victims of labor trafficking are found in every nation and are employed in a broad range of industries, from domestic servitude to carnivals (International Labour Office & Walk Free Foundation, 2017; Polaris, 2014c). Labor traffickers use a variety of coercive tactics to exploit labor, including withholding wages; withholding documents; physical, sexual, and emotional violence; debt bondage; and threats toward family members.

While victims and perpetrators are hidden from law enforcement and the public, the products of forced labor are in our homes, schools, electronics, and the foods we eat. The demand for cheap goods and labor is a significant contributing factor to the persistence of labor trafficking (Bales, 2012). The U.S. Department of Labor (2016) identified 139 goods from 75 countries produced using forced labor or involuntary child labor. If you own a cell phone, for example, it was almost certainly produced using forced labor in columbo-tantalite mines (also known as "coltan" mines). The dangerous working conditions in these mines lead to substantial worker injury and premature death (Dizolele & Applewhite, 2009).

Unfair Practices Versus Labor Trafficking

Most victims of labor trafficking are subject to unfair or illegal civil labor practices. Unfair civil labor practices are situations where an employer financially gains from participating in the illegal treatment of employees. In the U.S., unfair labor practices are defined in the 1935 **National Labor Relations Act (NLRA)** and include paying someone less than the minimum wage, paying less than an agreed on or contracted amount, wage theft, illegal deductions, or other violations of local labor laws. The NLRA does not define certain categories of workers, such as agricultural workers and domestic workers, as "employees." This limits workers' rights and prevents them from being able to organize together for fair treatment (Bales, Fletcher, & Stover, 2004). International standards vary, but as depicted in

Table 9.1, the International Labour Organization (ILO) outlines four core standards in eight conventions with varying degrees of ratification from its member countries (International Labour Organization, 2014c).

While unfair labor practices are criminal acts, without the presence of force, fraud, or coercion, unfair labor practices are not a form of labor trafficking. The key distinction between labor trafficking and unfair civil labor practices has to do with whether the worker is voluntarily staying in his or her job. If workers are subject to unfair civil labor practices, they are free to leave this situation of their own will. When an employer exerts control over individuals so that they have no choice but to accept these practices, this constitutes labor trafficking.

To understand labor trafficking more precisely, it is helpful to examine each of its components, which include forced labor, debt bondage, and involuntary child labor. These concepts are related but legally distinct. Many organizations recognize forced labor as an umbrella term that includes debt bondage and involuntary child labor. Figure 9.1 provides an overview of how these terms are related.

Forced labor is any involuntary work conducted as the result of coercion. Particularly in international reports, *forced labor* is sometimes used synonymously with *labor trafficking*. Forced labor is characterized by an involuntary, coercive

Table 9.1 Ratifications of ILO Core Labor Standards

ILO Conventions According to the Core Labor Standard They Represent	Ratified by How Many Countries (Possible = 187)	Ratified in Full by the U.S.
Freedom of association and the right to collective bargaining		
Convention 87: Freedom of Association and Protection of the Right to Organize	154	No
Convention 98: Right to Organize and Collective Bargaining	165	No
Freedom from forced labor		
Convention 29: Forced Labor	178	No
Convention 105: Abolition of Forced Labor	175	Yes
Freedom from child labor		
Convention 138: Minimum Age Convention	170	No
Convention 182: Worst Forms of Child Labor	181	Yes
Freedom from discrimination at work		
Convention 100: Equal Remuneration	173	No
Convention 111: Discrimination (Employment and Occupation)	175	No

Data source: International Labour Office, 2014c.

Figure 9.1 Labor Trafficking, Child Labor, and Unfair Labor Practices

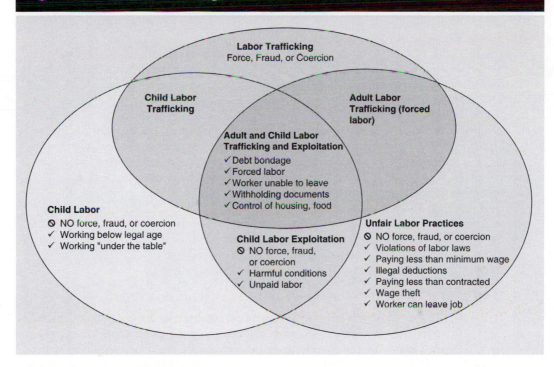

Labor Trafficking
Force, Fraud, or Coercion

Child Labor Trafficking

Adult Labor Trafficking (forced labor)

Adult and Child Labor Trafficking and Exploitation
✓ Debt bondage
✓ Forced labor
✓ Worker unable to leave
✓ Withholding documents
✓ Control of housing, food

Child Labor
⊘ NO force, fraud, or coercion
✓ Working below legal age
✓ Working "under the table"

Child Labor Exploitation
⊘ NO force, fraud, or coercion
✓ Harmful conditions
✓ Unpaid labor

Unfair Labor Practices
⊘ NO force, fraud, or coercion
✓ Violations of labor laws
✓ Paying less than minimum wage
✓ Illegal deductions
✓ Paying less than contracted
✓ Wage theft
✓ Worker can leave job

Data source: Owens et al. (2014).

relationship between an employer and worker where the worker feels he or she has no choice other than to continue working. It is not based on working conditions, even if they are hazardous; on the type of work performed; or on whether the work is legal (International Labour Office & Walk Free Foundation, 2017; U.S. Department of State, 2016). Most human rights organizations distinguish three types of forced labor: state-imposed forced labor, privately imposed forced labor, and forced child marriage. In this chapter, we will focus on state and privately imposed forced labor (forced child marriage is discussed in Chapter 13). Government- or state-imposed **forced labor** may be perpetrated by a military or paramilitary organization, in prisons that do not meet international standards, or in schools, where students' work is greater than would be needed for their educational training.

Debt bondage, or **bonded labor**, is a specific method of coercion used by labor traffickers. Employers create a situation where a worker is in financial debt and then use that debt as leverage to force that person to work for them until the debt is repaid. For example, an employer may offer a small amount of money to help a worker meet his or her immediate needs when beginning a new job. Employers generally apply fees and add hidden costs over time, and ultimately it is impossible for the worker to leave. The value of the victim's labor typically exceeds the value of the debt. Debt bondage is illegal in the United States and identified as a form of coercion in the United Nations trafficking in persons protocol (International Labour Office & Walk Free Foundation, 2017; Trafficking Victims Protection Act, 2000; United Nations General Assembly, 2000c).

Though today's consumer demand for cheap products is a primary driver of labor trafficking, labor trafficking is hardly a phenomenon that started because everyone wanted a smartphone in their hand. Institutionalized forced labor and debt bondage are historically rooted systems in many nations, which is a significant barrier to eradicating modern slavery. The Atlantic slave trade from 1526 to 1867 brought over 10 million African men, women, and children to North and South America and the Caribbean, where they were forced into slavery. Ten percent of the men, women, and children brought from Africa died in transit alone. The Indian Ocean slave trade spanned an estimated 1,300 years, not ending until the 20th century, and though outlawed, persists in some countries even today. Other examples of institutionalized forced labor in nations around the world are abundant. Forced labor was prevalent during the British occupation of India, the Arab occupation of Spain, and the Nazi occupation of Germany and Poland. Bonded labor is also rooted in many country's histories. Traditionally, bonded labor was an employer–creditor relationship in which debts were passed on through generations of families. This traditional form of bonded labor is still fairly common practice in many countries, primarily India, Pakistan, Bangladesh, and Nepal.

Child labor trafficking, put simply, is labor trafficking of a minor. Child labor trafficking is distinguished from child labor by the presence of force, fraud, or coercion.[1] For children, force, fraud, or coercion must be applied by someone other than the child's parents to the child or his or her parents to make the child work or to keep the child from leaving his or her employment. Child labor without an element of coercion from a third party, even if it is in hazardous conditions or the child is below the legal age of employment in a country, no matter how reprehensible, is sometimes referred to as child labor exploitation but does not constitute child labor trafficking (International Labour Organization, 2012).

Portrait of Labor Trafficking in the U.S.

Prevalence

Information on labor trafficking in the U.S. is compiled from a few sources: law enforcement data, data from the **National Human Trafficking Resource Center (NHTRC)**, and data from federally funded direct service providers. We can also turn to research organizations that use these sources as well as collect their own data to fill in gaps in our understanding of labor trafficking. Data from all of these sources agree in some areas, such as in which states labor trafficking is most prevalent, which industries are involved in labor trafficking, and which populations are most at risk, but diverge in others, such as how prevalent labor trafficking is.

It is estimated that at any given time, upwards of 10,000 people in the U.S. are victims of labor trafficking (Bales et al., 2004; Walk Free Foundation, 2018). Law enforcement data find that labor trafficking constitutes 11% of all known cases of human trafficking in the U.S., but federal grantees serving victims of human

---

[1] Child soldiering is a form of child labor trafficking. We discuss child soldiering in detail in Chapter 11.

trafficking report that 64% of their caseload is labor trafficking victims (Banks & Kyckelhahn, 2011). Another study found that 55% of prosecuted human trafficking cases in the U.S. contained an element of labor trafficking, but just 29% of cases contained charges for labor trafficking (Farrel et al., 2012).

The states with the most known cases of labor trafficking are California, Texas, Florida, New York, and Georgia. Labor trafficking is known to occur in at least 90 U.S. cities (Polaris, 2017), though some research has estimated that labor trafficking occurs in at least 116 U.S. counties (Newton, Mulcahy, & Martin, 2008).

The industries with the most cases of labor trafficking in the U.S. are domestic work in private homes, agricultural work, and factory work. Labor trafficking in the U.S. is also found in sales crews, restaurants, construction, carnivals, and the health and beauty industry (Bales et al., 2004; Polaris, 2017).

The National Human Trafficking Resource Center provides recent statistics based on calls to their hotline. In 2016, the NHTRC identified 1,064 cases of labor trafficking involving at least 2,785 victims in 2016. Each case reported by the NHTRC may include multiple victims, but they have victim information only if the caller provides it. Of the 1,064 cases in 2016, there were roughly equal numbers of male and female victims, 843 were adults and 211 were children, and 694 were foreign nationals and 153 were either U.S. citizens or lawful permanent residents (Polaris, 2017).

Labor trafficking victims have been identified as coming from over 40 countries into the U.S. Most often, labor traffickers are of the same ethnicity as their victims. Department of Justice reports on federally prosecuted cases of labor trafficking indicate that many labor traffickers are newly naturalized U.S. citizens with close ties to their country of origin. It is also common for recruiters of labor trafficking to be based in other countries and work with domestic traffickers (Clawson, Dutch, Lopez, & Tiapula, 2008).

As mentioned, data from the NHTRC provide insight into the demographic characteristics of trafficking victims. This information, shown in Table 9.2, is available only for cases that are reported to the hotline. For reported instances of labor trafficking, we know that the majority of labor trafficking victims are adults, females, and foreign nationals. Foreign nationals are individuals who have come to the United States but have citizenship in another country, also referred to as immigrants.

Laws

Laws and statutes provide us with an understanding of how law enforcement, and to some extent direct service providers, might conceptualize labor trafficking. Anti-trafficking and anti-slavery laws are key to protecting victims and prosecuting traffickers, but legislation in a broad range of fields is used to prevent and stop trafficking. For example, labor laws set standards for fair treatment of workers and the legal age for child labor. Trade laws can be used to prevent importation of goods made with forced labor. Labor supply chain reporting laws can force companies to identify the source of their labor, consequently "naming and shaming" corporations that use forced labor.

In the past two decades, the U.S. and global communities have enacted landmark anti-trafficking legislation. Just because a law is enacted, however, does not signal the end of the issue it seeks to address. It takes many years to effectively implement new policies or legislation. The Emancipation Proclamation in 1863, for example, is often considered the statute that "freed the slaves" after the Civil War. In reality, the Emancipation Proclamation did not free any slaves. In 1865, the government passed the Thirteenth Amendment stating that "neither slavery

	Number of Cases in 2015	% of Cases in 2015
Age		
Adults	581	80.6%
Minors	114	15.8%
Gender		
Females	411	57%
Males	333	46.2%
Transgender Females	3	0.4%
Transgender Males	3	0.4%
Gender-Nonconforming	<3	N/A
Citizenship Status		
U.S. Citizens or Legal Permanent Residents	107	14.8%
Foreign Nationals	453	62.8%

*Statistics are noncumulative. Some cases had multiple victims.

Source: National Human Trafficking Resource Center, 2016.

Focus On
The 13th Amendment

Neither slavery nor involuntary servitude, except as a punishment for a crime whereof the party shall have been duly convicted, shall exist within the United States, or any place subject to their jurisdiction.

In the United States, prisoners earn as little as $0.02 per hour for full-time work in agriculture, manufacturing, food preparation, and other industries. Some activists suggest that this constitutes forced labor. The documentary *13th* (DuVernay, 2016) recently brought greater public attention to this topic.

nor involuntary servitude . . . shall exist within the United States." Even still, African men, women, and children were forced to work in sharecropping, domestic servitude, convict leasing, and chain gangs for nearly eight decades following the end of the Civil War (Blackmon, 2009).

U.S. Law

Most modern federal human trafficking legislation is rooted in the 13th Amendment, including the **Trafficking Victim Protection Act of 2000 (TVPA)**.

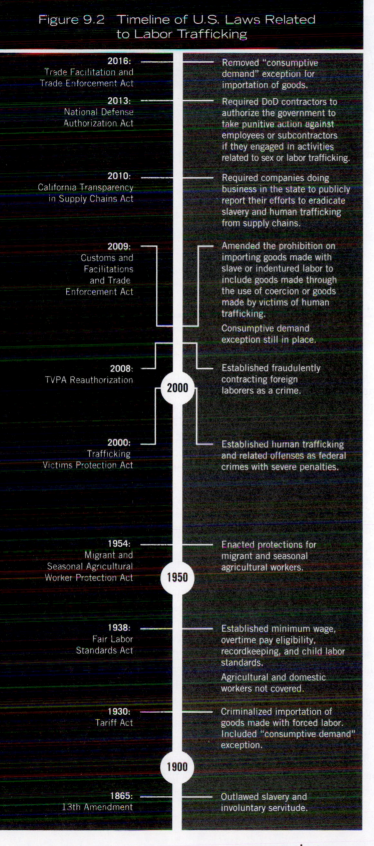

Figure 9.2 Timeline of U.S. Laws Related to Labor Trafficking

2016:
Trade Facilitation and Trade Enforcement Act
— Removed "consumptive demand" exception for importation of goods.

2013:
National Defense Authorization Act
— Required DoD contractors to authorize the government to take punitive action against employees or subcontractors if they engaged in activities related to sex or labor trafficking.

2010:
California Transparency in Supply Chains Act
— Required companies doing business in the state to publicly report their efforts to eradicate slavery and human trafficking from supply chains.

2009:
Customs and Facilitations and Trade Enforcement Act
— Amended the prohibition on importing goods made with slave or indentured labor to include goods made through the use of coercion or goods made by victims of human trafficking.
Consumptive demand exception still in place.

2008:
TVPA Reauthorization
— Established fraudulently contracting foreign laborers as a crime.

2000

2000:
Trafficking Victims Protection Act
— Established human trafficking and related offenses as federal crimes with severe penalties.

1954:
Migrant and Seasonal Agricultural Worker Protection Act
— Enacted protections for migrant and seasonal agricultural workers.

1950

1938:
Fair Labor Standards Act
— Established minimum wage, overtime pay eligibility, recordkeeping, and child labor standards.
Agricultural and domestic workers not covered.

1930:
Tariff Act
— Criminalized importation of goods made with forced labor. Included "consumptive demand" exception.

1900

1865:
13th Amendment
— Outlawed slavery and involuntary servitude.

The TVPA is considered the cornerstone of U.S. anti-trafficking legislation. The TVPA defines labor trafficking as "the recruitment, harboring, transportation, provision, or obtaining of a person for labor or services, through the use of force, fraud or coercion for the purpose of subjection to involuntary servitude, peonage, debt bondage or slavery."

The TVPA has since been reauthorized in 2003, 2005, 2008, and 2013. The 2008 reauthorization was particularly significant for labor trafficking efforts because it outlawed fraudulent foreign labor contracting, making it illegal to bring a foreign worker to the U.S. for work under false pretenses about the conditions of their employment.

Whoever knowingly and with intent to defraud recruits, solicits or hires a person outside the United States for purposes of employment in the United States by means of materially false or fraudulent pretenses, representations or promises regarding that employment shall be fined under this title or imprisoned for not more than 5 years, or both.

The TVPA is not the only federal legislation used to identify labor traffickers and labor trafficking victims. The Tariff Act of 1930 outlawed importation of goods made with forced or child labor, except in the case of consumptive demand. This consumptive demand exception allowed for the importation of goods produced with forced labor if U.S. supply was not meeting domestic demand for the goods. It was not until 2016 when President Obama enacted the **2015 Trade Facilitation and Trade Enforcement Act** that the U.S. prohibited the importation of any goods produced with forced labor without exception.

State law is also important to anti–labor trafficking efforts. In the U.S., the Tenth Amendment grants states "police powers," or the right to enact laws that protect the welfare of their residents when it is not explicitly prohibited by the federal government. This means states can prosecute any labor trafficking cases that do not fall under federal jurisdiction. As of 2014, all states and the District of Columbia had a human trafficking law with a labor trafficking statute. This means that in every state, it is a crime to compel someone through force, fraud, or coercion to provide labor or services (Polaris, 2014c). In 2010, California passed landmark legislation requiring companies in the state to report their efforts to remove forced labor and slavery from their supply chains. The U.S. Congress as well as governments in several other countries have since drafted federal legislation modeled after this law.

Despite the presence of these various laws and statutes, prosecution of labor trafficking varies substantially by state, and the overwhelming majority of labor trafficking violations continue to be prosecuted at a federal level (Farrell et al., 2012). Studies find that local, state, and federal agencies have a substantial knowledge gap when it comes to labor trafficking. One nationally representative study found that law enforcement, prosecutors, and direct service providers were unable to accurately define labor trafficking or to distinguish it from other forms of trafficking or smuggling and were unfamiliar with local statutes pertaining to labor trafficking (Newton et al., 2008). In this study, half of investigators and 44% of prosecutors did not even know their state had a statute specific to labor trafficking (Newton et al., 2008).

Law enforcement agencies do not allocate significant resources to the identification and prosecution of labor trafficking cases. For example, there are no positions in local law enforcement agencies dedicated to labor trafficking at the state level. At the federal level, the Department of Labor reports almost no involvement in identifying instances of labor trafficking (Banks & Kyckelhahn, 2011).

Migrant Workers in the U.S.

Though labor traffickers target U.S. citizens as well as noncitizens, foreign nationals are at an elevated risk, particularly those working in agriculture (Bales et al., 2004; Polaris, 2014c). Agriculture is a highly profitable industry in the U.S. Demand for U.S. agricultural products has increased substantially, which has driven the high levels of forced labor in this industry. More than 1 million migrant workers contribute to the agricultural work force in the U.S. each year (Bales et al., 2004).

Many people come to the U.S. in hopes of securing stable employment and earning money for their families. These individuals do not think they have the same opportunity for economic prosperity in their home countries. Recruiters and traffickers take advantage of this. They may convince victims that the conditions they are subject to are far better than any other employment they could secure. Traffickers may pay for visa application fees and transport costs, then use this debt to coerce victims to stay in an abusive environment. Employers may also take advantage of the complexity of the visa application process, a worker's lack of English fluency, and unfamiliarity with local culture to deceive workers (Polaris, 2015d). Traffickers may not let workers contact their family or service providers. This makes it harder still to escape an exploitive situation. Workers who do contact legal services are often placed on blacklists and unable to return for work in subsequent seasons (Bauer, 2007).

In the U.S., labor traffickers commonly use immigration status as a mechanism of control. One study among migrant workers in the U.S. found that about 71% of noncitizen victims of labor trafficking entered the country on a temporary work visa, but by the time of their escape, 69% of these workers were unauthorized (Owens et al., 2014; Polaris, 2015d). Because most temporary work visas are tied to a single employer, traffickers use workers' visa status as a point of coercion. Further, traffickers frequently do not allow workers to leave when their visas expire. After visas are expired, traffickers threaten to report now-unauthorized workers to Immigration in order to maintain control over them (Owens et al., 2014; Polaris, 2015).

> *When the supervisor would see that a person was ready to leave the job because the pay was so bad, he would take our papers from us. He would rip up our visa and say, "You don't want to work? Get out of here then. You don't want to work? Right now I will call immigration to take your papers and deport you."*

—H-2B forestry worker (as cited in Polaris, 2015d)

The structure of the temporary work visa programs in the U.S. put many workers at risk. In particular, temporary work visas that are specific to a single employer facilitate coercive and exploitive practices. Since employers know that a worker cannot obtain employment anywhere else and cannot afford to return home without earning money, they can use this to exploit workers for financial gain. Some visas permit employers to control food and housing for their workers. If workers try to speak out against abusive practices, they may have nowhere to live, no money for food, and no resources to return home.

Table 9.3 outlines the temporary work visas most commonly held by victims of labor trafficking in the United States. A feature of many of the temporary work visas that is highly conducive to trafficking is that they are tied to a single

Table 9.3 Summary of Temporary Work Visa Programs in the U.S.

Visa Type	Description	Specific to a Single Employer
H-2A: Temporary agricultural workers	Permits individuals to work in temporary or seasonal agricultural jobs	Yes
H-2B: Temporary nonagricultural workers	Permits individuals to work in a diverse range of industries on a temporary or seasonal basis	Yes
J-1: Exchange visitor program	Permits individuals to participate in a diverse range of work and study exchange programs	No, but the visa sponsor must approve a change in employer
A3: Diplomats and foreign government officials	Permits entrance for up to three years for employees of diplomatic and diplomat-affiliated visa holders (A1 and A2)	Yes
G-5: Employee of international organization and NATO	Permits entrance for employees of individuals who work for international organizations	Yes
B-1: Temporary business visitors	Permits foreign nationals to enter the United States for business on behalf of a foreign employer. The B-1 visa is temporary and is not a work visa	No

Source: U.S. Department of State (N.D.); Owens, C., et al. (2014); Polaris (2015).

employer. Workers may fear leaving their employer because they will have no way to return home or remain in the U.S. legally.

Among individuals with temporary work visas reporting trafficking to the NHTRC, most arrived to the U.S. on an H-2B or H-2A visa (see Figure 9.3).

The H-2A visa is for temporary or seasonal agricultural workers. There are also a few categories of specialized labor that are included in the H-2A visa. The H-2A visa affords several important legal rights to workers, which are outlined in Table 9.4.

The H-2B visa is designed for temporary and seasonal workers not working in industries covered by the H-2A visa. Trafficking victims known to the NHTRC with H-2B visas are most commonly employed in landscaping, hospitality, and forestry but also work in food service, construction, and traveling carnivals. These victims are predominantly male, and their primary country of origin is Mexico (Polaris, 2015d). H-2B visa holders do not have the same protections mentioned above that are granted to H-2A holders, as shown in Table 9.4 (Bauer & Stewart, 2013).

The J-1 visa permits foreign nationals for a broad variety of opportunities, from participating in student or teacher exchange programs to working in summer camps or as au pairs. Each of the 14 subcategories of the J-1 visa is regulated distinctly. Foreign nationals with a J-1 visa may apply to have their employer changed, but it is an arduous process and they must have sign-off from their sponsor. Victims reported to the NHTRC with J-1 visas were in a broad range of industries. Roughly half of the victims were female, in contrast to other visa programs, and J-1 visas were the only category where

Focus On

History of Temporary Work Visa Programs in the U.S.

Today, most temporary workers enter the U.S. under the **H visa program**, but this program evolved from several immigration policies before it. From 1790 to 1882, U.S. borders were open to immigrants from all over the world under the Naturalization Act. During this time, immigrant workers substantially contributed to U.S. expansion and economic growth. During the Mexican American War from 1846 to 1848, the U.S. acquired over 500,000 square miles of land from Mexico. After the war ended, huge numbers of Mexican workers continued to come to the U.S. for work, returning home after the work season ended. It was not until 1924, when the U.S. Border Patrol was established, that these workers were unauthorized to enter the U.S. Even still, legal immigration, particularly for temporary and seasonal work, remained common practice.

During the Great Depression, however, workers from Mexico were deemed a threat to American jobs, and the U.S. forcibly deported over half a million Mexican workers. When the U.S. entered World War II, the economy once again needed additional workers, and the United States reopened its borders to Mexican laborers. The U.S. and Mexico established the Bracero Program, which would allow Mexican workers to fill jobs in the U.S., similar to the current H-2 visa program. Though the program offered substantial protections to workers, they were not informed of their rights, and information about the program was provided only in English. Employers commonly stole the 10% of employee wages that was required to be placed in a pension plan for the employees in Mexico. Today, lawsuits have been filed on behalf of Mexican workers from the Bracero Program totaling hundreds of millions of dollars. The Bracero Program was used to exploit hundreds of thousands of workers. The U.S. program officer in charge of the program deemed it "legalized slavery." The program was so cruel and unfair that Cesar Chavez launched protests of the program. The Bracero Program ended in 1964, and today workers can enter the U.S. under the H-2 visa program.

Source: Adapted from Bauer (2007).

Figure 9.3 Total Labor Trafficking and Labor Exploitation Victims Reported to the NHTRC and BeFree Textline

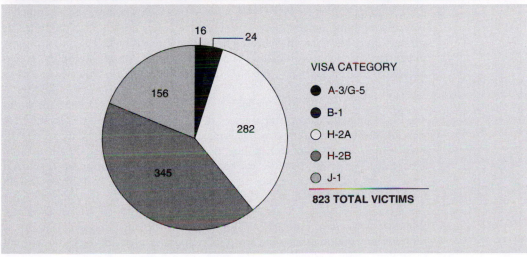

VISA CATEGORY

● A-3/G-5

◐ B-1

○ H-2A

◉ H-2B

◔ J-1

823 TOTAL VICTIMS

Source: Polaris Project's National Human Trafficking Resource Center, 2015d.

Table 9.4 Legal Rights for H-2A and H-2B workers

Legal Right	Description	H-2A	H-2B
Three-fourths guarantee	Employers must offer workers at least 75% of the hours guaranteed in their contract.	Yes	No
Free housing	Employers must offer housing in good condition for the duration of workers' contracts.	Yes	No
Workers' compensation benefits	Employers must cover medical costs and costs of lost time at work for job-related injuries.	Yes	No
Reimbursement for travel	Employers must pay for the costs of transportation, including food for workers at the beginning and end of their contract.	Yes	No
Federally funded legal services	Legal services must be made available to workers for issues related to their H-2A work.	Yes	No
50% rule	Employers must hire qualified U.S. employees before the second half of the season.	Yes	No

Source: Adapted from Southern Poverty Law Center (SPLC) (2007).

victims reported sex trafficking in addition to labor trafficking. A-3 and G-5 visas allow foreign government officials to employee foreign nationals, typically in domestic work. These visa programs account for a small proportion of work visas and accordingly a small proportion of human trafficking victims overall, but these cases tend to be highly publicized when they are uncovered. Victims known to the NHTRC with A-3 or G-5 visas are typically females working in domestic servitude. The B-1 visa is not a work visa program; its primary purpose is to allows foreign nationals to visit the U.S. for business purposes. It also, however, allows U.S. citizens living abroad to employ foreign nationals. Victims known to the NHTRC with B-1 visas are typically female as well (Polaris, 2015d).

Many victims of laboring trafficking work in private homes as domestic workers. When migrants gain a temporary work visa to work as domestic servants, it is typically tied to a single employer. This makes workers less likely to report abuses, because they do not want to risk their visa status. In some cases, diplomats from other countries bring domestic workers and exploit them for cheap or unpaid labor. These traffickers are protected by diplomatic immunity against prosecution for use of forced labor.

In addition to visa laws and diplomatic immunity, U.S. labor laws put domestic workers at risk. The NLRA does not identify domestic workers as "employees," limiting their ability to report abuse or organize for better and fair treatment.

Case Study

H-2B Visa

Angela was studying psychology in the Dominican Republic when she decided to become a guest worker in a New Orleans hotel, in part to earn money to pay medical bills for her cancer-stricken mother.

Like most guest workers, Angela was promised plenty of work. She would need it, because she had taken on $4,000 in debt to pay the fees necessary to obtain the job and the nine-month H-2B visa.

"Every one of us took out a loan to come here," she said. "We had planned to pay back our debt with our job here. They told us we would have overtime, that we could get paid double for holidays, that we would have a place to live at low cost, and it was all a lie."

When she arrived in New Orleans in April 2006, she was given a desk job at the hotel, earning $6 an hour. She worked full-time, with some overtime, for the first month. But then her hours started dwindling; soon she was working only 15 to 20 [hours] per week, earning an average of $120 per week. She hardly had enough money to eat three meals a day after paying for housing and transportation.

"We would just buy Chinese food because it was the cheapest. We would buy one plate a day for

about $11 and share it between two or three people. Sometimes we would eat bread and cheese. Sometimes we would make rice."

Her visa did not allow her to seek other employment, not even a part-time job, and she fell deeper in debt.

She felt trapped by debt and by the promise she had made: She and her mother had signed a guarantee that she would finish the contract—or pay $10,000. If she could not pay, the recruiters would take her mother's belongings.

"I felt like an animal without claws—defenseless. It is the same as slavery."

"There are some people that believe the guest worker program is a good idea, but it is not. . . . You put all your savings and hope into what this work promises and you accept the small amount of hours they give, the poor working conditions, and the low pay."

Angela's plans are ruined. "I cannot even talk to my mother about all of the troubles I have been having because I don't want her to worry and feel sicker. This is the other part that I have to swallow. It's like you are in hell and you are closed in and you don't know where the exit is. It's terrible."

Source: Bauer and Stewart, 2013.

Portrait of Labor Trafficking Globally

Prevalence

The ILO estimates that there are 16.4 million victims of labor trafficking worldwide, including 14.2 million victims of privately imposed forced labor and 2.2 million victims of government- or state-imposed forced labor (International Labour Office & Walk Free Foundation, 2017).

Figure 9.4 shows the number of victims of labor trafficking in state and privately imposed settings by geographic region. The highest prevalence of forced labor is in Asia and the Pacific, followed by Africa, Latin America and the Caribbean, Central and Southeastern Europe, Developed Economies and the European Union, and the Middle East.

The proportion of labor trafficking victims has steadily increased each year, from 32% in 2007 to 38% in 2014, the most recent year of available data. The increase in the proportion of labor trafficking victims is due, in part, to increased

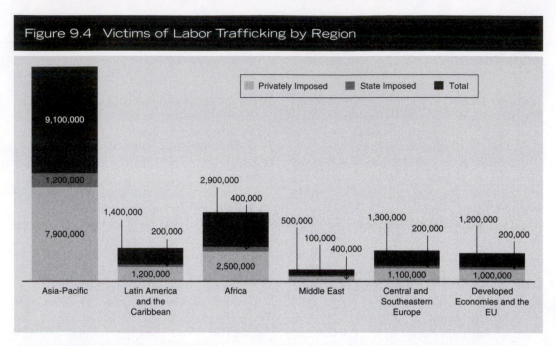

Figure 9.4 Victims of Labor Trafficking by Region

Legend: Privately Imposed | State Imposed | Total

Asia-Pacific	9,100,000 / 1,200,000 / 7,900,000
Latin America and the Caribbean	1,400,000 / 200,000 / 1,200,000
Africa	2,900,000 / 400,000 / 2,500,000
Middle East	500,000 / 100,000 / 400,000
Central and Southeastern Europe	1,300,000 / 200,000 / 1,100,000
Developed Economies and the EU	1,200,000 / 200,000 / 1,000,000

Source: International Labour Office (2016).

Challenge Yourself 9.2

Our knowledge of labor trafficking is limited to the information available to us. Often, data on labor trafficking are compiled using information provided by governments, data on prosecutions of traffickers, and data from victim-serving organizations. In some cases, these data may be supplemented by in-depth studies.

knowledge surrounding labor trafficking and better reporting (UNODC, 2018a). The proportion of labor trafficking cases relative to other types of trafficking varies by region. As shown in Figure 9.5, in North Africa, about 69% of trafficking victims are victims of labor trafficking, compared to just 5% in North America.

Revenue

Like other forms of trafficking, labor trafficking engenders substantial profits. Forced labor generates an estimated $51.2 billion worldwide: $9 billion from forced labor in agriculture, $8 billion from forced domestic labor, and $34 billion from other industries such as construction, manufacturing, and mining. Further, the costs associated with forced labor are estimated to be about $21 billion: $19.6 billion in underpaid wages and $1.4 billion in illegal recruitment fees (International Labour Office, 2014). When this is translated to profits per victim, forced labor in construction, manufacturing, mining, and utilities generates an annual $4,800 per victim; in agriculture, forced labor generates $2,500 per victim annually; and in domestic work, forced labor generates $2,300 per victim per year.

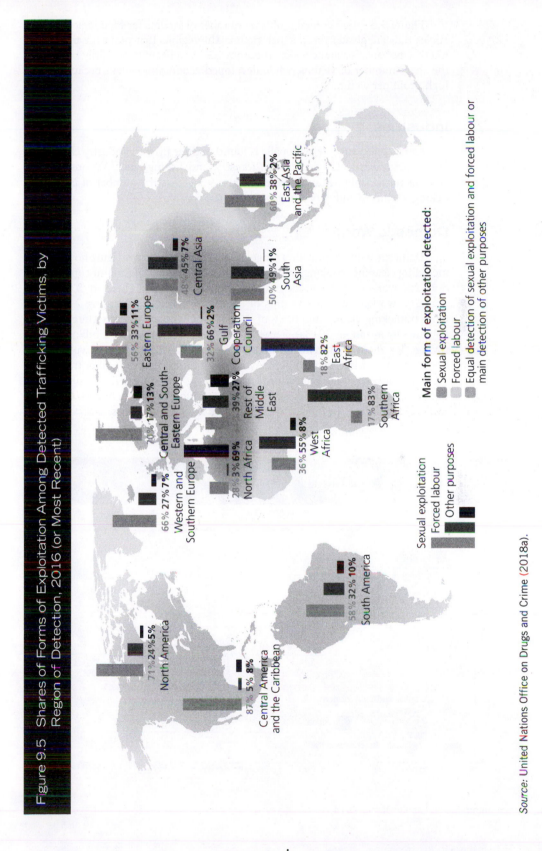

Figure 9.5 Shares of Forms of Exploitation Among Detected Trafficking Victims, by Region of Detection, 2016 (or Most Recent)

Main form of exploitation detected:

Sexual exploitation
Forced labour
Equal detection of sexual exploitation and forced labour or main detection of other purposes

East Asia and the Pacific 60% 38% 2%

Central Asia 48% 45% 7%

South Asia 50% 49% 1%

Eastern Europe 56% 33% 11%

Gulf Cooperation Council 32% 66% 2%

Central and South-Eastern Europe 70% 17% 13%

Rest of Middle East 39% 27%

East Africa 18% 82%

West Africa 36% 55% 8%

Southern Africa 17% 83%

North Africa 28% 3% 69%

Western and Southern Europe 66% 27% 7%

North America 71% 24% 5%

Central America and the Caribbean 87% 5% 8%

South America 58% 32% 10%

Sexual exploitation
Forced labour
Other purposes

Source: United Nations Office on Drugs and Crime (2018a).

Figure 9.6 shows annual profits by number of victims for each region. Larger circles indicate greater revenue per victim. The regions that profit the most from forced labor are Asia and developed economies. Asia benefits primarily because of the sheer number of victims, while developed economies benefit because of the high profit per victim.

Industries

Labor trafficking internationally is found in three primary industry categories: (1) domestic work; (2) agriculture, forestry, and fishing; and (3) construction, manufacturing, mining, and utilities. Figure 9.7 shows the number of labor trafficking victims by industry and geographic region.

Domestic Work

Domestic workers provide a range of services related to managing households, including cleaning, cooking, and taking care of children. It is not uncommon for domestic workers to live in the house with their employer. There are 3.8 million domestic workers who are victims of labor trafficking, representing 24% of all labor trafficking victims and 6.5% of all domestic workers globally (International Labour Organization, 2013a). These victims generate roughly $8 billion in cost savings for their traffickers. Domestic workers may be trafficked within their home country or internationally. Many factors facilitate domestic labor trafficking, including poverty, weak protections for workers at the country level, cultural and linguistic isolation of workers, and physical isolation in private homes. Domestic workers are also not covered under labor laws in many countries.

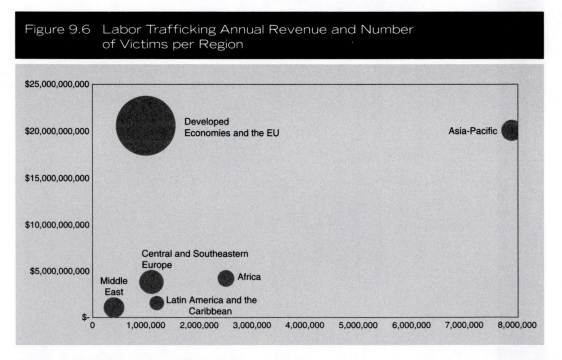

Figure 9.6   Labor Trafficking Annual Revenue and Number of Victims per Region

Data source: International Labour Office, 2014.

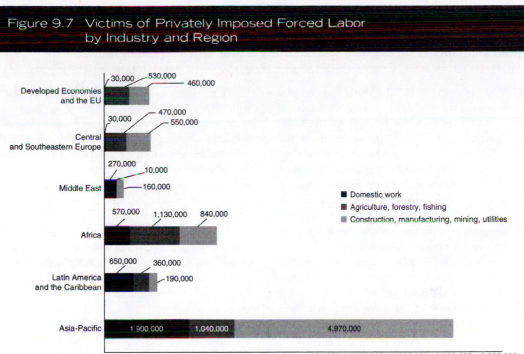

Figure 9.7 Victims of Privately Imposed Forced Labor by Industry and Region

Developed Economies and the EU: 30,000 / 530,000 / 460,000

Central and Southeastern Europe: 30,000 / 470,000 / 550,000

Middle East: 270,000 / 10,000 / 160,000

Africa: 570,000 / 1,130,000 / 840,000

Latin America and the Caribbean: 650,000 / 360,000 / 190,000

Asia-Pacific: 1,900,000 / 1,040,000 / 4,970,000

Legend:
- ■ Domestic work
- ■ Agriculture, forestry, fishing
- ■ Construction, manufacturing, mining, utilities

X-axis: 0, 1,000,000, 2,000,000, 3,000,000, 4,000,000, 5,000,000, 6,000,000, 7,000,000, 8,000,000, 9,000,000

Data source: International Labour Office, 2014.

Saudi Arabia, one of the world's largest employers of domestic workers, employs over 1.5 million domestic workers. Saudi Arabia and other Gulf countries including Bahrain, Kuwait, Oman, Qatar, and the United Arab Emirates permit foreign workers under the *Kafala* (Arabic for *sponsorship*) system. Under the Kafala system, domestic workers from foreign countries cannot leave the country, quit, or change employment without permission from their male employer. Workers who quit their job without permission typically must be deported from the country, often spending time in prison first (Human Rights Watch, 2008; Motaparthy, 2015). As a result of the coercive Kafala system and lack of protections for domestic workers under labor laws, abuse and exploitation of domestic workers are commonplace in Saudi Arabia and other Gulf countries (Human Rights Watch, 2008). Oman, another country operating under the Kafala system, is so infamous for abusive treatment of domestic workers that some countries have prohibited their citizens from migrating there, and the Human Rights Watch deemed the treatment of domestic workers *de facto slavery*. This means that while slavery is outlawed, the policy landscape facilitates, for all intents and purposes, enslavement of some groups of individuals (Human Rights Watch, 2016).

Forced domestic labor generates substantial profits. The estimated 3.4 million victims of labor trafficking in the domestic sector generate $7.9 billion in stolen wages. On average, these victims earn about 40 cents of every dollar of their earned wages. As shown in Table 9.5, forced domestic work generates $2,300 per victim, on average. Parallel to trends in forced labor overall, profits from forced domestic work are much higher in Asia, developed economies, and the EU (International Labour Organization, 2013a).

Case Study

Qatar Commits to Strengthen Workers' Rights for Two Million Migrants

With the upcoming 2022 FIFA World Cup in Qatar, many around the world have turned their focus to the labor rights of the country's migrant workers after widespread reports of their mistreatment. In fact, since 2014 there has been a complaint against Qatar at the International Labour Organization (ILO) alleging non-observance of ILO conventions related to forced labor and occupational safety inspections. In response, Qatar has taken initial steps to strengthen its compliance with international labor standards and implement extensive labor reforms.

On November 8, ILO's tripartite representatives (governments, employers, and workers), including the United States, agreed to close the complaint in partial recognition of Qatar's agreement to a three-year cooperation program in which they have committed to institute further reforms. Most importantly, Qatar pledged to reform its kafala (sponsorship) system, under which unskilled migrant workers cannot change employers or leave the country without the consent of their sponsor. The kafala system is in place in many countries throughout the Gulf region, and so reforms to the system in Qatar would mark a significant achievement in improving labor standards in the region.

The ambitious technical cooperation program with ILO will include reforms aimed at "improvement in payment of wages, enhanced labor inspection and Occupational Safety and Health (OSH) systems, refinement of the contractual system that replaced the kafala system and to improve labor recruitment procedures, increased prevention, protection and prosecution against forced labor, and promotion of the workers' voice." In addition, Qatar agreed to introduce a minimum wage for the first time, to establish a fund that will guarantee payment of late wages, and to work directly with migrant workers to renew residence permits.

The U.S. government delivered a plenary statement supporting the new agreement but also emphasizing the need to hold Qatar accountable to implementing and reporting regularly on these reforms. The United States also will seek to encourage Qatar to build on reforms such as Law No. 21 of 2015, which removed some constraints on migrant workers trying to change employers and freely exit the country. The new ILO cooperation program has the potential to be an effective tool in reforming migrant workers' rights in Qatar and serving as a positive example for the region.

Source: Moody, 2017.

Table 9.5 Profits From Forced Domestic Work by Region

	Annual Profits (in millions)	Total Victims	Profit per Victim
Asia-Pacific	$6,300	1,900,000	$3,300
Latin America and the Caribbean	$ 500	650,000	$ 800
Africa	$ 300	570,000	$ 600
Middle East	$ 400	270,000	$1,400
Central and Southeastern Europe	$ 100	30,000	$1,700
Developed Economies and the EU	$ 200	30,000	$7,500
Total	$7,900	3,440,000	$2,300

Data source: International Labour Office, 2014.

Agriculture, Forestry, and Fisheries

The victims of labor trafficking in the agricultural, forestry, and fishery sectors number 1.7 million individuals, accounting for 11% of forced labor victims globally. These victims generate $9 billion in profits for traffickers. Several factors facilitate labor trafficking in the agricultural sector. First, as in domestic work, there are weak labor protections for agricultural workers in many countries (International Labour Office, 2014). Weak labor protections in addition to remote locations of employers make it difficult for agricultural workers to organize for fair treatment. Further, traditional forms of bonded labor and slavery continue to be common practice in South Asia and Africa. In some cases, entire families are forced to work in exchange for inadequate food and housing. Families are unable to generate enough money to pay back imposed debts from recruiters and employers, and this debt is passed down through generations. Traffickers also take advantage of residents in rural areas who lack employment and educational opportunities. In Latin America, for example, workers from areas of socioeconomic disadvantage are transported to logging camps and fields, where they are often exploited and unable to earn enough money to return home (International Labour Office, 2014).

Many migrant workers are recruited to work at long distances on fishing ships. Since these workers are completely isolated offshore, exploitive work conditions and labor trafficking often go undetected (International Labour Office, 2014; International Labour Organization, 2013a). Figure 9.8 shows the processes that facilitate labor trafficking on fishing boats.

In 2012, a study of roughly 500 fishing ships in Thailand found that one in five workers was a victim of forced labor. In 2015, however, the Thai government reported that no cases of labor trafficking were identified in their inspections of roughly 500,000 ships. Victims are coercively recruited to work on the ships, or forced to work without pay once they are offshore (Human Rights Watch, 2018).

As shown in Table 9.6, forced labor in agriculture, forestry, and fisheries generates $2,500 per victim, on average. Profits per victim are highest in developed countries and the EU.

Construction, Manufacturing, Mining, Utilities, and Hospitality

Nearly half (47%) of labor trafficking victims work in construction, manufacturing, mining, utilities, or hospitality. These victims generate over $34 billion per year, accounting for roughly one-third of profits from human trafficking globally. Labor trafficking in these industries takes on many forms. For example, in South Asia, debt bondage is used to force work in brick kilns (Anti-Slavery International, 2017). Brick kiln employers pay family units per 1,000 bricks made. By paying only male heads of the family, females and children are never paid or formally reported as employees. Additionally, nearly all brick kiln workers take loans from their employer that their family ultimately cannot pay off. These loans keep the families coming back each year to endure long hours of work for little pay. About one-third of brick molders in India are children. These children work 10 to 12 hours per day throughout the year and consequently do not attend school (Anti-Slavery International, 2017).

As shown in Table 9.7, forced labor in industries other than agriculture generates $4,800 per victim. Parallel to trends in agriculture and labor trafficking overall, profits per victim are highest in developed countries and the EU.

Figure 9.8   Labor Trafficking in Fisheries

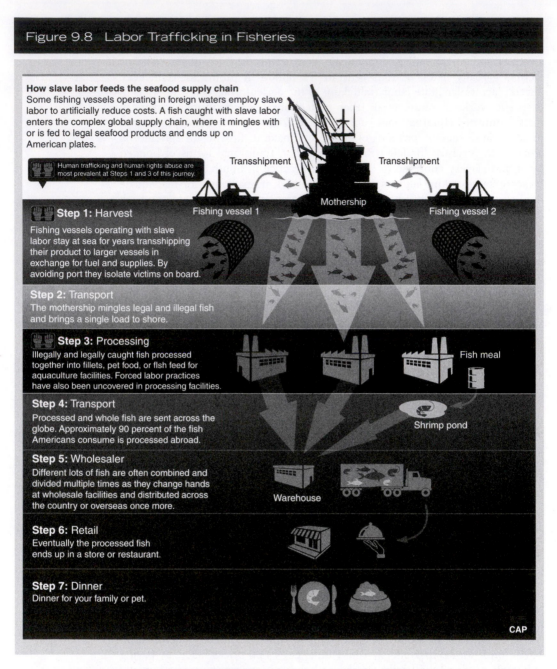

How slave labor feeds the seafood supply chain
Some fishing vessels operating in foreign waters employ slave labor to artificially reduce costs. A fish caught with slave labor enters the complex global supply chain, where it mingles with or is fed to legal seafood products and ends up on American plates.

Human trafficking and human rights abuse are most prevalent at Steps 1 and 3 of this journey.

Transshipment   Transshipment

Fishing vessel 1   Mothership   Fishing vessel 2

Step 1: Harvest
Fishing vessels operating with slave labor stay at sea for years transshipping their product to larger vessels in exchange for fuel and supplies. By avoiding port they isolate victims on board.

Step 2: Transport
The mothership mingles legal and illegal fish and brings a single load to shore.

Step 3: Processing
Illegally and legally caught fish processed together into fillets, pet food, or fish feed for aquaculture facilities. Forced labor practices have also been uncovered in processing facilities.

Fish meal

Step 4: Transport
Processed and whole fish are sent across the globe. Approximately 90 percent of the fish Americans consume is processed abroad.

Shrimp pond

Step 5: Wholesaler
Different lots of fish are often combined and divided multiple times as they change hands at wholesale facilities and distributed across the country or overseas once more.

Warehouse

Step 6: Retail
Eventually the processed fish ends up in a store or restaurant.

Step 7: Dinner
Dinner for your family or pet.

CAP

Source: This figure was created by the Center for American Progress (www.americanprogress.org).

Data source: International Labour Office (2013).

International Laws

International organizations like the ILO and the UN establish conventions around human rights, including policies specific to labor trafficking. Member countries agree to enact and enforce laws that meet certain standards outlined in these policies. While individual nations' policies around labor trafficking vary substantially, we can examine these international statutes to better understand the global political landscape.

Table 9.6 Profits From Forced Labor in Agriculture, Forestry, and Fisheries, by Region

	Annual Profits (in millions)	Total Victims	Profits per Victim
Asia-Pacific	$ 400	1,040,000	$ 400
Latin America and the Caribbean	$ 200	360,000	$ 700
Africa	$ 1,100	1,130,000	$ 1,000
Middle East	$ 20	10,000	$ 2,900
Central and Southeastern Europe	$ 700	470,000	$ 1,400
Developed Countries and the EU	$ 6,400	530,000	$12,200
Total	$ 8,900	3,540,000	$ 2,500

Data source: International Labour Office, 2014.

Case Study

Labor Trafficking in the United Kingdom

Tim lost his job in 2009 and was on the edge of destitution when a couple recruited him to work in their construction business, offering him housing and three meals a day. When he arrived at the couple's property, however, he found workers were living in a crowded and dirty trailer. The couple shaved his head, took his clothes, and confiscated his phone and identification. They held him captive, physically and verbally abused him, and forced him to work laying cement driveways. Eventually, the traffickers were arrested and Tim was released.

Source: United States Department of State (2016).

Table 9.7 Profits From Forced Labor in Construction, Manufacturing, Mining, Utilities, Hospitality, and Other Nonagricultural Industries

	Annual Profits (in millions)	Total Number of Victims	Profits per Victim
Asia-Pacific	$13,400	4,970,000	$ 2,700
Latin America and the Caribbean	$ 800	190,000	$ 4,100
Africa	$ 2,800	840,000	$ 3,300
Middle East	$ 600	160,000	$ 3,600
Central and Southeastern Europe	$ 3,000	550,000	$ 5,400
Developed Countries and the EU	$14,000	460,000	$30,400
Total	$34,500	7,170,000	$ 4,800

Data source: International Labour Office, 2014.

The 1815 Declaration Relative to the Universal Abolition of the Slave Trade was the first international law to establish slavery as a condemnable practice. During the abolitionist movement between 1815 and 1957, over 300 international agreements were established to abolish slavery. None of these agreements was completely effective (Office of the High Commissioner for Human Rights [OHCHR], 2002).

Today, the ILO has 183 conventions that describe protections for workers aiming to achieve four core principles: the elimination of forced labor, freedom of association, the abolition of child labor, and the ending of discrimination in employment. ILO conventions relevant to labor trafficking are outlined in Table 9.1 at the beginning of this chapter.

The United Nations International Bill of Human Rights also outlines protections against forced labor in each of the following sections: the Universal Declaration of Human Rights; the International Covenant on Economic, Social and Cultural Rights; and the International Covenant on Civil and Political Rights. Specifically:

- Article 4 of the Universal Declaration of Human Rights states, "No one shall be held in slavery or servitude; slavery and the slave trade shall be prohibited in all their forms" (Office of the High Commissioner for Human Rights [OHCHR], 2002).

- Article 6 of the International Covenant on Economic, Social and Cultural Rights guarantees the right to work, including "the right of everyone to the opportunity to gain his living by work which he freely chooses or accepts" (OHCHR, 2002).

- Article 8 of the International Covenant on Civil and Political Rights prohibits slavery and forced labor explicitly: "No one shall be required to perform forced or compulsory labour" (OHCHR, 2002).

The primary international regulation pertaining to labor trafficking, however, is the trafficking in persons protocol, formally known as the Protocol to Prevent, Suppress and Punish Trafficking in Persons Especially Women and Children, Supplementing the United Nations Convention Against Transnational Organized Crime. The protocol criminalizes labor trafficking and other forms of human trafficking. The protocol also encourages countries to address factors that facilitate labor trafficking, such as poverty.

There are also international policies pertaining to labor trafficking among the most vulnerable populations (OHCHR, 2002):

- The **Convention on the Elimination of All Forms of Discrimination Against Women** requires countries to reduce or eliminate trafficking among women and girls. General recommendation number 9 defines trafficking as a specific form of violence against women because trafficking puts women at an elevated risk of physical and sexual violence.

- The **Convention on the Rights of the Child (CRC)** prohibits trafficking in children, including forced labor. The CRC also establishes mandatory education for children and mandatory access to physical and mental health services, both of which are jeopardized in the case of child labor trafficking.

- The **Optional Protocol on the Sale of Children, Child Prostitution and Child Pornography** also outlaws child trafficking, including labor trafficking.

Vulnerabilities and Demographics of Labor Trafficking Victims

The relationship between labor supply and demand provides a straightforward explanation for the persistence of labor trafficking (see Figure 9.9). As reviewed previously, labor trafficking in every industry is a lucrative business for traffickers. Demand for goods and services typically increases the cost of labor. Traffickers bypass the increased cost of labor supply by forcing individuals to work for little or no wages. In the case of labor trafficking, labor is unwillingly supplied by victims because of threats, force, or coercion from traffickers. Traffickers' ability to produce goods or services at such a low cost further increases the demand for cheap goods and services.

To understand vulnerabilities to labor trafficking, then, we must examine the factors that contribute to the supply of forced laborers. Some examples of vulnerabilities at each level of the ecological spectrum are shown in Figure 9.10. Many people are unwilling to work in industries where labor trafficking predominates for any number of reasons, such as hazardous conditions, low wages, or distance from their families. Thus, the individuals most vulnerable to labor trafficking are those that are in dire need of income and few employment opportunities. Accordingly, individuals living in extreme poverty, historically marginalized groups, children, migrant workers, and those with low education or literacy are more at risk for labor trafficking.

Our understanding of the populations affected by labor trafficking is limited to populations that have been studied. That is, if a population is vulnerable to

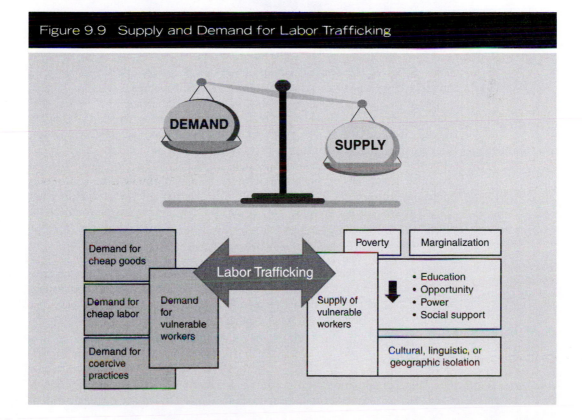

Figure 9.9 Supply and Demand for Labor Trafficking

Figure 9.10 Vulnerabilities to Labor Trafficking

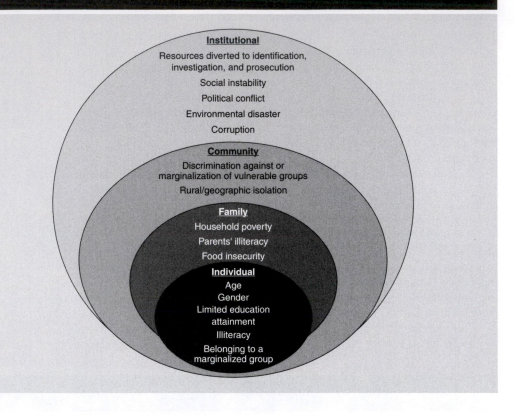

labor trafficking but lives in a country for which no survey or research has been conducted, we won't have information about them. Nonetheless, we have reliable information on vulnerabilities to labor trafficking victimization for several specific characteristics. Individuals are more vulnerable to labor trafficking if they are migrant workers (within their own country or across countries), they are younger, they are male, they have less than a primary school education, and/or they are poor (UNODC, 2016a). Further, the U.S. State Department and the United Nations note that historically marginalized groups, such as indigenous populations, religious minorities, and LGBTQ individuals, are at greater risk for labor trafficking. Children are also a vulnerable population, but specific groups of youth are at greater risk, including runaway youth, youth involved in child welfare systems, and indigenous youth (UNODC, 2016a; U.S. Department of State, 2016).

Most labor traffickers have characteristics similar to those of their victims: They are typically the same gender, the same ethnicity, and live in the same area. Gender and ethnic match facilitate trust between victims and traffickers, making it easier for traffickers to recruit victims (UNODC, 2016a). Chapter 5 describes characteristics of traffickers in more detail.

Migration

Whether within one's own country or across borders, migration is a significant risk factor for labor trafficking in all industries. Individuals who leave their primary area of residence to find work are at risk for a variety of coercive practices, including taking loans to cover their transportation costs, having passports withheld, and being isolated from their home with nowhere to go but to continue working. Most victims of labor trafficking, particularly those from low-income countries, are exploited in their home country (International Labour Office, 2014). This is in part because migration is expensive, and many individuals living in extreme poverty cannot afford to migrate outside their country. When labor trafficking victims cross international borders, they are most likely to move from their original place of residence to an area similarly impoverished. The exception to this is that traffickers in high-income countries are more likely to exploit workers from low-income countries or areas (International Labour Office, 2014; UNODC, 2009a). When workers travel to new cultures, they may be unaware of local laws and regulations and unable to speak the language, making them more vulnerable to dishonest and coercive practices from employers (International Labour Office, 2014; UNODC, 2009a; U.S. Department of State, 2018b).

The trafficking in persons protocol recognizes the vulnerability of migrant workers and designates specific protections for these victims:

- Article 7 states that countries should allow trafficking victims to stay lawfully in the country where they were trafficked. Further, individuals at risk of trafficking or who have been trafficked might be eligible for refugee protections under the United Nations' Convention Relating to the Status of Refugees.

- Article 8 states that countries should return immigrants to their country of origin in a safe way, and ideally that immigrants should be returned only voluntarily. The International Covenant on Civil and Political Rights also states that anyone should be allowed to return to their country of origin.

Age

Labor trafficking victims are all ages. In general, adult victims of forced labor tend to be younger than individuals working freely. Children comprise a greater proportion of trafficking victims in low-income countries relative to higher-income countries (U.S. Department of State, 2016). Among children, those in forced labor and those in free labor tend to be about the same age (International Labour Office, 2014; U.S. Department of Labor, 2016).

Gender

Males are disproportionately likely to be victims of labor trafficking, accounting for 63% of labor trafficking victims overall. Labor trafficking and trafficking of men are both likely to be underreported, so males may be at even greater risk of labor trafficking than current estimates suggest (International Labour Office, 2014; U.S. Department of State, 2016). Women who are subjected to labor trafficking are more likely than their male counterparts to also be subjected to sex trafficking. There is more accurate reporting of sex trafficking than labor trafficking, which may facilitate identification of female victims.

Trends in gender differences in labor trafficking vary substantially by industry and region. As shown in Figure 9.11, females constitute the majority of labor trafficking victims in East Asia and roughly half of victims of labor trafficking in North America.

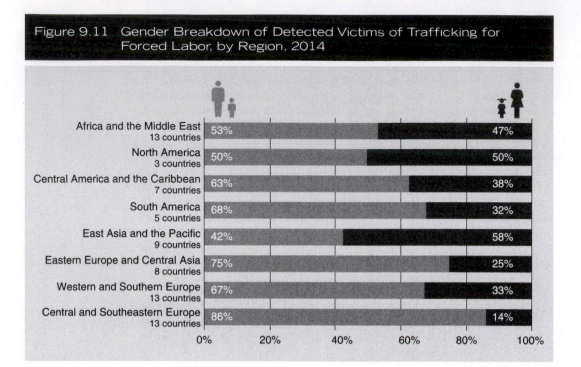

Figure 9.11 Gender Breakdown of Detected Victims of Trafficking for Forced Labor, by Region, 2014

Region	Male	Female
Africa and the Middle East (13 countries)	53%	47%
North America (3 countries)	50%	50%
Central America and the Caribbean (7 countries)	63%	38%
South America (5 countries)	68%	32%
East Asia and the Pacific (9 countries)	42%	58%
Eastern Europe and Central Asia (8 countries)	75%	25%
Western and Southern Europe (13 countries)	67%	33%
Central and Southeastern Europe (13 countries)	86%	14%

Source: United Nations Office on Drugs and Crime, 2016.

Males represent nearly all victims of labor trafficking in mining and are more likely than women to be trafficked in construction, begging, manufacturing, and agriculture. Females, on the other hand, are much more likely than men to be trafficked in restaurants, hospitality, and domestic work than are males.

Further, women and men tend to be subject to different forms of coercive practices. As shown in Figure 9.12, women are more likely to experience sexual violence or have their passport withheld than are men. Men are more likely than women to be exploited by being kept drugged or geographically separate from their home.

Education and Literacy

Victims of labor trafficking, whether they are adults or children, have lower levels of education than workers in free labor. Further, the parents of child victims of labor trafficking have lower levels of education than parents of children in free labor. Victims of labor trafficking are also less likely to have a literate head of household (International Labour Office, 2014; UNODC, 2016).

Poverty

Victims of labor trafficking are disproportionately likely to live in poverty (International Labour Office, 2014; UNODC, 2009a; U.S. Department of State, 2016). For example, a survey of workers in Nepal found that only 9% of victims of forced labor reported having food security compared to 56% of free laborers. Families who experience declines in household income are more likely to have members who become victims of labor trafficking (International Labour Office, 2014).

Figure 9.12   Gender Breakdown in Coercive Practices for Forced Labor

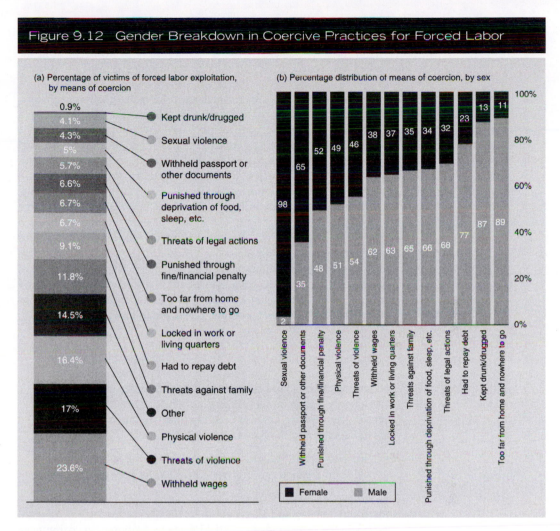

(a) Percentage of victims of forced labor exploitation, by means of coercion

(b) Percentage distribution of means of coercion, by sex

Source: International Labour Office & Walk Free Foundation, 2017.

Marginalized Populations

LGBTQ and gender-nonconforming individuals are vulnerable to labor trafficking because in many countries worldwide, there are no laws to prevent discrimination against these populations. The absence of anti-discrimination laws is only one indicator of a broader problem of ingrained societal and cultural stigma and discrimination, which is a greater contributor to their increased vulnerability. For example, they may have weaker and fewer ties to family and other support groups, and they are more likely to be abused as youth, to run away as youth, or to be homeless. Further, discrimination limits employment prospects and may therefore increase their vulnerability to coercive labor practices. Crimes are also less likely to be prosecuted when individuals are LGBTQ and/or gender-nonconforming. Further, these individuals are more likely to be injured, abused, or even prosecuted for behaviors related to their own victimization (U.S. Department of State, 2016).

One study in the U.S. and Canada found that 20% of homeless youth had been victims of trafficking, about 15% had been sex-trafficked, 8% had been labor-trafficked, and 3% had been victims of both sex and labor trafficking. This study also found that 8% of LGBTQ youth and 10% of youth with a foster care history had been victims of labor trafficking. Youth with a history of involvement in the foster care system accounted for 26% of all labor trafficking victims (L. T. Murphy, 2016).

Indigenous populations are also particularly vulnerable to labor trafficking. Relative to nonindigenous persons, indigenous people are more likely to live in poverty, are less likely to have official citizenship or documentation in their home country, have more limited access to education, and experience lower financial returns of education due to discrimination and linguistic and geographic isolation (Duncan et al., 2013; Forrest, 2014; U.S. Department of State, 2016). Though research is limited on labor trafficking among indigenous people, the ILO conducted an in-depth study in Bolivia, Paraguay, and Peru and found that indigenous people were at an increased risk of forced labor, particularly bonded labor, and initiated a new program to combat bonded labor among indigenous people in these areas (ILO, 2008). A study conducted in Guatemala found that at least one in four indigenous households had a member who was a victim of forced labor, and 65% of domestic workers in Guatemala are indigenous girls and adolescents (ILO, 2014a; Duncan et al., 2013). Forced labor among indigenous populations is pervasive in many countries; below are a few examples (Duncan et al., 2013).

- In Namibia, forced domestic servitude of indigenous San girls is disguised as adoption. High rates of physical and sexual abuse are documented among girls in these positions, and they are often subsequently sold to employers or sex traffickers in other parts of the country. This practice has also been documented among indigenous girls in Ecuador and the Batwa people in Uruguay.

- In Colombia, reports indicate that armed groups force domestic servitude of indigenous girls as well as physically and sexually abuse them.

- Indigenous Tamang and Magar youth in Nepal account for 58% of child laborers in the carpet industry and 51% of child laborers in coal mines.

Indigenous people are protected in all the ILO conventions and international laws pertaining to labor trafficking mentioned above, but in 1989 the ILO ratified a new convention specific to protecting indigenous people, the **Indigenous and Tribal Peoples Convention**.

Child Labor Trafficking

Child labor trafficking, or forced child labor, occurs when a child engages in work or provides services under the threat of force, fraud, or coercion from a third party (not their parents). This includes children who are forced to work because their parents are forced to work, such as in the case of debt bondage, in which children may be born into a situation of forced labor. Other forms of child labor, including hazardous working conditions, are not technically child labor trafficking, though they still represent a threat to children's livelihood and well-being (International Labour Office, 2017).

Case Study

Forced Labor in North Korea

Group 114 is a committee [created by the government in North Korea] tasked with restricting what the government considers impure media. Its primary function is to censor content and investigate individuals who have allegedly obtained access to foreign media. This group not only prevents outside information from entering the DPRK but also scrutinizes officials to prevent confiscated products from being resold or consumed. The committee secretly monitors North Korean markets and surveils defectors living in China. According to media reports, Group 114 agents are responsible for kidnapping defectors who escape into China and sometimes even South Korean and Chinese individuals involved in human rights activities. If captured, these individuals are either executed or sent into the political prison camp system, where serious human rights abuses such as torture, deliberate starvation, forced labor, and sexual violence are systematized as a matter of State policy.

Source: U.S. Department of State, 2018a.

Case Study

Forced Labor of Talibés

Senegalese boys and girls are subjected to domestic servitude, forced labor in gold mines, and sex trafficking. Internal trafficking is more prevalent than transnational trafficking. In Senegal, it is a traditional practice to send boys to Koranic schools, called daaras, for education. However, instead of receiving an education, many students, known as talibés, are forced to beg by their teachers, known as marabouts. The marabouts take the talibés' earnings and often beat those who fail to meet the daily quota. The talibés often live in overcrowded, unsanitary conditions, receive inadequate food and medical care, and are vulnerable to physical and sexual abuse. They typically come from rural areas in Senegal and from neighboring countries, sometimes as a result of human trafficking. In June 2016, President Macky Sall announced and launched an initiative to remove tailbés from the street and prosecute marabouts that perpetrate crimes against their students; however, in 2016, no marabouts were prosecuted. As of November, the government conducted 57 operations, removing 1,186 children from the streets and reuniting 1,086 of them with their families, although some of these children were eventually returned by their parents to daaras. A 2014 daara-mapping study estimated that 30,000 of the estimated 54,800 talibés in Dakar are forced to beg, and a 2016 study found that 9,000 of the estimated 14,000 talibés in one region of Senegal are also forced to beg. A variety of factors remain as barriers to education, forcing some students to quit school. These barriers include school-related fees, a lack of birth registration documents, a lack of teachers, and rural schools. Some girls reportedly quit school due to sexual harassment, including by teachers, and as a result of early pregnancy.

Source: Bureau of International Labor Affairs, 2017.

About 218 million children are employed worldwide. Among these, 152 million children, constituting one-tenth of all children, are in exploitive working conditions. An additional 73 million children work in a hazardous environment. An estimated 4.3 million children are victims of forced labor, comprising about 18% of all labor trafficking victims. Of these 4.3 million, about 1 million are exploited in the sex industry. Right now, we will focus on the 3 million children in nonsexual forced labor imposed by private actors and 300,000 children in nonsexual forced labor imposed by governments (International Labour Office, 2017; International Labour Office & Walk Free Foundation, 2017). These estimates do not include forced labor of children imposed by armed groups, though country-specific reports, particularly in conflict zones, find that armed groups commonly force children to work as domestic servants and as child soldiers (International Labour Office & Walk Free Foundation, 2017). Government-imposed forced labor of children often includes governments forcing children to perform public services during school, even when these services exceed what would be considered appropriate for their education. This practice is highly prevalent among children in North Korea, for example (International Labour Office & Walk Free Foundation, 2017).

Vulnerabilities to child trafficking include severe poverty, lack of opportunity for economic advancement, and death of parents. Additionally, marginalized populations such as LGBTQ youth, gender-nonconforming youth, youth in the child welfare system, and migrant youth are at an elevated risk for labor trafficking.

Risk factors specific to youth's country of residence may also increase vulnerability to labor trafficking. For example, the HIV epidemic in West Africa has a high mortality rate, leaving many children without parents. Further, border patrol agents throughout West Africa often passively or actively facilitate child labor trafficking. Consequently, child labor trafficking is a paramount issue in this region. Girls as young as three in Togo are sold into domestic servitude, where they are subject to sexual abuse and at risk of HIV infection. Boys in Togo are also forced into labor, often through debt bondage, in cotton fields, agriculture, and factories throughout West Africa (J. Cohen, 2003).

Consequences of Child Labor Trafficking

Child labor trafficking has devastating effects on individuals, on families, on communities, and at the global level. Many of the consequences of child labor trafficking are similar to those of child labor; some of these consequences are outlined in Figure 9.13. Child victims of labor trafficking are at risk of significant physical and mental health complications, including chronic respiratory issues, loss of limbs, sexually transmitted infections, gastrointestinal illnesses, exhaustion, malnutrition, and death (U.S. Department of Labor, 2017). The severe trauma that accompanies child labor trafficking puts victims at risk for post-traumatic stress disorder, chronic anxiety, depression, and other mental health issues. Victims of child labor trafficking are less likely to attend school, and those who do are more likely to underperform and drop out. Victims of child labor trafficking experience decreased employment opportunities and lower lifetime earnings overall. These children are more likely to have chronic illnesses and disabilities as adults, and their children are more likely to be victims of labor trafficking. This has consequences at a societal level; the adult labor force is less healthy and less skilled. Studies have also found that rates of forced child labor in developing countries are associated with country-level indicators, including the adolescent morality rate, level of undernourishment in the population, and infectious disease (Roggero, Mangiaterra, Bustreo, & Rosati, 2007; U.S. Department of Labor, 2017). Globally, the workforce is less productive and countries are more vulnerable to economic shocks (U.S. Department of Labor, 2017).

Figure 9.13   Outcomes of Child Labor

Outcomes of Child Labor

How the Plight of an Individual Child Becomes a Global Burden

Child	Family	Country	World
• Negative effects on physical and mental health	• Chronic illness and disability in adulthood	• Less healthy adult labor force	• Reduced productivity in global workspace
• Underperfomance in school and more susceptible to drop out	• Increased likelihood of next generation becoming child laborers	• Unskilled labor force willing to work for low wages or even forced to work for none	• Uneven playing field for all workers and businesses
• Decreased opportunity to obtain decent work	• Persistent poverty caused by a lifetime of jobs with depressed wages	• Social vulnerability, marginalization, inequality	• Greater susceptibility to economic shocks, resulting in irregular global migration patterns

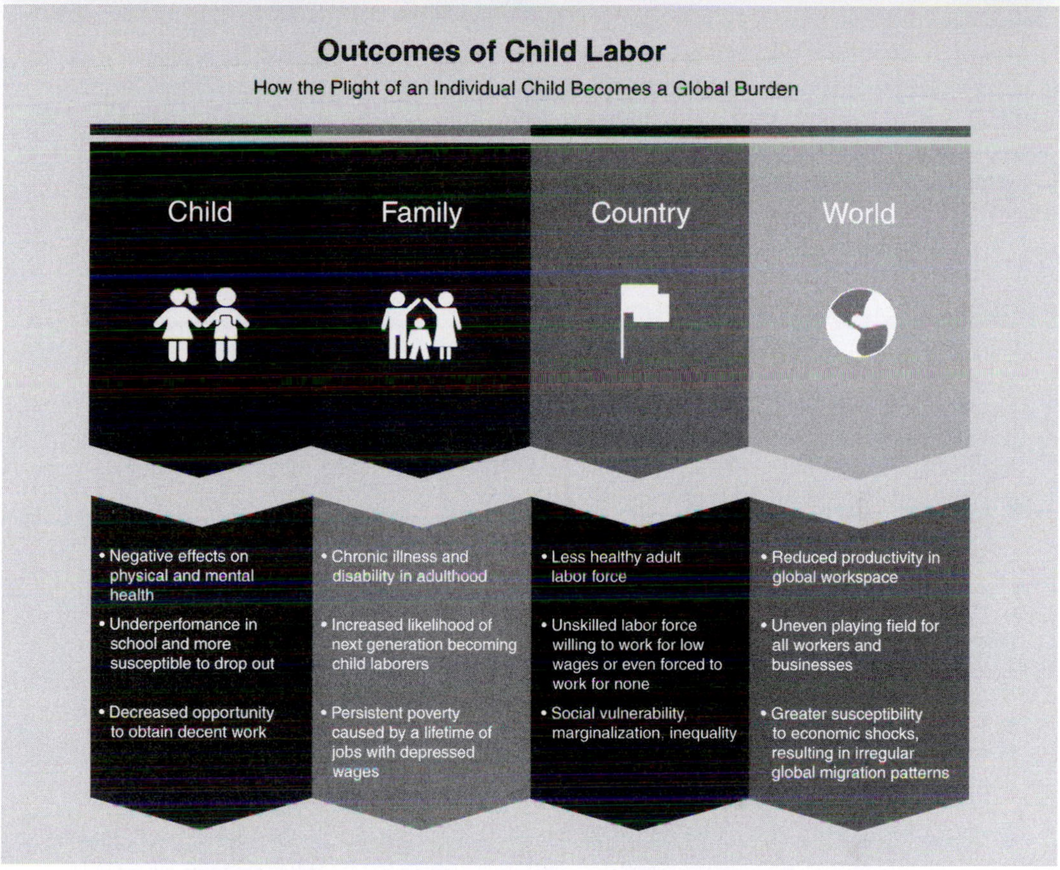

Source: U.S. Department of Labor (2019) 2016 FINDINGS ON THE WORST FORMS OF CHILD LABOR. Retrieved from https://www.dol.gov/sites/default/files/documents/ilab/reports/child-labor/findings/TDABook.pdf

Data Sources: Edmonds, E. GLM-LIC Working Paper No.11: Economic Growth and Child Labour in Low Income Economies; April 2016. LO. Children in Hazardous Work. Geneva, 2011.

Conclusion

Labor trafficking affects millions of men, women, and children worldwide. Traffickers operate in nearly every industry, including domestic work, construction, agriculture, mining, fishing, and hospitality. Many of these industries are geographically isolated, which makes it harder to identify victims and prosecute traffickers. Labor trafficking and poverty share many of the same risk factors, so interventions and policies that break the cycle of poverty may also help to prevent labor trafficking. Although labor trafficking looks different in each country and in each industry, marginalized populations are consistently at greater risk. We need better data to help protect migrant workers, indigenous population, and sexual minorities. We also need to examine structural-level policies that may facilitate labor trafficking, such as our temporary work visa programs and laws that limit protections for domestic workers. As President Obama stated in the quote that began the chapter, we must insist on the dignity of all human beings to put an end to labor trafficking.

KEY WORDS

DISCUSSION QUESTIONS

1. What are three ways historical and institutionalized racism and classism may facilitate labor trafficking and work as barriers to anti-trafficking efforts?

2. Did you know that slavery or involuntary servitude was allowable as a punishment for a crime in the U.S.? Do you think prison labor constitutes forced labor? What other countries permit forced labor as a punishment for a crime?

3. What similarities do you find between the current H visa program and the Bracero Program?

   - How are these programs different?

   - What characteristics of these programs facilitate labor trafficking?

   - How did national events influence the United States' treatment of foreign workers in the past?

   - How do current national events influence policies toward foreign workers?

   - How can national attitudes toward foreign nationals facilitate labor trafficking?

4. Identify one country you are interested in: What kinds of things might influence or bias estimates of forced labor in that country?

5. What are some vulnerabilities to being trafficked on fishing boats?

6. Who are the people involved in trafficking on fishing boats? What are their roles?

RESOURCES

- Video on trafficking in Thai fishing ships: https://www.hrw.org/report/2018/01/23/hidden-chains-rights-abuses-and-forced-labor-thailands-fishing-industry

- History of the work visa program: https://humantraffickinghotline.org/sites/default/files/Close%20to%20Slavery%20-%20SPCL.pdf

FULL-LENGTH CASE STUDIES

- Kafala system: https://www.hrw.org/report/2008/07/07/if-i-am-not-human/abuses-against-asian-domestic-workers-saudi-arabia

- North Korea: https://www.hrw.org/news/2012/06/13/north-korea-economic-system-built-forced-labor

- Talibés in Senegal: https://www.hrw.org/sites/default/files/reports/senegal0410webwcover.pdf

- Thai fishing industry: https://www.hrw.org/report/2018/01/23/hidden-chains-rights-abuses-and-forced-labor-thailands-fishing-industry

Responses to Labor Trafficking

Human trafficking crosses cultures and continents. I've met survivors of trafficking and their families, along with brave men and women in both the public and the private sector, who have stood up against this terrible crime. All of us have a responsibility to bring this practice to an end. Survivors must be supported and their families aided and comforted, but we cannot turn our responsibility for doing that over to nongovernmental organizations or the faith community. Traffickers must be brought to justice. And we can't just blame international organized crime and rely on law enforcement to pursue them. It is everyone's responsibility. Businesses that knowingly profit or exhibit reckless disregard about their supply chains, governments that turn a blind eye or do not devote serious resources to addressing the problem, all of us have to speak out and act forcefully.

—Hillary Clinton, 2010

Reactions to Labor Trafficking

In Chapter 9 we discussed labor trafficking and its consequences. In this chapter, we will review responses to labor trafficking. "Responses" broadly refers to the ways that individuals, nongovernmental agencies (NGOs), law enforcement, and government agencies work to prevent labor trafficking, stop it where it continues to exist, and serve and protect victims.

Perhaps not surprisingly, NGOs and government agencies alike face significant barriers to reducing the burden of labor trafficking. Before we dive too far into the responses to labor trafficking, let's review why some of the anti-trafficking efforts used to combat other forms of trafficking are not as successful for combating labor trafficking (see Figure 10.1).

Unlike some other forms of human trafficking, such as sex trafficking and organ trafficking, the average person cannot avoid being involved in labor trafficking by avoiding one industry or activity. As consumers, we drive the demand for forced labor, yet the average consumer rarely knows anything about the supply chain of the goods they buy or the materials in them. More knowledgeable consumers may have a good sense of the types of products that are commonly made with forced labor, but we rarely have the option to simply not purchase any product in one of those hundreds of categories. It would be nearly impossible to navigate a job or personal life without using a phone or computer, for example.

Figure 10.1 Common Anti-trafficking Approaches to Labor Trafficking

	INDIVIDUALS	*Don't participate in the industry affected by labor trafficking*	• Not informed about how goods are made • Can't "just avoid" the more than 100 goods that may be produced by forced labor, including food, clothing, and technology
	LAW ENFORCEMENT	*Set up a sting operation*	• Labor traffickers operate within legal industries • In most places, it is not the role of law enforcement to conduct workplace inspections
	VICTIM SERVICE PROVIDERS	*Conduct specific outreach to labor trafficking victims*	• Service providers have little information about which groups are affected; harder to tailor services to these individuals

Challenge Yourself 10.1

Slaveryfootprint.org describes your contributions to human trafficking using an interactive online quiz about your daily routine. I consider myself a conscientious consumer, and I found that I have "37 slaves working for me." Take the quiz online at http://slaveryfootprint.org/.

• What parts of your daily routine includes use of forced labor?

• What are three things you could do to reduce your contribution to forced labor?

As we reviewed extensively in Chapter 9, victims and perpetrators of labor trafficking are, for the most part, hidden within legitimate industries. This makes it difficult for law enforcement to set up sting operations as they might, for example, in a massage parlor or brothel. Law enforcement is not responsible for workplace inspections, so it is unlikely that they will become aware of illicit treatment of workers. Occupational safety organizations, which may be more likely to come in contact with victims, are not trained to identify labor trafficking. This means that there are no oversight mechanisms that might routinely identify labor traffickers or victims.

Victim service providers can only tailor services to the extent that they are aware of the characteristics of victims. If males are rarely referred for services, for example, then service providers will tailor their outreach and services to females. Male survivors are more likely to view their experience with forced labor as "bad luck" or a personal failure to provide for their families (U.S. Department of State, 2016). Most victim service providers do not have services to meet the needs of men and boys specifically. In particular, most organizations that provide emergency shelter do not provide beds for adult males (U.S.

Department of State, 2016). Many of the most vulnerable groups we discussed in Chapter 9, such as undocumented individuals, indigenous populations, and homeless individuals, are also less likely to receive services, and consequently victim service providers are not as equipped to serve their unique needs (U.S. Department of State, 2016).

How, then, can we work to eliminate labor trafficking? What, if anything, is being done already? As we will discover throughout this chapter, individuals in nearly every industry can help combat labor trafficking. We will review theories underlying anti-trafficking responses, standards for basic human rights outlined in international statutes, and how current responses to labor trafficking may facilitate but in some cases prevent these human rights from being achieved. We will also describe new and innovative approaches to anti–labor trafficking efforts using the 4R framework.

Theoretical Frameworks Guiding Existing Responses to Labor Trafficking

At a high level, theories guiding labor trafficking responses are the same as those guiding responses for other forms of trafficking. There are two primary philosophies for responding to trafficking: a **human rights approach** and a **labor approach**. We will discuss each of these and how they are applied in the case of labor trafficking.

The human rights approach, easily remembered as the **3P paradigm**, emphasizes prevention, prosecution, and protection, and more recently a fourth *p*, partnership (United Nations General Assembly, 2000c). Each of the *p*'s in the framework is interrelated with the others. Additionally, each *p* takes a victim-centered approach. Proponents of this framework suggest, for example, that when prosecution is victim centered, it is more likely to be successful, and successful prosecution will deter future trafficking by removing an active trafficker and sending a message to other traffickers, potentially deterring their future behavior as well. This deterrent effect will aid prevention efforts. This 3P framework has been adapted by nearly all the major anti-trafficking organizations, including the United Nations and U.S. Department of State.

Human Rights Approach

Critics of the 3P paradigm suggest that the approach is too focused on individual victims to be applied to labor trafficking. Because labor trafficking pervades a diverse range of industries, prevention, prosecution, and protection strategies would be too narrowly focused to make a large impact on the problem. By focusing on individual victims, critics argue, responses treat labor trafficking as a rare occurrence that can be dealt with on a person-by-person basis. In reality, trafficking is pervasive, and this paradigm, critics suggest, fails to address root causes of labor trafficking and consequently serves too few victims (Shamir, 2012). Others argue that the 3P paradigm is too broad and has led many nations to emphasize criminal justice measures to reduce trafficking. An emphasis on criminal justice tactics is often harmful to victims, leads to an emphasis on sex trafficking over labor trafficking, and does not address the root causes of trafficking (Baer, 2015).

Labor Approach

An alternative approach treats trafficking as a labor issue. By addressing structural factors, anti-trafficking efforts can lead to large-scale changes in institutions and communities that allow trafficking to persist. For example, (financially) incentivizing fair treatment of employees may reduce demand to use coercive practices, or improving public knowledge about businesses' supply chains may lead consumers to stop supporting companies that utilize forced labor.

Using the labor market framework, to eliminate labor trafficking, we must address structural conditions in labor markets that facilitate human trafficking. For example, the demand for cheap goods and services is a driving force in labor trafficking, and a lack of regulations, or limited oversight and enforcement of regulations that do exist, creates an environment where traffickers can profit (International Labour Office & Walk Free Foundation, 2017; Shamir, 2012). A major drawback of the labor market approach is that its macro view may fail to meet the needs of victims at an individual level. Changes to federal, state, and local policies, corporate practices, or consumer behavior do not address victims' needs for shelter, food, and stable employment.

In application, there is no reason that the human rights and labor market approaches operate in conflict with one another. Both viewpoints are useful in addressing labor trafficking. Accordingly, in line with both human rights and labor market approaches, we categorize responses to labor trafficking using the **4R framework**: research, recovery, resources, and restoration (see Figure 10.2).

Figure 10.2 The 4R Framework

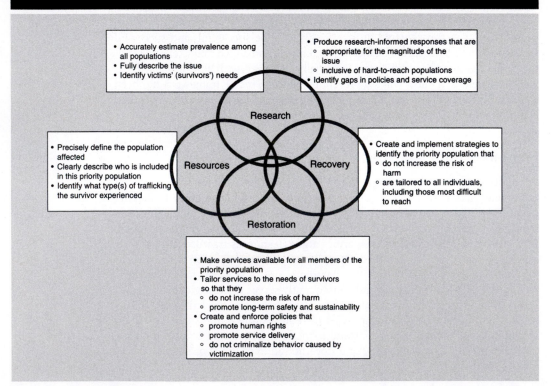

Review of Human Rights Guaranteed by International Statutes

The Universal Declaration of Human Rights (United Nations General Assembly, 1948) outlines human rights standards for all nations. Those particularly relevant to labor trafficking are outlined in Table 10.1.

Forced labor may violate each of these human rights guaranteed under international statute. Responses to labor trafficking, at a fundamental level, should seek to reinstate these rights to survivors and prevent them from being violated for others in the future.

Unfortunately, in the case of labor trafficking, many country-level policies, even those explicitly aiming to combat labor trafficking, jeopardize victims' fundamental human rights. For example, many countries' attitudes and policies around immigration facilitate an environment where law enforcement focuses on criminalizing unauthorized foreign nationals without screening them as potential victims of labor trafficking. Further, many countries have implemented stricter oversight of migration in the name of anti-trafficking efforts without instituting measures to prevent fraudulent recruitment or coercive labor practices (Baer, 2015).

For example, a commonly cited argument among those with more conservative political affiliations in the U.S. is that immigration harms the U.S. economy because immigrants take jobs from American workers. Research finds quite the opposite; immigration is associated with economic growth and growth in innovation (Hoban, 2017). We learned in Chapter 9, though, that foreign nationals are at a heightened risk for labor trafficking in the U.S. and globally. Policies and

Table 10.1 UN Declaration of Human Rights Articles That Pertain to Labor Trafficking

Right	Article Number
The prohibition of discrimination on the basis of race, color, sex, language, religion, political or other opinion, national or social origin, property, birth, or other status	Article 7
The right to life, liberty, and security	Article 3
The right not to be submitted to slavery, servitude, forced labor, or bonded labor	Article 4
The right not to be subjected to torture, and/or cruel, inhuman, degrading treatment or punishment	Article 5
The right to associate freely	Article 20
The right to freedom of movement	Article 13
The right to the highest attainable standard of physical and mental health	Article 25
The right to just and favorable conditions of work	Article 23
The right to an adequate standard of living	Article 25
The right to social security	Article 25
The right to special protection for children	Article 25

Source: United Nations. General Assembly. (1995). The universal declaration of human rights (Vol. 1). United Nations Dept. of Public Information.

ideology that criminalize noncitizens can be harmful to victim recovery efforts in several ways. First, they contribute to traffickers' ability to use immigration status as a coercion tactic. Second, cultures that emphasize the criminalization of immigrants create hostile environments where victims may be afraid to leave exploitive conditions, or afraid to seek help if they do escape (Farrell & Pfeffer, 2014; Zatz & Smith, 2012). Third, if victims come into contact with government agencies only to be punished through detention, deportation, or fines, this worsens the risk factors that made them and their families vulnerable to trafficking to begin with.

As we reviewed in the previous chapter, institutional factors such as the structure of work visas also facilitate labor trafficking (Polaris, 2015d). Workers who hold visas tied to a single employer are not allowed to change jobs once they arrive in a new country. If the employer refuses to return their documents, they cannot even return to their country if they want to, and over time their visa expires. Employers can then use their unauthorized status as a threat and additional means of coercion. In extreme cases, such as in countries with kafala laws, workers must be jailed and deported to leave employment if their employer refuses to authorize their departure. Fortunately, many countries are addressing these weaknesses in their work visa programs. Some Gulf countries are also considering changing their kafala visa system. One simple change the U.S. has made is to provide workers' rights to them in pamphlets in their own language upon arrival in the United States.

Throughout the rest of the chapter, we will review responses to labor trafficking following the 4R framework.

Research

Research refers to the systematic collection and analysis of data to describe patterns and relationships.

In climates increasingly focused on accountability for appropriately allocating limited resources, service providers and policy makers alike are focused on identifying and implementing what works. Unfortunately, when it comes to labor trafficking, the field does not have a lot of information about what works. We know that higher standards for fair civil labor practices, mandatory education for children, and policies that promote equity in the workforce may help reduce the burden of labor trafficking. However, in contrast to our understanding of other public health and criminal justice problems, we have not identified an intervention that definitively works to prevent or stop labor trafficking (CdeBaca & Sigmon, 2014; Steiner, Kynn, Stylianou, & Postmus, 2018; United Nations Office on Drugs and Crime [UNODC], 2009a). This lack of evidence is a primary indicator that labor trafficking is an underresearched area. Without sufficient research, we cannot develop evidence-informed interventions or evaluate those interventions.

Research allows us to estimate the prevalence of labor trafficking, identify the populations affected, understand the ways that traffickers recruit, coerce, and exploit their victims, and assess how well prevention and intervention strategies work. Research also informs policy and public awareness of labor trafficking as an issue. We saw in Chapter 9 that research on labor trafficking has several limitations. Nearly any report on labor trafficking is presented with the caveat that the magnitude of the problem is underestimated. If we lack sufficient data, how do we arrive at estimates at all? Researchers use complex methodologies to estimate as precisely as possible the extent of trafficking. Quantitative estimates are often supplemented by case studies, victim interviews, and expert input.

Figure 10.3 describes how research can play a role in the labor trafficking response for different audiences.

With issues such as labor trafficking that confer devastating consequences on individuals and communities, it can be tempting to overestimate the magnitude of the problem. Some people perceive that policy makers and humanitarian organizations will focus more on issues that affect a greater number of people. Inflating the prevalence of labor trafficking or misrepresenting its influence on particular populations, however, does more harm than good. If labor trafficking truly affects only 100 people in an area, we should create a response best suited for 100 people, not 100,000. The severity of labor trafficking alone is adequate to justify the need for a response. Diverting more resources than needed to one area is arguably unethical, given that excess resources could be used somewhere else. Overestimation also threatens the credibility of all research (Tyldum & Brunovskis, 2005).

Figure 10.3   The Role of Research in Anti-trafficking Efforts

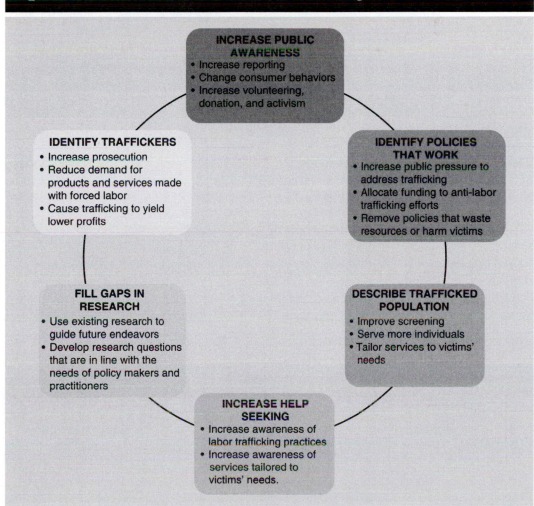

INCREASE PUBLIC AWARENESS
- Increase reporting
- Change consumer behaviors
- Increase volunteering, donation, and activism

IDENTIFY TRAFFICKERS
- Increase prosecution
- Reduce demand for products and services made with forced labor
- Cause trafficking to yield lower profits

IDENTIFY POLICIES THAT WORK
- Increase public pressure to address trafficking
- Allocate funding to anti-labor trafficking efforts
- Remove policies that waste resources or harm victims

FILL GAPS IN RESEARCH
- Use existing research to guide future endeavors
- Develop research questions that are in line with the needs of policy makers and practitioners

DESCRIBE TRAFFICKED POPULATION
- Improve screening
- Serve more individuals
- Tailor services to victims' needs

INCREASE HELP SEEKING
- Increase awareness of labor trafficking practices
- Increase awareness of services tailored to victims' needs.

Although we lack the type of data that might be ideal for best understanding labor trafficking, many data sources can be used to glimpse one aspect of the issue. Table 10.2 lists a few publicly available data sources that provide information on labor trafficking.

Data-Driven Responses to Labor Trafficking

In addition to these publicly available sources, recent innovative approaches to combating labor trafficking use financial data and "**big data**" to identify traffickers.

Use of Financial Services Data

The goal of labor trafficking is to generate profits; this means traffickers must leave a money trail in some form or another. Accordingly, financial institutions are becoming increasingly involved in anti-trafficking efforts. Financial institutions are uniquely suited to help combat labor trafficking because they routinely monitor for suspicious activity, such as money laundering. There are many places where traffickers may leave a money trail, including in payment for recruitment or transportation or in compensation (or lack thereof) of workers. One red flag that many financial institutions are now tracking is the use of funnel accounts,

Table 10.2   Publicly Available Data Sources Related to Labor Trafficking

Data Source	Description
CIRI Human Rights Data	Data from 202 countries, annually from 1981 to 2011, about governments' respect for internationally recognized human rights
Freedom House	Excel data sheet on "Freedom in the World" and annual reports on an array of human rights topics
Gap Minder	Aggregate of data sets related to the UN Millennium Development Goals; MDG 8 and 16 are particularly relevant to labor trafficking
Human Rights Data Analysis Group	Reports and publicly available data sets pertaining to global human rights issues
Quality of Government Institute	Several publicly available data sets about governance and corruption globally
ICPSR	Allows search for data sets used in articles, or by variable; data sets are publicly available; some require application for restricted access

Challenge Yourself 10.2

Identify one question you have about labor trafficking. Answer that question using a publicly available data set from the list in Table 10.2.

- How easy or difficult was it to answer your question?

- What, if any, additional data would you like to have?

accounts where money is deposited in one location and made immediately available in a different location (D. L. Rogers, 2016; Financial Crimes Enforcement Network, 2014). These types of accounts are used by many criminal organizations, including traffickers. Anti-trafficking partnerships between financial institutions, information technology (IT) companies, and businesses are already being implemented in the U.S., European Union (EU), and Canada.

In Canada, for example, a partnership between financial institutions and IT companies has developed mechanisms to identify suspicious activity. This partnership reports all suspicious activity to a national oversight organization. This oversight organization vets the claims and refers them to law enforcement agencies focused on human trafficking when appropriate (Financial Action Task Force, 2011; Government of Canada, 2012).

In the U.S., the Financial Crimes Enforcement Network released a guidance document in 2014 for financial institutions to use to identify potential human trafficking and human smuggling. A shortened version of appendix B from this report, shown in Table 10.3, describes red flags for human trafficking at each stage in the trafficking process.

Table 10.3   Human Trafficking Red Flags in Financial Data

No one transaction or red flag by itself is a clear indicator of human trafficking; accordingly, financial institutions may consider applying these red flags in combination with other factors, such as a customer's profile and expected transaction activity.

Transactional Red Flags: Behaviors Observed as Part of Account Activity	Who Would Most Likely See the Red Flag? When Would It Be Most Likely to See the Red Flag?
When: Exploitation Stage	
Substantial deductions to wages. To the extent that a financial institution is able to observe, a customer with a business may deduct large amounts from the wages of its employees, alleging extensive charges (e.g., housing and food costs), where the employees receive only a small fraction of their wages; this may occur before or after the payment of wages.	Who: Banks, credit unions, check cashers, prepaid card providers
When: Exploitation Stage	
Cashing of payroll checks where the majority of the funds are kept by the employer or are deposited back into the employer's account. This activity may be detected by those financial institutions that have access to pay stubs and other payroll records.	Who: Banks, credit unions, check cashers, prepaid card providers, money transmitters
When: Recruitment, Transportation, and Exploitation Stages	
Frequent outbound wire transfers, with no business or apparent lawful purpose, directed to countries at higher risk for human trafficking or to countries that are inconsistent with the customer's expected activity.	Who: Banks, credit unions, money transmitters
When: Recruitment, Transportation, and Exploitation Stages	
A customer's account appears to function as a *funnel account*, where cash deposits occur in cities/states where the customer does not reside or conduct business. Frequently, in the case of funnel accounts, the funds are quickly withdrawn (same day) after the deposits are made.	Who: Banks, credit unions

(Continued)

Table 10 3   (Continued)

When: Exploitation Stage	
Transactions conducted by individuals, escorted by a third party (e.g., under the pretext of requiring an interpreter), to transfer funds (that may seem to be their salaries) to other countries.	Who: Banks, credit unions, money transmitters, check cashers
When: Exploitation Stage	
Frequent transactions, inconsistent with expected activity and/or line of business, carried out by a business customer in apparent efforts to provide sustenance to individuals (e.g., payment for housing, lodging, regular vehicle rentals, purchases of large amounts of food).	Who: Banks, credit unions, money transmitters, prepaid card providers
When: Recruitment, Transportation, and Exploitation Stages	
Inflows are largely received in cash, where substantial cash receipts are inconsistent with the customer's line of business. Extensive use of cash to purchase assets and to conduct transactions.	Who: Banks, credit unions, money transmitters, check cashers

Source: Adapted from Financial Crimes Enforcement Network, 2014, appendix B.

Internationally, the Financial Action Task Force (FATF) also released a guidance document in 2018 for financial institutions working to combat human trafficking. Annex B in this document lists red flags, also broken down by the stage of the trafficking process. The FATF notes that trends in money laundering by traffickers varies substantially by country and by purpose of labor trafficking. Accordingly, they provide specific indicators for separate regions and countries. A few examples of financial indicators of labor trafficking identified in the report include:

- A high percentage of income withdrawn quickly after receipt in the accounts

- A property, when looked at on Google Street View, could only comfortably accommodate two or three people at the most, but seems to have more people living there

- Analysis of ATM activity shows that their ATM usage often occurred at the same machine at the same time suggesting that a third party is in control of their cards

- Customer displaying a poor standard of dress and personal hygiene

- Lack of living expenses such as food, petrol, utilities and rent (one utility may be set up for the purposes of confirming ID for account opening)

- No evidence of payment of taxes or of other payments to a tax authority or other government or regulatory body typically associated with legitimate full-time employment of workers

- One-way flight purchase from high-risk country by non-family member

- Payment for visa by non-family member

- Payments to labour agencies, recruiters or employment websites, especially if those entities are based overseas

- Personnel numbers and costs, if known through the provision of information by the entity, is not in line with wages paid out, or what you know of the entity

- Repeated (at least weekly) transfers of funds to the same third party (where known), often in round amounts

- Reports or indication of cheap labour or unfair business practices towards an entity. (FATF, 2018)

Reports note that financial institutions are more successful at identifying traffickers and providing sufficient evidence to convict them than are law enforcement agencies (European Commission, 2016; FATF, 2018). The FATF, however, found that the majority of its member countries do not have a specialized unit investigating money laundering by traffickers (FATF, 2011). A financial report from the European Union similarly noted that financial investigation of labor trafficking (and other forms of trafficking) remains "worryingly low" and has called on member countries to increase financial investigations of traffickers (European Commission, 2016).

Use of Big Data to Identify Traffickers

Definitions of big data vary (Press, 2014), but typically, when people discuss big data, they are referring to a range of new, large-scale data that have become available as individuals and businesses increasingly use and rely on the Internet to conduct their personal and professional business. Traffickers are heavily reliant on the Internet and web-based applications to recruit, transport, and advertise. Partnerships between data scientists and anti-trafficking organizations leverage traffickers' reliance on the Internet (see Table 10.4).

Table 10.4 Big Data Solutions to Labor Trafficking

Challenge	Solution
✕ Individuals are sold or traded between individuals or businesses online, avoiding detection by law enforcement.	✓ Data scientists can match pictures, names, descriptions on advertisements with those in missing persons reports.
✕ Traffickers avoid detection from law enforcement by changing their transportation routes and keeping victims isolated.	✓ Data scientists can map victim locations using emergency room data and reports from law enforcement to identify the areas where traffickers may work and move.
✕ Lack of oversight, insufficient oversight, or corruption among oversight entities prevents detection of employers using forced labor.	✓ Data scientists can employ network analysis using social network data to map out probabilistic real-life connections, which can be used to identify victims and traffickers.

Source: Konrad et al., 2017.

The **Global Emancipation Network** is working to bring together individuals in data science, information technology, and anti-trafficking. It has created an open database of trafficking information that can be shared with researchers, law enforcement, and service providers; groups have not historically shared human trafficking data. The Global Emancipation Network brings together data from a variety of sources in 22 countries and more than 70 cities. It scrapes for information such as text messages and images on both the open and deep web and supplements this data with public records. It also securely stores trafficking data from its partners. In partnership with intelligence analytics firms, it uses these data to identify patterns in traffickers' behavior, locate sites used by traffickers to facilitate their business, and assist law enforcement in action plans that are likely to successfully identify traffickers. The Global Emancipation Network also allows registered partners in the hospitality, transportation, and financial sectors to check whether trafficking is in place in their own businesses to make sure their service isn't being taken advantage of by traffickers. The Global Emancipation Network has successfully identified traffickers and victims and influenced modern trafficking legislation. The Global Emancipation Network also works to train individuals fighting human trafficking who are not sufficiently technologically proficient to use web data in their investigations.

Data source: Global Emancipation Network, n.d.

Recovery: The Identification of Traffickers and Victims

There are significant barriers to identifying labor trafficking victims and perpetrators, including little or no training specific to labor trafficking for law enforcement, few resources devoted to prosecution, victims' fear of seeking services, victims' being trafficked in isolated settings, and victims' often being "hidden populations."

Research has found that the majority of law enforcement officers, prosecutors, and direct service providers are unable to identify key characteristics of labor traffickers and victims.

In the U.S., every state has anti–labor trafficking laws, yet most prosecutors do not have enough information or experience to prosecute these cases. Consequently, even when labor trafficking cases are identified, the majority are referred to the federal government for prosecution. This is in part because law enforcement agencies have limited resources. To train law enforcement to identify labor traffickers and subsequently to devote time to investigating and prosecuting them would require incredible resources. It is easier and less resource intensive to pass all labor trafficking cases to federal agencies. This approach leads to states handling labor trafficking incidents on a case-by-case basis rather than having procedures in place to identify and prosecute traffickers on an ongoing basis (Clawson, Dutch, Lopez, & Tiapula, 2008). Given what we know about how prevalent labor trafficking is, this system does not lend itself to systematically combating labor trafficking.

Although most labor trafficking cases are referred to the federal government, local law enforcement is more likely to encounter actual victims. Another barrier that law enforcement faces in identifying labor trafficking, however, is that victims are typically exploited in legitimate industries. Law enforcement tends to rely, therefore, on reports of potential trafficking, creating a reactive rather than a proactive response. This stands in direct contrast to sex trafficking, which occurs (for the most part) in an illegal industry, allowing police to set up sting operations.

Prioritize Prosecution of Civil Labor Violations

One way to identify labor traffickers and victims is to prioritize the prosecution of civil labor violations. Many labor trafficking victims are subject to civil labor violations, but these go unreported or unprosecuted. Consistently prosecuting civil labor violations would constitute a shift in structural conditions that facilitate trafficking. If employers think it is likely that they may get caught, they may be less willing to engage in unfair labor practices, including labor exploitation and trafficking.

Increase Investigation Efforts

Countries that make concerted efforts to increase investigation and prosecution of traffickers are often successful. This may sound like a no-brainer, but a barrier to many anti–labor trafficking efforts is the perception that it would be too difficult to gather enough evidence to prosecute. Governments must weigh the time and resources that it takes to secure a prosecution of a labor trafficker against the demand for other investigations and prosecutions. It may be easy to decide in favor of prosecution of other crime types where there is more certainty of a positive outcome.

For example, in Brazil, efforts to combat the pervasive use of forced labor in agriculture, construction, and manufacturing began in the mid-1990s. The Brazilian Ministry of Labour and Employment launched Special Mobile Inspection Groups in 1995. These groups were charged with combating forced labor, particularly forced child labor, using unscheduled visits and investigations. Following political changes in 2002, including the election of Luiz Inácio Lula de Silva and a public criminal complaint from a victim of labor trafficking against the Brazilian government, additional efforts were put in place to combat labor trafficking.

Focus On
Justice at Work

Justice at Work (previously Friends of Farmworkers) initially provided legal services to migrant workers in Pennsylvania. Over time, however, they realized that many of their clients were actually victims, not just of labor violations, but of labor trafficking. In response to the massive number of trafficking victims they served, they decided to intentionally target and serve victims of labor trafficking. Today, they work with victims to recover unpaid wages, connect with direct service providers, and obtain permanent residency in the U.S. for victims and their families. They also work with law enforcement, when victims are willing, to prosecute traffickers.

Data source: Justice at Work, n.d.

In particular, the National Commission to Eradicate Slave Labor was established in 2003. This commission provides plans for the government, businesses, and the public to work to eradicate labor trafficking. Between 1995 and 2012, these groups rescued 44,000 victims of labor trafficking. As of 2015, the government had started using drones to monitor harder-to-access areas (Feasley, 2015).

Some NGOs are helping to increase prosecutions of traffickers. The Human Trafficking Legal Center, for example, connects victims of human trafficking with free legal services. It also maintains a database of federally prosecuted human trafficking cases. Since 2012, it has trained over 3,200 attorneys internationally, connected victims with free legal services in more than 250 cases, and educated over 14,000 community leaders on victim's rights. The center estimates that it has generated millions of dollars in free legal services (Human Trafficking Legal Center, n.d.).

Involve Health Care Providers

Health care providers are uniquely positioned to identify and support labor trafficking victims. Studies find that between 50% and 80% of all trafficking victims (not specific to labor trafficking) access at least one health care professional while they are being trafficked. Labor trafficking victims preferentially access urgent care clinics and emergency departments for medical services but have also

Case Study

When Traffickers Have Diplomatic Immunity

Under the 1961 Vienna Convention on Diplomatic Relations, it was essentially impossible to prosecute diplomats guilty of forced labor because they maintained immunity. In a 2006 case known as the **Swarna decision**, however, the court ruled that diplomats who leave their post may be prosecuted for trafficking crimes committed while they were diplomats.

Swarna filed a case against a Kuwaiti diplomat and his wife in 2002, who, Swarna noted, had tricked her into going with them to the U.S., then held her captive in their apartment, forced her to work as a domestic servant, and took away her passport. The male employer raped her on multiple occasions. The court dismissed her case because her employers had diplomatic immunity. In their decision, however, the court noted that the employers might not have diplomatic immunity if they ever left their post. Swarna filed a second case in 2006 when the couple moved to Paris. In this case, the court decided that the husband and wife did not qualify for "residual immunity."

Because Al-Awadi's employment of Plaintiff [Swarna] as a personal domestic servant was not an official act performed in the exercise of his diplomatic functions for Kuwait, the district court correctly held that Al-Awadi is not entitled to residual diplomatic immunity from Plaintiff's claims. Because AlShaitan, as Al-Awadi's spouse, did not hold a position at the Kuwait Mission to the United Nations, her employment of Plaintiff could not be an official act, and the district court correctly held that she is not entitled to residual diplomatic immunity. (State Department, as quoted in Vandenberg & Levy, 2012, p. 90)

This case marked the end of residual immunity for diplomat traffickers in the United States.

Data source: Vandenberg & Levy, 2012.

been identified by oncologists, podiatrists, endocrinologists, obstetricians, and gynecologists (Baldwin, Eisenman, Sayles, Ryan, & Chuang, 2011; Schwarz et al., 2016). This means that health care providers may be one of the only professionals who interact with victims while they are still being trafficked, but they may see victims just one time. Health care providers may be viewed as less intimidating than criminal justice practitioners, making it more likely that victims will trust and confide in them (Dovydaitis, 2010).

In line with this information, and in response to the severe medical consequences associated with trafficking, the medical and public health fields have set guidelines for screening and serving labor trafficking victims (Advocates for Human Rights, 2017; Dovydaitis, 2010). Health care providers are used to referring patients for additional services that address the underlying cause of their illness, so screening patients for human trafficking and subsequently referring them to services is a fitting role for these providers. To adequately serve victims, however, health care providers need effective screening tools and protocols for identifying victims and linking them to coordinated care.

In response to this need in the U.S., the Office on Trafficking in Persons and the Office of Women's Health developed a curriculum for health care, public health, behavioral health, and social work providers to identify and serve victims of human trafficking. The curriculum, **SOAR to Health and Wellness**, trains health care providers in responding to trafficking (Administration for Children and Families, n.d.b). Professional organizations have also administered guidelines for screening and responding to human trafficking, including the American Medical Association, the American Academy of Pediatrics, and the American Public Health Association (American Public Health Association, 2015; Chaet, 2017; J. Greenbaum, Bodrick, & Committee on Child Abuse and Neglect, 2017). The International Organization on Migration has also created a guidance document for health care providers to better serve victims of human trafficking (International Organization for Migration, Global Initiative to Fight Human Trafficking, & London School of Hygiene and Tropical Medicine).

Case Study

Health Care Provider Identifies Labor Trafficking Victim

Some medical conditions may begin as minor issues but become serious when left untreated. In a civil trafficking case brought in Washington, D.C., *Mazengo v. Mzengi*, a Tanzanian diplomat and his wife held a young woman in domestic servitude for four years, paying her nothing. During this time, the victim suffered severe ingrown toenails that went untreated for years. She was unable to wear shoes or walk without pain. Traffickers finally allowed her to see a doctor; her condition required surgery to remove the ingrown toenails. The doctor told the victim that if she had waited any longer to seek medical treatment she might have lost her toes. According to the complaint, the victim's traffickers forced her to return to work immediately following surgery. The court awarded the victim over $1 million in damages from the defendants.

Source: Bessell, Baldwin, Vandenberg, & Stoklosa, 2017.

Transparency in Supply Chain Laws, aka "Name and Shame"

A newer category of legislation seeks to combat labor trafficking by placing the pressure on businesses to eradicate forced labor and slavery from their supply chains. A **supply chain** is a network, or a sequence of processes used to create and distribute a product. Ultimately, if it is no longer beneficial to companies to use forced labor, or to remain ignorant about whether it is used, it will reduce the demand for labor trafficking. The idea behind supply chain transparency is that companies report what efforts they take to eradicate slavery from their supply chains in a place readily available to the public. If consumers do not feel these actions are in line with their beliefs or values, they can stop supporting the company. This type of reporting may also incentivize large companies to make a public effort to combat human trafficking, but this would be a positive externality. In many countries, companies have been encouraged to provide information about their supply chain voluntarily. In some places, however, businesses are required to report.

In 2010, California passed the **Transparency in Supply Chain Act**, making it a requirement for companies to report information about efforts they are taking to eradicate slavery from their supply chains. The law, which went into effect in 2012, applies only to companies doing business in California who gross at least $1 billion in revenue per year (Harris, 2015). Specifically, these companies must report in an obvious place on their website's home page:

- Efforts to evaluate and address potential human trafficking and forced labor in their supply chain, including whether a third party conducted this evaluation

- Whether the company conducts audits of suppliers' compliance with their company's standard for forced labor

- Whether the company requires its suppliers to certify that materials in its products comply with standards for forced labor in the country where they were produced

- What the company's internal accountability system is for when employees or suppliers fail to meet standards for forced labor

A small loophole to this law continues to threaten true supply chain transparency, however. The attorney general in California stated that California cannot release the list of companies that are required by law to report on supply chain transparency. As with similar supply chain transparency laws, companies are not required to take any action beyond reporting, so the burden falls on consumers to make informed choices about where they spend their money, and to change their purchasing habits based on their values. No other state has passed similar legislation, but the federal government is considering a similar bill, the **Business Supply Chain Transparency on Trafficking and Slavery Act** (2017–2018), which would require companies in all states to comply by reporting their efforts to eradicate slavery from their supply chains to the Securities and Exchange Commission.

The United States has also passed related legislation at the federal level. Section 1502 of the Dodd-Frank Act requires companies to report if they are using "conflict-minerals" from a war-torn part of Africa. Specifically, this law sought to reduce

U.S. involvement in and financial support of columbo-tantalite mines ("coltan") in the Congo that use slave labor. Columbo-tantalite is used in many electronics, including video game systems, computers, televisions, and nearly every cell phone that is manufactured or sold in the U.S. The law, though well intentioned, is limited by the fact that many corporations do not directly contact mineral-sourcing companies (Dizolele, 2017). Before corporations can purchase columbo-tantalite, the mineral must be processed into tantalum, where it is then distributed for use. Manufacturers have very little control over or knowledge of where these processers get these minerals. This further means that manufacturers are the only companies covered under this law. Many of the top tech companies do not manufacture their own products, so Sony, Apple, and Microsoft are not covered by the law. Following the passage of this law, there was also substantial pushback from businesses who thought it would be a significant burden to comply. This law was delayed for a few years and currently faces being repealed.

An alternative approach to helping companies comply with human rights standards in their supply chains is the **Responsible Minerals Initiative**. This initiative, which began in 2008, provides companies with an audit of the smelters (the companies that process minerals such as columbo-tantalite into other materials such as tantalum). It also publishes a publicly available database that lists responsible smelters. This allows companies to use smelters that use only responsibly sourced minerals in their supply chains. The initiative also provides workshops and technical assistance for companies trying to remove forced labor from their supply chains and identify emerging risks.

The United Kingdom also passed supply chain transparency legislation in its Modern Slavery Act in 2015. Like the California bill, the Modern Slavery Act requires any businesses (foreign and domestic) generating over £36 million in the UK to report their efforts to eradicate slavery from their supply chain on a "prominent place" on their website.

Brazil takes a somewhat different approach to supply chain transparency. Beginning in 2004, Brazil has published a "**Dirty List**" that includes the names of every employer that has been found to use "conditions analogous to slavery." The list is updated every six months, is searchable, and contains the name of the owner of the company, where the offense happened, what product was being produced, and how many workers were victimized (Feasley, 2015; Pierce, 2015). A company is monitored for two years following placement on the list. To be removed from the list after two years, a company must have paid fines and not committed any further acts of forced labor. The Dirty List is only a feasible approach in Brazil because beginning in the 1990s, Brazil underwent major legislative reform to identify and prosecute traffickers. Without an investigative system in place to identify traffickers and determine that they are guilty in a review court, the Dirty List would not be as helpful. Penalties for being on the Dirty List are more extreme than deterring potential consumers. Public and private financial institutions in Brazil refuse to grant loans or credit lines to companies on the Dirty List. Dirty List organizations cannot compete for public funding, and a newer bill allows the government to seize land without compensation from companies that use forced labor. The government reports that the financial consequences matter most to the businesses. In addition to these financial consequences, however, international human rights organizations have created a **National Pact for the Eradication of Slave Labour**. About 30% of businesses in Brazil have joined this pact. If the businesses are found to be in contact with a business on the Dirty List, their image in the international community is damaged (Feasley, 2015; Pierce, 2015).

This section focuses on allegations of forced labor in factories in China and on the actions taken in response by one major U.S. electronics company. The descriptions of working conditions ranged from being forced to work very long hours and live in cramped and insufficient accommodations to being forced to pay for accommodations and food and prevented from leaving the facility.

Business Responses to the Issue

The U.S. company in question responded with a statement within three days of the allegations. The U.S. company took steps to investigate the allegations through extensive factory visits and worker interviews. It published a report on its website within six weeks of the initial media coverage. In the report, the company stated that an audit team sent to the factory was made up of staff from its human resources, operations, and legal departments, and that the evidence gathered was cross-checked against many sources of information from employees, management, and staff records. The company stated that, as a result of its findings, the supplier was changing its policy to ensure compliance with the weekly overtime limits. In addition, the company noted that improvements to the sleeping facilities were required but that the supplier was in the process of acquiring more land to build further facilities. The supplier was quoted as being satisfied that the U.S.

company's report cleared up the allegations about working conditions in its factory. It is interesting to note that the Business and Human Rights Resource Centre, which has a policy of requesting responses from companies cited in human rights abuse allegations, records this particular case in its summary as having been resolved prior to the company responding. It is the only case that appears with this indicator.

Initial Lessons from the Issue

The U.S. company in question was using around 15% of the total workers employed by the factory in China. Nevertheless, this percentage share did not limit the access the company had in producing its audit findings. The story also highlighted the Electronics Industry Code of Conduct, a sector-specific tool and initiative that brings together over 40 (as of September 2008) companies working in the electronics industry. This initiative is aimed at improving working conditions in the industry supply chain. This case demonstrates that by acting quickly and being thorough in its response, the company quelled concern about the particular working conditions involved in the manufacture of key products. Nevertheless, the case highlights the difficulties in ensuring compliance with company codes in situations where there is extensive outsourcing.

Source: Adapted from International Labour Organization, 2015, p. 6.

Resources and Restoration

Resources refers to providing survivors of trafficking with the services they need to move toward restoration. *Restoration* refers to providing survivors with the services they need to lead healthy, stable lives and to prevent revictimization.

Increased recovery of survivors of labor trafficking must coincide with increases in support services for these individuals. For victims to move toward restoration, we must identify their needs and ways to fulfill them. Figure 10.4 describes a hierarchy of labor trafficking survivors' needs and services.

Typically, the first step toward restoration is to provide victims with tangible services such as food, housing, medical services, clothing, and safety from their trafficker. Then, victims need mental health services such as counseling and

Figure 10.4 Labor Trafficking Survivors' Needs

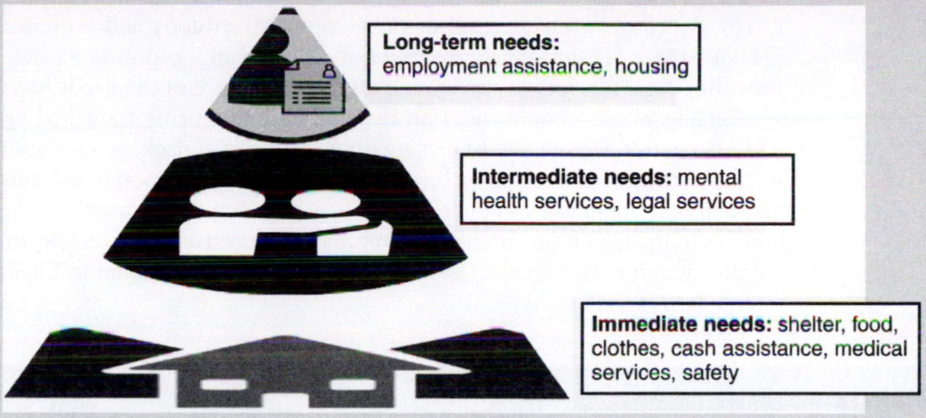

Long-term needs: employment assistance, housing

Intermediate needs: mental health services, legal services

Immediate needs: shelter, food, clothes, cash assistance, medical services, safety

legal services. In the long term, survivors need to be able to live stable, independent lives. Services to help toward this goal include job training, education, and employment assistance (Clawson & Dutch, 2008).

Meeting the immediate needs of victims requires significant coordination of case management, typically across a variety of partners. Not all recovered victims will require immediate services, however. A study of labor trafficking in the U.S. found that victims typically escaped on their own and lived for months or years before being connected to specialized services (Owens et al., 2014). Victims of labor trafficking may be reluctant to seek help for a multitude of reasons, including fear of retribution from traffickers, fear about immigration or visa status, lack of clarity about their rights in their current country of residence, lack of a support network, inability to speak the predominant language in the country where they have been trafficked, or simple lack of awareness of the services available (if they are even available; Office of Refugee Resettlement, 2012; Owens et al., 2014; U.S. Department of State, 2016).

A variety of legal services are critical for survivors, including services to help them regain unpaid wages; maintain or obtain legal residency for themselves and their families in the country where they have been trafficked or else return home safely, based on their preferences; and attain criminal prosecution of their trafficker (Office of Refugee Resettlement, 2012). In many countries, foreign national survivors of trafficking can gain assistance to remain lawfully in a country because they were victims of trafficking. In the U.S., this process is called certification, and it grants trafficking victims the right to legally remain in the U.S. and to receive government benefits and services. Figure 10.5 shows the process for becoming a certified trafficking survivor for adults in the United States. Foreign child victims of trafficking do not need to apply for certification. To become certified, adult victims must agree to participate in the investigation and prosecution of their trafficker. This requirement is waived if the survivor is deemed too psychologically or physically traumatized to assist. A T visa is granted to survivors who wish to stay in the U.S. T visas grant survivors "nonimmigrant status," which means they can live and work legally in the United States for four years, at which time they may apply for lawful permanent resident status

(Office of Refugee Resettlement, 2012). Continued presence is granted from the Department of Homeland Security and allows foreign national survivors of trafficking to remain lawfully in the United States for one year so they can assist with the trafficking investigation (U.S. Immigration and Customs Enforcement, 2010). As you can imagine, all of these steps are arduous and require a great deal of paperwork and timely oversight of different application processes. Thus, providing legal services to survivors is an essential piece of the needs hierarchy.

Finally, efforts should focus on the prevention of being trafficked again by addressing risk factors for trafficking such as poverty, lack of education, and unemployment. Survivors must be empowered to resist coercion in the future and assisted with obtaining legal, fair employment. Foreign survivors who bring their families to the U.S. from another country may also need assistance with childcare, employment for their spouse, and other needs, such as education in English as a foreign language.

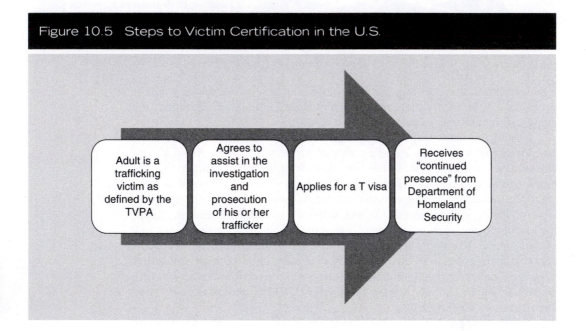

Figure 10.5   Steps to Victim Certification in the U.S.

Adult is a trafficking victim as defined by the TVPA → Agrees to assist in the investigation and prosecution of his or her trafficker → Applies for a T visa → Receives "continued presence" from Department of Homeland Security

Case Study

Recovery and Restoration for Natalia

Born and raised in a small village in Ghana, Natalia's family was struggling to pay the school fees for their children's education and welcomed the opportunity for Natalia to receive an education in the United States.

Shortly after she arrived in the U.S., the father she was living with began to physically and sexually abuse the young girl, creating a constant environment of fear for Natalia. For the next six years she

was forced to clean the house, wash clothes, cook, and care for their three children, often working 18 hours a day while receiving no form of payment. She was never allowed to enroll in school as the family had promised, go outside, or even use the phone. One day, after she was severely beaten, Natalia saw an opportunity to run away from the home and a neighbor called the police. She was then taken to a local hospital for medical care. The nurse assisting Natalia was aware of the National Human Trafficking Resource Center and referred her to Polaris New Jersey.

The Polaris New Jersey team met Natalia at the local hospital and immediately coordinated emergency services including clothing, a safe shelter, counseling, emotional support, and case management. Within a month, Natalia was enrolled in

school as she had always dreamed, living in transitional housing and beginning to feel like herself again. Now, nearly a year later, she is volunteering at a local animal rescue shelter, participating in a weekly poetry workshop, and is pursuing her education to become a nurse. Natalia is one of the many examples of the reliance and courage of survivors who have redefined their future and are working towards achieving their long-term goals.

Source: Polaris, 2015f.

Conclusion

There remain significant gaps in our response to labor trafficking. It remains difficult to successfully identify and prosecute traffickers, who continue to operate behind the veil of legitimate businesses, successfully isolate their victims, and prey on marginalized or hidden individuals. There remains an extreme shortage in services for male victims, even for things as basic as emergency shelter. Most urgent, perhaps, is that primary risk factors for labor trafficking such as poverty and marginalization are far from being addressed.

Nonetheless, ongoing responses to labor trafficking provide many reasons for optimism. Anti–labor trafficking efforts are leveraging more data and more types of data than ever before. Policy makers are starting to hold corporations accountable for their business practices. Practitioners in a wide variety of fields, from data science to public health, are engaged in anti–labor trafficking efforts. This increase in information means that the era where anyone can claim ignorance about the presence of labor trafficking is ending and will hopefully be paralleled by a shift in consumer behavior. As stated in the opening quote for this chapter by Hillary Clinton, "all of us have a responsibility to bring this practice to an end."

KEY WORDS

3P paradigm 245
4R framework 246
big data 250
Business Supply Chain
  Transparency on Trafficking
  and Slavery Act 258
Dirty List 259

Global Emancipation
  Network 254
human rights approach 245
labor approach 245
National Pact for the
  Eradication of Slave
  Labour 259

Responsible Minerals
  Initiative 259
SOAR to Health and Wellness 257
supply chain 258
Swarna decision 256
Transparency in Supply Chain
  Act 258

DISCUSSION QUESTIONS

1. What are some barriers presented to individuals, law enforcement, and victim service providers with respect to anti-

trafficking approaches to labor trafficking, and what are some of the challenges in overcoming those barriers?

2. Explain in detail the two primary theories for responding to trafficking, in particular, the 3P paradigm and the 4R framework, and the challenges encountered with each framework.

3. What role do research and data play in anti-trafficking efforts?

4. In what ways are financial institutions helpful in anti-trafficking efforts?

5. What are some of the challenges in identifying labor trafficking victims?

6. You completed a quiz to identify how many slaves work for you. You also learned about the challenges faced in reducing exploitation within supply chains. Research a company that has issues in its supply chain. What is it doing to reduce exploitation? Could it do more?

RESOURCES

- Global Emancipation Network: https://siliconangle.com/2017/10/02/noble-nerds-fight-human-trafficking-data-blockchain-analytics-splunkconf17-womenintech/; https://www.globalemancipation.ngo/

- Human Trafficking Legal Center and HEAL Trafficking, "Fact Sheet: Human Trafficking and Healthcare Providers": https://healtrafficking.org/wp-content/uploads/2017/11/Medical-Fact-Sheet-Document_FINAL_NOVEMBER-20–2017.pdf

- International Labour Office, Combating Forced Labour: A Handbook for Employers and Businesses, http://www.ilo.org/wcmsp5/groups/public/---ed_norm/---declaration/documents/publication/wcms_101171.pdf

- Justice at Work, "Fighting Labor Trafficking": https://www.justiceatworklegalaid.org/service-areas/special-initiatives/services-for-victims-of-labor-trafficking/

- Polaris, "Survivor Story: Promised an Education, Forced to Work Instead": https://polarisproject.org/blog/2015/06/17/survivor-story-promised-education-forced-work-instead

- Slavery Footprint: https://slaveryfootprint.org/

Other Forms of Human Trafficking

In this section we will review less prevalent, though equally severe, forms of human trafficking including organ trafficking, child marriage, and child soldiering. These categories of trafficking are often only brought to public attention through significant events that make news headlines but unfortunately are often forgotten once the news cycle changes. These less prevalent forms of human trafficking impact the most vulnerable but are often perpetrated by individuals with substantial power. For example, organ trafficking victims are typically individuals in severe poverty, desperate to earn money to support themselves or their families or to pay off debts. Organ traffickers, on the other hand, often include medical personnel as well as organ recipients wealthy enough to pay tens of thousands of dollars or more for an organ. Consequences for each of these forms of trafficking are severe, including increasing victims' likelihood of premature death. As you read this section, think about the structural factors that are conducive to these forms of trafficking and what the ideal points for prevention and intervention might be.

Child Soldiers

Most evidence suggests that ordinary children, faced with the extraordinary circumstances of combat, are capable of learning to kill and to kill repeatedly.

—Michael Wessells, *Child Soldiers: From Violence to Protection* (2009)

Case Study

Junior Nzita Nsuami

My name is Junior Nzita Nsuami and I am a former child soldier. My story is long and difficult to tell. My childhood was not like other children's. It was stolen, confiscated, and deprived of the love of my mother and the protection of my country.

In 1996, I left the home of my parents who were living in Goma, the capital of North Kivu in the Democratic Republic of the Congo, in order to continue my studies in Kiondo, a remote village. It was there that my friends and I were surprised one day by the soldiers of the Alliance of Democratic Forces for the Liberation of Congo (Alliance des Forces Démocratiques pour la Libération du Congo—AFDL), who forced us to join their ranks.

Without my consent, or that of my parents, I became a soldier at the age of twelve, forced to fight the regime of Mobutu Sese Seko. Soon after our forced recruitment, my friends and I were transferred to a training camp where we were taught how to use guns, how to kill, and how to hate our fellow human beings.

One year later, in 1997, Mobutu was removed from power. The AFDL had fulfilled its mission, but mine continued. I was still a child soldier. After having been moved to Matadi, a port city in Bas-Congo, the desire to resume my studies and have a normal school life began to overwhelm me daily. I asked my commander if I could be put on extended leave and in 2000, I was able to go back to school. I had been forced to leave school when I was twelve years old. I was now fifteen and had spent three long, difficult years in another world, carrying a gun instead of a book bag, a bayonet for a pen, and ammunition instead of school books.

My reintegration into society was painful. I had to learn again how to live a normal life, to change my habits and to think differently. I had to become a citizen who respects his neighbors, his friends and his community. It was a major change. After having spent years witnessing abuse of all kinds, I realized that it was time to protect the land, the richness and beauty of my country, and to work to reconstruct my nation.

In October of 2001, I had the good fortune to be adopted by a family who were able to offer me a stable and supportive living environment as I resumed my studies. Four years later, I graduated with a degree in Social Sciences. In 2006, when the national commission for Disarmament, demobilization and reintegration arrived in Matadi to urge all former child soldiers to leave the army and reintegrate into normal life, I was ready. Off I went to sign my official demobilization papers. Ten years had passed between my recruitment and my demobilization.

Source: Junior Nzita Nsuami (29 May 2013). Junior Nzita Nsuami: A Former Child Soldier Rebuilds His Life. Special Representative of the Secretary-General for Children and Armed Conflict. Retrieved from https://childrenandarmedconflict.un.org/junior-nzita-former-child-soldier/.

Child soldiers are not inherently violent. They are trained, misled, and brainwashed to be this way. This chapter will explore what a child solider is. What regions of the world are they most often found? What are the risk factors for and consequences of such violent experiences during a vulnerable period of child development? Finally, what is currently being done to control and eliminate this terrible practice, and what challenges do we face in doing so?

Historical Context

The concept of the involvement of children in war is not new (Bower, 2008; Laband, 2017; Robinson, 2018; Tiefenbrun, 2007). The use of children in military combat stems back several centuries (Laband, 2017). As presented by Bower (2008, p. 6), even in more modern times, children have been integral to war. Drummer boys fought alongside soldiers in the American Civil War. In World War II, Hitler used children as spies and soldiers (Bower, 2008; Kaplan, 2005; Tiefenbrun, 2007). The **Hitler Youth movement** indoctrinated kids into taking the Nazis' position on politics and social issues alike. Although abduction was not the primary means of recruitment, as it is with many of today's child soldiers, propaganda, brainwashing, and manipulation were all strategies used by Hitler and continue to be used today to gain the cooperation of child soldiers. Also during World War II, women and young girls were recruited by the Japanese to sexually service the soldiers (Alfredson, 2001). The Vietnamese army also used children during their civil war in the late 1960s through the early 1970s. Finally, coming into present times, child soldiers continue to be used in civil and territorial conflicts, primarily in Asia and Africa.

Definition

When one hears the term *child solider*, images immediately come to mind. Perhaps you are imagining young African boys, heavily armed, forlorn or angry looking. These images are not inaccurate, although they may not fully encompass the breadth of who becomes child soldiers.

The generally agreed upon definition of a child soldier, as described by the United Nations Children's Fund (UNICEF), is a child associated with an armed force or armed group—any person under the age of 18 years old who is or has been recruited or used by an armed force or armed group in any capacity, including but not limited to fighters, cooks, porters, spies, or for sexual purposes (UNICEF, 2007a). Child soldiers can be male or female.

The U.S. Child Soldiers Prevention Act of 2007 (2008) defines the term *child soldier* as follows:

i.   any person under 18 years of age who takes a direct part in hostilities as a member of governmental armed forces;

ii. any person under 18 years of age who has been compulsorily recruited into governmental armed forces;

iii. any person under 15 years of age who has been voluntarily recruited into governmental armed forces; or

iv. any person under 18 years of age who has been recruited or used in hostilities by armed forces distinct from the armed forces of a state.

The term *child soldier* includes any person described in subsections 2, 3, or 4 who is serving in any capacity, including in a support role, such as a "cook, porter, messenger, medic, guard, or sex slave."

Both the U.S. definition and UNICEF's align closely with the United Nations' Optional Protocol to the Convention on the Rights of the Child on the Involvement of Children in Armed Conflict (United Nations General Assembly, 2000a), discussed in more depth later in the chapter.

Photo 11.1 More than 30,000 children have been kidnapped to serve as soldiers and slaves by the rebel Lord's Resistance Army in its 20-year war against the Ugandan government. Boys in captivity are forced to loot and burn villages and torture and kill neighbors. Abducted girls are routinely raped and become sex slaves or "wives" of rebel commanders. This drawing, presented in the 2009 Trafficking in Persons Report, expresses the traumas of war experienced by Ugandan children who have returned home.

Focus On
Definitions

Several terms are critical in comprehending the full experience of child soldiers. A child does not just become a soldier. There is typically some process, or strategy, behind it. As in other forms of human trafficking, recruitment strategies are central to the identification of child soldiers. UNICEF (2007a) defines *recruitment* as "compulsory, forced, and voluntary conscription or enlistment of children into any kind of armed force or armed group" (p. 7).

Unlawful recruitment refers to recruitment strategies that attract children under the age stipulated in international treaties and/or national laws. Child soldiers can be recruited by both **armed forces** and/or **armed groups**. Forces are those sponsored by the state, whereas groups are those militarized groups not representing the state. Examples would include rebel groups or other oppositional groups unrelated to the state government.

There are several important terms relating to the end of a child's experience as a soldier. UNICEF (2007a) defines **release** as the "process of formal and controlled disarmament and demobilization of children from an armed force or armed group as well as the informal ways in which children leave by escaping, being captured or by any other means." (p. 7). This release is the first step in disassociating from military life and transitioning to civilian life. After release, **child reintegration** must take place. UNICEF describes this as "the process through which children transition into civil society and enter meaningful roles and identities as civilians who are accepted by their families and communities in a context of local and national reconciliation" (p. 7). Several conditions must be in place for this reintegration to occur, relating to stable and just political, legal, economic, and social conditions. Children must have available to them formal and nonformal forms of education, family unity, and safety from harm. These conditions can be especially unattainable in countries ridden with conflict and the continued use of child soldiers. More detail on these terms is presented throughout this chapter.

Where Are Child Soldiers Found?

As with other forms of human trafficking, estimates of child soldiers are difficult to assess and thus somewhat unreliable (Bower, 2008). While sources can provide information regarding where child soldiers are found, as described below, understanding the specific numbers and demographic descriptors of this hidden population can be more challenging.

What is certain is that the number of children acting as soldiers across the world is startling. Tiefenbrun (2007) reports that "the recruitment of children into armed conflict has claimed the lives of more than two million children, left more than six million children maimed or permanently disabled, caused one million children to be orphaned, afflicted ten million children with serious psychological trauma, and made 12 million children refugees" (p. 421).

Two-thirds of United Nations member states have laws in place to protect youth (under age 18) from forced participation in military forces and groups. These laws, described in more detail later in the chapter, have resulted in a global decline in the use of child soldiers. Nevertheless, children are still routinely used as soldiers in those countries that are involved in armed conflict (Child Soldiers International, n.d.a; Withers, 2012).

Youth involvement goes beyond national armies. Children are found in paramilitaries, civil defense forces, and state-allied armed groups (J. Becker, 2005). Research conducted by Child Soldiers International provides some understanding of the distribution of child soldiers across different affiliations and roles (Withers, 2012). Between 2010 and 2012, Child Soldiers International found evidence of the use of child soldiers in 20 countries and in various roles, including in national armies, paramilitaries, and opposition groups. Table 11.1 highlights the specific types of combatant groups children were associated with and in which countries. During that two-year period, child soldiers were most often found in national armies or paramilitaries, civil defense forces, police, and other branches of state security forces. Sudan had child soldiers identified in several difference groups, including national armies, paramilitaries, irregular paramilitaries, and opposition groups. Yemen also had children involved in combat from various groups, including national armies, paramilitaries, and irregular paramilitaries.

Table 11.1 Identification of Child Soldiers, 2010–2012

	National Armies[1]	Official Paramilitaries, Civil Defense Forces, Police, and Other Branches of State Security Forces	Irregular Paramilitaries, "Self-Defense" Militias, and Other Armed Groups That Are Not Part of Official State Security Forces but Are Supported by or Otherwise Allied to Governments	Armed Opposition Groups Operating in Other Countries With the Support of or as Proxy Forces of Governments	Children, While not Actually Recruited, Were Used Informally by State Armed Forces in Situations of Armed Conflict
Afghanistan		X			X
Central African Republic (CAR)			X		
Chad	X			X[2]	
Colombia					X
Cote d'Ivoire	X		X		
Democratic Republic of the Congo (DRC)	X	X			
Eritrea				X[3]	
Iraq		X			
Israel					X
Libya	X	X			
Myanmar	X	X			
Philippines		X			X
Republic of South Sudan		X			
Rwanda				X[4]	X
Somalia	X		X		
Sudan	X	X	X	X[5]	
Syria					
Thailand		X			
Yemen	X	X	X		

[1]In addition, several under-18s have been inadvertently deployed in the British armed forces in recent years, including at least one in 2010.

[2]Sudan armed opposition groups.

[3]Somali armed opposition groups.

[4]DRC armed opposition groups.

[5]Chad armed opposition groups.

Data source: Withers, 2012.

The UN and the U.S. Department of State assess the extent to which specific countries are using child soldiers. In its 2018 report, the UN General Assembly Security Council (2018) verified 21,000 violations of human rights around the world in 2017, including the recruitment of child soldiers. The report lists seven countries (Afghanistan, Myanmar, Somalia, South Sudan, Sudan, Syria, and Yemen) and 56 nonstate armed groups as recruiting and using child soldiers. The UN reports an increase in the 2017 number of child soldier–related violations as compared to 2016. This increase in violations occurred specifically in the Central African Republic and the Democratic Republic of the Congo (General Assembly Security Council, 2018). The annual UN report also indicated a high number of verified cases of child soldiers in the following locations during 2017: Somalia (2,127), South Sudan (1,221), the Syrian Arab Republic (961), and Yemen (842). The report also showed evidence of increased killings and maimings of children during 2017.

The U.S. Department of State has been reporting on the use of child soldiers by country since the 2002 Trafficking in Persons (TIP) Report. In that report, child soldiers were not defined but simply noted as a form of trafficking occurring in the following countries: Sri Lanka, Sudan, and Tanzania. The 2004 report (U.S. Department of State, 2004) introduced child soldiers as a form of human trafficking in its introductory material. It provided a description of the experiences of child soldiers as well as the contexts in which child soldiers are typically found. The 2009 report (U.S. Department of State, 2009), which reported on data prior to enactment of the Child Soldiers Prevention Act (CSPA), described UN data indicating that there were 57 armed groups and forces using children in 2007, up from 40 armed forces and groups in 2006. Starting in 2010, the TIP Report provided more specific information on child soldiers, thanks to the CSPA. Starting in the 2010 TIP Report, the CSPA was introduced and countries using child soldiers were listed (U.S. Department of State, 2010). Figure 11.1 lists all countries included in

Figure 11.1   CSPA List, 2010–2018

2010, 2011	2012	2013[1]	2015	2016	2017	2018
☐ Burma	☐ Burma	☐ Burma	☐ Burma	☐ Burma	☐ DRC	☐ Burma
☐ Chad	☐ DRC	☐ CAR[3]	☐ DRC	☐ DRC	☐ Mali	☐ DRC
☐ DRC[2]	☐ Libya	☐ Chad	☐ Nigeria	☐ Iraq	☐ Nigeria	☐ Iran
☐ Somalia	☐ South Sudan	☐ DRC	☐ Somalia	☐ Rwanda	☐ Somalia	☐ Iraq
☐ Sudan	☐ Somalia	☐ Rwanda	☐ South Sudan	☐ Somalia	☐ South Sudan	☐ Mali
☐ Yemen	☐ Sudan	☐ Somalia	☐ Sudan	☐ South Sudan	☐ Sudan	☐ Niger
	☐ Yemen	☐ South Sudan	☐ Syria	☐ South Sudan	☐ Syria	☐ Nigeria
		☐ Sudan	☐ Yemen	☐ Sudan	☐ Yemen	☐ Somalia
		☐ Syria		☐ Syria		☐ South Sudan
		☐ Yemen		☐ Yemen		☐ Syria
						☐ Yemen

[1]The CSPA list in 2014 was identical to the 2013 list, except for the removal of Chad in 2014.

[2]Democratic Republic of the Congo

[3]Central African Republic

Source: U.S. Department of State, 2010.

the CSPA list since its inclusion in the TIP Reports in 2010. As apparent in the figure, there is not a lot of variation in the list from year to year. The 2013 list was slightly expanded, perhaps due to a new trend in the use of child soldiers, noted in the 2013 TIP Report (U.S. Department of State, 2013). During 2013, the use of child soldiers seemed to go beyond state-associated militaries. Children were being found in oppositional groups for the purposes of fighting and acting as porters, spies, and prostitutes. While likely this had been going on well before 2013, the expanded use of child soldiers was acknowledged during this time period, at least by the Department of State.

While understanding where child soldiers are being used is important from a preventative standpoint, a demand for action is unlikely without a closer look into what is happening on the ground. Examples of the status of child soldiers in select countries are provided below.

Country-Level Examples

Sierra Leone struggled through a civil war between 1991 and 2002. During this extensive time in conflict, over 25,000 children were forced to become soldiers for state-run armed forces as well as oppositional groups (Tiefenbrun, 2007). At one point in the war, 40% to 50% of oppositional groups and 20% of state forces were children (Bradley, 2017).

Similarly, the Democratic Republic of the Congo (DRC) seems to be using children in multiple aspects of fighting—and not sparingly. In 2003, observers described the overabundance of young fighters, calling them "armies of children" (J. Becker, 2005).

Over 6,000 children have been recruited by armed forces and groups in Somalia since 2011. It is estimated that approximately 50% of soldiers in the militant group al-Shabab (the group fighting against the UN-backed Somali government) are children (Dallaire Initiative & Dalhouse University, 2018). In fact, *al-Shabab* means *the youth* in Arabic (Felter, Masters, & Sergie, 2018). The UN identified two armed groups and one state group that recruit children into armed conflict. Evidence shows that children as young as nine have been found using weapons in Somalia (Dallaire Initiative & Dalhouse University, 2018).

There are reports like this coming out of many countries. These examples simply highlight the problem.

The next section will discuss child soldiers in the context of human trafficking. Understanding child soldiers in this context can contribute to an understanding of how to reduce the use of child soldiers globally.

Is This Human Trafficking?

As a reminder, human trafficking, or

> "trafficking in persons[,]" shall mean the recruitment, transportation, transfer, harbouring or receipt of persons, by means of the threat or use of force or other forms of coercion, of abduction, of fraud, of deception, of the abuse of power or of a position of vulnerability or of the giving or receiving of payments or benefits to achieve the consent of a person having control over another person, for the purpose of exploitation. (United Nations General Assembly, 2000c)

Child soldiers experience similar risk factors, undergo similar recruitment tactics, and have equally challenging transitions out of their trafficking experiences as victims of other forms of human trafficking.

Risk Factors

As with other forms of trafficking, both individual-level and structural factors explain the large supply of children vulnerable to forced recruitment into armed forces and groups. The risk factors identified in Chapter 4 of this text apply as much to child soldiers as to any other trafficking victims. Nevertheless, the following section briefly reviews these risk factors as they apply specifically to child soldiers.

Age Blindness

Age is an inherent risk factor for becoming a child soldier. In all countries, participation in state militaries is not unlawful once an individual is of consenting age. One particular challenge faced by vulnerable children is the dismissal or unavailability of age information by army recruiters. This "**age blindness**" occurs in countries that ignore the concept of age (such as the DRC and Yemen) or have no infrastructure in place to document age (Withers, 2012). Countries such as Uganda, Afghanistan, and the Philippines do not routinely provide birth registrations to infants, resulting in the possible, if not likely, participation of youth in state armed forces. Other instances of age blindness occur when laws do not specifically prohibit the voluntary participation of children in combat. Both the United States and the UK have policies that permit 16- and 17-year-olds to voluntarily enter state militaries. While tracking procedures are meant to ensure that children are not placed in hostile environments, Child Soldiers International found rare instances where tracking failed and youth were deployed to combat situations (J. Becker, 2005; Withers, 2012). Children who routinely participate in military schools may also become victim to age blindness or the dismissal of age. Evidence from Mexico shows children from military schools participating in the war on drugs. There is debate over whether this war should be considered armed conflict, but the risk to children in military schools being recruited to participate in state military activity is concerning (Withers, 2012).

Structural Factors

Child soldiers' vulnerabilities largely stem from infrastructure weaknesses. Unstable governments, poverty, violence, and conflict explain all forms of human trafficking, including child soldiers. Extreme poverty exists in nations where child soldiers are most likely to be found, as well as cultural values that condone

Challenge Yourself 11.1

Compare the child soldier definition to what you know about human trafficking. Do you see similarities? Do you support the notion that forced recruitment of children into armed forces and groups constitutes human trafficking?

the practice of using child soldiers (Achvarina & Reich, 2006; J. Becker, 2005; Somasundaram, 2002; Tiefenbrun, 2007; Withers, 2012). Public health issues such as AIDS and the traumatic effects of living in conflict zones also drive the supply of child soldiers (Kaplan, 2005).

Individual-Level Factors

As with other forms of trafficking, poverty, limited access to education, family structure, and peer groups can all increase the likelihood of a child becoming a soldier (Achvarina & Reich, 2006; Bloom, 2018; Kaplan, 2005; Robinson, 2018; Somasundaram, 2002; Tiefenbrun, 2007). These factors especially make children more vulnerable to abduction tactics and indoctrination tactics, both commonly used methods of recruitment.

For more information on the risk factors associated with becoming victims of human trafficking, including child soldiers, refer to Chapter 4.

Case Study: Child Soldiers in Africa

A Synopsis of *Armed & Underage,* an Exposé of Child Soldiers in Africa

The *New York Times Upfront* magazine published an exposé on child soldiers in Africa. The article describes the context and consequences of governments employing the use of children (Gettleman, 2010). The article begins by describing Awil Salah Osman, a normal-looking 12-year-old boy except for the massive (10-pound) gun he is carrying and his affiliation with the Somali armed forces (which are partly supported by the United States government). The Somali government is known to indoctrinate soldiers as young as nine years old. The author estimates that Awil is one of more than 200,000 child soldiers worldwide.

Moving away from Awil's personal story, the article transitions into an analysis of how children may become vulnerable to becoming soldiers and why countries employ the use of youth as a war tactic. The article quotes a Chad military commander: "Child soldiers are ideal . . . they don't complain, they don't expect to be paid—and if you tell them to kill, they kill" (p. 6). Poor education and exposure to traumatic events make children vulnerable targets and easily conditioned for war.

Gettleman ties in the historical use of children in warfare, citing the Nazis' use of children during World War II and the use of children in the Iran-Iraq war in the 1980s. While acknowledging the use of child soldiers in Colombia, Myanmar, Afghanistan, Southern Thailand, and the Philippines, Gettleman believes the worst region in the world for child soldiers is Africa. This is partially due to conflicts morphing from "cause-driven struggles, like ending colonial rule, to criminal drives led by warlords whose goals are nothing more than plunder, greed, and power" (p. 7). The article notes that the standards the Somali government uses to select soldiers are limited to the individual's ability to carry a gun.

The article concludes with an encouraging assessment of the international justice system's attempts to serve justice to those who have been employing the use of child soldiers in various countries. One major case mentioned by Gettleman (2010) involved Charles Taylor, the former Liberian president. He was accused of "sponsoring a brutal rebel group that routinely forced children into combat during wars in Liberia and Sierra Leone from 1989 to 2003" (p. 9). These prosecutions are hopefully setting examples to other countries, showing them that there are consequences for using child soldiers. However, there is still progress to be made in addressing governments' use of child soldiers.

The Experiences of Child Soldiers

The recruitment tactics, traumatic experiences, and escape difficulties of child soldiering all echo much of what has been described for other forms of human trafficking, with some features being unique to child soldiers.

Recruitment

Recruitment of child soldiers is not very different from that used in other forms of human trafficking. Force, fraud, and coercion entrap young people and result in them becoming child soldiers. Force is common in the recruitment of child soldiers, perhaps more so than in other forms of trafficking. A systematic review of former child soldier mental health outcomes found abduction to be the most common method of children becoming involved with armed forces and groups (Betancourt et al., 2013). This is especially the case in Sub-Saharan Africa.

Fraud and coercion are also common tactics in recruiting child soldiers. Even those who seemingly volunteer are influenced by manipulation and deception (Bloom, 2018; Tiefenbrun, 2007). Recruiters capitalize on the vulnerabilities of their potential victims, particularly in the Middle East and Asia (Betancourt et al., 2013; Bloom, 2018; Kohrt et al., 2016). Propaganda and manipulation tactics are used to convince families that their children should be part of the military effort. Evidence shows that in schools controlled by the Islamic State in Iraq and Syria (ISIS) and other oppositional groups in the Middle East, families typically volunteer their children to join the army (Bloom, 2018). In this region, children are also sold by parents. Pakistani officials reported children being sold for between $7,000 and $14,000 to become suicide bombers. Similar reports of the sale of children to terrorist groups occurred in the Philippines (Bloom, 2018).

A common strategy for recruiting and keeping youth affiliated with armed forces and groups is to promise protection (Bloom, 2018; Kohrt et al., 2016; Robinson, 2018). This is an especially powerful tactic for girls and children coming from impoverished backgrounds. Girls have been told that joining the army will protect them from rape at border crossings. A study of Nepali child soldiers indicated that girls were more likely than boys to have joined the military voluntarily (Kohrt et al., 2016). As noted by former child soldier "Shova," the military promises girls escape from their perceived obligations to their family. "Shova" reports:

> I was thirteen years old. I was a very shy girl who wouldn't speak with people other than my mother. . . . In our village, people used to come to ask my hand in marriage even when I was very young. Even a mention of marriage gave me a headache. I hated it! I wanted to avoid marriage in any way possible . . . at the time, many Maoist [communist party of Nepal] activities used to take place in our village. . . . I liked their cultural program. . . . What a wonderful life—I would often think—I would have if I became a Maoist. I would travel a lot and wouldn't have to be forced into marriage. . . . (Kohrt et al., 2016, p. 9)

Evidence shows that for "Shova" and girls like her, Maoism did provide some protection from traditional gender roles and an empowering experience. Unfortunately, in other parts of the world, joining armed forces and groups has offered little protection from forced marriage, sexual exploitation, and rape (Elezi, 2011; Tiefenbrun, 2007).

Living as a Child Soldier

When examining the experiences of child soldiers, there are some consistencies across regions and some variations. Across all regions, children's roles in the military will vary, but they often include both labor and sex exploitation. Labor exploitation may include work as porters, cooks, guards, servants, messengers, or spies, in addition to traditional fighters. Both girls and boys may be sexually abused and risk contracting sexually transmitted diseases. Girls have been known to be forced to act as "wives" to male combatants (Elezi, 2011; Tiefenbrun, 2007).

Child soldiers are exposed to the most violent and immoral treatment. Tiefenbrun (2007) writes about unimaginable treatment used to keep children obedient and compliant, including being boiled alive, eating human flesh, smearing themselves with the blood of those they killed, beatings, and threats to the children and their families. Torture such as this, abduction, brainwashing, forced drug use, sexual exploitation, and exposure to violence result in young, focused, fearless killing machines. Child soldiers become violent to their core, conditioned to kill without restraint (Kaplan, 2005; Tiefenbrun, 2007).

Exposure to Violence and Sexual Exploitation

Exposure to violence and **sexual exploitation** are especially common features of being a child soldier (Alfredson, 2001; Bloom 2018; Human Rights Watch, 2003; Somasundaram, 2002; Withers, 2012).

If you join the paramilitaries [the United Self-Defense Forces of Colombia,] your first duty is to kill. They tell you, "Here you are going to kill." From the very beginning, they teach you how to kill. I mean when you arrive at the camp, the first thing they do is kill a guy, and if you are a recruit they call you over to prick at him, to chop off his hands and arms.

—Human Rights Watch (2003, p. 95)

Sexual exploitation is commonly experienced by both male and female child soldiers, albeit more so by females (Alfredson, 2001; J. Becker, 2005). Routine "servicing" of both men and boy soldiers is a common role for girls serving as soldiers (J. Becker, 2005; Tiefenbrun, 2007). Interestingly, when the definition of victimization is expanded to include forced perpetration of sexual assault, boys are more often found to be exploited. Evidence shows that during Sierra Leone's civil war, boys were forced to commit sexual violence (Alfredson, 2001).

Forced participation in violent actions, whether of a sexual nature or not, can have damaging and long-term effects on children. Child soldiers have extreme and constant exposure to violence, a fact that must be acknowledged for those soldiers fortunate enough to reach the release and reintegration stages.

Reintegration

As discussed in previous chapters, separation from the trafficking experience can be dangerous and difficult. Generally, fear of deportation, lack of documents, and so forth may keep labor trafficking victims in their trafficking situations. Drug addiction, fear, perceived feelings of love, and lack of other opportunities keep sex trafficking victims in their situations. Child soldiers have other, yet equally

Case Study

Boko Haram

Child soldiers are captured not just to be fighters. They take on many roles, in some cases overlapping with other forms of human trafficking. **Boko Haram** provides a good example of using child soldiers in multiple ways. Abduction is the group's primary means of getting children (United Nations Children's Fund, 2018b). In Aisha's case, she was captured by Boko Haram and forced to marry one of the group's fighters. In Abdul's case, he was forced to act as a spy and participate in combat missions, killing many civilians.

Aisha was at a friend's wedding when she was abducted by Boko Haram, along with her sister, the bride, and the bride's sister. They were taken to a camp, where her friends were forcibly married to Boko Haram fighters. Aisha, at 19 years old, had to learn how to fight; she was trained how to shoot and kill, detonate bombs, and execute attacks on villages. She was forced to participate in armed operations, including against her own village; those who refused were buried in a mass grave. Aisha saw more than 50 people killed, including her sister, before she managed to escape (U.S. Department of State, 2015, p. 39).

Boko Haram attacked Abdul's village and kidnapped him when he was 14 years old. They trained him to handle assault weapons such as machine guns, anti-aircraft guns, and rocket-propelled grenades. The group kept him and forced him to carry out various operations, during which he was forced to kill 18 civilians. They also forced Abdul to gather intelligence on government forces, where he risked being recognized and prosecuted as a Boko Haram member. After being forced to fight for three years, Abdul decided to flee while on a spying mission but was recognized as Boko Haram and arrested when he entered an internally displaced persons camp to look for his parents (U.S. Department of State, 2017c, p. 21).

---

powerful, reasons for staying in their forced-combat lifestyle. A lack of family to go home to, revenge, anger, and fear all play into their commitment to their armed forces or groups (Betancourt et al., 2013). Upon surviving the trafficking situation, reintegration is critical to victims' leading successful lives and not returning to their traffickers.

Because the tactics used to keep victims in their trafficking experience are so powerful, reintegration out of the trafficking experience must be well thought out and include wraparound strategies. The limited research available shows common reintegrative efforts include interim care centers, educational support, job skills training, and employment programs. All of these services are combined with mental health support. Although little is known about how these services are offered and whether or not they are effective, preliminary research and anecdotal evidence are encouraging (Betancourt et al., 2013, Kohrt, Jordans, & Morley, 2010).

Junior Nzita Nsuami, the young man introduced at the beginning of this chapter, personifies the reliance and strength of former child soldiers. He is not alone. Research is starting to challenge the notion that child soldiers are "lost boys" incapable of rehabilitation and reintegration into civilian lives (Bower, 2008). Psychiatrist Jon Shaw converted a Catholic school in Mozambique to rehabilitate young men abducted into the rebel armies in that nation in the 1980s. The center offered sports, art, and music. The boys resided in the center for six months before returning to their villages. The boys had to undergo cleansing rituals to be forgiven and accepted back into their communities. Of the 40 boys who entered the rehabilitation center, most grew up to own their own homes, get married, and have children. Only three of the boys were never able to successfully reintegrate. One died in a police shooting, and another suffered from alcoholism. The third, who had suffered more trauma than Dr. Shaw had ever seen in a patient, struggled throughout his life with emotional challenges and an inability to relate to others. This individual had been abducted at the age of six after watching his parents' murders and his family home burn down (Bower, 2008).

Responses to the Use of Child Soldiers

The experiences of child soldiers resonate well with our understanding of human trafficking. As with other forms of human trafficking, there must be international guidance and pressure for countries to put into place and enforce legislature that prevents the use of child soldiers and protects former child soldiers. This is a basic first step but will not be sufficient in ending the use of child soldiers. Even with the treaties described in this section, child soldiers continue to be routinely used. After a review of the international response to child soldiers, a discussion of the current challenges to implementing these policies is presented.

International Responses

The recruitment of child soldiers is considered one of the UN's "six grave violations" affecting children the most during times of war (Office of the Special Representative of the Secretary-General for Children and Armed Conflict, 2013b). The UN's focus on this crime has driven a global outcry on the issue. Several international treaties tackle the use of child soldiers, as described in Table 11.2 (Druba, 2002). The **Geneva Conventions**, the earliest treaty to focus on child soldiers, provide 17 provisions aimed at children. While the conventions do not specify or define policy relating to the recruitment of children into armed forces and groups, **Additional Protocols to the Geneva Conventions**, enacted in 1977, offer more specific direction in regard to the recruitment of child soldiers (Druba, 2002). Many argue, however, that these Additional Protocols are not stringent enough because they allow the recruitment of children as young as 15 years old into military service. The weak language of Additional Protocol I, which requires "all feasible measures" to be taken to avoid a direct part in hostilities, is also criticized (Druba, 2002). Additional Protocol II is more explicit in its prohibition of direct and indirect participation of children under the age of 15 in conflict and hostilities.

The **Convention on the Rights of the Child**, enacted in 1989, does little to improve on the Additional Protocols to the Geneva Conventions. It retains the age-15 minimum in spite of the UN's defining a child as a person under age 18. It also fails to further clarify "all feasible measures" (J. Becker, 2005; Druba, 2002).

By 1990, the **African Charter on the Rights and Welfare of the Child** was enacted and ratified by 15 African states (Druba, 2002). As noted in Table 11.2, the charter prohibits the recruitment and direct participation in hostilities of children under the age of 18 years old. Of the 54 member states of the African Union, all but eight have become party to the African Charter (Withers, 2012).

The 1999 **Convention Concerning the Prohibition and Immediate Action for the Elimination of the Worst Forms of Child Labour**, adopted by the International Labor Organization (ILO), prohibits recruitment and directed

Table 11.2 International Treaties on Child Soldiers

Treaty	Refers to	Age Limit for Recruitment	Prohibition of Direct Participation	Prohibition of Indirect Participation
Geneva Conventions (1949)	Conflicts of an international nature	No	No	No
Additional Protocol I to the Geneva Conventions of 1949 (1977)	Conflicts of an internal nature, such as fighting against colonial domination or alien occupation	15 years; priority shall be given to those who are the oldest	"All feasible measures" to prevent children from taking a direct part in hostilities	No
Additional Protocol II to the Geneva Conventions of 1949 (1977)	Conflicts of an internal nature, such as conflicts between state armies and organized armed groups	15 years	Yes	Yes
Convention on the Rights of the Child (1989)	State parties, which are to take special care and to provide protection for children	15 years; priority shall be given to those who are the oldest	Yes	No
African Charter on the Rights and Welfare of the Child (1990)	Members of the Organisation for African Unity	18 years	Yes	No
ILO Convention 182 (1999)	Members of the ILO	18 years for forced or compulsory recruitment	Yes	Prohibition of "dangerous work"
Optional Protocol to the Convention on the Rights of the Child on the Involvement of Children in Armed Conflict and on the Sale of Children, Child Prostitution and Child Pornography (2000)	State parties, which are to take special care and provide protection for children	18 years for recruitment into nongovernment entities; at least 16 years for voluntary recruitment into governmental forces	Yes	No

Source: Druba (2002). Reprinted with permission.

participation in hostilities but not voluntary enlistment of children under the age of 18 (Druba, 2002). As of 2012, 175 states had agreed to this convention.

One of the most thorough forms of legislation, and the one still used to measure a country's practices in relation to child soldiers, is the **Optional Protocol to the Convention on the Rights of the Child** on the Involvement of Children in Armed Conflict (the Optional Protocol), enacted in 2000 (Druba, 2002; Withers, 2012). It prohibits the recruitment of youth under the age of 18 for governmental and nongovernmental armed forces or groups. Further, it specifies a minimum age for voluntary enlistment, as noted in Table 11.2. As of 2012, 147 states are party to the Optional Protocol and thus agree to a minimum age of 18 for forced recruitment into state armed forces. More than 100 of these countries have also agreed to a minimum age of 18 for voluntary recruitment (Withers, 2012).

The **Paris Commitments** and the accompanying Principles and Guidelines on Children Associated With Armed Forces or Armed Groups have the endorsement of 100 UN member states as of 2012 (Withers, 2012). The Paris Commitments were first drawn up by UNICEF in 2007, in coordination with other UN agencies and NGOs (UNICEF, 2007a; Withers, 2012). The policy focuses not only on reducing the unlawful recruitment of youth under the age of 18 for combat but also on their safe and successful reintegration into civilian life.

Improvements to Existing Policy

Advocates offer several suggestions for how to improve existing policies relating to the prohibition of the recruitment of child soldiers (Druba, 2002; Withers, 2012). Specifically in regard to the age of forced participation, progress is being made. This is likely related to the specification of age 18 for recruitment purposes in the Optional Protocol. In 2000, Sierra Leone raised the legal age to bear arms from 17 to 18. Colombia, in 1999, raised the legal age permissible to become a soldier to 18 years old. At that time, nearly 800 children were released from the Colombian army and other military forces (J. Becker, 2005). In 2003, the legal age for recruitment in Afghanistan was changed to 22 years old.

More attention must now be given to the age of voluntary recruitment. The minimum age for voluntary recruitment should be raised to age 18. This is the age of adulthood, as defined by the UN (J. Becker, 2005). As noted above, even voluntary participation in armed forces is associated with some form of coercion and deception. Advocates argue that the surest way to protect children is to raise the minimum age for voluntary participation to 18 years old.

In addition to age minimums, more can be done to ensure the protection of children. Ten years after the Optional Protocol was enacted, Child Soldiers International (a UK nonprofit) assessed the status of the law and its effectiveness in preventing the use of child soldiers (Withers, 2012). The law provides the most comprehensive expectations of states to end the use of child soldiers in state armed forces and nongovernmental armed groups. The results of this research indicate that while over 75% of states are party to the treaty and have laws in place to protect youth under the age of 18 from being forced into armed forces and groups, many states struggle in implementing these laws and effectively protecting children. Child Soldiers International suggests the following strategies must be in place to properly enforce existing laws relating to child soldiers:

- Independent verifiable proof of age for every child;
- Effective processes to verify the age of new recruits;
- Independent monitoring and oversight of military recruitment processes;

The following 10 questions can be asked of countries to assess whether children are at risk of being used by armed forces or groups as child soldiers (Withers, 2012).

Child Soldier Use by State Armed Forces

1. Are children prohibited in law from participating in hostilities?

2. Has 18 years been established in law as the minimum age for compulsory and voluntary recruitment?

3. Does every child have independently verifiable proof of age?

4. Are there effective processes to verify the age of new recruits?

5. Are military recruitment processes subject to independent monitoring and oversight?

6. Are unlawful child recruitment and use criminalized in national law?

7. Does the criminal justice system have the capacity to effectively investigate and prosecute allegations of unlawful recruitment and use?

Child Soldier Use by State-Allied Armed Groups

8. Are legal and practical safeguards in place to prevent recruitment and use of children by any armed groups allied to the state?

Arms Transfers and Security Sector Reform Assistance

9. Are measures in place to ensure that international arms transfers and other forms of military assistance do not contribute to or facilitate the unlawful recruitment and use of children as soldiers in recipient states?

10. Are safeguards set out in this checklist reflected in national security sector reform (SSR) programs and in SSR assistance programs?

Source: Questions and their headings from Withers, 2012.

- Criminalisation of child recruitment and use in law;

- Capacity within the criminal justice system to effectively investigate and prosecute allegations of unlawful recruitment and use. (Withers, 2012, p. 12)

The report is especially explicit in making states responsible for the use of child soldiers by nongovernmental armed groups. The state must protect children from all groups motivated to arm children and place them in hostile environments.

The U.S. Child Soldiers Prevention Act

The **United States Child Soldier Prevention Act (CSPA)** not only defines and prohibits the use of child soldiers in the United States but also permits the Department of State to police countries around the world on their use of child soldiers. As a result, this law holds international significance. Annually, in the Department of State's Trafficking in Persons (TIP) Report, the U.S. government lists countries they believe to be using child soldiers. The basis for placement on this list includes several forms of evidence. Should U.S. government personnel observe the use of child soldiers, that would justify including a country on the CSPA list. Additional sources of evidence could include United Nations agencies, international organizations, NGOs, and international media outlets (U.S. Department of State, 2011).

Those countries on the list run the risk of losing certain forms of U.S. military assistance, including international military education and training, foreign military financing, excess defense articles, section 1206 assistance, and the issue of licenses for direct commercial sales of military equipment (U.S. Department of State, 2011). Human Rights Watch believes that the CSPA has influenced governments such as Chad, the DRC, and Rwanda to curb child recruitment (J. Becker, 2018).

The United States' Failed Opportunity

While the CSPA has the potential to reduce the use of child soldiers around the world, it is not without controversy. To advocates, the implementation of the law is frustrating. As with the TIP Report, advocates question the role of politics in the creation and enforcement of the CSPA's annual list. As mentioned above, the CSPA mandates that all listed countries lose forms of military assistance. However, presidential waivers routinely exempt countries from these consequences.

In 2016, President Obama provided full or partial waivers to every country on the CSPA list in the name of U.S. national security (Chadwick, 2016; Ravinsky & Lumpe, 2016; Rogin, 2016). In 2016, $14 million was transferred from the U.S. to the Congo for peacekeeping initiatives. One hundred million dollars went to Somalia and approximately $30 million went to South Sudan in 2016. All of these countries were listed on the 2016 CSPA list.

Another controversy stems from which countries make it onto the list. The U.S. has a major loophole in the CSPA relating to its limited acknowledgment of what is considered government-supported armed groups. Take, for example, a controversial issue, well described by media outlets in 2016 (e.g., Chadwick, 2016; Ravinsky & Lumpe, 2016; Rogin, 2016). In 2015, the UN identified 48 soldiers in Afghanistan. More than a quarter of them were working for state-run military groups, including the Afghan National Army, the Afghan Local Police (ALP), and the Afghan National Police (Chadwick, 2016; General Assembly Security Council, 2016). In spite of this finding, the U.S. did not list Afghanistan in its mandated reporting of foreign governments identified as having governmental armed forces or government-supported armed groups that recruit and use child soldiers. The Department of State did acknowledge some disturbing practices in Afghanistan, stating in the 2016 TIP Report the following:

> In 2015 and 2016, the UN, *The New York Times* and other media outlets, and credible NGOs reported on the recruitment and sexual abuse of children under the age of 18 by the Afghanistan Local Police (ALP). Although the ALP is a government security force in Afghanistan, it falls outside of the armed forces of the country as defined by the CSPA. Though Afghanistan has not been listed under the CSPA, these incidents raise concerns regarding the protection of children and warrant further remedial action by the Government of Afghanistan. (U.S. Department of State, 2016, p. 25)

Using this loophole in the CSPA, the U.S. gave $470 million to the ALP in 2016, while still acknowledging their use of child soldiers (Chadwick, 2016). This occurred even as the Afghani government publicly criminalized the recruitment of child soldiers. In spite of this law, evidence has shown that children were being recruited and inserted into defense forces at all levels, from the Taliban to the local police, as recently as 2017 (J. Becker, 2018). Further, the Afghan Ministry of Interior Affairs reports that it does consider the local police and armed defense force as part of the national government (Chadwick, 2016). The purpose of the police is to fight insurgencies. If this is the case, it seems reasonable to group the Afghan Local Police with other categories of "government-supported armed groups" that are prohibited from receiving military assistance and aid when identified as using child soldiers. By continuing to support the Afghan Local Police, the United States is funding an organization that traffics children. Certainly, this is not consistent with the U.S.'s general policies and beliefs about the prevention of human trafficking, especially as it involves children.

Photo 11.2 Another picture published in the 2009 Trafficking in Persons Report. Also in the report, a former child soldier from Chad is quoted as saying, "If you see a young person wearing military clothes, carrying a gun, these are children who have lost their lives. Fighting is the last thing that a child should be doing" (p. 20).

Human rights advocates vocally argue for revisions and amendments to the CSPA. Clearer language needs to be in place to ensure that simply changing the name of a militia does not take the country off the list of countries using child soldiers. These loopholes have resulted in the United States' list of countries using child soldiers to be inconsistent with the UN's lists. The UN's more comprehensive definition of what can land a country on this list includes all governmental and nongovernmental armed forces, including the police. According to Chadwick (2016), the UN has published a consistent list of 14 countries using child soldiers since 2010. On the contrary, the U.S. listed only six countries in 2010. That number rose to 11 countries by 2018.

In addition to tightening up a relatively loose law—the CSPA—the U.S. can do more to treat child soldiers like other victims of human trafficking. Since 2000, the U.S. has created 11 laws to better define and strengthen reactions to human trafficking. During that same time, the CSPA has weakly communicated the U.S.'s condemnation of the use of child soldiers. Perhaps even worse than its weak wording, it gives executive privilege to the president to either partly or fully waive the prohibition against military assistance (Ravinsky & Lumpe, 2016).

Child soldiers are not eligible for the same special U.S. visas that are available to sex and labor trafficking victims, nor are victim services available to them as they are to other victims of human trafficking. Further, there seems to be little relationship between the Department of State's ranking system and the CSPA list. For example, in 2016, Congo, Iraq, Nigeria, and Rwanda were all on the CSPA list but were not ranked as Tier 3 countries in the TIP Report (Ravinsky & Lumpe, 2016). All were ranked as Tier 2 or Tier 2 Watch List (U.S. Department of State, 2016). There seemed to be more correlation between the TIP Report rankings and the CSPA list in 2018. Of the 11 CSPA countries, all but four were ranked as Tier 3 or Special Cases (U.S. Department of State, 2018b). The remaining four (Iraq, Mali, Niger, and Nigeria) were ranked as Tier 2 Watch List.

Consequences

"I was forced literally to kill my best friend as an initiation process into the army. That's something I will never forget and I still fight with every single day" (U.S. Department of State, 2017c, p. 21). This quote, from a former child solider in the DRC, is quintessential in understanding the trauma child soldiers experience.

Psychological Consequences

Research consistently shows the horrific psychological damage caused by child soldiering as well as encouraging information about the resilience of many of those who experienced such trauma (Betancourt et al., 2013; Kizilhan & Noll-Hussong, 2018; Klasen et al., 2010; Somasundaram, 2002). A systematic review of existing literature focuses on the mental health outcomes of former child soldiers. The review includes 14 observational studies, 5 intervention studies, and 2 prospective studies (Betancourt et al., 2013). Nearly 4,000 children were analyzed across the 20 studies, of whom 30% were girls. Findings of mental health problems were inconsistent; however, this could have been due to weak methodologies and unvalidated measures and assessments. That being said, in the three studies using comparison groups, former child soldiers had higher rates of post-traumatic stress disorder (PTSD) than civilian children. More recent research examining former child soldiers for the Islamic State in northern Iraq also showed higher rates of PTSD and other negative mental health outcomes among former child soldiers as compared to a control group (Kizilhan & Noll-Hussong, 2018). Other studies using comparison groups have found exposure to violence to be more predictive of PTSD than child soldier status (Betancourt et al., 2013).

Betancourt and colleagues (2013) generally found, through their systematic review, that length of time in combat does not predict PTSD or other forms of maladjustment. However, exposure to violence, specifically torture, witnessing the death of a family member, participating in the killing of others, and sexual violence were predictive of negative mental health outcomes.

Gender differences in negative outcomes were also found in samples of child soldiers, albeit not consistently (Betancourt et al., 2013; Klasen et al., 2010). Studies using comparison groups found former female child soldiers to be at a greater risk of experiencing PTSD than former male child soldiers, when compared to civilian girls and boys, respectively (Betancourt et al., 2013). Klasen and colleagues (2010) found no gender differences in mental health outcomes among a sample of Ugandan former child soldiers.

Fortunately, research indicates that some protective factors mediate the consequences of being a child soldier and exposure to violence, including family support and acceptance upon leaving combat (Betancourt et al., 2013). Returning or beginning an education program as well as entering the labor force also reduce depression and improve confidence and empowerment.

Community Acceptance

Former child soldiers, particularly females, experience rejection from their former communities when they return home. This can be particularly traumatic after exiting lives as soldiers. Stigma, often related to assumptions that girls lost their virginity, result in rejection from their families and communities (Betancourt et al., 2013; Child Soldiers International, n.d.b; Robinson, 2018;

Withers, 2012). Another cause for rejection is the misperceived notion that child soldiers are adults and treatment of them as such. Rather than receiving treatment and rehabilitation, some child soldiers have been known to be punished for war crimes in the same manner as adult soldiers (General Assembly Security Council, 2018; Tiefenbrun, 2007). In countries such as Uganda and Rwanda, child soldiers have been punished for genocide and rebel causes and incarcerated (Tiefenbrun, 2007).

Other Forms of Human Trafficking

A particularly disturbing consequence of child soldiering is the retrafficking of children. Child who are at grave risk for becoming child soldiers, such as those in Somalia in 2012, often migrate to neighboring countries to avoid becoming a child soldier. However, age and migrant status leave these youth especially vulnerable to other forms of human trafficking, specifically sex and labor trafficking (U.S. Department of State, 2013). In 2012, children were desperate to protect themselves from the militant group al-Shabaab. This group was well known for forcing children into combat and/or prostitution. Unfortunately, after escaping to Kenya, these youth were often placed into forced prostitution and forced labor as herders (U.S. Department of State, 2013).

Moving Forward

There is ample agreement in the global community that the use of child soldiers is immoral and against international law. Nevertheless, the demands of war will continue to drive the use of child soldiers (J. Becker, 2005; Somasundaram, 2002; Tiefenbrun, 2007). Even those countries that implement laws prohibiting the recruitment of children into armed forces continue to violate their own laws. Similarly, opposition groups that publicly pledge to no longer recruit children appear to do so for the sake of public relations. In practice, children continue to be recruited and used in times of war (J. Becker, 2005). Several responses must be put into place, beyond laws and treaties, to truly reduce the use of children in war. Even in the United States, a country that ratified the Optional Protocol in 2002 failed to meet its obligations to this treaty. Evidence indicates that 50 U.S. soldiers under the age of 18 were inadvertently sent to Iraq in 2003 and 2004 (J. Becker, 2005). Every country on every continent can do better.

Raising global awareness about the experiences of child soldiers could be a powerful means of change. As with other forms of human trafficking, there is a misunderstanding about the brutality and trauma victims face. With more awareness, embarrassment and shame will be felt by countries that condone, or don't condemn, the use of child soldiers. Further, support of NGOs on the ground in countries with child soldiers will help to change the culture from within.

Challenge Yourself 11.2

There is general agreement that the use of child soldiers is bad. What actions can an individual in the developed world take to make an impact on this crime?

Sierra Leone offered many firsts for the international community's response to child soldiers. The peace accord ending its civil war was the first to mention the reintegration of child soldiers. It was the first time the UN included a child protection officer in a peacekeeping mission. The Special Court, discussed in this box, was the first international tribunal to convict individuals of war crimes including the use of child soldiers (Shepler, 2016).

The following excerpt comes from the 2015 TIP Report (U.S. Department of State, 2015, p. 39).

Special Court of Sierra Leone: Accountability at the Highest Level for Child Soldiering Offenses

The Special Court for Sierra Leone (SCSL) was established in 2002 by agreement between the Government of the Republic of Sierra Leone and the United Nations to try those most responsible for crimes against humanity, war crimes, and other serious violations of international humanitarian law, including conscripting or recruiting children under the age of 15 years, committed in the civil war. Since its inception, the Special Court has handed down several important decisions in cases involving allegations related to the conscripting or enlisting of children under the age of 15 years into armed forces or armed groups. During Sierra Leone's civil war, all parties to the conflict recruited and used child soldiers. Children were forced to fight, commit atrocities, and were often sexually abused. Former Liberian President Charles Taylor was convicted by the SCSL on 11 counts of crimes against humanity and war crimes for his role in supporting armed groups, including the Revolutionary United Front, in the planning and commission of crimes committed during the conflict. In a landmark 2004 decision, the Court held that individual criminal responsibility for the crime of recruiting children under the age of 15 years had crystallized as customary international law prior to November 1996. In June 2007, the Court delivered the first judgment of an international or mixed tribunal convicting persons of conscripting or enlisting children under the age of 15 years into armed forces or using them to participate actively in hostilities.

In 2013, the Special Court reached another milestone by upholding the conviction of former Liberian President Charles Taylor. The judgment marked the first time a former head of state had been convicted in an international or hybrid court of violations of international law. Taylor was convicted, among other charges, of aiding and abetting sexual slavery and conscription of child soldiers. After more than a decade of working toward accountability for crimes against humanity and war crimes committed in Sierra Leone, the SCSL transitioned on December 31, 2013, to a successor mechanism, the Residual Special Court for Sierra Leone, which will continue to provide a variety of ongoing functions, including witness protection services and management of convicted detainees. Its work stands for the proposition that the international community can achieve justice and accountability for crimes committed, even by proxy, against the most vulnerable—children in armed conflict.

Enforcement of laws and prosecutions will also be an effective way to reduce the use of child soldiers. Those who abduct and indoctrinate children to become child soldiers require severe and certain sentencing, thereby increasing the risks associated with their actions (Tiefenbrun, 2007). With the enforcement of laws, however, needs to come acknowledgment of the role child soldiers play. Child soldiers are victims of war, not perpetrators. They must be exempt from prosecutions and punishment. Rather, laws must be put into place and enforced that protect child soldiers from prosecution and provide them with rehabilitative services and opportunities for reintegration. Sierra Leone, as highlighted in the Focus on Sierra Leone box (see page 286), has found a solution to prosecuting war criminals but not children (Tiefenbrun, 2007).

Research

In addition to advocacy and law enforcement, improved research can go a long way in improving the world's reaction to child soldiers. Academically speaking, little is known about child soldiers (Alfredson, 2001; Betancourt et al., 2013; Druba, 2002). Case studies are plentiful. But high-quality quantitative research is lacking. Take, for example, a meta-analysis of mental health outcomes for former child soldiers (Betancourt et al., 2013). Using a systematic review approach, the authors searched for quantitative studies focused on the mental health outcomes of former child soldiers. Opinion pieces, editorials, and qualitative publications were excluded. Their findings identified only 20 studies that fit their specifications, of which only eight were high quality. Most studies suffered from cross-sectional designs and lacked comparison groups. Without improved data on who is most at risk to become child soldiers as well as the most effective ways to reintegrate these kids back into civilian life, we stand little chance at being effective in eliminating this human rights violation. While qualitative data and methodologies should not be underestimated—they are most certainly important for improving our understanding of child soldiers—high-quality quantitative data is of equal importance and currently lacking.

Several factors can explain why research is limited. One particularly challenging aspect of conducting research on this population is sampling. Child soldiers are not an easily identifiable population (Betancourt et al., 2013). This, combined with ethical and human subject concerns, may dissuade researchers from collecting data on this population. Proper assessments tools are also critical for understanding the effects of being a child soldier and are underdeveloped. In their systematic review, Betancourt and colleagues (2013) found publications using assessments and screening tools not validated for the population. As discussed in regard to male sex trafficking victims (see Chapter 7), improper screening tools and assessments limit the accuracy of the information gathered. If questions are not asked properly for the population, the subjects may not give accurate responses.

Conclusion

In the developed world, individuals are incensed by gun and gang violence, and rightfully so. They mourn the loss of innocence that comes with each mass shooting or truck carelessly trampling people as if they were pebbles on a road. While citizens of the developed world adjust to the inundation of images of pain and anger in their communities while still convincing themselves that violence won't touch them, families and children in the Middle East, Africa, and Asia take in these images as normal and unavoidable. Violence, instability, and terrorism are defining features of daily living in many parts of the world. This chapter reviews an atrocious consequence of constant war and conflict—child soldiers. While (inexcusable) oversights result in American and British children getting sent to war on occasion, children are routinely put on the battlefields in many poor, underdeveloped countries. The global community must respond to a call to action. They must put pressure on those countries that don't condemn the use of child soldiers and focus on protecting and reintegrating former child soldiers. As actor Forest Whitaker (2017) said in a blog post:

> We may take a child out of an army, but unless we do more for him— help him re-enter society, enroll him in a good school, teach him a useful trade—we have not set him free. For so many of these children, war and violence are all they have ever known, and if we do not take it upon ourselves to teach them something new, then they are just soldiers-in-waiting. And when another war breaks out five or ten years in the future, they will be the first ones recruited to go back to the battlefield.

> We must act to prevent this. Not only because these children deserve the chance to live normal, healthy lives, but also because we have an opportunity to avert future violence. If we can make these children emotionally whole again and restore a sense of normalcy to their lives, then they will be able to put down their arms for good, and, instead of perpetuating vicious cycles of violence, they will help build a peaceful future for their country. (paras. 6–7)

KEY WORDS

Additional Protocols to the Geneva Conventions 278
African Charter on the Rights and Welfare of the Child 278
age blindness 273
armed forces 268
armed groups 268
Boko Haram 277
Convention Concerning the Prohibition and Immediate Action for the Elimination

of the Worst Forms of Child Labour 278
Convention on the Rights of the Child 278
exposure to violence 276
Geneva Conventions 278
Hitler Youth movement 267
Optional Protocol to the Convention on the Rights of the Child 280
Paris Commitments 280

child reintegration 269
release 269
sexual exploitation 276
United States Child Soldier Prevention Act (CSPA) 281

DISCUSSION QUESTIONS

1. History sets the foundation for the current use of child soldiers. How are the current recruitment practices and use of children similar and different from those employed during historical wars?

2. Visit the Child Soldiers World Index (https://childsoldiersworldindex.org/). Identify patterns in the use of child soldiers that you find most interesting or surprising. What did you learn about those regions after conducting

a brief web search of the region's use of child soldiers?

3. Ample legislation exists protecting youth from being forced into combat. And yet children continue to be used as child soldiers. What have you learned about other forms of human trafficking that help to explain the continued use of child soldiers? Do you see any differences between child soldiers and victims of other forms of human trafficking?

RESOURCES

- Child Soldiers World Index: https://childsoldiersworldindex.org/

- "The Making, and Unmaking, of a Child Soldier": https://www.nytimes.com/2007/01/14/magazine/14soldier.t.html

Organ Trafficking

A black market in human organs is not only a grave threat to public health, it reserves lifesaving treatment for those who can best afford it at the expense of those who cannot. We will not tolerate such an affront to human dignity.

—**U.S. Attorney Paul J. Fishman (United Nations Office on Drugs and Crime, 2018b)**

Organ trafficking is often distinguished as one of the most invisible forms of human trafficking (Office of the Special Representative and Co-ordinator for Combating Trafficking in Human Beings, 2013). While it used to be a phenomenon discussed only in rumors and hyperbolic cautionary tales, our understanding of organ trafficking has vastly improved in recent years. This chapter will review the history of organ transplantation, definitions of distinct types of organ trafficking, legal frameworks and considerations related to organ trafficking, and the prevalence of trafficking globally and in the U.S. We will also discuss factors that facilitate vulnerability to trafficking, characteristics of traffickers, and responses to organ trafficking.

Brief History of Organ Transplantation

Organ transplantation revolutionized medical care for patients with chronic organ failure. This procedure has the potential to improve patients' quality of life and extend life expectancy (United Nations Office on Drugs and Crime [UNODC], 2015a). The first successful organ transplant in 1954 took place in the United States, where a man received a kidney from his twin brother. Following this transplant, doctors could transplant organs only between genetically close relatives. Advances in the medical field in the 1980s, particularly the use of immunosuppressant drugs, allowed genetically unrelated adults to donate and receive organs without an elevated risk of the recipient rejecting the donated organ. Following these advances, there are now three categories of eligible living donors: genetically related, emotionally related, and unrelated/anonymous (Office of the Special Representative and Co-ordinator for Combating Trafficking in Human Beings, 2013; UNODC, 2015a). Since 2012, about half of live donors have been genetically unrelated to recipients. Living donors can transplant one kidney, half of a liver, or a lobe of the lung (United Network for Organ Sharing [UNOS], 2016).

Organs can also be transplanted from deceased donors after brain or circulatory death. Depending on a country's policies, donors either opt in to or opt out of consent to organ donation after they die. As the name suggests, in the opt-in system, donors must provide explicit consent, whereas with an opt-out system, consent is assumed unless the individual requests otherwise (UNODC, 2015a).

In 2015, 31,812 donors, or about one-quarter of donors, were deceased. A deceased donor can provide lungs, a liver, a pancreas, bowels, a heart, and kidneys (UNOS, 2016). Despite advances in transplant procedures, the need for organ donors greatly surpasses the availability of deceased donors, making live donors crucial to filling this gap (Shimazono, 2007; UNODC, 2015a).

According to UNOS, transplants have increased by 20% in the past five years. International reports based on information from roughly 90% of the global population indicate that there were 126,670 organ transplants performed in 2015; about 67% were kidney transplants, 22% were liver transplants, 6% were heart transplants, 4% were lung transplants, and 2% were pancreas transplants (Global Observatory on Donation and Transplantation [GODT], n.d.). These global patterns parallel U.S. trends; in 2015, 30,974 transplants were performed in the United States, of which about 60% were kidney transplants, just over 20% were liver transplants, and less than 10% were another organ (UNOS, 2016).

Despite these impressive numbers, less than 10% of the global need for organ transplants is being met today. The need for kidney transplants is most urgent; in 2015, 11,000 people on a waiting list for a kidney died (Shimazono, 2007). Globally, over 180,000 patients are estimated to be waiting for a kidney transplant each year (GODT, n.d.).

Brief History of Trafficking in Organs

The earliest reports of **organ commercialization** are from the 1980s, when Indian citizens in extreme poverty sold their kidneys to foreign patients, primarily from Persian Gulf coast countries (UNODC, 2015a). One journal article reported that over 100 patients traveled with their doctors to Bombay to pay for kidneys and undergo transplantation. Selling organs was not yet outlawed in India, so the primary concern was that many donors experienced significant complications after the procedure (Bos, 2015). Selling organs was outlawed in the 1994 Indian Transplantation of Human Organs Act, but records indicate that at least 300 Indian citizens sold kidneys between 1994 and 2000 (Goyal, Mehta, Schneiderman, & Sehgal, 2002). Western countries, which claim that they do not allow payment for organs, also have a history of trafficking in organs. In the U.S. and the European Union (EU), there is documentation of surgeons inviting foreign patients to their facilities to receive priority organ transplants as early as 1984 (Bos, 2015). A high-profile case of trafficking in organs in 1988, when a Turkish citizen died during a transplant in a private London clinic, was a contributing factor leading to the establishment of the UK Human Organ Transplant Act in 1989, which outlawed trafficking in organs in Britain (Bos, 2015; UNODC, 2015a).

The World Health Organization's official guidance is that to prevent exploitation of economically vulnerable individuals, donors should not be paid for organs. Despite this, there exists a black market for organs, though we do not know the full scope of this market. Given that organ transplantation is a complex activity requiring a donor, patient, medical professional, and medical facilities, experts believe that these black-market networks are highly organized criminal enterprises (Office of the Special Representative and Co-ordinator for Combating Trafficking in Human Beings, 2013; UNODC, 2015a).

Forms of Trafficking in Organs

Despite increases in donors and advancements in the transplant process, there is still a huge gap between demand for organs and donor supply. Estimates suggest that donor transplants meet just 10% of the global demand (Shimazono, 2007). Accordingly, desperate patients turn to the black market when they are unable to obtain a legitimate, altruistic donation. Trafficking in organs encompasses a range of illicit activities that aim to profit from human organs and tissues, including trafficking of persons with the intent to remove their organs; trafficking in organs, tissues, and cells; and transplant tourism.

Trafficking in human beings with the intent to remove their organs includes exploitation of human beings for the purpose of organ removal. Victims of trafficking whose organs are removed may be exploited for other forms of trafficking as well. Trafficking in humans is a crime where exploitation of the human is the central issue, and three elements must be present: action, means, and purpose. Consequently, trafficking in humans for the purpose of organ removal can be committed only if the organ donor is living. Living organ trafficking victims are typically referred to as "victim donors." Trafficking in human beings for organ removal is described in the trafficking in persons protocol supplementing the UN Convention Against Transnational Organized Crime:

> Trafficking in persons shall mean the recruitment, transportation, transfer, harbouring or receipt of persons, by means of the threat or use of force or other forms of coercion, of abduction, of fraud, of deception, of the abuse of power or of a position of vulnerability or of the giving or receiving of payments or benefits to achieve the consent of a person having control over another person, for the purpose of exploitation. Exploitation shall include, at a minimum, the exploitation of the prostitution of others or other forms of sexual exploitation, forced labour or services, slavery or practices similar to slavery, servitude or the removal of organs. (United Nations General Assembly, 2000b)

This definition is used by all major anti-trafficking organizations, including the United Nations (United Nations General Assembly, 2001) and the Organization for Security and Co-operation in Europe (2003), and was included in the European Convention on Action Against Trafficking in Human Beings in 2005 (Council of Europe, 2005).

Trafficking in organs, tissues, and cells involves commercial transactions including organs, tissues, or cells that have already been removed from a living or deceased donor (Bos, 2015). Trafficking in organs, tissues, and cells is a crime where organs or tissues and their use are the key elements. It doesn't matter whether the organ was taken from a living or deceased donor, because there is no human element to this crime. Trafficking in organs, tissues, and cells can occur if the donor is deceased or if no illegal means were used to procure the organ from a living donor but sale of the organ violates the law. Because trafficking in organs, tissues, and cells does not include a living victim, it is not punishable as a crime of trafficking in human beings. It is punishable as a crime of profiting from the human body or its parts, which is prohibited in most countries and in international regulations (Council of Europe, 1997).

Transplant tourism includes patients traveling across jurisdictional borders to obtain an illegal transplant from a paid donor. Transplant tourism is often considered a subtype of trafficking in persons that includes the intent to remove their organs, because paying a donor for their organs is considered a form of exploitation. The crime associated with transplant tourism is typically related to the recipient who paid for the organ. **Transplant tourism** is distinguished and defined as a subtype of organ trafficking in the 2008 Declaration of Istanbul on Organ Trafficking and Transplant Tourism:

> Travel for transplantation is the movement of organs, donors, recipients, or transplant professionals across jurisdictional borders for transplantation purposes. Travel for transplantation becomes transplant tourism if it involves organ trafficking and/or transplant commercialism or if the resources devoted to providing transplants to patients from outside a country undermine the country's ability to provide transplant services for its own population. (Steering Committee of the Istanbul Summit, 2008)

In transplant tourism, the recipient pays a willing donor, who is typically extremely poor, for his or her organ. Paying individuals living in extreme poverty for their organs is considered exploitation of an economic vulnerability, in which case consent is no longer based on an autonomous or voluntary decision. Further, in many cases, victim donors are defrauded or misled about the payment and also do not receive adequate care after the procedure.

The Declaration of Istanbul further states that transplant tourism is distinct from *traveling for transplantation*, in which a patient, donor, or medical professional travels across jurisdictional borders for an organ transplant. When traveling for transplantation, the organ comes from an altruistic, consenting donor. Many patients travel for transplantation to areas with better medical facilities.

This brief overview of the types of trafficking in organs shows how blurry the lines can be between not only the different types of trafficking in organs but also between a legitimate organ transplant from a consenting donor and organ trafficking. One of the easiest ways to distinguish legitimate organ donation from organ trafficking is to assess whether anyone financially profited from the transaction. If any middleman, broker, or donor is paid for the procedure, this constitutes trafficking. Similarly, if medical personnel or facilities are paid above and beyond the required payment for the transplant itself, this likely includes trafficking (UNODC, 2015a). The "Guiding Principles on Human Cell, Tissue and Organ Transplantation" of the World Health Assembly, the decision-making body of the World Health Organization (WHO), emphasize that patients must be able to provide consent for a medical procedure without coercion or abuse of a vulnerability (WHO, 2010). A vulnerability exists when the person has no practical alternative but to consent; such vulnerabilities include economic circumstances. It is generally assumed that, given other options to generate money, no adult would voluntarily sell his or her organs (Office of the Special Representative and Co-ordinator for Combating Trafficking in Human Beings, 2013; UNODC, 2015a).

Figure 12.1   Types of Organ Trafficking and Travel for Transplantation

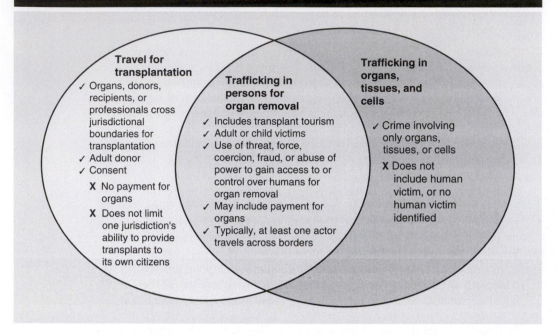

The run-through of different types of trafficking may also raise another question: Is it necessary to distinguish between trafficking in persons for the purpose of organ removal; trafficking in organs, tissues, and cells; and transplant tourism? These acts are defined separately because the legal response to trafficking in organs varies depending on whether a living human is involved or not.

Legal and Ethical Frameworks Pertaining to Trafficking in Organs

Guiding Instruments

A variety of international documents provide guidance and requirements pertaining to organ transplantation. Guiding documents include the previously mentioned "Guiding Principles on Human Cell, Tissue, and Organ Transplantation" (WHO, 2010) and Declaration of Istanbul on Organ Trafficking and Transplant Tourism (see Steering Committee of the Istanbul Summit, 2008).

The World Health Assembly (WHA) first identified a need for standards on organ transplantation in 1987 via "Resolution WHA40.13" and in 1989 "Resolution WHA42.5 on Preventing the Purchase and Sale of Human Organs." In response to these, the WHA endorsed its original "Guiding Principles on Human Cell, Tissue, and Organ Transplantation" in 1991. These guiding principles help to conceptualize the differences between organ trafficking and organ donation (UNODC, 2015a). Table 12.1 summarizes these principles as they relate to deceased and living donor donations.

Table 12.1 Summary of WHO Guiding Principles

	Deceased Donor	Living Donor
Consent	• Need consent or lack of objection	• Need informed, voluntary consent • Minors and legally incompetent adults may not consent
Conflict of Interest	• Medical personnel who determine the death of a potential donor cannot be involved in removing the organ of the donor • Medical personnel who determine the death of a potential donor cannot be involved in the care of the recipient	• Medical personnel should not participate in organ transplants if the organs are obtained through exploitation or coercion, including monetary payment to the donor • Health insurers should not cover such procedures • All health care facilities and medical personnel should be prohibited from receiving payment that exceeds the cost for services rendered
Coercion	• Harvesting organs from deceased donors without their consent should not be permitted	• Buying, attempting to buy, or selling human organs should be banned • Donors should not receive any monetary payment aside from reimbursement for expenses incurred • It should be illegal to advertise the need for or availability of organs or broker payment for organs (excludes advertising legal, altruistic donation)

Source: UNODC, 2015.

The Declaration of Istanbul on Organ Trafficking and Transplant Tourism was adopted at the International Summit on Transplant Tourism and Organ Trafficking in 2008 (UNODC, 2015a). The Istanbul Declaration states that each country should establish legal and professional guidelines to govern transplantation. To help achieve this goal, the Istanbul Declaration further states, countries should establish regulatory organizations to monitor and ensure safe and ethical transplant processes. Further, each country should take measures to meet the transplant needs of its citizens.

The key takeaway from these guidelines is that donors should freely consent to organ donation. When individuals are paid for their organs, or coerced or exploited in other ways, then the donation moves from being altruistic and legitimate to organ trafficking. Thus, if a living donor agrees to sell an organ, this constitutes trafficking, because the monetary payment is coercive. If the individual did not need the money, he or she would not be selling his or her organ.

Legally Binding Instruments

The WHO guiding principles and the Istanbul Declaration are examples of guiding instruments, or suggestions to countries for reducing the burden of organ trafficking and working toward ethical and safe legal transplants. Legally binding international agreements include the United Nations trafficking in persons protocol; the United Nations Optional Protocol to the Convention on the Rights of the Child on the Sale of Children, Child Prostitution and Child Pornography; and the Council of Europe Convention on Action Against Trafficking in Human Beings (Council of Europe, 2005; Office of the Special Representative and Co-ordinator for Combating Trafficking in Human Beings, 2013; United Nations General Assembly, 2000b, 2000c; UNODC, 2015a). The trafficking in persons protocol identifies the removal of organs as a form of trafficking in persons:

> "Trafficking in persons" shall mean the recruitment, transportation, transfer, harbouring or receipt of persons, by means of the threat or use of force or other forms of coercion, of abduction, of fraud, of deception, of the abuse of power or of a position of vulnerability or of the giving or receiving of payments or benefits to achieve the consent of a person having control over another person, for the purpose of exploitation. Exploitation shall include, at a minimum, the exploitation of the prostitution of others or other forms of sexual exploitation, forced labour or services, slavery or practices similar to slavery, servitude or the *removal of organs*. (United Nations General Assembly, 2000c, emphasis added)

The Council of Europe's 2005 Convention on Action Against Trafficking in Human Beings adopted the trafficking in persons protocol definition, which includes the removal of organs as a form of trafficking in persons and has an additional amendment that prohibits profiting from the sale of human body parts as well as organs and tissue trafficking (Sembacher, 2005).

In the United States, the Trafficking Victims Protection Act of 2000 (TVPA) also adopts the same definition of trafficking in persons as the United Nations trafficking in persons protocol, including organ removal as a form of exploitation. The U.S. has additional legislation pertaining to organ trafficking as well. The 1984 National Organ Transplant Act prohibits the sale of organs, establishes a task force on organ transplantation, and provides grant funding for organ procurement organizations. As part of this legislation, the U.S. had to create a regulatory framework to inform local, regional, and national policy decisions related to allocating organs, including the formulas used in allocations for the U.S. Organ Procurement and Transplantation Network. The core principles of this framework are similar to those found in the Istanbul Declaration: (1) utility, (2) justice, and (3) respect for persons (Organ Procurement and Transplantation Network, Final Rule, 2003).

In 2015, the U.S. passed an amendment to the TVPA, the Strategy to Oppose Predatory Organ Trafficking Act (L. W. Rosen, 2016). This act states that the U.S. will prioritize combating organ trafficking and promote a voluntary organ donation system with "effective enforcement mechanisms." It also required that the state department report on organ trafficking and updated the definition of trafficking in persons to include living or deceased victims. This is distinct from international legislation for which trafficking in persons must include a living victim (L. W. Rosen, 2016).

Case Study

Harvesting Organs From Prisoners in China

Below is congressional testimony in support of HR 3694, the Strategy to Oppose Predatory Organ Trafficking Act, a bill that amended the U.S. Trafficking Victims Protection Action of 2000. The bill requires more action to stop organ trafficking and requires the State Department to report on the issue.

The fact that the evidence we have now examined shows much larger volumes of transplants than the Government of China has asserted points to a larger discrepancy between transplant volumes and Government of China–identified sources than we had previously thought existed. . . . That increased discrepancy leads us to conclude that there has been a far larger slaughter of practitioners of Falun Gong for their organs than we had originally estimated.

—David Matas, senior legal counsel for B'nai B'rith Canada

In a visit to Riyadh, Saudi Arabia, the physician sitting next to me at dinner told me of this incident: a 14-year-old girl underwent a kidney transplant in Tianjin, China, and returned home to Saudi Arabia ill. This patient underwent a biopsy of a kidney transplant to discover the kidney was obsolescent, scarred, certainly not suitable for transplantation . . . it had been obtained from an executed prisoner. This patient subsequently developed a viral infection that should've been prophylactically treated at the time of the transplant in China. This 14-year-old girl died within weeks of her transplant because of that derelict care.

—Dr. Francis L. Delmonico, professor of surgery at Harvard Medical School

In the event of brain dead organ recovery, the warm ischemic time is very minimal, because the heart stops only moments before the organs are cooled. With "brain death" not practicable, and almost no explainable, legitimate cause of death, then why did almost all organ procurements have such short warm ischemia times, with many of them even being under a minute? We know that these were not voluntary donors, and we know that the operation was scheduled in advance, because the recipient was already ready for the organ (given the short cold ischemic times.) This required blood-matching. Thus, the donors must have been killed for the purpose of having their organs removed. This is mass murder.

—Dr. Charles Lee, spokesperson for the Global Service Center for Quitting the Chinese Communist Party

Source: U.S. House of Representatives.

Prevalence of Organ Trafficking

It is hard to determine the true scope of organ trafficking because we do not have reliable data. Indeed, the most prominent international reports on organ trafficking emphasize that we do not have sufficient data to describe the scope of this problem. According to the 2018 Global Report on Trafficking in Persons, organ trafficking is estimated to account for less than 1% (0.3%) of all known human trafficking cases (UNODC, 2018a). This report also emphasizes that this calculation is likely an underestimate. The Global Report has identified trafficking in persons for organ removal in 25 countries worldwide. Estimates in this report suggest that up to 10% of all kidney and liver transplants use illegally obtained organs (UNODC, 2018a).

Table 12.2 Transplant Websites Available in 2007

Name of Organization	Location of Transplantation	Transplant Package
BEK-Transplant	China	Kidney: $70,000 Liver: $120,000 Pancreas: $110,000 Kidney and pancreas: $160,000
China International Transplantation Network Assistance Center	China	Kidney: $65,000 Liver: $130,000 Lung: $150,000 Heart: $130,000
Yeson Healthcare Service Network	China	Kidney, liver, heart, and lung: No price provided
Aadil Hospital	Pakistan	Kidney: No price provided
Masood Hospital	Pakistan	Kidney: $14,000
Renal Transplant Associates	Pakistan	Kidney: $20,500
Liver4You	Philippines	Kidney: $85,000

Source: Adapted from Shimazono, 2007.

The WHO estimates that upward of 10% of kidney transplants involve kidneys that have been paid for ("commercialized") and that between 5% and 10% of all kidney transplants are the result of transplant tourism (Office of the Special Representative and Co-ordinator for Combating Trafficking in Human Beings, 2013; Shimazono, 2007). Other estimates suggest that more than 10,000 illicit organ transplants take place per year, a number equivalent to more than one black-market organ transplant per hour. The president of the Transplantation Society has stated that 5,000 people sell organs each year (Office of the Special Representative and Co-ordinator for Combating Trafficking in Human Beings, 2013; Shimazono, 2007).

Transplant tourism is the most common form of organ trafficking. Frequently, intermediaries or middlemen facilitate transplant tourism by advertising to patients online. These online advertisements and websites offer "transplant packages." A systematic review found that the cost of a kidney transplant package ranges from $70,000 to $160,000. Other research has found that patients will pay more than $200,000 for donor organs; typically victim donors receive less than $5,000 (Shimazono, 2007). The 2018 Global Report on Trafficking in Persons similarly found that patients paid about $200,000 for an illegally obtained organ, while donors received about $10,000 (UNODC, 2018a).

Causes of Organ Trafficking

Many of the root causes of supply for black-market organs are similar to the root causes of other forms of trafficking in human beings, such as poverty, low education, few or no employment prospects, and belonging to a marginalized group. Vulnerable people have a hard time not agreeing to sell organs, often due to financial desperation, but sometimes also due to other forms of threat, force, or fraud.

The causes leading to an increased demand for black-market organs are somewhat distinct from causes of other forms of trafficking. These include too few

Figure 12.2 Root Causes of Organ Trafficking

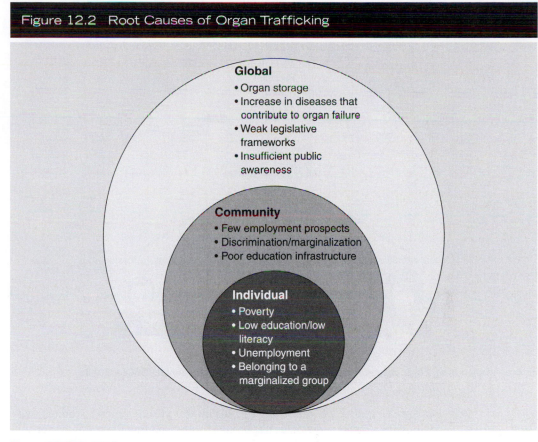

Global
- Organ storage
- Increase in diseases that contribute to organ failure
- Weak legislative frameworks
- Insufficient public awareness

Community
- Few employment prospects
- Discrimination/marginalization
- Poor education infrastructure

Individual
- Poverty
- Low education/low literacy
- Unemployment
- Belonging to a marginalized group

Source: UNODC, 2015.

altruistic donors to meet the need for transplants and the increased presence of diseases that contribute to organ failure (UNODC, 2015a).

Unlike other forms of trafficking, organ trafficking necessarily requires a high degree of organization and multiple actors, including professionals such as medical doctors (Office of the Special Representative and Co-ordinator for Combating Trafficking in Human Beings, 2013).

Structure of Organ-Trafficking Operations

Local Middlemen/Recruiters

Local recruiters are the individuals who find victim donors ("organ sellers"). They may be involved in other forms of human trafficking in addition to organ trafficking. Typically, local recruiters operate in one geographic area. They may be former victim donors (organ sellers), but in some cases they are corrupt government officials such as police officers. Local recruiters are paid on commission for each organ they provide for transplantation. In some trafficking networks, there are a myriad of local middlemen that facilitate the organ-selling process. There may be individuals who accompany the victim donor on

Figure 12.3 Organ Trafficking Networks

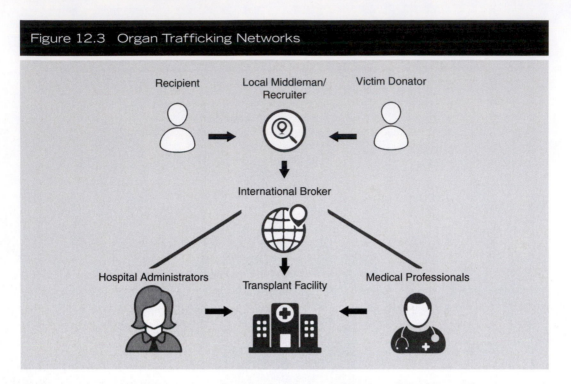

Source: Adapted from: Fig 3. Organization for Security and Co-operation in Europe (OSCE). 2013.

any travel, individuals whose job is to ensure that victim donors go through with selling their organ, individuals responsible for transporting the victim donor, and interpreters who translate for the victim donor and medical personnel.

International Coordinators/Brokers

International coordinators, commonly referred to as brokers, are the individuals responsible for establishing and coordinating organ trafficking networks. These individuals may be independent individuals with strong business savvy, medical providers, or hospital administrators. Brokers have extensive knowledge of different stakeholders, such as medical personnel and facilities willing to perform illegal organ transplants. Sellers do not have these same connections, so the brokers play an important role in organ trafficking networks: connecting sellers, patients, and medical personnel. Brokers set prices for black-market organ transplants and make offers to organ recipients. They also set payments to transplant facilities, medical providers, and other involved individuals.

Medical Professionals

Organ transplants necessarily include a variety of medical providers, including surgeons, nephrologists, anesthesiologists, nurses, and medical assistants. In some cases, doctors act as international brokers, but it is more common for the medical providers to simply be open to performing an illegal transplant for financial gain. In other cases, medical staff may have no idea that the transplant is illegal and the broker falsifies a relationship between the victim donor and recipient.

Case Study

Medical Professional Acts as International Coordinator

Levy Izhak Rosenbaum, aka "Isaac Rosenbaum," 60, admitted that from January 2006 through February 2009, he conspired with others to provide a service, in exchange for large payments, to individuals seeking kidney transplants by obtaining kidneys from paid donors. Specifically, Rosenbaum admitted to arranging three transplants on behalf of New Jersey residents that took place in December 2006, September 2008, and February 2009. Rosenbaum admitted that he was paid approximately $120,000, $150,000, and $140,000, respectively on behalf of these three recipients.

Rosenbaum's kidney business was exposed through the use of cooperating criminal defendant Solomon Dwek and an undercover FBI agent (the "UC") who was posing as an employee of Dwek and who represented to Rosenbaum that her uncle was in need of a kidney transplant. Dwek and the UC first met with Rosenbaum in mid-February 2008 at which time Rosenbaum informed them that "[i]t's illegal to buy and sell organs," but assured them that "I'm doing this a long time." Rosenbaum explained to Dwek and the UC that he would help the recipient and the donor concoct a fictitious story to make it appear that the transplant was the product of a genuine donation and that he would be in charge of babysitting the donor upon the donor's arrival from overseas. Rosenbaum also informed Dwek and the CW that he would charge $150,000 to arrange the transplant, explaining that the high price was due in part to payments that would be made to individuals in Israel for their assistance in locating the donor. At a July 2009 meeting, Rosenbaum informed the UC that he had been arranging kidney transplants like the one to be done on behalf of her uncle for a period of 10 years, the most recent only two weeks earlier.

During his guilty plea, Rosenbaum admitted he had told recipients that he could locate individuals who would donate their kidneys in exchange for money. Rosenbaum admitted that he arranged for blood samples to be drawn from the potential recipients so that appropriate donors could be located. He also acknowledged that he assisted each paid donor and recipient with fabricating cover stories in order to fool hospital employees into believing that the transplant in question was the product of a genuine donation.

Rosenbaum was sentenced to 2.5 years in prison in what experts said was the first U.S. federal conviction for profiting from the illegal sale of human organs. Rosenbaum also agreed to forfeit approximately $420,000 by the date of sentencing—consisting of the $410,000 he accepted for brokering the transplants and the $10,000 down payment he accepted from Dwek.

Source: U.S. Attorney's Office, 2011.

Medical Facilities and Administrative Staff

Donor–recipient matching as well as transplantation require access to a medical facility. Thus, medical staff and administrative staff may be involved at a variety of stages in the organ trafficking process.

Lab Technicians

There are blood tests that must take place prior to a transplant. Experts believe these often take place in labs connected to the hospitals where the transplant will take place, but they may also take place in other labs. Thus, lab technicians may facilitate organ trafficking by helping traffickers bypass legal or ethical standards, or they may help to match victim donors to recipients. It is also possible that lab technicians serve as brokers by advertising organ selling and making connections with brokers.

Administrative Health Officials

These individuals may facilitate organ trafficking networks by turning a blind eye to criminal activity, providing paperwork and licenses to allow traffickers to operate, and possibly by forging medical licenses or authorizations for transplants. It is rare for administrative staff to be convicted in organ trafficking cases, however.

Health Insurance Companies

Expert working group meetings on organ trafficking have found evidence that health insurance companies encourage patients to travel abroad for transplant surgery if it will be considerably cheaper in another country. They may be, knowingly or unknowingly, promoting the purchasing of organs from victim donors. There is no substantial evidence regarding the role of health insurance companies, however, to definitively state the extent to which this phenomenon occurs.

Corrupt Government Officials

All types of human trafficking are sometimes facilitated by corrupt government officials, particularly corruption in law enforcement, and organ trafficking is no exception. Some medical professionals establish close relationships with law enforcement to make sure they do not enforce laws pertaining to transplants.

Focus On
A Medical Facility Involved in Trafficking

Netcare Kwa-Zulu (Pty) Limited, "Netcare[,]" pled guilty to 102 counts related to charges stemming from having knowingly allowed its employees and facilities to be used for what amounted to the trafficking of persons for their organs, constitut[ing] one of the first such cases to make its way before a court of law. In so doing, the agreement implicated and effectively prosecuted the hospital involved, St. Augustine's Hospital.

In addition to Netcare, a number of other charges were laid against the St. Augustine's Hospital, located in Durban, South Africa[;] the CEO of Netcare, Richard Friedland[;] and eight others: four transplant doctors, a nephrologist, two transplant administrative coordinators, and an interpreter. The admission of guilt related to 109 illegal kidney transplant operations that took place between June 2001 and November 2003. The scheme involved Israeli citizens in need of kidney transplants who would be brought to South Africa for transplants performed at St. Augustine's Hospital.

While the kidneys supplied originally came from Israeli citizens, "later Romanian and Brazilian citizens were recruited as their kidneys were obtainable at a much lower cost." The broker, Ilan Perry, was the individual in charge of the recruitment of both kidney suppliers and recipients and was not South African and has not been charged. He set a fee of between $100,000–$120,000 for recipients and paid the original suppliers of kidneys $20,000. However, later on in the scheme, Romanians and Brazilians received on average of $6,000. Netcare received payments from the broker and it then disbursed payment "to the other accused and service providers; including the surgeons for their services." While Netcare was paid up-front for its participation in the illegal kidney transplants, the people supplying the healthy kidneys were paid after the fact and in cash.

Ilan Perry used recruiters to source individuals ready to supply kidneys; two of these, Captain Ivan Da Silva and Gaby Tauber, had

---

been imprisoned in Brazil for their roles in the affair. Blood screening of prospective kidney suppliers was done in-country and again in South Africa; those deemed suitable were "accommodated and chaperoned" and "given documents to sign falsely indicating that they were related to each other."

Netcare plead[ed] guilty [to] using five minors as organ suppliers in violation of the Human Tissue Act 1983 and received separate charges for receiving money for transplants from minors. In regard to the 102 transplant operations that did not include minors, the company pleaded guilty to its employees having received money, the proceeds of an unlawful activity.

Netcare had to pay the USD 466,839 that they gained from the illegal transplants, plus an additional USD 493,875 in fines.

Source: Queen's University, School of Law, n.d.

Victim Donors

Victim donors are not part of the criminal organ trafficking network. They are exploited individuals in need of protection. Factors that increase vulnerability to being a victim donor include:

- Living in a poor country

- Extreme poverty

- Belonging to a marginalized population

- Being undocumented in the country of residence

- Being a refugee

- Low education or illiteracy

- Lack of awareness of potential consequences associated with having an organ removed

- Being young (18–30)

- Being male

- Living in a country with a poor legal framework for addressing organ trafficking and/or with high levels of corruption

Victim donors tend to be from countries where a large proportion of the population lives below the national poverty level. As with other types of trafficking in persons, there is no single profile of an organ trafficking victim: victims may be men, women, or children of any age. However, victim donors tend to be relatively young (under 30), have low levels of education, and come from extremely low socioeconomic backgrounds.

Outcomes for Donors

There is incredibly limited information about outcomes for victim donors. Victim donors typically do not receive the full amount of money they are promised before selling their organ. Some victims receive no money, and some only a portion of the money. In extreme cases, victims do not even agree

Table 12.3 Consequences of Paid Kidney Donation: Summary of Three Studies

	Location	% Male	Economic Status	% Reporting Negative Effect on Health	Changes to Financial Status
Study 1	Egypt	95	Not available	78	78% spent the money within five months 73% reported being less able to perform labor-intensive jobs
Study 2	India	29	Almost three-quarters below poverty line: primarily laborers or street vendors	86	Nearly all sold their kidney to pay off debt, but three-quarters were still in debt afterward
Study 3	Iran	71	Nearly one-third unemployed	58	65% reported negative effects on employment status

Source: Adapted from Shimazono, 2007, table 4.

to sell their organ and it is taken against their will. Existing research suggests that victim donors are unlikely to receive postoperative care and are subsequently at heightened risk for health complications following the transplant surgery (Shimazono, 2007). Their worsened health status makes it more difficult for them to obtain or maintain employment and subsequently worsens their financial well-being. Many victim donors also report mental health disorders such as anxiety, depression, and loss of bodily integrity. In some cases, victim donors are stigmatized, shamed, and isolated for selling their organ (UNODC, 2015a).

Organ Recipients

There has been no significant research into the characteristics of organ recipients. The information we have is based on case studies and interviews with known recipients, which are limited and may not be generalizable to all recipients. Organ recipients, or buyers, are of all ages and typically wealthy. Even when buyers are not wealthy, they are generally in much better economic situations than victim donors and sellers. Ultimately, organ recipients provide funding for the whole organ trafficking network. Other characteristics that have been identified as contributing to the likelihood of an individual buying an organ include:

- Long wait times for altruistic donation

- Not qualifying to be on a waiting list because of a health condition

- Wanting a preemptive transplant (before organ failure)

- Not having related donors or not wanting to ask family for donation

Notably, no differences have been found between individuals engaged in transplant tourism versus other forms of organ trafficking. There is limited evidence that some ethnic groups have an increased demand for organ purchasing because of the high prevalence of diabetes among those exposed to a "Western diet."

Outcomes for Recipients

Patients who receive transplants abroad may be at increased risk for infection or other postoperative complications. One research synthesis conducted by the WHO found that "nonlocal" recipients had shorter survival periods and an increased likelihood of complications such as HIV and hepatitis B and C. Experts also suggest that patients who purchase organs may have a shorter survival period. Recipients of illegally obtained organs often have little information about the victim donor and his or her health status. After a transplant, patients require medical care. There are no reports of medical providers reporting their patient for illegally obtaining an organ after returning from the transplant (Office of the Special Representative and Co-ordinator for Combating Trafficking in Human Beings, 2013).

There is little information about prosecutions of organ recipients. In the Focus on a Medical Facility Involved in Trafficking box (see page 302) earlier in this chapter, a recipient was charged with illegal organ purchase and required to pay a fine. As mentioned in a quote under Case Study: Harvesting Organs From Prisoners in China (see page 297), one recipient was a 14-year-old girl who ultimately died. The recipient was charged, but ultimately charges were dropped.

Case Study

Doctor Charged With Organized Crime: The Medicus Clinic
· ·

The involvement of transplant doctors in organized, illegal transplant operations was revealed in 2008 at the "Medicus Clinic" in Pristina, Kosovo. Throughout 2008, a network consisting of transplant surgeons, anesthesiologists, urologists, other medical doctors and their staff, as well as organ brokers and local "fixers," that is people who helped to match possible organ suppliers and recipients, recruited approximately 30 persons from Russia, Moldova, Kazakhstan and Turkey who were transported to the Medicus Clinic in Kosovo for the removal of their kidneys. The victims were given false promises of up to USD 20,000 for their kidneys. Their organs were transplanted into foreign patients, who paid up to USD 200,000.

A transplant surgeon, who allegedly performed up to 3,000 commercial transplants between unrelated donors and recipients, played a key role in the

(Continued)

(Continued)

syndicate, flying into Kosovo regularly to perform most of the transplantations. In 2010 the Special Prosecution Office in Kosovo charged seven persons, amongst which was also a government official, with trafficking in persons, participation in organized crime, unlawful exercise of medical activity, abusing official position or authority, grievous bodily harm, fraud and falsifying (official) documents.

In 2013 five of the seven accused were convicted, including the clinic's director (a medical doctor) for trafficking in persons and organized crime, with prison sentences. The head of the clinic was found guilty on charges of organized crime, trafficking in persons and co-perpetration. He was sentenced to a punishment of eight years['] imprisonment and a fine of EUR 10,000. He was prohibited from exercising as a professional urologist for the period of two years. Also his son (an economist) was found guilty on charges of trafficking in persons and organized crime. He was sentenced to seven years and three months['] imprisonment and a fine of EUR 2,500. Three medical doctors were found guilty on the count of grievous bodily harm. They were sentenced to imprisonment between one and three years. One was prohibited from practicing as [an] anesthesiologist for the period of one year.

To obtain the convictions, the investigating authorities carefully secured, collected and corroborated evidential materials, such as flight records, as well as anesthesiology, laboratory and surgery records and utensils, so as to document, as complete[ly] as possible, medical interventions and the arrival and departure by plane and presence at the clinic of alleged organ suppliers, organ recipients and doctors. They examined and collected [forensic] evidence from operating [rooms] . . . investigated the clinic's licensing history. They also traced and examined electronic mail communication, e.g. between the local head of the clinic and the foreign surgeon; they moreover sought international legal assistance from the countries involved.

What triggered the investigations into this case and the raid of the Medicus Clinic was the collapse of a 23-year-old man, who fainted in front of customs officials at Pristina (Kosovo) airport in November 2008, while waiting for his international flight. When officials raised his shirt they discovered a fresh scar on his abdomen.

Source: United Nations Office on Drugs and Crime, 2015a.

Organ Trafficking as Organized Crime

Individuals interested in studying organ trafficking have investigated potential links between organ trafficking networks and traditional forms of organized crime. There is some evidence to suggest that recruiters, enforcers, and other local participants in organ trafficking networks may also be involved in other types of human trafficking or other forms of organized crime (Bos, 2015; Office of the Special Representative and Co-ordinator for Combating Trafficking in Human Beings, 2013). There is no evidence that traditional organized crime networks have taken up the "business" of organ trafficking. Many argue, however, that the operation of organ trafficking networks meet the characteristics of an organized crime network. Article 2(a) of the UN organized crime convention (United Nations General Assembly, 2001) states than an organized criminal group is

> a structured group of three or more persons, existing for a period of time and acting in concert with the aim of committing one or more serious crimes or offences established in accordance with this Convention, in order to obtain, directly or indirectly, a financial or other material benefit.

The 2014 Global Report on Trafficking in Persons (UNODC, 2014) characterizes three types of trafficking operations (see Table 12.4).

Table 12.4 Types of Trafficking Operations

Small Local Operations	Medium Subregional Operations	Large Transregional Operations
Domestic or short-distance	Within the subregion or neighbouring subregions	Long distance between different regions
One or few traffickers	Small group of traffickers	Traffickers involved in organized crime
Small number of victims	More than one victim	Large number of victims
Limited investment and profits	Some investments and some profits depending on the number of victims	High investments and high profits
No travel documents needed for border crossing	Border crossings with or without travel documents	Border crossings always require travel documents
No or very limited organization required	Some organization needed depending on border crossings and number or victims	Sophisticated organization needed to move large number of victims long distance

Source: United Nations Office on Drugs and Crime, 2014.

Challenge Yourself 12.2

Review each of the case studies in this chapter. For each, would you characterize the organ trafficking network as a small, medium, or large operation?

Research

Research refers to the systematic collection and analysis of data to describe patterns and relationships.

Research on organ trafficking has increased substantially in the past two decades, in part due to high-profile cases of organ trafficking but also because of contributions of victim advocates, journalists, and researchers. As described throughout this chapter, however, we have insufficient information about the prevalence of organ trafficking, the ways organ trafficking networks operate, and the characteristics of victim donors and recipients.

Research is critical to prevention efforts. As with other forms of trafficking, in order to prevent organ trafficking, we must address the root causes of vulnerability to engaging in organ selling. We know that poverty is a root cause of organ trafficking, as many victim donors sell their organs because they are financially desperate. Research can help identify, develop, and evaluate programs that promote economic self-sufficiency.

Public health practitioners and researchers can also help to prevent trafficking by reducing demand for illegal organs. This can be done, in part, by promoting healthy life choices that can ultimately prevent organ failure. Additionally, countries can work to reduce demand for illegally sourced organs by using living and deceased donors, if they have not already done so.

Additional research is also needed on reduction and control of existing organ trafficking efforts, including research on best practices for law enforcement. For example, there is almost no information about how recipients obtain organs, or on how the money flows between recipients, brokers, hospitals, and medical staff.

The United Nations (UNODC, 2015a) recommends that, at every level of government, additional data collection should take place pertaining to:

- Trafficking in persons for organ removal

- Long-term outcomes associated with illegal organ transplants

Economic Approaches

Some economists have called for legalizing the buying and selling of organs. They argue that the benefits of institutionalizing the organ trade outweigh the risks. Consider the following facts about kidney transplantation in the United States. Each day, about 13 individuals die waiting for a kidney. Those who remain on the waiting list require dialysis. Dialysis costs about $75,000 per year, and most of this is covered by a taxpayer-funded End Stage Renal Disease Program (part of Medicare). Individuals who receive a transplant are healthier for much longer than individuals on dialysis. Also, one economist estimated that a kidney transplant yields $90,000 in cost savings to taxpayers (Matas & Schnitzler, 2004). Based on this calculation, providing a transplant for each individual on the waiting list in the U.S. would save billions of dollars per year, or paying donors $90,000 would allow the country to break even. As detailed throughout the chapter, there are serious ethical and bioethical concerns with allowing donors to sell their organs.

Pilots of various extremes of the idea of institutionalized organ selling have yielded some information about the effectiveness of each in terms of reducing transplant waiting lists.

Proponents of an open organ market (G. S. Becker & Elias, 2007; Hippen, Ross, & Sade, 2009; Knoc, 2008) argue:

- We already sell things such as sperm, eggs, and blood, so selling organs is not much of a leap.

- It improves length and quality of life for recipients who are removed from organ waiting lists.

- Economically vulnerable people do dangerous things for money all the time.

- If medical professionals value autonomy, this should include allowing patients to decide whether they want to sell their organs.

- Poor people are already selling their organs out of desperation. A regulated market could ensure equitable compensation and increase safety for donors.

One study found that when Americans were told the benefits of a regulated organ market, approval for this type of market increased nearly 20% (Elias, Lacetera, & Macis, 2015).

Iran has legalized selling organs since the 1990s. Within a decade, the government claims to have eliminated the waiting list for organ recipients and created competitive demand among potential donors, who were paid the equivalent of about $3,500 at the outset of the program. This amount has not increased with inflation, however, and donors today receive approximately the equivalent of $350. In the Iranian model, donors go to a volunteer-run regional office and are matched with recipients based on their blood type. Donors must pass a health and psychological screen before the transplant. If the recipient can't afford the payment for the kidney, the government covers the costs. Male donors are exempt from military service requirements.

Iran has run into some problems with their system. For example, government funds in rural areas run out quicker, giving rural recipients inequitable access to transplants. There is some evidence of a stigma associated with kidney donation as well, so donors leave incorrect contact information, making it impossible for doctors to follow up with them for postoperative care. There is an effort in Iran to help overcome the stigma of organ donation and to connect donors with social and economic support (Rosenberg, 2015).

Economists have also argued for a less extreme option; compensating donors for the costs associated with donation. For living donors, proponents argue that the current transplant system in many countries, including the United States, favors those who are more economically well off. The quickest way off a waiting list for an organ is for a friend or family member to donate. In general, people who can donate an organ are at least moderately financially stable. Organ donation incurs substantial costs, and economists suggest that donors should be partially compensated for these costs to narrow the total costs associated with donation (Gaston et al., 2006).

Challenge Yourself 12.3

Consider the following quote:

> Perhaps "altruistic unrelated living donation," as we currently know it, is just a legal fiction that conceals commercial transactions more often than not. (Epstein, 2008)

Write a short (one-paragraph) response. Why do you agree or disagree with this statement?

Table 12.5 Suggested Compensation for Organ Donors

Cost to Donor	Suggested Compensation
One-year life insurance policy with a death benefit of $1,000,000	$1,300–$3,300
Health insurance	$15,000–$20,000
Reimbursement of out-of-pocket expenses/lost wages related to donor evaluation or transplant	$225–$4,500
Compensation for inconvenience, anxiety, and/or pain	$5,000 or $10,000 tax deduction
Total cost estimate per donor	$23,525–$32,800

Source: Adapted from Gaston et al., 2006. Reprinted with permission.

Other more widely accepted approaches to reducing the demand for organ donations include promoting chain donation. Chain donation, shown in Figure 12.4, works as follows: If you want to donate to your relative but you are type A and she is type B, you are matched with another donor who wants to donate their relative: this donor is type A and their relative is type B. This sort of coordination greatly increases the number of organ transplants that can take place (UNODC, 2015a).

Another common, and feasible, approach is to increase awareness around organ donation, particularly in countries with an opt-in system, such as the United States. For example, in New York, only 1 in 10 people is an organ donor. Awareness campaigns can help to demonstrate the advantages of organ donation and encourage people to opt in to the organ donation system.

Finally, principle 6 of the Istanbul Declaration provides guidance on another feasible way to reduce organ trafficking and transplant tourism: Ban any type of advertising or solicitation of human organs. This policy recommendation is meant to protect the most vulnerable, such as those living in poverty, from being financially coerced into organ donation (Steering Committee of the Istanbul Summit, 2008).

Figure 12.4 The Kidney Donor Domino Effect

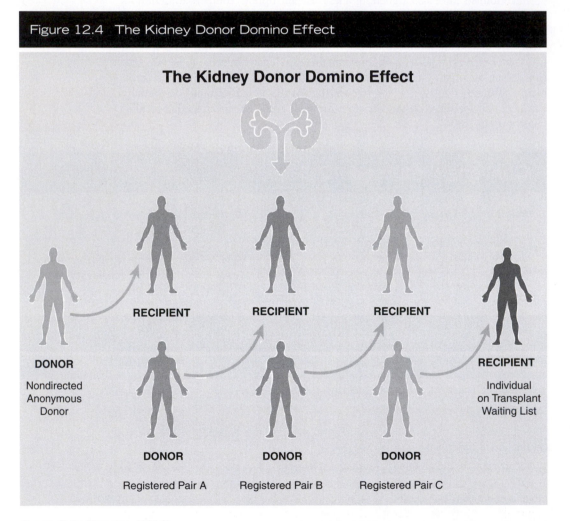

The Kidney Donor Domino Effect

RECIPIENT RECIPIENT RECIPIENT

DONOR

Nondirected Anonymous Donor

RECIPIENT

Individual on Transplant Waiting List

DONOR DONOR DONOR

Registered Pair A Registered Pair B Registered Pair C

Source: Pulse Magazine. (2016).

Recovery

Identification of Traffickers and Victims

As with other forms of trafficking, a primary challenge for detecting perpetrators is that the actors operate covertly. There are significant challenges associated with identifying the various members of organ trafficking networks.

For example:

- Organ trafficking may take place in legitimate industries

- Victim donors are afraid to report traffickers to law enforcement because of possible retaliation from traffickers

- Uninvolved medical staff who suspect colleagues of participation in organ trafficking are afraid to "whistle-blow" because of possible retaliation from traffickers

- Individuals who interact with victim donors are unable to identify them as victims

- Each actor in the organ trafficking networks may operate in a different country, making it difficult to identify one specific "crime scene" or one law enforcement agency that would be able to tie the pieces of the network together

Efforts to identify traffickers typically focus on local actors and medical professionals, in part because these are the easiest to identify. Law enforcement local to one jurisdiction or country can see an investigation through to the end with local perpetrators. It is much more difficult to identify international brokers because they may not reside in the country where the network operates. Unfortunately, with international brokers still in place, it would be easy to reestablish another organ trafficking network with new local recruiters and medical staff.

Identifying organ traffickers and victims usually requires international coordination. Law enforcement personnel are the primary agents positioned to identify traffickers, but because trafficking networks cross jurisdictional boundaries, a variety of law enforcement agents must work together to identify traffickers and victims. Police officers, customs agents, and immigration and border officials should be trained to identify signs of trafficking. Border and custom officials are uniquely situated to search bags without consent, which can provide evidence against traffickers, such as medical supplies or medical records. Law enforcement should also be trained to investigate online and print advertisements for organ selling and buying.

Countries can also launch awareness campaigns to prevent actors at all stages of organ transplantation from unknowingly becoming involved. Additionally, awareness campaigns can help inform potential victims of the costs and risks associated with organ selling. Signs of trafficking in persons for organ removal include:

- No documentation of the donor's consent

- No documentation of social or psychological reports for the donor

- An individual flying on an airplane within two days of surgery

- Immigration authorities noticing a substantial number of invitation letters from one specific hospital

- Individuals reporting that they are traveling for medical purposes without any documentation or medical records

- Any individual in an airport carrying large amounts of cash

- A large increase in the number of transplants at a hospital

Policy Measures

The medical community has made significant efforts to clarify ethical guidelines for organ transplants in an attempt to prevent illegal organ transplants. These guidelines put more responsibility on medical professionals and make it more difficult for them to turn a blind eye to evidence of organ trafficking. Such guidelines include evaluation of potential donors and providing them with complete information, including risks, recipient outcomes, and alternatives (American Medical Association, 2016). They also recommend appointing an advocate to the donor. Donor advocates minimize conflicts of interest. Transplant centers should use two separate staff members: one who conducts evaluation assessments and informed consent and another who performs the transplant. This way, the sole responsibility of one of the medical professionals is to advocate for the donor.

Guidance statements are not legally binding, however. Accordingly, the following measures have been recommended (UNODC, 2015a) pertaining to medical professional involvement in human trafficking:

- Stricter reporting requirements for donor evaluation

- Accountability for violations

- Raising awareness among medical professionals about the signs of organ trafficking

- Systems for anonymous reporting of suspicious activity or other protections for whistle-blowers

The trafficking in persons protocol establishes organ trafficking as a form of trafficking in persons. Thus, countries that have ratified this protocol need to ensure that their national and local legislation criminalizes organ trafficking. In addition, laws should clarify that consent to organ removal doesn't matter in the presence of threat, fraud, or coercion.

Resources and Restoration

Resources refers to providing the survivors of trafficking with the services they need to move toward restoration. *Restoration* refers to providing survivors with the services they need to lead healthy, stable lives and to prevent revictimization.

It is critical to assist and protect victims of organ trafficking. Victim assistance can facilitate successful prosecution of traffickers, help to prevent revictimization, and help victims lead self-sufficient lives, preventing them from becoming organ brokers themselves. International guidance from the WHO and UN suggests that governments provide the following minimum services to victims of organ trafficking (Office of the Special Representative and Co-ordinator for Combating Trafficking in Human Beings, 2013; UNODC, 2015a):

Immediate Safety: When a victim is identified, he or she should be referred to special protection and assistance services. This requires that there be direct service providers available to provide these services, which is not always the case. National governments can persuade direct service providers to tailor their services for organ trafficking victims through conditions in funding.

Mental and Physical Health: It is critical that victim donors receive physical and mental health support, which will likely require medium- to long-term attention. A designated case manager can help victims navigate the health care system and access services.

Legal Support: Victims should be encouraged to participate in prosecution of their trafficker, if they want. Victims may need access to pro bono legal support. Further, victims should not be prosecuted for having a role in the organ trafficking network.

The United Nations recommends that anyone who comes in contact with a potential donor victim should collect the following information to facilitate securing of immediate safety, service provision, and legal support:

- Are you injured? If yes, where and how are you injured?

- Do you need help?

- Does anyone else need help?

- Tell me what happened.

- Do you have a passport or other piece of identification?

- Is anyone threatening you? Has anyone threatened you?

- What were you told would happen? What actually did happen?

- Have you been asked to do anything you did not want to do?

- Are you alone here?

- Where are you staying? Who are you staying with? (UNODC, 2015a)

Conclusion

Organ transplantation has transformed life prospects and quality of life for individuals with organ failure. Unfortunately, the supply of donor organs does not come close to meeting the demand for organ transplants. Unlike other forms of organ trafficking, organ trafficking typically requires the participation of professionals such as medical staff and administrative personnel at medical facilities.

Similar to other forms of trafficking, organ trafficking victims are individuals who are marginalized, vulnerable, and left with no alternative but to sell their organs. In extreme cases, organs are taken forcibly from victim donors.

The lines can be somewhat blurred between trafficking in organs, tissues, and cells; transplant tourism; and trafficking in human beings for the purpose of organ removal. It may be more helpful to consider the elements of an ethical transplant and to note that if any of these elements is missing, then trafficking is likely occurring. First, organ donors should be legal adults. Second, nobody in the transplant process (donors, medical personnel, health insurance companies, medical facilities) should financially profit from the transplant. That is, they should not earn above and beyond what they would normally be paid for an altruistic donation.

Prosecuting members of organ trafficking networks is difficult. Law enforcement agencies typically focus on identifying members of the network that are in their jurisdiction. This means that local recruiters and medical staff are somewhat easier to identify. However, a variety of other evidence can point to networks that may be more widespread. This may involve comparing the number of transplants performed at a facility against records of consent forms, tracking payment for performing organ transplants, and identifying individuals traveling with medical supplies and no documentation of previous or planned surgeries. International brokers, who coordinate different members of a trafficking network, are much less likely to be caught. This is problematic, because the network can be reestablished as long as the international broker has not been stopped.

Serving victims of human trafficking is also difficult. Because organ trafficking constitutes a low proportion of all incidences of trafficking, victim service providers do not typically tailor services for these victims. There is incredibly limited research on the long-term needs of organ trafficking victims, but limited research shows that these victims have unique needs. Many need access to postoperative follow-up care, long-term health and psychological care, and help dealing with the stigma of selling organs in their communities. Some victims may need to be relocated if the stigma is so high that it prevents their ability to work.

KEY WORDS

organ commercialization 291   organ transplantation 290   transplant tourism 293

DISCUSSION QUESTIONS

1. Discuss the supply and demand factors that result in organ trafficking.

2. List and describe the different forms of organ trafficking. Make sure to distinguish between them.

3. Explain the multilevel factors that cause organ trafficking. In which countries is organ trafficking most common? What is the impact of these multi-level factors in those countries?

RESOURCE

Human Harvest documentary: http://www.humanharvestmovie.com/

13

Forced and Child Marriage

Case Study

Talamt

I was sold in 2007 after coming to visit my sister Chilek, the wahaya of Soho Dan Amali from Sokoto. My sister had also been sold by our father in Sokoto. Then I was sold to an old neighbourhood marabout [spiritual guide] called Malam Bouwèye. . . .

I was sold by my own father who made a lot of money. . . . I had come to Sokoto with my father. He then went back to Tambaye and left me with my older sister. During my stay, I became very ill for about 35 days. I had awful nightmares in which I thought I was being strangled. After I recovered, my sister told me to return home. She promised to give me money for my transport, because I was about to be sold. That's when my father returned. He spoke with the other two men, then he got the money and left. Next, I was sent "to the mill." As I didn't know the neighbourhood, I was told to go to the house of the old marabout, Malam Bouwèye, as I would find the mill there. I was naive.

Once in the courtyard, I was locked in and told that I would now be the wife (wahaya) of this old marabout, who was as old as my father. I would say that not only was I forced into this situation, but I was also abducted. I wanted to cry for help but I didn't want to cause trouble for my father. But I said that I had to see my sister to understand what was happening. I was told to wait for Malam.

That evening after the maghrib, the dusk prayer, my sister came and took me to a room and told me not to make a fuss as our father had already taken the money and left. She told me to accept the situation because it was better that our father should get the money from selling us, rather than being sold by our mother's masters. I spent the whole night crying. My sister spent the night with me to comfort me, explaining that it would be better to live in Sokoto with an old man than to live in the bush with a young man. The old man also made many promises and said he would pay for my father to go on pilgrimage to Mecca in 2010. So that's how I ended up as the wahaya of the old man Malam Bouwèye. All hope of marrying a young man of my choice vanished. But I have decided that I will leave here sooner or later. . . .

There is a kind of harmony between me and Malam's legitimate wives. His first wife is already old. The second wife is young, but we get along well. I get along especially well with the first wahaya. She does everything for me; she's really nice to me. Although they are my co-wives, I am very well-liked by the two mistresses. I think of them as my mothers; I always tell them the truth, and I do anything they ask of me happily. . . . Also, the two women see me as their daughter and encourage me to stay, saying that God is in control of everything. They say they want me to stay so that they can teach me the Qur'an and religious practice. I think it's because these women are educated and have studied the Qur'an a great deal that they are not like other mistresses.

But as for my husband, I don't like him for various reasons. I am only living with this marabout because I don't have a choice—I was sold by my own father. First, I was supposed to marry a young man from my village whom I really loved. Secondly, I am ashamed of my status as a wahaya, mainly because of how people perceive me. There was no religious marriage ceremony. And finally, he is so old for me; too old to be my husband.

However, he loves me very much. He does things for me that he doesn't do for his legitimate wives. He is negotiating with me so that I stay with him, but I'm looking for a way out. As soon as I get the chance, I'll leave. We're kept like prisoners. It's only because the guard knows that Malam Bouwèye has gone to Mecca that I'm able to talk to you; otherwise the guard would be in trouble. He is a fanatical man.

Source: Abdelkader and Zangaou, 2012, p. 22.

A unique form of slavery still exists in Niger in which the victims are labeled *wahayu* (*wahaya* is the singular term). Although slavery is expressly prohibited in the African nation, a lack of enforcement of the existing laws, combined with limited efforts to combat human trafficking, result in the persistence of slavery, often under the auspices of cultural tradition (Abdelkader & Zangaou, 2012).

Wahayu are female victims of human trafficking. They typically come from slave descent and are sold by their parents' masters or by their parents directly to a new master. Their purpose, once sold, is to serve their masters' households, including performing sexual acts for the master when desired (Abdelkader & Zangaou, 2012). This practice is most often found in Niger and Nigeria, with most wahayu coming from the Tahoua region of Niger. Unlike the children of other female slaves in the region, babies birthed from wahayu are considered legitimate. Wayahu are generally assumed to be the fifth wife of the master (although it is technically legal for the master to have only four wives) (Mathewson, 2012; U.S. Department of State, 2017c). While labeled a "wife," a wahaya has none of the rights given to legal wives.

There has not been a lot of attention to this practice. Much of our information comes from a study conducted by **Anti-Slavery International**, an anti-trafficking nongovernmental organization (NGO; Abdelkader & Zangaou, 2012). The NGO interviewed 165 wahayu. This research found that 85% of those interviewed were sold before they were 15 years old. One wahaya described being sold to her master at the age of 12 years old for 240,000 francs (about $483). She became one of 11 wives, eight of whom were wahayu (Abdelkader & Zangaou, 2012)! Talamt's story in the Case Study box (see page 315) provides a detailed account of a young wahaya's experience in slavery.

In addition to serving as wahayu, girls from Niger commonly enter into arranged marriages abroad. Due to their forced marriage, these girls are at an increased risk for sexual exploitation should they escape their marital enslavement (U.S. Department of State, 2017). Although the prevalence of child marriage is reviewed later in this chapter, it is worth noting that Niger has the highest rate of child marriage in the world. Seventy-six percent of girls are married before they are 18 years old and 28% before they are 16 years old (Dormino, n.d.).

Forced marriage is analogous to other forms of trafficking. This is particularly clear when dealing with the marriage of children. As with sex, a child typically cannot consent to marriage. However, also as with sex, the lines may seem blurred when it comes to whether marriage is considered forced versus consensual. In contrast to norms regarding sex, however, there is less consensus regarding the acceptability of forced and child marriages.

After a review of the prevalence of this form of trafficking, the chapter will focus primarily on child marriage. Child marriage is both simple and complicated at the same time. At its most basic level, it is simple—an underage child forced to marry another individual. However, the cultural rituals surrounding child marriage, combined with the normative nature of the practice in parts of the world, make the issue more complicated. This chapter will consider pervasive questions that surround the topic of child marriage. What is child marriage? Is child marriage a form of human trafficking? (Since an entire chapter of this book is dedicated to it, you can probably guess the authors' answer to this question!) Is child marriage inherently wrong, or are Western opinions shadowing this traditional practice? Where is child marriage occurring? What are the risk factors? The consequences? Finally, what do we do about it, if anything?

The Fundaments of Forced and Child Marriage

Men, women, boys, and girls can be forced to marry. **Forced marriage** involves individuals who are forced to marry against their will or forced to stay in their marriage against their will (Unchained at Last, n.d.; U.S. Citizenship and Immigration Services, n.d.a). In these cases, emotional abuse, deception, and threats are instrumental. Any marriage entered into with a child is typically considered forced, since a child is too young to consent (International Labour Office & Walk Free Foundation, 2017; Nour, 2009). **Child marriage** has also been referred to as early marriage, or child brides (Erulkar, 2013; Greene, 2014; Nour, 2009). The practice more often describes the marriage of girls, but boys have also been known to be married as children. Oftentimes, never meeting their new husband prior to the wedding, young girls are married off by their parents. The girl moves in with her husband's family and becomes his responsibility (Nour, 2009).

Note that arranged marriages are not necessarily considered forced. While families may be involved in both forced and *arranged* **marriages**, in the case of arranged marriages, the individuals being married are permitted to choose whether or not to be married and when they will marry (U.S. Citizenship and Immigration Services, n.d.a). Nevertheless, the line between arranged and forced marriages can be blurry. Arranged marriages often come with intense family pressure and even threats of harm (Unchained at Last, n.d.). Unchained at Last, a U.S.-based nonprofit focused on assisting women and girls escape forced marriages, considers forced and arranged marriages indistinguishable. While, inherently, the terms have different definitions, in reality, arranged marriages often look very similar to forced ones.

Take for example, the case of a young Pakistani man. *The Guardian* newspaper recounts his story of being locked in a room by his father after refusing to marry. His father would enter the locked room daily to abuse the boy, breaking bones and sexually abusing the child (Hill, 2010).

A telltale sign of forced marriage is the inability to leave the marriage. More indicators are listed in Table 13.1. Those who attempt to leave will experience many barriers, including social isolation and possible violence (Unchained at Last, n.d.). Social customs, religious law, and potential immigration barriers (when the forced participant is married outside her home country) pose serious barriers to escaping the marriage. This is especially true for women and girls attempting to leave forced marriages. In many regions, women do not have the same rights as men when it comes to divorce, such as in Orthodox Jewish communities where only men can grant a divorce (Unchained at Last, n.d.).

Challenge Yourself 13.1

Do you see any benefits or detriments to the different terms used to refer to child marriage (e.g., early marriage, child brides)? What sorts of messaging might terms such as these imply?

Table 13.1 Indicators of Forced Marriage

You feel you do not or did not have a choice regarding whom to marry or when to marry
You are experiencing or are being threatened with abandonment, isolation, or physical or emotional abuse if you do not marry or if you attempt to leave a marriage you did not concent to
You are afraid of the consequences of saying no to a marriage, including physical harm or being cut off from your family
You are being closely monitored in an effort to prevent you from talking to others about the pressure you are facing
You feel you cannot refuse to marry or leave a marriage you did not consent to because it would shame or harm you or your family
You believe that you or people you care about would be hurt or even killed if you refuse to marry or attempt to leave a marriage you did not consent to
You have had your travel documents, identification, communication devices, or money taken away from you and will not get them back unless you agree to marry or remain in a marriage you did not consent to

Source: "Forced Marriage", n.d.

The Prevalence of Forced and Child Marriage

The U.S. Department of State's Trafficking in Persons (TIP) Reports acknowledge child marriage, highlighting the practice in Egypt, Iraq, and Syria (U.S. Department of State, 2017; U.S Department of State, 2018). In these countries, the issue of "temporary" marriages has come to attention. In this context, **temporary marriages** are forced marriages of women for the purposes of sexual exploitation and commercial sex (Turner, 2013). While these brief mentions in the most recent TIP Reports are not reflective of the magnitude of the issue globally, they indicate some recognition of the problem. This is notable, as it is only in the last several years that this issue has been brought to light. For this reason, many of the numbers presented in this chapter are likely gross underestimates. Methodologies for collecting data on this topic are imperfect, to say the least, resulting in only a surface understanding of the magnitude of the practice (International Labour Office & Walk Free Foundation, 2017). The International Labour Office (ILO) and Walk Free Foundation's (2017) forced-labor data are considered one of the more methodologically sound data sources on forced marriage. The methodology to create their estimates can be examined in further detail in their full report. Their estimates of forced marriage will be presented in this chapter.

According to the ILO and Walk Free Foundation (2017), approximately 15.4 million people were living in forced marriages in 2016. As noted in Table 13.2, females and children were most likely to enter into forced marriages (3.5 women per 1,000 persons and 2.5 children per 1,000 persons, respectively). Based on the ILO and Walk Free Foundation estimates (2017), forced marriage was overwhelmingly more likely to occur in Africa than in other regions of the world (4.8 individuals per 1,000 persons in Africa, as compared to the Americas, Arab states, Asia and the Pacific, and Europe and Central Asia with 0.7, 1.1, 2.0, and 1.1 individuals experiencing forced marriage per 1,000, respectively).

Table 13.2 Estimates of Forced Marriage

Forced marriage

Number and prevalence of persons forced into marriage, by sex, age, and region

		Number (000s)	Prevalence (per 1,000 persons)
World		15,442	2.1
Sex	Male	2,442	0.6
	Female	13,000	3.5
Age Grouping	Adult	9,762	1.9
	Children	5,679	2.5
Region	Africa	5,820	4.8
	Americas	670	0.7
	Arab States	170	1.1
	Asia and the Pacific	8,440	2.0
	Europe and Central Asia	340	1.1

Source: ILO and Walk Free Foundation, 2017, p.43. Licensed under CC BY 3.0 IGO, https://creativecommons.org/licenses/by/3.0/igo/.

Figure 13.1 illustrates the percentage of individuals forced into marriage around the world. However, these calculations, as well as those in Table 13.2, may be misleading due to a lack of data in certain regions, such as the Arab and Central Asia regions. What researchers are confident in is the fact that most forced marriages are occurring in Africa and South Asia (Pandey, Karki, Murugan, & Mathur, 2017; Raj, 2010). While South Asia has the highest number of reported marriages, prevalence is highest in Sub-Saharan Africa (ILO & Walk Free Foundation, 2017).

The following sections explore the gender and age breakdowns for forced marriage.

Gender

According to ILO and Walk Free Foundation (2017) data, 84% of all victims of forced marriage are women and girls. Women and girls are impacted more by forced marriage than by any other form of forced labor, including commercial sexual exploitation. Girls are overwhelmingly more likely to be forced to marry as children than boys.

Although women and girls are the most typical victims of forced marriage, men and boys are certainly not immune (de Groot, Kuunyem, & Palermo, 2018; ILO & Walk Free Foundation, 2017; Strochlic, 2014). According to the United Nations Population Fund (UNFPA), 16% of those forced into marriage are male. Approximately 4% of boys in low- and middle-income countries marry before age 18, and less than 0.5% marry before the age of 15. The UNFPA reports that in 10 countries (Madagascar, Pakistan, the Central African Republic, the Lao People's Democratic Republic, Comoros, Honduras, the Marshall Islands, Nauru, Nepal, and Guatemala) the rate of child marriage of boys is greater than 10% (UNFPA, 2018).

Figure 13.1   Forced Marriage Across Regions

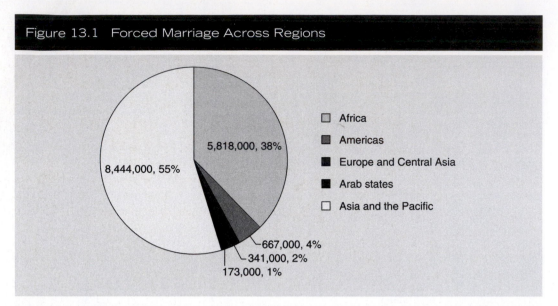

Source: ILO and Walk Free Foundation, 2017, p. 43. Licensed under CC BY 3.0 IGO, https://creativecommons.org/licenses/by/3.0/igo/.

Anecdotal evidence suggests, however, that official estimates may be inaccurate. Patriarchal cultures may prevent males forced or manipulated into marriages from coming forward, due to shame and embarrassment (e.g., Hill, 2010; S. Yu, 2017). This results in boys and men remaining in forced marriages, undetected, and sometimes being exposed to further exploitation, as highlighted by Shahid Sandhu's story (see Case Study: Slave Grooms on page 321).

Throughout this chapter, descriptions of forced and child marriage will focus on women and girls, as this is the population most impacted by the practice and the one most focused on in the existing research. However, don't take this to mean that men and boys are not also impacted by forced marriage. More attention must be given to this population in terms of research, identification, and prevention in order to have an informative discussion on the topic.

Age

Child marriage is an especially disturbing yet relatively common practice. The ILO and Walk Free Foundation (2017) estimate that 37% of those living in forced marriages are children, and of those, 44% are forced to marry before the age of 15. The United Nations Population Fund (n.d.) reports that, globally, one in five girls marries before reaching 18 years old. The rates are even higher in the developing world, with the UNFPA reporting 40% of girls being married prior to age 18 and 12% marrying prior to age 15. It is worth noting that child marriage may not always be considered forced marriage (in certain regions of the world) and thus may not be properly reflected in the data. Global estimates, such as those presented by the ILO and Walk Free Foundation (2017), are reliant on what is reported by survey respondents. If the respondent does not recognize child marriage as forced, the data will be impacted.

Research using the National Family Health Survey (nationally representative sample of women in India) indicates that 90% of women ages 20 to 24 reported being married before the age of 20. Nearly three-fourths of the sample were married before the age of 18 (Raj, 2010). Interestingly, the age of the child had a

Case Study

Slave Grooms

S. Yu (2017) published an exposé of a disturbing trend in Hong Kong. South Asian men are coming to Hong Kong, a wealthy, advanced city, tricked into arranged marriages. Once they arrive in Hong Kong, their brides' families force these men into exploitive labor. It is believed that most of these men arrive in Hong Kong from Pakistan and India as well as other South Asian countries such as Bangladesh and Nepal. Yu recounts Shahid Sandhu's experience:

> The nightmare Sandhu found himself living is a far cry from the charmed lifestyle the 34-year-old had imagined when he was approached by a matchmaker about marrying a Hong Kong–born Pakistani woman. Hearing about her wealthy family helped seal the deal for Sandhu and his impoverished parents, who are farmers in the Punjab region of Pakistan. Sandhu, who has a university degree in commerce, had a respectable job at a bank in Pakistan, but his salary was meagre and the prospect of a prosperous life in Hong Kong meant financial security for his parents. He married his bride in Pakistan, arriving in Hong Kong months later on a dependant visa.
>
> The post-wedding bliss vanished immediately. Sandhu's in-laws and wife locked away his passport and identity papers for "safe keeping"—something that is against the law—then informed him that he would be working overtime at a construction site six days a week to earn money for his bride and her entire family. Every night, and on his one day off each week, he would do the domestic work. Whenever Sandhu complained, verbal and physical abuse kept him in his place.
>
> "My in-laws were always bullying me. Although I am a university graduate, I was always called illiterate and a jungle man. Once I shouted back at them and they beat me. After that I was resigned to my fate and work," he said.
>
> Broken though he was, Sandhu did manage to reach out to Richard Aziz Butt, a sought-after immigration consultant in the South Asian community, having got his number from a work colleague. "I need to get out," Sandhu told Butt. However, Sandhu was not willing to go to the police. Like many other slave grooms, he feared deportation, repercussions from his in-laws and shame.
>
> "I would call him a slave groom," said Butt. "His marriage was arranged so that he could be brought here to work as a machine to earn money for the bride's family. All these things are elements of slavery," Butt said. "The [victims] are monitored 24 hours [by their tormentors]. These people will not talk [to the police] even if they are abused.
>
> "These men are from male-dominated [patriarchal] countries. If they say to someone that they were treated like slaves, people will laugh at them and call them cowards, useless and lazy. Therefore, they dare not say anything to anyone."
>
> A week ago, Sandhu was famished at the end of an 18-hour construction shift and decided to get some food. That angered his younger brother-in-law, who gives him just enough money for transport. He beat Sandhu for disobeying him.
>
> Sandhu's salary from construction goes into his bank account, but that is controlled by his brother-in-law and wife, who take all his money. "They only put some travel money on my Octopus card and every day she checks on her phone how much money I have on my card. And where I spent it," he said.
>
> His wife and in-laws threatened to kill him if he tried to escape. "Now I am trapped," he said. (Yu, 2017)

negative effect on the impact of the marriage. As children married younger (25% reported marrying at 14 to 15 years old), they experienced more spousal violence, less prenatal and postnatal care, and more child deaths, among other negative effects, compared to those who married closer to age 20 (Raj, 2010).

The remainder of the chapter will focus mostly on child marriage. Child marriage is not considered forced marriage by law in many places. While overlap exists between the causes of forced and child marriage, child marriage has received specific attention. The next several sections will aim to understand specific trends in child marriage, what it looks like around the globe, and how to remove cultural and structural barriers delegating girls to marry as children.

The Condemnation of Child Marriage

While there may be cultural support for the practice of child marriage, the evidence unequivocally shows the practice to be detrimental to children—physically, mentally, socially, and developmentally (e.g., Onagoruwa & Wodon, 2017; Turner, 2013). Further, there is little evidence of children happily and willingly entering into marriage. The marriage is typically arranged, forced, or at a minimum, occurs under great amounts of pressure on the child (Erulkar, 2013).

The United Nations condemns the practice of child marriage, labeling it a human rights and child rights violation (Nour, 2009). This belief is supported by nearly all countries, as indicated by ratification of both the **Convention on the Rights of the Child** and the **Convention on the Elimination of All Forms of Discrimination Against Women.** These two treaties are two of the most broadly endorsed human rights agreements, having been ratified by all but one country (UNFPA, n.d.).

If Condemnation Isn't Universal, Is Child Marriage So Wrong?

Unfortunately, country-level laws are not always consistent with international views. In many countries, child marriage is legal. This leads to the question: If child marriage is legal, is it forced? If it is so widely condoned in some regions of the world, is it truly wrong? Is it possible that the developed world is simply placing judgment on those less developed countries without a basis? The United Nations Population Fund fields questions like these regularly, so much so that the following question is listed in its frequently asked questions: "Is it insensitive to interfere with other countries' religious or cultural traditions around child marriage?" The UNFPA (2018) response speaks for itself:

> There are no major religious traditions that require child marriage. Yet child marriage persists, across many cultures and religions. But it would be wrong to say that child marriage warrants protection as a cultural or religious practice. Governments around the world have overwhelmingly, and independently, decided that child marriage is a grave violation of human rights.

> In places where child marriage persists, evidence about its harms are usually convincing to policymakers, community leaders, religious leaders and parents. In fact, there are many examples of cultural and religious leaders taking a strong stance against child marriage. But prohibitions themselves are not always sufficient; because child marriage is typically

the result of a lack of choices, and because it is viewed as the norm, families and communities also need alternatives.

There is evidence throughout the world of girls being abducted for the purposes of marriage (e.g., see Hodal, 2017, to learn more about bride trafficking to China, where a shortage of women is increasing the demand for international brides). Some argue that child marriage is used as a strategy to mask child exploitation (ECPAT International, 2014; Turner, 2013). Anti-Slavery International (a leading anti-slavery NGO) points out that the 1926 Slavery Convention, considered international law, defines slavery as "the status or condition of a person over whom any or all of the powers attaching to the right of ownership are exercised" (Turner, 2013, p. 16). If a child is forced to marry, forced to have children, and fully under the control of his or her spouse and spouse's family, does this equate to ownership? Also consider whether the child is unable to leave the marriage. Does the spouse and family, for all intents and purposes, own the child? Is this slavery?

The role of consent also plays into our definitions of slavery. It is a theme throughout this text. Without consent, the act of marriage is forced marriage. If a child is getting married, does he or she have the ability to consent? Should his or her parents? Further, if money is exchanged for a bride, as is often the case (think bride prices and dowries), does this make child marriage slavery?

Global Perspectives of Child Marriage

Child marriage is occurring all over the world. This next session will explore the context of the practice in different regions of the world. Following this global review, the general risk factors for and consequences of child marriage are reviewed.

Asia

South Asia has the highest number of child brides as compared to any other region in the world. Research coming out of Nepal helps us to understand the practice of child marriage in this region. Data from the 2011 Nepal Demographic and Health Survey, a nationally representative survey, indicates that a majority of women (approximately 80%) were married during their teen years (Pandey et al., 2017). While the average age at the time of marriage was 17 years old, nearly 35% were married by age 15. Pandey and colleagues (2017) noted specifically that the disempowerment of women in Nepal, namely through child marriage and a lack of education, was a major risk factor for child mortality.

Nepal sets the minimum legal age of marriage for men and women at 20 years old. Marriages can occur at age 18 with parental consent. However, enforcement is minimal, with many simply not registering their marriages (Pandey et al., 2017).

Nepal is not unlike other South Asian countries, a region where nearly half of all child marriages occur (Nour, 2009). Child marriage is condoned, and laws prohibiting the practice are ignored and unenforced. Cultural and social values seem to be the primary driver of child marriage in the region (Nour, 2009; Verma, Sinha, & Khanna, 2013). Families who believe premarital sex to be shameful are typically eager to marry their girls off before the opportunity for sex presents itself. Further, in Asian culture, wives are meant to be subservient and trainable. Young girls are believed to fit these expectations as opposed to older women (Pandey et al., 2017).

One specific group that may be able to impact the rates of child marriage in South Asia is priests. Pandey and colleagues (2017) report priests being involved in nearly all child marriages. Educating and training local priests on the dangers associated with this practice may be impactful in terms of reducing the numbers of child marriages in the region.

Africa

Sub-Saharan Africa continues to have the highest prevalence of child marriage in the world. Trends indicate that efforts to reduce the practice are slow (Petroni, Steinhaus, Fenn, Stoebenau, & Gregowski, 2017; Raj, Jackson, & Dunham, 2018; UNICEF, 2018a). In Sub-Saharan Africa, one in 10 girls is married before the age of 15. Four in 10 girls are married before the age of 18 (Erulkar, n.d.).

Focus On
India: Efforts to Reduce Child Marriage

The United Nations Children's Fund (2017b) reports 7% of girls in India marrying by age 15 and 27% of girls marrying by age 18. Girls Not Brides (n.d.c), a global partnership of more than 900 civil society organizations from over 95 countries committed to ending child marriage, reports that the rates of child marriage are as high as 69% in some regions of India. On the whole, India has more child brides than any other country in the world. Although the 27% estimate represents a significant decline from a decade ago, the cultural and structural barriers oppressing women make it unlikely that child marriage will end anytime soon. The patriarchal society, coupled with the economic burden of girls, gender discrimination, and stigma surrounding female sexuality, creates an environment prime for marrying off young daughters (Girls Not Brides, n.d.c).

More innovative programs including cash incentive programs (also known as conditional cash transfer programs), empowerment programs, and awareness-raising initiatives have also been impactful (Girls Not Brides, n.d.c). The first cash incentive program, **Apni Beti Apna Dhan (ABAD)**, was developed in 1994 by the Government of Haryana (Nanda, Datta, & Das, 2014). The program provided impoverished households and disadvantaged caste groups two monetary transfers. The first (500 Indian rupees) occurred within 15 days of delivery of an eligible girl. Within three months of the birth, should the parents enroll in the program, the government would purchase a savings bond worth ₹2,500 in the name of the daughter, redeemable on the daughter's 18th birthday, assuming she was not married.

The conceptual framework for the ABAD program and similar programs is illustrated in Figure 13.2.

Preliminary research on these programs has shown somewhat mixed results. While higher

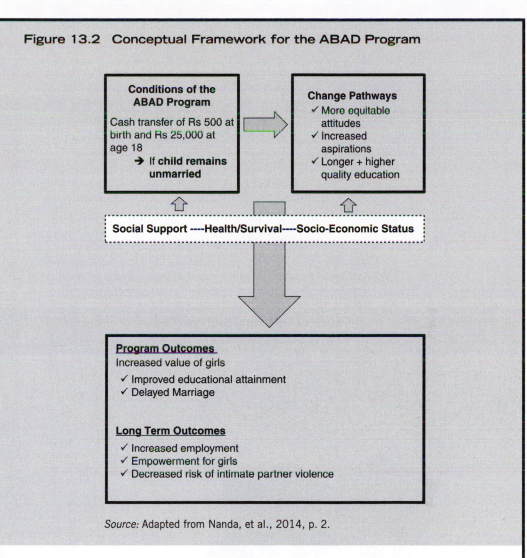

Figure 13.2 Conceptual Framework for the ABAD Program

Conditions of the ABAD Program

Cash transfer of Rs 500 at birth and Rs 25,000 at age 18

→ If **child remains unmarried**

Change Pathways

✓ More equitable attitudes
✓ Increased aspirations
✓ Longer + higher quality education

Social Support ----Health/Survival----Socio-Economic Status

Program Outcomes
Increased value of girls

✓ Improved educational attainment
✓ Delayed Marriage

Long Term Outcomes

✓ Increased employment
✓ Empowerment for girls
✓ Decreased risk of intimate partner violence

Source: Adapted from Nanda, et al., 2014, p. 2.

levels of educational attendance and attainment were observed, barriers to girls' education still occurred due to cultural views of the role of females (Khan, Hazra, Kant, & Ali, 2016; Nanda et al., 2014). Research has not shown these programs to have a positive impact on child marriage. In fact, some families appeared to be incentivized by the program to marry their daughters off as soon as they turned 18. Research indicates that girls involved in the program were more likely to be married at age 18 than girls not involved in the program. The money earned at age 18 was used to pay dowries and other marital expenses (Girls Not Brides, 2016). For programs like this to be more effective, they need to be implemented with other socially focused programs, empowering girls and shifting deeply embedded cultural views of women (Kalamar, Lee-Rife, & Hindin, 2016; Khan et al., 2016; Krishnan, Amarchand, Byass, Pandav, & Ng, 2014; Nanda et al., 2014; Nanda, Datta, Pradhan, Das, & Lamba, 2016).

Child marriage is a common practice in this region, to say the least. Research done by the Population Council found that, in this region:

- Early marriage is extremely common, virtually always arranged, and girls have little foreknowledge of their marriage or their husband. Of the girls surveyed 95% did not know their husband before marriage, and 85% were not told that they were going to be married.

- Marriage effectively forces girls into having unwanted sexual relations with a stranger.

- More than two-thirds of married girls report that they had not yet started menstruating when they had sex for the first time.

- Many of these marital unions are unstable, and 12% of girls in Amhara aged 10–19 are divorced.

- Girls experienced significant trauma during these transitions as well as social isolation and lack of support following marriage. (Erulkar, n.d.)

Figure 13.3 Prevalence of Child Marriage Before Age 18 in West and Central Africa

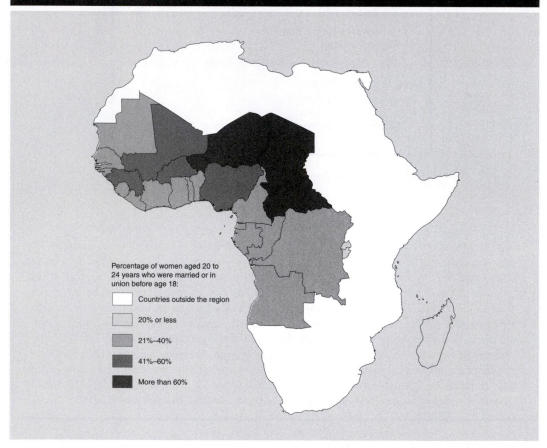

Percentage of women aged 20 to 24 years who were married or in union before age 18:

- Countries outside the region
- 20% or less
- 21%–40%
- 41%–60%
- More than 60%

Source: UNICEF (2017b).

These findings were confirmed in other studies showing that girls in this region are more likely to be married before age 18 than not. Further, the effects of these marriages are detrimental to the girls' physical and mental health, their education level, and their perceptions of control over their own lives (e.g., Atim, 2017; de Groot et al., 2018; Girls Not Brides, n.d.b). What becomes apparent when reviewing countries in this region is that child marriage is often restricted by law. However, the custom is condoned and widely practiced.

In 2017, the United Nations Children's Fund (UNICEF) provided an overview of West and Central Africa (UNICEF, 2017a). Girls from this region of Sub-Saharan Africa have the highest chance of marrying before age 18 of anywhere in the world. In fact, of all child brides in the area, one in three marries before age 18. Six of the 10 countries from this region have the highest prevalence of child marriage in the world. Additional detail highlighting the most egregious countries is depicted in Figure 13.3.

West and Central Africa have unique circumstances that will make reducing the practice of child marriage more challenging. The region has a higher prevalence of child marriage than other regions of the world combined with a slow rate of decline in such marriages. In fact, the trend predicts an increase in the number of girls by 2050. The current rate of decline, combined with the influx of girls in the region, has UNICEF (2017a) estimating a potential increase in the rate of child marriage without renewed accelerated efforts to end the practice. UNICEF (2017a) predicts that at the current rate of progress, it will take over 100 years to end child marriage in the region.

While Sub-Saharan Africa is still one of the more troublesome spots when it comes to child marriage, there is some encouraging progress in Ethiopia, Senegal, and North Africa (Petroni et al., 2017; UNICEF, 2018a).

A Comparison of Child Marriage Hot Spots

When one thinks of child marriage, Africa and Asia come to mind, for good reason. Data show the practice to be most concentrated in these regions. A recent qualitative study, however, indicates that the context surrounding child marriage looks different in South Asia and Sub-Saharan Africa. While in Asia, child marriage is believed to occur to prevent girls from engaging in premarital sex, it seems that in parts of Africa (specifically, Zambia, Uganda, and Kenya), sexual activity is less unusual among the 15- to 19-year-old demographic. There appears to be less of a relationship between age at time of first sexual intercourse and age at time of marriage. In the three African countries under review, the median age of first sexual activity was at least a year earlier than the median age at the time of marriage (Petroni et al., 2017). In these countries, there was a closer relationship between pregnancy and child marriage. Pregnant girls were more likely to marry and drop out of school. The study noted that access to contraception appeared to delay age at time of marriage by delaying pregnancy. Additional research also supports the belief that a lack of contraception results in higher fertility rates and a higher number of lifetime births among child brides (Onagoruwa & Wodon, 2017). Population growth could be slowed in overpopulated developing nations by delaying marriage and using contraception.

There are similarities in the drivers of child marriage on the two continents as well. As in South Asia, gender discrimination and limited access to education are the primary drivers of child marriage in Africa. When access to education (including health-related education) and means for women to support themselves become available, child marriage is likely to decline in both regions (Petroni et al., 2017).

The variations in the practice of child marriage within regions further highlight the possibility that the practice can be slowed, if not eliminated, even in the most vulnerable of communities. In other words, not every country in Africa has a high rate of child marriage. Therefore, it is possible to reduce the rates of other countries in the region.

Research on Ghana shows that there can be variations in the practice of child marriage even within countries. Better understanding of the patterns of child marriage, even down to the country level, can improve our ability to target hot spots with resources. UNICEF indicates that Ghana is one of five countries in West and Central Africa with the greatest decline in child marriage, show-

ing that progress is possible even in countries where the practice is common (UNICEF, 2017a).

In Ghana, around a quarter of girls report being married before age 18. Most children married before age 18 are female, but 2.3% of males also report being married as children. Child marriage is more common in the northern regions of Ghana and mostly impacts impoverished, undereducated girls in rural communities.

The child marriage trends in Ghana are interesting and demand further attention. While the rates of child marriages decreased in the central and southern regions from 2011 to 2014, rates increased in the northern regions (see Figure 13.4). These statistics highlight the increasingly divergent trends in child marriage within Ghana (de Groot et al., 2018).

Figure 13.4 Change in Rates of Child Marriage in Ghana, 2011 to 2014

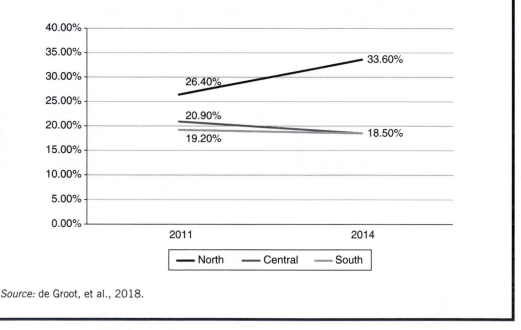

Source: de Groot, et al., 2018.

The Americas

Forced and child marriages don't happen in the United States, right? Wrong! In fact, children as young as 15 years old have been found in forced marriage situations in the U.S. The practice is common within many communities, including, but not limited to, Orthodox Jewish, Muslim, Mormon, Sikh, Asian, African, and Hmong (Unchained at Last, n.d.). Unchained at Last estimates that there are hundreds of thousands of women and girls in the U.S. living in forced marriages (Unchained at Last, n.d.).

More than six of every 1,000 children included in the American Community Survey for 2010–2014 had ever been married. Rates were highest in Hawaii, West Virginia, and North Dakota and lowest in Maine, Rhode Island, and Wyoming. Immigrant children were more likely to have been married than U.S.-born children, as were children of American Indian or Chinese descent (Koski & Heymann, 2018).

Forced marriage is expressly condemned by the United States. Child marriage is considered a form of child abuse. The legal age to marry in most states is 18 years old. Unfortunately, multiple exceptions allow for child marriage to essentially be legal in 25 states. These exceptions most often include parental consent and judicial approval. In some states, even with these exceptions, there is still a minimum age in place. However, in others, exceptions to the minimum age law allow children of any age to get married (Johnson, 2018; Tahirih Justice Center, 2018).

A recent assessment of U.S. state laws on the minimum age of marriage indicate that we have a ways to go in the U.S. to eradicate this practice (Tahirih Justice Center, 2018). Results of this assessment specify that while many states do have age floors set by statute, in most states, exceptions are permitted to allow children under the set age to marry. Regarding the state statutes on child marriage, results show:

- Only one state—Delaware—sets the age floor at the age of majority, age 18, with no exceptions.

- Twenty states do not set an age floor by statute, though some (e.g., Massachusetts) may set an age floor through case law.

- Five states require parties to be legal adults: Delaware (age 18 or older), Texas and Virginia (age 18 or older, or age 16–17 and emancipated by court order), and Kentucky and New York (age 18 or older, or age 17 and emancipated upon grant of petition for permission to marry).

- Six states require parties to be at least age 17: Florida, Kentucky, Nebraska, New York, Oregon, and Tennessee. Nebraska also requires parental consent until age 19, that state's age of majority.

- Fifteen states require parties to be at least age 16: Alabama, Arizona, Connecticut, Georgia, Illinois, Iowa, Minnesota, Montana, North Dakota, South Carolina, South Dakota, Texas, Vermont, Virginia, and Wisconsin. The District of Columbia also requires parties to be at least age 16.

- In 10 states, clerks alone—without judges—can issue marriage licenses for all minors: Florida, Maryland, Nebraska, North Dakota, Oregon, South Carolina, South Dakota, Tennessee, Vermont, and Wisconsin. The District of Columbia also does not involve judges.

- Only 13 states require all minors to go before a judge before they can marry: Alabama, California, Connecticut, Georgia, Iowa, Kentucky, Massachusetts, Minnesota, Montana, New Hampshire, New York, Texas, and Virginia. Some of these judicial processes are bare-bones, while others set several criteria for approval.

- In states with judicial approval requirements that apply at least to younger minors or under certain circumstances, only 17 states require judges to consider the minors' best interests.

- Statutes in a handful of states—Arkansas, Mississippi, New Hampshire, and Ohio—either set different age floors or set different conditions for approval based on a party's gender.

Figure 13.5 Minimum Age for Marriage in the United States

No Floor	Age 13	Age 14	Age 15	Age 16	Age 17	Age 18
• Arkansas • Arizona • California • Colorado • Delaware • Florida • Idaho • Kentucky • Louisiana • Maine • Massachusetts • Michigan • Mississippi • Missouri • Nevada • New Jersey • New Mexico • Ohio • Oklahoma • Pennsylvania • Rhode Island • Tennessee • Washington • Wyoming • West Virginia	• New Hampshire	• Alaska • North Carolina	• Hawaii • Indiana • Kansas • Maryland • Utah	• Alabama • Connecticut • District of Columbia • Georgia • Illinois • Iowa • Minnesota • Montana • North Dakota • South Carolina • South Dakota • Vermont • Wisconsin	• Nebraska • New York • Oregon	• Texas • Virginia

Data source: Johnson, 2018.

In 2011, the Tahirih Justice Center (TJC) published a report based on the findings of the first-ever national survey of forced marriage as a problem in the U.S. (Tahirih Justice Center, 2016). Nearly every state reported instances of forced marriage, mostly of girls under age 18. Victims came from 56 different countries of origin as well as multi-generational U.S.-born families. These disturbing results prompted TJC to implement the **Forced Marriage Initiative.** Working with other nonprofits and leaders committed to ending forced and child marriage, TJC has made strides to end the practice of forced and child marriage in the United States. Some of its achievements include:

- Creation of the **National Forced Marriage Working Group,** which includes more than 40 members from all over the country

- Creation of the **National Network to Prevent Forced Marriage,** which includes more than 7,000 advocates and allies to produce a coordinated national response

- Identification of six priority areas for legal and policy changes

- Conduction of a national awareness tour, gaining significant media attention

- Creation of a national dialogue on key issues surrounding forced and child marriage

- Conduction of high-level policy meetings at the White House

- Provision of technical assistance

- Seven states expressly permit pregnancy to lower the minimum marriage age: Arkansas, Indiana, Maryland, New Mexico, North Carolina, Ohio, and Oklahoma.

Figure 13.5 displays the minimum age of marriage by state, once again reflecting the long road the U.S. has to ending the practice of child marriage. It is important to note that one would need to examine each state individually to fully understand any exceptions permitted to allow for marriage outside the state statute.

Europe

Most readers won't associate Europe with child marriage. While the prevalence is certainly lower than in other regions of the world (recall Figure 13.1), child marriage is notably more common among certain marginalized subpopulations in Europe (BoÅnjak & Acton, 2013). The Roma are one such group. An estimated 5.2 million Roma reside in Central and Eastern Europe. Research on the group has repeatedly shown them to be marginalized and discriminated against, resulting in numerous disparities, including in health, education, and access to other resources (e.g., Cook, Wayne, Valentine, Lessios, & Yeh, 2013; Hotchkiss, Godha, Gage, & Cappa, 2016; McFadden et al., 2018; Tugwell, Patrick, Idzerda, Schrecker, & Adams, 2011). It goes without saying that this population is particularly vulnerable to many forms of exploitation, including child marriage.

Serbia offers an informative comparison of the general population of the country versus the Roma communities residing within it (e.g., BoÅnjak & Acton, 2013; Hotchkiss et al., 2016; Tugwell et al, 2011). Marrying at a young age is

Figure 13.6 Percentage of Women Ages 20 to 24 Who Report First Marrying Before Ages 15 and 18

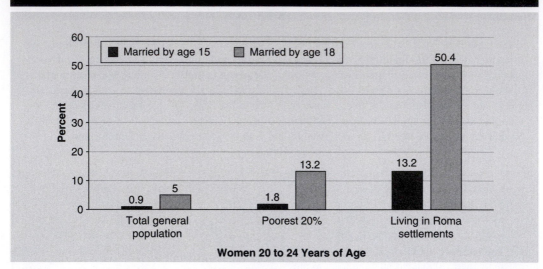

Source: Hotchkiss, et al., 2016, p. 10. Licensed under CC BY 4.0, https://creativecommons.org/licenses/by/4.0/.

characteristic of Roma communities and more common in those communities than in Serbia more generally (BoÅnjak & Acton, 2013). Women are still expected, in Roma culture, to take on the tradition roles of mother, wife, and homemaker. Virginity is an expectation at time of marriage. As in other regions of the world (e.g., Asia), this intense focus on virginity helps to explain the young age of marriage for Roma girls. According to the Statistical Office of the Republic of Serbia and UNICEF (2014), 57% and 17% of Roma girls were married before age 18 and age 15, respectively. As a comparison, only 7% of the general female population of Serbia was married before age 18 and less than 1% of the general population was married before age 15. At the time of data collection, the percentage of women age 15 to 19 who were married was 43% among the Roma in Serbia and 3.5% among the general female population.

The high rates of child marriage among the Roma can be explained by socioeconomic and geographical characteristics. For example, research on Roma child marriage shows a negative relationship between level of education and age at time of marriage (Hotchkiss et al., 2016). Using data among 20- to 24-year-old Roma females in Serbia, 22% with no formal education and 12.6% with primary education reported marrying at age 14. Roma living in rural locations were also more likely to marry young. However, additional factors, such as tradition, also play a role. As illustrated in Figure 13.6, in a comparison of women ages 20 to 24 years old in 2010, Roma individuals had higher rates of child marriage than even the poorest 20% of women in the general population (Hotchkiss et al., 2016).

What Fuels Child Marriage?

Several factors have proven to be risk factors for forced and child marriage (see Figure 13.7). Poverty and culture are two of the main reasons for forced and child marriages reviewed in this section (Atim, 2017; ILO & Walk Free Foundation, 2017; Nour, 2009). Additional reasons are also discussed below.

Figure 13.7 Vulnerabilities and Consequences of Child Marriage

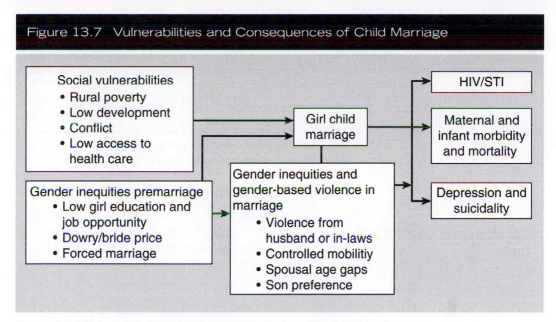

Source: Raj, 2010, p. 933. Reproduced with permission from BMJ Publishing Group Ltd.

Gender inequality interacts with all of the vulnerabilities described below. When resources are limited, girls are typically the ones most likely to lose out. For this reason, girls are typically less educated and receive less medical care (Raj, 2010). Girls are seen as burdens on their families.

Poverty

Poverty fuels child marriage, perhaps more than any other factor (ILO & Walk Free Foundation, 2017; Nour, 2009; Raj, 2010; Turner, 2013; UNFPA, n.d.; Verma et al., 2013). The regions with the highest rates of child marriage are characterized by high levels of poverty. In fact, the highest rates of child marriage are in countries where 75% of the population lives on $2 per day or less (Turner, 2013). Raising girls in these regions is often considered a financial burden. The marriage of a girl comes with a dowry to the girl's family. Even when families are not keen on selling their daughter into marriage, the burden of a girl is considered a poor investment, as girls will eventually get married and leave their families. Families that have the opportunity to match their girl with a more well-off family ensure the girl's financial security while also relieving the burden of providing for the girl themselves (ILO & Walk Free Foundation, 2017; Nour, 2009; UNFPA, n.d.). Oftentimes the new husband is considerably older than the girl. The expectation for a high dowry typically results in this large age difference (Nour, 2009).

Further supporting the link between poverty and the practice of child marriage, evidence shows that rates of child marriage decline as the economy of impoverished countries improves, as highlighted in Korea, Taiwan, and Thailand (Nour, 2009).

Culture, Religion, and Social Norms

Culture plays a large role in forced and child marriages. This is especially the case in developing nations where, due to cultural, religious, and normative beliefs, individuals may be forced to marry (ECPAT International, 2014; UNFPA, 2018).

Menstruation

The age at which a girl begins to menstruate has been shown to be linked to her age at time of marriage. This is primarily due to the belief that once a girl begins to menstruate, she is ready to enter her childbearing years (Atim, 2017; Mason et al., 2013; Tellier & Hytell, 2017).

Country-Level Conflict and Instability

There is also evidence of girls being kidnapped in countries with high conflict to marry fighters and of marriage being used to settle family disputes and/or debt (ILO & Walk Free Foundation, 2017; Raj, 2010). In developed countries, individuals may be forced to marry in order to secure another person's entry into the country.

Other Forms of Exploitation

Those forced into marriage, especially children, are at a higher risk of other forms of exploitation, including sexual labor and domestic servitude (ILO & Walk Free Foundation, 2017).

Research indicates that child marriage occurs in nearly all religions (Tahirih Justice Center, 2011). Family honor, the stigma of premarital sex, and societal pressure to have large families are additional norms that drive child marriage (Turner, 2013). In these situations, parents truly believe they are doing right by their children by marrying them off at an early age. More research must be conducted to better understand specific cultural traditions that encourage child marriage.

The Consequences of Child Marriage

Limited Education

Getting married as a child typically signals the end of a girl's education (Atim, 2017; Erulkar, 2013; Hotchkiss et al., 2016; Verma et al., 2013). Some may question the time order of the relationship between education and child marriage (Atim, 2017; Petroni et al., 2017; Onagoruwa & Wodon, 2017). While it seems entirely possible to see education and marriage as somewhat codependent, there is evidence of children staying in school until a proper match is made. Once a spouse is identified, the girl is removed from school (Atim, 2017). However, in those communities where the schooling of girls is not considered essential, marriage does not necessarily inhibit girls' educational opportunities. Their gender has already done that (Kalamar et al., 2016). Further, as girls progress through school, they may be required to board at their school due to the location being a long distance from home. Fears of premarital sex often result in parents not allowing their daughters to continue on in schools that require boarding (Atim, 2017).

A Call for Education and Empowerment

As with other forms of trafficking, the practice of child marriage can be understood in terms of supply and demand. One way to reduce the supply of young girls to be married off is to increase their level of education. Impressing upon parents in countries with high rates of child marriage the importance of educating girls will go a long way in lowering the rates of child marriage. Education has been shown not only to delay marriage and childbearing age but also to improve girls' understanding of the risks associated with sexual behaviors (Nour, 2009; Pandey et al., 2017; Turner, 2013; Verma et al., 2013).

Research in Senegal showed that increasing access to education for girls delayed marriage (Petroni et al., 2017). However, more than cultural shift must occur. There are structural barriers in place in many regions of the world that prevent girls (and boys, for that matter) from attending school. Secondary school completion is critical for girls. This education must be free. When resources are limited, girls are typically the first to miss out on education. Further barriers to education relate to girls' menstrual cycles. While it may seem common practice in more developed regions of the world, access to sanitary napkins, clean underwear, and private bathrooms in schools will allow girls to go to school regularly after puberty (Petroni et al., 2017). Girls who already are married and have children also require resources, including education, emotional and physical support, and postpartum medical care.

Finally, girls in developing nations feel a loss of control over their lives. Gender discrimination and cultural assumptions limit girls' abilities to do more than act as wife and mother. With proper education and awareness of reproductive health and contraception, girls can be empowered to demand control over their futures and potential (Abdullah, Qureshi, & Quayes, 2015).

Exposure to Domestic Violence

Girls are typically more likely to experience violence (physical, sexual, and psychological in nature) in their homes, at the hands of their husband or his family (Abdullah, Qureshi, & Quayes, 2015; Atim, 2017; Erulkar, 2013; Yount et al., 2016). Girls Not Brides (n.d.d) reports that girls who marry before age 15 are 50% more likely to experience physical or sexual violence at the hands of a partner. The organization estimates that ending child marriage would reduce intimate-partner violence by more than 10% in certain African nations.

Sexual Health

The concept of child marriage for the purposes of protection from the consequences of premarital sex was introduced earlier in this chapter. While this seems logical, research indicates the opposite to be true. Girls married as children have a higher risk of being infected with HIV/AIDS (Nour, 2009; UNFPA, n.d.). Evidence of this comes out of several African countries where the likelihood of HIV/AIDS infections is higher for married girls than single girls. The explanation of this phenomenon is that married girls have frequent intercourse with their older husbands in an effort to become pregnant quickly and frequently. Their older husbands have often had previous sexual partners and/or continue to have multiple partners while trying to impregnate their child wife. These husbands are more likely to pass on sexually transmitted diseases, including HIV/AIDS (Nour, 2009). Physical immaturity on the part of the young wife may also result in an increase in STDs due to an increased likelihood of hymenal, vaginal, and cervical lacerations (Nour, 2009).

Pregnancy

Pregnancy among married young girls also promotes health risks. Pregnant girls in malaria-ridden areas are more likely to be infected with malaria than girls who are not pregnant. The co-occurrence of malaria and HIV is especially problematic in areas including central Africa and the east coast of the continent (Nour,

Case Study

Aysheh

The story below, published by the United Nations Population Fund, recalls the story of a 15-year-old forced into marriage by her parents and the way she escaped and improved her life.

DOHUK, Iraq

Aysheh was only 15 years old when she and her family fled Qamishli, northeastern Syria, to find refuge in Iraq in 2014. They ended up in Domiz 1 camp in Iraq's Kurdistan region.

Built rapidly and with little planning to accommodate the large numbers of refugees fleeing northern Syria in 2012, Domiz 1 is now home to 5,608 Syrian refugee families. They contend with overcrowding, and live in shelters in need of upgrading. And livelihood opportunities are scarce.

The dearth of options in the camp compelled Aysheh's father to travel to Europe in search of better job prospects.

"I was devastated," Aysheh told UNFPA. "Not only had I lost my friends and home, but now my father was leaving. I remember consoling myself that day and saying that at least I was fortunate to continue my education. I had plans to obtain a degree and then, when we return home, to work on rebuilding my community and country."

But two years later, as the family continued to struggle, Aysheh's stepmother decided to take her out of school and marry her off to a 45-year-old man. As Aysheh's new husband, she hoped, he would support the family financially.

While the number of child marriages occurring among Syrian refugees in Iraq is not available, research conducted among Syrian refugees elsewhere suggests a link between the poverty and instability facing displaced families like Aysheh's, and rising pressure for girls to get married. Feeling helpless, Aysheh sought help from the UNFPA-supported Zahrat Al-Yasamin women's social centre in the camp.

After Aysheh told her story to the centre's social workers, they reached out to her stepmother and explained the risks of child marriage and the repercussions it would have for an adolescent girl. They convinced her to allow Aysheh to go back to school and complete her education.

"I would not be exaggerating if I said that was the best day of my life. I couldn't believe it. I had given up on the idea of having a normal life again," Aysheh recalled. "I felt my life had meaning again."

The Zahrat Al-Yasamin centre is one of 140 women's centres supported by UNFPA as part of its emergency response throughout Iraq. In the Domiz 1 camp, UNFPA also supports a reproductive health unit within the Domiz hospital, as well as a youth centre.

These facilities provide a spectrum of support and care for the camp's women and young people. Services includes family planning, maternal health care, as well as counselling, psychosocial support, awareness sessions, recreational activities and life-skills courses.

After the successful intervention that got her back to school, Aysheh became a regular at the women's centre, attending all the sessions on offer. When a part-time volunteering opportunity arose, she applied and was selected to shadow social workers, gaining the practical experience to take up the work herself.

"I feel content when I help women who are going through hard times," said Aysheh. "They talk to me; I listen and advise them."

"Besides," she added, "the sum I get in return helps me support my sibling and our family."

Now 19, Aysheh is determined to continue her work to help other girls and women. "My goal right now is to advocate against early and child marriages through the awareness sessions and activities conducted at the centre," she said. (Tayeb & Moussa, 2018)

2009). In addition to the health risks of the mother, the pregnancy and unborn child are also put at risk by these dangerous infections. Pregnant girls are less likely to respond to anti-malaria medications, and malaria has also been shown to increase the transmission of HIV between mother and child (Nour, 2009).

The physical immaturity of the young mother also creates grave risks during labor and delivery. Their small pelvises (remember, these girls can be as young as 10 to 15 years old) result in a greatly increased chance of obstetric fistula. Research has shown the risk of this occurring with this population to be approximately 88% (Nour, 2009). Complications during pregnancy and birth are the leading causes of death among older adolescents, according to the UNFPA (n.d.).

Focus On
Obstetric Fistulas

Obstetric fistula is a pregnancy-related disability most often occurring due to poor nutrition and pregnancy at a young age (EngenderHealth & UNFPA, 2003). Annually, 50,000 to 100,000 women experience this labor and delivery-related disability (World Health Organization, 2018). It occurs during obstructed labor when a cesarean section is not available. In these cases, women can be in labor upwards of five days. "If the obstruction is not interrupted in a timely manner, the prolonged pressure of the baby's head against the mother's pelvis cuts off the blood supply to the soft tissues surrounding her bladder, rectum, and vagina, leading to tissue necrosis" (EngenderHealth & UNFPA, 2003, p. 4). In these situations, the baby often dies and the mother is left with a fistula. The fistula results in continuous leakage of urine and/or incontinence, depending on the fistula's location.

The social consequences of obstetric fistula are potentially as serious as the physical. Rejection by one's spouse and community due to constant wetness and a humiliating stench divest the mother of her emotional and financial support system. The physical consequences of fistula go beyond incontinence and smell. Infections and kidney failure are common consequences of fistulas that can lead to premature death (EngenderHealth & UNFPA, 2003). Obstructed labor accounts for up to 6% of all maternal deaths (World Health Organization, 2018).

Poverty, stigma, and serious, if not fatal, health consequences leave women with obstetric fistulas in dire situations (World Health Organization, 2018). However, with proper treatment, fistulas are completely preventable and repairable. Prevention involves avoiding childbirth at a young age as well as receiving proper nutrition and obstetric care (EngenderHealth & UNFPA, 2003; World Health Organization, 2018). Increased awareness of these preventive strategies in areas where obstetric fistulas are most common, Africa and Asia, could greatly reduce this traumatizing and potentially deadly disability.

Awareness and resources should also be dedicated to the treatment of fistulas in these regions. The cost of fistula repair ranges from $100 to $400. This is certainly a lot of money for those suffering from a fistula, as women living in poverty are more likely to experience this disability. However, the repair, combined with proper postoperative care and successful reintegration into the community, can be very successful. Success rates associated with repair are typically around 90% and can allow future childbearing if so wanted (EngenderHealth & UNFPA, 2003; World Health Organization, 2018).

Obstetric fistulas are nearly unheard of in Europe and North America, where child marriage is far less common and the education rates of women are higher. With proper accessible obstetric and medical care, obstetric fistulas can be prevented and affordably treated.

The Edna Adan Hospital, located in Somaliland (a self-declared state recognized as an

(Continued)

autonomous region of Somalia) offers an inspiring example of extending affordable and accessible prenatal and postnatal care to mothers across the Horn of Africa. The hospital runs as a nonprofit charitable institution built by its namesake, a World Health Organization retiree who donated her pension and other assets to help women and

children in the region. The hospital offers surgical, medical, and pediatric services; diagnostic laboratories and emergency blood banks; and options for diagnosing and treating sexually transmitted diseases, including HIV/AIDS.

The hospital touts its achievements, including "basic and comprehensive obstetric care, human resource development, and the reduction of the rate of maternal and child mortality" (Edna Adan Hospital, n.d.). It reports receiving support from both governmental and nongovernmental organizations, volunteers, and individual donors. Fees to patients are minimal. Those who cannot pay are treated free of charge.

More information on this exemplary facility can be found at http://www.ednahospital.org/.

© Edna Adan Hospital

| **Photo 13.1 Edna Adan Hospital in Somaliland.**

Perhaps not surprisingly, there are also consequences to the newborn child in the case of a very young mother (Atim, 2017; S. H. Yu, Mason, Crum, Cappa, & Hotchkiss, 2016). The rate of infant mortality is higher when a mother is under the age of 18. Preterm deliveries and low birth rates are also more common (Atim, 2017; Nour, 2009). Even moving into toddlerhood, there is an increased risk of death among young children born to very young mothers. Research in Nepal indicated that women married by 15 years old were three times as likely to experience the death of a child before the child reached one month of age and twice as likely to have their child die before age five (Pandey et al., 2017). This is primarily due to a young mother's inability to provide good nutrition and a lack of physical and emotional maturity.

Mental Health

Child marriage takes a toll on the emotional well-being of children, resulting in feelings of hopelessness, suicidality, and loss of control (Atim, 2017; Gage, 2013; Nour, 2009). Child marriage takes children away from their families. Their husbands' families may live in different towns, states, or countries. Their cultural practices may be different. These factors can result in the child feeling depressed and isolated. The age differences between husband and wife can further exacerbate these feelings, as can the intense pressure to have and care for children (Nour, 2009). In some cases, polygamy is acceptable, causing further feelings of rejection and depression in the girl.

Girls entering into marriage often feel as if it limits their opportunities. Evidence of increased levels of suicidality was found among girls who had ever been married, promised marriage, or received marriage requests among a sample of 10- to 17-year-old Ethiopian girls (Gage, 2013). Those with marriage requests were twice as likely to attempt suicide as those without requests. Girls who grew up in communities that protected them from child marriage were less likely to be suicidal.

Responding to Forced and Child Marriage

Responding to child marriage, and more broadly, forced marriage, requires a collaborative effort. Governments, NGOs, and communities must work together to eradicate this practice (Atim, 2017; ECPAT International, 2014; Sharpe & Wright, 2016; UNFPA, n.d.; UNICEF, 2017a; Verma et al., 2013). Fortunately, awareness of the detrimental effects of this practice are growing, resulting in an increase in efforts around the world to end it (Petroni et al., 2017; UNICEF, 2018a).

International Response

An immediate international response could be the implementation of country-level laws raising the minimum age of marriage to 18 years old, without exception (Girls Not Brides, n.d.a; Inter-Parliamentary Union & World Health Organization, 2016; UNFPA, n.d.). Doing so would be a powerful first step toward ending the practice of child marriage. It would not be sufficient by any means, but a start nonetheless. Several international organizations are working toward this goal as well as other goals associated with ending child marriage.

The UNFPA (n.d.) is the United Nations reproductive health and rights agency, formally named the United Nations Population Fund. Much of their research has been cited through this chapter. One of their primary purposes is to end child marriage around the world. They do this through "evidence-based, girl-centered investments that empower girls with the information, skills and services they need to be healthy, educated and safe, helping them make a successful transition into adulthood" (UNFPA, n.d., para. 3). The organization also supports married girls by providing family planning and maternal health.

The UNFPA works with governments, NGOs, and other organizations at all levels to support the protection of girls and promote their access to opportunity. One example of their work is their collaboration with UNICEF to design the **UNFPA-UNICEF Global Programme to Accelerate Action to End Child Marriage.** The program began in 2016 to support married and unmarried girls in 12 countries across Africa, Asia, and the Middle East. The program targets child marriage from multiple angles, including increased access to education and health care for girls, education for parents and communities on the dangers of child marriage, economic incentives to families, and advocacy for the creation and enforcement of laws against child marriage (Sharpe & Wright, 2016).

UNICEF, also focused on the global issue of child marriage, promotes a similar message. They cite four specific strategies that must be implemented to end child marriage: (1) empowering girls, (2) changing attitudes and behaviors among families and communities, (3) providing services to girls at risk of becoming child brides as well as those already married, and (4) implementing and enforcing laws that protect child from child marriage (UNICEF, 2017a).

NGOs also play an important role in combating child marriage. As of 2016, 1,861 nongovernmental organizations (NGOs) were identified as working to combat human trafficking across 168 countries (Limoncelli, 2016). Seventy percent of these organizations focused on sex trafficking. Over half of those ($n = 702$) focused on particular issues related to child sex trafficking, including child marriage. This specific focus was especially found in India and some Sub-Saharan African countries. Focus on Reducing Child Marriage in Ethiopia: A Promising Intervention (see page 340) powerfully illustrates the contributions NGOs can make.

Berhane Hewan. It means "Light for Eve" in Amharic (Erulkar, 2013). The program, supported by the Population Council, focuses on preventing the marriage of young girls in Ethiopia, specifically girls under 15 years old. Its focus is on education. To keep girls unmarried and in school, the program provides school supplies and a goat or sheep to the family. The animal is given to the family only if their daughter remains unmarried and in school for two years (Erulkar, n.d.). It also educates communities on the consequences of child marriage and attempts to change attitudes at a community level. An evaluation of the program showed that after two years of implementation, girls in the program were less likely to be married and more likely to be in school as compared to a control group (Erulkar, n.d.; Erulkar & Muthengi, 2009). Girls in the program were also more likely to be using family-planning methods than were married girls in a control site. The program, one of the more rigorously evaluated programs of its kind, focuses on directly engaging the girl, her family, and her community. The tri-pronged approach seems to be especially effective.

To better assess which part of the program was most effective, the Population Council expanded the program to additional locations, including Burkina Faso and Tanzania. Program evaluation focused on the following components:

- Informing communities about the dangers of child marriage using community meetings and the engagement of religious leaders.

- Supporting girls' education with cost-effective efforts, such as providing girls with school supplies or uniforms, making it easier for families to send girls to school.

- Providing conditional economic incentives for families for keeping girls unmarried. For example, girls received chickens or a goat if they remained unmarried and in school for the two-year duration of the project.

- Combining all of these approaches. (Erulkar, n.d., para. 10)

Findings in Ethiopia included the following:

- In communities where girls were offered educational support, girls aged 12–14 were 94% less likely to be married at endline than were girls in that age range at baseline.

- In communities where girls were offered two chickens for every year they remained unmarried and in school, girls aged 15–17 were half as likely to be married at endline than were girls in that age range at baseline.

- In communities that were engaged in conversations about the value of educating girls and the harms of child marriage, girls aged 12–14 were two-thirds less likely to be married at endline than were girls in that age range at baseline.

- In communities where all the strategies were employed, girls aged 15–17 were two-thirds less likely to be married at endline than were girls in that age range at baseline. (Erulkar, n.d., para. 11)

The results in Tanzania were similar; however, the effect of interventions to keep girls ages 12 to 14 unmarried and in school did not reach significance. When 12–14- and 15–17-years-olds experienced all three interventions (educational support, economic incentives, and community engagement), positive effects on child marriage were evident.

Cost-effectiveness was also assessed as part of the evaluation of the Berhane Hewan program. As indicated in Table 13.3, the cost (per girl per year) was not substantial, in terms of U.S. dollars.

Data on program effectiveness is still being collected in Burkina Faso.

Berhane Hewan has undergone fairly rigorous evaluation (as compared to other programs). Its recommendations, listed below, could prove

Table 13.3 Berhane Hewan: Cost per Girl by Intervention

Intervention	Ethiopia	Tanzania
School supplies	$17	$22
Community conversations	$30	$11
Conditional economic incentives	$32 (two chickens)	$107 (one goat)
Full model	$44	$117

beneficial in reducing child marriage in Sub-Saharan Africa and potentially beyond:

- Recognize the economic elements of child marriage
- Invest in the tough areas (child marriage hotspots)
- Tailor programs by age and gender
- Avoid duplicating efforts (most regions with high levels of child marriage are receiving developmental support. Efforts must be made to use resources efficiently and not duplicate efforts). (Erulkar, n.d., para. 17)

Source: Erulkar, 2018.

Predicting the Future of Child Marriage

The UN has set a goal to end all practices of child, early, and forced marriage by 2030 as well as all other forms of violence against women, including trafficking and exploitation (UNICEF, 2018a; United Nations Entity for Gender Equality and the Empowerment of Women, n.d.). Reaching this goal has proved to be a challenge.

Forced marriage is similar to other forms of human trafficking. Similar vulnerabilities, including poverty, gender discrimination, and unstable governments (resulting in violence), drive individuals into arrangements that are ultimately forced marriages. Child marriage is the result of the same vulnerabilities. But the consequences of this practice are especially damaging and long term. Encouraging data from the UNFPA (n.d.) and UNICEF (2018a) indicate that child marriage appears to be on the decline. In 2000, one in three women ages 20 to 24 reported having been married as a child. Today that number is one in five (UNFPA, n.d.; UNICEF, 2018a). Much of this success comes from targeted efforts to reduce child marriage, as indicated in India (UNICEF, 2018a).

As depicted in Figure 13.8, the trend indicates a decline in child marriage worldwide. Just 10 years ago, nearly 50% of women were married before age 18. Today that number is down to 30%. It is anticipated that the percentage will decline even more by 2030—to around 15% (UNICEF, 2018). Unfortunately, while South Asia is making strides, the practice seems to be making less progress in parts of Africa. As noted in Figure 13.8, South Asia had the most progress to make, but the lag in Africa is concerning. Take for example, Eastern and Southern Africa. Twenty-five years ago, approximately 45% of girls reported being married before the age of 18. The projected percentage for that region in 2030 is still more than 25%. This slow progress, combined with a near lack of progress in Latin America and the Caribbean, result in an unlikely chance of meeting the goal to eliminate this practice by 2030.

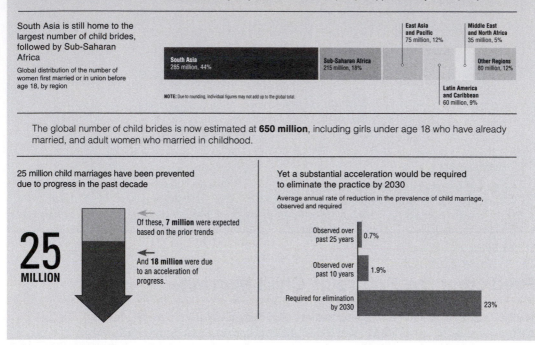

Figure 13.8 Evidence of a Decline in Child Marriage

The practice of child marriage has continued to decline around the world. During the past decade, the proportion of young women who were married as children **decreased by 15 per cent**, from 1 in 4 (25%) to approximately 1 in 5 (21%).

South Asia is still home to the largest number of child brides, followed by Sub-Saharan Africa

Global distribution of the number of women first married or in union before age 18, by region

South Asia 285 million, 44%

Sub-Saharan Africa 215 million, 18%

East Asia and Pacific 75 million, 12%

Middle East and North Africa 35 million, 5%

Other Regions 80 million, 12%

Latin America and Caribbean 60 million, 9%

NOTE: Due to rounding, individual figures may not add up to the global total.

The global number of child brides is now estimated at **650 million**, including girls under age 18 who have already married, and adult women who married in childhood.

25 million child marriages have been prevented due to progress in the past decade

25 MILLION

Of these, **7 million** were expected based on the prior trends

And **18 million** were due to an acceleration of progress.

Yet a substantial acceleration would be required to eliminate the practice by 2030

Average annual rate of reduction in the prevalence of child marriage, observed and required

Observed over past 25 years 0.7%

Observed over past 10 years 1.9%

Required for elimination by 2030 23%

Source: UNICEF, 2018, p. 2.

In fact, unless dramatic actions are taken to better understand and eradicate the practice of child marriage (as noted in Figure 13.8, and more in depth in Figure 13.9), there is no reason to expect the practice to end. According to some more dismal views, it may likely become more common, especially in developing countries (Erulkar, 2013; World Health Organization, 2013). Take, for example, the trend reported by UNICEF (2018) indicating an increase in child marriage in Sub-Saharan Africa. While 25 years ago the proportion of girls being married before age 18 was one in seven, the proportion is now closer to one in three. The World Health Organization estimates that if efforts aren't made to reduce the number of child marriages worldwide, the numbers will likely reach 39,000 children daily forced into marriage (World Health Organization, 2013). The UNFPA (n.d.) expects that, without action, the numbers will increase by 2030 rather than decrease. UNICEF (2018) reports that no region in the world is on track to meet the 2030 deadline. Progress would need to be 12 times faster than the rate over the past 10 years, which is sadly unlikely.

What does this action look like? The UNFPA (2018) recommends focusing on laws—both creation and enforcement are critical. In the case of forced marriage, there is no law to support this practice. But without enforcement of existing law,

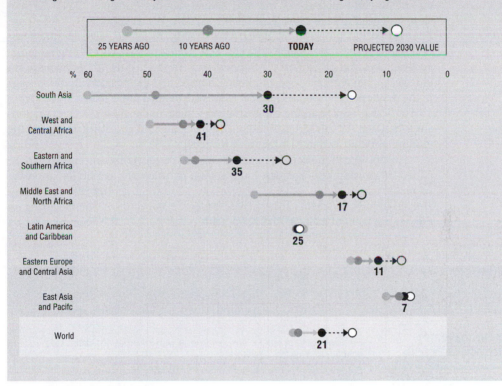

Figure 13.9 Projections of Child Marriage in 2030

Despite a marked reduction in child marriage, especially in South Asia, no region is on track to eliminate the practice by 2030
Percentage of women aged 20–24 years who were first married or in union before age 18, by region

25 YEARS AGO   10 YEARS AGO   **TODAY**   PROJECTED 2030 VALUE

% 60   50   40   30   20   10   0

South Asia — 30
West and Central Africa — 41
Eastern and Southern Africa — 35
Middle East and North Africa — 17
Latin America and Caribbean — 25
Eastern Europe and Central Asia — 11
East Asia and Pacifc — 7
World — 21

Source: UNICEF, 2018, p. 3.

there is little to prevent it. For child marriage, laws exist that permit the marriage of children. The legal age of marriage should be 18 years old in every country around the world (Inter-Parliamentary Union & World Health Organization, 2016; UNFPA, 2018).

Legislation, even enforced legislation, would not by itself eliminate the practice of child marriage. Efforts must be made to provide girls with more access to education, health information, and life skills training. Access to these resources acts as a protective factor against child marriage (UNFPA, 2018). Additionally, already-married girls should not be overlooked. Reproductive health services, family planning, and access to education can all improve the chances of the married child remaining healthy, delaying pregnancies, and improving her life in general. Providing increased opportunities to girls, married and unmarried, will result in healthier families, less gender discrimination, and stronger societies and economies (UNFPA, 2018).

Community engagement is also critical. As in countries with human trafficking laws, without cultural shifts, laws will not be sufficient to end the practice of child marriage.

As insinuated above, even with a focus on at-risk girls and the communities they live in, combined with the enforcement of laws, the world is unlikely to see an end to child marriage in the next several decades (Greene, 2014). Current strategies need to be reenvisioned (UNFPA, 2018; Verma et al., 2013). The Ford Foundation has proposed an investment strategy meant to eradicate the practice of child marriage (Greene, 2014). Their strategy, based on existing research, encompasses four categories: (1) Support and empower girls, (2) promote norm change, (3) advocate for legal and policy change, and (4) position child marriage in the development agenda. These categories are defined more succinctly in Figure 13.10. Those implementing these strategies must understand the interrelationships between the categories. Additionally, investment in girls must always be the guiding principle within each category (Greene, 2014).

Specific attention should be given to the last category, making child marriage a focus in development agendas. Ending child marriage is a step in the improvement of human rights, poverty eradication, abolishing gender discrimination, and social justice (Greene, 2014). These issues are all priorities when focusing on the development of nations. Another notable point made by the Ford Foundation

Figure 13.10 Ford Foundation Investment Framework for Ending Child Marriage

A. SUPPORT AND EMPOWER GIRLS
- Empower girls at risk for early marriage with information, skills, safe spaces, and support networks
- Enhance girls' access to school and the quality of that education
- Offer economic support and incentives for girls and families to delay
- Mitigate impact on married girls

B. PROMOTE NORM CHANGE
- Focus on girls and gatekeepers
- Educate and mobilize parents of potential brides and grooms
- Engage men and boys, including fathers and religious leaders

C. ADVOCATE FOR LEGAL AND POLICY CHANGE
- Foster an enabling legal and policy framework (human rights approach)
- Conduct segmentation analysis of marriage patterns within high-prevalence countries

D. POSITION CM IN DEVELOPMENT AGENDA
- Demonstrate the macroeconomic impact of child marriage
- Situate child marriage (CM) in emerging post-2015 development

Source: Green, 2014, p. 8. Licensed under CC BY 4.0, https://creativecommons.org/licenses/by/4.0/.

was to challenge the "cultural defense" argument for child marriage. No other issue is defended on a cultural basis as intently as child marriage. However, culture is no justification for a practice so convincingly proven by research to be harmful.

Conclusion

Child marriage is occurring all over the world, in underdeveloped and developed countries. The causes of child marriage are similar to the causes of other forms of trafficking and exploitation. Like those other forms, legislative, cultural, and structural initiatives must all be put in place to eradicate the practice. Evidence shows that culture does not justify child marriage. Child marriage is detrimental and damaging to children. The good news is that it is possible to end child marriage. The bad news is that how long it will take remains an unanswered question.

KEY WORDS

Anti-Slavery International 316
Apni Beti Apna Dhan (ABAD) 324
arranged marriage 317
Berhane Hewan 340
child marriage 317
Convention on the Elimination of All Forms of Discrimination Against Women 322

Convention on the Rights of the Child 322
forced marriage 317
Forced Marriage Initiative 331
National Forced Marriage Working Group 331
National Network to Prevent Forced Marriage 331

obstetric fistula 337
temporary marriage 318
UNFPA-UNICEF Global Programme to Accelerate Action to End Child Marriage 339
wahayu 316

DISCUSSION QUESTIONS

1. What are the key differences between child marriage, forced marriage, and arranged marriage? How does temporary marriage play a part in the aforementioned types of marriages?

2. List three social factors that create situations in which it is in a family's best interest to marry off daughters. Explain how a family may rationalize social factors in carrying out this practice.

3. Compare and contrast some of the differences regarding child marriages in Africa and Asia. What are the driving factors of child marriages in each region?

4. What negative consequences do women exposed to child marriage experience? Which negative consequence do you believe is most concerning?

5. Education is a proven way to reduce the occurrence of child marriage. Using information found in this chapter as well as the resources listed below, describe the relationship between education and child marriage and provide examples of how education reduces the occurrence of child marriage.

RESOURCES

- Anti-Slavery Organization: https://www .antislavery.org/

- Edna Hospital: http://www.ednahospital .org/

- Girls Not Brides: https://www .girlsnotbrides.org/

- Trafficking in Persons Reports: https:// www.state.gov/bureaus-offices/under- secretary-for-civilian-security-democracy- and-human-rights/office-to-monitor-and- combat-trafficking-in-persons/

- United Nations Population Fund (UNFPA): https://www.unfpa.org/; https://www.unfpa .org/data/dashboard/adolescent-youth; https://www.unfpa.org/child-marriage- frequently-asked-questions#are%20 boys%20ever%20involved%20in%20 child%20marriages

- Unchained at Last: http://www .unchainedatlast.org/

- World Health Organization on child marriage: http://www.who.int/ mediacentre/news/releases/2013/child_ marriage_20130307/en/

Conclusion

The root causes of the crime are deeper than any one of its facets and relate to larger systemic conditions such as poverty, forced migration, racism, and discrimination, among many others. Understanding human trafficking in its local context is critical to developing a meaningful response.

—2018 Trafficking in Persons Report
(U.S. Department of State, 2018)

Trafficking is a rapidly growing criminal enterprise that confers substantial profits to traffickers. Contrary to misconceptions about trafficking, it is not an isolated act that happens among a few people on the outskirts of society, and there is no uniform profile of a trafficker or a victim. Anti-trafficking approaches will be most effective if multiple sectors are engaged and coordinated in their responses.

In this book, we reviewed human trafficking in its various forms. In this concluding chapter we will review common themes from across the previous chapters. We will then discuss emerging issues in the human trafficking field and innovative solutions to combat trafficking.

Overview

Trafficking victims may be exploited into performing sexual acts, working without pay, or removing an organ. Children are additionally exploited through forced marriages or being forced to become soldiers. In some cases, traffickers exploit victims in multiple ways. The case studies we reviewed in each chapter show that each instance of trafficking can vary drastically from another. There are, however, some commonalities across types of trafficking, including (1) defining elements, (2) root causes, (3) research quality, (4) barriers to identifying traffickers and victims, and (5) resources and restoration available for victims.

Challenge Yourself 14.1

Write a definition of human trafficking. How does this compare to the one you wrote while reading Chapter 2?

Defining Elements

In Chapter 1, we reviewed definitions of human trafficking, which we came to understand as

> the recruitment, transportation, transfer, harboring or receipt of persons, by means of the threat or use of force or other forms of coercion, of abduction, of fraud, of deception, of the abuse of power or of a position of vulnerability or of the giving or receiving of payments or benefits to achieve the consent of a person having control over another person, for the purpose of exploitation. Exploitation shall include, at a minimum, the exploitation of the prostitution of others or other forms of sexual exploitation, forced labor or services, slavery or practices similar to slavery, servitude or the removal of organs. (United Nations General Assembly, 2000c)

By now, you may more easily recognize this definition in the form of the action, means, and purpose model (see Figure 2.3 in Chapter 2). At least one element in each category (action, means, and purpose) is present in cases of human trafficking.

Within each section, we then focused on the specific definitions and typologies of trafficking. Often, the lines are blurry when it comes to identifying the type of trafficking or whether something constitutes trafficking at all. Consider prostitution, sexual exploitation, and child sexual exploitation. Table 6.2 in Chapter 6 showed us the differences between prostitution and sex trafficking. As an additional reminder, children are considered victims of sex trafficking if they are involved in any form of commercial sex, due to their age.

Consider labor trafficking. How do you differentiate between unfair labor practices and forced labor? As we reviewed in Chapter 9, unfair civil labor practices are situations where an employer financially gains from participating in

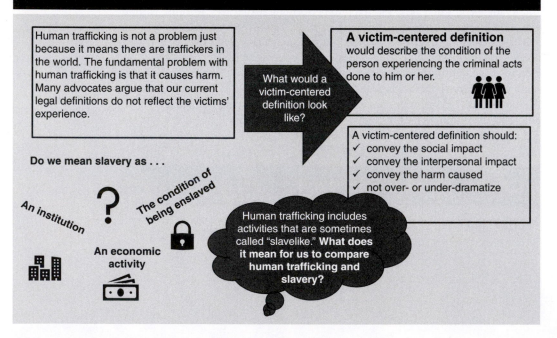

Figure 14.1 Considerations for a Victim-Centered Definition of Human Trafficking

Write your own victim-centered definition of one type of human trafficking reviewed in this book.

How does this definition vary from the definition you wrote before (in Chapter 2 or earlier in this chapter)?

the illegal treatment of employees. While unfair labor practices are criminal acts, without the presence of force, fraud, or coercion, unfair labor practices are not a form of labor trafficking.

Definitions also vary by country or locality due to differences in legal policies related to trafficking. Variations in definitions by country are a contributing barrier to broad anti-trafficking efforts. Victims' rights advocates argue that the standard definition of human trafficking centers too much around criminal justice. One issue with a criminal justice–focused definition is that it implies that the problem with human trafficking is that there are "criminals" in society getting away with breaking the law. Advocates of a victim-centered definition argue that the real problem with human trafficking is the harm it causes people, families, and societies, as described in Figure 14.1. Further, a victim-centered definition would allow for a common definition of trafficking across regions.

Root Causes

As reviewed in Chapter 3, promising theoretical models (1) take an integrated approach to understanding risk factors for trafficking across ecological levels and (2) consider the role of traffickers as well as victims.

One common vulnerability that traffickers exploit is victims' desire to migrate. Often victims want to migrate because of the push and pull factors listed in Figure 3.1 in Chapter 3, including poverty, lack of human rights, lack of economic opportunity, conflict, instability, civil unrest, war, or natural disasters. Traffickers take advantage of victims, offering to facilitate their move only to employ coercive tactics once they arrive in a new country or region.

Recall that while poverty is a contributing risk factor to trafficking, it is not the sole determining risk factor. Traffickers' ultimate goal is to make money, and it is easiest to exploit the most vulnerable individuals, including those living in extreme poverty. This does not mean that traffickers and victims all hail from impoverished backgrounds. Consider, for example, the role of medical professionals in organ trafficking networks, or the role government officials can play in forced domestic servitude.

Social factors in some areas may also increase vulnerability to trafficking. For example, the devaluation of women, girls, gender-nonconforming individuals, and LGBTQ populations increases their vulnerability to trafficking.

Given these root causes, trafficking prevention strategies tend to focus on:

- Reducing vulnerability through social and economic empowerment

- Public awareness campaigns and education

- Discouraging use of the services of trafficked persons

- Preventing corruption in government officials

- Border control

Navigate to one of the following sites:

> https://migrationdataportal.org/themes/
> human-trafficking

> http://www.humantraffickingdata.org/

1. What is one limitation of the data available on this site? What is one positive attribute of the data available?

2. Select a country you are interested in other than the country where you live. Are you able to find a prevalence estimate for human trafficking in that country? What is one country-level factor that may explain why you were or were not able to find data for that country?

Research

A third common thread throughout these chapters is that we simply don't have the level or quality of data that we would like for any form of trafficking. For example, we don't know the true extent of trafficking globally. It is hard to collect data and study trafficking because:

- Traffickers exploit the most vulnerable populations

- Traffickers operate covertly

- Victims are isolated (geographically, linguistically, and/or culturally)

- Victims are stigmatized

- Traffickers may operate across jurisdictional lines

- Definitions around human trafficking are inconsistent

- Barriers exist to sharing information about traffickers across jurisdictional lines

Despite these roadblocks to research on trafficking, there are promising innovations in human trafficking research on the horizon. Financial analytics, big data, new data collection efforts, and complex computer programming offer creative ways to identify traffickers and victims.

Identifying Traffickers

A fourth common theme discussed throughout each chapter is that it is incredibly difficult to identify traffickers. One reason for this is that anti-trafficking is a somewhat new field relative to intimate-partner violence, sexual assault, and traditional organized crime. Official laws outlawing trafficking are less than two decades old. Law enforcement providers are not thoroughly trained on all forms of trafficking or on how to identify victims and traffickers. Even when law enforcement providers are trained, if traffickers leave their jurisdiction, it can be hard to continue pursuing their case. Lawyers also have limited information about trafficking. Most trafficking cases in the U.S. are prosecuted at the federal level because of limited capacity at local levels.

Fortunately, human trafficking awareness has increased in the past two decades. This is due in large part to a few factors:

- The passage of the UN trafficking in persons protocol, the Trafficking Victims Protection Act, and other national anti-trafficking legislation

- Broad public awareness campaigns

- Media coverage of high-profile instances of trafficking

- The use of research to generate a deeper understanding of the scope of the problem

The general public is still unlikely to be able to spot the signs of trafficking in an individual. Fortunately, many more direct service providers are being trained to do just this: Social workers, medical professionals, domestic violence service providers, and others have all moved toward trauma-informed care models and specific trainings on spotting trafficking in persons. Most jurisdictions still need a continuity-of-care system that allows these professionals to safely transition victims into safe, secure, care away from their traffickers.

It is hard to identify traffickers, in part because there is no single typology of a trafficker. Some traffickers operate independently, and others are part of organized networks, as is typically the case in organ trafficking. Traffickers, or members of trafficking networks, can be government officials, medical personnel, friendly strangers, farmers, teachers, caregivers, mothers, fathers, or hotel managers, and may be victims themselves. Traffickers are motivated by making profits, even when it comes at human expense. Traffickers are successful because there is a demand for what they are selling. Whether it is produce, clothes, sex, organs, or ideology, there are people willing to buy it.

Where Do We Go From Here?

Many more organizations are beginning to take a public health approach to human trafficking. Public health approaches focus on addressing the root causes of an issue and implementing solutions that prevent future incidences of trafficking, identifying trafficking where it exists, and reducing the harm caused when trafficking has already happened. A public health approach to human trafficking has several advantages. First, it informs which actors can and should be involved in anti-trafficking efforts. A public health approach extends beyond law enforcement and direct service providers and looks for individuals who can prevent trafficking in all sectors. It is key to the public health approach in that survivors are engaged and inform anti-trafficking efforts.

A public health approach also informs how we tackle human trafficking by focusing on available research and addressing risk factors. Public health approaches do not assume that one intervention strategy will work with all populations. Research identifies which populations are the most vulnerable, and then strategies are developed with each population in mind. A good analogy for human trafficking is cancer. There is not just one type of cancer, and each type of cancer has unique risk factors. Further, some individuals have an elevated risk for certain types of cancer because of their behaviors, their environment, and family risk factors. No medical professional would suggest the same approach to preventing or treating different types of cancer or even the same cancer in different individuals. Thus, we must recognize that trafficking occurs in the context of other forms of violence and trauma and apply approaches that are culturally sensitive and tailored to victims' needs.

Finally, a public health approach focuses on informing policy and practice. In public health, the work isn't finished after victims and traffickers are identified and vulnerable populations are educated. A public health approach focuses on researching the intervention, determining whether it works and how it works, and using that information to develop programs and policies that work on a broader level.

Case Study

"Now I Dare to Speak": SYSTERM Students Reflect on the Project's Impact

There is a certain symphony to the way the Development and Education Programme for Daughters and Communities Centre (DEPDC) hums to life most mornings: the archetypal rooster does indeed crow one yard over; children scamper up and down the stairs squealing and shouting (usually accompanied by an exasperated call from a teacher nearby); birds chirp outside in the pasture as they try to pry their way into the rice field; the same Thai playlist makes its usual circuit through the kids' favorite songs. It is a rhythm, something one comes to memorize, proof of the vivacity, energy, and joy that still courses through DEPDC's veins.

On this particular morning, a new and significant voice crescendoed into DEPDC's harmony: that of a young girl from Shan State, Myanmar, who stood in front of her fifty-two peers, pressed her lips against a black microphone, and began speaking . . . Thai. Boldly, confidently, calmly. While she was simply describing her experience during the internship phase of DEPDC's new leadership program, her testimony contained so many more unspoken triumphs.

She was a member of SYSTERM, a group of young adults between the ages of thirteen and twenty-seven who had the opportunity to leave their rural villages in Shan State and travel to Thailand to learn about human rights, leadership skills, non-profit management, and the realities of undocumented migration.

The Shan Youth Safety Training to End Risk Migration program was initiated in reaction to atrocious Myanmar behavior towards its minority groups in an effort to train Shan State's next generation on how to advocate and protect their people from suppression during large movements of people from one location to another. The expectation was four months of education on human rights and Thai language, one month of internships, one month of a project report, and then a return home to put the newfound skills into practice. The reality: an education . . . and an utter transformation in character, confidence, and motivation of fifty-three young adults.

Just two weeks before, this same girl was interviewed about her experience in SYSTERM. She specifically mentioned a rising confidence speaking in front of other people. "Before when I would go in front of a microphone, I had no confidence," she described. "No words would come out. I couldn't do it. But now, now I dare to speak."

Many of the youth who arrived on DEPDC's doorstep five months ago had never been taught how to speak in front of a crowd, had never been given a leadership position, and had never even been aware of their own human rights or broad global issues. Moreover, their own primary schooling required all children to learn in Burmese and take English as their alternative language, even though Thailand was the biggest destination for migration and business and the majority of the children only spoke Tai (Shan language). Up until about five years ago, any efforts to teaching in Tai could have been punishable by death or the notification of a "missing person." This factor led to a turbulent education for the majority of the SYSTERM members: if they even managed to pass primary and secondary school with limited Burmese, they often could not pass the competitive exam in order to complete high school. This was partly due to corrupt graders who would fail students if they recognized their Shan name. Many children simply stopped learning by ten or eleven to work their family farms instead. The result? Undereducated, vulnerable generations of Shan people who were never provided the tools to even know *how* to advocate for themselves.

For many students, a desire to change this stagnancy was the driving force behind their decision to come to DEPDC. "My monastery told me about the opportunity, and I was 50% sold, 50% nervous and wanting to stay home," one student describes. "But then I thought that if I stayed here, I would have nothing. Just the same situation. So I knew I had to go."

Some had never been to another country before; some had never been beyond their immediate village. All, however, recognized their limitations without education. "I had never learned about leadership before," another student explained, "and I knew that the only way I could improve my country would be to learn how to be a good leader."

DEPDC chose to tackle this learning gap with several key techniques: mind-mapping, learning by doing, group activities, and educational trips. The students camped in the mountains to understand what it was like to survive in nature while migrating, gave talks to their peers on global issues like trafficking and plastic pollution, and were forced to slowly integrate Thai into their journaling and presentations. They also were given leadership positions during their one-month internship in nonprofits and businesses across Mae Sai, and they underwent a rigorous, three-day critique exercise of the flaws of each member. While perhaps this sounds like an unconventional way of teaching humility, the exercise was actually a favorite part of SYSTERM training for many.

"We would start each critique by telling them that we loved them and that we knew them well after four months of being together and that we were friends," one student explained. "Then, we would tell them where they fell short and needed more work. After we finished, the person in the middle would respond by thanking us for being honest." The student explained this was a crucial turning point in his definition for a good leader. "In daily life, when you do something wrong, someone should come tell you. We have to be open-minded to other people, especially leaders. You have to let people criticize you in order to grow."

Additionally, many students valued SYSTERM's emphasis on equality, a value championed by DEPDC's founder, Sompop Jantraka. "We used to have 'my ethnic, your ethnic,'" the SYSTERM peer-elected president described. "We saw Thai people, Myanmar people, and other minority groups and could not see them as our equals. We were either above or below them. But Ajaan Sompop is open to every background and treats everyone the same. And I think back home we should do that."

Looking back on his journey through SYSTERM, the president admitted it had changed his whole outlook to his purpose when he returns home. "I want to help more people. I am not only Shan. I am human. I want to be more open to every ethnic group." As for the others, SYSTERM has been a wake-up call to realizing that they could indeed make change in their communities. "I used to live like everyone else," one student explains. "No vision. No target. But then I came here, and now I have something to get me up in the morning. I have a purpose. I have action. I have creativity. I know how far hard work can get you now."

When asked about what the students plan to do when they return home, almost all the answers were the same: education. Many wanted the SYSTERM curriculum to be taught in Shan State, others wanted to open schools that teach in Tai rather than Burmese, but all agreed that something must be done to tell their people about their rights, the importance of education, and the future it can unlock. "When I go back, I will have to change education in my village first," a student explicated, "and if I can change education in my village first, I can change education in Shan State."

The students planned for this campaign for education to extend beyond the classroom. For one

(Continued)

(Continued)

girl, she wanted to share the importance of learning Thai and English with older generations in order to be able to simply look up information on the internet. One of the boys wanted to travel around Shan State and videotape his culture in an effort to teach others about Shan State culture on a global level. Another was dedicated to teaching farmers about the environment and the detrimental effects of deforestation and pesticides, as well as spread the importance of teaching IT to children in a world of increasing technology reliance.

Each student also recognized the danger in their projected initiatives, some of which could result in threats, violence, and pushback from the Burmese government, but they were dedicated to their mission. "We are like a banana tree," one explained. "They will come to chop off the limbs, but we will keep growing. The first time there will always be problems. It will be the hardest. But we will keep growing."

Source: DEPDC/GMS, 2018.

Remaining Issues in the Field of Human Trafficking

There is an almost overwhelming number of possible approaches to combat trafficking: public service campaigns, advocacy, policy changes, service provision, research, monitoring, and evaluation of existing programs. While there are no evidence-based responses to human trafficking, there are many promising approaches along the continuum of prevention. Given the plethora of responses to trafficking, we will group them according to the public health–based continuum of prevention (see Figure 14.2).

Primary prevention approaches aim to stop trafficking before it happens. Examples of primary prevention strategies include educational programs for populations vulnerable to trafficking, public awareness campaigns, and demand reduction programs. *Secondary prevention* aims to identify trafficking where it exists. Secondary prevention approaches to combat trafficking include training programs for professionals who may come into contact with victims as well as screening tools. Finally, *tertiary prevention* aims to minimize the harm done in cases where trafficking has already taken place. This includes ensuring safety for identified victims, providing services and resources to survivors, and prosecuting traffickers.

Primary Prevention Efforts

Educational Programs

At the individual level, programs that provide job training and life skills training can help reduce vulnerability to trafficking. It is particularly important to provide these trainings to the most vulnerable populations (e.g., youth who are neither in school nor working and homeless populations).

Demand Reduction Efforts

For sex trafficking specifically, there is some research indicating that mandating individuals who pay for prostitution services to attend a program that teaches about the consequences of prostitution, healthy relationships, empathy, and toxic

Figure 14.2 Public Health–Based Continuum of Prevention

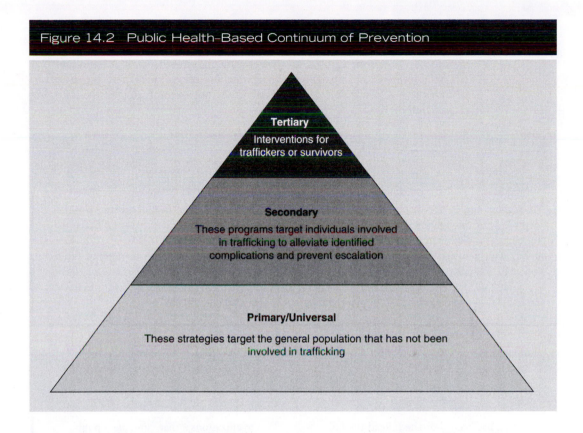

Tertiary
Interventions for
traffickers or survivors

Secondary
These programs target individuals involved
in trafficking to alleviate identified
complications and prevent escalation

Primary/Universal
These strategies target the general population that has not been
involved in trafficking

Focus On
"I Am Little Red"

Watch the 10-minute video *I Am Little Red* (Mazzio, Sokolow, Osorio, & Pierart, 2017):

> *I Am Little Red* is a 10-minute animated short aimed at children most at-risk for sex trafficking (e.g. foster-care, runaway, LGBTQ, homeless, and adopted children), with the goal of prevention and awareness. The film, narrated by Academy Award nominee Jessica Chastain (English) and Aislinn Derbez (Spanish), animated by Academy Award winners Gabriel Osorio and Pato Escala from Punkrobot, and written by 10 survivors of sex trafficking (aged 14–21) along with Alec Sokolow (Academy Award nominated writer of *Toy Story*) and Mary Mazzio, is a contemporary re-imagining of the classic fairy tale, Little Red Riding Hood. *I Am Little Red* addresses the four tactics a "wolf" (trafficker/pimp) will typically use to lure a Little Red off her path. (Mazzio, n.d.)

masculinity can help reduce demand for exploitative services. Men who complete these programs are less likely to reoffend. There is limited research on the value of outreach services, but less rigorous preliminary research finds that programs specifically tailored to the populations they serve are promising approaches.

Public Awareness Campaigns

Throughout this book, we have reviewed a few public awareness campaigns. You may have seen a public awareness campaign in person. It is important that public awareness campaigns for anti-trafficking efforts be responsible, however. To achieve a responsible campaign, advocacy organization suggest the following guidelines.

Focus On
John Schools

Throughout the course of this year, about 400 men will walk through the doors of an unassuming church in Nashville, sentenced to attend an all-day course designed to change their actions and their attitudes toward women. These men are johns, all arrested for solicitation. If they pay a $300 fine and spend eight hours listening to former prostitutes, health experts, psychologists, district attorneys, and police officers, their records will be expunged.

Listen to the interview on NPR at https://www.npr.org/2011/05/24/136617710/john-school-teaches-about-ills-of-sex-solicitation (Conan, 2011).

Focus On
Responsible Public Awareness Campaigns for Anti-trafficking

This blog has been shortened. Read the full version here: https://combathumantrafficking.org/2017/02/the-importance-of-responsible-public-awareness-campaigns-for-human-trafficking/

First, Do No Harm

The purpose of public awareness campaigns for human trafficking is to bring attention, compassion, and resources to the plight of trafficked persons. However, decisions about which aspects of the crime are portrayed versus which are left out can create critical misconceptions about the scope of human trafficking and the methods needed to combat it. Issues may also arise from campaigns that are so compelling that they drive a wrong, vigilante call to action. In these cases, the campaign's audience may feel inspired to "rescue" or "save" victims on their own. This approach can endanger both the "rescuers" and the victims, as well as interfere with ongoing law enforcement investigations.

Organizations that pursue public awareness campaigns must be acutely aware of these potential outcomes, and plan calls to action that discourage a well-intentioned public from taking matters into their own hands.

The Lived Experience of Human Trafficking Survivors

Human trafficking public awareness campaigns should always be grounded in the lived experiences of human trafficking survivors and oriented towards systemic solutions. Human trafficking is on the extreme end of a continuum of labor exploitation that affects vulnerable people. The strengths of campaigns aimed at promoting workers' rights must be rooted in the leadership of workers and survivors of all forms of abuse along this continuum. Public awareness campaigns must recognize this and approach the issue with systemic causes in mind. Promising practices to create and disseminate an effective public awareness campaign must include a survivor-centered approach. Survivors should be empowered to control their own narrative. Within the current narrative, survivors lack both control and consent over the public framing of their very personal, diverse experiences. Instead of rescuing a helpless victim, the narrative approach should move towards survivorship and how to support survivors.

Accessing Resource Networks

It is imperative for public awareness efforts to ensure that individuals know how to appropriately refer victims to the services they need. (Laboratory to Combat Human Trafficking, 2017)

Source: This blog is written by the Laboratory to Combat Human Trafficking, combathumantrafficking.org. Read the full version here: https://combathumantrafficking.org/2017/02/the-importance-of-responsible-public-awareness-campaigns-for-human-trafficking/.

Secondary Prevention Efforts

One area that lacks substantial evidence and innovation is the development and use of screening tools. There are a variety of screening tools available, but none have been formally validated. Screening tools can be used by anyone with the appropriate training to identify potential victims. It is becoming more common for medical personnel to receive training with these tools because they are the professionals most likely to come in contact with victims.

Tertiary Prevention Efforts

Victim/Survivor Services

As reviewed throughout the chapters in this book, human trafficking survivors need a wide variety of services, and often these needs vary by the type of trafficking and by individual.

Prosecuting Traffickers

Understandably, substantial attention has been paid to providing victims with resources to facilitate recovery. Further, prevention programs targeting priority populations have also become more common to reduce vulnerability to trafficking victimization. To stop trafficking, however, we must focus on the traffickers. You wouldn't suggest that the best way to stop drunk driving is to tell the general public to stop driving when there could be drunk drivers on the road. Similarly, we cannot focus all of our attention on preventing victimization. The number of convictions of traffickers has grown but has not kept pace with growing awareness of human trafficking. Many of the risk factors for becoming a trafficker are similar to those for being victimized: poverty and a lack of economic opportunities. Thus, addressing societal risk factors such as access to education and poverty may be promising approaches to reducing trafficking. Many victims are also recruited to become traffickers themselves. Although men commit the overwhelming majority of crime overall, women constitute a substantial proportion of traffickers. We still do not have a lot of information about the role of women as traffickers, however.

Pick the field from the list below that best fits the career you would like to have or currently have.

1. Identify how individuals in this field can contribute to anti-trafficking efforts.

    - Law enforcement
    - Social workers
    - Psychologists
    - Researchers
    - Victim advocates

    - Medical personnel
    - Bankers
    - CPAs
    - Programmers
    - Data scientists
    - Truckers

    - Programmers
    - Data scientists
    - Truck drivers
    - Taxi or ride share drivers

Traffickers are motivated by profits, however, and unfortunately there will likely always be people willing to exploit others for financial gain. Thus, the most certain ways to stop traffickers are to increase the likelihood that they will be caught and prosecuted, and to remove the profits associated with trafficking.

While there is plenty of work to be done, there are also ongoing, innovative efforts that are making a difference in combating trafficking. One strength of anti-trafficking efforts is that people in all fields can contribute to reducing the burden of trafficking, including truck drivers, data scientists, medical professionals, and bankers.

Final Remarks

As a reader of this text, you now have more expertise on this topic than most other citizens of the world. While *human trafficking* and *slavery* may be words people can define, the complicated nature of the crime and the devastating consequences to the victims are widely misunderstood and unacknowledged. By reading this book, you now know. You know that no town, city, state, country, or continent is immune to human trafficking. It may look and feel different, but the exploitation of others occurs everywhere. You also know that trafficking does not spare any gender, race, ethnicity, religion, or age group. While others may be able to convince themselves that trafficking doesn't occur where they live, readers of this book know differently.

You also know that many of the items you purchase are touched by slavery. Whether it be clothes, jewelry, household items, food, or electronics, readers of this book know that consumers must demand better from producers of commercial goods.

Whether it be the trafficking of children or adults, transgender individuals or homeless people, it is all bad and warrants our attention. Prostitution is not a victimless crime. Labor exploitation is not okay. Forcing children into marriage or armies, manipulating individuals into giving up organs—all of these actions impede on human rights. All levels of government, all over the world, must come together to create like definitions of human trafficking, aggressively react to all forms of trafficking, and compassionately serve victims of this deplorable crime.

As readers of this book, you now know all of this. You can now make a difference. It is as simple as sharing something you learned from this book with your family, friends, neighbors, and so forth. Plan a community awareness event. Intern or volunteer with an organization working to combat trafficking. Further your education on the topic. There is so much you can do now that you have this knowledge.

Human trafficking will continue until the citizens of the world demand that it stops. Coordinated preventive and reactive efforts are required on a global scale. The momentum is growing. Awareness is spreading. Demands are being made. The exploitation of others, in all forms, is unacceptable and must be stopped. Perhaps you, the reader of this book, will be the one to stop it.

References

Abdelkader, G. K., & Zangaou, M. (2012). Wahaya: Domestic and sexual slavery in Niger. Retrieved from http://www.antislavery.org/wp-content/uploads/2017/01/wahaya_report_eng.pdf

Abdullah, S., Qureshi, H., & Quayes, S. (2015). The adverse effect of child marriage on women's economic well being in Bangladesh—Can microfinance help? *Journal of Developing Areas, 49*(4), 109–125.

Achilli L. (2016). *Tariq al-Euroba: Displacement trends of Syrian asylum seekers to the EU* (MPC RR 2016/01). San Domenico di Fiesole (FI): European University Institute, Robert Schuman Centre for Advanced Studies.

Achvarina, V., & Reich, S. F. (2006). No place to hide: Refugees, displaced persons, and the recruitment of child soldiers. *International Security, 31*(1), 127–164.

Adams, W., & Flynn, A. (2017). *Federal prosecutions of commercial sexual exploitation of children cases, 2004–2013* (NCJ 250746). Retrieved from https://www.bjs.gov/content/pub/pdf/fpcsecc0413.pdf

Adepoju, A. (2005). Review of research and data on human trafficking in sub-Saharan Africa. *International Migration, 43*, 75–98. doi:10.1111/j.00207985.2005.00313.x

Administration for Children and Families. (n.d.a). Resource guide to trauma-informed human services: Resources specific to victims of human trafficking. Retrieved from https://www.acf.hhs.gov/trauma-toolkit/victims-of-human-trafficking

Administration for Children and Families. (n.d.b). SOAR to health and wellness training. Retrieved from https://www.acf.hhs.gov/otip/training/soar-to-health-and-wellness-training

Administration for Children and Families. (2013, September 13). Guidance to states and services on addressing human trafficking of children and youth in the United States. Retrieved from https://www.acf.hhs.gov/sites/default/files/cb/acyf_human_trafficking_guidance.pdf

Advocates for Human Rights. (2017). Labor trafficking protocol guidelines. Retrieved from https://www.theadvocatesforhumanrights.org/uploads/labor_trafficking_protocol_guidelines_final.pdf

Agnew, R., Brezina, T., Wright, J. P., & Cullen, F. T. (2002). Strain, personality traits, and delinquency: Extending general strain theory. *Criminology, 40*(1), 42–72.

Agnew, R., Cullen, F. T., Burton, V. S., Evans, T. D., & Dunaway, R. G. (1996). The new test of classic strain theory. *Academy of Criminal Justice Sciences, 13*(4), 681–704.

AIDS InfoNet. (2014, April 21). AIDS myths and misunderstandings. Retrieved from http://www.aidsinfonet.org/fact_sheets/view/158

Akbas, H. (2009). *Application of situational crime prevention to female trafficking for sexual exploitation in Turkey.* Doctoral dissertation. Retrieved from http://rave.ohiolink.edu/etdc/view?acc_num=ucin1258724618

Akee, R., Bedi, A., Basu, A. K., & Chau, N. H. (2010). Transnational trafficking, law enforcement and victim protection: A middleman's perspective (IZA Discussion Paper No. 6226). Retrieved from http://ftp.iza.org/dp6226.pdf

Aleem, Z. (2015, March 13). 16 years since decriminalizing prostitution, here's what's happening in Sweden. *Mic.* Retrieved from https://mic.com/articles/112814/here-s-what-s-happened-in-sweden-16-years-since-decriminalizing-prostitution#.yJRGeJ2iH

Alfredson, L. (2001). Sexual exploitation of child soldiers: An exploration and analysis of global dimensions and trends. *Child Soldiers Newsletter*, No. 2, 6–9.

Allen, E. (2007). *Domestic minor sex trafficking in America: How to identify America's trafficked youth.* Washington, DC: Shared Hope International, 2007.

American Hospital Association. (2018). Human trafficking: A trauma-informed health care response [Webinar]. Retrieved from https://www.aha.org/education-events/human-trafficking-trauma-informed-health-care-response

American Medical Association. (2016). Chapter 6: Opinions on organ procurement and transplantation. In *AMA principles of medical ethics.* Retrieved from https://www.ama-assn.org/sites/ama-assn.org/files/corp/media-browser/code-of-medical-ethics-chapter-6.pdf

American Psychological Association. (2014). *Report on the task forces on trafficking of women and girls.* Retrieved from http://www.apa.org/pi/women/programs/trafficking/report.pdf

American Public Health Association. (2015). Expanding and coordinating human trafficking–related public health research, evaluation, education, and prevention. Retrieved from https://www.apha.org/policies-and-advocacy/public-health-policy-statements/policy-database/2016/01/26/14/28/expanding-and-coordinating-human-trafficking-related-public-health-activities

Amnesty International. (2016). Amnesty International policy on state obligations to respect, protect, and fulfil the human rights of sex workers (Pol 30/4062/2016). Retrieved from https://www.amnesty.org/en/documents/pol30/4062/2016/en/

Anti-Slavery International. (2017). *Slavery in India's brick kilns & the payment system.* Retrieved from http://www.antislavery.org/wp-content/uploads/2017/09/Slavery-In-Indias-Brick-Kilns-The-Payment-System.pdf

Antonopoulos, G. A., & Winterdyk, J. A. (2005). Techniques of neutralizing the trafficking of women. *European Journal of Crime, Criminal Law, and Criminal Justice, 13*(2), 136–147.

Anwar, A. (2007, November 8). Criminalizing the customers: Prostitution ban huge success in Sweden. *Spiegel Online.* Retrieved from http://www.spiegel.de/international/europe/criminalizing-the-customers-prostitution-ban-huge-success-in-sweden-a-516030.html

Arizona State University, Center for Problem-Oriented Policing. (n.d.). Twenty five techniques of situational prevention [Table]. Retrieved from https://popcenter.asu.edu/sites/default/files/library/25%20techniques%20grid.pdf

Aroma, K. (2007). Trafficking in human beings: Uniform definitions for better measuring and for effective counter-measures. In Savona & Stefanizzi (Eds.), *Measuring human trafficking: Complexities and pitfalls.* New York, NY: Springer. Retrieved from http://public.eblib.com/choice/publicfullrecord.aspx?p=302152

Aronowitz, A., Theuermann, G., & Tyurykanova, E. (2010). *Analysing the business mode of trafficking in human beings to better prevent the crime.* Vienna, Austria: OSCE Office of the Special Representative and Coordinator for Combating Trafficking in Human Beings.

Arsovska, J., & Zabyelina, Y. G. (2014). Irrationality, liminality and the demand for illicit firearms in the Balkans and the North Caucasus. *European Journal on Criminal Policy and Research, 20*(3), 399–420. doi:10.1007/s10610-014-9231-0

Arthur, A. (2018, February 22). MS-13 and sex trafficking [Blog post]. Retrieved from https://cis.org/Arthur/MS13-and-Sex-Trafficking

Atim, G. (2017). Girls not brides: Ending child marriage in Nigeria. *Journal of Gender, Information and Development in Africa, 6*(1–2), 73–94.

Austin, R., & Farrell, A. (2017). Human trafficking and the media in the United States. *Oxford Research*

Encyclopedia of Criminology. Oxford University Press. doi:10.1093/acrefore/9780190264079.013.290

Ayikukwei, R., Ngare, D., Sidle, J., Ayuku, D., Baliddawa, J., & Greene, J. (2008). HIV/AIDS and cultural practices in western Kenya: The impact of sexual cleansing rituals on sexual behaviours. *Culture, Health and Sexuality, 10*(6), 587–599. doi:10.1080/13691050802012601

Baarda, C. S. (2016). Human trafficking for sexual exploitation from Nigeria into Western Europe: The role of voodoo rituals in the functioning of a criminal network. *European Journal of Criminology, 13*(2), 257–273.

Baer, K. (2015). Debate—The Trafficking Protocol and the Anti-Trafficking Framework: Insufficient to address exploitation. *Anti-Trafficking Review.* Retrieved from http://www.antitraffickingreview.org/index.php/atrjournal/article/view/98

Baldwin, S. B., Eisenman, D. P., Sayles, J. N., Ryan, G., & Chuang, K. S. (2011). Identification of human trafficking victims in health care settings. *Health and Human Rights, 13*(1), 36–49.

Bales, K. (2012). *Disposable people: New slavery in a global economy.* Oakland: University of California Press.

Bales, K. (2016). *Blood and earth: Modern slavery, ecocide, and the secret to saving the world.* New York, NY: Spiegel & Grau.

Bales, K., Fletcher, L., & Stover, E. (2004). Hidden slaves: Forced labor in the United States. UC Berkeley, Human Rights Center. Retrieved from https://escholarship.org/uc/item/4jn4j0qg

Bales, K., & Soudalter, R. (2010). *The slave next door.* Oakland, CA: University of California Press.

Bandyopadhyay, R. (2013). A paradigm shift in sex tourism research. *Tourism Management Perspectives, 6,* 1–2.

Banks, D., & Kyckelhahn, T. (2011). Characteristics of suspected human trafficking incidents 2008–2010 (NCJ 233732). Retrieved from http://www.bjs.gov/index.cfm?ty=pbdetail&iid=2372

Barbagiannis, E. (2017). Protecting victims of human trafficking: Creating better residency visas. *Cardozo Journal of International and Comparative Law, 25*(3), 561–593.

Barnard, A. (2014). The second chance they deserve: Vacating convictions of sex trafficking victims. *Columbia Law Review, 114*(6), 1463–1501.

Barnert, E. S., Abrams, S., Azzi, V. F., Ryan, G., Brook, R., & Chung, P. J. (2016). Identifying best practices for "safe harbor" legislation to protect child sex trafficking victims: Decriminalization alone is not sufficient. *Child Abuse and Neglect, 51,* 249–262. doi:10.1016/j.chiabu.2015.10.002

Barnert, E., Iqbal, Z., Bruce, J., Anoshiravani, A., Kolhatkar, G., & Greenbaum, J. (2017). Commercial sexual exploitation and sex trafficking of children and adolescents: A narrative review. *Academic Pediatrics, 17*(8), 825–829. doi:10.1016/j.acap.2017.07.009

Barrett, N. (2013). *An assessment of sex trafficking in Canada.* Retrieved from https://www.canadianwomen.org/wp-content/uploads/2017/09/NB-Nov-14-FINAL-REPORT-Assessment-of-Sex-Trafficking-in-Canada.pdf

Batsyukova, S. (2007). Prostitution and human trafficking for sexual exploitation. *Gender Issues, 24*(2), 46–50.

Bauer, M. (2007). *Close to slavery: Guestworker programs in the United States.* Retrieved from https://humantrafficking hotline.org/sites/default/files/Close%20to%20Slavery%20-%20SPCL.pdf

Bauer, M., & Stewart, M. (2013). *Close to slavery: Guestworker programs in the United States.* Retrieved from https://www.splcenter.org/20130218/close-slavery-guestworker-programs-united-states

Bayhi-Gennaro, J. (2008). *Baton Rouge/New Orleans area assessment: Identification of domestic minor sex trafficking victims and their access to services.* Retrieved from http://sharedhope.org/wp-content/uploads/2012/09/BatonRouge-NewOrleans_PrinterFriendly.pdf

Bazelon, E. (2016, May). Should prostitution be a crime? *New York Times Magazine.* Retrieved from https://www.nytimes.com/2016/05/08/magazine/should-prostitution-be-a-crime.html

Beah, I. (2007). *A long way gone.* New York, NY: Sarah Crichton Books.

Becker, C. (2008). Impact of statelessness in Thailand: Universal human rights violations in relation to U.S. foreign policy. *UWB Policy Journal.* Retrieved from https://uwbpolicyjournal.files.wordpress.com/2012/06/impact-of-statelessness.pdf

Becker, G. S., & Elias, J. J. (2007). Introducing incentives in the market for live and cadaveric organ donations. *Journal of Economic Perspectives.* Retrieved from http://www.atyponlink.com/AEAP/doi/pdf/10.1257/jep.21.3.3?cookieSet=1

Becker, J. (2005). Child soldiers: Changing a culture of violence. *Human Rights, 32*(1), 16–18.

Becker, J. (2018, June 29). A better US list of countries using child soldiers. Retrieved from https://www.hrw.org/news/2018/06/29/better-us-list-countries-using-child-soldiers

Bessell, S., Baldwin, S., Vandenberg, M., & Stoklosa, H. (2017). *Human trafficking and health care providers: Lessons learned from federal criminal indictments and civil trafficking cases.* Retrieved from https://healtrafficking.org/wp-content/uploads/2017/11/Medical-Fact-Sheet-Document_FINAL_NOVEMBER-20–2017.pdf

Betancourt, T. S., Borisova, I., Williams, T. P., Meyers-Ohki, S. E., Rubin-Smith, J. E., Annan, J., & Kohrt, B. A. (2013). Research review: Psychosocial adjustment and mental health in former child soldiers—a systematic review of the literature and recommendations for future research. *Journal of Child Psychology and Psychiatry, 54,* 17–36.

Bhabha, J. (2005, March 1). Trafficking, smuggling, and human rights [Feature]. Retrieved from http://www.migrationpolicy.org/article/trafficking-smuggling-and-human-rights

Blackmon, D. A. (2009). *Slavery by another name: The re-enslavement of black Americans from the Civil War to World War II.* New York, NY: Anchor Books.

Bloom, M. (2018). Child soldiers in armed conflict. *Armed Conflict Survey, 4*(1), 36–50.

Blumenthal, M. (2018, April 24). Inside human trafficking investigations [Blog post]. Retrieved from https://www.wearethorn.org/blog/what-human-trafficking-investigations-look-like/

BoÅnjak, B., & Acton, T. (2013). Virginity and early marriage customs in relation to children's rights among Chergashe Roma from Serbia and Bosnia. *International Journal of Human Rights, 17*(5–6), 646–667. doi:10.1080/13642987.2013.831697

Bos, M. (2015). *Trafficking in human organs.* Retrieved from http://www.europarl.europa.eu/RegData/etudes/STUD/2015/549055/EXPO_STU%282015%29549055_EN.pdf

Bouché, V. (2017). *An empirical analysis of the intersection of organized crime and human trafficking in the United States.* Retrieved from https://www.ncjrs.gov/pdffiles1/nij/grants/250955.pdf

Boukli, A., & Renz, F. (2018). Deconstructing the lesbian, gay, bisexual, transgender victim of sex trafficking: Harm, exceptionality and religion–sexuality tensions. *International Review of Victimology.* doi:10.1177/0269758018772670

Bower, B. (2008). Lost are found: Child soldiers can reenter, thrive in former community. *Science News, 173*(18), 5–6.

Bradley, O. (2017, November 5). 10 facts about child soldiers in Sierra Leone [Blog post]. Retrieved from https://borgenproject.org/10-facts-about-child-soldiers-in-sierra-leone/

Brents, B., & Hausbeck, K. (2001). State-sanctioned sex: Negotiating formal and informal regulatory practices in Nevada brothels. *Sociological Perspectives, 44,* 307–332. Retrieved from https://faculty.unlv.edu/brents/research/socpersp.pdf

Brents, B., & Hausbeck, K. (2005). Violence and legalized prostitution in Nevada: Examining safety, risk, and prostitution policy. *Journal of Interpersonal Violence, 20,* 270–295. Retrieved from http://journals.sagepub.com.proxy-um.researchport.umd.edu/doi/pdf/10.1177/0886260504270333

Brents, B., & Hausbeck, K. (2006). What is wrong with prostitution? Assessing exploitation in legal brothels: Paper presented at the American Sociological Association Annual Meetings, Montreal, August 2006. Retrieved from https://faculty.unlv.edu/brents/research/Stereotypes%20Brothels%20ASA06.pdf

Brewer, D. (2009). Globalization and human trafficking. *Human Rights, 11,* 46–56.

Brunovskis, A., & Surtees, R. (2012a). Coming home: Challenges in family reintegration for trafficked women. *Qualitative Social Work, 12*(4), 454–472.

Brunovskis, A., & Surtees, R. (2012b). *Out of sight? Approaches and challenges in the identification of trafficked persons.* Oslo, Norway: Allkopi AS.

Bureau of International Labor Affairs. (2017). Senegal. In *2016 findings on the worst forms of child labor.* Retrieved from https://www.justice.gov/eoir/page/file/1011616/download

Bureau of Public Affairs. (2004, November 24). The link between prostitution and sex trafficking. Retrieved from https://2001-2009.state.gov/r/pa/ei/rls/38790.htm#4

Burnette, M. L., Lucas, E., & Ilgen, M. (2008). Prevalence and health correlates of prostitution among patients entering treatment for substance abuse disorders. *Archive of General Psychiatry, 65,* 337–344.

Bush, M. A. (2010). Afghanistan and the sex trade. In K. A. McCabe and S. Manian (Eds.), *Sex trafficking: A global perspective* (pp. 111–118). Lanham, MD: Lexington Books.

Business Supply Chain Transparency on Trafficking and Slavery Act of 2018, H.R. 7089, 115th Cong. (2017–2018).

Canadian Blood Services. (2016). How kidney donation works. Retrieved from http://pulse.blood.ca/2016/04/how-kidney-donation-works/#.WzTCf9JKg2w

Capaul, A. J. (2013). *An examination of prostitution and sex trafficking laws within the United States* (Honors

thesis). Retrieved from http://digitalcommons.hamline.edu/cgi/viewcontent.cgi?article=1003&context=dhp

Carpenter, A., & Gates, J. (2016). *The nature and extent of gang involvement in sex trafficking in San Diego County.* Retrieved from https://www.ncjrs.gov/pdffiles1/nij/grants/249857.pdf

Castles, S., & Miller, M. J. (2009). Migration in the Asia-Pacific region. Retrieved from https://www.migrationpolicy.org/article/migration-asia-pacific-region

CdeBaca, L., & Sigmon, J. N. (2014). Combating trafficking in persons: A call to action for global health professionals. *Global Health: Science and Practice, 2*(3), 261–267.

Centers for Disease Control and Prevention. (n.d.). HIV/AIDS. Retrieved from https://www.cdc.gov/hiv/basics/index.html

Chadwick, L. (2016, August 3). Afghan forces use child soldiers, and the U.S. still gives them money. *Foreign Policy.* Retrieved from https://foreignpolicy.com/2016/08/03/afghan-forces-use-child-soldiers-and-the-u-s-still-gives-them-money/

Chaet, D. H. (2017). AMA Code of Medical Ethics' opinions related to human trafficking. *American Medical Association Journal of Ethics, 19*(1), 43–44.

Chambliss, W. (1996). Towards a political economy of crime. In J. Muncie, E. McLaughlin, & M. Langan (Eds.), *Criminological perspectives. A reader* (pp. 224–231). London, England: SAGE.

Chemin, M., & Mbiekop, F. (2015). Addressing child sex tourism: The Indian case. *European Journal of Political Economy, 38,* 169–180. doi:10.1016/j.ejpoleco.2015.02.005

Child Soldiers International. (n.d.a). Child soldiers world index. Retrieved from https://childsoldiersworldindex.org/

Child Soldiers International. (n.d.b). South Sudan. Retrieved from https://www.child-soldiers.org/south-sdan

Child Welfare Information Gateway. (2015). Child welfare and human trafficking [Brief]. Washington, DC: Author.

Child Welfare Information Gateway. (2016). Definitions of human trafficking [Factsheet]. Retrieved from https://www.childwelfare.gov/pubPDFs/definitions_trafficking.pdf

Child Welfare Information Gateway. (2017). Human trafficking and child welfare: A guide for child welfare agencies (Bulletin for Professionals). Washington, DC: Author.

Children's Bureau. (n.d.). At risk for sex trafficking: Youth who run away from foster care. Retrieved from https://library.childwelfare.gov/cwig/ws/library/docs/capacity/Blob/100462.pdf?r=1&rpp=10&upp=0&w=+NATIVE%28%27recno%3D100462%27%29&m=1

Cho, S.-Y. (2016). Liberal coercion? Prostitution, human trafficking and policy. *European Journal of Law and Economics, 41*(2), 321–348. doi:10.1007/s10657-015-9519-7

Cho, S.-Y., Dreher, A., & Neumayer, E. (2013). Does legalized prostitution increase human trafficking? *World Development, 41*, 67–82.

Cho, S.-Y., Dreher, A., & Neumayer, E. (2014). Determinants of anti-trafficking policies: Evidence from a new index. *Scandinavian Journal of Economics, 116*, 429–454. doi:10.1111/sjoe.12055

Chronology—Who banned slavery when? [Timeline]. (2007, March 22). Retrieved from https://www.reuters.com/article/uk-slavery-idUSL1561464920070322

Clarke, R. V. (1995). Situational crime prevention. *Crime and Justice, 19*, 91–150. Retrieved from http://www.jstor.org/stable/1147596

Clarke, R. V., & Cornish, D. B. (2001). Rational choice. In R. Paternoster & R. Bachman (Eds.), *Explaining criminals and crime: Essays in contemporary theory*. Los Angeles, CA: Roxbury.

Clawson, H. J., & Dutch, N. (2008). Case management and the victim of human trafficking: A critical service for client success. Retrieved from https://aspe.hhs.gov/system/files/pdf/75416/ib.pdf

Clawson, H. J., Dutch, N., Lopez, S., & Tiapula, S. (2008). *Prosecuting human trafficking cases: Lessons learned and promising practices*. Retrieved from https://www.ncjrs.gov/pdffiles1/nij/grants/223972.pdf

Clinton Foundation & Bill and Melinda Gates Foundation. (2015). No Ceilings: The Full Participation Project [Website]. Retrieved from http://www.noceilings.org/

Cockbain, E., Brayley, H., & Laycock, G. (2011). Exploring internal child sex trafficking networks using social network analysis. *Policing, 5*(2), 144–157. doi:10.1093/police/par025

Cockbain, E., & Wortley, R. (2015). Everyday atrocities: Does internal (domestic) sex trafficking of British children satisfy the expectations of opportunity theories of crime? *Crime Science: An Interdisciplinary Journal, 4*(1), 1–12. doi:10.1186/s40163-015-0047-0

Cohen, J. (2003). *Borderline slavery: Child trafficking in Togo*. Retrieved from https://www.hrw.org/report/2003/04/01/borderline-slavery-child-trafficking-togo

Cohen, L., & Felson, M. (1979). Social change and crime rate trends: A routine activity approach. *American Sociological Review, 44*(4), 588–608. Retrieved from http://www.jstor.org/stable/2094589

Comacho, F. (2013). Sexually exploited youth: A view from the bench. In J. L. Goodman & D. A. Leidholdt (Eds.), *Lawyer's manual on human trafficking: Pursuing justice for victims* (pp. 141–148). Supreme Court of the State of New York & New York State Judicial Committee on Women in the Courts. Retrieved from https://www.nycourts.gov/ip/womeninthecourts/pdfs/lmht.pdf

Conan, N. (2011, May 24). John School teaches about ills of sex solicitation. *NPR Talk of the Nation*. Retrieved from https://www.npr.org/2011/05/24/136617710/john-school-teaches-about-ills-of-sex-solicitation

Connell, T. (2013). ILO: Child labor declines, worst forms will remain by 2016. Retrieved from http://www.aflcio.org/Blog/Global-Action/ILO-Child-Labor-Declines-Worst-Forms-Will-Remain-by-2016

Consumer Goods Forum. (2016). The consumer goods forum's board-approved resolutions & commitments. Retrieved from https://www.theconsumergoodsforum.com/wp-content/uploads/2017/11/2018-CGF-Resolutions-and-Commitments.pdf

Consumer Goods Forum. (2017). Business actions against forced labour. Retrieved from https://www.theconsumergoodsforum.com/wp-content/uploads/2017/11/2018-CGF-Resolutions-and-Commitments.pdf

Cook, B., Wayne, G., Valentine, A., Lessios, A., & Yeh, E. (2013). Revisiting the evidence on health and health care disparities among the Roma: A systematic review 2003–2012. *International Journal of Public Health, 58*(6), 885–911.

Cornish, D. B., & Clarke, R. V. (Eds.). (1986). *The reasoning criminal: Rational choice perspectives on offending*. New York, NY: Springer-Verlag.

Cornish, D. B., & Clarke, R.V. (2003). Opportunities, precipitators, and criminal decisions: A reply to Wortley's critique of situational crime prevention. *Crime Prevention Studies, 16*, 41–96.

Council of Europe. (1997). Convention for the protection of human rights and dignity of the human being with regard to the application of biology and medicine: Convention on human rights and biomedicine (CETS 164). Retrieved from https://rm.coe.int/168007cf98

Council of Europe. (2005, May 16). Council of Europe convention on action against trafficking in human beings (CETS 197). Retrieved from https://rm.coe.int/168008371d

Council of Europe. (2017). *6th general report on GRETA's activities*. Retrieved from https://ec.europa.eu/anti-trafficking/sites/antitrafficking/files/greta_2017_7_web_6gr_en.pdf.pdf

Council of Europe Portal. (n.d.). Action Against Trafficking in Human Beings: About the convention. Retrieved from https://www.coe.int/en/web/anti-human-trafficking/about-the-convention

Counter Trafficking Data Collaborative. (2017). Counter-trafficking data brief 081217.pdf. Retrieved from https://www.iom.int/sites/default/files/our_work/DMM/MAD/Counter-trafficking%20Data%20Brief%20081217.pdf

Countryman-Roswurm, K., & Bolin, B. (2014). Domestic minor sex trafficking: Assessing and reducing risk. *Child and Adolescent Social Work Journal, 31*(6), 521–538. doi:10.1007/s10560-014-0336-6

Courture, T. (2017, March 30). A dangerous journey north [Blog post]. Retrieved from https://polarisproject.org/blog/2017/03/30/dangerous-journey-north

Covenant House. (n.d.). Labor and sex trafficking among homeless youth. Retrieved from https://covenanthousestudy.org/landing/trafficking/?_ga=2.190526507.1019278852.1527195575-1467842975.1527195575

Cray, A. (2013, May 29). 3 barriers that stand between LBGTQ youth and healthier futures. Retrieved from https://www.americanprogress.org/issues/lgbt/news/2013/05/29/64583/3-barriers-that-stand-between-lgbt-youth-and-healthier-futures/

Cray, A., Miller, K., & Durso, L. E. (2013, September 26). Seeking shelter: The experiences and unmet needs of LGBT homeless youth. Retrieved from https://www.americanprogress.org/issues/lgbt/reports/2013/09/26/75746/seeking-shelter-the-experiences-and-unmet-needs-of-lgbt-homeless-youth/

Curtis, R., Terry, K., Dank, M., Dombrowski, K., & Khan, B. (2008). *Commercial sexual exploitation of children in New York City: Vol. 1. The CSEC population in New York City: Size, characteristics, and needs* (NCJRS Document No. 225083). Retrieved from https://www.ncjrs.gov/pdffiles1/nij/grants/225083.pdf

Dallaire Initiative & Dalhouse University. (2018). The Roméo Dallaire Child Soldiers Initiative: Annual report 2017. Retrieved from https://www.childsoldiers.org/wp-content/uploads/2018/09/RDCSI_AnnualReport_2017_14x8-5_V6_full_web.pdf

Dang, M. (2014, October 2). Language matters: Defining human trafficking and slavery [Blog post]. Retrieved from http://www.endslaverynow.org/blog/articles/language-matters-defining-human-trafficking-and-slavery

Dank, M., & Johnson, M. (2014). The hustle: Economics of the underground commercial sex industry. Retrieved from http://apps.urban.org/features/theHustle/index.html

Dank, M., Khan, B., Downey, P. M., Kotonias, C., Mayer, D., Owens, C., . . . Yu, L. (2014, March 12). Estimating the size and structure of the underground commercial sex economy in eight major US cities [Research report]. Retrieved from https://www.urban.org/research/publication/estimating-size-and-structure-underground-commercial-sex-economy-eight-major-us-cities

Dank, M., Yu, L., Yahner, J., Pelletier, E., Mora, M., & Conner, B. (2015, September 29). Locked in: Interactions with the criminal justice and child welfare systems for LBGTQ youth, YMSM, and YWSW who engage in survival sex [Research report]. Retrieved from https://www.urban.org/research/publication/locked-interactions-criminal-justice-and-child-welfare-systems-lgbtq-youth-ymsm-and-ywsw-who-engage-survival-sex

Darlington, S. (2017). Transgender women at risk of sex trafficking. Retrieved from https://www.cnn.com/2017/01/02/americas/transgender-san-jose-costa-rica/index.html

D'Cunha, J. (2002). Trafficking in persons: A gender and rights perspective. Retrieved from http://www.un.org/womenwatch/daw/egm/trafficking2002/reports/EP-DCunha.PDF

de Groot, R., Kuunyem, M. Y., & Palermo, T. (2018). Child marriage and associated outcomes in northern Ghana: A cross-sectional study. *BMC Public Health, 18*, 285–297.

de Pérez, J. L. (2015). Contrasting the conceptualisation of victims of trafficking for sexual exploitation: A case study of Brazilians in Spain and Portugal. *European Journal on Criminal Policy and Research, 21*(4), 539–563.

Deady, G. M. (2011). The girl next door: A comparative approach to prostitution laws and sex trafficking victim identification within the prostitution industry. *Washington and Lee Journal of Civil Rights and Social Justice, 17*, 515–555. Retrieved from http://scholarlycommons.law.wlu.edu/crsj/vol17/iss2/7

DEPDC/GMS. (2018, July 3). "Now, I dare to speak": SYSTERM students reflect on the project's impact [Blog post]. Retrieved from https://depdcblog.wordpress.com/2018/07/03/now-i-dare-to-speak-systerm-students-reflect-on-the-projects-impact/

Dey, B., & Roy, R. (2016, May 27). Strength in numbers: Sex worker collectives in India. Retrieved from https://www.amnesty.org/en/latest/news/2016/05/rita-roy-and-bharati-dey-sex-worker-testimony-india/

Dizolele, M. P. (2017). Dodd-Frank 1502 and the Congo Crisis. Retrieved from https://www.csis.org/analysis/dodd-frank-1502-and-congo-crisis

Dizolele, M., & Applewhite, N. (Producers). (2011, January 6). Congo's Bloody Coltan [Video file]. Retrieved from https://pulitzercenter.org/reporting/congos-bloody-coltan

Dormino, M. (n.d.). Niger. Retrieved from https://www.girlsnotbrides.org/child-marriage/niger/

Dottridge, M. (2006). *Action to prevent child trafficking in south eastern Europe: A preliminary assessment.* Retrieved from https://www.unicef.org/ceecis/Assessment_report_June_06.pdf

Dovydaitis, T. (2010). Human trafficking: The role of the health care provider. *Journal of Midwifery and Women's Health, 55*(5), 462–467.

Drexler, J. N. (1996). Governments' role in turning tricks: The world's oldest profession in the Netherlands and the United States. *Penn State International Law Review, 15*, 201–236.

Druba, V. (2002). The problem of child soldiers. *International Review of Education, 48*(3/4), 271–277.

Dudley, S. (n.d.). Human trafficking in the Middle East and North Africa Region. *Topical Research Digest: Human Rights and Human Trafficking.* Retrieved from https://www.du.edu/korbel/hrhw/researchdigest/trafficking/MiddleEast.pdf

Duncan, B., Sommarin, C., Brandt, N., Aden, A. D., Briones, C., Barragues, A., . . . Anicama, C. (2013). *Breaking the silence on violence against indigenous girls, adolescents and young women: A call to action based on an overview of existing evidence from Africa, Asia Pacific and Latin America.* Retrieved from http://www.unfpa.org/sites/default/files/resource-pdf/VAIWG_FINAL.pdf

Dutton, D. G., & Painter, S. (1981). Traumatic bonding: The development of emotional attachments in battered women and other relationships of intermittent abuse. *Victimology: An International Journal, 1*, 139–155.

Dutton, D. G., & Painter, S. (1993). Emotional attachments in abusive relationships: A test of traumatic bonding theory. *Violence and Victims, 8*, 105–120.

DuVernay, A. (Writer & Director). (2016). *13th* [Documentary film]. United States: Kandoo Films.

Echavez, C., Bagaporo, J. L., Pilongo, L. W., & Azadmanesh, S. (2014). Why do children undertake the unaccompanied journey? Motivations for departure to Europe and other industrialised countries from the perspective of children, families and residents of sending communities in Afghanistan. Retrieved from https://www.unhcr.org/548ea0f09.pdf

ECPAT International. (2014). *The commercial sexual exploitation of children in Africa: Developments, progress, challenges, and recommended strategies.* Retrieved from http://www.ecpat.org/wp-content/uploads/legacy/Regional%20CSEC%20Overview_Africa.pdf

ECPAT International. (2018, December 6). Summit concludes with renewed commitment to protecting children in travel and tourism. Retrieved from http://www.ecpat.org/news/summit-concludes-with-renewed-commitment-to-halting-traveling-child-sex-offenders/

ECPAT International & Interpol. (2018). *Toward a global indicator on unidentified victims in sexual exploitation material: Summary report.* Retrieved from http://www.ecpat.org/wp-content/uploads/2018/02/TOWARDS-A-GLOBAL-INDICATOR-ON-UNIDENTIFIED-VICTIMS-IN-CHILD-SEXUAL-EXPLOITATION-MATERIAL-Summary-Report.pdf

Edmonds, E. V. (2016). Economic growth and child labour in low income economies (GLM/LIC Working Paper No. 11). Retrieved from https://glm-lic.iza.org/wp-content/uploads/2017/06/glmlic-wp011.pdf

Edna Adan Hospital. (n.d.). [Website] Retrieved from http://www.ednahospital.org/

Edwards, J. M., Iritani, B. J., & Hallfors, D. D. (2006). Prevalence and correlates of exchanging sex for drugs or money among adolescents in the United States. *Sexually Transmitted Infections, 82*, 354–358.

Edwards, O. (2015, July 10). The secret victims of sex trafficking [Blog post]. Retrieved from http://www.endslaverynow.org/blog/articles/the-secret-victims-of-sex-trafficking

Elezi, A. (2011). Fighting human trafficking. *Curentul Juridic / Juridical Current / Le Courant Juridique, 44*, 77–91.

Elias, J. J., Lacetera, N., & Macis, M. (2015). Sacred values? The effect of information on attitudes toward payments for human organs. *American Economic Review, 105*(5), 361–365.

Emerson, J., Kroman, J. L., Mogulescu, K., & Sartori, L. S. (2014). Obtaining post-conviction relief for survivors of human trafficking [PowerPoint]. Retrieved from https://www.americanbar.org/content/dam/aba/directories/pro_bono_clearinghouse/ejc_2014_182.authcheckdam.pdf

EngenderHealth & United Nations Population Fund. (2003). *Obstetric fistula needs assessment report: Findings from nine African countries.* Retrieved from https://www.unfpa.org/sites/default/files/pub-pdf/fistula-needs-assessment.pdf

Enos, O. (2015, August 10). *A call to review evaluation methods in the Trafficking in Persons Report*. Retrieved from http://www.heritage.org/crime-and-justice/report/call-review-evaluation-methods-the-trafficking-persons-report#_ftn1

Epstein, M. (2008). The Declaration of Istanbul on Organ Trafficking and Transplant Tourism: An important international achievement with one disturbing loophole. *BMJ, 336*, 1377. Retrieved from https://www.bmj.com/rapid-response/2011/11/02/declaration-istanbul-organ-trafficking-and-transplant-tourism-important-in

Equality Now. (n.d.). Trafficking survivor stories: Grace. Retrieved from https://www.equalitynow.org/campaigns/trafficking-survivor-stories/grace

Erulkar, A. (n.d.). Building an evidence base to delay marriage in sub-Saharan Africa. Retrieved from http://www.popcouncil.org/research/building-an-evidence-base-to-delay-marriage-in-sub-saharan-africa

Erulkar, A. (2013). Adolescence lost: The realities of child marriage. *Journal of Adolescent Health: Official Publication of the Society for Adolescent Medicine, 52*(5), 513–514. doi:10.1016/j.jadohealth.2013.03.004

Erulkar, A., & Muthengi, E. (2009). Evaluation of Berhane Hewan: A program to delay marriage in rural Ethiopia. *International Perspectives on Sexual and Reproductive Health, 35*, 6–14.

European Commission. (2016). Report on the progress made in the fight against trafficking in human beings. Retrieved from https://ec.europa.eu/anti-trafficking/sites/antitrafficking/files/report_on_the_progress_made_in_the_fight_against_trafficking_in_human_beings_2016.pdf

European Parliament & Council of the European Union. (2011). Directive 2011/92/EU of the European Parliament and of the council of 13 December 2011 on combating the sexual abuse and sexual exploitation of children and child pornography, and replacing council framework decision. *Official Journal of the European Union*. Retrieved from https://eur-lex.europa.eu/legal-content/EN/TXT/?uri=celex%3A32011L0093

Fair Girls. (n.d.a). Our mission. Retrieved from https://www.fairgirls.org/our-mission/

Fair Girls. (n.d.b). Vida Home. Retrieved from http://www.fairgirls.org/vida-home/

Fargues, P. (2016). Uptick in African refugees expected to continue. *Cipher Brief*. Retrieved from https://www.thecipherbrief.com/article/europe/uptick-african-refugees-expected-continue-1093

Farley, M. (2009). Theory versus reality: Commentary on four articles about trafficking for prostitution. *Women's Studies International Forum, 32*, 311–315.

Farley, M., & Barkan, H. (1998). Prostitution, violence, and posttraumatic stress disorder. *Women and Health, 27*(3). Retrieved from http://www.prostitutionresearch.com/Farley%26Barkan%201998.pdf

Farrell, A., McDevitt, J., Pfeffer, R., Fahy, S., Owens, C., Dank, M., & Adams, W. (2012). *Identifying challenges to improve the investigation and prosecution of state and local human trafficking cases*. Retrieved from https://www.urban.org/research/publication/identifying-challenges-improve-investigation-and-prosecution-state-and-local-human-trafficking-cases

Farrell, A., & Pfeffer, R. (2014). Policing human trafficking: Cultural blinders and organizational barriers. *Annals of the American Academy of Political and Social Science, 653*(1), 46–64.

Feasley, A. (2015). Deploying disclosure laws to eliminate forced labour: Supply chain transparency efforts of Brazil and the United States of America (Criminal Justice, Borders and Citizenship Research Paper No. 2732885). *Anti-Trafficking Review* (Special Issue: Forced Labour and Human Trafficking, No. 5). Retrieved from https://papers.ssrn.com/sol3/papers.cfm?abstract_id=2732885

Febry, A. (2013, March). Reevaluating the Trafficking Victims Protection Act [Blog post]. Retrieved from http://thehill.com/blogs/congress-blog/civil-rights/274800-reevaluating-the-trafficking-victims-protection-act

Federal Bureau of Investigation. (n.d.). Crime in the United States: 2016. Retrieved from https://ucr.fbi.gov/crime-in-the-u.s/2016/crime-in-the-u.s.-2016/tables/table-21

Fedina, L., Williamson, C., & Perdue, T. (2016). Risk factors for domestic child sex trafficking in the United States. *Journal of Interpersonal Violence, 34*(13), 2653–2673.

Felter, C., Masters, J., & Sergie, M. A. (2018). Al-Shabab. Retrieved from https://www.cfr.org/backgrounder/al-shabab

Fernandez, M. (2012). For many illegal entrants into U.S., a particularly inhospitable first stop. *New York Times*. Retrieved from http://www.nytimes.com/2012/05/27/us/for-many-illegal-entrants-into-us-a-particularly-inhospitable-first-stop.html?_r=0

Figlewski, B. M., & Brannon, L. W. (2013). Trafficking and the commercial sexual exploitation of young men and boys. In J. L. Goodman & D. A. Leidholdt (Eds.), *Lawyer's manual on human trafficking: Pursuing justice for victims* (pp. 149–168). Supreme Court of the State of New York & New York State Judicial Committee on Women in the Courts. Retrieved from https://www.nycourts.gov/ip/womeninthecourts/pdfs/lmht.pdf

Financial Action Task Force. (2011). Annual report 2010–2011. Retrieved from http://www.fatf-gafi.org/media/fatf/documents/reports/FORMATTED%20ANNUAL%20REPORT%20FOR%20PRINTING.pdf

Financial Action Task Force. (2018). *Financial flows from human trafficking.* Retrieved from https://www.fatf-gafi.org/media/fatf/content/images/Human-Trafficking-2018.pdf

Financial Crimes Enforcement Network. (2014, September 11). Advisory: Guidance on recognizing activity that may be associated with human smuggling and human trafficking—financial red flags (FIN-2014-A008). Retrieved from https://www.fincen.gov/sites/default/files/advisory/FIN-2014-A008.pdf

Finckenauer, J. O., & Chin, K. (2010). Sex trafficking: A target for situational crime prevention? In K. Bullock, R. Clarke, & N. Tilley (Eds.), *Situational prevention of organised crime* (pp. 58–80). Oxfordshire, UK: Willan.

First amendment—Ministerial exception—Ninth circuit avoids constitutional question, holding that ministers did not state a claim that church of scientology violated Trafficking Victims Protection Act.—*Headley v. Church of Scientology Int'l*, 687 F.3d 1173 (9th Cir. 2012). (2013). *Harvard Law Review, 126*(7), 2121–2130. Retrieved from http://www.jstor.org/stable/23415069

Flores, T. L., with Wells, P. (2010). *The slave across the street: The true story of how an American teen survived the world of human trafficking.* Boise, ID: Ampelon.

Forrest, A. (2014). *The Forrest review: Creating parity.* Commonwealth of Australia, Department of the Prime Minister and Cabinet. Retrieved from https://www.pmc.gov.au/sites/default/files/publications/Forrest-Review.pdf

Franklin, C.A. (2008). Women offenders, disparate treatment, and criminal justice: A theoretical, historical, and contemporary overview. *Critical Journal of Crime, Law and Society, 21*, 341–360.

Franzblau, K. (2013). Sex trafficking: Looking at demand. In J. L. Goodman & D. A. Leidholdt (Eds.), *Lawyer's manual on human trafficking: Pursuing justice for victims* (pp. 299–304). Supreme Court of the State of New York & New York State Judicial Committee on Women in the Courts. Retrieved from https://www.nycourts.gov/ip/womeninthecourts/pdfs/lmht.pdf

Gage, A. (2013). Association of child marriage with suicidal thoughts and attempts among adolescent girls in Ethiopia. *Journal of Adolescent Health, 52*(5), 654–656. doi:10.1016/j.jadohealth.2012.12.007

Gallagher, A. T. (2010). Improving the effectiveness of the international law of human trafficking: A vision for the future of the US trafficking in persons report. *Springer Science Business Media, 12*, 381–400.

Garcia, A. D. (2013). Voodoo, witchcraft and human trafficking in Europe (New Issues in Refugee Research, Research Paper No. 263). Retrieved from https://www.ecoi.net/file_upload/1930_1382531731_526664234.pdf

Gaston, R. S., Danovitch, G. M., Epstein, R. A., Kahn, J. P., Matas, A. J., & Schnitzler, M. A. (2006). Limiting financial disincentives in live organ donation: A rational solution to the kidney shortage. *American Journal of Transplantation, 6*(11), 2548–2555.

Gates, H. L. (2014, February 10). Slavery, by the numbers. Retrieved from https://www.theroot.com/slavery-by-the-numbers-1790874492

Gausman, J., Chernoff, M., Duger, A., Bhabha, J., & Chu, H. (2016). *When we raise our voice: The challenge of eradicating labor exploitation.* Retrieved from http://freedomfund.org/wp-content/uploads/FINAL-When-We-Raise-Our-Voice-.pdf

General Assembly Security Council. (2016). *Children and armed conflict.* Retrieved from http://www.un.org/ga/search/view_doc.asp? symbol=s/2016/360&referer=/english/&Lang=E

General Assembly Security Council. (2018). *Children and armed conflict.* Retrieved from http://undocs.org/s/2018/465

Gettleman, J. (2010). Armed and underage. *New York Times Upfront.* Retrieved from http://www.derrickalums.com/learning/wp-content/uploads/2011/01/NYTimes_Upfront2010_10_04forclass.pdf

Gezinski, L. B., Karandikar, S., Levitt, A., & Ghaffarian, R. (2016). "Total girlfriend experience": Examining marketplace mythologies on sex tourism websites. *Culture, Health and Sexuality, 18*(7), 785–798. doi:10.1080/13691058.2015.1124457

Gianni, M. C., & Di Filippo, L. C. (2015). The trafficking in human beings prevention: A criminological perspective (part 2). *Lex Scientia International Journal, 2*(22), 122–140.

Gilsinan, K. (2015, October 29). The confused person's guide to the Syrian civil war. *The Atlantic.* Retrieved from http://www.theatlantic.com/international/archive/2015/10/syrian-civil-war-guide-isis/410746/

Girls Not Brides. (n.d.a). Child marriage and the law. Retrieved from https://www.girlsnotbrides.org/child-marriage-law/

Girls Not Brides. (n.d.b). Ending child marriage in Africa [Brief]. Retrieved from https://www.girls notbrides.org/wp-content/uploads/2015/02/Child-marriage-in-Africa-A-brief-by-Girls-Not-Brides.pdf

Girls Not Brides. (n.d.c). India. Retrieved from https://www.girlsnotbrides.org/child-marriage/india/

Girls Not Brides. (n.d.d). Violence against girls. Retrieved from https://www.girlsnotbrides.org/themes/violence-against-girls/

Girls Not Brides. (2016, October 17). Are economic incentives enough to prevent child marriage? Findings from Haryana, India. Retrieved from https://www.girl snotbrides.org/economic-incentives-enough-prevent-child-marriage-findings-haryana-india/

Glionna, J. M., & Panzar, J. (2015). In Nevada, there is little love left for brothels. *Los Angeles Times*. Retrieved from http://www.latimes.com/nation/la-na-nevada-brothel-20151014-story.html

Global Alliance Against Traffic in Women. (2010). Beyond borders: Exploring links between trafficking and gender (GAATW Working Papers Series 2010). Retrieved from http://www.gaatw.org/publications/WP_on_Gender.pdf

Global Emancipation Network. (n.d.). About. Retrieved 2017 from https://www.globalemancipation.ngo/global-emancipation-network-mission-offerings/

Global Observatory on Donation and Transplantation. (n.d.). Chart production: Information evidence and research. Retrieved from http://www.transplant-obser vatory.org/data-charts-and-tables/

Global Slavery Index. (n.d.). About the index. Retrieved from http://www.globalslaveryindex.org/about/

Global Slavery Index. (2018). Unravelling the numbers. Retrieved from https://www.globalslaveryindex .org/2018/findings/highlights/

Godwin, J. (2012). *Sex work and the law in Asia and the Pacific: Laws, HIV and human rights in the context of sex work*. Retrieved from http://www.undp.org/content/dam/undp/library/hivaids/English/HIV-2012-SexWorkAndLaw.pdf

Government of Canada. (2012). National action plan to combat human trafficking. Retrieved from https://www.publicsafety.gc.ca/cnt/rsrcs/pblctns/ntnl-ctn-pln-cmbt/ntnl-ctn-pln-cmbt-eng.pdf

Government of Canada. (2016). Protection and assistance for victims of human trafficking. Retrieved from https://www.canada.ca/en/immigration-refugees-citizenship/services/application/application-forms-guides/protection-assistance-victims-human-trafficking.html

Goyal, M., Mehta, R. L., Schneiderman, L. J., & Sehgal, A. R. (2002). Economic and health consequences of selling a kidney in India. *Journal of the American Medical Association, 288,* 1589–1593.

Gozdziak, E. M., & Bump, M. N. (2008). *Data and research on human trafficking: Bibliography of research-based literature*. Retrieved from https://repository .library.georgetown.edu/bitstream/handle/10822/551495/Data_research_%09trafficking.pdf? sequence=1

Green, S. L. (2002). *Rational choice: An overview.* Retrieved from https://business.baylor.edu/steve_green/green1.doc

Greenbaum, J., Bodrick, N., & Committee on Child Abuse and Neglect. (2017). Global human trafficking and child victimization. *Pediatrics, 140*(6), e20173138.

Greenbaum, V. J. (2014). Commercial sexual exploitation and sex trafficking of children in the United States. *Current Problems in Pediatric Adolescent Health Care, 44,* 245–269.

Greene, M. E. (2014). Ending child marriage in a generation: What research is needed? Retrieved from https://www.fordfoundation.org/media/1890/ending-childmarriage.pdf

Greve, A. (2014, September). Human trafficking: What about the men and boys? [Blog post]. Retrieved from http://humantraffickingcenter.org/men-boys/

Gruner, W. (2006). *Jewish forced labor under the Nazis: Economic needs and racial aims, 1938–1944.* Cambridge, UK: Cambridge University Press.

Gupta, J., Raj, A., Decker, M. R., Reed, E., & Silverman, J. G. (2009). HIV vulnerabilities of sex-trafficked Indian women and girls. *International Journal of Gynecology and Obstetrics, 107*(1), 30–34. doi:10.1016/j .ijgo.2009.06.009

Guth, A., Anderson, R., Kinnard, K., & Tran, H. (2014). Proper methodology and methods of collecting and analyzing slavery data: An examination of the Global Slavery Index. *Social Inclusion, 2,* 14–22.

Half the Sky Movement. (n.d.a). Forced prostitution. Retrieved from http://www.halftheskymovement.org/issues/forced-prostitution

Half the Sky Movement. (n.d.b). Gender based violence. Retrieved from http://www.halftheskymovement .org/issues/gender-based-violence

Half the Sky Movement. (n.d.c). Sex trafficking. Retrieved from http://www.halftheskymovement.org/issues/sex-trafficking.html

Harris, K. (2015). The California Transparency in Supply Chains Act: A resource guide. Retrieved from https://oag.ca.gov/sites/all/files/agweb/pdfs/sb657/resource-guide.pdf

Hartinger-Saunders, R. M., Trouteaud, A. R., & Matos Johnson, J. (2016, March 17). Mandated reporters' perceptions of and encounters with domestic minor sex trafficking of adolescent females in the United States. *American Journal of Orthopsychiatry, 87*(3), 195–205.

Havocscope. (2015). *Prostitution: Prices and statistics of global sex trade* [Kindle DX version]. Retrieved from https://www.amazon.com/Prostitution-Prices-Statistics-Global-Trade-ebook/dp/B00ZZBFXO2

Hennigan, P. C. (2004). Property war: Prostitution, red-light districts, and the transformation of public nuisance law in the Progressive Era. *Yale Journal of Law and the Humanities, 16*, 123–197. Retrieved from http://digitalcommons.law.yale.edu/yjlh/vol16/iss1/5

Her Majesty's Government, UK Department of Justice, Scottish Government, & Welsh Government. (2017). 2017 UK annual report on modern slavery. Retrieved from https://assets.publishing.service.gov.uk/government/uploads/system/uploads/attachment_data/file/652366/2017_uk_annual_report_on_modern_slavery.pdf

Hersh, L. (2013). Sex trafficking investigations and prosecutions. In J. L. Goodman & D. A. Leidholdt (Eds.), *Lawyer's manual on human trafficking: Pursuing justice for victims* (pp. 255–270). Supreme Court of the State of New York & New York State Judicial Committee on Women in the Courts. Retrieved from https://www.nycourts.gov/ip/womeninthecourts/pdfs/lmht.pdf

Hill, A. (2010, June 30). More men seek help with forced marriages. *The Guardian*. Retrieved from https://www.theguardian.com/world/2010/jul/01/men-help-forced-marriages-rise

Hippen, B., Ross, L. F., & Sade, R. M. (2009). Saving lives is more important than abstract moral concerns: Financial incentives should be used to increase organ donation. *Annals of Thoracic Surgery, 88*(4), 1053–1061.

Hoban, B. (2017, August 24). Do immigrants "steal" jobs from American workers? [Blog post]. Retrieved from https://www.brookings.edu/blog/brookings-now/2017/08/24/do-immigrants-steal-jobs-from-american-workers/

Hobson, B. M. (1990). *Uneasy virtue: The politics of prostitution and the American reform tradition*. Chicago, IL: University of Chicago Press.

Hodal, K. (2017, August 26). "I hope you're ready to get married": In search of Vietnam's kidnapped brides. *The Guardian*. Retrieved from https://www.theguardian.com/global-development/2017/aug/26/ready-married-kidnapped-brides-vietnam-china

Hodge, D. (2008). Sexual trafficking in the United States: A domestic problem with transnational dimensions. *Social Work, 53*(2), 143–152. Retrieved from http://www.naswpress.org/publications/journals/sw.html

Hoke v. United States, 227 U.S. 308 (1913).

Hom, K. A., & Woods, S. J. (2013). Trauma and its aftermath for commercially sexually exploited women as told by front-line service providers. *Issues in Mental Health Nursing, 34*, 75–81.

Hossain, M., Zimmerman, C., Abas, M., Light, M., & Watts, C. (2010). The relationship of trauma to mental disorders among trafficked and sexually exploited girls and women. *American Journal of Public Health, 100*(12), 2442–2449. Retrieved from http://doi.org/10.2105/AJPH.2009.173229

Hotchkiss, D. R., Godha, D., Gage, A. J., & Cappa, C. (2016). Risk factors associated with the practice of child marriage among Roma girls in Serbia. *BMC International Health and Human Rights, 16*. Retrieved from https://bmcinthealthhumrights.biomedcentral.com/track/pdf/10.1186/s12914-016-0081-3

Hughes, D. M. (2000). The "Natasha" trade: The transnational shadow market of trafficking in women. *Journal of International Affairs, 53*(2), 625–651.

Hughes, D. M. (2002, June 19). *Foreign government complicity in human trafficking: A review of the State Department's 2002 Trafficking in Persons Report*. Testimony before the U.S. House Committee on International Relations, Washington, DC. Retrieved from https://digitalcommons.unl.edu/cgi/viewcontent.cgi?referer=https://www.google.com/&httpsredir=1&article=1027&context=humtraffdata

Human Rights Watch. (2003). *"You'll learn not to cry": Child combatants in Colombia*. Retrieved from https://www.hrw.org/reports/2003/colombia0903/colombia0903.pdf

Human Rights Watch. (2008). *"As if I am not human": Abuses against Asian domestic workers in Saudi Arabia*. Retrieved from https://www.hrw.org/report/2008/07/07/if-i-am-not-human/abuses-against-asian-domestic-workers-saudi-arabia

Human Rights Watch. (2016, July 13). Oman: Domestic workers trafficked, trapped. Reform system, laws to protect migrant women. Retrieved from https://www.hrw.org/news/2016/07/13/oman-domestic-workers-trafficked-trapped

Human Rights Watch. (2017, July 24). Thailand: Trafficking convictions important step forward. Retrieved from https://www.hrw.org/news/2017/07/24/thailand-trafficking-convictions-important-step-forward

Human Rights Watch. (2018). Hidden chains: Rights abuses and forced labor in Thailand's fishing industry. Retrieved from https://www.hrw.org/report/2018/01/23/hidden-chains/rights-abuses-and-forced-labor-thailands-fishing-industry

Human Smuggling and Trafficking Center. (2006). Fact sheet: Distinctions between human smuggling and human trafficking. Retrieved from https://www.state.gov/documents/organization/90541.pdf

Human Trafficking Legal Center. (n.d.). [Website]. Retrieved from http://www.htlegalcenter.org/

Human Trafficking Pro Bono Legal Center. (2016). Trafficking of persons with disabilities in the United States. Retrieved from http://www.ndrn.org/images/webcasts/2016/Trafficking-of-Persons-With-Disabilities-in-the-United-States-04.12.2016.pdf

Hume, T., Cohen, L., & Sorvino, M. (2013). The women who sold their daughters into sex slavery. Retrieved from http://www.cnn.com/interactive/2013/12/world/cambodia-child-sex-trade/

Hunt, J., & Moody-Mills, A. (2012, June 29). The unfair criminalization of gay and transgender youth: An overview of the experiences of LBGTQ youth in the juvenile justice system. Retrieved from https://www.americanprogress.org/wp-content/uploads/issues/2012/06/pdf/juvenile_justice.pdf

Ikeora, M. (2016). The role of African traditional religion and "Juju" in human trafficking: Implications for anti-trafficking. *Journal of International Women's Studies*, *17*(1), 1–18.

Institute for Human Rights and Business. (2011). Dhaka principles for migration with dignity. Retrieved from https://www.ihrb.org/uploads/member-uploads/DPs_-_English_Short_Version.pdf

Institute for Human Rights and Business. (2016). Leadership group for responsible recruitment. Retrieved from https://www.ihrb.org/employerpays/leadership-group-for-responsible-recruitment

Institute of Medicine & National Research Council. (2013). *Confronting commercial sexual exploitation and sex trafficking of minors in the United States*. Washington, DC: National Academies Press.

International Air Transport Association. (n.d.). Human trafficking (HT). Retrieved from https://www.iata.org/policy/consumer-pax-rights/Pages/human-trafficking.aspx

International Air Transport Association. (2018). Guidance on human trafficking. Retrieved from https://www.iata.org/policy/consumer-pax-rights/Documents/human-trafficking-guidelines-v1.pdf

International Civil Aviation Organization. (2018). Preventing human trafficking by empowering aircraft cabin crew. Retrieved from https://www.icao.int/Newsroom/Pages/Preventing-human-trafficking-by-empowering-aircraft-cabin-crew.aspx

International Civil Aviation Organization & Office of the High Commissioner for Human Rights. (2018). Guidelines for training cabin crew on identifying and responding to trafficking in persons (Circular 352). Retrieved from https://www.icao.int/safety/airnavigation/OPS/CabinSafety/Documents/Cir.352.alltext.en.pdf

International Labour Office. (2014). *Profits and poverty: The economics of forced labour*. Retrieved from http://www.ilo.org/public/libdoc/ilo/2014/485559.pdf

International Labour Office. (2017). *Global estimates of child labour: Results and trends, 2012–2016*. Retrieved from https://www.ilo.org/wcmsp5/groups/public/@dgreports/@dcomm/documents/publication/wcms_575499.pdf

International Labour Office & Walk Free Foundation (2017). *Global estimates of modern slavery: Forced labour and forced marriage*. Retrieved from http://www.ilo.org/wcmsp5/groups/public/---dgreports/---dcomm/documents/publication/wcms_575479.pdf

International Labour Organization. (n.d.a). Forced labour and human trafficking playlists [YouTube channel]. Retrieved from https://www.youtube.com/playlist?list=PL077D1DC843F1D3FD

International Labour Organization. (n.d.b). Forced labour, modern slavery and human trafficking. Retrieved from http://www.ilo.org/global/topics/forced-labour/lang--en/index.htm

International Labour Organization. (n.d.c). ILO conventions and recommendations on child labour. Retrieved from http://www.ilo.org/ipec/facts/ILOconventionsonchildlabour/lang--en/index.htm

International Labour Organization. (n.d.d). 2017 global estimates of modern slavery and child labour. Retrieved from http://www.ilo.org/global/topics/forced-labour/publications/WCMS_547398/lang--en/index.htm

International Labour Organization. (1997). *Private employment agencies convention, 1997* (No. 181).

Retrieved from https://www.ilo.org/dyn/normlex/en/f?p=
NORMLEXPUB:12100:0::NO::P12100_INSTRUMENT_
ID:312326

International Labour Organization. (2008). Forced labour, discrimination and poverty reduction among indigenous peoples in Bolivia, Peru and Paraguay. Retrieved from http://www.ilo.org/global/topics/forced-labour/WCMS_082040/lang--en/index.htm

International Labour Organization. (2012). ILO global estimate of forced labour: Results and methodology. Retrieved from http://www.ilo.org/global/topics/forced-labour/publications/WCMS_182004/lang--en/index.htm

International Labour Organization. (2013a). *Caught at sea: Forced labour and trafficking in fisheries.* Retrieved from http://www.ilo.org/global/topics/forced-labour/publications/WCMS_214472/lang--en/index.htm

International Labour Organization. (2013b). *ILO global estimate of forced labour 2012: Results and methodology.* Retrieved from https://www.ilo.org/global/topics/forced-labour/publications/WCMS_182004/lang--en/index.htm

International Labour Organization. (2013c). *ILO 2012 global estimate of forced labour: Executive summary.* Retrieved from http://ilo.org/wcmsp5/groups/public/@ed_norm/@declaration/documents/publication/wcms_181953.pdf

International Labour Organization. (2013d). *Marking progress against child labor: Global estimates and trends 2000–2012.* Retrieved from http://www.ilo.org/wcmsp5/groups/public/---ed_norm/---ipec/documents/publication/wcms_221513.pdf

International Labour Organization. (2014a). Action to prevent and prosecute human trafficking in Guatemala. Retrieved from http://www.ilo.org/global/topics/forced-labour/projects/WCMS_320413/lang--en/index.htm

International Labour Organization. (2014b). Protocol of 2014 to the Forced Labour Convention, 1930. Retrieved from https://www.ilo.org/dyn/normlex/en/f?p=NORMLEXPUB:12100:0::NO::P12100_ILO_CODE:P029#A1

International Labour Organization. (2014c). *Rules of the game: A brief introduction to international labour standards.* Retrieved from http://www.ilo.org/global/standards/information-resources-and-publications/publications/WCMS_318141/lang--en/index.htm

International Labour Organization. (2015). Combating forced labour: A handbook for employers and business. Retrieved from http://www.ilo.org/wcmsp5/groups/public/---ed_norm/---declaration/documents/publication/wcms_101171.pdf

International Labour Organization. (2016). General principles & operational guidelines for fair recruitment. Retrieved from https://www.ilo.org/wcmsp5/groups/public/---ed_norm/---declaration/documents/publication/wcms_536755.pdf

International Organization for Migration. (n.d.). International Recruitment Integrity System. Retrieved November 11, 2018, from https://iris.iom.int/

International Organization for Migration. (2008). *Human trafficking in Eastern Africa: Research assessment and baseline information in Tanzania, Kenya, Uganda, and Burundi.* Retrieved from http://publications.iom.int/system/files/pdf/kenyahumantraffickingbaselineassessment.pdf

International Organization for Migration. (2015). Addressing human trafficking and exploitation in times of crisis: Evidence and recommendations for further action to protect vulnerable and mobile populations (Briefing document). Retrieved from https://www.iom.int/sites/default/files/press_release/file/CT_in_Crisis_FINAL.pdf

International Organization for Migration. (2016). *Migrant smuggling data and research: A global review of the emerging evidence base.* Retrieved from http://publications.iom.int/system/files/smuggling_report.pdf

International Organization for Migration, Global Initiative to Fight Human Trafficking, & London School of Hygiene and Tropical Medicine. (2009). *Caring for trafficked persons: Guidance for health providers.* Retrieved from https://publications.iom.int/system/files/pdf/ct_handbook.pdf

International Organization for Migration, United Kingdom. (2016, October 18). Abuse, exploitation, and trafficking: IOM reveals data on the scale of the danger and risks that migrants face on the Mediterranean routes to Europe [Blog post]. Retrieved from https://unitedkingdom.iom.int/blog/news/abuse-exploitation-and-trafficking-iom-reveals-data-on-the-scale

Inter-Parliamentary Union & World Health Organization. (2016). *Child, early and forced marriage legislation in 37 Asia-Pacific countries.* Retrieved from http://archive.ipu.org/pdf/publications/child-marriage-en.pdf

Ireland Department of Justice and Equality, Anti–Human Trafficking Unit. (n.d.). Trafficking or smuggling? Retrieved from http://www.blueblindfold.gov.ie/en/BBF/Pages/Trafficking_or_Smuggling

Jackman, T. (2018, April 11). Trump signs "FOSTA" bill targeting online sex trafficking, enables states and victims to pursue websites. *Washington Post.* Retrieved from https://www.washingtonpost.com/news/

true-crime/wp/2018/04/11/trump-signs-fosta-bill-targeting-online-sex-trafficking-enables-states-and-victims-to-pursue-websites/? utm_term=.eb6d055dbc39

Jackman, T., & O'Connell, J. (2017, July 11). 16-year-old was found beaten, stabbed to death after being advertised as prostitute on Backpage. *Washington Post.* Retrieved from https://www.washingtonpost.com/local/public-safety/how-a-16-year-old-went-from-backpage-to-prostitution-to-homicide-victim/2017/07/10/72eca33c-5f55-11e7-a4f7-af34fc1d9d39_story.html? utm_term=.7a64640a96da&wprss=rss_crime

Jakobsson, N., & Kotsadam, A. (2013). The law and economics of international sex slavery: Prostitution law and trafficking for sexual exploitation. *European Journal of Law and Economics, 35,* 87–107.

Jani, N., & Anstadt, S. P. (2013). Contributing factors in trafficking from south Asia. *Journal of Human Behavior in the Social Environment, 23,* 298–311.

Jiang, B., & LaFree, G. (2016). Social control, trade openness and human trafficking. *Journal of Quantitative Criminology,* 1–27. doi:10.1007/s10940-016-9316-7

Johnson, E. W. (2018, March 16). Kentucky votes to ban child marriage [Blog post]. Retrieved from https://www.npr.org/sections/thetwo-way/2018/03/16/594253182/kentucky-votes-to-ban-child-marriage

Jones, L., Engstrom, D., Hilliard, P., & Sungakawan, D. (2011). Human trafficking between Thailand and Japan: Lessons in recruitment, transit, and control. *International Journal of Social Welfare, 20,* 203–211.

Jordan, A. (2004). *Human Trafficking and Globalization.* Washington, DC: Center for American Progress.

Jordan, J., Patel, B., & Rapp, L. (2013). Domestic minor sex trafficking: A social work perspective on misidentification, victims, buyers, traffickers, treatment, and reform of current practice. *Journal of Human Behavior in the Social Environment, 23*(3), 356–369. doi:10.1080/10911359.2013.764198

Justice at Work. (n.d.). Fighting labor trafficking. Retrieved from https://www.friendsfw.org/service-areas/special-initiatives/services-for-victims-of-labor-trafficking/

Kalamar, A. M., Lee-Rife, S., & Hindin, M. J. (2016). Interventions to prevent child marriage among young people in low- and middle-income countries: A systematic review of the published and gray literature. *Journal of Adolescent Health, 59,* 516–521.

Kamhi, A., & Prandini, R. (2017). T visas: What they are and how they can help your clients. Retrieved from

https://www.ilrc.org/sites/default/files/resources/t_visa_advisory-20170509.pdf

Kangaspunta, K. (2010). Measuring the immeasurable. *Criminology and Public Policy, 9*(2), 257–265. doi:10.1111/j.1745-9133.2010.00624.x

Kaplan, E. (2005, December 2). Child soldiers around the world. Retrieved from https://www.cfr.org/backgrounder/child-soldiers-around-world

Karlsson, M. (2013). Anti–sex trafficking institutions. *International Migration, 51*(4), 73–86. doi:10.1111/imig.12040

Kaufman, M. R., & Crawford, M. (2011). Sex trafficking in Nepal: A review of intervention and prevention programs. *Violence Against Women, 17*(5), 651–665. doi:10.1177/1077801211407431

Kennedy, M. A., Klein, C., Bristowe, J. K., Cooper, B. S., & Yuille, J. C. (2007). Routes of recruitment: Pimps' techniques and other circumstances that lead to street prostitution. *Journal of Aggression, Maltreatment and Trauma, 15*(2), 1–19.

Kenyon, S. D., & Schanz, Y. Y. (2014). Sex trafficking: Examining links to prostitution and the routine activity theory. *International Journal of Criminology and Sociology, 3,* 61–76.

Kessler, G. (2015, April 24). Why you should be wary of statistics on "modern slavery" and "trafficking." *Washington Post.* Retrieved from https://www.washingtonpost.com/news/fact-checker/wp/2015/04/24/why-you-should-be-wary-of-statistics-on-modern-slavery-and-trafficking/? utm_term=.90a03c735c3d

Khan, M., Hazra, A., Kant, A., & Ali, M. (2016). Conditional and unconditional cash transfers to improve use of contraception in low and middle income countries: A systematic review. *Studies in Family Planning, 47*(4), 371–383. doi:10.1111/sifp.12004

King, L. (2008). International law and human trafficking. *Human Rights and Human Welfare.* Retrieved from http://www.du.edu/korbel/hrhw/researchdigest/trafficking/InternationalLaw.pdf

Kizilhan, J., & Noll-Hussong, M. (2018). Post-traumatic stress disorder among former Islamic State child soldiers in northern Iraq. *British Journal of Psychiatry, 213*(1), 425–429.

Klasen, F., Daniels, J., Oettingen, G., Post, M., Hoyer, C., & Adam, H. (2010). Posttraumatic resilience in former Ugandan child soldiers. *Child Development, 81*(4), 1096–1113.

Kloer, A. (2010). Sex trafficking and HIV/AIDS: A deadly junction for women. *Human Rights Magazine, 37.* Retrieved from https://www.americanbar.org/publications/human_rights_magazine_home/human_rights_vol37_2010/spring2010/sex_trafficking_and_hiv_aids_a_deadly_junction_for_women_and_girls.html

Knoc, R. (2008). Should we legalize the market for human organs? *NPR.* Retrieved from https://www.npr.org/2008/05/21/90632108/should-we-legalize-the-market-for-human-organs

Kohrt, B., Jordans, M., & Morley, C. (2010). Four principles of mental health research and psychosocial intervention for child soldiers: Lessons learned in Nepal. *International Psychiatry, 7*(3), 57–59.

Kohrt, B., Yang, M., Rai, S., Bhardwaj, A., Tol, W., & Jordans, M. (2016). Recruitment of child soldiers in Nepal: Mental health status and risk factors for voluntary participation of youth in armed groups. *Peace and Conflict: Journal of Peace Psychology, 22*(3), 208–216.

Kolb, M. (2018). What is globalization? Retrieved from https://piie.com/microsites/globalization/what-is-globalization.html

Konrad, R. A., Trapp, A. C., Palmbach, T. M., & Blom, J. S. (2017). Overcoming human trafficking via operations research and analytics: Opportunities for methods, models, and applications. *European Journal of Operational Research, 259*(2), 733–745.

Kortla, K. (2010). Domestic minor sex trafficking in the United States. *Social Work, 55*(2), 181–187. Retrieved from http://www.naswpress.org/publications/journals/sw.html

Koski, A., & Heymann, J. (2018). Child marriage in the United States: How common is the practice, and which children are at greatest risk? *Perspectives on Sexual and Reproductive Health, 50*(2), 59–65. doi:10.1363/psrh.12055

Krishnan, A., Amarchand, R., Byass, P., Pandav, C., & Ng, N. (2014). "No one says 'No' to money": A mixed methods approach for evaluating conditional cash transfer schemes to improve girl children's status in Haryana, India. *International Journal for Equity in Health, 13*, 11. doi:10.1186/1475-9276-13-11

Kristof, N. D., & WuDunn, S. (2010). *Half the sky: Turning oppression into opportunity for women worldwide.* Vintage Books: New York.

Laband, J. (2017). The slave soldiers of Africa. *Journal of Military History, 81*(1), 9–38.

Laboratory to Combat Human Trafficking. (2017, February 13). Responsible public awareness campaigns for human trafficking [Blog post]. Retrieved from https://combathumantrafficking.org/2017/02/the-importance-of-responsible-public-awareness-campaigns-for-human-trafficking/

Laczko, F., & Gramegna, M. A. (2003). Developing better indicators of human trafficking. *Brown Journal of World Affairs, 10*(1), 179.

LasVegasNow.com. (2007, September 5). Many tourists think prostitution is legal in Las Vegas. Retrieved from http://www.lasvegasnow.com/news/many-tourists-think-prostitution-is-legal-in-las-vegas/81756115

Law, S. (2000). Commercial sex: Beyond decriminalization. *Southern California Law Review, 73*, 523–610.

Lederer, L. (2011). Religious persecution and human trafficking. *Prism Magazine*, p. 6. Retrieved from https://issuu.com/prismmagazine/docs/pages_from_sept-oct_2010_prism_religious_persecuti

Lee, S., & Persson, P. (2015). Human trafficking and regulating prostitution (New York University Law and Economics Working Paper 299). Retrieved from http://lsr.nellco.org/nyu_lewp/299

Leidholdt, D. A. (2013). Interviewing and assisting trafficking survivors. In J. L. Goodman & D. A. Leidholdt (Eds.), *Lawyer's manual on human trafficking: Pursuing justice for victims* (pp. 169–182). Supreme Court of the State of New York & New York State Judicial Committee on Women in the Courts. Retrieved from https://www.nycourts.gov/ip/womeninthecourts/pdfs/lmht.pdf

Lerch, M. (2015). The European year for development: Women and girls [Briefing]. Retrieved from http://www.europarl.europa.eu/EPRS/2015-02-05_03_EYD_women_and_girls.pdf

Levenkron, N. (2007). *"Another delivery from Tashkent": Profile of the Israeli trafficker.* Tel Aviv, Israel: Hotline for Migrant Workers. Retrieved from https://hotline.org.il/wp-content/uploads/Another_Delivery_From_Tashkent_Eng.pdf

Lillie, M. (2017). The connection between the Mara Salvatrucha (MS-13) and human trafficking. Retrieved from http://humantraffickingsearch.org/wp-content/uploads/2017/09/MS-13-Publication.pdf

Limoncelli, S. A. (2016). What in the world are anti-trafficking NGOs doing? Findings from a global study. *Journal of Human Trafficking, 2*(4), 316–328. doi:10.1080/23322705.2015.1135605

Lopez, S. (2016). Prostitution in Nevada has its advantages, experts say. *Las Vegas Review-Journal.* Retrieved from https://www.reviewjournal.com/local/local-las-vegas/downtown/prostitution-in-nevada-has-its-advantages-experts-say/

Lutya, T. M., & Lanier M. (2012). An integrated theoretical framework to describe human trafficking of young women and girls for involuntary prostitution [Open-access chapter]. Retrieved from http://www.intechopen.com/articles/show/title/an-intergrated-theoretical-framework-to-describe-human-trafficking-of-young-women-and-girls-for-invo

Lyneham, S., & Richards, K. (2014). Human trafficking involving marriage and partner migration to Australia (Research and Public Policy Series No. 124). Retrieved from https://aic.gov.au/publications/rpp/rpp124

Major, R. W. (2008). Paying kidney donors: Time to follow Iran? *McGill Journal of Medicine, 11*(1), 67.

Mann Act, 18 U.S.C., §§ 2421–24 (1910).

Marian, J. (2017). Prostitution laws in Europe. Retrieved from https://jakubmarian.com/prostitution-laws-in-europe/

Martinez, M. (2016, October 19). What to know about Nevada's legal brothels. Retrieved from http://www.cnn.com/2015/10/14/us/lamar-odom-nevada-brothels/index.html

Martinez, O., & Kelle, G. (2013). Sex trafficking of LGBT individuals: A call for service provision, research, and action. *International Law News, 42*(4). Retrieved from https://www.ncbi.nlm.nih.gov/pmc/articles/PMC4204396/

Mason L., Nyothach, E., Alexander, K., Odhiambo, F.O., Eleveld, A., Vulule, J., . . . Phillips-Howard, P. A. (2013). "We keep it secret so no one should know": A qualitative study to explore young schoolgirls attitudes and experiences with menstruation in rural Western Kenya. *PLoS ONE, 8*(11), e79132. doi:10.1371/journal.pone.0079132

Matas, A. J., & Schnitzler, M. (2004). Payment for living donor (vendor) kidneys: A cost-effectiveness analysis. *American Journal of Transplantation, 4*(2), 216–221.

Mathewson, S. (2012, December 2). Child bride or slave? The girls of Niger who are both. Retrieved from https://www.girlsnotbrides.org/child-bride-or-slave-the-girls-in-niger-who-are-both/

Mattar, M. (2004). Trafficking in persons, especially women and children in the countries of the Americas. A regional report on the scope of the problem and the governmental and non-governmental response. In *Human rights and trafficking in persons in the Americas: Summary and highlights of the Hemispheric Conference on International Migration*. Retrieved from https://repositorio.cepal.org/bitstream/handle/11362/6659/1/S0310675_en.pdf

Mazzio, M. (n.d.). I am Little Red. Retrieved from https://www.iamlittlered.com/

Mazzio, M., Sokolow, A., Osorio, G. (Directors), & Pierart, P. (Producer). (2017). *Little red*. United States: 50 Egg Films.

McCartin, E. (2016, January 5). The average age of entry myth [Blog post]. Retrieved from https://polarisproject.org/blog/2016/01/05/average-age-entry-myth

McCombs, E. (2018, May 17). "This bill is killing us": 9 sex workers on their lives in the wake of FOSTA. Retrieved from https://www.huffingtonpost.com/entry/sex-workers-sesta-fosta_us_5ad0d7d0e4b0edca2cb964d9

McFadden, A., Siebelt, L., Gavine, A., Atkin, K., Bell, K., Innes, N., . . . MacGillivray, S. (2018). Gypsy, Roma, and Traveller access to and engagement with health services: A systematic review. *European Journal of Public Health, 28*, 74–81.

Mehdiyev, F. (n.d.). Human trafficking: Russia as the country of origin. Retrieved from http://www.academia.edu/210605/Human_Trafficking_Russia_As_The_Country_Of_Origin

Mehlman-Orozco, K. (2017). Projected heroes and self-perceived manipulators: Understanding the duplicitous identities of human traffickers. *Trends in Organized Crime*. doi:10.1007/s12117-017-9325-4

Merton, R. (1938). Social structure and anomie. *American Sociological Review, 3*, 772–682.

Meshkovska, B., Siegel, M., Stutterheim, S. E., & Bos, A. R. (2015). Female sex trafficking: Conceptual issues, current debates, and future directions. *Journal of Sex Research, 52*(4), 380–395. doi:10.1080/00224499.2014.1002126

Michaels, K. (2017, August 24). Surviving as working class after Backpage [Blog post]. Retrieved from http://titsandsass.com/surviving-as-working-class-after-backpage/#more-23180

Migration to Europe: Death at sea [Blog post]. (2015, September 3). *The Economist*. Retrieved from http://www.economist.com/blogs/graphicdetail/2015/09/migration-europe-0

Miller, H. (2017, October 26). Mapped: The prostitution laws of every European country. Retrieved from https://matadornetwork.com/read/prostitution-laws-of-european-countries/

Miller, L. (2005). *Handbook of international adoption medicine: A guide for physicians, parents, providers*. Oxford, England: Oxford University Press.

Miller-Perrin, C., & Wurtele, S. K. (2017). Sex trafficking and the commercial sexual exploitation of children. *Women and Therapy, 40*(1–2), 123–151. doi:10.1080/02703149.2016.1210963

Missing Migrants Project. (2016). Migrant routes: America (Central America, Mexico, and U.S.) 2016. Retrieved from https://reliefweb.int/map/world/migrant-routes-americas-central-america-mexico-and-us-2016

Moody, S. (2017, November 20). Qatar commits to strengthen workers' rights for two million migrants [Blog post]. Retrieved from https://blogs.state.gov/stories/2017/11/20/en/qatar-commits-strengthen-workers rights-2-million-migrants

Moore, J. L., Hirway, P., Barron, C. E., & Goldberg, A. P. (2017). Trafficking experiences and psychosocial features of domestic minor sex trafficking victims. *Journal of Interpersonal Violence, 4*, 1–16. doi:10.1177/0886260517703373

Motaparthy, P. (2015, March 11). Understanding Kafala: An archaic law at cross purposes with modern development. Retrieved from https://www.migrant-rights.org/2015/03/understanding-kafala-an-archaic-law-at-cross-purposes-with-modern-development/

Motivans, M., & Snyder, H. N. (2018). Federal prosecution of human-trafficking cases, 2015 (NCJ 251390). Retrieved from https://www.bjs.gov/content/pub/pdf/fphtc15.pdf

Mullen, K., & Lloyd, R. (2013). The passage of the Safe Harbor Act and the voices of sexually exploited youth. In J. L. Goodman & D. A. Leidholdt (Eds.), *Lawyer's Manual on Human Trafficking: Pursuing Justice for Victims* (pp. 129–140). Supreme Court of the State of New York & New York State Judicial Committee on Women in the Courts. Retrieved from https://www.nycourts.gov/ip/womeninthecourts/pdfs/lmht.pdf

Murphy, L. S. (2010). Understanding the social and economic contexts surrounding women engaged in street-level prostitution. *Issues in Mental Health Nursing, 31*, 775–784.

Murphy, L. T. (2016). *Labor and sex trafficking among homeless youth.* Retrieved from https://www.covenant house.org/sites/default/files/inline-files/Loyola%20Multi-City%20Executive%20Summary%20FINAL.pdf

Mzezewa, T. (2017, April 17). Homeless youth at high risk of human trafficking. *New York Times.* Retrieved from https://kristof.blogs.nytimes.com/2017/04/17/homeless-youth-at-high-risk-of-human-trafficking/

Nanda, P., Datta, N., & Das, P. (2014). Impact on marriage: Program assessment of conditional cash transfers. Retrieved from https://www.icrw.org/wp-content/uploads/2016/10/IMPACCT_Hires_FINAL_3_20.pdf

Nanda, P., Datta, N., Pradhan, E., Das, P., & Lamba, S. (2016). Making change with cash? Impact of a conditional cash transfer programme on age of marriage in India. Retrieved from https://www.icrw.org/publications/making-change-with-cash-impact-of-a-conditional-cash-transfer-program-on-age-of-marriage-in-india/

Napier-Moore, R. (2011). FAQ2: Smuggling and trafficking intersections. Retrieved from http://www.gaatw.org/publications/Working_Papers_Smuggling/FAQ2_TraffickingandSmugglingIntersections.pdf

National Center for Missing and Exploited Children. (2017). Child sex trafficking. Retrieved from http://www.missingkids.com/theissues/trafficking

National Center for Prosecution of Child Abuse. (2012). Child protection laws regarding victims of commercial sexual exploitation. Retrieved from http://www.ndaa.org/pdf/Child%20Protection%20Laws%20Regarding%20Victims%20of%20Commercial%20Sexual%20Exploitation.pdf

National Coalition for the Homeless. (2009). *LGBTQ homelessness.* Retrieved from http://nationalhomeless.org/wp-content/uploads/2015/03/LGBTQ-Homelessness.pdf

National Crime Agency. (n.d.). National referral mechanism. Retrieved from http://www.nationalcrimeagency.gov.uk/about-us/what-we-do/specialist-capabilities/uk human-trafficking-centre/national-referral-mechanism

National Disability Rights Network. (2017, February 1). Disability rights advocates take aim at human trafficking of people with disabilities [Press release]. Retrieved from http://www.ndrn.org/en/media/releases/614-human-trafficking.html

National Human Trafficking Resource Center. (2015). Trauma-informed human trafficking screenings [Webinar]. Retrieved from https://humantraffickinghotline.org/resources/trauma-informed-human-trafficking-screenings

National Human Trafficking Resource Center. (2016, February). *2015 NHTRC annual report.* Retrieved from https://humantraffickinghotline.org/resources/2015-nhtrc-annual-report

National Institute of Justice. (n.d.). Human trafficking. Retrieved from https://www.nij.gov/topics/crime/human-trafficking/pages/welcome.aspx

National Institute of Justice. (2016). Improving the investigation and prosecution of state and local human trafficking cases. Retrieved from http://nij.gov/topics/crime/human-trafficking/pages/improving investigation-and-prosecution-of-human-trafficking-cases.aspx

National Organ Transplant Act, Pub. L. 98-507 (1984).

Neumann, V. (2015). Never mind the metrics: Disrupting human trafficking by other means. *Journal of International Affairs, 68*(2), 39–53.

New York State Unified Court System, Office of Policy and Planning. (n.d.). Problem-solving courts: Human trafficking intervention courts. Retrieved from https://www.nycourts.gov/courts/problem_solving/htc/index.shtml

Newman, W., Holt, B., Rabun, J., Phillips, G., & Scott, C. (2011). Child sex tourism: Extending the borders of sexual offender legislation. *International Journal of Law and Psychiatry, 34*(2), 116–121. doi:10.1016/j.ijlp.2011.02.005

Newton, P., Mulcahy, T., & Martin, S. (2008). *Finding victims of human trafficking.* Retrieved from https://www.ncjrs.gov/pdffiles1/nij/grants/224393.pdf

Nichols, A. (2010). Dance Ponnaya, dance! Police abuses against transgender sex workers in Sri Lanka. *Feminist Criminology, 5*(2), 195–222.

Niveau, G. (2010). Cyber-pedocriminality: Characteristics of a sample of Internet child pornography offenders. *Child Abuse and Neglect: The International Journal, 34*(8), 570–575.

Nour, N. M. (2009). Child marriage: A silent health and human rights issue. *Reviews in Obstetrics and Gynecology, 1,* 51–56.

O'Brien, J. E., Li, W., Givens, A., & Leibowitz, G. S. (2017). Domestic minor sex trafficking among adjudicated male youth: Prevalence and links to treatment. *Children and Youth Services Review, 82,* 392–399.

O'Connor, M., & Healy, C. (2006). *The links between prostitution and sex trafficking* [Ebook]. Coalition Against Trafficking in Women. Retrieved from https://ec.europa.eu/anti-trafficking/sites/antitrafficking/files/the_links_between_prostitution_and_sex_trafficking_a_briefing_handbook_en_1.pdf

Office for Victims of Crime, Training and Technical Assistance Center. (n.d.a). Mental health needs. In *Human trafficking task force e-guide.* Retrieved December 22, 2018, from https://www.ovcttac.gov/taskforceguide/eguide/4-supporting-victims/44-comprehensive-victim-services/mental-health-needs/

Office for Victims of Crime, Training and Technical Assistance Center. (n.d.b). Safe housing options. In *Human trafficking task force e-guide.* Retrieved from https://www.ovcttac.gov/taskforceguide/eguide/4-supporting-victims/44-comprehensive-victim-services/safe-housing-options/

Office for Victims of Crime, Training and Technical Assistance Center. (n.d.c). Using a trauma-informed approach. In *Human trafficking task force e-guide.* Retrieved from https://www.ovcttac.gov/taskforceguide/eguide/4-supporting-victims/41-using-a-trauma-informed-approach/

Office for Victims of Crime, Training and Technical Assistance Center. (n.d.d). Victims with physical, cognitive, or emotional disabilities. In *Human trafficking task force e-guide.* Retrieved from https://www.ovcttac.gov/taskforceguide/eguide/4-supporting-victims/45-victim-populations/victims-with-physical-cognitive-or-emotional-disabilities/

Office of Refugee Resettlement. (2012). Fact sheet: Labor trafficking. Retrieved from http://www.acf.hhs.gov/programs/orr/resource/fact-sheet-labor-trafficking-english

Office of the High Commissioner for Human Rights. (n.d.). Escaping the bonds of human trafficking: Pamela's story. Retrieved November 11, 2018, from https://www.ohchr.org/EN/NewsEvents/Pages/EscapingBondsOfHumanTrafficking.aspx

Office of the High Commissioner for Human Rights. (2002). Abolishing slavery and its contemporary forms. Retrieved from http://www.ohchr.org/Documents/Publications/slaveryen.pdf

Office of the High Commissioner for Human Rights. (2014). *Human rights and human trafficking* (Fact Sheet No. 36). Retrieved from https://www.ohchr.org/Documents/Publications/FS36_en.pdf

Office of the High Commissioner for Human Rights. (2016, September 15). Debt bondage remains the most prevalent form of forced labour worldwide—New UN report. Retrieved from https://ohchr.org/EN/NewsEvents/Pages/DisplayNews.aspx?NewsID=20504&LangID=E

Office of the High Commissioner for Human Rights. (2018). How to train cabin crews to identify trafficking victims. Retrieved from https://www.ohchr.org/EN/NewsEvents/Pages/AviationGuidelinesOnTrafficking.aspx

Office of the Special Representative and Co-ordinator for Combating Trafficking in Human Beings. (2013). *Trafficking in human beings for the purpose of organ removal in the OSCE region: Analysis and findings.* Retrieved from https://www.osce.org/cthb/103393?download=true

Office of the Special Representative of the Secretary-General for Children and Armed Conflict. (2013a, May 29). Junior Nzita Nsuami: A former child soldiers rebuilds his life. Retrieved from https://childrenan darmedconflict.un.org/junior-nzita-former-child-soldier/

Office of the Special Representative of the Secretary-General for Children and Armed Conflict. (2013b). The six grave violations against children during armed conflict: The legal foundation (Working Paper No. 1). Retrieved from https://childrenandarmed-conflict.un.org/publications/WorkingPaper-1_SixGraveViolationsLegalFoundation.pdf

Office on Trafficking in Persons. (n.d.). Federal government efforts to combat human trafficking. Retrieved from https://www.acf.hhs.gov/otip/resources/federal-efforts

Office to Monitor and Combat Trafficking in Persons. (2007). Policy approaches to trafficking in persons. In *Trafficking in Persons Report*. Retrieved from https://www.state.gov/j/tip/rls/tiprpt/2007/82813.htm

Office to Monitor and Combat Trafficking in Persons. (2017a). Civilian security, democracy, and human rights: The 3Ps: Prevention, protection, and prosecution. Retrieved from https://www.state.gov/documents/organization/272970.pdf

Office to Monitor and Combat Trafficking in Persons. (2017b). Fact sheet: The vulnerability of LGBTI individuals to human trafficking. Retrieved from https://www.state.gov/j/tip/rls/fs/2017/272724.htm

Ohio Department of Developmental Disabilities. (2014). Fact sheet: Human trafficking of individuals with disabilities. Retrieved from http://dodd.ohio.gov/HealthandSafety/Documents/Human%20Trafficking%20Fact%20Sheet%2010%2017%2014.pdf

Oluga, M., Kiragu, S., Mohamed, M., & Walli, S. (2010). "Deceptive" cultural practices that sabotage HIV/AIDS education in Tanzania and Kenya. *Journal of Moral Education, 39*(3), 365–380.

Onagoruwa, A., & Wodon, Q. (2017). Measuring the impact of child marriage on total fertility: A study for fifteen countries. *Journal of Biosocial Science.* doi:10.1017/S0021932017000542

Organ Harvesting: An Examination of a Brutal Practice: Joint Hearing Before the Subcommittee on Africa, Global Health, Global Human Rights, and International Organizations & the Subcommittee on Europe, Eurasia, and Emerging Threats of the Committee on Foreign Affairs, House of Representatives, 114th Cong. (2016).

Organ Procurement and Transplantation Network, Final Rule, 42 C.F.R. 121 (2003).

Organisation for Economic Co-operation and Development. (2016). *Trafficking in persons and corruption: Breaking the chain.* Retrieved from https://doi.org/10.1787/9789264253728-en

Organization for Security and Co-operation in Europe Permanent Council. (2003). OSCE action plan to combat trafficking in human beings (PC.DEC/557). Retrieved from https://www.osce.org/actionplan?download=true

Outshoorn, J. (2005). The political debates on prostitution and trafficking of women. *Social Politics: International Studies in Gender, State and Society, 12*(1), 141–155.

Owens, C., Dank, M., Breaux, J., Bañuelos, I., Farrell, A., Pfeffer, R., . . . McDevitt, J. (2014). *Understanding the organization, operation, and victimization process of labor trafficking in the United States.* Retrieved from https://www.urban.org/sites/default/files/publication/33821/413249-Understanding-the-Organization-Operation-and-Victimization-Process-of-Labor-Trafficking-in-the-United-States.PDF

Padilla, M. B., & MPH. (2007). "Western Union Daddies" and their question for authenticity: An ethnographic study of the Dominican gay sex tourism industry. *Journal of Homosexuality, 53*(1–2), 241–275. doi:10.1300/J082v53n01_11

Pandey, S., Karki, Y. B., Murugan, V., & Mathur, A. (2017). Mothers' risk for experiencing neonatal and under-five child deaths in Nepal: The role of empowerment. *Global Social Welfare, 4*, 105–115.

Parmentier, S. (2010). Epilogue: Human trafficking seen from the future. *European Journal of Criminology, 7*(1), 95–100.

Pellerin, C. (2017, January 4). DARPA program helps fight human trafficking. Retrieved from https://www.defense.gov/News/Article/Article/1041509/darpa-program-helps-to-fight-human-trafficking/

Petroni, S., Steinhaus, M., Fenn, N. S., Stoebenau, K., & Gregowski, A. (2017). New findings on child marriage in sub-Saharan Africa. *Annals of Global Health, 83*, 782–791.

Pierce, S. (2015). Blacklisted: An overview of Brazil's "Dirty List." Retrieved from https://humantrafficking-search.org/blacklisted-an-overview-of-brazils-dirty-list/

Polaris. (n.d.a). The facts. Retrieved November from https://polarisproject.org/facts

Polaris. (n.d.b). Global safety net. Retrieved from https://polarisproject.org/initiatives/global-safety-net

Polaris. (n.d.c). More assistance. More action. 2016 statistics from the National Human Trafficking Hotline and BeFree Textline. Retrieved from http://polarisproject.org/sites/default/files/2016-Statistics.pdf

Polaris. (n.d.d). 2015 statistics. Retrieved from http://polarisproject.org/sites/default/files/2015-Statistics.pdf

Polaris. (2014a). A look back: Building a human trafficking legal framework. Retrieved from http://polaris project.org/sites/default/files/2014-Look-Back.pdf

Polaris. (2014b, November 8). Survivor story: He dreamed of working in the United States [Blog post]. Retrieved from https://polarisproject.org/blog/2014/11/08/survivor-story-he-dreamed-working-united-states

Polaris. (2014c). 2014 state ratings on human trafficking laws. Retrieved from https://polarisproject.org/sites/default/files/2014-State-Ratings.pdf

Polaris. (2015a). Breaking barriers: Improving services for LBGTP human trafficking victims. Retrieved from https://polarisproject.org/sites/default/files/breaking-barriers-lgbtq-services.pdf

Polaris. (2015b). Human trafficking issue brief: Safe harbor. Retrieved from https://polarisproject.org/sites/default/files/2015%20Safe%20Harbor%20Issue%20Brief.pdf

Polaris. (2015c). Human trafficking issue brief: Task forces. Retrieved from http://polarisproject.org/sites/default/files/2015%20Task%20Forces%20Issue%20Brief%20Final.pdf

Polaris. (2015d). Labor trafficking in the U.S.: A closer look at temporary work visas. Retrieved from http://polarisproject.org/sites/default/files/Temp%20Visa_v5%20%281%29.pdf

Polaris. (2015e). Sex trafficking in the U.S.: A closer look at U.S. citizen victimization. Retrieved from https://polarisproject.org/sites/default/files/us-citizen-sex-trafficking.pdf

Polaris. (2015f, June 17). Survivor story: Promised an education, forced to work instead [Blog post]. Retrieved from https://polarisproject.org/blog/2015/06/17/survivor-story-promised-education-forced-work-instead

Polaris. (2017). The typology of modern slavery: Defining sex and labor trafficking in the United States. Retrieved from https://polarisproject.org/sites/default/files/Polaris-Typology-of-Modern-Slavery.pdf

Polaris. (2018). On-ramps, intersections, and exit routes: A roadmap for systems and industries to prevent and disrupt human trafficking. Retrieved from https://polarisproject.org/sites/default/files/A%20 Roadmap%20for%20Systems%20and%20 Industries%20to%20Prevent%20and%20Disrupt%20 Human%20Trafficking%20-%20Transportation%20 Industry.pdf

Press, G. (2014, September 3). 12 big data definitions: What's yours? Retrieved from https://www.forbes.com/sites/gilpress/2014/09/03/12-big-data-definitions-whats-yours/#54e69b2513ae

ProCon.org. (n.d.). 100 countries and their prostitution policies. Retrieved from https://prostitution.procon.org/view.resource.php?resourceID=000772

Project Vic. (n.d.). Technology. Retrieved from http://projectvic.org/technology/

Queen's University, School of Law. (n.d.). State v. Netcare Kwa-Zulu Limited (UNODC No. ZA4002). Retrieved from https://www.unodc.org/cld/case-law-doc/traffickingpersonscrimetype/zaf/2010/state_v._net care_kwa-zulu_limited.html?tmpl=old

Quinnell, J., & Perri, S. (n.d.). Statelessness in Thailand. Retrieved from http://www.thethailandproject.org/who-we-help-stateless.html

Raj, A. (2010). When the mother is a child: The impact of child marriage on the health and human rights of girls. Archives of Disease in Childhood, 95(11), 931–935.

Raj, A., Jackson, E., & Dunham, S. (2018). Girl child marriage: A persistent global women's health and human rights violation. In S. Choudhury, J. T. Erausquin, & M. Withers (Eds.), Global Perspectives on Women's Sexual and Reproductive Health Across the Lifecourse (pp. 3–19). Cham, Switzerland: Springer.

Rand, A. (2009). It can't happen in my backyard: The commercial sexual exploitation of girls in the United States. Child and Youth Services, 31(3/4), 138–156. Retrieved from http://dx.doi.org/10.1080/0145935X.2009.524480

Rankin, J. (2016, May 19). Human traffickers "using migration crisis" to force more people into slavery. The Guardian. Retrieved from https://www.theguardian.com/world/2016/may/19/human-traffickers-using-migration-crisis-to-force-more-people-into-slavery

Raphael, J., Reichert, J., & Powers, M. (2010). Pimp control and violence: Domestic sex trafficking of Chicago women and girls. Women and Criminal Justice, 20(1–2), 89–104.

Ravinsky, J., & Lumpe, L. (2016, November 7). In the fight against human trafficking, child soldiers get ignored. Retrieved from https://www.opensocietyfoundations.org/voices/fight-against-human-trafficking-child-soldiers-get-ignored

RedTraSex. (n.d.). Our history. Retrieved from http://redtrasex.org/spip.php?rubrique41

Refugee Project. (n.d.). Retrieved from http://www.therefugeeproject.org/#/2015

Reid, J. A. (2010). Doors wide shut: Barriers to the successful delivery of victim services for domestically trafficked minors in a southern U.S. metropolitan area. Women and Criminal Justice, 20, 147–166. doi:10.1080/08974451003641206

Reid, J. A. (2011). An exploratory model of girl's vulnerability to commercial sexual exploitation in prostitution. *Child Maltreatment, 16*(2), 146–157.

Reid, J. A. (2016). Entrapment and enmeshment schemes used by sex traffickers. *Sex Abuse: A Journal of Research and Treatment, 28*, 491–511.

Reid, J. A., & Jones, S. (2011). Exploited vulnerability: Legal and psychological perspectives on child sex trafficking victims. *Victims and Offenders, 6*(2), 207–231. doi:10.1080/15564886.2011.557327

Reid, J. A., & Piquero, A. R. (2014). Age-graded risks for commercial sexual exploitation. *Journal of Interpersonal Violence, 29*, 1747–1777.

Reid, J. A., & Piquero, A. R. (2016). Applying general strain theory to youth commercial sexual exploitation. *Crime and Delinquency, 62*(3), 341–367.

Reiger, A. (2007). Missing the mark: Why the Trafficking Victims Protection Act fails to protect sex trafficking victims in the United States. *Harvard Journal of Law and Gender, 30*, 231–256.

Reuters. (n.d.). Disputed rankings [Table]. Retrieved from http://graphics.thomsonreuters.com/15/07/USA-TRAFFICKING-TIER3.jpg

Richards, K., & Lyneham, S. (2014). Help-seeking strategies of victim: Survivors of human trafficking involving partner migration. *Trends and Issues in Crime and Criminal Justice, 468*, 1–10.

Richards, T., & Reid, J. (2015). Gender stereotyping and sex trafficking: Comparative review of research on male and female sex tourism. *Journal of Crime and Justice, 38*(3), 414–433. doi:10.1080/0735648X.2014.1000560

Rijken, C., van Waas, L., Gramatikov, M., & Brennan, D. (2015). *The nexus between statelessness and human trafficking in Thailand.* Oisterwijk: Netherlands: Wold Legal Publishers.

Robinson, M. (2018, January 2). 10 shocking facts about child soldiers [Blog post]. Retrieved from https://borgenproject.org/shocking-facts-about-child-soldiers/

Roenigk, E. (2014, August 27). Unaccompanied minors are "uniquely vulnerable" to trafficking. Retrieved from http://www.huffingtonpost.com/emily-roenigk/unaccompanied-minors-uniq_b_5536501.html

Roe-Sepowitz, D., Gallagher, J., Hogan, K., Ward, T., & Denecour, N. (2017). *A six-year analysis of sex traffickers of minors.* Retrieved from https://www.mccaininstitute.org/wp-content/uploads/2017/04/asu-sex-traffickers-of-minors-six-year-study-full-report-april-20172.pdf

Rogers, D. L. (2016). Humanity's travesty: The trafficking and smuggling of humans as a commodity. Retrieved from http://files.acams.org/pdfs/2016/Humanitys_Travesty_The_Trafficking_And_Smuggling_D_Rogers.pdf

Rogers, T. (2014, December). Sex workers fight to get a leg up in Latin America. *Splinter.* Retrieved from https://splinternews.com/sex-workers-fight-to-get-a-leg-up-in-latin-america-1793844392

Roggero, P., Mangiaterra, V., Bustreo, F., & Rosati, F. (2007). The health impact of child labor in developing countries: Evidence from cross-country data. *American Journal of Public Health, 97*(2), 271–275.

Rogin, J. (2016). Obama's failed legacy on child soldiers. *Washington Post.* Retrieved from https://www.washingtonpost.com/opinions/global-opinions/obamas-failed-legacy-on-child-soldiers/2016/09/25/fe1b36ac-81b7-11e6-8327-f141a7beb626_story.html?utm_term=.b247005a051b

Rosen, E., & Venkatesh, S. A. (2008). A "perversion" of choice: Sex work offers just enough in Chicago's urban ghetto. *Journal of Contemporary Ethnography, 37*, 417–441.

Rosen, L. W. (2016, August 5). Trafficking in persons and U.S. foreign policy responses in the 114th Congress. Retrieved from https://digitalcommons.ilr.cornell.edu/cgi/viewcontent.cgi?referer=https://scholar.google.com/&httpsredir=1&article=2553&context=key_workplace

Rosenberg, T. (2015). Need a kidney? Not Iranian? You'll wait. *New York Times.* Retrieved from https://opinionator.blogs.nytimes.com/2015/07/31/need-a-kidney-not-iranian-youll-wait/?_r=0

Ross, J. (2015, September 11). The politics of the Syrian refugee crisis, explained. *Washington Post.* Retrieved from https://www.washingtonpost.com/news/the-fix/wp/2015/09/11/the-politics-of-the-syrian-refugee-crisis-explained/?utm_term=.2e2e9be39453

Samarasinghe, V. (2009). Two to tango: Probing the demand side of female sex trafficking. *Pakistan Journal of Women's Studies, 16*(1/2), 33–54.

Sampson, R. J., & Groves, W. B. (1989). Community structure and crime: Testing social-disorganization theory. *American Journal of Sociology, 94*, 774–802.

Sampson, R. J., Raudenbush, S. W., & Earls, F. (1997). Neighborhoods and violent crime: A multilevel study of collective efficacy. *Science, 277*, 918–924.

Schartz, R. (2017, March). Trafficking in Persons Report: 15 years later. *Harvard Political Review.* Retrieved from http://harvardpolitics.com/world/trafficking-in-persons-report/

Schmitt, V. (2016). Sex trafficking and LBGTQ youth. Retrieved from https://polarisproject.org/resources/sex-trafficking-and-lgbtq-youth

Schwarz, C., Unruh, E., Cronin, K., Evans-Simpson, S., Britton, H., & Ramaswamy, M. (2016). Human trafficking identification and service provision in the medical and social service sectors. *Health and Human Rights, 18*(1), 181.

Seals, M. (2015). Worker rights and health protection for prostitutes: A comparison of the Netherlands, Germany, and Nevada. *Health Care for Women International, 36,* 784–796.

Seelke, C. R. (2016). Trafficking in persons in Latin America and the Caribbean (Congressional Research Service report). Retrieved from https://www.fas.org/sgp/crs/row/RL33200.pdf

Sembacher, A. (2005). Council of Europe Convention on Action Against Trafficking in Human Beings. *Tulane Journal of International and Comparative Law, 14,* 435.

Shamir, H. (2012). A labor paradigm for human trafficking. *UCLA Law Review, 60,* 76.

Shared Hope International. (n.d.a). Facts and questions on domestic minor (child) sex trafficking: The USA | FAQs. Retrieved from https://sharedhope.org/the-problem/faqs/

Shared Hope International. (n.d.b). What is trafficking? Retrieved from https://sharedhope.org/the-problem/what-is-sex-trafficking/

Shared Hope International. (2016a). Non-criminalization of juvenile sex trafficking victims. Retrieved from http://sharedhope.org/wp-content/uploads/2014/04/JUSTRESPONSE-POLICY-PAPER-NON-CRIMINALIZATION-OF-JUVENILE-SEX-TRAFFICKING-VICTIMS.pdf

Shared Hope International. (2016b). 2016 end of year legislative progress report. Retrieved from http://sharedhope.org/wp-content/uploads/2012/09/PIC_2016End_of_Year_Report_August_2016-1.pdf

Shared Hope International. (2017). Protected Innocence Challenge: Toolkit 2017. Retrieved from https://sharedhope.org/wp-content/uploads/2017/11/2017-PIC-Toolkit.pdf

Shared Hope International & Center for Justice Advocacy. (n.d.). Protected Innocence Challenge: Toolkit 2018. Retrieved from http://sharedhope.org/wp-content/uploads/2012/09/PIC_2016End_of_Year_Report_August_2016-1.pdf

Shared Hope International Staff. (2014, March 28). Gang sex trafficking on the rise. Retrieved from https://sharedhope.org/2014/03/gang-sex-trafficking-rise/

Sharpe, M., & Wright, E. (2016). New multi-country initiative will protect millions of girls from child marriage—UNICEF/UNFPA [Press release]. Retrieved from https://www.unfpa.org/press/new-multi-country-initiative-will-protect-millions-girls-child-marriage-%E2%80%93-unicefunfpa

Shaw, C. R., & McKay, H. D. (1942). *Juvenile delinquency and urban areas: A study of rates of delinquency in relation to differential characteristics of local communities in American cities.* Chicago, IL: University of Chicago Press.

Shdaimah, C. S. (2017). Prostitution/human trafficking courts: Policy frontline as fault line. *Texas Law Review Online, 96,* 14–22.

Sheldon-Sherman, J. A. (2012). The missing "P": Prosecution, prevention, protection, and partnership in the Trafficking Victims Protection Act. *Penn State Law Review, 117,* 443–501.

Shepler, S. (2016). Sierra Leone, child soldiers and global flows of child protection expertise. In J. Knörr & C. Kohl (Eds.), *The Upper Guinea Coast in global perspective* (pp. 241–252). New York, NY: Berghahn Books.

Shimazono, Y. (2007). The state of the international organ trade: A provisional picture based on integration of available information. *Bulletin of the World Health Organization, 85*(12), 955–962.

Shively, M., Smith, K., Jalbert, S., & Drucker, O. (2017). Human trafficking organizations and facilitators: A detailed profile and interviews with convicted traffickers in the United States. Retrieved from https://www.ncjrs.gov/pdffiles1/nij/grants/251171.pdf

Siegel, D., & Nelen, J. M. (Eds.). (2008). *Organized crime: Culture, markets, and policies.* New York, NY: Springer.

Siegel, J. A., & Williams, L. M. (2003). The relationship between child sexual abuse and female delinquency and crime: A prospective study. *Journal of Research in Crime and Delinquency, 40,* 71–94.

Silbert, M. H., Pines, A. M., & Lynch, T. (1982). Substance abuse and prostitution. *Journal of Psychoactive Drugs, 14*(3), 193–197.

Simons, R. L., & Whitbeck, L. B. (1991). Sexual abuse as a precursor to prostitution and victimization among adolescent and adult homeless women. *Journal of Family Issues, 12*(3), 361.

Smith, L., Vardaman, S. H., & Snow, M. A. (2009). *The national report on domestic minor sex trafficking: America's prostituted children.* Retrieved from http://sharedhope.org/wp-content/uploads/2012/09/SHI_National_Report_on_DMST_2009.pdf

Smith, M. D., Grov, C., Seal, D. W., & McCall, P. (2013). A social-cognitive analysis of how young men become involved in male escorting. *Journal of Sex Research,* 50(1), 1–10. doi:10.1080/00224499.2012.681402

Somasundaram, D. (2002). Child soldiers: Understanding the context. *British Medical Journal, 324*(7348), 1268–1271.

Spagat, E. (2011, November). Cell phones aid in border smuggling. Retrieved from https://www.yahoo .com/news/apnewsbreak-cell-phones-aid-border-smug gling-214609369.html

Spencer, P., Peck, C., & Dirks, S. (2014). 2014 Las Vegas sex trafficking case study. Retrieved from https://www. mccaininstitute.org/wp-content/uploads/2017/02/las-vegas-sex-trafficking-report.pdf

Sprang, G., & Cole, J. (2018). Familial sex trafficking of minors: Trafficking conditions, clinical presentation, and system involvement. *Journal of Family Violence, 33*(3), 185–195. doi:10.1007/s10896-018-9950-y

Statelessness: Nowhere to call home. (2014, May 17). *The Economist.* Retrieved from http://www.economist. com/news/international/21602251-changing-face-worlds-non-citizens-nowhere-call-home

Statistical Office of the Republic of Serbia & UNICEF. (2014). Serbia multiple indicator cluster survey 2014 / Serbia Roma settlements multiple indicator cluster survey, key findings. Retrieved from https://mics-surveys-prod.s3.amazonaws.com/MICS5/Europe%20and%20 Central%20Asia/Serbia/2014/Key%20findings/Serbia%20 %28National%20and%20Roma%20Settlements%29%20 2014%20MICS%20KFR_English.pdf

Steele, S., L. (2010). Combating the scourge: Constructing the masculine "other" through U.S. government anti-trafficking campaigns. *Journal of Hate Studies, 9*(1), 33–64. Retrieved from http://journals .gonzaga.edu/index.php/johs

Steering Committee of the Istanbul Summit. (2008). Organ trafficking and transplant tourism and commercialism: The Declaration of Istanbul. *The Lancet,* 372(9632), 5–6.

Stein, A. (2012). Engendered self-states: Dissociated affect, social discourse, and the forfeiture of agency in battered women. *Psychoanalytic Psychology, 29,* 34–58.

Steiner, J. J., Kynn, J., Stylianou, A. M., & Postmus, J. L. (2018). Providing services to trafficking survivors: Understanding practices across the globe. *Journal of Evidence-Informed Social Work, 15*(2), 151–169.

Street Outreach Program. (2016). *Data collection study final report.* Retrieved from https://www.acf.hhs.gov/ sites/default/files/fysb/data_collection_study_final_ report_street_outreach_program.pdf

Strochlic, N. (2014, September 18). The sad hidden plight of child grooms. *The Daily Beast.* Retrieved from https://www.thedailybeast.com/the-sad-hidden-plight-of-child-grooms

Swedish Ministry of Industry, Employment, and Communications. (2004). Fact Sheet: Prostitution and Trafficking in Women. http://www.sweden.gov.se/content/ 1/c6/01/87/74/6bc6c972.pdf

Sykes, G. M., & Matza, D. (1957). Techniques of neutralization: A theory of delinquency. *American Sociological Review, 22,* 664–670.

Szep, J., & Spetalnick, M. (2015, August 3). Special report: State Department watered down human trafficking report. Retrieved from http://www.reuters .com/article/us-usa-humantrafficking-disputes-special-idUSKCN0Q821Y20150803

Tahirih Justice Center. (2011). Forced marriage in immigrant communities in the United States: 2011 survey results. Retrieved from https://www.tahirih.org/ wp-content/uploads/2015/03/REPORT-Tahirih-Survey-on-Forced-Marriage-in-Immigrant-Communities-in-the-United-States.pdf

Tahirih Justice Center. (2016, September 20). From shadows to spotlight: The birth and growth of a new U.S. movement. Retrieved from https://www.tahirih. org/news/from-shadows-to-spotlight-the-birth-and-growth-of-a-new-u-s-movement/

Tahirih Justice Center. (2018). *Understanding state statutes on minimum marriage age and exceptions.* Retrieved from https://www.tahirih.org/wp-content/ uploads/2016/11/2018-State-Marriage-Age-Require ments-Statutory-Compilation.pdf

Tayeb, S., & Moussa, S. (2018, June 4). Finding a way out of child marriage and towards a vocation. Retrieved from https://www.unfpa.org/news/finding-way-out-child-marriage-and-towards-vocation

Tellier, S., & Hyttel, M. (2017). *Menstrual health management in East and Southern Africa: A review paper.* Retrieved from http://esaro.unfpa.org/sites/default/ files/pub-pdf/UNFPA%20Review%20Menstrual%20 Health%20Management%20Final%2004%20June%20 2018.pdf

Thomas, S. E. (2011). *Responses to human trafficking in Bangladesh, India, Nepal and Sri Lanka.* Retrieved from http://www.unodc.org/documents/human-traf ficking/2011/Responses_to_Human_Trafficking_in_ Bangladesh_India_Nepal_and_Sri_Lanka.pdf

Thorn (n.d.a). [Website]. Retrieved from www .wearethorn.org/.

Thorn. (n.d.b). Spotlight. Retrieved from https://www.wearethorn.org/spotlight/

Tiefenbrun, S. (2007). Child soldiers, slavery, and the trafficking of children. *Fordham International Law Journal, 31*, 415–486.

Trafficking Victims Protection Act of 2000, 22 U.S.C. §§ 7101–10 (2000).

Tugwell, P., Patrick, J., Idzerda, L., Schrecker, T., & Adams, O. (2011). Access to primary healthcare services for the Roma population in Serbia: A secondary data analysis. *BMC International Health and Human Rights, 11*(1), 1–14. doi:10.1186/1472-698X-11-10

Turner, C. (2013). Out of the shadows: Child marriage and slavery. Retrieved from http://www.antislavery.org/wp-content/uploads/2017/01/child_marriage_final-1.pdf

Twis, M. K., & Shelton, B. A. (2018). Systematic review of empiricism and theory in domestic minor sex trafficking research. *Journal of Evidence-Informed Social Work, 15*(4), 432–456. doi:10.1080/23761407.2018.1468844

Tyldum, G., & Brunovskis, A. (2005). Describing the unobserved: Methodological challenges in empirical studies on human trafficking. *International Migration, 43*(1–2), 17–34. Retrieved from http://childhub.org/sites/default/files/library/attachments/107_19_EN_original.pdf#page=19

Unchained at Last. (n.d.). About arranged/forced marriage. Retrieved from http://www.unchainedatlast.org/about-arranged-forced-marriage/

United Nations. (2000). *Protocol against the smuggling of migrants by land, sea and air, supplementing the United Nations Convention Against Transnational Organized Crime.* Retrieved from https://www.unodc.org/documents/middleeastandnorthafrica/smuggling-migrants/SoM_Protocol_English.pdf

United Nations. (2016, January 12). 244 million international migrants living abroad worldwide, new UN statistics reveal [Blog post]. Retrieved https://www.un.org/sustainabledevelopment/blog/2016/01/244-million-international-migrants-living-abroad-worldwide-new-un-statistics-reveal/

United Nations Children's Fund. (2007a). The Paris principles: Principles and guidelines on children associated with armed forces or armed groups. Retrieved from https://www.unicef.org/emerg/files/ParisPrinciples310107English.pdf

United Nations Children's Fund. (2007b). *Promoting the rights of children with disabilities* (Innocenti Digest No. 13). Retrieved from https://www.unicef-irc.org/publications/pdf/digest13-disability.pdf

United Nations Children's Fund. (2017a). Achieving a future without child marriage: Focus on West and Central Africa. Retrieved from https://data.unicef.org/wp-content/uploads/2017/10/Child-Marriage-WEB.pdf

United Nations Children's Fund. (2017b). *The state of the world's children 2017: Children in a digital world.* Retrieved from https://www.unicef.org/publications/index_101992.html

United Nations Children's Fund. (2018a). Child marriage: Latest trends and future prospects. Retrieved from https://data.unicef.org/wp-content/uploads/2018/06/Child-Marriage-data-brief.pdf

United Nations Children's Fund. (2018b, April 13). More than 1,000 children in northeastern Nigeria abducted by Boko Haram since 2013 [Press release]. Retrieved from https://www.unicef.org/wca/press-releases/more-1000-children-northeastern-nigeria-abducted-boko-haram-2013

United Nations Development Programme. (2007). *Human trafficking and HIV: Exploring vulnerabilities and responses in south Asia.* Retrieved from https://www.unodc.org/documents/hiv-aids/publications/human_traffick_hiv_undp2007.pdf

United Nations Educational, Scientific and Cultural Organization. (2012). *World atlas of gender equality in education.* Retrieved from http://www.uis.unesco.org/Education/Documents/unesco-world-atlas-gender-education-2012.pdf

United Nations Entity for Gender Equality and the Empowerment of Women. (n.d.). SDG 5: Achieve gender equality and empower all women and girls. Retrieved from http://www.unwomen.org/en/news/in-focus/women-and-the-sdgs/sdg-5-gender-equality

United Nations General Assembly. (1948, December 10). Universal declaration of human rights (A/RES/3/217A). Retrieved from https://academic.oup.com/rsq/article/27/3/149/1514986

United Nations General Assembly. (1949, December 2). Convention for the suppression of the traffic in persons and of the exploitation of the prostitution of others (A/RES/4/317). Retrieved from https://www.ohchr.org/EN/ProfessionalInterest/Pages/TrafficInPersons.aspx

United Nations General Assembly. (2000a, May 25). Optional protocol to the Convention on the Rights of the Child on the involvement of children in armed conflict (A/RES/54/263). Retrieved from https://www.ohchr.org/en/professionalinterest/pages/opaccrc.aspx

United Nations General Assembly. (2000b, May 25). Optional protocol to the Convention on the Rights of the Child on the sale of children, child prostitution and child pornography (A/RES/54/263). Retrieved from https://www.ohchr.org/EN/ProfessionalInterest/Pages/OPSCCRC.aspx

United Nations General Assembly. (2000c, November 15). Protocol to prevent, suppress and punish trafficking in persons especially women and children, supplementing the United Nations Convention Against Transnational Organized Crime (A/RES/55/25). Retrieved from https://www.ohchr.org/EN/ProfessionalInterest/Pages/ProtocolTraffickingInPersons.aspx

United Nations General Assembly. (2001, January 8). *United Nations Convention Against Transnational Organized Crime and the Protocols Thereto* (A/RES/55/25). Retrieved from https://www.unodc.org/unodc/treaties/CTOC/

United Nations Global Initiative to Fight Human Trafficking. (n.d.). Trafficking of children. Retrieved from http://www.ungift.org/knowledgehub/en/about/trafficking-of-children.html

United Nations Global Initiative to Fight Human Trafficking. (2008). The Vienna Forum to Fight Human Trafficking 13–15 February 2008 (Austria Center Vienna Background Paper): 016 workshop: Profiling the traffickers. Retrieved from https://www.unodc.org/documents/human-trafficking/2008/BP016ProfilingtheTraffickers.pdf

United Nations Office on Drugs and Crime. (n.d.a). Case law database. Retrieved from https://sherloc.unodc.org/cld/v3/htms/cldb/index.html?lng=en

United Nations Office on Drugs and Crime. (n.d.b). Human trafficking. Retrieved from https://www.unodc.org/unodc/en/human-trafficking/what-is-human-trafficking.html

United Nations Office on Drugs and Crime. (n.d.c). Human Trafficking Knowledge Portal. Retrieved from https://www.unodc.org/cld/en/v3/htms/index.html

United Nations Office on Drugs and Crime. (n.d.d). Prosecuting human traffickers. Retrieved from https://www.unodc.org/unodc/en/human-trafficking/prosecution.html

United Nations Office on Drugs and Crime. (n.d.e). Trafficking in persons. Retrieved from https://www.unodc.org/unodc/data-and-analysis/glotip.html

United Nations Office on Drugs and Crime. (2002). *Results of a pilot survey of forty selected organized criminal groups in sixteen countries.* Retrieved from http://www.unodc.org/pdf/crime/publications/Pilot_survey.pdf

United Nations Office on Drugs and Crime. (2006). *Trafficking in persons: Global patterns.* Retrieved from https://www.unodc.org/pdf/traffickinginpersons_report_2006ver2.pdf

United Nations Office on Drugs and Crime. (2008a). *An introduction to human trafficking: Vulnerability, impact and action.* Retrieved from http://www.unodc.org/documents/human-trafficking/An_Introduction_to_Human_Trafficking_-_Background_Paper.pdf

United Nations Office on Drugs and Crime. (2008b). *Toolkit to combat trafficking in persons* (online ed.). Retrieved from https://www.unodc.org/unodc/en/human-trafficking/2008/electronic-toolkit/electronic-toolkit-to-combat-trafficking-in-persons---index.html

United Nations Office on Drugs and Crime. (2009a). *Global report on trafficking in persons.* Retrieved from http://www.unodc.org/documents/Global_Report_on_TIP.pdf

United Nations Office on Drugs and Crime. (2009b). *International framework for action to implement the trafficking in persons protocol.* Retrieved from https://www.unodc.org/documents/human-trafficking/Framework_for_Action_TIP.pdf

United Nations Office on Drugs and Crime. (2010). *The globalization of crime: A transnational organized crime threat assessment.* Retrieved from http://www.unodc.org/documents/data-and-analysis/tocta/TOCTA_Report_2010_low_res.pdf

United Nations Office on Drugs and Crime. (2011a). The role of corruption in trafficking in persons. Retrieved from https://www.unodc.org/documents/human-trafficking/2011/Issue_Paper_-_The_Role_of_Corruption_in_Trafficking_in_Persons.pdf

United Nations Office on Drugs and Crime. (2011b, October 10). UNODC launches first global database of human trafficking cases. Retrieved from http://www.unodc.org/unodc/en/frontpage/2011/October/unodc-launches-first-global-database-of-human-trafficking-cases.html

United Nations Office on Drugs and Crime. (2014). *Global report on trafficking in persons 2014.* Retrieved from https://www.unodc.org/res/cld/bibliography/global-report-on-trafficking-in-persons_html/GLOTIP_2014_full_report.pdf

United Nations Office on Drugs and Crime. (2015a). *Assessment toolkit: Trafficking in persons for the purpose of organ removal.* Retrieved from http://www.unodc

.org/documents/human-trafficking/2015/UNODC_Assessment_Toolkit_TIP_for_the_Purpose_of_Organ_Removal.pdf

United Nations Office on Drugs and Crime. (2015b). *The role of recruitment fees and abusive and fraudulent recruitment practices of recruitment agencies in trafficking in persons.* Retrieved from https://www.unodc.org/documents/human-trafficking/2015/Recruitment_Fees_Report-Final-22_June_2015_AG_Final.pdf

United Nations Office on Drugs and Crime. (2016a). *Global report on trafficking in persons 2016.* Retrieved from http://www.unodc.org/documents/data-and-analysis/glotip/2016_Global_Report_on_Trafficking_in_Persons.pdf

United Nations Office on Drugs and Crime. (2016b, December 20). Historic human trafficking resolution passed at UN Security Council [Press release]. Retrieved from https://www.unodc.org/unodc/en/press/releases/2016/December/historic-human-trafficking-resolution-passed-at-un-security-council.html

United Nations Office on Drugs and Crime. (2018a). *Global report on trafficking in persons 2018.* Retrieved from http://www.unodc.org/documents/data-and-analysis/glotip/2018/GLOTiP_2018_BOOK_web_small.pdf

United Nations Office on Drugs and Crime. (2018b). Module 3: Organized crime markets. E4J University Module Series: Organized Crime. Retrieved from https://www.unodc.org/e4j/en/organized-crime/module-3/exercises/case-studies.html

United Nations Population Fund. (n.d.). Child marriage. Retrieved 2018 from https://www.unfpa.org/child-marriage

United Nations Population Fund. (2018). Child marriage—Frequently asked questions. Retrieved from https://www.unfpa.org/child-marriage-frequently-asked-questions#how%20common%20is%20child%20marriage

United Nations Refugee Agency. (n.d.). Media backgrounder: Millions are stateless, living in legal limbo. Retrieved from http://www.unhcr.org/en-us/protection/statelessness/4e54ec469/media-backgrounder-millions-stateless-living-legal-limbo.html

United Nations Refugee Agency. (2015a). I am here, I belong: The urgent need to end childhood statelessness. Retrieved from http://www.unhcr.org/ibelong/wp-content/uploads/2015-10-StatelessReport_ENG16.pdf

United Nations Refugee Agency. (2015b). The sea route to Europe: The Mediterranean passage in the age of refugees. Retrieved from http://www.unhcr.org/en-us/protection/operations/5592bd059/sea-route-europe-mediterranean-passage-age-refugees.html

United Nations Refugee Agency. (2016a). *Global trends: Forced displacement in 2015.* Retrieved from http://www.unhcr.org/576408cd7.pdf

United Nations Refugee Agency. (2016b). *UNHCR age, gender, and diversity: Accountability report 2015.* Retrieved from http://www.unhcr.org/5769092c7.pdf

United Nations Treaty Collection. (n.d.). Penal matters. Retrieved from https://treaties.un.org/Pages/ViewDetails.aspx?src=TREATY&mtdsg_no=XVIII-12-a&chapter=18&lang=en

United Network for Organ Sharing. (2016). Providing more opportunity for transplant candidates: 2015 in review. Retrieved from https://unos.org/about/annual-report/2015-annual-report/

United States v. Ingalls, 73 F. Supp. 76 (1947).

United States v. Kozminski, 487 U.S. 931 (1988).

Urban Light. (n.d.). The start. Retrieved from https://www.urban-light.org/about-us#wherewestarted

U.S. Attorney's Office. (2011). Brooklyn man pleads guilty in first ever federal conviction for brokering illegal kidney transplants for profit. Retrieved from https://archives.fbi.gov/archives/newark/press-releases/2011/brooklyn-man-pleads-guilty-in-first-ever-federal-conviction-for-brokering-illegal-kidney-transplants-for-profit

U.S. Attorney's Office. (2014). Ashland man sentenced to 30 years in prison for labor trafficking conspiracy. Retrieved from https://www.justice.gov/usao-ndoh/pr/ashland-man-sentenced-30-years-prison-labor-trafficking-conspiracy

U.S. Child Soldiers Prevention Act of 2007, Pub. L. 110–457 (2008).

U.S. Citizenship and Immigration Services. (n.d.a). Forced marriage. Retrieved from https://www.uscis.gov/humanitarian/forced-marriage

U.S. Citizenship and Immigration Services. (n.d.b). Victims of human trafficking: T nonimmigrant status. Retrieved from https://www.uscis.gov/humanitarian/victims-human-trafficking-other-crimes/victims-human-trafficking-t-nonimmigrant-status

U.S. Customs and Border Protection. (2018, August 15). Stash house discovered by Laredo sector border patrol agents. Retrieved from https://www.cbp.gov/newsroom/local-media-release/stash-house-discovered-laredo-sector-border-patrol-agents

U.S. Department of Homeland Security. (n.d.). Blue campaign: What is human trafficking? Retrieved from https://www.dhs.gov/blue-campaign/what-human-trafficking

U.S. Department of Labor. (n.d.). Youth & labor. Retrieved from https://www.dol.gov/general/topic/youthlabor

U.S. Department of Labor. (2016). *List of goods produced by child labor or forced labor.* Retrieved from https://www.dol.gov/sites/default/files/documents/ilab/reports/child-labor/findings/TVPRA_Report2016.pdf

U.S. Department of Labor. (2017). *2016 findings on the worst forms of child labor.* Retrieved from https://www.dol.gov/agencies/ilab/our-work/child-forced-labor-trafficking

U.S. Department of State. (n.d.a). 3Ps: Prosecution, protection, and prevention. Retrieved December 22, 2018, from https://www.state.gov/j/tip/3p/

U.S. Department of State. (n.d.b). 2018 Trafficking in Persons Report. Retrieved from https://www.state.gov/j/tip/rls/tiprpt/

U.S. Department of State. (n.d.c). U.S. laws on trafficking in persons. Retrieved from https://www.state.gov/j/tip/laws/

U.S. Department of State. (2002). *Trafficking in persons report.* Retrieved from https://2009-2017.state.gov/documents/organization/10815.pdf

U.S. Department of State. (2004). *Trafficking in persons report.* Retrieved from https://2009-2017.state.gov/documents/organization/34158.pdf

U.S. Department of State. (2007). *Trafficking in persons report.* Retrieved from https://2009-2017.state.gov/documents/organization/82902.pdf

U.S. Department of State. (2009). *Trafficking in persons report.* Retrieved from https://2009-2017.state.gov/documents/organization/123357.pdf

U.S. Department of State. (2010). *Trafficking in persons report.* Retrieved from https://2009-2017.state.gov/documents/organization/142979.pdf

U.S. Department of State. (2011). *Trafficking in persons report.* Retrieved from https://2009-2017.state.gov/documents/organization/164452.pdf

U.S. Department of State. (2013). *Trafficking in persons report.* Retrieved from https://2009-2017.state.gov/documents/organization/210737.pdf

U.S. Department of State. (2015). *Trafficking in persons report.* Retrieved from https://2009-2017.state.gov/documents/organization/245365.pdf

U.S. Department of State. (2016). *Trafficking in persons report.* Retrieved from https://2009-2017.state.gov/documents/organization/258876.pdf

U.S. Department of State. (2017a, June 27). Human trafficking & migrant smuggling: Understanding the difference. Retrieved from http://www.state.gov/j/tip/rls/fs/2017/272005.htm

U.S. Department of State. (2017b). Paying to work: The high cost of recruitment fees. Retrieved from https://www.state.gov/documents/organization/272409.pdf

U.S. Department of State. (2017c). *Trafficking in persons report.* Retrieved from https://www.state.gov/wp-content/uploads/2019/02/271339.pdf

U.S. Department of State. (2018a). Report on serious human rights abuses or censorship in North Korea. Retrieved from https://www.state.gov/j/drl/rls/287984.htm

U.S. Department of State. (2018b). *Trafficking in persons report.* Retrieved from https://www.state.gov/wp-content/uploads/2019/01/282798.pdf

U.S. Department of Transportation. (n.d.). Blue Lightning Initiative. Retrieved from https://www.transportation.gov/administrations/office-policy/blue-lightning-initiative

U.S. Department of Transportation. (2016, December 19). Transportation Leaders Against Human Trafficking. Retrieved from https://www.transportation.gov/TLAHT

U.S. Federal Acquisition Regulation; Ending Trafficking in Persons, 80 Fed. Reg. 4967 (2015).

U.S. Government Accountability Office. (2016). *Human trafficking: Agencies have taken steps to assess prevalence, address victim issues, and avoid grant duplication.* Retrieved from http://www.gao.gov/assets/680/678041.pdf

U.S. Government Publishing Office. (2009a). *Title 18—Crimes and criminal procedure.* United States Code, 2009 edition. (Part I Chapter 67 Section 1384). Retrieved from https://www.gpo.gov/fdsys/pkg/USCODE-2009-title18/html/USCODE-2009-title18.htm

U.S. Government Publishing Office. (2009b). *Title 18—Crimes and Criminal Procedure.* United States Code, 2009 edition. (Part I Chapter 117 Section 2423). Retrieved from https://www.gpo.gov/fdsys/pkg/USCODE-2009-title18/html/USCODE-2009-title18.htm

U.S. Government Publishing Office. (2009c). *Title 18—Crimes and Criminal Procedure.* United States Code, 2009 edition. (Part I Chapter 95 Section 1952). Retrieved from https://www.gpo.gov/fdsys/pkg/USCODE-2009-title18/html/USCODE-2009-title18.htm

U.S. Immigration and Customs Enforcement. (n.d.a). Her story. Retrieved from https://www.ice.gov/features/human-trafficking-victim-shares-story

U.S. Immigration and Customs Enforcement. (n.d.b). Human smuggling. Retrieved from https://www.ice.gov/human-smuggling

U.S. Immigration and Customs Enforcement. (n.d.c). Human Smuggling and Trafficking Center. Retrieved from https://www.ice.gov/human-smuggling-trafficking-center

U.S. Immigration and Customs Enforcement. (2010). Continued presence: Temporary immigration status for victims of human trafficking. Retrieved from https://www.ice.gov/doclib/human-trafficking/pdf/continued-presence.pdf

Vandenberg, M. E., & Levy, A. F. (2012). Human trafficking and diplomatic immunity: Impunity no more. *Intercultural Human Rights Law Review, 7,* 77.

Vanwesenbeeck, I. (2013). Prostitution push and pull: Male and female perspectives. *Journal of Sex Research, 50,* 11–16.

Verma, R., Sinha, T., & Khanna, T. (2013, May 29). Asia child marriage initiative: Summary of research in Bangladesh, India, and Nepal. Retrieved from https://plan-international.org/publications/asia-child-marriage-initiative

Victims of Trafficking and Violence Protection Act of 2000, H.R. 3244, 106th Cong. (2000).

Vindhya, U., & Dev, V. S. (2011). Survivors of sex trafficking in Andhra Pradesh: Evidence and testimony. *Indian Journal of Gender Studies, 18,* 129–165.

Voronova, S., & Radjenovic, A. (2016). The gender dimension of human trafficking. *European Parliament Briefing.* European Union, European Parliamentary Research Service. Retrieved from http://www.europarl.europa.eu/RegData/etudes/BRIE/2016/577950/EPRS_BRI(2016)577950_EN.pdf

Walk Free Foundation. (2018). *The global slavery index 2018.* Retrieved from https://downloads.globalslavery-index.org/ephemeral/GSI-2018_FNL_180907_Digital-small-p-1560808612.pdf

Warchol, G., & Harrington, M. (2016). Exploring the dynamics of South Africa's illegal abalone trade via routine activities theory. *Trends in Organized Crime, 19*(1), 21–41.

Wasch, S., Wolfe, D. S., Levitan, E. H., & Fink, K. (2016). An analysis of safe harbor laws for minor victims of commercial sexual exploitation: Implications for Pennsylvania and other states. Retrieved from https:// fieldcenteratpenn.org/wp-content/uploads/2013/05/SafeHarborWhitePaperFINAL.pdf

Weiner, N. A., & Hala, N. (2008). *Measuring human trafficking: Lessons from New York City* (NCJRS Document No. 224391). Retrieved from https://www.ncjrs.gov/pdffiles1/nij/grants/224391.pdf

Weitzer, R. (2000). Prostitution control in America: Rethinking public policy. *Crime, Law, and Social Change, 32,* 83–102.

Wessells, M. (2009). *Child soldiers: From violence to protection.* Cambridge, MA: Harvard University Press.

Wheaton, E., Schauer, E., & Galli, T. (2010). Economics of human trafficking. *International Migration, 48*(4), 114–141. doi:10.1111/j.1468-2435.2009.00592.x

Whitaker, F. (2017). Securing a future for child soldiers [Blog post]. Retrieved from https://www.huffington-post.com/forest-whitaker/securing-a-future-for-child-soldiers_b_9190472.html

Wilber, D. Q. (2011). MS-13 gang is branching into prostitution, authorities say. *Washington Post.* Retrieved from https://www.washingtonpost.com/local/ms-13-gang-is-branching-into-prostitution-authorities-say/2011/11/04/gIQAAtOyIN_story.html? utm_term=.6af5e25cdd3e

Williams, R. (2017). Safe harbor: State efforts to combat child trafficking. Retrieved from http://www.ncsl.org/Portals/1/Documents/cj/SafeHarbor_v06.pdf

Williamson, C., & Prior, M. (2009). Domestic minor sex trafficking: A network of underground players in the Midwest. *Journal of Child and Adolescent Trauma, 2*(1), 46–61. Retrieved from http://dx.doi.org/10.1080/19361520802702191

Wilson, B., & Butler, L. D. (2014). Running a gauntlet: A review of victimization and violence in the pre-entry, post-entry, and peri-/post-exit periods of commercial sexual exploitation. *Psychological Trauma: Theory, Research, Practice, and Policy, 6*(5), 494–504. doi:10.1037/a0032977

Withers, L. (2012). *Louder than words: An agenda for action to end state use of child soldiers.* Retrieved from https://resourcecentre.savethechildren.net/node/6626/pdf/6626.pdf

Wonders, N. A. (2016). Just-in-time justice: Globalization and the changing character of law, order, and power. *Critical Criminology, 24*(2), 201–216. doi:10.1007/s10612-015-9305-4

Wonders, N. A., & Michalowski, R. J., Jr. (2001). Bodies, borders, and sex tourism in a globalized world:

A tale of two cities—Amsterdam and Havana. *Social Problems, 48*(4), 545–571.

Wooditch, A. (2011). The efficacy of the Trafficking in Persons Report: A review of the evidence. *Criminal Justice Policy Review, 22*(4), 471–493. doi:10.1177/0887403411386217

World Bank. (n.d.). Education overview. Retrieved from http://www.worldbank.org/en/topic/girlseducation/overview#1

World Health Organization. (2010). WHO guiding principles on human cell, tissue and organ transplantation. *Transplantation, 90*(3). Retrieved from https://journals.lww.com/transplantjournal/fulltext/2010/08150/WHO_Guiding_Principles_on_Human_Cell,_Tissue_and.1.aspx

World Health Organization. (2013). Child marriages: 39 000 every day [News release]. Retrieved from http://www.who.int/mediacentre/news/releases/2013/child_marriage_20130307/en/

World Health Organization. (2018). 10 facts on obstetric fistula. Retrieved from http://www.who.int/features/factfiles/obstetric_fistula/en/

Wright, E. (2015, April 17). Poverty and its contribution to human trafficking [Blog post]. Retrieved from http://borgenproject.org/poverty-contribution-human-trafficking/

Yates, A. (2016). An introduction to the world of sex tourism [Blog post]. Retrieved from https://kinsey confidential.org/sex-tourism-sex-tourists/

Yea, S. (2009). Human trafficking: A geographical perspective. *Geodate, 23*(3), 2–6. Retrieved from https://moodle.plc.nsw.edu.au/pluginfile.php/6379/mod_page/content/5/GeoDate_Vol_23_No_3_July_2010.pdf

Yount, K., Crandall, A., Cheong, Y., Osypuk, T., Bates, L., Naved, R., & Schuler, S. (2016). Child marriage and intimate partner violence in rural Bangladesh: A longitudinal multilevel analysis. *Demography, 53*(6), 1821–1852. doi:10.1007/s13524-016-0520-8

Yu, S. (2017, May 21). Slave husbands of Hong Kong: The men who marry into servitude. *This Week in Asia.* Retrieved from https://www.scmp.com/week-asia/society/article/2094868/slave-husbands-hong-kong-men-who-marry-servitude

Yu, S. H., Mason, J., Crum, J., Cappa, C., & Hotchkiss, D. R. (2016). Differential effects of young maternal age on child growth. *Global Health Action.* Retrieved from http://data.unicef.org/wp-content/uploads/2016/11/Paper-Child-marriage-and-nutrition-Global-Health-Action.pdf

Yuko, E. I. (2009). *Theories, practices and promises: Human trafficking laws and policies in destination states of the Council of Europe.* Unpublished master's thesis, Dublin City University, Dublin, Ireland.

Zatz, M. S., & Smith, H. (2012). Immigration, crime, and victimization: Rhetoric and reality. *Annual Review of Law and Social Science, 8*, 141–159.

Zhang, S. (2011). Woman pullers: Pimping and sex trafficking in a Mexican border city. *Crime, Law and Social Change, 56*(5), 509–528. Retrieved from http://dx.doi.org/10.1007/s10611-011-9333-2

Zimmerman, C., Hossain, M., Roche, B., Morison, L., Watts, C., Yun, K., . . . Kefurtova, A. (2008). The health of trafficked women: A survey of women entering post-trafficking services in Europe. *American Journal of Public Health, 98*(1), 55–59. doi:10.2105/AJPH.2006.108357

Zimmerman, C., Hossain, M., Yun, K., Roche, B., Morison, L., & Watts, C. (2006). *Stolen smiles: A summary report on the physical and psychological health consequences of women and adolescents trafficked in Europe.* London, England: London School of Hygiene and Tropical Medicine.

Zimmerman, C., Kiss, L., Hossain, M., & Watts, C. (2009). Trafficking in persons: A health concern? *Ciência e Saúde Coletiva, 14*, 1029–1035. doi:10.1590=S1413-81232009000400010

Index